Aeolian-Skinner Opus 1203
First Church of Christ, Scientist, Boston

THE AMERICAN CLASSIC ORGAN

A HISTORY IN LETTERS

CHARLES CALLAHAN

PUBLISHED IN 1990 BY
THE ORGAN HISTORICAL SOCIETY
RICHMOND, VIRGINIA

This book is dedicated to
the memory and genius of
G. Donald Harrison

Table of Contents

Illustrations

> The Diapason *graciously permits re-publication of photographs which appear on pages 7, 31, 40, 42, 49, 56, 61, 67, 103, 137, 139, 149, 162, 179, 186, 202, 209, 255, 268, 273, 280, 337, 387*

Subscribers

Leo Abbott, FAGO, ChM
Larry Abbott
Dan Abrahamson
Lester E. Ackerman, Jr.
Elizabeth J. Adair
Herbert P. Adams, Jr., FAGO
Gilbert F. Adams
W. Thomas Alderman
Marilyn Alexander, AAGO
Richard Alexander
Linda C. Allen
Jonathan Ambrosino
Paul D. Andersen
Arthur and Christine
  Anderson
J. Theodore Anderson
Karl F. Anderson
Dr. Robert T. Anderson
Norman A. André
Daniel L. Angerstein
John Apple
Jerry W. Archer
Joseph Armbrust
Susan Armstrong-Ouellette
D. Byron Arneson
Robert E. Arnold
Amory T. Atkins
Gordon Atkinson
Gordon S. Atkinchloss
Austin Organs Inc.
Richard M. Babcock
Frederik M. Bach
Fredrick W. Bahr
Samuel Baker
Charles F. Baker
Wayne H. Balch
Mary Ann Crugher Balduf
John G. Ballard
Cryder H. Bankes, III
Peter Baratta, Jr.
Nelson Barden
Barger & Nix Pipe Organs
Stephen M. Barker
Dale R. Barnes
David M. Barnett
Donald C. Barnum, Jr.
J. Michael Barone
Wilson Barry
Wayne Barton
Benjamin S. Basile
Peter Batchelder
Robert S. Bates
Ronald R. Bates
H. Thomas Baugh III
Rev. Richard M. Baxter
Victor W. Beck
Diane Meredith Belcher
Rex Bell
William H. Belliston
Benjamin W. Belton
Dr. Paul A. Bender
Bruce P. Bengtson, SMM,
  AAGO
Richard Bennett
R. Monty Bennett
Robert C. Bennett
E. Franklin Bentel
J. Peter Bercovitz
Gary J. Bergmark
Mary Lynn Bergsten
Dr. Robert L. Berkey
Leon C. Berry
Stephen H. Best
Benjamin H. Best, II
Jack M. Bethards
Michael L. Bigelow

Keith Bigger
David John Billeter
Dean W. Billmeyer
Fred W. Billmeyer, Jr.
Edgar Billups
L. Jeffries Binford, Jr.
Lawrence Birdsong, Jr.
The Bishop Organ Co.
David Alan Bishop
Lawrence E. Bishop, Jr.
Raymond A. Biswanger, III
Gustav Bittrich
Mr. & Mrs. Larry Blackburn
Harriet H. Blackman
Mrs. Homer D. Blanchard
Ted W. Blankenship, Jr.
J. D. Blatt
Burton Bluemer
E. A. Boadway
Bob Jones University
Willis Bodine
Charles F. Boehm
Bruce P. Bogert
Norman A. Bolton
Christopher A. Bono
Richard L. Bordelon
Boston Organ Club
David A. Bottom
Leslie W. Bouldin, Jr.
Jane A. Bourdon
Arnold E. Bourziel, AAGO
Richard G. Boutwell
Ruth H. Bowers
William Brach
E. William Brackett
James E. Brackett
Berenice Bragdon
William F. Brame
Anthony R. Brandelli
James M. Bratton
To E. Carter Breeze
  from the Classical String
  Quartet
Robert E. Breihan
Harry L. Brengel
Bridgewater College, VA
Colver R. Briggs
David C. Brock
John Brombaugh
Mark Brombaugh
David A. J. Broome
Dr. William J. Brosnan
John O. Brostrup
Peter A. Brown
Kyler W. Brown
Vernon Brown
Thomas Brown
Kenneth L. Brown
Mr. and Mrs. J. Pinoake
  Browning
Raymond J. Brunner
Fred N. Buch
Bruce Buchanan
Charles E. Buchner
Richard H. Buck
Nelson E. Buechner
Anthony A. Bufano
Prof. John M. Bullard
Jonathan C. Bumbaugh
Bill Bunch
Robert W. Bunn, Jr.
Bunn-Minnick Pipe
  Organs
Dr. J. Owen Burdick
Susan Burkhalter
Gregg F. Burks

Lawrence S. Burt
William G. Burt, Jr.
Mary R. Burton
James Busby
Donald Wallace Button
G. Huntington Byles
H. M. Cabot
James L. Caldwell
David Chas. Calhoun
  in loving memory of
  Randall Jay McCarty
Allen B. Callahan
Neal Campbell
David J. Campbell
Dr. John C. Campbell
Craig Cansler
Mr. & Mrs. Byron
  Christian Carlson
Carolyn Gage Carpenter
Troy Carpenter
The Rev. Thomas J.
  Carroll, S. J.
Brian T. Carson
Laurence Carson
Paul S. Carton
Casavant Frères Ltd.
Dr. Del W. Case
Catherine S. Casey
Don W. Cassel
Jackson H. Chadwell
David Chalmers
David Bieler Chamberlin
Terry Charles
Richard R. Charlett
Thomas R. Charsky
Dr. Robert Chase
Raymond & Elizabeth
  Chenault
Rev. James J. Chepponis
R. Craig Chotard
N. Francis Cimmino
Dr. Thomas R. Clark
Ken Clark
Elinor Clarke
William B. Clarke, Jr.
Dan Clayton
Marion L. Clemens
Kevin M. Clemens
Nelson A. Close
Charles N. Clutz, AIA
David L. Cogswell
Ann E. Colby
Norman A. Cole
R. E. Coleberd
Gary Coleman
Monte W. Coleman
Dr. Michael J. Collier
Adrian A. Collins
Columbia Organ Works
Henry M. Cook
Chester W. Cooke
Giles Cooke
Robert R. Cornelison
Raymond Correll
Kenneth H. Courtney
Fr. Peter Courtney
Allen E. Crandall
Douglas W. Craw
James W. Crawford
Paul Creasman
Ron Crider
Peter Crisafulli
James H. Crissman
Douglas C. Crocker
Daniel G. Cronenwett
H. Proctor Crow, Jr.

Ronald Sheley Crowl
Michael J. S. Cubbage
James Lynn Culp
Richard Cummins
Eldon R. Cunningham
Carlo Curley
Donald D. Curry
R. Donald Curry
The Curtis Institute of Music
  Library
Marilyn Baker Curtis
Messrs. Czelusniak et
  Dugal, Inc.
William F. Czelusniak
Thaddeus J. Czerkowicz
Kenneth G. Danchik
James S. Darling
Michael S. David
James Davies
Grahame Scott Davis
Merrill N. Davis III
Mark Davis, Organ
  Conservator
Grahame Davis
Hal M. Davison
Bradley M. Day
Harold de La Chapelle
Franklin A. de Lespinasse
Evelyn De Long
Ronald E. Dean
C. Robert Dean, MD
Francis P. Dean
John W. Decker
Herman W. DePriest
Carolyn Deuel
Di Gennaro-Hart Organ Co.
Pierce Dickens
Matt L. Dickerson
Robert C. Dickinson
William E. Didelius
Steven Dieck
E. J. Digneo
David R. Dion
Mark Dirksen
Lynn A. Dobson
Stephen Varick Dock
Mary Ann Dodd
Dr. Alan R. Dodds
Jack A. Dommer
Carol Doran
Alan Douglas
Charles W. Douglas
Joseph F. Douglas, Sr.
Arthur Allen Douglass, Jr.
Eugene & Janet Doutt
John H. Dower
John Francis Downing
Brock W. Downward
James M. Drake
Wayne P. Drake
Allen G. Dreyfuss
David Drinkwater
Hugh L. Dryden, Jr.
Dr. Robert DuBert
Peter DuBois
William N. Duck
Brantley A. Duddy
Wesley C. Dudley
Francis E. Dugal
Dr. Donald R. Du Laney
Malcolm D. Dutton
Randall Dyer & Assoc.
Joseph F. Dzeda
David E. Easler
Terry Byrd Eason
Charles Eberline

B. H. Elker
Larry D. Ellis
Ronald F. Ellis
David Elson
Stephen L. Emery
Richard E. Emmons
David P. Engen
Benjamin Epstein
Mildred Demaree Erhart
Rich Erickson
Joan M. Eschenbauch
Karen Eshelman and
  Charles Tompkins
Fr. Julio M. Espinosa, OAR
Broocke Eubank
David Evans
William Gregory Evans
Robert A. Eversman
Emory M. Fanning
The Rev. Jere T. Farrah
Tom Farrell
Charles J. Farris
George Faxon
Michael Fazio
David E. Fedor
Theodore Feldmann
James R. Feller
Donald K. Fellows
James H. Felten
James A. Fenimore, MD
Mr. and Mrs. James G.
  Ferguson, Jr.
Paul W. Fernald
Lee C. Ferrier
D. Thomas Ferris
Susan Ferré
Frank S. Fess
Fred W. Field
Thomas & Frances Finch
First Plymouth Congrega-
  tional Church, Lincoln, NE
Marty Fisher
Douglas Fizel
Lee Flathers
Gordon Flesher
James D. Flood
Wallace C. Flower
Maude Fluchere
Darrell K. Fluehr
Thomas C. Flynn
Stephen C. Foley
James P. Folkert
Davis Folkerts
Russell L. Followell
J. Tyson Forker, Jr.
Brian M. Fowler
G. Reese Fowler
Michael Alan Fox
David H. Fox
David F. Fraley
Burton E. Frank
Frederick P. Frank
Bruce Robert Frank
Arthur Frantz
Richard M. Frary Jr.
James E. Frazier
John L. Frederick
E. Carl Freeman, Jr.
Rubin Steele Frels
John Evans French
Roy E. Frenzke
Michael & Susan Friesen
Charles Frischmann
Paul B. Fritts
Thomas P. Frost
Wiatt Andrew Funk

David and Nancy Peckham
Peebles-Herzog, Inc.
William D. Peek
Pelland Organ Company
Michael D. Pelton
Robert E. Penn
John Peragallo
Richard L. Perham
Fred H. Persson
H. Wilfrid de B. Peters
John J. Peters
Peters-Weiland & Co.
G. James Petersen, Jr.
Roberta J. Peterson
Roger T. Petrich
Ellsworth Pettit
Petty-Madden Organbuilders
Thomas L. Peyton, Ph.D.
Lawrence I. Phelps
John D. Phillipe
Adrian W. Phillips
William M. Phillips, MD
Anthony Piaggi
Charles F. L. Pierpont
Harley V. Piltingsrud
Mr. & Mrs. Edgar L. Pinel
Stephen L. Pinel
Mark W. Pinnick
Keith E. E. Pittman
Gary W. Plantinga
Jay R. Plumb
John O. Porbeck
R. David Porper
Thomas V. Potter
Stephen Potter
John J. Potter
D. B. Prescott
Jules E. Prevost
Donald G. Pribble
Edgar E. Price
Steven A. Protzman
Larry R. Pruett
Thomas M. Pulsifer
Richard Purvis
Michael R. Quimby
Wylie S. Quinn, III
Forrest & Elin Radley
Douglas Rafter, AAGO
Jean B. Raitch
Charles W. Rakow
Gordon Clark Ramsey
Dr. Richard S. Rand, CFEI
John L. Randolph
R. M. Range
John G. Ranney
J. L. Ransford, CPA
William Osborn Rarich
Doris & Dave Rasche
George A. Rau
Leonard Raver
John E. Reber, IV
Roy A. Redman
Robert E. Reid
James R. Reid
Bert Reiter
Timothy P. Remsen
Richard Rensch
Martin Renshaw
William F. Reynolds
Robert G. Reynolds
C. Thomas Rhoads
Robert W. Rhynsburger
Ronald C. & Tracey R. Rice
Joyce Painter Rice
Luke H. Richard
James C. Richardson
Harriette Slack Richardson
Blaine Ricketts
Rowland Ricketts, MD

George Rico
Robert E. Ridgeway
Douglas E. Rife
Terry B. Rinkenberger
The Rev. Theodore W. Ripper
Drs. William and Charlotte Risinger
Myron Roberts
Albert F. Robinson
Bert J. Robinson
Joseph E. Robinson
F. Robert Roche
Lester V. Rockafellow
Richard C. Rogers
Jelil F. Romano
Edward Rook, J. P.
Gary Kendall Roper
Stephen M. Rosenberg
Paul Alan Rosendall
Rick Ross
Stephen William Ross
Joseph K. Rotella
Daniel Roth
Theodore J. Rowland
Mary-Julia C. Royall
Henry R. Ruby
Jack R. Ruhl
Stephen Rumpf
Carl F. Rupprecht
Allan H. Russcher
Victor Monte Russell
Harold Rutz
James Sadie
Kevin J. Sadowski
James Gillis Saenger
Paul Sahlin
The Saint Dunstan-Art Organ Works
The Salt Lake Mormon Tabernacle Choir
Mario Salvador
Mr. & Mrs. Luis Harold Sanford
Allen R. Savage
James J. Schaedle
John Schaefer
K. Thomas Schaettle
Schantz Organ Co.
Robert F. Scheiblhofer
Russell Schertle
The Rev. John L. "Jack" Schindler
Arthur E. Schleuter, Jr.
Tamara L. Schmiege
Elizabeth Towne Schmitt
Stephen J. Schnurr, Jr.
Lawrence L. Schoenstein
Schoenstein & Co., Organbuilders
Menno N. Scholten, AIA
Mark R. Scholtz
William J. Scholz, Jr.
Charles W. Schramm, Jr.
Carl E. Schroeder
Gaspar Schulek
Preston Schultz
David G. Schutt
Carl Clinton Schwartz
Jeffrey A. Scofield
Stylianos P. Scordilis
Robert A. Scott
Mark Scott
David C. Scribner
Robert E. Seamon
John P. Seiz
Selah Publishing Co.
Ronald T. Severin
William Henry Shambaugh II
Gerard S. Shamdosky

David R. Sharpe
Richard N. Shattuck
John H. Shaum
Dr. Ben A. Shaver
John R. Shaw
Harry Sherman
Rev. Timothy J. Shreenan
Courtney A. Shucker II
Enos E. Shupp, Jr.
Stewart Shuster
Jonathan Sibley
Sharon Sasse Silleck
Micki W. Simms
Irving Stacey Simpson
Larry A. Simpson
Paul D. Singleton
Lee Singleton
Robert L. Sipe
Hampson A. Sisler, MD, FAGO
Wayne D. Skinner
Edward F. Small
Richard A. Smid
Arnold E. Smith
Jeffrey Smith
Stoddart Smith
Timothy Edward Smith
Timothy Q. Smith
Wm. R. Smith
Nick Snow
James G. Snyder
William T. Snyder
David & Chris Snyder
Milton B. Snyder
David Solada
Hazel & Murray Somerville
George H. Sparks
David D. Speck, MD
Dr. John L. Speller
The Rev. Norman Spicer
Harry Spring
Henri M. St. Louis
Mr. Jack Staley
Margaret Stanbery
Thomas C. Stapleton
Carl B. Staplin, Ph.D.
Kenneth Starr
Stephen A. Steely
Charles W. C. Stein
C. Kenneth Stein
Rev. John W. Steiner
Dr. Phillip Steinhaus
Jack Steinkampf
C. Martin Steinmetz
Joseph Stephens
Bertram L. Sterbenz
Stephen M. Sterbenz
Karen Stewart
Timothy Glen Stewart
Ruth Elsa Stickney
Louis Sticks
Flaccus M. B. Stifel
Sunny Stiklius
Ray W. Stilwell
David H. Stockstill
John Albert Stokes
Frank G. Stoner
David Marshall Storey
Brent Stratten
A. Richard Strauss
Nelson A. Streett
Thomas Strickland
J. Bertram Strickland
Theron Strike
Lois Margaret Strother
Michael E. Sussman, MD
Norman A. Sutphin
Frederick Swann

Richard Thomas Swanson
Jean Swanson
Samuel John Swartz
Charles F. Swisher
George W. Swope
Henry Sybrandy
J. Richard Szeremany
A. Thomas Talbert
Eric B. Talbot
Ken Tate
Frank H. Taylor
Taylor Miller Organbuilders
Mark A. Thewes
Jon H. Thieszen
Kenneth L. Thomas
Ladd Thomas
Thornton W. Thomas
Kathleen Thomerson
Camille E. Thompson
Frank H. Thompson
Charles W. Thompson
Nicholas Thompson-Allen
F. Anthony Thurman
Gary W. Tidwell
Burton K. Tidwell
Timothy James Tikker
Bruce E. Tillberg
Stephen E. Tillotson
Paul Tindall
Adrienne M. Tindall, AAGO
Herbert Wills Tinney
Gary C. Toops
Jack Townsend
Ivan W. Traucht
The Rev. William B. Trexler
Peter Treybal
Trinity Cathedral Choirs, Little Rock
John Edward Trout
E. Rodney Trueblood
Lawrence Trupiano
Dr. Fred Tulan
John H. Tully
Alfred J. Turnbull
Thomas Turner
P. D. Tuttle
Robert A. Tuttle
Jonathan A. Tuuk
James G. Twyne, Jr.
John J. Tyrrell
Kenneth Udy
Donald C. Ulm
William E. Unbehaur
Richard Unfreid
Charles J. Updegraph
Kenneth W. Usher
Ralph B. Valentine
Charles H. van Bronkhorst
Bruce Van Horne
William Triplett Van Pelt III
John Veldhuyzen Van Zanten
Robert & Karen Van Zweden
Frank Bennett Vanaman
Nancy W. Vernon
Leonard G. Vernon
William M. Via
James Vinson
Arie M. Voskuil
Robert M. Voves
Mary Jane Wagner, OSF
Randall E. Wagner
Dr. David O. Wagner
Ted R. Wahlstrom
Leonard E. Walcott, Jr.
Robert W. Waldele
Roman Walek
Robert G. Walker
Charles Dodsley Walker

J. W. Walker & Sons Ltd
Lawrence Edward Wall, Jr.
Edward A. Wallace
Joseph Wallace, Jr., MD
Gary E. Waller
Robert E. Waller
Eric Walling
James L. Wallmann
John Powel Walsh
Matthew Walsh
Edna & Norman Walter
John Walter
Sally Slade Warner
Charles Wassberg
Karl Michael Watson
Barry U. Watson
James D. Weatherald
William Weaver
Harold W. Weaver
W. Kenneth Weaver
John Weaver
Scott C. Weidler
Jeff Weiler
John H. Welch
J. Ernest Wells, DC, JD
Steven Wente
George F. Wharton III
Tim Wheat
Harvey Wheeler
Larry L. Wheelock
Marshall Whisnant
Robert W. White
Robert Bruce Whiting
Douglas Alan Whitman
Bard B. Wickkiser
Harold D. Wiebe
Martin Wiegand
David K. Wigton
Russell L. Wilcox
James O. Wilkes
Bruce R. Wilkin
Walter G. Wilkins
Robert P. Wilkinson
Dr. B. McK. Williams
Craig Williams
Carmen Willoughby
David Judge Wilson
Dr. Charles D. Wilson
Todd & Anne Wilson
Clark Wilson
John Wilson
Walter E. Wilson
H. E. Wiltse
John Peyton Wise
Robert G. Withers
Henry D. Wolfgang
Barclay Wood
Charles R. Wood
Douglas M. Woodard
Charles Woodward
Ty Woodward
Robert Eugene Woodworth, Jr.
William J. Wright
Jonathan Wright
Robert Wyant
Dr. Stanley E. Yoder
Judith P. York
Rev. Carol Henry Youse
Laird D. Zacheis
Joseph Zamberlan
Richard Zamoyski
Robert D. Zay
James Zieba
Robert B. Ziegler
James M. Zima
Douglas E. Zimmer
Robert G. Zopfi, Sr.

"I have lived long enough to know that the whole truth is never told in history texts. Only the people who lived through an era, who are the real participants in the drama as it occurs, know the truth."

LILLIAN GISH
Noel Coward and His Friends

Preface

Pipe organs evolve slowly, and only the best examples advance the development of the instrument. To alter the course of American organbuilding with a single stroke is a rarity indeed—scarcely a handful of organs have done this in two hundred years. Boston has seen two such pivotal events: Walcker's 1863 Music Hall organ and Aeolian-Skinner's 1936 organ at the Church of the Advent.

Nestled at the foot of Beacon Hill on Brimmer Street, the Advent is a model Boston church: handsome Victorian architecture, stunning appointments, and acoustics that angels would love. In November of 1935, G. Donald Harrison of Aeolian-Skinner wrote to his friend and former employer Henry Willis III in London, "We have just received a contract for an organ in the Church of the Advent in Boston . . . we got the job without competition . . . moreover they gave me carte blanche within the funds available."

The organ was Aeolian-Skinner's Opus 940 with three manuals and 76 ranks, installed early in 1936. On April 23, Clarence Watters opened his dedicatory recital with Bach's "Wedge" Prelude and Fugue, playing the episodes on the sparkling, unenclosed Positiv division. Watters was one of the young "classical" organists, and during his program all 27 ranks of Advent mixtures came into play. Conservative Boston organists were not impressed. Compared to the majestic E. M. Skinner organs they knew so well, the Advent organ was full of "screaming mixtures." Few in the audience that night realized the significance of the event. Harrison's work was so novel that it took years for the full impact to be felt.

The Church of the Advent organ was neither the first nor the largest of its type. A sister instrument of 85 ranks had been installed in the Groton School chapel the previous fall. But in those days, Groton was two hours from the Aeolian-Skinner factory, while Beacon Hill was just 15 minutes away. The Advent organ became the ideal showcase, and a parade of prominent organists (including Albert Schweitzer) was converted by the crystalline sound. Thomas Stevens wrote in the British journal *The Organ*, "I was very much struck with this instrument . . . the Advent organ was probably the finest small modern organ that I have heard."

More than any other, the Brimmer Street church can be called the birthplace of the American Classic organ. As time passed, the impact on organbuilding became more impressive and profound. Harrison's influence soon eclipsed his contemporaries, and the resplendent and instantly recognizable American Classic tone was widely imitated in this country for decades.

As Harrison owed much to those who went before, so we owe much to him. He was not alone in working toward brighter, more cohesive ensembles, but he was the most conspicuous champion of the trend. Much of the historical orientation in today's organbuilding is due to his pioneering efforts. Figuratively speaking, present-day American organbuilders first walked in Harrison's footsteps and then stood on his shoulders to achieve a prominence of their own.

* * *

What do we know of G. Donald Harrison? His instruments say much for themselves, but little of him. Historians analyze his achievements, but tend to neglect the man. More than 30 years have passed since Harrison's death, and few people remember him well. Already, his thinking and his inner motivation seem lost. We are left with the historian's lament: it is easy to establish *what* happened, but it is far more elusive and challenging to find out *why*.

This book is the answer. At last, Harrison and the other creators of the American Classic organ speak for themselves, and we can listen in. The phrase is apt. Most of these letters were dictated to secretaries who typed a literal transcript, and the words leap from the page in the writer's own voice. Harrison and his friends share their adventures, doubts, triumphs and technical discoveries. There are fascinating revelations, a wealth of anecdote, penetrating commentary, and some wonderfully pungent and even offensive lines. In the interest of completeness and authenticity, and to preserve the extraordinary flavor of the letters, Dr. Callahan has made no attempt to suppress statements which today might be considered prejudiced or even untrue. He has acted as historian, not critic, and has performed a major service to his sources and to us.

Good biography illuminates character, but as this chronicle unfolds Harrison and his associates develop *personality*. We come to feel we know them well, and we admire them despite their faults. Scholars will undoubtedly analyze the contents of this book for decades. In the meantime, we can enjoy unprecedented illumination of the American Classic organ and the lives of those who made it. Seldom in organ history has there been such enticement, entertainment, and, above all, such enlightenment in reading other people's mail.

Nelson Barden

Acknowledgments

A book of this nature could not appear in print without tremendous assistance. My greatest debt is to the letter-writers themselves, who have given us a front-row seat to over thirty years of organbuilding on both sides of the Atlantic.

An equal debt is owed to those who saved and shared letters. This book would not have been possible without the significant contributions of Mr. Henry Willis, 4. The support and encouragement of Michael and Stephen Harrison through many years of research is greatly appreciated. Jonathan Ambrosino, Nelson Barden, Ralph Downes, and Carl Weinrich have given much of their time and talents. And my parents have been consistently encouraging in so many ways.

Many others who helped did not live to see the completion of this book. It is my firm belief that they are making splendid music with the heavenly band.

My thanks to those whose names follow for their part in bringing this story to you.

Charles Callahan
Boston, Massachusetts
December, 1989

Stephen Adams	Michael Gariepy	William Rosser
Thomas H. Anderson	Donald M. Gillett	Royal College of Organists
Donald Austin	Catharine Crozier Gleason	Alexander Schreiner
Henry Karl Baker	Robert M. Harrison	William Self
Jack Bethards	John Hendricksen	John H. Steinkampf, Jr.
Mrs. E. Power Biggs	David Junchen	Anna Steinmeyer
Arthur Birchall	Alexander McCurdy	George Steinmeyer
Mabel Birdsong	Mary McGaffigan	Paul Steinmeyer
William F. Brame	Grace McGinness	Johnston Stewart
Bruce Buchanan	Jason McKown	Flora Symons
Paul Callaway	Joseph Morgan	William C. Teague
Neal Campbell	Charles Moseley	Sir George Thalben-Ball
Douglas Carrington	Granville Munson	Robert M. Turner
Dulwich College	Thomas Murray	John J. Tyrrell
Robert Covell	Robert Noehren	Edward A. Wallace
James Culp	Arnold Ostlund	William Watkins
Robert Cundick	Barbara Owen	Karl M. Watson
William F. Czelusniak	Roy Perry	Clarence Watters
Phillip C. Dodson	Bynum Petty	Raymond Whalon
Francis E. Dugal	Lawrence I. Phelps	Joseph S. Whiteford
George Faxon	Henriette Willis Ravet	Nora Williams
John Ferris	Mrs. Emerson Richards	J.C. Williams
John Fesperman	Thomas Richner	John Sinclair Willis
Mildred Fox	Albert Robinson	Charles Woodward
Edward B. Gammons	Rodgers Organ Company	
Gerald Gardner	Edward Rook	

Introductory Notes

The majority of the letters in this book are located at the Willis firm in a file labeled "American Correspondence." Not only did Henry Willis III save the letters from his American correspondents, but carbon copies of his replies as well. Of the hundreds, if not thousands of letters in the file, only those pertinent to the American Classic organ have been included here.

The Willis collection has been augmented by letters from the collections of William King Covell and E. Power Biggs, now located in the E. Power Biggs Organ Library at Boston University; and from Carl Weinrich, Ralph Downes and others. Sources are identified in the appendix following the Index of Letters.

The majority of the original letters were typed by secretaries from dictation; some were typed by the writers and others handwritten. Spelling has been generally standardized, as have the positions of inside addresses, salutations, closes, reference initials, etc. Punctuation has not been standardized but, for the sake of clarity, has occasionally been modified without comment.

About the Correspondents

Ernest M. Skinner 1866-1960

Ernest Martin Skinner is as important to American organ history as Father Willis is to English organ history. Skinner was not the only distinguished builder in the early 20th century, but his work was an important element in American organ evolution, just as Willis advanced the organ in the United Kingdom. These two men left legacies which typify the periods in which they lived.

Born in Clarion, Pennsylvania, Skinner had only a grade school education before apprenticing with George Ryder of Reading, Massachusetts. By 1893, Skinner joined the Hutchings firm as a draftsman. With this well-respected company, Skinner was involved with installations at the Mission Church, Roxbury, Massachusetts, and Symphony Hall, Boston. He also designed the first electric action that Hutchings built, for St. Bartholomew's Church, Manhattan. Shortly before Skinner left to form his own company (Skinner and Cole, 1901), Hutchings was awarded the contract for a new four-manual organ at Woolsey Hall, Yale University. This instrument was to become Hutchings' most prominent instrument, and a generation later one of the great organs of the world, after its rebuilding first by Steere and then by Skinner in 1929.

Ernest Skinner severed the connection with Cole and incorporated his own company in 1905, with the help of investors from Worcester, Massachusetts. His engaging and forthright personality secured several large contracts. Fine craftsmanship and solid construction characterized these early instruments, with tonal schemes typical of the period — a wide variety of unison stops and reduced emphasis on ensemble. Skinner had visited England in 1898, and was overwhelmed by Willis high pressure chorus reeds. He was welcomed at the Willis factory, and given information regarding the construction and voicing of their chorus reeds. Skinner remained unimpressed by the rest of the Willis ensemble, however, and upon his return began developing reed voicing and mechanical improvements.

A significant early organ which helped establish Skinner's reputation was the 1910 instrument for the Cathedral of St. John the Divine, Manhattan — the first of several collaborations and collisions between Skinner and the architect Ralph Adams Cram. The organ included cement swell boxes and fundamental diapasons, but was crowned by magnificent solo and chorus reeds, and ethereal soft stops unequalled by any other builder. These sounds quickly won a wide following.

Willis was one inspiration for these sounds, but another was the orchestra, to which Skinner was passionately devoted. At the time, Mahler, Ravel and Strauss were all contemporary masters, and they were Skinner's favorites. His love of orchestral effects led to his development of symphonic color and expression in the organ. Skinner's efforts had the approval of all leading organists during the era, when color, refinement and subtlety were paramount. Further, Skinner developed electropneumatic stop and key action, sensitive swell shade action and superb pitman chests. Coupling this superior mechanism to his elegant and well-appointed consoles, Skinner developed an entirely new style of organ.

These factors made Skinner the high priest of his profession, and established his instruments as the Rolls-Royce of organs. But Skinner was an artist, not an entrepreneur. He was so determined to create quality that the company finances suffered. During one of Skinner's minor financial crisis in 1919 (in part due to the post-War slump) he sold control of his business to Arthur Hudson Marks, a wealthy Manhattan financier. Marks knew Skinner's work, and had a Skinner residence organ in his home. The Skinner Company was reorganized with Marks as president, and Skinner and William Zeuch, a well-known organist and salesman, as vice-presidents. Later, Marks purchased the former Steere Organ Company of Westfield, Massachusetts, ran it independently for awhile, then merged it into the Boston operation. Marks also brought George Catlin into the company, who functioned in an administrative role.

In 1924, Ernest Skinner was at the height of his personal fame and influence. He had built nearly 500 organs, many of them large four-manual instruments in prominent institutions and churches. In addition, he had developed an ingenious automatic player mechanism, which allowed miniature Skinners into affluent homes. A well-earned European holiday was in order. In Paris, he inspected French organs and met Louis Vierne and Marcel Dupré. But it was Skinner's return to England after a 26-year absence that had the strongest effect. This time, Skinner was as mesmerized with the Willis diapason ensemble as he had been with the Willis reeds in 1898. When he returned to Boston, he began to make changes in his tonal designs to accommodate his new-found love of ensemble. And he invited Henry Willis III to America to help him.

Henry Willis III 1889-1966

Henry Willis III was the grandson of Father Willis, the illustrious founder of the firm which built many of England's most important organs. Toward the end of his life, Henry Willis I was given the name "Father" Willis by the editor of the *Musical Times*, who compared the Willis dynasty and its work to that of the 17th-century builder "Father" Smith. Willis' two sons, Henry II and Vincent, became partners in the family business in 1878. Vincent left the firm in 1894, and upon Father Willis' death in 1901 at the age of 79, Henry II assumed control of the company. In June 1910, he took into partnership his own son, Henry III, who was then 21 years old.

Due to the ill health of his father, Henry III gradually assumed direction of the firm. One of his first organs was built for the Lady Chapel of the new Liverpool Cathedral (1910), and its success assured that the mammoth organ in the Cathedral itself would be a Willis. By the time G. Donald Harrison first met Willis III in 1914, a significant percentage of the Liverpool Cathedral pipework had been completed in the factory. World War I service for both men intervened; between periods of active duty, Willis kept busy voicing the pipework which had been stored pending the end of war. The Liverpool Cathedral organ was finally dedicated in October, 1926. This instrument and the grand organ of Westminster Cathedral, London, completed in 1932, were among Willis III's greatest achievements.

A man of small physical stature but immense vitality and commanding presence, Willis III had apprenticed in every department of the factory. He combined an intimate knowledge of the practical details of organ building with a broad overview of its various national schools. Many visits to the Continent had given him detailed perceptions unequalled by any other organ builder of the day. Although he was broad-minded in introducing mechanical innovations to the factory, he inclined toward pomposity when it came to organ tone. Henry Willis, 4, his son and present head of the Willis firm, comments, "My father was a man of very definite opinions. He basically thought that anyone who did not agree with everything he did was a bloody fool. The alarming thing is that he was usually right."

This assessment is particularly revealing in light of Willis' letters regarding the work of Ernest Skinner and Donald Harrison. In his opinions, Willis was trenchantly outspoken. His concept of the ideal organ varied only slightly over the years.

G. Donald Harrison 1889-1956

George Donald Harrison's parents were both products of strict Victorian upbringing. His father, George Harrison (1857-1938), started work at age 10 in a cotton factory in Lancashire, England. Recognizing the lad's intelligence, his parents paid two pence a week to send him to night school. Later, he received a scholarship to study engineering at Owen's College, now Manchester University. George's grandfather had been an inventor, designing steam-pumping engines. During his college days, the boy worked inspecting steam boilers and then as sub-editor of a technical journal.

Before moving to London to become a chartered patent agent, George Harrison married Edith Leach, a young lady from his hometown, Oldham. Edith was the daughter of a stern Methodist minister. George and Edith had three children: Eric, who was wounded in the Royal Flying Corps in World War I and recovered to become a medical doctor in Sussex; a daughter, Renée; and George Donald, born April 29, 1889, in Huddersfield, Yorkshire.

The boy soon became known as "Don," and evidenced an interest in the organ at an early age. This resulted, in his own opinion, from listening to the excellent three-manual Lewis organ in the family church. At London's Dulwich College, he studied organ seriously enough to become an assistant organist in the chapel, which housed a George England organ. Dating from the 1790s, the organ had been carefully restored by the Lewis firm, under the direction of Dr. Edward John Hopkins, longtime organist of the Temple Church. It featured light-pressure diapasons, a mounted cornet and reverse-color keyboards. Harrison took his first lessons on this instrument and also used it for practice. He said later that it left a strong impression on him, and that his particular interest in mixtures began during his Dulwich days.

Also at college, he studied mechanical engineering. After graduation, he served an apprenticeship in the machine and drafting shops of J. Hopkinson and Co., a large Huddersfield engineering firm. At this time, Don studied organ with Arthur Pearson, organist of the four-manual Father Willis in Huddersfield Town Hall. After his apprenticeship, Harrison passed law examinations in order to work in his father's firm as a patent attorney. The Lewis firm had discouraged him from a career in organbuilding — "There is no money in it" — so Harrison contented himself with weekend visits to organs with the Rev. Noel Bonavia-Hunt, an organ enthusiast; Stuart Archer, a well-known organist, and Henry Willis III. Each instrument would be carefully examined, inciting lively discussions about the various tone colors and their blending properties. As Harrison later said, this was a remarkable course in ear-training.

During World War I, Harrison and Willis were active in His Majesty's Service. In 1919, Willis was instrumental in obtaining Harrison's demobilization and offered him a position at Willis and Sons. Harrison's mechanical training, fine ear and quiet, engaging personality made him popular with the Willis staff. In 1921, he was elected a director of the firm. His association with Willis III was a close one, for they were friends at work and at play. Harrison developed a profound respect for Willis' knowledge of voicing. During this period, many important organs were built and rebuilt, and Willis constantly experimented with all kinds of pipes and voicing methods. In an article in *The American Organist* in February, 1937, Harrison wrote:

> In England, so much organ work consists of rebuilding old instruments or using old pipes; those from practically all the famous English builders from Father Smith on passed through the Willis factory for revoicing during my time there; also there was one large organ from Cavaillé-Coll. Extraordinary changes in some cases were made to the pipes. I remember one set, which had been a flute for fifty years, was turned into a powerful 'cello.

A factor in Harrison's development was lifelong friendships with some of the century's finest organists. His personal friendship with Marcel Dupré dated from that organist's visit to England in 1920. Subsequently, Harrison made many trips to Paris and apparently grew deeply interested in Cavaillé-Coll organs. Later friendships with Lynnwood Farnam, Clarence Watters, Carl Weinrich, Ernest White and others focused his view of organbuilding more and more on the requirements of organ literature.

In 1927, the birth of Henry Willis, 4, signaled the continuation of the Willis dynasty, and Harrison realized that his opportunities for advancement were limited. He had met Ernest Skinner in 1924 when the American visited England, and had learned more about the Skinner Company from Willis, who had visited Boston in 1924, 1925 and 1926 as a consultant. In the spring of 1927, Arthur Hudson Marks visited the Willis factory, and offered Harrison a position on the Skinner staff. While Marks was either unwilling or unable to start Harrison as a director, as Harrison had been with Willis, it is apparent that even at this date, Marks was planning for the future and Ernest Skinner's eventual retirement.

On St. Patrick's Day, 1914, Harrison had married Dora Lang at St. Martin in the Fields. Dora was the daughter of Dr. Jackson Lang, a prominent physician active in London musical and sporting circles. After following Harrison to Boston in 1927, Dora left him abruptly less than two years later. She returned to England with their two young sons, Michael and Stephen and obtained a divorce. In 1945, she married Henry Willis III, whose wife had died during World War II.

Senator Emerson Richards 1884-1963

At the age of seven, most little boys can barely reach the pedals of an organ. Nonetheless, Emerson Lewis Richards, who was big for a seven-year-old, had his first lessons in 1893 on a Roosevelt organ in a Catholic Church near his parents' home on the boardwalk in Atlantic City, New Jersey. Emerson was an only child. His parents, of Welsh and French heritage, had amassed considerable real estate and business holdings, including a profitable bath-house in the resort town.

Richards received the L.L.B. from the University of Pennsylvania in 1906 and was admitted to the bar a year later. In 1911, he was elected to the New Jersey Assembly. His forceful personality and high intelligence, apparent even at the beginning of his political career, led to his appointment as Assembly Leader in 1912. After a single term in the Assembly, he ran successfully for the State Senate.

During World War I, Richards served concurrently as a Major in the Army and as Republican Majority Leader of the New Jersey Senate. His role in revising the State's laws in 1918 won him the reputation of being second only to Woodrow Wilson in his impact on the statute books. The following year, Richards had to leave the Senate when the Attorney General ruled that military officers could not hold legislative posts. In 1922, after overseeing financial disbursements pursuant to the construction of the Holland Tunnel connecting New Jersey with New York City, Richards was elected to the Senate once again. He remained in office for twelve years, during which he served twice as President of the Senate and once, briefly, as Acting Governor. In 1934, at the age of fifty, he retired from public office.

Richards' musical interests were broad, and like those of Ernest Skinner, encompassed the orchestral and operatic repertoire. For many years, Richards attended the Metropolitan Opera each Tuesday night of the season, and as many Philadelphia Orchestra concerts as his busy schedule would allow. But the pipe organ was his lifelong passion. He had a profound love for the instrument, a deep knowledge of its history and construction, and a desire to improve its status among musicians. Beginning in 1899, he installed in the family residence a series of increasingly larger organs. These included a 1914 Estey of 35 stops, voiced by William Haskell.

As a young organist, Richards' organ repertoire had been mainly orchestral transcriptions. His self-proclaimed "god" was W. T. Best, the leading English organist of the Victorian era and arranger of countless orchestral and operatic works for organ. In a letter to William King Covell, Richards recalled that "anytime I could wind up the Third Act of *Lohengrin* on one of Skinner's Dulcets, I was pretty sure to have the audience going. . . . The War *[World War I]* broke in on my playing and when I came back, most of my technical facility had disappeared. I plunged into the building of the Holland Tunnel and from that back into politics, until my days and nights have been so pre-empted that sometimes weeks go by without even as much as my touching the keyboard."

In the 1920s, Senator Richards began a series of trips to Europe to study historic organs, often in company with organbuilders Henry Willis III and Hans Steinmeyer. At that time few other Americans had done so, and the tonal and technical details of old European instruments were virtually unknown in this country. Richards began to see and hear why he had been dissatisfied with the performance of Bach on American organs, and thus began his early interest in ensemble, mixture-work and unenclosed Choir divisions. Over the following 35 years, he published a long series of articles (principally in *The American Organist*) on old European organs, which exerted enormous influence over the course of American organbuilding.

Only in the heady atmosphere of America in the Roaring Twenties could political and musical circumstances combine to produce the situation whereby Senator Richards was retained by Atlantic City as architect of the colossal Atlantic City Convention Hall organ. With seven manuals and 455 ranks, it was the largest organ in the world. The gigantic size and many unusual features indicated the exceptional scope of Richards' ambition, imagination, and technical expertise.

Lynnwood Farnam 1885-1930

Lynnwood Farnam was born in Sutton, Quebec, Canada. After early training with his mother, he went to England to complete his musical education. Returning to North America, he served as organist and choirmaster of Emmanuel Church, Boston, where he designed and supervised the installation of what was then Casavant Frères' largest organ.

Following World War I, Farnam moved to New York, where he served briefly at Fifth Avenue Presbyterian Church before accepting the post at Church of the Holy Communion. The organ, a 1910 Ernest Skinner, opus 185, was transformed by Farnam's magical registrations. Both Donald

Harrison and Alexander McCurdy are quoted as saying, "The organ is all wrong, but when he plays it, it's all right!"

Farnam's recitals throughout America and Europe established his reputation as one of the world's greatest organists. Dedication to his art and an unassuming, friendly nature endeared him to his fellow organists, who, with the general public, held him in high esteem. Clarity of line, impeccable and seemingly effortless technique, brilliant and colorful registration, and unflagging rhythm were the hallmarks of Farnam's style. He became the first head of the organ department at the Curtis Institute of Music, and edited for publication many compositions by early as well as modern composers. His pupils included Robert Cato, Robert Noehren, Alexander McCurdy, Carl Weinrich and Ernest White.

Carl Weinrich 1904-

Carl Weinrich was born in Paterson, New Jersey, in 1904. After earning his B.A. from New York University in 1927, he studied for three years with Lynnwood Farnam at the Curtis Institute. Weinrich also studied piano with Abram Chasins, and organ with Marcel Dupré.

After succeeding Farnam at the Church of the Holy Communion in Manhattan, Weinrich taught at Westminster Choir School (now College) from 1934 to 1940 and at Columbia University from 1942 to 1952. In 1943, Weinrich became organist and director of music at the Princeton University Chapel, a position which he held for 30 years.

Early in his career, Weinrich became identified with the classic organ. Although he played from an exceptionally broad repertoire, his tastes were patrician. His recordings of Bach were among the first records of classical organ music available in America.

William King Covell 1904-1975

William King Covell became interested in the organ in the 1920s when Ernest Skinner and his ideals dominated American organbuilding. Yet Covell was interested in organs from an historical viewpoint and watched the arrival of Donald Harrison with enthusiasm. From his undergraduate rooms at Harvard (A.B. 1928, A.M. 1930), he began a secondary career in letter-writing that continued unabated for almost half a century.

His letters to Harrison inquiring about Aeolian-Skinner organs often solicited the Englishman's opinions. Harrison's polite, reserved replies form a unique commentary on his own work. Harrison obviously thought well of Covell's writing; as early as 1932, Covell's description of the new Harvard organ appeared in the dedicatory program. And yet, the relationship between the two men remained formal for decades. Only in the last few years of their correspondence does Harrison begin "Dear King" instead of "Dear Mr. Covell."

Covell taught American History in the Newport, Rhode Island, high school. His other interests included steamboats and antiquities. But his life-long passion was the pipe organ. From his sprawling 1869 residence on Washington Street in Newport, he wrote frequent articles for organ journals on both sides of the Atlantic and corresponded regularly to organ friends such as Ned Gammons of the Groton School, Ed Flint of the Brooks School, Walter Holtkamp and Senator Emerson Richards.

Letters

Letters

1 Henry Willis to Ernest Skinner

Ernest M. Skinner Esq.
The Skinner Organ Co. Ltd
Dorchester
Boston Mass. U.S.A.

26th March 1924

Dear Mr. Skinner,

I hope that you had an interesting time in France and particularly that you called on Albert Dupré at Rouen and saw the Cavaillé-Coll at St. Ouen there.

As regards your visit here — it was all too short. You did not give me the chance to show you as much as I would have liked to for I was anxious to take you to try and hear small instruments as well as large ones to demonstrate that the same tonal build-up is present in all — thus ensuring correct ensemble.

Reference Washington Cathedral — I would very much like to see the specification for possibly I could make a few suggestions that would create an ensemble on "Willis" lines, and I would send you pipes indicating the scales and voicing & treatment that I would employ if I were doing the organ. I take it that the Tuba, Clarion, Mixture etc., would be used for Washington, so be sure to give the pitch. If so, I would also suggest my sending you at least C's of the complete Diapason chorus — leading up to the mixture.

Please ask for exactly what you want and you shall have it. Let me know the best way to consign goods so as to minimize freight tariff charges your end.

Now I want the following please!:

Sample magnet complete in chest. Samples of outside and inside primaries. Samples of exhaust diaphragm units — with drawstop action for both "straight" and "compound" sliderless chests. Samples of all electric action parts, complete drawings of electric key action at console showing couplers and cut outs. Drawing showing manual and pedal piston touch, full size drawings showing complete two- three- and four-manual consoles. Eight-station electric swell engine complete with balanced pedal and contacts, drawings of electro-pneumatic relay as used for pedal actions, i.e. one wire from pedal touch box and say eight out. Samples of the various units used in your combination action. Sample of reversible action.

French Horn 8ft complete — the type you consider your best — voiced on the pressure you consider the most suitable — French pitch i.e.

A 435. Sample pipes of the following stops — all the C's:

Corno d'Amour	Flauto Dolce
Gamba Celeste	Erzahler
Flute Celeste	English Horn
Orchestral Oboe	Gross Gedeckt
Bassoon	Heckelphone

all voiced on the pressure you consider best.

Would it be too much to ask for a complete sliderless chest of the "compound" type for an 8ft Tuba — scale to be 8ft.? This would be of enormous value and much more informative than drawings.

I hope that this list will not frighten you, but you told me to ask for what I wanted.

Will you please send the magnet first giving all electrical data as I want to have some made at once — what do they cost you to make?

I hope to be able to visit you in September.

Kind regards from all here.

Yours very sincerely,
Henry Willis

P. S. Reference 8 Station Swell Engine may I have <u>the complete unit</u> as well as the drawing?

Albert Dupré at Rouen — father of Marcel Dupré

---

2 Ernest Skinner to Henry Willis

June 9, 1924

Henry Willis, Jr.,
234 Ferndale Road,
Brixton, London,
S.W.9.

My dear Willis:

Placing the armature above the magnet favors the magnet by twice the weight of the armature. In the one case you have the weight of *[the]* armature helping the magnet, in the other, the weight of the armature is <u>against</u> the magnet. The difference between +1 and -1 is 2. Also, when the armature is below, dirt falls into it. In a 30 days test on an automatic test we hitched up 30 armatures above magnet and 30 below. We put sawdust into the magnet chamber. We got over 50 ciphers on the one and none on the other. The magnets were operated by automatic circuit breakers. You will be surprised if you put a 6" pressure or even less on the box, at what the armature will lift. Push down on it with a ½" wire nail and you will see it will lift the nail and a lot beside.

I would very much like the drawings of the zinc rolling machine. Send it as soon as you can conveniently.

Our pitch is 440A.

I note a French Horn in the Liverpool scheme. Good work. Are you going to give me credit for it?

This thought has occurred to me. I am quoting your work exclusively and making as much as possible of your Mixtures which I am going to follow up with some articles on my trip to England.

What do you say to a statement that we have entered into an artistic alliance? We are each in the premier position in our country. It cannot fail to be of help to both of us. The thought is very pleasant to me. I have no thought of claiming anything for myself, whatever influence I may have on anything you do over there. It will be entirely in your hands to regulate as you think best. I feel that the idea will help us both, but of course I want you to agree to any statement of this sort, or I cannot make it, however true.

I want a complete 16' Swell reed such as you put in Westminster Cathedral. I want also to know if you can get a good result with it on a 7½" pressure.

I made a Chorus Mixture exactly as you told me, but to my great surprise I could get no power out of it with that cut up. I had to cut it up considerably more before it would sound with the clang I heard at Westminster.

I have all the models ready to ship. I am sorry that the chest will not show the standard construction of chest with the channels above the wind. The interchangeable chest shows channels below, but you can probably get it from the drawings.

Send me that Mixture and one of the triangular Flutes.

I expect to ship the models as soon as the sample pipes are done.

There is a spring in the secondary of the stop action which stops any pipes sounding when wind comes on. The switches and magnets are fastened to the model of the keyboard for convenience only. If any of the "tracker touch" pins falls out in shipment you can put them in again.

The movies came out fine. I had a wonderful trip but Holy Moses what a condition in France!

Please take note of the dip of touch and height of sharp, also that sharps are plumb on sides instead of inclined. This gives more room between keys and also the small height of sharps made possible by the 5⁄16 dip of key makes it easy to play what are, with the older type, somewhat difficult positions.

Can you send us a four-manual set of your thick ivory keys from the model or drawings we are sending, keeping exactly our design or what do we have to do to get a four manual set every set alike?

Sincerely yours,

E.M.S.

EMS/HML

P.S. Damn Hope-Jones

N.B. By a statement of an artistic alliance I mean on such occasions as we may find it helpful or useful or anyway you perhaps may like to suggest. You may depend on my keeping within the lines that you suggest. I am not looking for any appearance of showing you how to do it. If you think that ever I'll biff you on the nose. But don't return the compliment! E.M.S.

Armature above the Magnet — It was Skinner practice to mount chest magnets upside down.

Our Pitch is 440A — International Pitch was established as A440 at 68° F., except for the United States, which is A440 at 70° F., at two international conferences held in London in 1938 and '39.

French Horn in the Liverpool Scheme — this stop was one of Ernest Skinner's proudest developments.

Damn Hope-Jones — Robert Hope Jones (1859-1914), an inventive organbuilder born in England, where he premiered the use of electric action and movable consoles. He later emigrated to the United States and worked briefly for Austin in Hartford and Skinner in Boston before establishing his own firm and, later, developing the unit orchestra. Traditional organbuilders such as Skinner and Willis found it difficult to counteract Hope-Jones' tonal influence, which embraced complete unification, orchestral scaling and total enclosure.

---

3 George Catlin of Skinner firm to Henry Willis

December 26, 1924

Mr. Henry Willis
c/o Henry Willis & Sons
  and Lewis & Co., Ltd.
234 Ferndale Road
Brixton,
London, Eng.
Dear Willis,

Received your fine letter written on the steamer. Intended to reply before this date but have been waiting to get a few things in shape to enclose.

In the first place, regarding our factory organization, I submit the following, which will probably serve to refresh your memory, as you no doubt will recall practically all of these facts when you see them in writing.

The factory is divided into ten departments as follows:

Department	Foreman
Mill & Lumber Storage	Weston
Chest, Pedal, Bass & Wood Pipes	Larson
Action, Console and Reservoir	Eklund
Small parts for stock	Goddard
Frames & Sills and Casework	Sivertsen
Finish & Painting	Morrill
Assembling	Westhaver
Pipe Setting	Rooney
Reed Voicing	Bolton
Flue Voicing	Goodman

As you probably know, Bolton and Goodman report directly to this office as to schedule, and to Mr. Skinner, of course, as to the technical end of the work.

A production chart, a copy of which is enclosed, is placed in each department to be recorded daily by the foreman. A master chart of the same form is maintained in the superintendent's office and also in this office, which shows the organs in process and percentage of completion from day to day and week to week.

A chart, also the same form, is kept in the lumber storage room showing the weekly inventory and daily consumption and incoming stock.

A reservoir chart is kept in the action room and superintendent's office showing reservoirs required for organs and production so that reservoirs made on stock orders may be ordered in time to meet the rest of the organ on the assembly floor.

A wood pipe stock chart is kept in the chest department and superintendent's office for the same purpose as the reservoir chart.

A so-called factory bible showing the organ production and schedule dates of shipments is sent out by the superintendent to each foreman at least once a month with a copy to the storekeeper and engineering department.

Also at the same time a shortage list of supplies needed is sent to this office, engineering department and storekeeper. This list not only shows the shortage of supplies and organ parts necessary for production but also shows the shortage of information required from the engineering department, specifying the particular part of the particular organ for which this information is needed.

The superintendent has a weekly meeting of the foremen on each Monday at 11 a.m. in which matters of production and other matters of interest to the employees are discussed.

Once a month and sometimes oftener, as sales conditions make it necessary, the general manager makes up a schedule of organ shipments, furnishing copies to the sales department, superintendents, engineering department and Mr. Hanley.

Also once a week we have a short meeting in which Mr. Martin, representing the engineering department, Mr. Black, superintendent, Mr. Keating, as purchasing agent and the writer takes up each organ in process of production to have a general check up as to information, outside purchases, etc. so that there will be no passing of the "buck" from one department to another and no misunderstanding as to the actual conditions of each organ in process.

Regarding a works superintendent, I am afraid it would be very difficult to find a man fulfilling all of your specifications. In other words, it would be an exceptional man who had been trained as a draftsman and organ builder and could also be an efficient organizer. If you would be satisfied to get simply an organ builder capable of laying out jobs and at the same time a fair draftsman, the former works manager of the Steere Plant at Westfield, Mass., H.F. VanWart, would answer that description. I could not recommend him however as an efficient organizer, as he had a way of carrying a great deal of information under his hat and though he was very clever as an organ builder and had considerable inventive genius, he ran things in the shop by rule of thumb methods rather than modern methods. Of course he would be helpful on electric action, as he thoroughly understands it.

He left us about a year and a half ago as he got into trouble with his wife and left the State of Massachusetts in order to avoid legal service. Not long ago he applied to us for reinstatement but we have no place for him now. I do not know where he can be reached at the present time, but if you wanted to get in touch with him [I] believe we might be able to locate him. If you should seriously consider getting him, I would want you to understand all about him in advance. I imagine he would be glad to get to England and could probably be secured at a very reasonable rate considering his knowledge of organ building, but I would not recommend him as an organizer.

Answering your question on the subject of salesmen, I will briefly outline the general policy of our company.

As you probably surmise, very few spectacular jobs are contracted for without an inquiry being sent to the Skinner Organ Company. These inquiries, whether they come to our New York office or Boston, are turned over to Mr. Skinner or Mr. Zeuch, who handle them by correspondence until it becomes advisable to make a visit to the committee or persons in charge of the prospect. As you could easily see, Skinner and Zeuch work

Henry Willis III

with fine harmony on these things and Zeuch does much more traveling than Skinner. As they both have so many friends all over the country, we often get advance notice of projects through these friends.

We also receive a great many inquiries from small churches who know of our reputation but have no acquaintance with anyone in the organization. These inquiries are usually handled by Mr. Kingsbury at the New York office working directly under Mr. Marks' supervision and sometimes he goes out himself to call on the purchasers. Other times he sends Mr. Cameron, whom you may also have met at our New York office, who knows the organ pretty thoroughly and is also a good draftsman.

The inquiries we receive from the South and Southwest, which do not run into organs costing over $20,000.00, are usually handled by an agent we have in the South under the direction of Mr. Kingsbury. This agent works on a commission basis averaging about seven percent and pays all his own traveling expenses etc. out of this commission. He is a pretty good salesman and sells pretty nearly enough small organs to keep our Westfield Plant in operation. We have a few more agents around the country including a couple on the Pacific Coast, but when they get on to a real big job usually Skinner or Zeuch will go out to close up the contract and be sure that the specifications are satisfactory to Skinner's artistic standpoint.

We hope that during 1925 Skinner will not have to be away from the factory so much, and we have plans already drawn and working drawings made and approved for the extension over our office here and we have hopes of going ahead with this work this year.

We are making up models of the new console mechanism designed by Skinner, and we have hopes that this new mechanism will be practical and efficient so that we can adopt it very soon.

We recently received your order for further material in connection with the electric action and I hope to give you something definite about shipments of all this material within a few days, but as I have been trying for about two weeks to get off this letter to you, I am not going to hold it up any longer.

I am glad to say that we have been favored with quite a number of new contracts this month totaling almost $150,000.00 in value, so with these added to what we already have booked in advance we feel very optimistic about 1925.

Just received your note enclosing copy of your letter to Mr. L. which I will simply hold in my personal file awaiting any developments.

I feel that I have not made a very good start as to promptness in answering your letters but I hope to improve my reputation in this respect.

With very best regards.

> Very truly yours,
> George Catlin

GLC:MEC
Encls.

An agent we have in the South — Harjung Tchakarian (1882-1959) known as "Uncle Chick," a loquacious, likeable Armenian who had trained with Ingraham in Scotland. He migrated to the U.S., became one of Skinner's best salesman, and set a record by selling four four-manual organs in one day — opus 470, 471, 472 and 473.

H.F. VanWart — Harry VanWart worked at Hutchings and was an early investor and manager in E.M. Skinner's company. Apparently because of disagreement with another investor, VanWart left Skinner for the Steere factory in Westfield. When A.H. Marks purchased Steere in 1921, VanWart moved to New Jersey to operate a chain of movie theatres. In 1929, Siebert Losh hired him to supervise the work on the Atlantic City Convention Hall Organ.

new console mechanism — an improved combination action allowing more pistons

---

4 Ernest Skinner to Henry Willis

December 26, 1924

Mr. Henry Willis
c/o Henry Willis & Sons and Lewis & Co., Ltd.,
234 Ferndale Road
Brixton, London, Eng.
My dear Mr. Willis:

I now rise to break my long silence occasioned by extended absences from this office and lack of opportunity when at the office.

The first thing I have to say is with regard to the swell engine, which you are kind enough to approve. The success of these swell engines depends on other features outside the engine itself, but before mentioning these outside features I want to say a word about the regulation of the engine.

First, it should have plenty of wind pressure; second, the valves exhausting the motors should be choked so that the motors cannot exhaust in less than one second of time — a second and a quarter would probably be better. Another rule of thumb which may be followed in adjusting these valves is that there should be no slam when the folds close — not using any air cushion, the slam can be taken entirely out without making them slow in response.

You will find the magnets numbered. Number one operates first and number two second, etc. This tends to keep the levers level and to make them operate generally level and it reduces the effect of angularity on them.

The motor serves to close the shades and a spring should be used to open them. The spring should have a long draw without a material increase in the pull. In other words, the spring should have a good length so that the last inch of pull does not develop a resistance materially greater than the first inch. The spring should be located on the action as near the shutters as possible. While this increases the friction throughout the train of mechanism it eliminates all backlash for reasons which will be obvious to you. If the shutters are too thick and heavy you will not be able to obtain the Sforzando effects which are otherwise possible. Our standard thickness of shutters is as shown on the blueprint which I send.

This is a question of inertia. We make the shades vertical. They ride on a metal point resting on metal of another kind which makes them well-nigh frictionless, which is not the case where they are horizontal and rest on a pin at both ends.

Kindly note the shape of the toggle on this shade which opens to an angle of 45. You will note that the motion of the toggle is one-half each side of a line which is at right angles with the shutters. This makes each movement of the motor of equal value except that the lap of the folds softens the preliminary portion of the opening at which point the effect is most apparent. The bevel on the edge of the fold has been planned to make the most effective closure and to discount the effect of warping as far as possible, which in the case of the rabbeted shades used by some organ-builders has no offset whatever. I do not feel that I need to go into this point further with a builder of your calibre, as reference to the point will be apparent and sufficient. The spring should be at the lightest possible tension that will work the folds. It will probably not be necessary to choke more than eight of the valves out of the sixteen, the same being numbers one to eight inclusive. This varies with the case depending on conditions.

The old type of toggle, which is used where the folds open square, is not satisfactory in connection with this motor for the reason that the first opening opens the shades so much more than with the toggles shown in the drawing, unless some offsetting device is employed in the train of mechanism, which I will not go into, but it increases complication and puts leverage on both the spring and the motor at a disadvantage. Of course in small organs where there is not much in the swell box to hold back, a thinner shade can be used than where the swell is of the calibre of Westminster Cathedral although the distance from that swell to the congregation will cause shades to be more effective than where the swell is in close proximity to the congregation, because the small amount of sound that gets out around the shutters will not travel as far as the big amount that comes out when they are open, which you have undoubtedly found by experience, the same as I have.

If you will follow my directions to the letter, it may save you some time in experimenting and also help our motor to give a good account of itself at the outset. After learning what you can from following these directions, you can go ahead from that point according to your necessities.

The angle at the edge of the fold previously referred to is plotted to accomplish several things. If the angle is too flat the folds are apt to become locked and if it is too sharp they are apt to slam; also in the latter case, the increase in the sound when the shades begin to open is not in correct proportion. The angle shown is the best for all purposes and quite important.

The mixtures are working out wonderfully. I do not know which I like best, the French V rank Cornet or the English Quint Mixture. They are both an extraordinary improvement on anything we ever had here and are doing wonders for the ensemble.

Your magnet has not yet arrived. Shall be glad to see it when it does get here. Wish I could put more 'go' into the idea of using rolling machines and hard zinc, but as I have found on previous occasions it is very hard to get an innovation of this kind started.

Upon what pressure is the Diapason 8' C you sent us supposed to speak? We found it best at 5". The strings you sent are very fine in quality but softer than we are accustomed to in a Salicional. Upon what pressure were they voiced? The Diapason has some very agreeable qualities but I think our larger toned ones are more effective in standing up to the Willis type reed than the wide mouth Diapason. I am reserving judgment on it until I know it better. I feel that I have so far gotten more out of the contact between the other side than you have with contact with this side, speaking tonally, for the reason that I think I form opinions less hastily than you do. I do not reject a thing at the outset simply because it is not like what I am

Ernest M. Skinner, center; Arthur Hudson Marks, right; Chandler Goldthwaite and an unidentified person.

accustomed to. I get better acquainted with it and see how it fits in with other material before I form an opinion. You know I am of English descent. I think your mind works more like that of an American in haste in forming opinions. At least I got the distinct impression that you didn't care much for our tone, unless you were, as usual, trying to string me, or rag me as you call it.

With regard to the pressure reducing valve, of which we made a model when I was in your works, I made one about the same size recently, which gave me the same trouble that the one did over there, namely, it set up a vibration. I found a complete cure for this in cutting out a ring of leather which I glued around the hole, fuzzy side up. This made a soft seat for the valve which completely killed the vibration.

Shall be glad to see the sample reed you talked of sending, one of which I think was an Oboe.

We found it about twice as difficult to voice the Trumpets for the Florida organ on 12" than is customarily the case on 10" and under. Haven't had time to look into this yet to find out why.

We have just received a contract to build a very large organ for a Masonic Hall in Detroit and another for the Peabody Conservatory of Music, Baltimore.

I am glad to be able to squeeze this letter into the small amount of time at my disposal. Regards to Mr. Harrison, Goss-Custard and the rest of my friends over there.

Are you reading Audsley's interminable words in <u>The American Organist</u> on the "Behavior of Organ Pipes?" Perhaps if he knew more about it he could say it in fewer words.

Sincerely yours,

Ernest M. Skinner

EMS:MEC

Encls. (1)

With regard to the swell engine — The Skinner whiffletree Swell Engine consisted of 16 pneumatic motors tied together with levers resembling a whiffletree, the pivoted swinging bars used to attach teams of horses to a wagon. Properly adjusted on heavy wind pressure, whiffletree engines made possible smooth crescendos as well as sharp accents without slamming the shades.

Your magnet — In electro-pneumatic action, keys, pedals and other console devices operate small electric magnets located inside the organ chests. Each magnet contains an air valve that energizes the action. There are hundreds of magnets in a small organ; large instruments contain thousands. Skinner's magnets were reliable but expensive.

Rolling machines and hard zinc — American bass pipes employed soft annealed zinc shaped by hand; Willis used hard zinc shaped by machine.

The Florida organ — Skinner opus 501, four-manual, Auditorium of the University of Florida, Gainesville.

Audsley's interminable words — George Ashdown Audsley (1838-1925) was an organ enthusiast and critic, best remembered for his two volume work *The Art of Organ Building* (1905) and *The Organ of the Twentieth Century* (1919).

12

PERSONAL
26th May 1925

Mr. Ernest Skinner
Skinner Organ Co.
Dorchester
Boston, Mass. U.S.A.

My dear Skinner,

Thanks for yours of the 24th April — but I am sure that I do not know what I have done that you should "Mr." me!

Your remarks re: swell engines are very interesting. I do not agree with the thin shades you favor. Of course thin and light shades help the engines, but I do not consider that the crescendo can be so good. As I think I told you I use boxes and shades 2" thick to contain stops speaking on pressures up to 6" — 3" thick on pressures above that. At Liverpool the swell boxes are 4" thick with 3" thick shades.

I have done some very successful swell engines recently both whiffle-tree and concertina — with my uncle's floating lever control — all connected with a cam action to get a slow first opening.

I am glad that you are getting on all right with the mixtures — Farnam writes enthusiastically about your work in this connection.

I am surprised to learn that you find it "very hard to get an innovation of this kind started" (referring to rolling machines for hard zinc). I felt sure that you would be able to go straight for it.

I will send you one of our magnets as soon as I can spare one! This sounds ludicrous but supplies come in so slowly that the works manager is crying for magnets all the time. However you will have one soon.

I am sending per S.S. "Scythia" 5 rank Mixture exactly as the Grand Chorus at Westminster Cathedral but voiced on 5" instead of 4". It was voiced on the machine you sent over and I had no difficulty about cut up which was normal. You have to cut up more on account of your absolutely flat <u>lower lips</u> which I hold to be a bad form of construction except for very small Diapason work voiced on pressures not exceeding 3" it being the early English type.

The sample pipes sent to you were voiced on 5" wind as mentioned in letter to Catlin dated 13/2/25. The power of a Salicional is not a defined thing over here — every firm has a different idea of what it should be. I sent you an average treatment.

I am sorry to have to disagree with you entirely upon the subject of diapasons — the leathering of diapasons etc., kills their blending properties. I can get all the power that can possibly be required by suitable scaling and pressure. I put in a whopper at Eton College last year CC 7⅝" 4th mouth on 10" wind that has its harmonics fully developed and so <u>blends</u>. You do not want diapasons to "stand up" to the reeds but to blend with them, and this effect cannot be obtained with very foundational diapasons. Shall I send you one of these big diapasons — same scale as the No.2 8ft Diapason on the Great at Liverpool Cathedral voiced on 10" wind or 12" if to stand on a chest with reeds? I think that it would convert you; say from tenor C up.

As regards forming opinions hastily — well, a man who knows what he wants and hears what he doesn't want ought to form an opinion at once. Anything that does not conduce to perfect ensemble (except of course certain solo stops) I consider wrong. To be quite candid, as I was when over with you, you don't get a <u>true</u> ensemble and won't until you adopt the necessary design, forms of construction, and voicing that are necessary to obtain this result.

To merely add proper mixtures is not sufficient though a step in the right direction. I have got a lot from you mechanically and I want you to <u>get</u> all I can give you tonally.

I am at a loss to understand why you found the trumpets on the Florida Organ more difficult to voice on 12" than on 10" — we find that the higher the pressure, the easier on our system it becomes. I suppose your voicer increased the brass weights one size?

No, I only skim through Audsley's tosh — it's hardly worth the reading.

I see Elliot has transferred his allegiance to the Welte-Mignon.

Yours very sincerely

Henry Willis

I see Elliot — Robert Pier Elliot (1871-1941) was the first Vice President of the Austin Organ Company in 1898, founder of the Kinetic Engineering Co. (1904), president of the Hope-Jones Organ Co. (1909), eastern manager of the Kimball Organ Co. (1914), general manager of Robert Morton Co. (1916), general manager of the Kimball Organ Co. (1918), and from 1925 to 1927 general manager of the Welte Organ Company. Subsequently he held similiar positions with Aeolian and Wurlitzer before returning to the Kimball Co. from 1929 to 1933. A polished gentleman and acknowledged expert, Elliot corresponded widely.

6 George Catlin to Henry Willis

July 1, 1925

Mr. Henry Willis
234 Ferndale Road
Brixton, London, England.
Dear Willis:

Your letter of June 15th received, and am very glad you have decided to come over again this fall. You really ought to see what our winters are like, for I certainly suffered enough during two winters during the War in your otherwise delightful country.

Mr. Skinner has gone off on what he says will be a short trip to California. Otherwise he would want me to send you his regards. Zeuch is here and wants to be remembered to you.

With best regards, I am,

Very truly yours,
G.L. Catlin

GLC/HML

---

7 Henry Willis to George Catlin

PRIVATE
25th May 1926

Mr. George L. Catlin Esq.
Skinner Organ Co.
Dorchester
Boston, Mass. U.S.A.
Dear George,

In January you said that in a few days you would be sending me a tremolo and sforzando pedal! Where are they? If not dispatched don't bother about them, but just send blueprints.

I wrote a letter to Zeuch on 15th March and asked him to show it to you — did he and what about it? Bill Zeuch is a rotter at writing.

I enclose a copy of letter received from Skinner and copy of my reply. Skinner is hopeless and, I am afraid, will not progress. It is the same old trouble. "You can't teach an old dog new tricks."

What you need is somebody to take Skinner's place when he is away and be in charge of the artistic side of production in Boston. I wrote to Bill and said that my chap Harrison would "fill the bill" — what about it? You must have someone to take Skinner's place when the inevitable happens. I could spare Harrison as I have some young men coming along. Did Bill Zeuch show you my letter and acquaint you with my suggestions?

All being well and assuming that you want me I propose to sail for Boston on October 23rd next. Try and persuade Bill to come over this summer.

Cheerio — write me all the news.

Yours ever,

H.W.

H.W./K.C.

when the inevitable happens — In 1926, Skinner would turn 60 years old. His personal popularity and professional standing had helped establish him as the leading organbuilder of his generation. But he was not without critics, particularly among younger organists returning from European study. Arthur Hudson Marks, president of the Skinner company, and the management wanted to keep options open on future development.

---

8 George Catlin to Henry Willis

June 11, 1926

Mr. Henry Willis
Rotunda Organ Works,
234 Ferndale Road,
Brixton, London, England
Dear Henry,

Your letter of May 25th enclosing certain correspondence received.

Regarding Harrison, I find that he made a very good impression on both Mr. Marks and Ernest and we would like to have him in our organization. We could not however start him in at or near the top, for this would only make trouble all around. If he would be willing to come over here and go into our drafting room directly under Perry Martin, depending on his ability and diplomacy to work out his future, we would like the idea first rate.

I believe, as you do, that there would be a good future for him here, provided he was willing to be in a receptive mood for the first year or two until he became thoroughly acquainted with American practices and conditions and that the plan might work out well for all concerned. We of course could not pay any fancy salary without also making trouble, but his future would be dependent pretty much on himself and, from all accounts, his ability would have a tendency to make him more and more valuable as time goes on.

Would appreciate it if you would talk over this matter with him and give us a line on his reaction to this proposition and also tell us about what amount in salary you think would interest him to start in with the Skinner Company, under the conditions outlined above.

Bill is talking quite seriously about coming over this Summer and I would not be a bit surprised if he really got there, though he will probably write you himself a little later on this subject.

Our sales are running just about the same as last year and I believe our production for the year will be the same, or possibly a little more than 1925.
...

[George Catlin]

[The close and signature do not survive; the letter may be incomplete.]
Bill is talking — William Zeuch

---

9 G. Donald Harrison to Ernest Skinner

17th September, 1926

Mr. E.M. Skinner
215 Sidney Street,
Dorchester, Mass. U.S.A.
My Dear Mr. Skinner,

In further reference to my letter of the 8th instant; our selection of records by The Gramophone Co. has been forwarded per parcel post as per settled invoice enclosed herewith. I was unfortunately unable to secure trade terms and the prices charged are at the ordinary retail price.

The Columbia Co. state that under agreement they are not allowed to send records to America unless instructed to do so by the New York House. They also state that there is an exchange of records and that you are almost sure to be able to obtain those you require without delay from their Boston House. Anyway, they will be able to get them for you.

Willis sends his best wishes and says don't trouble to send over a cheque for the above as you can give it to him when he goes over to America.

We are running a special train from London to Liverpool and back on the 23rd Oct. so as to give organists here a chance of attending the recital in the afternoon. It is causing some wild excitement. I want to fix a Tuba on the front of the locomotive voiced 200 lbs. per sq. inch!

You must have had a busy but interesting time at the conventions. How did you like the big Austin there?

With kindest regards,

Very sincerely yours,
G.D.H.

GDH/TH

a special train — Willis hired a train to transport London organists to Liverpool for the dedication of the Cathedral organ, the largest instrument in England.

The big Austin — a large four-manual Austin built for the Sesquicentennial Exposition in Philadelphia, now in Irvine Auditorium, University of Pennsylvania.

---

10 George Catlin to Henry Willis

December 30, 1926

Mr. Henry Willis
   234 Ferndale Road,
     Brixton, London
       England

Dear Henry:

Received your personal letter and also the full report on your visit and believe we shall really do something in connection with your recommendations before another six months even rolls by.

Regarding Mr. Harrison, I appreciate your friendly tip and Mr. Marks is definitely planning to come over in connection with this subject in the early Spring, so I trust Mr. Harrison will not make any commitments before he has a talk with Mr. Marks.

Furthermore, Mr. Marks has another subject of a larger caliber which he will want to discuss with you when he arrives.

I am sending a check for the balance of your expenses, etc., next week, which I trust will be satisfactory.

Wishing you a really prosperous 1927, I am

                   Yours very truly,
                   George

GLC/W

subject of a larger caliber — Arthur Hudson Marks wanted to merge with or buy out the Willis Company. When he broached the subject, Willis is said to have replied, "Buy the Willis Company? You might buy Westminster Abbey more easily!"

2nd May, 1927

Mr. George L. Catlin
E.M. Skinner Organ Co.
Crescent Avenue
Dorchester, Mass. U.S.A.

Dear George,

I am delighted that Harrison has accepted Mr. Marks' offer and decided to join you. He is a fine chap and exactly the type you want. He will be sure to have a big future with you.

Now a chap called Pickett, our Liverpool Foreman (our Liverpool works compares with London just as Westfield compares with Dorchester) wants to go to America now: he came to me immediately after the War and got on so well and impressed me so considerably that I selected him to be transferred to Liverpool to be in charge of the erection of the Cathedral organ, which he was and since its completion he has been in charge of the job, mechanism, tuning, charging plant, everything, so is an all round man. If he passes the doctor in July would you have a job for him? He would make an excellent erector for about a year, then would be thoroughly conversant with methods (in fact a week in the factory would do that really), then would be fitted for better things. Pickett doesn't drink and therefore is ideally suited to the United States, but he smokes and drinks milk!

Let me know and what his pay would be. If he goes over I would rather he went to you and you told me that you had room for tip-top men.

<u>Send</u> Bill over this summer, it will pay the Skinner Co.

No news of Skinner; I thought he was coming over!

Harrison sails on 5th July for New York.

All the best,

Yours ever,

H.W.

H.W./K.C.

ideally suited to the United States — Prohibition was in effect.

11th May, 1927

Mr. William E. Zeuch
c/o The Skinner Organ Co.
Crescent Avenue
Dorchester, Mass.
U.S.A.

My dear Bill,

Really glad to get your letter. Awfully glad that Harrison will be going to you. You two fellows will get on splendidly.

As Harrison will be over in July, you will be able to turn over your prospects to him and come over here. Book your passage and so commit yourself definitely.

I know the troubles and the people you are up against.

Don't forget that certain basic errors have been made in the use of mixtures etc.; an ensemble must be retained. In spite of what dear old Skinner writes (can he think it?), a mixture is not an independent effect like a celeste (or a tuba) and everything has got to be right to go with it. A brilliant mixture against thick toned reeds is simply silly. To take the Westminster Cathedral big mixture, lop off the top rank (29) and use it, is simply silly. But you know this. Harrison will help you guide Skinner's feet which stray from the straight and narrow path!

St. Patrick's Cathedral looks like a cert for Balbiani unless you go behind Yon to the authorities, why not? Yon will never be any use to you so down him.

St. Vincent Ferrer is the foulest thing ever.

Glad you have made it up with Courboin.

Yes, Elliot and Co. seem to be "in the soup."

Cheerio — all the best,

Yours ever,
H.W.

H.W./K.C.

a cert for Balbiani . . . go behind Yon — Pietro Yon, the organist of St. Patrick's Cathedral, wanted the Italian organbuilder Balbiani to build the cathedral organ. Willis advises Zeuch, who sold many large jobs for Skinner, to circumvent Yon and approach the church authorities directly.

St. Vincent Ferrer — A Manhattan church on Lexington Avenue with a 1924 Balbiani, which Willis had visited the previous fall.

Elliot and Co. — the Welte-Mignon Corporation was nearing bankruptcy, in the first year of Elliot's tenure there.

13 Arthur Thompson of Welte firm to Henry Willis

Septemper 1, 1927

Mr. Henry Willis
234, Ferndale Road,
Brixton, London, ENGLAND
Dear Willis:

I have delayed for some time answering your letter of July 5th and owe you all kinds of apologies.

You will be interested in knowing that Reginald Goss-Custard put over a magnificent recital in St. Louis. It was one of the best things I have ever heard done in the country. Everybody was tremendously pleased and complimented his work highly.

Harrison seems to be taking a hold very well up at Skinners and seems to be perfectly happy — a thing which he has no doubt told you. I heard a good many jobs on the trip and am thoroughly convinced now that the real organ building lies between ourselves and Skinner, but of course they have a tremendous advantage in selling because of their old tradition. Kimball's do excellent mechanical work and beautiful pipe work, but there is absolutely no tone direction to the place.

Our studio organ is finished and is very satisfactory. Whitelegg is head voicer now and works very hard. He has broken up some bad tendencies we had at first, due to other men in the department. It is now turning out real diapasons much better than those in Boston. The reeds are very good — free and yet no trace of Cor Anglais tone as is common in American bright chorus stops.

Mr. Elliot is out at present but I know he sends his best regards and I do the same.

Sincerely yours,

Arthur Thompson

AJT:FG.

Whitelegg is head voicer — Like Harrison, Richard Whitelegg worked for Henry Willis before emigrating to the United States. Before World War I he trained at several English organ works, including Harrison and Harrison. After the war, Whitelegg worked as a voicer and finisher for Willis, and was involved with the Liverpool Cathedral and Westminster Cathedral organs. He came to America first as a London representative for Aeolian, then as head voicer for Welte, and finally as a voicer for Möller, where he became Tonal Director. For this firm, he created many organs on Willis lines which still exist today. He died in 1945.

14 Stephen Stoot of Casavant to Henry Willis

September 8th, 1927

Mr. Henry Willis,
   234, Ferndale Road,
      BRIXTON, LONDON, S.W.9, England

Dear Mr. Willis:

I received your letter of July 4th and after reading the last paragraph about Donald Harrison going to Skinners, on a visit as I understood, I made arrangements at the office to have them get in touch with me (in the event of my being away) as soon as any message arrived from him. I was on my vacation for two weeks in Michigan, and then returned to Toronto for two weeks. In Toronto I attended a recital of Healey Willan, and just after it began I was surprised to find Goss-Custard sitting in the same pew with me. I asked him where Harrison was, and he said he believed he had returned. Perhaps he misunderstood my question, but imagine my amazement when I arrived home and saw in the September <u>Diapason</u> that he had gone to Skinners to stay. I hope he will be happy there. . . .

I trust you have plenty of business, and with kind regards, I remain,

Yours very sincerely,
Stephen Stoot

SS/SC

Stephen Stoot — Casavant's Tonal Director and an Englishman

---

15 Robert P. Elliot of Welte Organ Co. to Ernest Skinner

September 19, 1927

Mr. Ernest M. Skinner,
Skinner Organ Co.,
Crescent Ave.,
Dorchester, Mass.

Dear Ernest:

I had quite a visit with Stokowski today. He drifted in and tried the organ. Probably Gibson put him up to it after trying it himself Monday. He liked it very much, but that won't interest you equally with the following.

Dr. Noble came along and we went over to St. Thomas' Church where he had a good go at that organ. Stokowski told me to tell you he thought it the most magnificent instrument he had played in America. Now that's what I call a high authority.

I had told him that you were in the other night when Goss-Custard played and he told me if I saw you soon to give you his best regards and say he remembered well the old days at St. Bartholomew's.

Which is about all for the present. Regards to Don.

Cordially yours,

Robert P. Elliot

RPE:MD

Stokowski — Leopold Stokowski, well-known conductor of the Philadelphia Orchestra 1913-36, was organist of St. James's Piccadilly in 1900 and of St. Bartholomew's, New York in 1905.

Dr. Noble — T. Tertius Noble, organist at St. Thomas

Gibson — S. Archer Gibson, well-known residence organist from about 1910 until his death in 1952. His society patrons included the Vanderbilts and Rockefellers, as well as oil magnates Charles E. Schwab, Henry C. Frick and steel tycoon Andrew Carnegie.

St. Thomas Church — Manhattan, Skinner opus 205, four-manual, 1913, 83 ranks — one of Skinner's favorites

---

16 Henry Willis to Stephen Stoot

20th September 1927

Mr. Stephen Stoot
Casavant Freres
Organ Builders
St. Hyacinthe P.Q.
Canada

Dear Mr. Stoot,

Glad to hear from you again.

It was interesting your meeting Goss-Custard in Toronto.

Yes, Harrison has gone to Skinners — he didn't feel there was enough scope in this country. He left with my blessing and I am sure that he will make good. . . .

Things are slow here — aftermath of last year's Coal and General Strike I suppose. Still we worry along.

Yours very sincerely,

H.W.

HW/KC

Stephen Stoot, Henry Willis III, G. Donald Harrison

---

17 Henry Willis to T. Scott Buhrman

22nd September, 1927

Mr. T. Scott Buhrman,
Organ Interests Inc.
467, City Hall Station
New York, U.S.A.
Dear Mr. Scott Buhrman,

   Thanks for your letter of the 8th instant, just to hand.

By all means, reproduce the drawing of the Macpherson-Willis inclined manuals, as appeared in the April <u>Rotunda</u>. Please consider yourself free to reproduce any photo or drawing which appears in the "Rotunda" with the usual acknowledgement.

The No. 1 Vol. II is now in the press and you will have a copy shortly.

Yes, I noted with interest the announcement of the third generation of Möllers. I trust in their case as my own that the youngest representative of the house will be a better organ builder than his forebears!

Alas! I am so occupied here that a visit to the States this year is out of the question. I hope for better luck next year for I greatly enjoyed all my visits and the many interesting contacts made. I have not been afraid to acknowledge much interesting and useful information gained in U.S. but judging by some curiously worded articles that have appeared in the <u>American Organist</u> and <u>The Diapason,</u> acknowledgement of information gained on your side from me does not seem to be forthcoming! I don't mind this. It only amuses me. I prophesy that American organ building will rapidly attain a much higher artistic level than it held in the past and I advise you to keep an eye on the productions of the Skinner Co. in particular — great advances are being made there on "Willis" lines.

Yours very sincerely,
H.W.

H.W./K.C.

April *Rotunda* — *The Rotunda* was the journal of the Willis firm in the late '20s and early '30s, named after the Rotunda Works in Camden Town, the Willis factory from the late 1860s until 1905. It featured articles on new Willis instruments and other items of interest to organists. During the same period, the Skinner Company produced *Stop, Open and Reed*, a similar publication.

T. S. Buhrman — T. Scott Buhrman, editor of the *American Organist*. He began the magazine in 1917.

---

18 Charles Courboin of Wanamaker to Henry Willis

November 26, 1927

Mr. Henry Willis,
c/o H. Willis & Son
Rotunda Organ Works,
234 Ferndale Road,
Brixton, London, S.W.9.
Dear Willis:

The question of the high pressure unit for the big Philadelphia Organ has now come up for discussion.

Without going into details, we would like to ask you to give us an immediate reply on the following questions:

#1 — Would it be possible for you to furnish us with six C's starting from 16 foot lower C on 100 inch wind, which would give us an idea of the qualities and intensities of a tuba section?

If you have an experimental chest and regulator in the factory which you use for this purpose, could you send it along? If this is not possible, we will furnish our own apparatus over here.

#2 — What sort of financial arrangement would you want, to make these experimental pipes for us?

If we come to a mutual agreement, we would like to hear these pipes in the Grand Court at the earliest possible opportunity. They would be placed in an enclosed section, which you know is essential in the Court.

Please let us hear as quickly as possible about this.

Most sincerely yours,
Charles M. Courboin

CMC/MU

high pressure unit — The Stentor Division of the Wanamaker organ was planned as a large enclosed section of high pressure diapasons and reeds on the ninth floor of the Grand Court. Courboin and the others involved wanted a 100" pressure reed for this division. However, neither the Stentor organ nor the 100" reed was ever installed.

Charles M. Courboin — A Belgian native, Courboin was a popular recitalist. With Dr. Alexander Russell, then director of music at Princeton Chapel, and others, Courboin was instrumental in developing the immense Wanamaker Grand Court Organ. Courboin later became organist of St. Patrick's Cathedral, New York.

---

19 Emerson Richards to Henry Willis

December 3, 1927

Mr. Henry Willis,
    34, Ferndale Road,
        Brixton, London, S.W.9.

My dear Willis:

It is a long time since I have heard from you and imagine that you are not contemplating a visit to us this year. My own plans to get to England have all miscarried, partly because political matters have not admitted so long an absence from home, and more largely because the Courts never seem to cease to operate and professional engagements have been extremely heavy.

Did get a few days off in August and had the pleasure of meeting Goss-Custard and his family, and had the pleasure of a few hours visit with them here in Atlantic City.

Have been retained by the municipality to design the organ for the Convention Hall, and in as much as I would like to employ pressures up to 100" on two of the manuals and one of the pedal reeds, I would like to have a serious talk with you on the behavior of the high pressure reed at Liverpool, so that I hope, before anything is done, to get over in the spring.

I note that there was a recent issue of the Rotunda. We have not received it. Is it possible that our subscription miscarried? If so, please send us another bill, because I do not want to miss this very interesting publication.

With kindest regards, I am,

Cordially yours,
Emerson Richards

ER H

pressures up to 100" — Richards' and Courboin's inquiries regarding 100" pressures were made within a fortnight of each other.

---

20 E. M. Skinner's Open Letter in *The Diapason*, January, 1928, and in *Stop Open & Reed*, Volume 5, Number 1, 1929

December 21, 1927
<u>G. DONALD HARRISON</u>

This is by way of introducing my friend and co-worker, Donald Harrison, whom I first met on the occasion of my visit to the factory of Henry Willis, in 1924.

I had with me at that time a set of blueprints of various mechanisms, which I thought might be regarded, in some measure, as an exchange for time given to me in showing the Willis work. I explained them at some length to Mr. Willis, but received the impression at the moment that he was not especially intrigued by them, which I afterward became aware, was but a characteristic reserve. Mr. Willis was called away for a few moments, whereupon Mr. Harrison seized the opportunity to tell me not to take Mr. Willis' aloofness to heart, that he was more interested than he seemed. A sense of humor had, however, carried me along well enough, as I had nothing to sell, but the occasion gave me an illuminating viewpoint toward Harrison.

My previous meetings with "Father Willis" and his son, whom I met at Liverpool thirty years or so ago, at the time the St. George's Hall organ was being rebuilt, had left me with a sense of obligation toward the House of

G. Donald Harrison

Willis, so I invited him to America, saying that such a visit would save him twenty years of experimentation and expense in the development of electrical mechanism and chest design, as there was nothing, as far as I knew, but tracker pneumatic and tubular work in vogue in England, and France was, and is, in a hopeless state of antiquated stagnation on mechanical questions.

The business outlook was such that Mr. Willis could see no prospect of such a visit, so I said to Harrison from the open window of a train as I was leaving, "You come."

As it happened, Mr. Willis and Mr. Harrison both came, but Mr. Willis came first and Mr. Harrison later.

Mr. Harrison decided, after looking us over, that he would like to carry on in America. This is our great good fortune. He is a modern by temperament and inclination. His musical taste is of the highest order. His experience as an artist brought him in intimate contact with all the recent great work of Willis, including Dunedin, Westminster and Liverpool Cathedrals, of which the latter is regarded as the greatest example of the art of organbuilding anywhere.

Mr. Harrison is fully acquainted with the great French masterpieces and has, in short, that wide knowledge of the art and its historical foundation without which no work of distinction can be created. Mr. Harrison is destined to be a great figure in the art of organbuilding in America.

He was born April 21, 1889 at Huddersfield, Yorkshire, England; he is a graduate of Dulwich College, near London. In 1912 he passed the qualifying examination of the chartered institute of patent agents and joined his father's firm. He later in 1914 did some work as Patent Attorney for Henry Willis. He married Dora Jackson Lang, only daughter of the late Dr. Jackson Lang, well-known in musical and sporting circles. During the War he served for over three years in the Royal Air Force, being attached to the Sixth Brigade.

He studied organ with Arthur Pearson, and also played Cornet in Dulwich Military band. All his spare time in boyhood days he studied the organ, and on leaving college he tried to get into the Lewis firm, but Mr. Lewis discouraged the idea, saying "There is no money in it." "I therefore took to my second love, engineering, until I met Henry Willis just before the War."

He acted as salesman to Willis and studied voicing methods, afterward becoming a director of the Willis firm. He had made an especial study of ensemble and mixtures, more especially as related to the conspicuous examples of Father Willis, Cavaillé-Coll and Schulze. Mr. Harrison has the most profound knowledge of tonal structure, commonly described as "specifications" of anyone I have ever met. My confidence in his judgment stands at 100%, which is somewhat better than I rate my own, to be perfectly frank about it.

I welcome with relief one with whom I can, in the fullest confidence, share the responsibility of bringing to a state of perfection such great undertakings as we are carrying out at the present time.

Ernest M. Skinner

---

21 Lynnwood Farnam to Henry Willis

(Written on train, excuse writing)
49 W. 20 St., New York
March 14, 1928

Dear Henry:

I never received any response from the Westminster Cathedral authorities regarding the letter you so kindly wrote them about my recital fee. I am very sorry to trouble you about this again but could you give me the address of the individual to whom I might write in order to get the matter cleared up.

It is a great pleasure to see Donald Harrison now and then and I am so glad that Mrs. Harrison was able to get over here recently.

Kindest remembrances to you and Mrs. Willis and all your family.

Sincerely yours,
Lynnwood [Farnam]

22 Henry Willis to Lynnwood Farnam

12th April, 1928

Mr. Lynnwood Farnam
49 West 20th Street
New York, U.S.A.
My Dear Chap,

Reference Westminster Cathedral. I have done all I can in the matter but get referred from one Monsignor to another without result. I do not care to trouble them further so send you cheque for £10.10.0. Please send a receipt "Received from Henry Willis & Sons Ltd., the sum of £10.10.0 by cheque being payment of fee for recital given at Westminster Cathedral on ----------" there is a chance that I might get repayment someday!

Thanks for your views on the specifications I sent you.

Firstly, for an <u>ideal</u> organ specification to play organ music upon there should be no difference between that for a church or residence. I am glad you noted that.

I am, frankly, horrified that you recommend total enclosure of a Great Organ, and assume that the replacement of the Gemshorn by the Harmonic Flute is in that connection.

You say that you miss a Clarinet on *[the]* Choir and would omit the Nazard to have it. Yet one of the many purposes of the Nazard is to enable a synthetic Clarinet tone to be built up — to say nothing of many other colours of entrancing beauty. You have not tried my latest mutations or you would see the point of retaining the Nazard and also of taking the Tierce right down in stopped metal pipes.

All best,

Yours ever,
H.W.

H.W./K.C.

---

23 Lynnwood Farnam to Henry Willis

49 West 20 St., New York
May 1, 1928

Dear Henry:

Thank you very much for your letter and the enclosed check for £10.10.0 which I am returning herewith as I could not dream of allowing you to pay for that Westminster Cathedral appearance of mine. It is most generous of you, but if the authorities cannot pay for it, we'll just let the matter drop.

Yes, I felt you would be somewhat shocked at my stand on totally enclosed Greats, but I am convinced by using a number of them, in spite of

Lynnwood Farnam

myself. I shall be eager to hear your latest achievements when I go over in 1930, for one thing the Synthetic Clarinet. 999 times out of 1000, though, off-unisons in the bass are ugly for solo purposes and for music in two or three voices.

Pardon train writing. With warmest regards,

Very sincerely yours,

Lynnwood

---

24 Emerson Richards to Henry Willis

June 6th, 1928

Mr. Henry Willis,
234, Ferndale Road,
Brixton, London, S.W.9,
My dear Willis:

I am very much afraid that you have brought upon yourself a rather undesirable and perhaps useless reply to your request for a criticism of the specification that you sent me.

However, you know enough of my ideas to realize that I would not be satisfied with the type of organ suggested, when there is something which, to my mind, is so much better just around the corner.

I can understand and appreciate your difficulties from a business standpoint, and that you would hardly care to advocate something which seems so radical. But as I have said in the enclosed, it is largely a matter of experience. As you know, I have done more to compel American organ builders to listen to the word "Diapason Chorus" than any one else over here, to the extent that we really are making progress. But as Goss-Custard said to me last summer, American organs do excel in the multitude of soft and refined effects that seem to be characteristic of our instruments. They could be easily added at small cost to your fine ensembles, and that is what I am trying to indicate in the enclosed.

As you note, I have not disturbed the "guts" of your design, just added some ornamentations to it. It would cost a little more to build, not very much, but for concert work would certainly excel the straight design.

A multitude of business matters again stands in the way of the long deferred trip to England. I may have better luck in the late summer or fall.

The design of the Convention Hall organ is nearing completion and the specifications will be offered to the builders probably within the next six weeks. I think you told me that you did not believe that you could compete, but you are welcome to the opportunity if you desire.

The hall itself is fairly well along, but three of the great arches remain to be placed. Some space to fill. 500 feet long, 350 feet wide, 138 feet to the ceiling — 11,000,000 cubic feet, and a possible audience of 41,000.

With kindest personal regards, I am,

Cordially yours,
Emerson Richards

ER H
Enc.

Some space to fill — The auditorium was actually 487 feet long, had a volume of 15,500,000 cubic feet, and cost some $15 million to build.

---

25 Henry Willis to Emerson Richards

20th June, 1928

Senator Emerson Richards
Atlantic City
N.J.
U.S.A.
My dear Senator,

Thanks for yours of the 6th instant, and for going to so much trouble.

I am sorry that you suggest any form of extension or unification on the manuals — I am unalterably opposed to anything of the sort.

If Goss-Custard said that American organs excel in the multitude of soft and refined effects, he was pointing out in his usual charming way that such effects were produced before the true organ tone was properly developed.

You really must come over here and study these matters.

Thanks very much, but I would not be interested in the Convention Hall organ, certainly not "in competition" with American builders or to any specification but one with which I was wholly in sympathy. The fact is that I only care to work to my own specifications; I am always willing to consult the organist interested in a scheme and even to accommodate him on comparatively trivial matters, but generally speaking I feel that I could not do myself justice in any other way. I would be very glad to see a copy of your Convention Hall scheme when ready.

Yours sincerely,
H.W.

H.W./K.C.

---

26 Emerson Richards to Henry Willis

July 2nd, 1928

Mr. Henry Willis,
   34, Ferndale Road,
      Brixton, London, S.W.9,
My dear Willis:

Have your letter of the 20th. Under the law, in this state, we are compelled to submit all municipal contracts to competitive bids. I am hoping to take care of this situation by providing that only builders of certain skill, experience and financial standing may compete. We are not at liberty to select any particular builder as a private individual might do.

Harrison has done a very fine job at Princeton. I am quite sure you would like the organ.

Relative to the specification as I proposed it, I fully believe that with the possible exception of the extension of the Great reed, none of the proposed unifications would affect the ensemble, and for this reason cannot be objectionable. On the other hand, they provide much in the way of flexibility and tone colors not obtainable except at great expense in the ordinary way.

I am very much with you in opposing unification that does in fact, not theory, affect the ensemble. For example, the Dulciana extension has no effect whatever on the ensemble, yet in itself provides a very delightful effect — one that is being widely copied over here; while a very soft 4' and 2' are very useful in combination with the other choir material. Why not have them, when the expense is so trifling and the result so gratifying? We would not put them in as single stops. It would be unnecessary, and whatever is unnecessary is not good art.

When the Convention Hall scheme is finally adopted, I will be glad to send you a copy of the complete specifications.

I am looking longingly towards September and a possible attempt to get over, but alas there is a presidential campaign in the offing and that makes it very difficult.

Very truly yours,
Emerson Richards

very fine job at Princeton — Skinner opus 656, four-manual, the first significant job from the Skinner Company after Harrison's arrival. Ralph Downes was its first organist.

specification as I proposed it — the experimental scheme Willis and Richards have been discussing

---

27 Henry Willis to Emerson Richards

28th January, 1929

Senator Emerson Richards
Atlantic City
N.J.
U.S.A.
Dear Senator,

Many thanks for your letter of the 13th instant, enclosing a copy of specification for the Convention Hall Organ and offer to hold matters up so that I could "bid."

For many reasons I am unable to do so. In any case it would be quite impossible for me to build such an organ *[in]* under five years.

You will permit me to remark, in the friendliest possible manner, that I cannot imagine any builder of repute agreeing to work under the conditions mentioned which appear to me as not only intolerable but impossible.

I anticipate your receiving "bids" from:

    1) Wurlitzer's   2) Kimball's   3) Austin
    4) Midmer-Losh,

and venture to "back" No.4 as the "winner!"

In any case the result will be extremely interesting.

Yours sincerely,
H.W.

H.W./K.C.

venture . . . the "winner" — Willis' guess was ultimately correct. See letter 31.

February 8th, 1929

Mr. Henry Willis,

    234, Ferndale Road,

      Brixton, London, S.W.9.

My dear Willis:

This acknowledges your letter of the 28th. You were wrong about the bids. Of the four you picked only Kimball bid, and their proposal was for $853,646.41. The low bidder, however, was Welte at $550,000. and in as much as I have grave doubts concerning their financial stability, all the bids were rejected and new proposals will be asked in the near future.

I am also making some cuts in the number of voices in order to reduce somewhat the cost and find better lay-out conditions. The 64' Diaphone has to go in this arrangement. It simply crowds everything else out of the way.

None of the prominent builders except Austin complained about the conditions. You must remember that this was a municipal contract, that it had to conform to the same laws relating to contracts and the giving of work that obtain in all other municipal matters. Admittedly not ideal conditions for an organ proposal but inevitable. Of course, much depends on the interpretation of the specifications by the architect, and which would not have resulted in undue hardship.

Many of the builders were frightened at the 100" wind pressure and others at the double languids, but as you know there is nothing impossible about either.

Am still hoping to get over this spring.

           Cordially yours,

           Emerson Richards

64' Diaphone has to go — In the final specification, this rank was included.

double languids — adding a second languid to obtain great power in flue pipes was an invention of Vincent Willis, uncle of Henry Willis III, who left the firm in 1894 and set up on his own account.

---

29 Lynnwood Farnam to Henry Willis

May 3, 1929

Dear Henry:

For a long, long time I have intended sending you a line. It is a great delight to me to note the results Donald Harrison's coming has produced in Skinner's work. The new Grace Church, New York instrument is simply splendid with its fine build-up, cohesion, brilliance, bearded Pedal Open and other fine points. I was particularly delighted to see the picture of you and your bonny little son. How well he is coming on.

Could you send me one or two more copies of the <u>Rotunda</u> containing Havergal Brian's "Contrasts or Affinities" (September, 1928). I enjoy your publication and am very grateful to you for sending me presentation copies.

Remembrances to Mrs. Willis and all your family. See you, I hope, in 1930.

Sincerely as ever,

Lynnwood

Havergal Brian (1876-1972) was born in Dresden, Staffordshire, England. He enjoyed some success as a composer in Britain before World War I. Thereafter, his music became neglected until revivals of interest in the 1950s and again following his death. His works include 32 symphonies, five operas, and over 100 songs.

---

30 Ernest M. Skinner to *The American Organist*

May 6, 1929

The American Organist,
    467 City Hall Station,
        New York City, N.Y.

Gentlemen:

I would like to make reference to your editorial in the issue of May 1929, with special attention to your statement regarding the organ for the Atlantic City Auditorium, i.e. "I believe the reason more bids were not entered was that most of our competent builders gave it too little actual study." I can assure that this was not the case with respect to ourselves. The fact that we did give it study was one of the reasons why we did not submit a bid, but only one of them.

I might mention another of the reasons was that the specifications, without taking into account any remote control combinations or special construction or two consoles, called for 1242 stops and stated that there was $300,000 available, which reduced to $241.00 a stop, something less than the pre-war price for average construction, with no 32's, 64's or 100" wind pressure to consider. As it now stands, the specification calls for 1042 stops and the contract, I believe, was let for $340,000.00. This leaves about the average pre-war price of an 8' stop. The number of stops and the sum available would prohibit the Skinner Company from entering the competition, as I have no doubt it did others.

I might name another reason, provided we agreed with the specifications in toto and the price was sufficient to allow us to build the organ at a fair profit; the organ with its unusual features, remote control combinations and double consoles, could not be built in less than one year by the

Skinner organization, which would cut us off from any other business for at least a year, which would be in some cases a very unfortunate position in which to place ourselves. I would rather build the organ for the National Cathedral at Washington of 100 stops than to build the Atlantic City Auditorium of 1,000 stops, regardless of price. The Atlantic City job might shut us out of a chance to build others.

Contrary to what Mr. Richards says, it is not the question of losing one's nerve, or the size of the instrument, or insuring ourselves against our own ignorance, nor is it a question of exposing bunk, but it is a perfectly straightforward matter of choice and common sense. Neither is it a question of meeting a perfectly definite standard common to competitors. There is no minuteness of detailed exactness or design of construction or insistence of painstaking care that the Senator could possibly set down that would equal the normal quality of the output and standards of construction that the Skinner Company have set for themselves. The Senator should not forget that the Skinner Company are organ architects and have more than theoretical background. They have not only a practical background but have built several hundred organs that are finer in detail and design than anything ever specified by the Senator or our old friend Audsley or any other architect.

If the Senator will point out one detail in his specifications that has so discouraged the builders, in his opinion, I will point out ten details in the normal Skinner construction that are not mentioned in his specifications. I regret the Senator has fallen into the error that Audsley invariably made. He bundled all the organ builders into one group which he described as "groove-loving tradesmen," and similar characterizations and never mentioned the fact that there were exceptions and to those exceptions belong the credit of making the organ the king of instruments, of their own volition and not because they were pounded into it by any organ architect. A great work of art in the shape of a painting is not made so because someone stands behind the painter with a club. No more is a great organ a work of art because someone stands behind the builder with a club. Great organs are created only by artistic organ builders and organ builders who want to make them great organs for love of the art.

The Senator says his specifications call for nothing that has not been done before, but I will point out one little item that has not been done before, nor will it be done in the present instance, and that is to build an organ under present conditions at the rate of $241.00 per stop. We will hear more of this later.

I am indebted to Senator Richards for giving me credit for my French Horn, in which connection he says everybody makes them now, without giving Skinner credit for it. I would like to amend this slightly by saying that nobody makes the Skinner French Horn except the Skinner Company. I have heard most of the attempts and not one of them really approaches the Skinner French Horn, or shall we say the orchestral instrument of that name.

There is one other Skinner device that is spoken of in these specifications, and that is the pitman windchest, for which the Senator does not give the Skinner Company credit. The pitman windchest is one Skinner device which threatens to become universal. It is used by the great majority of the American builders and one English builder and I believe it has now found its way into France.

I hope the above explanation will make it clear that failing to bid on the Atlantic City organ is not an evidence of loss of nerve or the size of the job or the fact that we were disinclined to live up to definite specifications, especially the latter. The Skinner organ is built under the most exacting specifications to which any builder has ever been committed.

Very truly yours,
Ernest M. Skinner

---

31 Emerson Richards to Henry Willis

May 30th, 1929

Mr. Henry Willis,
234 Ferndale Road,
Brixton, London, S.W.9,
My dear Willis:

You were right after all. Losh did get the contract for the big organ. Personally, I had hoped and expected that Kimball would get it, but the best they could do was to carry off the consolation prize for the organ in the ballroom, $47,550. Losh's bid was about $100,000 below that of Kimball and in as much as he had been successful with the High School organ, there was no justification for not awarding him the contract.

As you may have heard, the Welte Company, which has just completed a very modern factory with over $175,000 of machinery and equipment, is bankrupt, and Losh has bought the entire equipment from the Receiver and will operate the factory, which is situated in New York City, in conjunction with the Merrick factory for the time being. This will mean a much quicker delivery for us, since he not only has the additional facilities but can carry on his other work from the Welte factory.

You will recall this was the venture that was inaugurated by Elliot, and that he had Harry Willis and Whitelegg with him.

In making up some of the double languids, Losh's voicers are having some difficulty in determining just where the false languids should be located. The drawings you gave me are not accurate on this point, and the double languids at the Welte factory made by Harry Willis do not show the same location as in your drawing.

I am wondering whether you care to give me personally the information as to the relative positions of the mouth, the false languid, and the true languid. Is there any advantage in pocketing the true languid or running it back on an angle? Also you told me that something special had to be done to the lip in the case of the string double languids. I think some sort of a slight hump, and you also told me where this should occur, but I have forgotten the exact proportion.

I am sending under separate cover a copy of the specifications as revised. The bid was $347,200.

The Convention Hall itself will be dedicated tomorrow, May 31st. Expect to have part of the organ playing from a temporary console by mid-summer; the brass wind section now being complete in the factory. The reeds are voiced without any leather on the eschallots and are very quick.

I am anxious to hear this particular division, because of the extent to which we have carried the reed mutation.

Am really planning and expect to make a rather quick trip your way in September.

With kindest regards, I am,

Cordially yours,
Emerson Richards

ER H

Harry Willis — Harry Vincent Willis (1890-1973), son of Vincent Willis and a cousin of Henry Willis III. Robert Pier Elliot brought Harry to Welte in hopes that the Willis name and inventive genius would lend the firm prestige, and Siebert Losh soon hired him to work on the Atlantic City organ.

---

32 William H. Barnes to Henry Willis

August 26, 1929

Mr. Henry Willis
234 Ferndale Road,
London, England.
Dear Willis:

. . .The only large and interesting organ that is going forward in this country at the present time that has many unusual features, is the one that is being built for the Atlantic City Municipal Auditorium. I understand that they are having great success with the double languid diapasons and double languid strings in this organ and that they are highly delighted with this

William H. Barnes

type of pipe and expect to use a great many more than were originally called for in the scheme, which you no doubt have seen in the <u>American Organist</u> or <u>Diapason</u>.

There is much about the scheme that I do not like, particularly the unifying, in an organ of this size. The 100" pressure seems also problematical at this time and I believe unnecessary. However, as I have been appointed as Senator Richards' successor to see that this organ is finished in case anything happens to the Senator, I have been following their operations rather closely and though I am perfectly satisfied that either the Kimball Company or Möller, who were the only other two bidders, could have done a much better job than our friend Losh, I think there is considerable likelihood of his completing the job in some sort of shape. Though under the very trying conditions that exist in placing a large organ, (you might say) in the middle of the Atlantic Ocean, as it will be out on the end of a pier extending into the ocean, that an almost endless amount of mechanical trouble may be expected from an organ of this size by such a builder. However, we shall hope for the best, but I can almost be sure that not all of this organ will ever be in working condition at the same time.

Our plans for a European trip are somewhat indefinite but hope to get over there late this fall or in the spring.

With kindest regards to yourself, I am

Very sincerely yours,

William H. Barnes

on the end of a pier — Actually, the Convention Hall sits on the Boardwalk of Atlantic City on dry land.

33 Henry Willis to William H. Barnes

Mr. William H. Barnes
Messrs. A.R. Barnes & Co.
1100 South Wabash Avenue
Chicago, Ill.
U.S.A.

6th September 1929

Dear Barnes,

. . . I am awaiting with interest the completion of the Atlantic City organ, and trust eventually to be able to try it, or as much as may be working!

I have just returned from an interesting trip touching Norway, Sweden, Esthonia, Dantzig, Denmark etc, and have seen and tried many organs both old and new, the old being the best. Oliva Cathedral near Dantzig quite an extraordinary old job, built by a monk, Johann Wolf in 1603 (not quite sure of the date) and rebuilt <u>once</u> — in about 1840. The organist played the Hallelujah Chorus to me but it sounded so dreadful that I didn't recognize it until half-through. Roskilde Cathedral in Denmark an old job dating back to 1562 and many of the old stops practically untouched — effect quite grand, etc. etc.

All the best,

Very sincerely yours,
H.W.

H.W./K.C.

---

34 Robert Pier Elliot to Henry Willis

September 16, 1929

My dear Willis:

. . . I haven't much news. It has been slow through July and August, but people are home again and I am busier than I find quite comfortable. I shall do very well presently.

I hear little direct news from the east, but it is rumored via the Toronto convention and otherwise that Don chafes a little. I hazard a guess that they press standardization and cheapening processes beyond his liking, tho' they still build a very fine organ, and there is no doubt it is better tonally, and markedly so, since your influence was felt, and later Don's direct work. They continue busy. . . .

Dupré to play the Barton Abomination in the Stadium. Can you imagine that? I sent you a poster-program of it some weeks ago — of the organ, I mean.

Robert Pier Elliot

I'm glad to hear from you. Write when you can. I have been too busy to write much, lacking my capable secretary. I appreciated that girl when she was with me, and more than ever now that she isn't.

Cordially,
R. P. Elliot

Don chafes a little — Donald Harrison

Dupré to play the Barton Abomination — A six-manual unit theatre organ in the Chicago Stadium built by the Barton Organ Company on 10" to 35" pressure. *The Diapason* reported that 10,000 people attended the recital, and that the tone of the organ was "overwhelming" and "too abundant to be artistic," noting that "even the most ardent addict of, shall we say, chocolate soda, would hardly care to be thrown into a swimming pool filled with it."

---

35 Henry Willis to Robert Pier Elliot

Mr. Robert Pier Elliot
220 Kimball Hall
Chicago, Ill.
U.S.A.

30th September, 1929

My Dear Elliot,

. . . Just had William E. Zeuch here for ten days. We had a good time together. . . .

Terrible to hear that Dupré is to play that Barton job in the Stadium — managers do such things.

Very busy here. Just finishing the Alexandra Palace job which will be, beyond any doubt, the finest concert organ in this country.

Yours ever,

H.W.

H.W./K.C.

Alexandra Palace — A large London concert hall housing a four-manual Father Willis, then recently rebuilt by Willis III. The organ was rained and snowed upon after the building was damaged early in World War II. Later in the war, the organ, except for 32' stops and the case, was removed and stored. Henry Willis, 4, bought the organ, moved it to his factory, and later rebuilt it for the restored "Ally Pally."

---

36 Emerson Richards to Henry Willis

October 3rd, 1929

Mr. Henry Willis,

234, Ferndale Road,

Brixton, England, S.W.9.

My dear Willis:

The arrival of the <u>Rotunda</u> yesterday reminded me that I have not answered your last letter. Between the date of my inquiry about the double languids and the arrival of your reply, the situation had changed, as you may know indirectly. Henry Vincent Willis had, in the mean time, joined the Midmer-Losh organization, and, of course, he had all of the information and experience that we already did not have, and had double languids already in construction when your letter arrived, so that there was no reason for troubling you further in the matter. I had neglected to tell you in my original letter that Donald Harrison had already given me the same information that I had requested of you, but I wanted to check it up.

You will undoubtedly be interested to know that we have since produced these double languids in all their tonalities — diapasons, strings, open and stopped flutes — with very fine success. We have about half a dozen sets now playing in the second String Organ, and besides the greatly increased power, [they] give a refinement of tone that makes it very well worthwhile. We have produced three Diapasons of immense power and scale, but which are not yet on the wind in the organ. The medium one I did place on the 20-inch wind at the High School (where the flute stood) and find that its power and brilliance is such that it is more than a match for the unenclosed tuba, which you will probably remember. The fine thing is that these stops are quite bright and have no phonon reaction. The stopped and open flutes are both extremely interesting, and of course we are getting immense power from them. All of which is necessary in this immense building.

We have the Brass Wind and the second String Organ playing, and the Brass Wind is a great success. The reed and flue mutation works in wonderfully well. The reeds have been treated as trombones and the whole division as a single ensemble, which gives quite a remarkable effect. Bill Barnes was here the other day and was extremely enthusiastic. If we have anything like the same amount of luck with the other material we will have quite an organ to show you the next time you get over.

Have added two more 32's to the job — a slim scale double languid Violone which goes in with the Echo, and a Trombone which is extended to form a 16-8-4 foot unit to go with the Gallery Diapasons and is situated in the other Echo chamber directly above them. Work is pretty well along and we are getting some results from some of the interesting mechanical features. The String Organ is equipped with duralium swell shades, lightning fast in their operation, so that a quicker accent can be gotten on this division. Think you will be interested in them when you see them.

Have been tied up with some important business details and a terrible amount of professional work, and it looks as if I am hooked again as far as my intended vacation abroad is concerned; although the skies might clear within the next two or three weeks.

With kindest personal regards, I am,

Cordially yours,
Emerson Richards

ER H

no phonon reaction — no undue fundamental tone
duralium swell shades — Duralium was an early alloy of aluminum promoted for decorative and architectural use.

---

37 Ernest Skinner to G. Donald Harrison

November 23, 1929

Dear Don:

I felt some embarrassment when Marcel [Dupré] handed me that testimonial so personal to myself regarding the Princeton organ, and I can imagine you may not have been without some feeling of being left out of it, so I want to say right here that I hold your contribution to the quality of that great instrument to be such that my opinion of you as an artist, publicly and privately expressed, is more than justified.

Cordially, and with great admiration,
Ernest M. Skinner

EMS:MSL

38 Lynnwood Farnam to Henry Willis

March 17, 1930

Henry Willis, Esq.,
234, Ferndale Rd., Brixton,
London, S.W. 9, England.
Dear Henry:

I am delighted as usual to read of the fine and interesting things you are doing. Skinner is going strong these days, and I never cease to be glad that he imbibed your influence and that Donald Harrison was able to come over to carry on his fine work.

I plan to sail for England July the sixth and shall be abroad in my usual way until September twentieth. If opportunities occur for me to play on any of your big new jobs, I shall be very glad to do so, especially St. Paul's or Alexandra Palace. Am very fond, also, of playing at Westminster Cathedral.

With kindest regards to you and Mrs. Willis and the children,

Sincerely yours,
Lynnwood

---

39 William H. Barnes to Henry Willis

March 25, 1930

Mr. Henry Willis,
234 Ferndale Road,
London, England S.W.9.
Dear Mr. Willis:

It has been a long time since I have heard from you and I think perhaps you will be interested in knowing that I am engaged in writing a work which I expect to call <u>Contemporary American Organ Building</u>. This book will deal largely with the mechanical side of organ building as practiced by the leading builders of America and I have secured shop drawings from many of the builders of their action, both console and chest and think it may be something of a contribution to the literature on organ building.

I have not devoted so much space to tonal matters and history but sufficient to make frequent reference to the remarkable pioneer work that your grandfather did in organ building, particularly in regard to chorus reed tone. I have given him, I hope, all the credit that is so rightly his due. I shall see that you get a copy of this book as soon as it is ready and think you will probably be interested in looking over the large collection of drawings that I am reproducing in this work.

The other parts of the book, of course, will be very old stuff to you and of no special interest. Some of the book will necessarily be elementary for educating the younger student of organ matters.

I visited the Atlantic City auditorium organ some two months ago and found that they are making considerable progress there, particularly in the matter of double languid pipes of all sorts. Harry Willis is doing some quite remarkable things.

You will be interested I think, in an anecdote of Seibert Losh. I don't know whether you met him when you were in this country but he is something of a "nut," to use American slang. One of the things that worried him most about building this organ was the one-hundred-inch-pressure tubas. By dint of much persuasion, some blower concern that makes vacuum cleaners or apparatus of this sort was finally induced to build a blower with a fifty horsepower motor to produce a small volume of air at 100" pressure. The best the machine would ever do, even turned at 3500 rpm, was 91" at the blower, which was some 400 feet from where the pipes are to sound.

Harry Willis has made a sample middle C pipe that will actually play tunes on this pressure, and they have a more or less experimental chest rigged up with two or three notes available. By calling up the power house and notifying them that they are going to start the blower they are enabled to hear the sound of this sample pipe, which isn't so much anyway. The reeds on 30" pressure seem just as good to me. When I inquired of Mr. Losh how he was getting along with the 100" pressure reeds he admitted that he was worried about them at first but now that he was "in production on them, there was nothing to it." The latest reports that I get from there is that this blower finally flew all to pieces, luckily doing no injury to anyone as it was placed in a reinforced concrete chamber under the stage. This would seem to indicate that "production" has ceased on 100" pressure, temporarily at least.

They are still debating and messing around over what they are going to do about the big console. The latest idea seems to be to use an individual solenoid for each stop key. If you are familiar with the workings of this type of combination action, you can imagine what a thousand of these stop keys moved at once would sound like. It seems to me that the ensuing clatter would probably cover the sound of double languid diapasons and 100" tubas.

With kindest regards, I am

Very sincerely yours,
William H. Barnes

WHB:Y

Contemporary American Organ Building — Barnes' book was eventually titled *The Contemporary American Organ*.

---

40 Henry Willis to Lynnwood Farnam

28th March, 1930

Mr. Lynnwood Farnam
49 West 20th Street
New York City
U.S.A.

My dear Chap,

Delighted to have your letter of the 17th inst. and to hear that you will be over this summer.

I think that it will be possible to fix you up a recital at the Alexandra Palace. Let me know by return please when you will be available. The job is really magnificent.

St. Paul's has hitherto been against recitals but Dr. Marchant is giving two early in July next, following the opening services in June, and it may be possible to get you there. I will have a try anyway — the fee, if any, would be very nominal but I don't think in that particular case you would worry about the fee. I will approach Dr. Marchant on those lines anyway.

It is good to hear that Don Harrison is carrying on the good work. Recent Skinner jobs must be <u>very</u> much improved. I hope to run over next year to hear all the latest jobs including the new Atlantic City monster, which should be finished by then.

Would be very happy indeed if you would stay with us when you are in London — Always a room for you.

All the best,

Yours ever,
H.W.

H.W./K.C.

Dr. Marchant — organist of St. Paul's Cathedral, London

41 Henry Willis to William H. Barnes

7th April, 1930.

Mr. W.H. Barnes
c/o Messrs. A.R. Barnes & Co.
1100-1118, South Wabash Avenue,
Chicago, Ill,
U.S.A.

Dear Barnes,

Thanks for yours of the 25th March; always very glad to hear from you.

I am looking forward to your new book <u>Contemporary American Organ Building</u>.

I was very interested to hear the news about the new big Atlantic City Organ. I quite fail to understand why they should have had such trouble raising 100" wind. When I was asked to submit a scheme in a certain quarter for a big Bombarde department embodying 100" work I went into the matter with the engineers and there did not appear to be any mechanical difficulty. If you care to pass on the information to Senator Richards I can put him in touch with my engineers who can provide that which is required.

As regards using solenoids for the big console, well why not? I am using them for my latest 1930 combination mechanisms and they are practically silent in operation.

Yours very sincerely,
H.W.

H.W./E.F.

submit a scheme in a certain quarter — Wanamaker's. See letter 18.

---

42 Edwin H. Lemare to Henry Willis

2200 Fairfield Avenue
Hollywood. Calif.
April 12. 1930.

Mr. Henry Willis
Rotunda Organ Works
London. N.W.

My dear Mr. Willis:

It has been brought to my notice that you have recently rebuilt and brought up to date the fine old Organ in the "A.P." — at which, as a boy, I often sat enthralled with the nobility and grandeur of its tone. Never have I ceased to proclaim it as your immortal Grandfather's masterpiece of tonal production. (N.B. As yet I have not had the opportunity of hearing what I am told is your masterpiece in Liverpool Cathedral)!

It seems almost certain that I again pay another visit HOME from September onwards to conduct the premier of my new Operetta (of a Gilbert and Sullivan humorous type!) and also make English Phonograph records, and I am wondering if you would care to arrange a series of recitals for me at the A.P.?

Judging by the many approaches from admirers in my old country (plus the unprecedented success of my 1922 tour) I am led to believe that my return — for a short visit — would be enthusiastically acclaimed by the press and public. At the moment I am uncertain as to whom I shall entrust my management; but will hope to soon find a "live-wire" man for this purpose — not alone for London but for other cities. Perhaps you may know of someone?

Edwin H. Lemare

If you have introduced into the old country — as doubtless you have — such things as master adjustable pistons (especially eight or ten "Generals" — controlling everything!) you will have done THE GREATEST THING FOR ENGLISH ORGAN PLAYING AND ORGAN BUILDING IN YOUR GENERATION!

The old fixed pistons have for many years been an inseparable barrier against a more artistic and comprehensive school of organ playing; as the player was unable, at the moment, to "set" his pistons so as to be instantly available according to his own particular requirements. Not alone this but, if he were a student of the orchestra, and conversant with the score, he was unable to give an approximate portrayal of same. It may interest you to know that on my first visit to Canada (1902), Casavant, at my suggestion, was the first to realize the importance and advantage of the master adjustable piston and henceforth adopted it as standard in all his instruments. The idea was afterwards copied by Austin, Skinner and others. It was about this time (1902) that I introduced to U.S.A. the original Willis Pedal-board — not Audsley's mutilation of same!

As far as I can see, you are the only really progressive organ builder left at home, and I wish you every possible success. It may take a long time to overcome old fashioned ideas, and you may have to struggle as "Henry Willis the Great" did with his pedalboard before I was able to <u>kill</u> the old College of Organists abortion of a pedal-board in England.

In conclusion, I would welcome the opportunity of again playing to my old musical public in London and elsewhere on some of your up-to-date instruments; as being fully conversant with the endless possibilities of "adjustables" etc. I know I could further a new standard of Organ playing (at least insofar as tone-colouring and registration are concerned!) in my own country.

Send me a line — will you?

Sincerely yours,

Edwin H. Lemare

CS-EHL

P.S. The above address (or Bohemian Club, San Francisco) will find me for the next two months when I return East to New York. The five-year contract in Chattanooga expired last June and was not renewed on my part, despite its financial attractions and the <u>really</u> fine organ built to my design by the Austin Co. The South, however, is hopeless — musically!

Edwin H. Lemare (1865-1934) — English organist, noted transcription artist and composer. Immediately after a scandalous divorce from his second wife in London, Lemare married an American woman and settled in the U.S. as municipal organist of San Francisco; Portland, Maine; and Chattanooga, Tennessee.

Audsley's mutilation of same — Audsley's variation of the Willis concave and radiating pedalboard. Lemare gave fullscale plans of the original design to E.M. Skinner in 1902.

43 G. Donald Harrison to Henry Willis

April 22, 1930

Mr. Henry Willis,
234 Ferndale Road,
Brixton,
London, S.W.9,
England.

My dear Henry:

Very many thanks for sending the sample of moleskin so promptly. Will you kindly have Messrs. Alfred Brown & Sons send us 50 yards of this material 36" wide as soon as possible.

Reference R. Rushworth Dreaper, there is absolutely no truth in the rumors which you have heard regarding these people obtaining information from us about wind chests, etc. We have had no correspondence with them whatever, and it must be from someone else. You will remember before I left England that Bob Elliot wrote to us about a practise reed organ, and we referred him to Rushworth's. It strikes me, therefore, that it is quite possible that they have communicated with him.

I was quite interested in the latest <u>Rotunda,</u> and am glad to hear that Reginald Goss-Custard has been appointed organist of the Alexandra Palace.

I would very much like to pay you a visit this year with my family, but it will be quite impossible as I have to go to California.

Sincerely,
Don

GDH:MGM

Rushworth & Dreaper — English organbuilders
have to go to California — perhaps on business related to Op. 818, Royce Hall, UCLA

---

44 Henry Willis to G. Donald Harrison

25th April, 1930

Mr. G.D. Harrison
Skinner Organ Co.
Crescent Avenue
Dorchester
Boston, Mass.
U.S.A.

Dear Don,

Thanks for yours of the 12th instant, and information therein which is very interesting. Kiln-dried timber has no use in this country for our purposes because the humidity is so high. Kiln-dried stock would absorb the natural moisture present in the atmosphere during manufacture and go on doing so. The only thing is to go on as we are and make every piece of mechanism capable of expanding and contracting by the use of spring washers etc. on the system we have used since 1925 as you know. Whereas hundreds of jobs built on the old system have given trouble under the trying "modern" heating conditions of cathedrals and churches, none of the jobs built by us 1925 onwards have given any trouble that could not be readily taken up by tightening a few screws.

The rehumidifying of cathedrals and churches involves an expense which, in the impoverished state of the Church today, simply cannot be entertained.

At Liverpool Cathedral the Lady Chapel organ commenced to give trouble during the Winter heating season shortly after the chapel was connected up to the main cathedral. This shrinkage has been overcome by fitting humidising pans on each side of the organ and during the past winter, with an average relative humidity of 59% the organ remained perfect.

The big job in the Cathedral was damaged very severely during the Arctic weather we experienced in this country in February 1929 when, in buildings heated to a reasonable degree for comfort, the relative humidity was very low. The result was, of course, severe shrinkage throughout the woodwork, splitting of soundboard tables, casting of upperboards, etc. I pleaded for a higher level of humidity and an attempt was made in the direction of re-humidisation; little good was done and it upset the general balance of the heating arrangements so that the authorities became "fed up" and claimed that the organ ought to have resisted "modern heating."

The fact is that the dried-up atmosphere of the Cathedral has been a subject of comment for some time. I was talking to Dr. Rhodes of Coventry Cathedral, who attended a conference of Cathedral Organists held at Liverpool during a winter and he remarked how dried up and "stale" the atmosphere was.

Anyway, the attitude of the authorities has been so "difficult" that I eventually and reluctantly offered to remake all the old slider soundboards and to adapt them as far as possible (screw washers, etc.) to stand the conditions, to guarantee the result, and to do it for nothing. But they want up-to-date sliderless chests fitted — a gigantic proposition and (you will scarcely credit it) have suggested very definitely that they expect me to stand half the cost!

Of the scores of cases where organs on our books suffered damage in February 1929 we have only had any trouble with four clients, two of these were Scottish (Aberdeen) Churches, one Welsh and the other Liverpool Cathedral. It's very trying.

The joke is that our new work is O.K. with the sliderless chests but Harrison & Harrison, Hill & Norman & Beard, Walkers, and Rushworth & Dreapers are still using the old type slider chests so they are bound to give trouble in time.

Yours ever,
H.W.

H.W./K.C.

big job in the Cathedral — The Liverpool organ is still fitted with its original electric-slider chests.

---

45 Emerson Richards to Henry Willis

May 2nd, 1930

Mr. Henry Willis,

   234 Ferndale Road,

      Brixton, London, S.W.9, England

My dear Willis:

Upon looking it up we have discovered that our subscription to the Rotunda has expired. Cannot find the subscription rate, but upon consulting my former remittance am sending the same amount, which will last, we presume for another year or thereabouts.

Have bound all the copies up to September, 1929. There appears to be a missing number. If so, may we have it forwarded to us with the present number and credited to the subscription account.

Have just completed the Kimball organ in the ballroom, which, because of its rather powerful seven-rank Mixture, is much more brilliant than Kimball organs usually are. It has some very fine solo reeds and quite a decent ensemble.

The big organ is coming along well, being nearly 50% completed and in operation. We are just putting in place the big metal 32. The low C is 24 inches in diameter and the metal is unannealed zinc ¼ inch thick. The pipe is fitted with double languids. We expect to have the wind on in a day or two and are quite anxious to find how they will come out.

At present we have playing the enclosed Choir, String Organ No. 2, the Brass Wind division, Gallery divisions 2, 3 and 4, and all of the Echo Organ, also part of the Fanfare Organ.

The Fanfare Organ has been considerably augmented. A family of three voices similar to Haskell's reedless tubas have been added called Gamba Tubas. The Clarion is in and playing and is an extremely powerful but fine stop. We have a 32' Trombone unit which plays on the manual at 32, 8 and 4, and of course also on the pedal at 32, 16 and 8.

If you will note these divisions, I think you will agree that this is quite the most interesting feature in the organ. Incidentally, this division was moved to a position in the central part of the hall.

The battery of double languid Diapasons (Gallery Division 2) are playing and give a perfectly enormous amount of very bright Diapason tone. The six stops quite fill the auditorium.

Am still trying to find time to make a dash across. This is pretty definitely settled now for early September or the latter part of August.

With kindest personal regards, I am,

Cordially yours,
Emerson Richards

ER H
Enc.

Kimball organ in the ballroom — the five-manual organ in the ballroom of Atlantic City Convention Hall.

---

46 Henry Willis to Emerson Richards

17th May, 1930

My dear Senator,

Many thanks for yours of the 2nd inst. The Publishing Department say that you have had all numbers including Vol. 3 No. 2 March 1930. If you let me know which one you have not got, and a copy is available, I will have one sent you. If you had said which one was missing it could have been sent at once.

Mayer of West Point was over recently and told me of the fine progress you are making at Atlantic City.

The big metal 32' you mention is on the lines of Liverpool Cathedral as regards diameter, material and thickness, but I did not use double languids — no need.

When will the job be finished? I want to run over again when it is done to hear it and other big new jobs built since I was last over in 1926.

I do trust that you will come over this year — much of interest for you to see and hear. The Alexandra Palace organ is magnificent.

Yours very sincerely,
H.W.

H.W./K.C.

Mayer of West Point — Frederick C. Mayer, organist of the Cadet Chapel, West Point Military Academy, New York.

47 Henry Willis to Edwin H. Lemare

16th July, 1930.

Mr. Edwin H. Lemare
2200, Fairfield Avenue
Hollywood
California
U.S.A.

Dear Mr. Lemare,

Your letter of the 12th April reached me eventually.

Reginald Goss Custard is the official organist at the Alexandra Palace and you will have to apply to him. He gives recitals on Sunday afternoons during the season — October-April/May.

Sorry — but there is no one over here who specializes as an Agent for Virtuoso Organists.

I have been using all-adjustable pistons for years — I quite agree with all you say about them.

Looking forward to seeing you over here,

I am,

Yours sincerely,
H.W.

H.W./K.C.

---

48 Lynnwood Farnam in Antrim Hotel, Liverpool, to Henry Willis

August 3, 1930

Dear Henry:

I was certainly sorry to hear you had an accident while taking a ride in your car, but hope that the change you are experiencing will restore you to your usual health. I am here for four days and had my pupils Cato and McCurdy along for part of the time. We came hurriedly and did not arrange far enough ahead to have a try on St. George's Hall, and Ellingford is away. But we all were thrilled by the Cathedral. They have spent a month in Salisbury and declare that full swell measures up to that one. Goss-Custard took several friends in to the Cathedral last evening and he and I played. It was a treat.

You very kindly gave me an invitation to visit you and I should enjoy being with you for a few days if you and Mrs. Willis find it convenient — perhaps toward the end of this month. I am taking things easier than formerly this trip, but if a single recital at Westminster can be arranged, say September 5 or 6, I should like to do it. I know you said you thought the time out of the question but circumstances might change! I plan on going to the Hereford Festival September 7 to 11.

With kindest regards as ever,

Sincerely yours,
Lynnwood

my pupils Cato and McCurdy — Robert Cato and Alexander McCurdy Jr., students of Farnam at the Curtis Institute.

---

49 Henry Willis to Charles M. Courboin of Welte-Tripp Organ Co.

9th September, 1930.

Dear Charles,

I could not fail to notice the Welte-Tripp advertisement in the September issue of the <u>Diapason,</u> part of which reads as follows:

"Welte voicers have voiced many of the most famous organs in Europe and America, including the organ in the renowned Westminster Cathedral."

Charles M. Courboin

While it may be understood in America the only way in which an average person over here can construe the above extract is that Welte Voicers voiced the Westminster Cathedral Organ.

I take exception to this for it is not true and, furthermore, indicates that I engaged Welte Voicers to voice the Westminster Cathedral Organ — this is damaging to my prestige.

I am aware that the one bare fact behind the statement is that Whiteby, when with me, voiced a few of the stops for Westminster Cathedral under

my close supervision. At the time he was a Willis voicer, <u>not</u> a Welte voicer.
. . .

I am sure that the advertisement was not meant to convey the impression that any English reader would obtain from it and that all it was meant to convey was that you had a voicer who had been with Willis.

I think that you will agree to make it clear in your Company's next advertisement the true circumstances and so avoid the necessity of doing so myself.

Why do you not make a point of stating that "our Mr. R.W. in charge of voicing, several years with Willis" or words to that effect? It would be correct and, I feel sure, have a greater advertising value than a reference to past Welte voicing, much of which is deplorable.

Senator Richards and I have been running around trying Organs and have had a great time together.

Yours ever,
H.W.

H.W./E.F.

Whiteby — actually, Richard Whitelegg. See note, letter 13.

---

50 Charles Courboin of Welte-Tripp to Henry Willis

September 17, 1930

Mr. Henry Willis
c/o Rotunda Organ Works,
234, Ferndale Road,
Brixton, London
My dear Henry:

I have your letter of September 9. I am terribly sorry, there must be some misunderstanding.

This advertisement was written by our former business manager, Mr. A.E. Lott, who was absolutely foreign to anything pertaining to organ building. He is no longer with us and has not been for the last two months, and what he meant I do not know. I showed the letter to Whitelegg who was very distressed by it; so was I, of course.

I am sure that the proper information was given Mr. Lott regarding Whitelegg and that it was never intended to have Whitelegg as a Welte voicer, having voiced your organs in England.

We are proud of the fact that we have a Willis voicer with us, and this fact certainly enhances our prestige.

As I am now in full charge of everything pertaining to the Welte Company, rest assured that this will not occur again, furthermore you may make use of this letter as you wish, and *[we]* would be very glad to have you do so. We do not intend to advertise our voicing department again, but I will make such redress as will be agreeable to you.

I wish I were with you and Senator Richards in London, we certainly would have a great time together. Please let me know how you want this matter adjusted to your entire satisfaction.

Yours ever,

Charles Courboin

---

51 Henry Willis to Charles Courboin

1st October, 1930

Mr. Charles M. Courboin
Welte-Tripp Organ Corporation
Sound Beach
Connecticut
U.S.A.

My dear Charles,

Thanks for yours of the 17th instant, I knew that you could not have been responsible for the advertisement in question.

I certainly think that you ought to make a feature of the fact that your voicing work is under the supervision of Whitelegg etc. A good point to make.

Have just returned from Belgium where I went with Senator Richards and Hans Steinmeyer to inspect the organs in the Antwerp and Liege Expositions. Unfortunately I have lost your sister's name and address or I would most certainly have called upon her when in Antwerp.

Hans Steinmeyer is the head of the firm of Steinmeyer. It was his brother Fritz whom we met at Passau as you may remember. Hans is an even better fellow than his brother as regards certain virtues essential to organ builders. In fact, he is "some boy!"

All the best,

Yours ever,

H.W.

H.W./K.C.

52 Henry Willis to Basil Austin

2nd October, 1930

Mr. Basil Austin
The Austin Organ Co.
Hartford
Conn.
U.S.A.
Dear Mr. Austin,

I have sent a letter addressed to your firm (in case of your absence) asking if you can make a four-row set of keys complete with couplers, coupler drawstop etc. and ship within three months. It's for a rebuild and wanted in a hurry. We are so full up with work that it would be a great help if you could do it for us.

The set you sent some years ago for a Hope-Jones rebuild works perfectly.

Yours very sincerely,
H.W.

H.W. K.C.

four-row set of keys — Austin cabled back, "YES CAN SUPPLY."

---

53 Bernard Laberge to Henry Willis

October 6, 1930

Mr. Henry Willis,
Henry Willis & Sons, Ltd.
234 Ferndale Road,
Brixton, London, S.W. 9,
England.
My dear friend:

A few words in haste to ask you for some very important information, that is, for me. I want you to kindly write me by return mail what you know about the German organ composer, Karg-Elert, whom I would like to bring to America for a transcontinental tour next season 1931-32, provided he can play. Nobody seems to be able to tell me about that here, and since he had the festival of his works in London last spring you surely can tell me if I could present him in an organ concert in which he could play a number of his works.

Does he play for instance as well as Hollins? I think that I could book him a very good tour here on account of his being widely known as a composer, but of course I must make sure beforehand that he himself can play well enough.

59

Thanking you very much for letting me have this information at your earliest convenience, and with always kindest regards and best wishes,

Sincerely yours,

Bernard R. Laberge

BOGUE-LABERGE CONCERT MANAGEMENT, INC.

Karg-Elert — Sigfrid Karg-Elert, German organist-composer (1877-1933)
Laberge — manager for Dupré, Gunther Ramin, Palmer Christian, and others

---

54 Emerson Richards to Henry Willis

October 16th, 1930

Mr. Henry Willis
234 Ferndale Road,
Brixton, London, S.W.9.
My dear Willis:

Caught the train all right and had plenty of time to wait before the ship sailed at 11:30. Never left Cherbourg until 8 P.M. But nevertheless we had a five-day passage, and landed 8 o'clock Monday morning. About 300 prominent Atlantic City people motored up to New York to be on hand when we arrived. It turned into a sort of all-day celebration.

Incidentally the ship was wet, but I calculated the reserve stock so that I took the last drink just as the boat docked.

I have had ample time to think over the very many kindnesses that you did for me while in England, and I want to assure you of my most grateful appreciation. All I can do is to wait until I get you over here to get even. Will you please give my regards to your good wife, and apologize for my abrupt departure.

I am sending you one of the action magnets and one of the stop action magnets, and I am also making an arrangement to get samples of the coupler and combination actions.

With kindest personal regards, I am,

Cordially yours,

Emerson Richards

ER H

the ship was wet — alcoholic consumption was allowed on board

Bernard Laberge

55 Henry Willis to Bernard Laberge

20th October, 1930

Mr. Bernard R. Laberge
250, West 57th Street,
New York City,
U.S.A.

My dear Laberge,

Reference yours of the 6th instant about Karg-Elert, he was over here about three months ago and I know him and his work. K.E. is utterly out of practice as a recitalist; he has no organ to preside over. On the other hand, K.E. has great gifts and if he had intensive practice beforehand would do well, if he could handle American consoles, which I doubt. K.E. was completely baffled by English consoles, so heaven knows how he would get on in America!

Candidly, I am afraid that he would be a complete "flop" unless he worked intensively in preparation for his tour and had ample time for rehearsal at every organ he was to play on.

Yours ever,

H.W.

H.W./E.F.

October 27th, 1930

Mr. Henry Willis
234 Ferndale Road,
Brixton, London, S.W.9.
My dear Willis:

Thank you for your letter enclosing the receipted bill. We are forwarding you this morning a sample of the Klann magnet made by August Klann, Waynesboro, Virginia, and the stop action frame as made by W. H. Reisner, Hagerstown, Maryland. The Klann magnet has the resistance of 400 ohms, the Reisner stop action 26 ohms.

I am engaged to write a series of articles for the <u>American Organist,</u> covering my recent organistic adventures with you and Steinmeyer. I shall discuss at some detail the organs I saw in England, and which will naturally feature your particular work.

I thought it was quite possible that you might wish me to use some illustrations, and if you have any photographs of any of the jobs that Buhrman has not already published, I am sure he would be glad to use them. Incidentally, I will make every effort to try and send you a copy of what I have written in advance, so that if there is anything to which exception might be taken, you could point it out to me. I am not sure whether the English articles will appear before the German ones.

I am arranging to obtain the sample rigs for the coupler and remote control combination actions. Of course this will take some time to make up, but will send them on to you as soon as I can get them together.

Found good progress on the work here. The big C of the 64' is laying up in the organ chamber and a very imposing sight. However, I have decided to mitre it, setting it up on its foot at the extreme back of the chamber and turning the bell over a matter of about 20 feet towards the grill. The C#, the D and the D# and E will all nest one right under the other. Being directional they ought to give a fine account of themselves.

Harry is working hard today regulating the 100" in time for the football game tonight. It will be its first appearance. It certainly is a magnificent tone. The extra pressure adds refinement. Showing, however, we are never satisfied, Harry now feels that it would be even better if the pressure was much greater.

Losh, thank fortune, is still away — Florida and then points west, and VanWart, Skinner's old superintendent, is in active command of the job and the work goes on merrily.

Trusting that the magnets will reach you OK, and with kindest regards to the family, I am,

Cordially yours,

Emerson Richards

ER H

P.S. — Note the no-impulse feature.

VanWart — see letter 3.

no-impulse feature — in combination actions, this device disengages the action behind idle knobs to reduce noise.

---

57 Ernest Skinner to Archibald T. Davison

November 8, 1930

Dr. Archibald T. Davison
22 Francis Ave.,
Cambridge, Mass.

Re: <u>Appleton Chapel, Harvard College</u>

My dear Dr. Davison:

In the opinion of one who knows as much about tone as the next man, if 45 years experience means anything, the Swell Diapason in your organ is the purest tone, and the Great No.1 is the next to it. The other two on the Great are of a more nasal variety that is supposed to make a better ensemble.

We, undoubtedly, went too far on the fluty side in years past; then along came an appreciation of the fact that the fluty side of the question was overdone, and that we should restore the mixtures and give more attention to the ensemble, but it so happens that it is just as easy to err on the too brilliant side as it is in the other direction.

The reason the Great Diapason No.1 is said not to blend is because it has something to say on its own account, and in effect, it cannot be entirely obliterated by the balance of the material on the Great organ. If you will pull out all the Great except the Diapasons and then draw Diapason numbers 2 and 3, you will find that they are very largely swallowed up by the upper work and the reeds.

This is all very well if one's musical aspirations are satisfied with contrapuntal music, but this is a long way from my idea of the musical wants that should attend a vocal accompaniment. I happen to know from personal contact that your Great Organ Diapason No.1 makes a beautiful blend with the voices because it has something in common with the voices. To say that that Diapason No.1 does not blend with the balance of the organ is equivalent to saying that your voices do not blend with the organ, because Diapason No.1 has a normal quality that is common to voices. It is a quality

63

neither on the sharp nor fluty side of the intermediate ground which makes the perfect diapason.

Youngsters like Covell and Gammons read up on these points and get the old world idea of an ensemble, also that of a contrapuntal specialist, and have nothing in common with the ear that loves a beautiful tone on account of its beauty. After all is said and done, I have put what you call a friendly characteristic in the organ which has given to it something of the warmth and temperamental qualities of other instruments. I have never agreed with the idea that the organ should be cold and unsympathetic, but I think it is a fair statement to say that it has been very largely of this description.

The German organ at Methuen, of which Covell thinks so much, is as hard as nails. It hasn't a decent reed or string in the entire outfit, and yet he thinks it is the greatest organ in America. Take a tip from me and don't rely too much on the infallible omniscience of the dilettante.

If that Great Diapason No.1 is changed, it will be over my dead body. If you would sit out in the gallery a little way from the Choir, where I sit, and hear it with the voices, you would know that it was an invaluable voice for your purpose.

Another thing of importance, as I see it, this type of diapason gives the Great organ a character distinct from that of the Swell or Choir, so that you not only have variation in the individual voices of given manuals, but you have manual distinction.

Frankly, we are being criticized at the present time because we have been turning out diapasons that were lacking in the body that the former examples had. I do not care too much for a blend that means being swallowed up. The lion and the lamb make a perfect blend, but the lamb is inside the lion. Your ensemble will be very nearly destitute of diapason quality if the Great organ Diapason No.1 is changed.

I will get over there and see you as soon as I can. In the meantime, the Philomela couples to the Great, the Solo Tuba couples to the Great, and all the stops of the organ respond to the couplers as they should.

I do not know whether I can improve the condition of the basses or not. I have pretty nearly exhausted my resources in that direction. The acoustics of some buildings exaggerate this windy element, which it did to a remarkable degree in the 4 upper notes of the 32' octave of the Fagotto. I practically eliminated this defect in these four pipes by doing something to these four notes which has never been done before in the history of the world, as far as my knowledge goes, and I never touched the reeds themselves.

Here's to our early meeting.

Yours very sincerely,
Ernest M. Skinner

EMS:MBL
cc to NYO & GLC

Archibald Davison.— Professor of music at Harvard University, eminent musicologist, choral director, and university organist

The German organ at Methuen — an 1863 Walcker organ, originally installed in the Boston Music Hall. Edwin F. Searles, a wealthy Massachusetts philanthropist, moved this organ to Serlo Hall in Methuen, a building he constructed especially for the organ. Skinner purchased Serlo Hall with the organ in 1929, and it was consequently rebuilt by Harrison in 1947.

cc to NYO & GLC — New York Office and George L. Catlin, Treasurer and General Manager of the Skinner Co.

---

58 Henry Willis to Emerson Richards

21st November, 1930

Senator Emerson Richards
800 Schwehm Building
Atlantic City
New Jersey
U.S.A.

My dear Richards,

Many thanks for your letter of the 27th instant.

I got and tried the Klann magnet. On test here the resistance only worked out to 226 ohms in place of the 400 you mentioned — this on 10 volts. However, it's a very neat unit and has given me an idea for a very useful "converter" magnet — exhaust to pressure. Our ordinary magnets deal with all pressures up to 30", which is as much as we normally use. All the same, the Klann relay magnet is very good. It would be better with a Bakelite base, armature cap etc.

The Reisner stop key magnet unit is their usual standard plus the no-impulse device. It draws a lot of current — momentarily.

If you let me know what photos you want, I will send at once. I believe the only important ones that Buhrman has not used are those of the Alexandra Palace. You can have any that have appeared in the Rotunda. What about Thornton Heath, the three-row job, all-enclosed, four swell boxes? This might be of interest and might demonstrate that I am not as "dyed in the wool" as some people (Barnes!) imagine.

I would like to go over any drafts on organs because I might help to avoid any error of fact.

I think you were wise to mitre your 64's. I am looking forward to hearing it in due course.

I have just received and glanced through Barnes' new book. It's all very ingenuous and typical of him. A pity he did not wait another five years for his opinions will be more mature then.

All the best,

Henry Willis

H.W. K.C.

his opinions will be more mature — Barnes published a second version of *The Contemporary American Organ* in 1933, and continued to produce new editions through the 1970s.

---

59 Henry Willis to James B. Jamison of Estey

21st November, 1930

My dear Jamison,

I was sorry not to have seen you again before you sailed. I trust that you had a good crossing and are glad to be back in harness again.

Take my tip and keep regular scaling on all your diapason work, halving it at the 16½ note is best all round. This is, I believe, the regular scale used in U.S.A. Don't make the 4' Principal one scale smaller than the Open and the 15th one scale smaller than the Principal — it leaves the upperwork too big and foundational and, with you, finishers would be forced to cut the power down, leaving flutey trebles which are dreadful.

Don't use 2/7 mouths on pressures higher than 4" nor ¼ mouths over 5" — they tend to become intractable and windy. Voicers then beard the basses, which is all wrong.

The safest all round is:

Mouth --

5	Double	16'	two scales small to Open 1
4	Open 1.	8'	scale to suit circumstances
4/4½/or 5	Open 2.	8'	two scales small to Open 1.
4½	Principal 1.	4'	two scales small to Open 1.
	Principal 2.	4'	two scales small to Open 2.
5	Twelfth	2⅔'	two scales small to 15th
5	Fifteenth	2'	two scales small to Principal 1.
5	<u>Mixtures</u>		unisons same scale as 15th

quints   "   "   " 12th and
25% softer than <u>unisons</u>
tierce ranks (17) — two scales small to
12th and 30% softer than <u>quints</u>

Cut-ups should be as regular as clockwork.

James B. Jamison

		Really resonant buildings	Non-resonant buildings
2/7	mouth	4 in 1	7 in 2
4	"	3 in 1	11 in 4
4½	"	11 in 4	5 in 2
5	"	5 in 2	9 in 4

Slightly more wind is required, of course, for the higher cut-ups in non-resonant buildings.

Don't use <u>flat</u> lower lips except for special circumstances, i.e. old English-type diapasons, as for a Choir Organ, when long flats on top and lower lips, nearly upright front to languid, knife cut nicks, etc.

For all diapason work the nicking on the lower lip should be half the depth of that on the languid and nicks on lower lip should be between those on languid to obtain proper wind diffusion. Don't allow double edge nickers to be used.

As regards the bevel on upper lips, don't overdo it. A bevel reducing thickness by 50% at an angle of 30° from the vertical is a sound treatment. More bevel, reducing thickness of edge of upper lip, increases the harmonic development a little and can always be done on the job when required to brighten up a stop. Of course if done the pipes will require quickening slightly.

Use this information as personal to you, for obvious reasons. You can, of course, make use of it, but take credit for any success yourself!

I will be glad to hear how you get on.

Two things you told me interest me greatly, and I would be really grateful for data concerning them. I refer to the pipes with inside cylinder to reduce height, and the particular form of adjustable combination action governed by <u>one</u> setter button your people use. I like to know what is being used.

Yours sincerely,

H.W.

My dear Jamison — James B. Jamison, Estey tonal designer interested in incorporating English ensemble ideas. At the time, he was working on a large organ he hoped would be a masterpiece: Bridges Auditorium, Claremont College, Claremont, Ca. Among other features, the instrument included complete diapason choruses and an imported tuba from the English builder Harrison & Harrison. See letter 78.

Take my tip — Willis later seems to deny that he supplied Jamison with this information. See letters 88 and 89.

pipes with inside cylinder — the patented Haskell invention frequently used for bass pipes. Jamison's reply is letter 73.

by one setter button — In England, few organ consoles were fitted with combination action using a setter button. Combinations were either fixed or chosen on a setter board. The Willis system did use a setter button, however.

---

60 Emerson Richards to Henry Willis

November 22nd, 1930

Mr. Henry Willis
    234 Ferndale Road,
        Brixton, S.W.9.
            London, England

My dear Willis:

Went over to hear Swinnen on the new Hook and Hastings organ in the new Rockefeller Church. Enclose a program. The organ is terrible. Swinnen had a fit. Told me that if he could have gotten out of it he would not have played.

While over there I heard some very sad news. As you know, Farnam was supposed to have been operated upon for gallstones about a month ago. He is still in the hospital — no one allowed to see him, and now his father, who was in attendance, admits that the operation disclosed the fact that he was suffering from a cancer and that there is no hope of his recovery. It would seem as if it is only a matter of days.

Saw Buhrman and am waiting for a reply to my last letter relative to the pictures before proceeding with the articles in the <u>American Organist</u>.

With kindest personal regards, I am

Cordially yours,

Emerson Richards

P.S. Will forward key and stop action in about 4 weeks.

Swinnen — Firmin Swinnen (1885-1972) Belgian concert organist who migrated to England in 1914 and the U.S. in 1916 to play in various New York City theatres. Later he became Pierre S. duPont's personal organist at Longwood Gardens, Kennett Square, Pennsylvania, where he supervised the Aeolian company's installation of a 177-rank 10,010 pipe organ in the conservatory ballroom.

the new Rockefeller Church — Riverside Church, New York City. The organ was later rebuilt by Aeolian-Skinner.

---

61 Henry Willis to Alexander Russell

25th November, 1930

Dr. Alexander Russell
Hotel Webster
40 W. 45 Street
New York City
U.S.A.

My dear Russell,

It was a dreadful shock to receive a cable this morning announcing Lynnwood's death and I took the liberty of cabling you, as enclosed confirmation, asking you to send a wreath for myself and my wife. Please let me know cost and I will remit at once. Thanks awfully for taking the trouble.

The poor chap was in bad health when with us over here, but we all thought it due to gastric trouble which he would overcome.

We got the impression that Lynnwood was bearing up after the operation but it was not so — a gap is left which simply cannot be filled. It has been a great thing to have known, intimately, so great a player.

We hope that Mrs. Russell had a pleasant journey back to the States; it was delightful seeing her here.

With our united regards,

Yours ever,

H.W.

H.W./K.C.

My dear Russell — Alexander Russell, the Director of Music at Princeton Chapel and Music Director of Concerts at the Wanamaker Store, Philadelphia.

Lynnwood's death — Farnam died in New York on November 23, 1930, at age 45.

3rd December, 1930

Senator Emerson L. Richards
Atlantic City,
New Jersey,
U.S.A

My dear Richards,

Thanks for yours of the 22nd inst. It is sad that the new Hook and Hastings in the Rockefeller Church is such a "flop."

It was a terrible shock to receive a cable on the 24th Nov. intimating that Lynnwood Farnam died on the 23rd. I hoped, as we all did, that he would get over the operation for <u>gallstones,</u> but as you say it turned out to be a cancer it was hopeless. Cancer is a terrible thing. This is a terrible loss to organ playing. Still it has been a great privilege to have known Lynnwood so intimately.

I have got Klann to make up that heavy-pressure relay magnet modified for "pressure-out." It is going to be very useful for "conversion" jobs of which we do a lot. Many thanks for putting me on to it.

When do you really anticipate having the Convention Hall job absolutely finished in every way? I suppose it would be certain to be finished by next fall. It is possible that I could make a trip in early October next following the completion of the St. George's Hall rebuild in September.

All the best,

Yours ever,
H.W.

H.W./E.F.

December 8th, 1930

Mr. Henry Willis
234, Ferndale Road,
Brixton, S.W.9.
London, Eng.

My dear Willis:

Thanks for your letter of November 21st. I am surprised about the test on the Klann magnet. I was taking his tests for granted and never checked them up myself. I will do so now.

Am very glad that you are sending the Alexandra Palace pictures; of the five big jobs I think it stands next to Liverpool as the best. Would very much like to have Thornton Heath, St. Thomas a'Becket, and in this case please send me the specification. I ought to have it in my bound copies of the <u>Rotunda</u>, but that might be the volume which is missing. I do not recall that Buhrman has published a picture of Westminster Cathedral, and if you happen to have handy a picture of St. Ann's, could use it also.

The key action contact rig is promised for the next two weeks and I will forward it immediately upon its completion. Almost ready to turn on the big 64'.

Losh just had me on the telephone and I spoke to him about the Klann magnets. He explained that you were right — that the magnet that I had picked up and sent to you is only a 200 ohm magnet. The 400 ohm magnet will not deal with the 100" pressure and the lower resistant magnet had to be used on this pressure. He is sending you a 400 ohm magnet by today's mail. This magnet was especially designed to be used for stop action and all other places where the magnet is on for any great length of time.

With kindest personal regards, I am,

Cordially yours,
Emerson Richards

ER H

P.S. The Alexandra Palace pictures arrived this morning.

---

64 Emerson Richards to Henry Willis

December 15th, 1930

Mr. Henry Willis
234 Ferndale Road,
London, England

My dear Willis:

Your letter of the 3rd came in this morning just as we were sending off the key coupler action. We have forwarded the same to you securely packed via parcel post. I trust it will turn up in good order.

This action as presently constituted was designed by George Losh and his engineers, but constructed by Klann who has all of the necessary dies for stamping out the various parts and is in a position to furnish you with parts or the whole action if you desire. The cardboard top has a spring clamp which makes it instantly removable.

We have mounted the key frame and this action on the tail of the keys as one unit and then permit it to rest in the grooves of two angle irons, one placed on each side, thereby permitting complete accessibility by simply sliding the whole unit out from the rear. This makes it a bit more accessible than by raising the key action up from the front. I will send a picture of the seven-manual console which shows the way this rig works.

This sample is for you. It seemed, however, unnecessary to make two of them for you and Steinmeyer, and therefore after you have looked it over carefully would suggest that you pass it on to Steinmeyer for his inspection with instructions that he then return it to you permanently. I am writing him accordingly, so that he will understand he is to return it to you.

A fairly long key tail naturally makes for a lighter action. If you want to use a tracker touch, of course it simply means putting another spring under the key in the usual manner. This rig with the remote control combination action admits of an all-electric console without any wind in it and with practically nothing except the stop knobs, a magnet to move the stop knobs and the cables, making a very light and small console possible where room is needed.

Note how the little contact springs are flattened out so as to lessen their resistance to the rotating contact bar, thereby making no appreciable difference in the touch no matter how many contacts are in service. Klann is making all the die stampings for the combination action and is going to assemble the sample and send it on in a couple of weeks, and I will forward it to you.

I anticipate that the organ will be finished by mid-summer at the outside. All of our experimental work is over and it is just plain sailing from now on. We have the big 32' 50" Diaphone playing and it certainly makes a noble <u>noise</u> in the hall.

It would be fine if you could get over in the fall. I am going to try and repeat my stunt of this year, getting away about the same time or possibly a week earlier, spend a few days in England, then the balance in Germany doing what did not get done this time. It will depend somewhat on my political engagements at that time, in which case your visit here would follow right along afterwards, perhaps even returning on the same ship. It would a fine time of the year to be here and an excellent opportunity for us to do some real motoring looking at the various jobs.

The cards have been shuffled recently and as a result both Maurice and Walter Hardy are now with Skinner and Skinner's western representative is now with Kimball.

Please give my best to Mrs. Willis and here is wishing you a very Merry Christmas and the most prosperous New Year.

Cordially yours,
Emerson Richards

ER H

the seven manual console — The five manual console at Atlantic City was of relatively modest design, but the seven manual console was large enough for several men to work inside, where the entire action was accessible. Despite the massive relays inside the organ, extensive key contacts were required for coupling. This action was mounted at the back of each manual, all seven of which could be separately removed for adjustment.

The cards have been shuffled — Maurice and Walter Hardy were formerly with Kimball.

---

65 Henry Willis to Emerson Richards

19th December, 1930

Senator Emerson L. Richards
800 Schwehm Building
Atlantic City, New Jersey, U.S.A
My dear Richards,

Many thanks for yours of the 8th instant.

Losh sent another Klann magnet, but it is almost exactly the same as the one you sent before — and nothing like 400 ohm resistance on 10 volts. The last one is 250 ohms. However, that is not material for it works on 30" wind comfortably.

I am sending you a copy of the <u>Rotunda</u> Vol. 3 No. 3, September 1930, which gives the St. Jude's Thornton Heath specification. I gave you a copy when you were here but you must have mislaid it.

If you check through your copies of the <u>Rotunda</u> you will note which number is missing and if you advise me I will send a copy, unless out of print.

I am looking forward to seeing the key action contact rig.

Publishing Department is looking up photos of St. Jude's Thornton Heath (2) and St. Thomas a Becket Wandsworth, and St. Anne's Soho for you.

Buhrman has already used a photo of Westminster Cathedral, at least I think so — same photo as appeared in the <u>Rotunda</u>. I am sending you photos for blockmaking as desired.

Yours ever,
Henry Willis

H.W. K.C.

---

66 Henry Willis to Emerson Richards

29th December, 1930

Senator Emerson L. Richards
800 Schwehm Building
Atlantic City, New Jersey, U.S.A
My dear Richards,

Many thanks for yours of the 15th inst. just to hand.

It will be most interesting to receive the model of the key coupler action, and I am looking forward to it, also, later on, the electric combination setter. Thanks for the information which has been noted. I will send the model over to Hans Steinmeyer and know that he will be as interested as I am. As you know, I have been using all electric consoles; they work beautifully but are costly to manufacture and there is no doubt about the greater economy of doing <u>everything</u> in the console including the combination action for an instrument of normal proportions. This means anything of the size we do or are likely to do over here. Of course at Atlantic City, remote control for the combination actions was an absolute necessity.

From your letter I take it that Losh has no objection to my utilising the designs wholly or in part, for you are good enough to say that Klann can furnish either the parts or the whole. As a matter of fact it may prove a blessing, for we are so full of work that our electrical departments are overwhelmed.

It will be nice if you can come over next summer in which case I will try and get over to Germany with you. It was maddening having to leave you at Liege this year.

I don't suppose that I will have anything new of note to show you in England — St. George's Hall will not be finished until the end of September and it is after the opening of that job that there is some hope of my being free to run over to the States for a quick run around. . . .

It is rather amusing that Skinner's western representative has gone over to Kimball — when Jamison, Estey's western representative was here, he was bewailing the fact that Skinner's chap had been . . . *[material lost]*

<u>Thornton Heath, St. Jude's</u>. "less loss of bloom in the (Great) Diapasons" — I hold that the treatment is such that there is no loss and quite thought you agreed — it is that fact which gives me more pleasure than anything else in that instrument.

<u>Westminster Bridge Rd. Christ Church</u>. It was this Lewis-Schulze Great Mixture and the 5 rank Willis one named "Grand Chorus" at Westminster Cathedral which took Skinner's breath away and converted him and Arthur Marks in 1924. Why not mention names? Skinner makes no secret about it.

<u>Electric action</u>. My electric mechanism are <u>accepted</u> here without any argument or difficulty on my part — since I standardised electric action in 1924 I have only lost one contract by insisting on that form of mechanism and that was for Paisley Abbey where, with a detached console etc, tubular action would have been ludicrous. General opinion here is now in favour of electric action properly done — but the efforts of some builders in this direction do not help!

<u>Liverpool Cathedral</u>. I agree to some extent with your comments about the Solo strings — they were made at a time when small scaled strings had

high popularity. If I did them again today they would be broader in tone and bigger.

H.W.

H.W. K.C.

Skinner makes no secret — See letter 77.

---

67 Emerson Richards to Henry Willis

January 8th, 1931

Mr. Henry Willis
34, Ferndale Road,
Brixton, S.W.9.
London, England
My dear Willis:

Your letters of the 19th and 29th arrived in the reverse order yesterday and today. The pictures and copy of the Rotunda arrived, and I am quite sure that Buhrman will be glad to use them.

By this time you should have received the key contact model. I am writing to Klann to find out why the combination action has not turned up as yet.

There will be no objection from Losh about the use of any part of the Klann rig, because it is understood that Klann may use the whole affair in view of the fact that he made all the dies at his expense.

Am having my hands full here at home, as my mother is very ill at the present time.

Making considerable progress on the big organ. The lower six notes of the 64' are completed and in place and we are expecting to get wind on the low C before the end of the week. Have all the Swell finished except the mixtures. I set the C's on them last week and we are certainly going to have some fireworks there. The end of this month will probably see the last of the great and solo chests in place, and from then on it will only be a question of the making and voicing of the pipe work for these two divisions, the completion of the consoles and the wiring.

With kindest personal regards, I am,

Cordially yours,
Emerson Richards

ER H

March 13th, 1931

Mr. Henry Willis
234, Ferndale Road,
London, England
My dear Willis:

Thank you for your letter and the corrected copy of the article on English organs.

Returned from Florida last week, making the trip from Palm Beach to Atlantic City, 1269 miles, in exactly two days and three hours, stopping overnight at Jacksonville and Raleigh. Fine time. Flew to Havana and had a good time over there; also to Nassau and return.

On the way down I stopped and saw Klann about the combination action. He is making up the whole action at one time, consequently the sample is no further advanced than the rest of the action. All of the frames are completed, the pneumatics placed and the lower movable elements inserted. The setter element, or center, was still in the process of manufacture, and the little movable dogs with the contact points were being assembled.

A letter from him says that he is shipping the sample to me about the 15th, followed by the regular elements themselves about the 29th. Therefore, I am hoping to have your sample ready to send to you before the end of the month.

In the mean time we have been testing out Voice #78, the Bugle, in the Solo division. This is a brass belled reed on 50" pressure. Due to the unusual treatment of the shallot and other points of interest, I thought you might be interested in a sample pipe and had an additional middle C made up. Figuring that you might not have 50" wind available for testing purposes, I also had an additional tongue curved suitable for 30". It goes on both pressures. You will find the regulation marked on the pipe. The resonator is tuned by moving the sliding stem up and down, and the tone regulation is adjusted the same as any other reed pipe. A different tuning on the resonator is required on the 30" and the 50" wind. That is marked and you will note. The 50" tongue is in the pipe, and the 30" tongue is packed in a little box which is placed in the bell of the pipe.

I think you will be interested in the tone quality. Of course, it is only useful in a big job, and am merely sending it on as a matter of interest and as an illustration of some of the funny things we are doing. The pipe, of course, was voiced in Losh's factory by Capaldi, his voicer of fancy reeds, after considerable experimentation which we did down here.

Am looking forward to receiving the magnets which have not yet arrived. The photos did arrive and will be used in the article on the English organs. Buhrman rather feels that we ought to clean up the German section first, which now starts in the April number, so that the publication may be deferred for two or three months, until we have the complete German stuff out of the way.

I will re-type the Wandsworth job so as to show both the model scheme and the organ as built. I will clean up the question of the possible loss of bloom in the Diapasons by saying that there is no apparent loss of bloom. It was to this that I agreed, although my own experiments prove that there must be a dampening of the harmonics when the pipe is located in a swell box. This does not mean that if the harmonics are suitably developed for the purpose, that they may not be put in a swell box and give the proper effect in the auditorium — simply that they must be exaggerated to do it.

In the Westminster Bridge case, I do not think it wise to mention Skinner's name in the article, the reason being that about two years ago in making a reference to Skinner which I thought was complimentary, Skinner took offense. So much so that he withdrew his advertising from the <u>American Organist</u>, and they have only just gotten it back. I do not feel like embarrassing Buhrman that way again.

I will change the article on the electric action to make it clearer, as per your suggestion. Perhaps my information was wrong, but I have heard both in England and over here that you were obliged to fight against the conservatism that had obsessed the English authorities against electric action.

Things are coming along pretty well down at the Convention Hall. The Swell organ is completed, and certainly is a rather thrilling affair. I would say that it is about as big as the Swell and Solo at the Alexandra Palace combined. Most of the Pedal on that side is also playing, and the big 32' Diaphone on 50" wind certainly does make a grand impression. The big Pedal mixture is also well worth the money. Practically all the Great and Solo chests are up, the 64' Octave of the Dulcian is completed and in place, and the only big job yet remaining is the balancing of the Great organ Diapasons. Of course that will be quite a job for me, and I am hoping that I will be clear of the heavy work in the Senate before I have to tackle it. However, it is almost immediately upon me, so I fancy that I will spend a few late hours in the Auditorium in the near future.

Will forward you the combination action as soon as it arrives, accompanied by a letter.

With kindest personal regards, I am,

Cordially yours,

Emerson Richards

ER H

the Wandsworth job — St. Thomas à Becket Church, a recent Willis three-manual

28th April, 1931

Senator Emerson L. Richards
800 Schwehm Building
Atlantic City, New Jersey
U.S.A
My dear Richards,

It is a long time since I wrote you. I have had a touch of 'flu and have been feeling very unwell for some time.

I am looking forward to receiving the sample of the combination action which I suppose will be along any day now.

Received the Bugle — a very interesting tonality— I tried it on 30".

Sorry that magnet was not sent you. I am now having it sent.

There is more in the handling of Diapasons on an enclosed Great Organ than merely encouraging a higher harmonic development. If that was done, the effect would be of Geigens. At Thornton Heath the whole Great Diapason structure was of special scale, treatment and voicing. I wish you could have heard the Great with all the shutters out — the effect was curious.

It is curious how thin-skinned "Ernest M." is. First he denounced the English Diapason's structure—then Don Harrison got it in, perhaps somewhat on exaggerated lines according to accounts I have heard, when Skinner at once took the credit. Now I hear that in deference to the tonally uneducated, he is opposing the use! Poor Harrison.

I trust you are keeping fit and that the Convention Hall job is now nearly complete.

Any chance of your coming over this summer?

Yours ever,
H.W.

H.W./K.C.

May 8th, 1931

Mr. Henry Willis
234, Ferndale Road,
Brixton, S.W.9.,
London, England
My dear Willis:

Received your welcome letter this morning. The flu is a mean thing and always has some unwelcome after-effects. Hope you are feeling much better by the time this reaches you.

As I explained in my last letter, the combination action went back to Klann for some slight changes and was only returned and set up for test this morning. It seems to work very well.

Will amplify the Thornton Heath Diapason matter before that article is printed. Have you seen the German articles thus far?

Yes, I am in pretty good shape. Have had a terribly hard winter except for the three weeks in Florida. The Senate work has been simply terrific. I seem never to get to bed any more. And today is the first time in the last five that I have even been able to answer letters. Professional work has also kept me quite busy.

Had a terrific row with Seibert Losh over the Convention Hall organ, due to some attempted monkey business on his part which resulted in my forcing him to resign as president and director of the company. He has been succeeded by Mr. Otto Strack, who is a thoroughly reliable and conscientious man of considerable means who will carry on until the job is completed. I do not know whether you have met Strack. He is a very fine old gentleman. An engineer of some note in New York and owns several loft properties of his own. His interest in organs is purely that of an amateur, but he has done considerable structural engineering on this job and feels morally responsible for its completion in that he urged the company to bid on the work originally.

Feel very much more comfortable now, as Losh had become entirely too erratic and unreliable to deal with. The company is well rid of him. My gain is likely to be your loss, as I understand Losh has threatened to take a trip to Europe. If so he will undoubtedly try to tell you how to build your organs, although as an organ builder he is an excellent salesman. So look out!

You must be having a lot of laughs over Jamison's advertisements in the Diapason. They have made those who know better very sore. I imagine it must burn Skinner up, but it is all very funny to me.

Have had a big job setting the C's on the Great Diapasons. When you are dealing with anything from 4" to 30" inch wind, you have a job on your hands — and then the mixtures as well. Spent nearly all night several nights getting through with it last week.

The Swell organ is finished and certainly does kick up a noble row. Just tackling the voicing of the 64', which is all in place. As a matter of fact, all of the chest work is now in place, mostly wired, and all winded. Looks as if we will have practically the whole organ playing by mid-July.

Yes, I am thinking of coming over for a short time this summer, probably about the same time as last year. The Majestic sails I think on August 21st.

Will forward the combination action in a very few days, just as soon as we are sure that it is not developing any defects.

With very kindest regards, I am,

Cordially yours,
Emerson Richards

ER H

the German articles — Richards' series in the *American Organist*
a terrific row with Seibert Losh — President of Midmer-Losh. According to Sam Hovsepian, organ technician at Atlantic City, Losh had become desperate with the mounting cost of the project and had attempted to use second-hand parts.
Jamison's advertisements — Jamison, the Estey designer and voicer, advertised the Claremont College organ heavily before the installation.

---

71 Henry Willis to Emerson Richards

19th May, 1931

Senator Emerson L. Richards
Atlantic City
New Jersey
U.S.A

My dear Richards,

Thanks for yours of the 8th inst and all the news.

I read your "German articles" with great interest and appreciation — am looking forward to sequelae.

Interesting about Losh, but not much of a surprise — you know my opinion of him. It will relieve you of worry in the finishing of your great conception at Atlantic City and ensure its being finished in every detail as you want it.

I will be interested to meet Losh over here — he will surely have some terrible things to say about you!

The Esteys' ads in the <u>Diapason</u> are a source of great joy — I wonder if such bunk will go down in the U.S.? I suppose that some of it will.

I note with satisfaction that you are coming over this year. I will be away with my family, unfortunately, end of August and early September — but we can get together later. I will make an effort to get St. George's Hall going, for you to hear before you go back. Let me know your plans and movements.

Am looking forward to having the combination action model.

Yours ever,
H.W.

H.W. K.C.

June 19th, 1931

Mr. Henry Willis
234, Ferndale Road,
Brixton, S.W.9.,
London, England
My dear Willis:

Your letter of June 8th came to hand this morning simultaneously with one from Steinmeyer under the same date. Steinmeyer's letter somewhat complicates the vacation situation because he says: "Yesterday I ordered my ticket for Bremen to New York. I am sailing on the North German Lloyd leaving Bremen June 28th and arriving in New York July 4th. I am planning to come back on the Columbus arriving New York August 16th."

As you know, he is coming over to personally finish a 65-stop organ that he is building for Altoona, Pennsylvania. Therefore, there is nothing doing with the German situation until he returns, and I hardly see how I could get away before the August 21st sailing of the Majestic.

Very possibly I could carry out the early part of my trip in England and northern Germany if there was a possibility of your joining us in Bavaria after you return on September 20th. I would have to figure on returning home about the first of October, as I am running for re-election in November and must be here in due season. Steinmeyer says in his letter that he is writing to you about coming to Bavaria after he returns.

I hope that your trip to the U.S. does not fall through, and I can assure you that we will put in the time to the best advantage. The latter part of October will be all right, although you can count on reasonably good weather through November.

The combination action has at last gone forward. It was held up pending my signing some necessary papers at the express office. I enclose the express company receipt and trust that the action reaches you in good order.

The reference to the pneumatic part of the combination action you will understand better when you see the mechanism. It is assumed that in the case of a remote control combination that the apparatus can be put in a position where wind is easily available, in which case magnets to pull the traces may be dispensed with. If this is not the case, then magnets instead of the pneumatics may be used, just as in pulling the traces in the coupler action, a sample of which I have already forwarded to you. The method is exactly the same in both cases.

We are making rather rapid progress now. All of the Pedal is wired, winded and the pipes in place. The Solo is in the same condition, and preliminary tuning going on there now. They are planting the pipes in the

Great Ancillary chests now. The Great chests are all winded and wired and a substantial part of the pipe work ready to be planted. The new type of aluminum shade is extraordinarily efficient. It begins to look as if we are getting near the end of our task.

I understand that Seibert Losh has married again and has already sailed for your shores with his new wife. He will talk the ears off you if you let him. And since Mr. Strack now is the majority stockholder of the organ company, and Losh's brother and his former wife are substantial shareholders, I would imagine that his interest in organs is more or less academic.

I don't know just what to say about any change in plans. It may be that Steinmeyer may be coming back earlier or that some friends of mine who usually sail on the Majestic about this time may try for the July 31st sailing. Of this I cannot be sure at this writing and will advise you a bit later, possibly right after Steinmeyer arrives.

With kindest personal regards, I am,

Cordially yours,
Emerson Richards

ER H

the organ . . . for Altoona — the Roman Catholic Cathedral in Altoona, Pennsylania
rather rapid progress — at Atlantic City

---

73 James B. Jamison of Estey to Henry Willis

June 21, 1931

My Dear Mr. Willis:

It seems to me that I have been something of a chump not to have sent this to you before now, but I have had to take time to realize it. I know you are interested, and you have been most kind to me, so here is the information relative to the Haskell type short length pipes.

Scale the outside cylinder exactly as you would a full length pipe. Suppose we take a 16' string pipe of metal, with a diameter of 5". The inside cylinder can be any length up to 7'. It must protrude above the edge of the outside one by about a third of its diameter. It must not reach down nearer than a foot from the upper lip of the outside pipe. While the relative lengths are flexible, the relative cross sectional areas are rigidly and most accurately fixed. The inner pipe must be exactly one half the cross sectional area of the outside one.

This, at first blush, looks like a rather complex and tedious problem to work out, but an easy way to do it is to figure that the area of a circle is .7854 times the square of its diameter. Thus Area = Diameter squared times

.7854. I have worked this problem out — and you must check my figures, and find that one diameter is 70.7% of the other. You can make a pair of dividers, with the arms pivoted by a pin, so as to realize this proportion. Then the scaling of inner and outer pipes is easy.

10"   *7.07*

Figure out where pin goes
check the 7.07 figure. I
am no great mathematician

The inner pipe can lie against the side of the outer one or rest anyplace inside it. It does not have to be centered. Hang it on the top edge of the outer one by a short iron hook. Its bottom has a sliding tuner, just like any Diapason slide, which can be worked up and down by a wire which runs to the top through guides like a fishing pole. Knocking down the wire of course lengthens the pipe and flattens it, and reverse.

A couple of flexible wire springs halfway down, soldered to inner tube, keeps it from rattling against outer pipe. These springs are simply bent wires that are fairly stiff, soldered to inner pipe.

This type of pipe is the best thing for low string tone there is. It does not work equally well above 8' C, but below that is wonderfully effective. The principle applies to wood flutes as well as metal pipes. Bonavia Hunt's book shows sketch of patented Pedal Diapason made this way. The half and half sectional areas must <u>always</u> be kept.

Beard the string basses of course, using large beards. Nicking can be coarse or fine according to what tone you seek. Just like full length pipes that way. But as a help to string tone the octave or first partial is accented and the speech is more prompt. We make metal 16' Diapasons that way and they are most excellent. By all odds the best I have ever heard. You avoid all mitering of course and it is most convenient where height is restricted, and in a box. These pipes need an extra large toe opening. Lots of wind. Don't forget to have the inner pipe protrude a third of its diameter above the outer one or you won't have any luck.

We have finished the California organ Great and have had about thirty or forty experts in to try it. All of them, including Courboin, say it is the best thing ever done in the country. We have not sought power at the expense of beauty of tone. We have the silver toppy quality without scream or coarseness. All the brilliancy in the world and a solidity that is most satisfying. I am very happy to have the commendation we are getting, but the country will take time to find it out and progress will be slow. I am prepared to be patient, but it is expensive and painful to wait.

If you acknowledge this, please address me care the "Brooks Hotel," Brattleboro, Vermont. I am doing this on my own and it would save embarrassment to say nothing about it. I want to repay you for what you did for me and I figure I am doing no one any harm. The patents on this side ran out some time ago.

With kindest regard, I am

Yours truly,

J. B. Jamison

short length pipes — see letter 59.
the California organ — Claremont College. Unfortunately, the organ was a failure and ruined Jamison's reputation. See letter 80.
what you did for me — see Willis' thorough discussion of scaling and voicing in letter 59.

---

74 Henry Willis to Emerson Richards

29th June 1931

Senator Emerson L. Richards
Atlantic City
N.J.
U.S.A.

Dear Richards,

I was in Paris a week ago and saw the rebuilt and enlarged Cavaillé-Coll at the American Cathedral. Whipp is the organist. The console is well done and all the electric work seems to work well. The tonal finishing is rough. I sent two stops — a Viol and a French Horn which are the best stops in the job. Also saw a six-rank unit Cavaillé-Coll in a private house, all electric stop key console with General Pistons that will not work properly on account of the voltage drop. Badly finished tonally.

The new Directorate of Cavaillé-Coll have decided to go back to tracker action and Barker lever — and this just as the men had learned to do electric action properly.

The state of affairs in France is terrible — there is no reliable builder to go to.

Am looking forward to receiving the combination action sample.

We must see how the dates work out for your trip. I will be, definitely, away August 29th onwards for 3 weeks.

Saw Losh. He is a 100% talker — he talks of you, kindly, as a nice but wayward individual! I took him to the Alexandra Palace and St. Paul's — he did not appear to be impressed in the least.

Yours ever,
H.W.

H.W./E.F.

---

75 Emerson Richards to Henry Willis

July 9th, 1931

Mr. Henry Willis
234 Ferndale Road,
Brixton, S.W.9.
London, England
My dear Willis:

Yours of the 29th received this morning just as I arrived back in town after a motor trip with Steinmeyer. He arrived on the Europa on Saturday afternoon. We flew down to Atlantic City, spent the evening in the Auditorium with the big organ, also Sunday. Monday did the Wanamaker organ, the Sesqui-Centennial organ now in the University of Pennsylvania, and Henry Fry's Austin. Then back for another night with the big job as well as to look at the Kimball and one in the High School.

Tuesday morning we left for Hagerstown, the Möller factory and the player, in which Steinmeyer was particularly interested. Arrived late yesterday afternoon in Altoona, where his organ in the Catholic Cathedral is all erected, and about half finished tonally. It sounded very good so far.

He is planning to leave the latter part of the month for St. Louis and Chicago and coming back here about the 8th of August and we are planning to motor up through New England to Skinner's and the Estey factory, as well as to see some other organs of interest. He will leave on the Europa on the 16th.

My plan was to leave here on August 24th on the Majestic, if I am able to go at all. This would bring me to London about the 31st, just after you left. However, I can see some things that I did not get to see on my former trip, and then plan to meet Steinmeyer at Hamburg with the intent of seeing some of the old north German organs as well as some of the newer ones. This means Hamburg, Lubeck and then gradually work our way south through the Bach country and then revisit some of the Bavarian organs which you did not see, like Ottobeuren and Weingarten.

If am going to see any of the French Cathedral cities, I could also do this before starting in on the German trip.

Hans Steinmeyer

Could you arrange to pick us up at the close of your other trip, say around the 20th of September? This would at least give us a chance to do south Germany together, or as much more as you could do with us. I will have to arrange to leave for home around the end of the month, as election is on November 3rd and as I am up for re-election it will be necessary for me to spend at least a month in campaigning.

I do hope that we can get together on the German proposition for a time at least, and so does Steinmeyer. We talked it over yesterday, and he is counting very much on having us both together, at least in Bavaria, and on the whole trip if possible, which would mean at least ten days.

Personally, I am very much interested in making a thorough investigation if possible of the Bach organs, as I believe that their tonal structure has a good deal to do with the proper interpretation of his music, and that of his predecessors.

I am getting this letter off at once with the hope I can get an answer from you with something definite in it before Steinmeyer leaves. We are sure to have a bully good time in Germany together, and it is an opportunity not to be missed if we can avoid it.

Of course, I am not entirely dead sure of my own plans at the moment, but I have every hope of being able to make the trip, unless some unforeseen emergency litigation intervenes.

I trust by this time that you have the combination action.

With kindest personal regards, I am,

Cordially yours,
Emerson Richards

ER H

Sesqui-Centennial organ — See note at end of letter 9.
Henry Fry's Austin — St. Clement's Church, Philadelphia.
the big job — Atlantic City
the Kimball — Atlantic City Ballroom
the High School — The Atlantic City High School housed a Midmer-Losh five-manual. The organ no longer exists at the school.

---

76 Henry Willis to Emerson Richards

20th July 1931

Senator Emerson L. Richards
Atlantic City
N.J.
U.S.A

My dear Richards,

I have carefully examined the combination action model and am of the opinion that it is a good, sound and reliable action admirably suited for remote control work. It is built on very sturdy lines and once set up properly should give no trouble. The Reisner stop keys are obviously better than the Klann units. Better make and work with more precision.

At Atlantic City this mechanism must occupy the space of a good sized room.

By the way, John Austin was very sniffy about this mechanism, which he appeared to have seen, and commented adversely upon it. He deems it clumsy and very bulky. Of course in comparison to his own forms of mechanism, operating in the way his does, it is bulky.

Austin admitted that the setting up of combinations by one setter button was superior to his system of holding piston in etc. but did not say if he proposed to amend it suitably.

I don't think it is worthwhile sending the model to Steinmeyer because he has a good system for remote control and will have seen it in action at Atlantic City.

All the best,

Yours ever sincerely,
H.W.

H.W. K.C.

July 29th, 1931

Mr. Henry Willis
234, Ferndale Road,
Brixton, S.W.9.
London, England
Dear Willis:

Your letters of the 18th and 20th arrived this morning. I am glad the combination action arrived safely and that you approve it. Of course Austin's action is very good and compact, but it cannot be worked with a setter button, as it depends on the pressure of the stop key to throw the dog, and if the action was made to throw the dogs automatically, then his action would be more bulky than most of the others of a somewhat similar description. Personally, I think the type developed by Möller is much superior mechanically to the Austin action.

The action I sent you appears more bulky in the sample than it would in actual practice. As I explained in my former letter, the space taken up by the pneumatics remains constant, while in a regular action the grid alone would extend.

Steinmeyer was here over the 4th of July. I drove him to Hagerstown and on to Altoona where his own organ was pretty well set up and partly finished. He completed it and the opening recital was on Friday, the 24th. He left immediately for St. Louis and Chicago. Will be back here on August 7th.

I am taking him by motor to see the Princeton organ, the Aeolian factory at Garwood, New Jersey, then to Boston where Skinner will join us. Inspect his factory and the old Walcker organ that was formerly in the Boston Music Hall that Skinner bought recently. Then we are going up into Maine, Moosehead Lake, to visit Buhrman, editor of the <u>American Organist</u>, who spends the summer on an island in the lake. Then back through the White Mountains to Brattleboro and the Estey Factory. Through the Connecticut valley to Hartford and Austin's and back in New York in time for the Europa on the 16th. A matter of about 1800 miles of traveling, but I think my new 16 will be quite equal to it.

In the meantime, Steinmeyer is mapping out our German trip, and we will keep you advised so that you can easily pick us up. I know both he and I will be mightily pleased to have you with us. Mrs. Steinmeyer has already determined where we will wind up — in a beer hall in Munich. Which isn't a bad place to wind up!

Work on the big organ is progressing. Practically all of the Solo is in and playing, as is the Woodwind section. The Enclosed Great pipes are being planted now, and part of the Unenclosed Great is about ready to go.

We had the 30" Diapasons playing last night. Also working on the 64'. *[I]* am using a Diaphone on the low notes, and the tongue is 2'8" long, 3" wide, 7/16" thick and with the weight weighs 14 lbs.

I shall probably come to London first. Will call on Aubrey for a chat, probably look around at some of the other organs that I did not see on my last visit. Shall make a trip into the provinces again, and may do a little looking around in France. Not very much, as I am not very keen about France. Then picking Steinmeyer up at Hamburg and working south.

If I may trouble you, I will have my mail addressed in care of your works, as it is the only place I know of that will be sure to reach me.

Looking forward to a bully good time with you in Germany, I am,

Most cordially yours,
Emerson Richards

ER H

to Hagerstown — the location of the Möller factory.
Moosehead Lake — Both Richards and Buhrman vacationed here. Advertisements for Moosehead Lake often appeared in the *American Organist* through the early '30s.
my new 16 — a 16 cylinder limousine
will call on Aubrey — Aubrey Thompson-Allen apprenticed with Willis 1922-28; he developed Willis' first all-electric consoles as well as the Infinite Speed and Gradation Swell Engine. He was elected a Director in 1932 and Managing Director in 1939.

---

78 Henry Willis to Robert Pier Elliot of Kimball

29th December, 1931

Mr. Robert P. Elliot
220 Kimball Hall
Chicago
Illinois
U.S.A

My dear Elliot,

Thanks for yours of the 30th November.

Up till a week ago we also have been all on full time but now the metal department is not working Saturdays. For years our metal department has been behind with production but several big rebuilds using comparatively few new pipes, St. George's Hall for instance, have enabled it to more than catch up.

I understand that the governing reason which Marks had in mind when taking over the Aeolian Company was probably the big Aeolian Residence Organ connection. Marks always had his eye on the development of that side of the business. Personally I would have thought it practically dead in these bad times.

Helen Hogan, now in America for a short trip, writes me that she met E.M. who said he was "broke" owing to the purchase of Methuen Hall etc. I gather from other sources that Marks will not have anything to do with it so that E.M. is left to hold the baby. It was a mad thing to have done anyway.

I will be glad to hear more news about Jamison's efforts in the direction of Diapason ensemble. As you say, the effect in the factory and in the job are two very different things.

About Second Baptist, Germantown, I cannot see how an 8' Harmonic Flute can do duty as a Third Diapason. Such stops also cannot blend with the Diapason structure to which they are foreign. For some years I have relegated Harmonic Flutes to the Choir or Solo as 4 fts., and one is enough.

I may be wrong, but I do not think that extension is even an economical method of obtaining effects. You have to have extended chests and all the action. Some people seem to think extension work is cheap — I doubt it except as regards the Pedal.

Reference Columbus, Ohio scheme I certainly agree that as a choice of evils extending the Great reed 16, 4 is preferable to Sub and Octave Couplers! The specification is a fine one.

At St. Jude's, Thornton Heath, the all-enclosed job, I put Sub and Octave Couplers on the Great for Solo effects, etc., but many players have sadly misused them.

You are quite right about John Connell — a very average player.

As regards pistons, it seems to me that the only ideal plan is to have separate pedal set-ups for Swell, Choir and Solo pistons brought on at will by a switch. I do this with the Octave Couplers also — i.e. "Pedal Combs. on Swell Pistons," "Octave Couplers on Swell Pistons." It gives the player absolute control but is very expensive — the best usually is.

Hooking up the Pedal combinations to manual pistons (other than the Great) is, of course, indefensible. One of the gadgets which has met with much approbation here is the Swell pedal switchplate which you gave me after I saw it at Kimball Hall. There is no doubt about its great utility on a job with three enclosed departments.

Who is Bill Barnes backing in these days? Any special Firm? He used to have a strange predilection towards Möller which I could not fathom. I predict that in a few years he will be a reactionary "dyed-in-the-wool" (as he terms those who think as I, and venture to say you do at heart) going for clean, straight, schemes and shuddering at 4' Harmonic Flutes on Great Organs!

What about Charlie Courboin — is his stock as a player as high as ever? What sort of a church job has he got?

Always glad to hear from you and to get all the intimate organ news.

Here's hoping that 1932 will see organ building, and the world, through the worst of its troubles. Nations are beginning to realise that if the Balfour Declaration of 1922 had been accepted, the present grave crisis would have been avoided.

Yours ever,
H.W.

H.W./K.C.

Helen Hogan—an American organ recitalist whose playing was popular in England and France

---

79 Emerson Richards to Henry Willis

January 15, 1932

Mr. Henry Willis
> 234 Ferndale Road,
>> Brixton, S.W.9.
>>> London, England.

My dear Willis:

It has been some time since we have heard from each other, and I thought you would like to have a report on the Karg-Elert recital in New York last Wednesday night. He was to inaugurate the Möller organ of 73 ranks in the Grand Ballroom of the new Hotel Waldorf Astoria. This organ has been voiced by John [sic] Whitelegg and was supposed to represent an improvement over general Möller practices. In addition, however, it had a harp, chimes, xylophone, orchestra bells and a piano.

The A.G.O. gave Karg-Elert a dinner and the Möller people issued elaborate invitations to all the musical people in New York and vicinity. About a thousand showed up, including of course a large number of well-known organists and other musicians.

The affair was a complete bust. Hans Steinmeyer characterized Karg-Elert as a harmonium player, which turned out to be somewhat of a libel on the harmonium! As a player he could not even sustain the rhythm of his own compositions, and he positively could not resist the toys in the organ.

He started out with a tribute to Lynnwood Farnam, including harp, chimes and the Vox Humana with a 2' Flute. The piano appeared in every number and mostly through all the numbers until it finally gave up the ghost in the last piece. Schulenberger of the Möller Company ordered the Post Horn cut off permanently after the first number and bitterly complained to me afterward that the recitalist had not discovered that there was a diapason in the organ. The Möller people were certainly burned up, and the musicians in the audience were shocked.

A number of them, including Courboin and Swinnen, came over to my apartment at the Ambassador to get the taste out of their mouths and to speculate on whether or not they had been mistaken about the caliber of his music. The Philadelphia people immediately cancelled their engagement, and I am very much afraid the tour is headed for the rocks.

This is all too bad, because judging from his compositions everybody expected something much better and different. They were not looking for a great virtuoso, but they thought that they would have a recitalist of taste, feeling and poetry.

Financial conditions are very bad here, with many bank failures and business entirely at a standstill. The Midmer-Losh Company is tied up, due to inability to collect for organs already installed, and work is almost at a standstill on the Convention Hall organ as a result.

Am wondering how the Liverpool job came off. I see by the <u>Musical Opinion</u> that you have two good-sized jobs in hand now, evidently since I left. Hope to send you a picture of the seven-manual console shortly. It is practically finished.

With kindest personal regards, I am,

Cordially yours,
Emerson Richards

ER H

the Karg-Elert recital — Karg-Elert's first recital on his tour. See letter 83.

---

80 Robert Pier Elliot of Kimball to Henry Willis

January 26, 1932

Mr. Henry Willis
Rotunda Organ Works
234, Ferndale Road
Brixton, London, S.W.9
England
My dear Willis:

Thanks for your prompt answer of December 29th. I went East immediately after receiving it and am taking a little time Sunday with my Dictaphone now that I am back. I just received a copy of the <u>Musical Standard</u> with another account of St. George's Hall organ. If you sent it, thank you. I wasn't sure of the writing and I have several courteous correspondents over there, or at least people on my mailing list who get our dedication programs, etc. and sometimes reciprocate in that manner.

There is some residence organ business. We have taken in two such contracts quite recently and expect another one next week. The church and auditorium business is largely four-manual organs with a few three-manuals. There is very little small organ business and practically none for the higher priced companies.

Yes, Ernest let his temper and his ideals run away from him and has been sorry. You know what he intended to do with that Methuen organ and shop I suppose? He may do it yet, at that, only he hasn't the capital, I believe, to go ahead and build a few more real Skinner organs before he dies, as he threatened.

Further reports on Jamison include such statements as "the field is widely divided on that job. It is hated or loved, depending upon how much leather you have in your ears." The truth seems to be that when it was shown in the factory the diapasons were on open chests right back of the console, very much the effect of a voicing machine. When it was put into the church with the diapasons in chambers, they failed to hold their own, with the consequence that the reeds and other work were forced and the organ is all out of balance. Attempts to raise the diapasons to their proper status seem to have failed. Davey, whom you used to know with me at Welte and later, says Jamison was forced to get Jim Nuttall to revoice all of the Estey reeds and regulate the Harrison Tuba, spending three days and nights on these before Christian would open the organ. He says that both Diggle and Wallace Sabin wrote their "blurbs" before the organ was finished and when the diapasons sounded pleasant enough, but the point had not been made that they were inadequate, and the reeds had not been voiced up to give them the volume they demanded. I certainly was ashamed of both men, and especially of Sabin who certainly knows better, for writing the guff he did.

The best Stanley Williams, the talented Englishman who is the Skinner representative in California, could say, was that "frankly it was the most disappointing organ." He says "the ensemble is terrific with a very poor blend. Reeds and mixtures dominate everything. The Diapason Chorus of which we read pages in the <u>American Organist,</u> absolutely failed to materialize." And a page more along that line. No judgment was used. Assuming Jamison took a Tyne Dock Diapason, voiced by Hunt, he hasn't got Tyne Dock acoustics, and then he shoves the stop into an organ chamber that is all cluttered with conductors and swell mechanism. I understand they had the usual pleasant Estey type of soft strings, etc., and also that they had a good many ciphers at the dedication.

Referring to your letter, I did not mean to say that a Harmonic Flute 8' could do duty as a Third Diapason. I meant that it was chosen instead of a Third Diapason, there being another 8' Flute. My own choice would run to one such Flute <u>and</u> the Third Diapason. This flute was not powerful enough to affect the Diapason structure. I agree with you in not caring whether there is a 4' Flute in the Great or not. . . .

You can see how much we care about extension work from the general run of our modern specifications. When we do it, it is usually a Choir Dulciana or a Swell Gedeckt, and in such cases there usually is an independent 8' string or corresponding [rank] in the Choir and an independent 8' basic Flute in the Swell, the unit being a very soft metal Gedeckt with high arched mouth — or a Rohrflöte ditto. I think the organ in Columbus is the finest of anything like its size I have heard. Herbert Hyde is just back from the dedication of the four-manual in Gray Chapel of Ohio Wesleyan University at Delaware, Ohio, twenty-four miles north of Columbus, and says that organ is better than Columbus, but confesses that it may be a more resonant room that influences his opinion.

You are right about combinations. That is the way we used to do it always, but finding Skinner took a short-cut that was much cheaper, we followed him, as of course the Great Man can do no wrong. Now and then we do it right, however, on important organs.

Barnes? Well, he veers with the winds of the season, but I think on the whole he would rather have us build an organ for which he was responsible, because we never let him down in any respect. He usually has nothing to criticize or to improve, and if he does, there is no argument about it, we do whatever is wanted — and that is an experience he does not have with others. I think he'll come back to absolutely sound organs, myself.

Courboin is not doing the work you heard when he played the Passacaglia for us the first time you heard the Wanamaker organ in New York. He is playing very well and in certain lines is unexcelled. He has a three-manual Welte organ of his own specification, nineteen sets of pipes with some unification, in a very beautiful church at Rye, New York. He gives a master class on that and one on our Germantown organ. I don't think he is entirely happy without the extra salary he had from Wanamaker or his organ connection, and at the time he did talk of going with Kilgen, during the New York Convention, but he could not stomach it. At the same time Al Kilgen has been flirting around with him since, and he may make some such jump. Otherwise, I think he is forced to give his work to us as the only people who will carry it out as he wants it. I don't think he has had any contracts to give out since he left Welte.

I am still sore about Oberlin going to Casavant, with five votes against it, three ours and two Skinner's. They are doing many things they said they would not. All the specifications I made, in complete harmony with the professional members of the committee, were for four-manual organs, and they are getting a five! They said all along they would not have an Echo organ — and they should not in that building — and they are getting one, and even putting in a fifth manual for it! The organ is not nearly so large, really, as when we were working on it. They cut the price down from $100,000.00 to $70,000.00, I understand, and I also understand they have been hearing plenty from laymen and professionals about giving the work out of the country when there were better builders in the country, and giving it out of the country at a time of such unemployment in the country. I hope they get a good organ for the benefit of my friends there, but I also hope that they hear all the things I hear about their action.

Of course you know Leet was the first one out after Skinner got control of Aeolian. In fact, it has been said, facetiously, that they bought the business for the sake of firing him. As a matter of fact, he had been taken out of the factory and transferred to the Sales Department before the blow fell. Zeuch, deposed from the vice-presidency he has held so many years, is unhappy, and I have yet to find anyone in the organization, on either side, who is pleased. And what they are doing to prices! We have a lot more money than they have, can stand it as long as they can, but we do not enjoy it while it lasts.

Cordially yours,
R.P. Elliot

RPE:MB

Ernest . . . has been sorry — By 1932, the alliance between Ernest Skinner and Arthur Marks had reached its nadir. Marks saw a future in Don Harrison, not in Skinner. Feeling angry and pushed out, Skinner planned to go into business for himself. But he had to wait until January of 1936, when his contractual committments to Aeolian-Skinner ran out, to move into the Methuen shop he had acquired in 1929 and begin operations as the Ernest M. Skinner & Son, Co.

reports on Jamison — refers to the Claremont College organ designed by Jamison at the Estey Organ Company

beautiful church at Rye, New York — Church of the Resurrection, Rye, New York

Leet was the first one out — Skinner seemed to hold a grudge against Leslie Leet, who had been a foreman/superintendent at Skinner's Westfield works in the early '20s. Leet left this job to work at Aeolian, and Skinner, or Skinner management, may well have considered Leet a traitor for having left.

---

81 Henry Willis to Emerson Richards

1st February, 1932

Senator Emerson L. Richards
Atlantic City, N.J., U.S.A.
My dear Richards:

Many thanks for your letter of the 15th January.

I am not surprised that Karg-Elert's show was a "flop" — I warned Laberge to try to keep a tight controlling hand on K.E. and to insist on adequate rehearsal on each instrument but I suppose he cannot dictate K.E.'s choice as regards the stops.

Some time ago K.E. sent me a long article, intended for the <u>Rotunda</u>, extolling "unification" and giving examples which indicated his being a deep-ender of the worst type.

It is a great pity that the Midmer-Losh financial difficulties are holding up the completion of your great Atlantic City organ. I was under the impression that if they got into trouble the job would be finished by a Surety.

St. George's Hall Liverpool is marvellous now — only one fly in the ointment — I wanted to put in a new 32' reed but it was cut out of the scheme so I was forced to revoice the old one on 20" — CCCC wooden tube 8⅜" square at the top — i.e. the scale of an average 16'!

Things are getting slack here. I have nothing big on except the new 4-row for Sheffield City Hall and that job is well on the way toward completion.

The Aeolian-Skinner merger is interesting, but from an English point of view curious — the effect of a similar merger in England would be bad, but I hope Marks knows his own business. In effect, of course, it means the wiping out of the Aeolian influence except from a sales point of view.

We have had a most curiously mild Winter so far — quite extraordinary — but I suppose we will have a week or so of what we call severe weather before it's over.

Any chance of your coming over this Summer?

I will have St. George's Hall and Sheffield to show you — also, if you cared, you could hear the York Minster job following Harrison & Harrison's last go at it.

Yours ever,
Henry Willis

H.W./K.C.

---

82 Bernard Laberge to Henry Willis

February 25, 1932

Mr. Henry Willis, Pres.
Henry Willis & Sons Ltd.
Rotunda Organ Works
234 Ferndale Road
Brixton, London, England
My dear Chap:

Many thanks for your letter of February 12th received.

RE: KARG-ELERT: Well, I admit that what you told me was right and he did in fact practise a lot, but he is so temperamental and nervous that he is really difficult to handle, although he means well. I can tell you I will be happy when he sails March 24th, because it is a great responsibility for me while he is here.

RE: GERMANI: My friend Fernando would be quite distressed if this tour did not take place, after having submitted the contents of your last letter to him. He does not expect to make any money and he would be satisfied, for this time, if he simply met his living and railroad expenses while in England. As to making a hit, there is not the slightest doubt in my mind because he is not only a very fine musician but a great virtuoso. If I remember correctly, both Courboin's and Farnam's English tours took place between June and October. Please, my dear Henry, (I ask this as a personal favor) do take this up with Mr. Verne at once, and let me know as quickly as you can, if something can be arranged for a few appearances. As I wrote you before, Germani would make this first tour for publicity's sake and because he knows that he can come back later on a different basis. The only thing he wants, and which I think is reasonable, is to get the few necessary pounds to pay his expenses in England, which cannot amount to much. Maybe our friend Mr. Custard would have him at his house in Liverpool (Germani is a delightful chap) and his railroad from Liverpool to Folkestone would not amount to much, second class. Now, my dear friend, please look into this at once, because Germani must make definite plans soon. . . .

[Bernard Laberge]

Mr. Verne — Battigan Verne, the editor of *The Rotunda* and Willis employee
Mr. Custard — Reginald Goss-Custard, organist of Liverpool Cathedral

---

83 Henry Willis to Bernard Laberge

16th March 1932

Mr. Bernard R. Laberge
Graybar Building
420 Lexington Avenue
New York
My dear Laberge:

Thanks for your letter. In reply to that of the 25th inst.

Germani. I have given the matter close consideration and have talked it over with Verne. There is not the slightest hope of arranging Recitals, for fees, at the time projected. If he comes over and offers his services gratuitously there would be no difficulty in fixing him up. Farnam often came over out of season but played without fee. Courboin's recital tour was in season but proved a loss.

The fact is that, even in season, Germani could not make money here, nor even expect to pay expenses. Strange as it may seem to you, his name is practically unknown here and it would take an expensive advertising campaign to make it so. Even the fees would be too low to make a tour worthwhile. We had the same experience with Charles Courboin. I am sorry, but facts are facts.

Myself. I have decided to postpone this matter until 1933 when the world may be over the worst of the existing depression.

Karg-Elert. I have not heard from him. I read your letter with interest and it most certainly would appear to be perfectly clear that you have done your best for him under most difficult conditions.

If I may say so, I think it was an error of judgment to let him give that first recital at the Waldorf-Astoria within 48 hours of his landing and with little time at the instrument. I am glad that you do not blame me at all!

Yours ever,
H.W.

H.W./K.C.

---

84 Bernard Laberge to Ernest Skinner

March 22, 1932

Mr. Ernest Skinner
Vice President,
Aeolian Skinner Organ Company
Boston, Mass.
My dear Mr. Skinner:

According to my promise I am sending you herewith Dr. Karg-Elert's address in Leipzig. It is as follows:

> Dr. Sigfrid Karg-Elert
> 111 Elisen Strasse,
> Leipsig, Germany.

The Doctor played yesterday at Wanamaker's and it was heart breaking for him because the organ was in such a terrific condition that he had to stop twice on account of ciphers and finally had to give up the concert entirely. I did fully sympathize with him, but must say that he was a good sport about it.

I take pleasure in telling you that we have settled our differences amicably and I am glad of it because the only thing I get out of this tour is the satisfaction of having presented someone I consider a very great artist and a most artistic soul. Next season I shall bring Gunther Ramin and then American audiences will be able to enjoy a straight organ virtuoso.

I thank you for your kindness toward the whole thing and for what you did for Dr. Karg-Elert. He leaves these shores with the idea that you are a great man and I fully agree with him.

With my kindest regards,

Always sincerely yours,
Bernard R. Laberge

BRL:mp

what you did for Dr. Karg-Elert — Skinner had arranged a recital at St. Thomas' Church, Manhattan, so that Karg-Elert could hear American organists perform his works.

---

85 Emerson Richards to Henry Willis

April 11, 1932

Mr. Henry Willis
234 Ferndale Road,
Brixton, S.W.9.
London, England.
My dear Willis:

The <u>Rotunda</u> arrived last week, and that reminds me of several things. One that I promised Aubrey that I would write an article for the <u>Rotunda</u>. I think he suggested a subject, but I have forgotten what it was now. Perhaps you better give me a choice of two or three, so that I can select the one that appeals the strongest. Don't know when I can promise to do it, as I haven't even gotten started on the new German series for Buhrman as yet.

This has been a most strenuous winter, ever since I stepped off the gangplank on my return from England. Terrible business conditions and bank difficulties have kept me stirring. Two of the largest of the beachfront hotels are in the hands of receivers, and I am acting for them.

But my chief difficulty has been the Senate. I hold the position of majority whip, which entails more responsibility than it would under your system, since I am virtually the party leader as well. The result is that I am never home and never seem to get a chance to get any rest. Am thoroughly tired out.

I hope to get this all cleaned up within the next month. The A.G.O. Convention is to be in Boston the latter part of June, which would be a dandy time for a trip over here. In as much as the ocean rate-war is on, it would also be opportune. Do you think you can make it? We could take two or three weeks off for a motor trip, doing New England and the Midwest as well.

I see that Liverpool is safely off your hands. Apparently things are looking up, judging from the new contracts you appear to have. The organ business here is just about at a standstill. Nobody has any work, and the prices are the lowest in years.

The big job is coming along slowly. The Losh firm has also been suffering financially and has been working with a reduced force of men. The big console is about completed. The combination action is working all right. A most agreeable and unaccountable thing is that with every stop on, the general cancel only drops the voltage one volt.

The Great flue chorus is truly remarkable. When the whole chorus is on from 32' up to Mixtures, even the 50 inch reeds have no chance with it in power and brilliance. A demonstration that reeds are unnecessary except for a change in color.

I am sending you pictures of the big console, consisting of a front view and the two side cheeks. Also a photo of the 100 inch [pressure] reeds — the Trumpet in front, the Tuba immediately back of it. Note that even the [treble] flues take the 100 inch wind. Also the heavy reinforcement on the Tuba. This is one-quarter inch thick organ metal. You can also note on the Tuba the reinforcements with organ metal at the node.

In anticipation of Aubrey's questions, I enclose a description of the console. I think we can safely say that the organ will be complete if you can come over in June.

With kindest personal regards, I am,

Cordially yours,
Emerson Richards

ER H
Encs.

---

reeds are unnecessary — before long, both Richards and Harrison agreed that reeds were superfluous on the Great division, and many of Harrison's designs omitted them.

organ metal — a mixture with a large proportion of lead used for the construction of flues and reeds to encourage strong fundamental tone.

9th May 1932

Mr. R.P. Elliot
W.W. Kimball Co., Organ Builders,
Kimball Hall
Chicago, Ill., U.S.A.
Dear Elliot:

Reference your cable I replied as follows:

"Whitelegg voiced twenty-three flue stops for Liverpool Cathedral no Reeds." I would say that Whitelegg voiced no reeds when with me. He was a flue voicer and regulator.

The complete list of the stops that Whitelegg did for Liverpool is as follows: Where marked RW/HW (Richard Whitelegg/Henry Willis) it means that the voicing was carried out under my direct personal supervision, i.e. I voiced and set the Cs and Whitelegg "filled in" between. Where RW only it means that Whitelegg voiced the stops to exact and written particulars given him by me and the stop was finished by me in the Organ.

Liverpool Cathedral

Dept.	Name of Stop	Pitch	Pressure	Notes	Voiced by-Date	
Great	Twelfth	2⅔	5"	61	RW/HW	7/7/24
Pedal	Violon	16	6"	32	RW	-/5/24
Pedal	'Cello	8	6"	32	RW	-/5/24
Pedal	Dolce	16	6"	32	RW	-/5/24
Pedal	Geigen	16	6"	32	RW	-/5/24
Swell	Mixture	5 rks	5"	305	RW/HW	22/9/24
Pedal	Contra Basso	16	10"	32	RW/HW	22/9/24
Great	Contra Violone*	32	6"	61	RW/HW	1924

(* - done partly in Works, partly in Cathedral)

Dept.	Name of Stop	Pitch	Pressure	Notes	Voiced by-Date	
Great	Contra Tibia*	16	5"	61	RW/HW	1925
Great	Tibia*	8	5"	61	RW/HW	1925
Solo	Contra Viole	16	10"	61	RW/HW	-/8/25
Solo	Viole de Gambe	16	10"	61	RW/HW	11/7/25
Solo	Viole d'Orchestre	8	10"	61	RW/HW	-/6/25
Solo	Viole Celestes	8	10"	56	RW/HW	-/6/25
Solo	Octave Viole	4	10"	61	RW/HW	-/8/25
Solo	Violette	2	10"	61	RW/HW	-/8/25
Solo	Cornet de Violes	3 rks	10"	183	RW/HW	-/8/25
Great	Fourniture	5 rks	5"	305	RW/HW	22/7/25

In addition Whitelegg re-regulated the Pedal Octave Flute 8ft and Pedal Double Open Diapason unit (32, 16, 8, and 4ft) so I have credited him with 23 stops.

Whitelegg was a good voicer but required close supervision. When he was voicing the Solo Violes I had to stand over him practically all the time. He, at first, admitted that he could not carry out my instructions so I had to voice all the C's personally to show him how they could and were to be done.

Whitelegg voiced no reed stop while he was with me.

Let me say that Whitelegg was a most careful and painstaking man and once he grasped exactly what I wanted he could carry out flue voicing as well as anybody. Further he was a most excellent regulator and finisher.

I want to make it quite clear that all my voicers work to the minutely detailed instructions that I draw up and divergence in any way is not permitted. I give an example from the Liverpool Cathedral Flue Voicing Book —

"Fourniture 5 ranks Great. 5"   C. 517.

CC to Tenor G	19,22,24,26,29	20 notes
Tenor G# to Middle G	12,15,17,19,22	12 notes
Mid. G# to Treble G	5, 8,10,12,15	12 notes
Treb.G# to Top C	3, 5, 8,12,15	17 notes

8,15,22 & 29   No.4 scale.   Length Mixture rod correct.
                                             Tip Open 4. ¾ 8ve full.

5,12,19 & 26   No.7 scale.   Length Mixture rod correct.
                                             Tip Open 4. ¼ 8ve full.

3,10,17 & 24   No.10 scale   Length Mixture rod correct.
                                             Tip Salicional 12.one 8ve full.

All spotted metal cone tuned.

                              RW/HW.   22/7/25."

All the above particulars mean something very definite and there is no room for divergence. The C's were all voiced to the above and "passed" by me — then the voicer "filled in."

In explanation I would say that over here we do not use the American method of talking about scales — but the numbers are constant — i.e. a No.4 scale is a No.4 scale whatever pitch it is used in — the relation being to the unison 8ft. A No.4 8ft Diapason being the equivalent of your No.44.

"5th mouths" means the width of the mouth is ⅕th of the circumference.

"Length Mixture rod correct" means that the standard rod for the pitch in question is used.

"Tip Open 4. ¾ 8ve full" means that the standard tip scale Open 4 is used but bigger by ¾ octave. The tip scales show the Cs and F#s and it is easy to gauge between.

Richard O. Whitelegg

"Cut up 9 in 4/ 10½ in 4" means that the height of the mouth is in that proportion to the width — 9 in 4 being half way between 2 in 1 and 5 in 2. The reference 9 in 4/ 10½ in 4 means that the bass part with ears is cut up 9 in 4 and the treble part without ears 10½ in 4, being slightly less by reason of the fact that there is no ear shading.

"Medium bevels and nicking" means something very definite, there being standard patterns. I might say, for instance "long bevels — sharp top lips" as indicating the requirements for a Viole, also "Fine" or "Medium-fine" nicking etc. All of which have a definite reference to the nature of the stop. "Fine" nicking having a different meaning for a Diapason and a Viole it being "fine" proportionately to the nature of the stop. "Broad nicking" on a Viole de Gambe would be equivalent C to C to "Fine" nicking on a Diapason and so forth.

In the U.S.A. the voicers always seem to me to be given a tremendous amount of latitude which seemed most astounding.

Thanks for your views on adjustable combination systems. Of course the "capture" system is the best. I would be glad of details of the new type combination action (remote control) which you advertise.

For "duplexing" we do not do it pneumatically — dropped that long ago.

Yours ever,

H.W.

H.W./K.C.

103

May 20, 1932

Mr. Henry Willis
Rotunda Organ Works,
234 Ferndale Road,
Brixton, London, S.W. 9, England.
Dear Sir Henry:

Yours of the 3rd instant is received and demands an immediate reply inasmuch as you intimate there is a possibility of your coming over this June for the convention here in Boston. I cannot tell you how anxious I am that this may eventuate. The convention will be more than usually interesting. Some of the best of the younger organists are giving recitals, and I feel sure that there will be playing and program making of a very high order of excellence. As soon as the printed program is received, I will send you a copy. Our company is hoping to be host with the Austin Company to the delegates of the convention in a little journey from Boston to Hartford to have a recital on the Austin organ in Bushnell Hall, followed by another recital on Don's new job at Trinity College. At the present writing there is a slight misunderstanding, and we are not entirely sure that the Austin Company will join with us. Even if they don't, I think that we will go through it alone provided the Guild is willing to accept our invitation.

It is good news to know that your internal volcano is quiescent. Let us hope that it will remain so indefinitely.

I am greatly interested in your all-electric console and as well your Compensating Amplifier, and will expect to hear more about them when and if you come over this June.

Things are picking up with us, and we have booked sufficient orders in the last several months to justify our increasing the force to over one hundred men in the factory. This has a salutary effect not only on the morale of the men, but very definitely also on the operating expense as it naturally reduces the overhead percentage appreciably. We have several large contracts that are practically sure to come to us so that we will have production assured for the balance of the year. If the improvement expected in business next fall materializes, we will then come through this depression without any loss. Not many concerns can say as much.

Please once more do try and come over this summer. I think you will find the trip worthwhile, and it goes without saying that we will all endeavor to make your visit a real pleasure to you.

My best,

As ever,
Bill

WEZ:MGM

Dear Sir Henry — Willis was not actually knighted; this was a term of endearment used by Zeuch.

your internal volcano — gastric trouble

Compensating Amplifier — a metal hood or cowl fitted to the top of flue or reed pipes to focus and project the tone. Many of the Atlantic City stops were so designed by Harry Willis.

---

88 G. Donald Harrison to Henry Willis

May 20, 1932

Mr. Henry Willis
Rotunda Organ Works,
234 Ferndale Road,
Brixton,
London, S.W.9,
England

Dear Henry:

Many thanks for your letter of May 9th. I am awfully sorry that your son has been so sick, but am delighted to learn that the crisis is over and that he is on the mend. I hope he will soon be perfectly fit again.

Many thanks for sending me a copy of your letter of May 9th addressed to R.P. Elliot. The information contained therein may be useful to us in certain cases. There is one thing very funny about the whole situation, and that is, when Whitelegg worked for Elliot at the Welte Company, Elliot himself made the wildest claims about Whitelegg's work both at Westminster Cathedral and at Liverpool Cathedral. Far greater in fact than Möller. Now the shoe is on the other foot, however, and he thinks quite differently.

In a way I am sorry you included so many particulars about the Great Fourniture as Elliot is quite a dangerous man to provide with information. He will certainly use what you have given him and your name in his high-pressure sales talks.

The information Jamison obtained from Harrison and Harrison, Compton and yourself, as you know from their ads, was tremendously exaggerated, and was quite a nuisance to us. Luckily it all fell flat, and Estey's are in such poor financial shape that I do not think it matters very much. However, I would be awfully glad if you would refrain as far as possible from giving any tonal information to American builders in view of your association with this company and our personal association. I would not think, for example, of sending Walkers any dope.

Kimballs are making a tremendous bid in the East here to get church work, and have closed a few contracts at ruinous prices. This is terribly bad for trade, as you can well imagine. Their organs are costly to build, and they are quoting as much as 25 to 30 percent below our cut prices. They got the Madison Avenue M.E. Church, New York City, purely on price. These people wanted a Skinner organ, and at the final meeting they sent a representative around to see Mr. Marks to inquire whether we would not build the instrument for them for several thousand dollars more than Kimball were offering. We turned it down stating that it was unfair to other clients to give organs away, so they finally gave the job to Kimball. They did not get more than $30,000 for the job, and you know it was a mighty big one and has two consoles and a duplexed Antiphonal.

Elliot has never been able to get a decent price in any company he has worked for, and has always been a price-cutter. In his sales talk he also does many unethical things, including the handing of a list to the intending purchaser of Skinner organs which are supposed to be unsatisfactory, and suggesting that they write to the owners of these installations.

Business is picking up here to some extent, and we have closed quite a few important contracts. You doubtless noticed the specification for the Harvard job in the Diapason, and since then I have closed a contract with the Church of St. Mary the Virgin, New York City, for quite an interesting job (which will be on the west wall of the church), and we have also received the contract for the new organ for the University of Minnesota.

You will remember the All Saints Church, Worcester where they had a buried Choir Organ, and you went over there with Skinner to see what could be done about it. This church burned down and Bill Zeuch is about to sign the contract for a new organ!

As it will not be possible for me to get to England this summer in view of so much important work which I have to attend to personally, I am very delighted to read that you may be over here in June.

Yours as ever,
Don

GDH:MGM

new organ . . . University of Minnesota — Aeolian-Skinner opus 892, Northrop Auditorium, a large 4 manual of over 100 ranks with four 32' stops.

All Saints Church — Aeolian-Skinner opus 909, 4 manual. William Self was organist at the time this instrument was installed and later went to St. Thomas Church, New York.

30th May 1932

Mr. G. Donald Harrison
Aeolian-Skinner Co.
677 Fifth Avenue
New York
U.S.A.

Dear Don,

Thanks for yours of the 20th instant. Am glad to say that "Son" is quite all right again and now recuperating at a farm in Sussex with Clara. I was down there yesterday and the boy looks splendid.

Ref: Elliot and my letter of the 9th instant. The "details" of the L.C.O. Great Fourniture are practically meaningless without the "context." I do take care not to give information of any real value to other American firms. As regards Jamison, the real facts are that he did not approach me, saying later that in view of the close contact between me and Skinners he had thought it hopeless. Harrisons had given him a lot of "bunk" information and, to unsettle him I explained what rot most of it was — my object being to thoroughly unsettle him by telling him enough of the truth to leave him thoroughly confused.

As regards the relations between myself and the Skinner organization, apart from the personal equation I really don't know what it is! Rightly or wrongly I feel that the balance of the interchange of ideas is in favor of your side. I in no way discount the importance of the result of Skinner's visit here in 1924 and my own to America later in the year. It decided us upon the complete change over of methods etc. I cannot help feeling, however, that the revolution in the Skinner tonal methods which was the result of cooperation, clinched by your going to them, was the greater, and that we are "all square" and more.

We do not now seem to be in close touch as regards developments, on the other hand I do receive interesting particulars of progress and developments from other firms which keeps me in touch with what is going on on your side, and occasionally has definite value. For instance, Richards put me onto the relay magnet which has proved most useful for "conversion" jobs. I have, of course, conversed quite freely with Richards upon the subject of tonal balance etc. but have not given him any concrete examples in the form of pipes.

There is a tendency for business to pick up here. We have enough to go on with — regular stuff — nothing very big.

How fortunate All Saints Worcester was burned down! You will now be able to do something fine there.

Unfortunately I will not be able to run over in June as there are two rather important contracts pending and I must be here until they are settled.

Yours ever,

H.W.

H.W./K.C.

"**conversion jobs**" — converting Barker lever or tubular-pneumatic action instruments to electro-pneumatic.

---

90 Ernest M. Skinner to Henry Willis

June 13, 1932

Mr. Henry Willis
c/o Henry Willis & Sons, Ltd.
Rotunda Organ Works,
234 Ferndale Road,
Brixton, London, S.W.9, England.

My dear Henry:

I would appreciate a line from you telling what width mouth you use on Diapasons as a general rule. If you have three Diapasons on the Great, how would you mug it? I would also like to know what you would use on the Swell. What is your conventional Great organ wind pressure?

Have you given up using the pocketed shallot that your father gave me for use on Tubas and Trombones?

Very sincerely yours,

Ernest M. Skinner

EMS:MBL

---

91 Henry Willis to G. Donald Harrison

27th June, 1932

Mr. G. Donald Harrison   <u>Private.</u>
c/o Aeolian-Skinner Co.
677 Fifth Avenue
New York, U.S.A.

My dear Don:

I enclose copy of letter in reply to Skinner's.

I fail to understand why he writes me. I hope all is O.K. between you and him.

Yours ever,

H.W.

H.W./K.C.

108

27th June, 1932

Mr. Ernest M. Skinner
Aeolian-Skinner Organ Co.
Boston,
U.S.A.

My dear Skinner:

In answer to your letter and query about width of mouths used for Great Diapasons, and "conventional" wind pressures etc. I have no standard, every job having its scales, mouth widths and pressures designed to suit the acoustical properties of the building and the same applies to wind pressures, but in respect to the latter, 4½" is the pressure which, on the average, is most used for Great Diapasons.

Reference scales, mouth widths and pressures I give you details of some typical jobs:

Westminster Cathedral
"Good acoustically"

Great		scale	mouth	wind
Open Diapason No.1	8ft	7⅜"	4½"	12"
Open Diapason No.2	8ft	6½"	2/7	4½"
Open Diapason No.3	8ft	5⅞"	5	4½"

Sheldonian Theatre Oxford "Medium acoustically"
(Not a Theatre but a semi-rotunda University Hall)

Great				
Open Diapason No.1	8ft	7⅛"	4	6½"
Open Diapason No.2	8ft	6½"	4½	3½"
Open Diapason No.3	8ft	5⅜"	2/7	3½"
Open Diapason No.4	8ft	4⅜"	4	3½"

Sheffield City Hall
"bad acoustically — reverberation period <u>empty</u> ½ second"

Great				
Open Diapason No.1	8ft	7⅜"	4½	10"
Open Diapason No.2	8ft	6⅛"	2/7	5"
Open Diapason No.3	8ft	5⅜"	5	5"

and so I could go on. There is no standard design etc. depends entirely upon the needs of the building. Generally speaking it is safe to say that the use of 2/7 mouths is unwise for high pressures (over 5") or for buildings with a low reverberation period.

In addition each Diapason has its own special treatment as regards its construction whether the lower lip is "punched," "half-rounded," "flat," or "long flat." Also languids vary in type and thickness according to requirements.

Reference Swell Organs: for moderate sized 3 manuals I often place all on one pressure which may be 5", 6" or 7" according to requirements — those of the reeds governing the pressure for there is no difficulty in adjusting the flue work to suit. When I want the chorus reeds on 8" or more I use a lower pressure for the flue work, 5" being a nice pressure.

By "pocketed shallot" you mean what we call "filled in." Yes, I use this type of shallot when refinement is called for. 16ft Waldhorns nearly always have filled in reeds, unenclosed Tubas for medium sized buildings generally filled in reeds, families of Great Trombas usually have filled in reeds — Trumpets never.

Don knows all this and was perfectly conversant with the reasons governing the selection of scales, mouth widths and pressures for Diapasons — also the use of filled in reeds.

Yours ever,
H.W.

H.W./K.C.

---

93 Ernest Skinner to William King Covell

February 8, 1933

Mr. Wm. King Covell,
c/o Brown, Shipley & Co.,
123 Pall Mall,
London, S.W.1,
England
Dear Mr. Covell:

Thanks for your good letter. I read your first installment of the description of the Methuen organ in The Organ, and enjoyed it very much, and shall be glad to have the balance of it. Thank you for the five copies you are sending. I hope you will have enough printed because I imagine they will be in great demand. The organ is growing in public interest. Mr. Alexander McCurdy of the Second Presbyterian Church in Philadelphia gave a recital on November 5th on the Methuen organ. It was one of the most delightful recitals I ever attended. The house was full and the program perfectly and marvelously played. In point of fact there were two encores at the conclusion of the program. You will read about it in the Diapason. Mr. Stone is still at Methuen.

We are doing nothing to the organ at this moment, nor have we done anything except add the strings which you know of. I am going to add some orchestral color alternately and enrich the string section, if these times don't knock the money out of the old pocket altogether.

Someone told me that you and Mr. Gammons were complaining that I was likely to do damage to this masterpiece. Now if I actually do damage to it, all well and good. I took on this load to save this old masterpiece, and I point out to you the unlikelihood of my doing any damage. I hope my 45 years' experience as an organbuilder, which has brought much more money to other people's pockets than it ever did to mine, will enable me to treat the instrument with respect. If I do make any substitutions, you may be sure that I will keep any pipes that may be removed where they may be replaced if my attempts do not meet with the approval of people who are competent to judge, to say nothing of my own opinion. Mr. Tietjen at the Convention, on St. Thomas organ, played a chorale of Bach's called "O Lord Have Mercy Upon Me." The accompaniment was played on the Kleine Erzähler and the melody or chorale voice on the English Horn, with a Dulciana on the Pedal, I believe. Without using either Tremolos or expression boxes, he achieved one of the most beautiful performances that I have ever heard, which opinion was also shared by every person present. I am sure that Bach would concur in this opinion, though not one of the stops used was in existence in Bach's time. There are no stops in existence in French, English or German organs that could have approached the results of these exclusively American developments — more particularly my own. When you are back home again Mr. Tietjen will be glad to play this for you as he has for me since the Convention. I agree with you that Father Willis's work is superior to present examples. I got all my ideas of reeds of the Trumpet family from Father Willis. If you will try the organ in Colston Hall, I think at Bristol (but you can verify this), I think you will agree with me that Father Willis himself once in a while ran rather wild on reeds. This organ, however, has some of the most magnificent 32' fronts I ever saw, although they are not of English tin.

Very sincerely yours,
Ernest M. Skinner

EMS:MGM

the Methuen organ — see note, letter 57
St. Thomas organ — see note, letter 15

February 8, 1933

Mr. William King Covell,
15 Summer Road
Cambridge, Mass.

Dear Mr. Covell: Re: <u>Harvard University</u>

Herewith are scales of important stops and particulars of mixtures for your proposed article.

In view of my connection with the Aeolian-Skinner Company, it is inadvisable to give the scales of mixtures, etc. This is special knowledge which cannot be handed over to competitors in this day and age!

I designed all the mixtures specially for Harvard with the exception of the Solo Fourniture. A similar stop was used in the St. Bartholomew Dome organ.

I find it absolutely essential to do this in every organ to obtain correct results. The scaling and mouthing vary to suit the acoustics and general location. The layout of each Mixture is designed not merely as an individual stop, but in relation to the other mixtures in the scheme, and particularly in relation to other mixtures, stops and mutations on the same department.

I believe you will find these mixtures an interesting study, and discover that a good deal more thought has been put into them than used to be the case even with the best of the older builders. For example, except for the number of ranks, a Plein Jeu was a Plein Jeu to Cavaillé-Coll. Everything always the same. I have developed a method of studying the tonal structure of the flue chorus, and a way of designing the mixtures. If you will experiment a little at Harvard by, say, drawing all flue stops and running up or down a chromatic scale from top to bottom, you will find a remarkably even and smooth result particularly when you consider the bold treatment of the mixtures. This means that the melodic line in any part of a contrapuntal composition runs smoothly and evenly at all times, thereby making it possible for the listener to hear all voices clearly in any section of the compass.

Schulze's work is very poor from this angle. At Armley, for instance, one hears a glorious brilliance, but you cannot pick out what is going on with the inner voices as they pass over the crude breaks in the mixtures.

I have a special way of regulating the individual ranks during the finishing process which also helps to obtain general smoothness.

I believe these are the reasons why the organ at St. Mary's sounds clearer to me than any other. The slightly improved results over Trinity and Harvard are due, in my opinion, to the superior location and acoustics. Harvard and Trinity are just as clear actually. The mixtures are quite different in each case. I am not claiming to have discovered anything new, nor am I boasting about results! You know me better than that. I do feel, however, that the long hours spent on the design and finishing of these organs were not entirely wasted. It means a more even result in the effectiveness of various organs, and reduces the hit and miss results to the minimum.

The finishing means so much. During this process I find it a great help to have an organist around of the "Watters" type who will play some fugues, etc. from time to time while I walk about the church. You can then pick up details which might escape attention.

Your letter received this morning informs me that you are interested in this subject, and I will be glad to discuss it with you in the near future. I believe it would create interest if some of these points were brought out in your article. They are rarely appreciated by even the best organists.

Now about your Cymbale: Harmonics above the 36th are of doubtful value, and it would be far better to start an octave lower. Personally I am not at all fond of the flat seventh in a Cymbale. You need not fear the grave ranks at the top. A Cymbale should never be used unless there are other mixtures in the scheme, and they will take care of 8' harmonic series perfectly. The Cymbale is a kind of "chink" filler taken in connection with the other mixtures, and further it adds point at the lower part of the compass and rounds out the upper octaves so they do not become too "spikey."

I'm sorry you didn't try the Yale Cymbale — it works in exceedingly well. It repeats every octave starting as follows:

19 - 22 - 26 - 29 - 31 - 33 - 36

This makes the top octave

$21\frac{1}{3}$ - 16' - $10\frac{2}{3}$' - 1 - 3 - 5 - 8

I have to leave town today. Will you kindly tell Doc I will attend to the finishing up of the remaining details on Monday. I will also bring your pipe along then.

Sincerely,
G. Donald Harrison

GDH:MGM
Encls.

St. Bartholomew Dome Organ — Skinner Opus 651, St. Bartholomew's Episcopal Church, New York City. A five-manual instrument last revised in 1927 with a fifth manual prepared for the Celestial division in the dome. This was added in 1930.

St. Mary's . . . Trinity . . . Harvard — in chronological order, opus 851, Trinity College Chapel, Hartford; opus 886, Appleton Chapel, Memorial Church, Harvard University, Cambridge; opus 891, Church of St. Mary the Virgin, New York. All were large installations over which Harrison had full tonal supervision for the first time. St. Mary's has been altered; the other two have been replaced.

organist . . . of the "Watters" type — Clarence Watters, the French-trained organist of Trinity College Chapel, Hartford, who specialized in music of the Classical period.

Yale Cymbale — opus 722, Woolsey Hall, Yale University. This instrument, a rebuild of Steere's enlargement of a Hutchings-Votey, now with 196 ranks, remains unaltered.
kindly tell Doc — Archibald T. Davison, Harvard University professor and organist

---

95 G. Donald Harrison to William King Covell

March 28, 1933

Mr. William King Covell,
15 Summer Road,
Cambridge, Mass.
Dear Mr. Covell:

Thanks for your letter of yesterday's date. I am glad to hear that you have sent a reply to Compton's recent letter in the <u>Musical</u> <u>Opinion</u>. The only thing to do is to keep hammering away at these people.

Many thanks for your kind remarks regarding the 32' reed at Harvard. I have felt that it would be just right providing the acoustics were at all decent, but I do agree that at present in certain spots it appears to be far too heavy for the rest of the organ. This is due to the fact, of course, that with all tone absorbing materials the higher frequencies suffer the most, while the lower ones are hardly affected. I believe that if the wooden screen could be removed and the ceiling and walls treated with a skim coat of hard plaster that the general effect of the organ when heard from the Nave would be fine and satisfying and in proper balance.

I expect to do some tuning at the Chapel tomorrow, and I am going to look into the Swell eight rank Mixture as there is one little spot which did not show up very well in Mr. Watters' recital. It is only for six notes, but as it happened, it gave an unfortunate series of consecutive fourths during the opening of the G Minor Fantasia. The rank that is creating this fault is at the point where the Double Quint appears for the first time. It sticks out far too prominently. This can be readily cured by introducing the Double at this point instead of the Double Quint, and introducing the Double Quint for the first time at the next break where it is quite inoffensive since it is covered by the Double.

I am telling you this because if you are giving the composition of this Mixture in your article, you will doubtless want to amend it so as to have everything absolutely correct.

Sincerely yours,
G. Donald Harrison

GDH:MGM
P.S. I hope friend Gammons is out of the wood by now.

114

Compton's recent letter — John Compton, an English builder whose hallmark was designing church organs with extensive and effective unification.

Mr. Watters' recital — Clarence Watters dedicated the Harvard Aeolian-Skinner on March 7, 1933.

---

96 G. Donald Harrison to William King Covell

April 26, 1933

Mr. William King Covell,
15 Summer Road,
Cambridge, Mass.

Dear Mr. Covell:

Thanks for your letter of yesterday's date.

I am glad to hear that Ned Gammons is now almost well. He appears to have had quite a bad time.

I was very much pleased to get Frank Bozyan's reaction to the Harvard organ as he is one of the coming young fellows. Baumgartner I cannot understand since he apparently has good musical taste judging by some of his compositions, and yet the only thing that seems to interest him in the organ is the combination action. You have, no doubt, heard the atrocious instrument he had built for himself in New Haven. I cannot agree with him regarding the combination mechanism at the Chapel. I do not believe I have ever heard smoother registration than Watters obtained at his recital. One was never conscious of the mechanical side of the instrument, and he did not use all the accessories by a long way. For example, he never touched the Crescendo Pedal, as he does not believe that this device is an artistic one.

I have been drawing up some specifications recently, and hope within the near future to put over a contract embodying the latest developments! I feel that I have learned quite a little from the Harvard organ and the organ at the Church of St. Mary the Virgin in New York City. You, at least, will be glad to know that my ideas all the time are tending towards Baroque ideas and low pressures and independent Pedal Organs!!

With kindest regards,

Yours sincerely,
G. Donald Harrison

GDH:MGM

Frank Bozyan — a well-known harpsichordist who taught at Yale University

Baumgartner I cannot understand — Hope Leroy Baumgartner of New Haven had a three-manual Aeolian-Skinner built for a new building of Church of the Redeemer, New Haven in 1951. Harrison may refer to an "atrocious instrument" as that built by the Hall Organ Co. of West Haven for the United Church in New Haven, where Baumgartner had been the organist.

September 6, 1933

Mr. William King Covell,
72 Washington Street,
Newport, Rhode Island.
Dear Mr. Covell:

Answering your letter of September 2nd, I believe that Melville Smith is at his mother's place in Leverett, Massachusetts. . . .

What do I think of the Harvard organ? That indeed is quite a big question, and honestly and frankly, especially since I have had about three weeks to think it over, I must say that I hardly know what to think.

There are so many conflicting conditions surrounding the installation of this fine big organ that a fair judgment is probably not possible on my part. In judging the instrument I am trying to put myself in the place of its builders and know full well that I would be quite bewildered at the prospect of finding a solution. Heard in the chancel particularly, but also in the body of the chapel, when the various manual departments are reduced to their strictly functional parts and superfluous material is left out of the ensemble, the effect is quite good.

With the whole works turned on, and since you ask the question: What do I think of the Harvard organ, I must say that to my ears it is not entirely musical. This of course is just a personal opinion and must be taken as such. To me, the tone is too direct and inflexible. The voices are TOO closely knit. I admire the courage of you gentlemen who were in on the planning, and I certainly take my hat off to Mr. Harrison for the precise and smooth finishing of the organ. Would that I could do as well.

I find the interest in stricter organ tone to be on the increase and it is a very welcome sign. While there seems to be a definite stand-patism apparent among some of the builders and quite a number of organists, their ranks are weakening and I have every confidence that "our" side will win out much to the good of the building and playing professions.

Trusting that you shall succeed in getting in touch with Mr. Smith before he leaves the East, I am with best regards,

Sincerely yours,
Walter Holtkamp
THE VOTTELER HOLTKAMP SPARLING ORGAN COMPANY

Mr. Smith — Melville Smith (1898-1962), organist, Cleveland Orchestra and at Western Reserve University; Director of the Longy School in Cambridge, Mass., 1941-62

Walter Holtkamp — Harrison was not alone in progressing beyond the English idea of ensemble to a more Classic design. Walter Holtkamp (1894-1962) introduced an unenclosed Positiv division in the Cleveland Museum of Art organ, a rebuild of a 1920 Skinner.

April 20, 1934

Mr. William King Covell,
72 Washington Street,
Newport, R. I.
Dear Mr. Covell:

I have just come to the office for a few minutes before going over to Worcester, and found your kind letter of the 17th awaiting me, and while I have not time at the moment to go into all you say in detail, I would like to thank you, and to say how glad I am that you think so highly of the All Saints organ.

Of course, it is not in its finished state, and some of the smaller criticisms you made have already been rectified or will be rectified, for example, in changing the lower three octaves of the Choir Nazard, which did not turn out as I had hoped, and the Choir Piccolo is being loudened. The other mutations are large scale, much larger than used at Harvard, for example, and blown fairly lightly.

Regarding the Swell reed, you are probably not aware that during the building of the church a small two manual organ, which was to form part of the present instrument, was placed in Huntington Hall, and the stops which were inserted in this instrument were not built under my supervision, but I was obliged to use some of them in the large organ. The Second Trumpet on the Swell is one of these stops, although it has been entirely revoiced with new shallots.

I think you would be quite surprised if you heard one rank of either the Great Fourniture or Cymbal alone. The tone is very broad, and one might even say that it is on the flutey side. Personally I feel that the lowering of the wind pressure to 3" or 3¼" would meet the case, and the next chance I have I am going to try this out. I wonder if you noticed how snappy the action is on light pressure. I cannot see the slightest difference between that and stops which were on heavier wind.

Yes, the Pedal organ is a joy to listen to.

Regarding the chorus reeds, after hearing the full flue work with no reeds in the organ I felt quite sorry that reeds had to be installed. Although the Clarions are not yet playable, perhaps the one criticism I have received from good organists is that, if anything, the reeds are underdone. This is a very difficult problem since it consists in blending old and modern ideas. One does not like to go back to the old brown paper type of reeds, and at Worcester I have tried to make a compromise, using modern methods on comparatively light pressures. The highest pressure used in the organ is 10" for the Solo reeds. The Pedal reeds are only on 8". By the way, the latter have only been roughed in, and I think when finished will be just right.

After all, for those who do not care for so much reed tone, they do not have to use all the reeds. Probably when finished, the best full organ effect from your point of view will be the full flue work, the Pedal reeds, the Choir reeds, and perhaps the Swell, leaving out the Great and Solo reeds. All these reeds just mentioned are on the thin side, and will, therefore, be the best blenders.

Directly when the instrument is finished, I hope you will arrange to pay another visit.

I was interested in your summing up of the Auditorium organ, and it agrees with the impression I received at the dedication.

What a frightful specification at Holy Cross.

I have thought of using the Hunt chest for Pedal 16' Octaves, and as a matter of fact before I read his book I had enlarged all the valves and put in very big cavities below the pipes, which resulted in an improvement in speech, and may be worth while to go still further. I do not at all agree with Hunt's idea of increasing pressure in the bass, and feel that it should be lighter if anything.

Thanks for the particulars of the Holy Cross Cathedral organ, which I find most interesting.

Hoping to see you soon, and with best wishes,

Sincerely,
G. Donald Harrison

GDH:MGM

the Auditorium organ — probably Harrison refers to the Worcester Memorial Auditorium, a four-manual Kimball of 106 ranks, dedicated November 6, 1933 by Palmer Christian, prominent recitalist and teacher of organ at University of Michigan.

frightful specification at Holy Cross — may refer to Holy Cross College in Worcester where the chapel housed Casavant Op. 1025 of 1924, a 3-manual of 27 stops.

Holy Cross Cathedral — in Boston, the 3 manual E. and G.G. Hook and Hastings Op. 801 of 1875.

---

99 G. Donald Harrison to William King Covell

June 8th, 1934

Mr. King Covell,
Newport, R. I.
Dear Mr. Covell:

It was very kind of you to send me a report about the latest Möller organ in New Jersey. Another friend had already given me some idea as to the tonal work in this instrument, and I understand that the Möller people gave Whitelegg his head in this particular instance.

The West End location for an organ is undoubtedly the ideal, and even also when the instrument contains those things which we think it should contain, as I have found in cases where powerful mixtures are located in chambers one does not obtain the clarity that would result in an open location.

I am sending you the program of the opening recital at Grace Cathedral, which I trust you will find interesting. The program is not one which will excite you greatly, but Mr. Lewis, the organist of the Cathedral, had to prepare it on very short notice, as there was a hitch in the arrangements with Mr. Warren Allen, who had planned to play a very classical program.

The organ itself is, I think, very successful. It is the first opportunity we have had of placing one of the newer type instruments in a real Cathedral with proper acoustics. The instrument is, of course, along the lines of the one at All Saints Church, Worcester, but, owing to the large capacity of the building and the fine acoustics, it sounds a great deal better and is undoubtedly the best organ of this kind we have turned out to date. The Diapasons on 3¾ inch wind are particularly successful. The general effect and impression that one receives is that the instrument lies some-where in between the work of T.C. Lewis and Father Willis. The Swell, for example, is very close to the older type of Willis with a very powerful mixture, while the Great flue work resembles to some extent the Lewis organ of Southwark Cathedral, only having a great many more ranks in the mixtures. However, the ensemble is more complex and complete.

My one regret is that this instrument is not in Boston or New York, where more people in the East would have a chance of hearing it.

I will save all the many details until we meet again, which, I trust, will be shortly after my return in the middle of the month.

Very sincerely yours,

G. Donald Harrison

GDH-T

opening recital at Grace Cathedral — The Grace Cathedral Aeolian-Skinner was dedicated June 3, 1934.

7th May, 1935

Mr. Henry Willis
Rotunda Organ Works,
234 Ferndale Road,
Brixton, London S.W.9,
England.

My dear Henry:

Very many thanks for your long letter of April 1st, and also for your promise to do all you can for Palmer Christian. I hope you have heard from him by now. I would like to tip you off to the fact that Christian is a great friend of Mr. Skinner's, so that you can bear this in mind during your conversations with him.

With reference to our new swell shades, we have so far only used them in one organ for the National Broadcasting Company Studio in New York, and have not come to any decision as to whether we will make the design standard or not. As a matter of fact, we are at present experimenting with a much lighter type of shade, and when we are through with that we will be in a better position to come to a decision as to the general arrangement.

Roughly speaking, the arrangement with N.B.C. consists of a series of swell shades which when closed stand at an angle of 45 degrees to the plane of the frame. In other words, when they are closed they present both inside and outside a corrugated effect. During the opening alternate shades move in opposite directions. In other words, Nos. 1,3,5,7 and 9 swing open in one direction, and Nos. 2,4,6,8 and 10 in the other direction. You will readily realize with a long arm pivoted in the center with the two trace rods connected at either end that this is readily accomplished. When the shades are fully opened they stand at 90 degrees to the plane of the frame. In other words, edge on to the sound waves. With this arrangement you will readily see that there is no general deflection of the sound waves either right or left or up or down according to whether you have vertical or horizontal shades, and although on the face of it this does not appear very important, it makes a surprising result in practice, particularly I think in rooms in which the ceiling and walls have highly absorbent qualities, such as broadcasting studios. The engineers at the N.B.C. have found with these rooms that the high frequencies deflected are absorbed and lost.

I was quite astonished at the result when we changed the original shades to this new type at their request as I did not believe that it would make any difference. Not only was the tone during the opening much more brilliant, but at full opening the stops had the effect of unenclosed ranks.

The above will give you a general idea of the scheme, but naturally there are a lot of details regarding the way the shades overlap when closed, and should we find on further experiment that it would be worth while to make all our shades this way, I will send you detailed drawings. We thought well enough of it to make a patent application.

Regarding reservoirs, you are perfectly right about the wind sag, and naturally this is a much more important matter when one is dealing with light pressures than with heavy pressures. We have been aware of the difficulty for some time, but did not really tackle it successfully until we started using light pressures regularly. Now these reservoirs are all checked over in the job when the organ is erected on the floor, and all wind sag eliminated. It was not long before we found the right type of spring that prevents this, and other details which are necessary to have right, to help to prevent this trouble.

We naturally have our lightest pressure on the Great flue work, and it is our standard practice in organs of any size at all to place all the pipes that stand on bass chests on a separate reservoir. This naturally prevents any robbing of the trebles by the bass, and at the same time puts very little demand on the main reservoir even when playing full. We have increased tremendously the size of our wind trunks, and use very large gates in the reservoirs, and consequently the top of the reservoir hardly drops when playing an enormous chord with all stops drawn.

They are tested in the shop by wind gauges, and we open a hole in the chest sufficiently large to account for about 100% more wind loss than is ever accounted for by actual playing. Even under these conditions the reservoir does not drop more than ½", and there is little difficulty in getting springs which will compensate for so small a drop.

It will naturally occur to your mind that a very large gate is liable to cause a dithering of the top of the reservoir since a very minute opening of the valve causes an extremely quick recovery of the reservoir. This is true, but is overcome quite simply by an apparatus which, for want of a better name, we call a wind bag, which is inserted inside the reservoir in the following manner. The bag consists of a cylinder of leather treated with a rubber solution to make it wind tight, and provided at either end with a plywood collar. One collar is screwed to the underside of the valve, and the other collar to the bottom plate of the reservoir. The diameter of these wind bags is usually somewhat less than the diameter of the gate, for instance, on a 12" gate we would use about a 10" wind bag. A hole of about ⅞" in diameter is bored through the bottom plate to the interior of the wind bag. The action is as follows: The wind bag relieves the pressure of the incoming wind from the underside of the gate or valve, and due to the atmospheric air, which is inside the wind bag and is in communication with the atmosphere through the small hole in the base plate of the reservoir, a snubbing action on the valve is also obtained quite similar in effect to the snubbers on motor car springs. This prevents jerky and erratic action of the gate, and it has the added advantage that it does not interfere at all with Tremolos. You will readily see that this is an extremely simple device, and one requiring no adjustment whatever, and at the same time will retain the very simple wind regulator or reservoir. This is not a new device. It was used by both Aeolian and the Welte people.

Another point in our general windage system is that it is standard practice to have basement reservoirs for every pressure, which enables one to control the wind pressures in the various main wind trunks, so that they remain constant under varying loads. In other words, if there is no basement reservoir, and the wind is coming direct from the blower, if you are using but one or two stops, the pressure in your main wind trunks is much higher than when you are making a real demand on the blower. You will readily see how the basement reservoirs enable you to control this condition.

During my experiments with a great number of jobs along these lines I found that a tremendous margin in the size of the wind trunks is essential in eliminating a great many windage troubles, and also the close proximity of the reservoir to its work. This has resulted in our using a great many reservoirs in our organs. In fact, Verne was quite surprised at the number he found in an organ like All Saints' Church, Worcester. It may sound quite expensive, but these reservoirs with our methods of manufacture do not cost us very much to build, and we have found that to have things right when they leave the shop saves all kinds of money spent in fooling around on the outside. I am sure when you are able to come over here that you will find that all our recent jobs are absolutely perfect as regards wind sag.

Regarding wind pressures, I saw Senator Richards the other day, and he told me that he had included in a recent letter to you a statement that our action would work on 1½", and that you replied saying "what for." Your remark is to the point. However, I do not intend to use 1" pressure, but it is comforting to know that the action would work perfectly on such a pressure. I found it out entirely by accident during an experiment in the shop. I was trying various types of springs, and during the experiment there were no springs on the reservoirs at all, and to my surprise I found the action was working even without pipes standing on the chest. The chest had five stops and continued to work with all the draw stops opened. I then got a wind gauge and found that the pressure was 1", obtained solely by the weight of the reservoir top. Naturally, I voiced a pipe on this pressure, and found that the articulation was excellent.

As you know, we have been making the pitman chests here for a great many years, and I think Carl Larsen, our chest foreman, is A-#1 at the job. It is only necessary to tell him that you are going to work on 2", and you can bet your last dollar that the chests will work. He works with extraordinary accuracy, and I do not remember an occasion where we have had to open up a chest to correct a fault in manufacture.

Regarding the valve springs, I have checked up with Larsen and find that we do still place the conical springs in position in the manner you describe — that is to say, a slight rotary movement of the thumb, but the tension is very very slight. Of course, this work is done by girls in our factory who become extremely expert at operations of this kind. I think their fingers are more adapted to work of this nature. Our chests are well nigh perfect, and I just hesitate changing them even in small details.

While on this subject, you will be interested to know that we do not use the double primary any longer, and have a magnet with a much larger exhaust port than the original Skinner. These magnets will exhaust a chest pouch quite comfortably, and in fact we are using such an arrangement on borrowed Pedal actions. That is to say, where a stop standing on a manual chest is borrowed to the Pedal. There is merely an additional set of magnets on the bottom board of the chest, which have a separate boring extending into the underside of the pouch.

Regarding wind pressures generally, with recent jobs I have gradually lowered those of the unenclosed departments, and would say that the standard for Great Organs now lies between 3" and 3¾". The recent organ at Trinity Church, New Haven has a pressure of 3¼" on the Great Organ. In larger churches where the pressure is desired for the reeds I use 5" on the Swell, and about 3¾" on the Choir, although I find with the French type of shallot which we are using extensively that 3¾" even on the Swell is all that is necessary for quite sizable places.

I am sure you will be interested in the enclosed specification which is for an organ for Groton School Chapel — a wonderful place for sound. You will note the very complete and independent Pedal Organ, and the unenclosed Positif on 2½" wind. This section will go in the old organist's gallery which juts out from the case of the organ, the whole being elevated about 15' from the Chancel floor level.

You ask about Baroque stops, and will note that this Positif includes a Koppel Flöte. I may have to experiment a little to get a proper scale for this, and if you have the actual particulars from Germany, I would greatly appreciate it if you would send me the measurements and details as soon as possible, and I will be glad to reciprocate in any way you wish.

The classical organ is going very strongly in this country, and although we are obliged to build some of the more normal pattern, there is an ever-increasing demand for the classical organ, particularly the straight Pedal Organ. I must confess that after working with a straight Pedal I have absolutely no use at all for the extended type or for the type which is based on the Wood Open. With the properly developed straight Pedal one can dispense with the use of the Great to Pedal couplers with contrapuntal work, which is naturally a tremendous advantage.

I am sorry to hear that Cavaillé-Coll are all through. Organbuilding is certainly at a low ebb in France.

Business has taken a sudden spurt for the better, and I hope it is not merely a temporary affair.

I am glad to see that Alcock at least is supporting the straight organ in England, and hope that business will soon pick up there.

It looks as though I am going to have a very busy summer personally, and fear that my often suggested trip home will have to be deferred.

All the best,

As ever,
Don

GDH:MGM
Encl.

[handwritten] P.S. I am using the Silbermann scale as standard for all Rohr Flötes, wide metal chimneys, etc. They are delightful.

P.P.S. My chorus scaling (which by the way I keep in the dark for obvious reasons) is as follows:

The 4' Major Octave is the largest scale of the chorus. The major 8' Diapason and all the unison and quint mutations also mixture ranks except Tierces are based on one scale smaller than the octave. In other words, the chorus is hung around the octave, which after all is more the centre of things than the unison. It certainly holds everything together. The mixture ranks are larger than anything else that's in the treble since they are based on a scaling ratio which halves on the 19th pipe. They are not tubby, merely full and clear. Cut up on mouth between ⅕th and ¼th. Tierces are usually Gemshorns. All this is perhaps unscientific, but it is the only way to get the effect I'm after, i.e. a really satisfying full organ without reeds and one on which counterpoint stands out clearly as it does in an orchestra.

Verne — Battigan Verne, a former Willis assistant
Trinity Church — Opus 927, a three-manual installed in early 1935
the organ for Groton School Chapel — Opus 936, a three-manual Aeolian-Skinner
at Groton School, Groton, Massachusetts, featured Harrison's first unenclosed Positif.

101 Henry Willis to Emerson Richards

17th May, 1935

Senator Emerson L. Richards
Atlantic City
N.J. U.S.A.

My dear Richards,

Following your letter of the 22nd April, Don has sent me the specification for the Groton School job. 'Pon my word it's fine, but so complete a "swing-back" that I marvel that even the most enlightened will stand for it.

The Great with 11 ranks of mixtures and 4 mutations in addition reads superbly but, of course, all depends upon the composition of the mixtures, strength, balance and so forth.

The straight Pedal is a delight — I rejoice to see the 4ft reed.

If I was to put such a scheme forward in this country people would think that I was mad!

I am a little disturbed at Don's statement that he is basing the scaling of the Great Diapason Chorus on the Octave (4ft), also by one or two other points. It seems to me to be unwise to go back 200 years completely — those old Baroque jobs are only for the connoisseur and student, not for duplication today.

I hear Verne has set up as an Organ Architect. Ye Gods and Little Fishes. V can draw up specifications all right — so can dozens of other amateurs, but an architect is expected to specify scales, treatment, pressures etc. which Verne is incapable of doing by direct experience — for while with me he had nothing whatsoever to do with the technical side. Let him write you — and tell me the fun!

Yours ever,
H.W.

H.W./E.F.

---

102 Henry Willis to G. Donald Harrison

21st May, 1935

G. Donald Harrison Esq.
c/o Aeolian-Skinner Corp.
Crescent Avenue, Dorchester,
Boston, Mass.
U.S.A.

My dear Don,

Thanks for yours of the 7th inst.

Koppel Flute. Attached are the measurements and working directions for 2ft C. You will like the lovely tone. I will send you C's if you wish.

I have working particulars of all Baroque stops and if you want any measurements etc. you have only to ask.

Swell Shades. The type you name may have value for the broadcasting salon you mention, but otherwise I fail to see any advantages in the design. When desired there is no difficulty in making shutters to swing full open but in normal cases that offers no advantage.

Regulators. All you say noted — of course huge trunks and big gates essential — but you say "does not drop more than ½", and there is little difficulty in getting springs which will compensate for so small a drop." On this point I cannot go all the way with you. No spring can sustain its pressure when slackened however little (without a compensating device) and it is this ½" drop that is so unfortunate resulting as it does in a wind-sag of 3/16" on 4" wind — enough to be unpleasant to the trained ear. I will try the "wind-bag" business.

Magnet machines. Glad you have dropped the primary and secondary arrangement and exhaust direct. As regards "borrowed" pedal actions — our "duplex" magnet takes care of such derivations — one magnet doing the job.

Groton School. Specification most excellent.

Rohr Flutes. Silbermann scale is very good — but to get the Silbermann effect you must use rich thin metal.

Koppel Flutes. This Baroque stop belongs to the half-stopped variety.

Pipes from 4ft C up should be made of thin but rich metal — not less than 55% tin — planed: can be hard rolled zinc below (baked zinc is useless).

Measurements etc. of 2ft C attached.

The canister sliding top must be made an accurate fit without leather or paper packing or the peculiar tone is impaired.

Scaling halves at the 16½ pipe.

Wind pressure should not exceed 3½" but 2¾" is very suitable.

The scale works out very large in the bass — but this is correct and typically Baroque.

Koppel Gedackt. 4ft G is same scale as 2ft Koppel Flute but sliding canister top is sealed.

Diapason Chorus scaling. I admit that you surprise me, basing the scaling on the Octave being a sheer swingback. I hope you get away with it.

Yours ever,
H.W.

H.W./K.C.

primary and secondary arrangement — Skinner chests used double valves; Harrison had simplified the action, using only one valve exhausted directly by the magnet.

duplex magnet — a magnet with multiple windings. They were usually used to make the same rank of pipes available on two or more divisions of an organ, each winding corresponding to one division.

---

103 Henry Willis to G. Donald Harrison

20th June, 1935

G. Donald Harrison Esq.
c/o Aeolian Skinner Corp.
Crescent Avenue,
Dorchester,
Boston, Mass.
U.S.A.

My dear Don,

I don't think that I sent you the details of the Dulzian 16ft. I used for Hereford Cathedral — very lovely and I recommend you to try it for a small Swell or as a soft Pedal reed.

<u>Dulzian 16ft</u> Normal construction no bells

CCC	16ft	Scale at top	5³⁄₃₂"	Length of tube	15' 1½"
CC	8ft	" " "	3½"	" " "	7' 4½"

Capped like an Oboe. Zinc lower 11 notes, rest spotted metal.

B. set unfilled reeds C.517   3½" wind.

CCC tongue thickness .025   CC ditto .020

"   Weight No. 20   "   Weight No. 9

A smaller scale of the small type as used for Contra Dulciana basses where no room for flue pipes to stand, carried down Dulciana or Salicional tone perfectly.

CCC 16ft   Scale 3³⁄₃₂"   CC 2"

"   "   Length 14' 2"   Length 6' 9"

Tongue .018   Tongue .012

C.51   4½" wind

I have "got away" with this quite successfully.

Yours ever,

H.W.

H.W./E.F.

June 24, 1935

Mr. Ernest M. Skinner
78 Beacon Street
Chestnut Hill,
Massachusetts
My dear Mr. Skinner:

Enclosed please find check for Six Thousand Five Hundred Dollars ($6,500.00) to cover the cost of the Methuen organ pipes which you so kindly offered to sell to the Cathedral.

It is understood that you will have these pipes stored for our account and properly insured, sending us, if you will, a memorandum of the same — where they are stored, and in what company and for how much they are insured. The policy should be made out in the name of the "Protestant Episcopal Cathedral Foundation of the District of Columbia;" and we should know the date of expiration, so that in every contingency the policy will be renewed at the proper time.

Thanking you again for your courtesy in this matter, I am

Faithfully yours,
G.C.F. Batenahl

GCFB:W
Encl.
P.S. I am leaving for Gloucester this morning.

1st July, 1935

Mr. G. Donald Harrison
Aeolian-Skinner Organ Co.
Crescent Avenue, Dorchester,
Boston, Mass. U.S.A.
My dear Don,

Herewith are typical scales of Baroque stops. I say typical because there are many differing scales but I consider those I have given you as most typical.

I consider the most characteristic to be the Koppelflöte and Spillflöte as these are examples of half-stopped pipes, then the Koppel Gedackt, Quintade and Blockflöte.

The conical Nachthorn scale was often used for Nasards and practically all the old Nasards were wide-scale conical open pipes. Personally I generally use a small scale Lieblich for a Nasard and an open pipe for the Terz.

There are literally swarms of varieties — the German builders of the 16th and 17th centuries seem to have gone out of their way to design and make stops with pipes of comic shapes — conical wooden pipes both open and stopped, wooden pipes normal but with a retreating front flank etc. all of little use or interest.

In Germany they are exaggerating the Baroque scales absurdly — also using copper basses for Gedackts etc.

No special tips about voicing Baroque Diapason work — thin rich metal, thin languids, low cut-up, slight bevel, sparse knife cut nicks and low pressure give the characteristic tone.

Yours ever,

H.W.

H.W./E.F.

BAROQUE STOPS TYPICAL SCALES

<u>KOPPEL FLÖTE</u> 4 or 2 ft as sent. *[See letter of 21 May 1935]*

<u>KOPPEL GEDACKT</u> 8 and 4ft. Use Koppel Flote scale and general method of manufacture — the open parallel — conical sliding canister top to have solid top — 4ft G (G in 4ft octave) will be same scale etc. as a Koppel Flute.

<u>QUINTADE</u> 16, 8, 4ft.   Diameters   ¼ mouth

16' CCC	6½"	Solid canister tops
8' CC	3⅞"	Cut up 4 in 1 to top of arch
4' C	2⅜" (1/64 bare)	Bar below ears.

<u>SPILLFLÖTE 2ft</u> Open conical.   Diameter at mouth 2ft C   1 13/16"

"   "   middle "   1 13/16"

"   "   top   "   ⅞"

These pipes are parallel ½ way up, then conicality commences — construction similiar to a Koppel flöte. Total length of 2ft C — 1' 8¼" overall. The top of parallel portion is 9½" from mouth — conical slider top has its parallel part 4" long giving desired overlap. ¼ ordinary mouths, cut up 4 in 1 top arch. This stop is often made all in one piece but tuning is then by a slot and it spoils the characteristic tone.

<u>BLOCKFLÖTE</u> 4 and 2ft. Conical

2ft C diameter at mouth 2⅜" Length 2' 1"

"   "   "   " top   1 9/32"

¼ ordinary mouths cut up 4 in 1 top arch.

Baroque stops often made parallel (not conical)

NACHTHORN 4 and 2ft (can be used 8ft) Open, not conical.

4ft C	4$\frac{1}{16}$"
2ft C	2$\frac{29}{32}$"

SCHWEIGEL 2ft   2$\frac{5}{32}$"

SIFFLÖTE 2ft   2$\frac{19}{32}$"

NASARD 2$\frac{2}{3}$ft   3$\frac{17}{32}$"

TIERCE 1$\frac{3}{5}$ft   2$\frac{9}{32}$"

All the above ordinary mouths, cut up 4 in 1 top arch.

All the above stops have more interest and character if made conical i.e. top $\frac{2}{3}$ diameter of mouth.

QUERFLÖTE 2ft (harmonic)   2$\frac{3}{8}$"

SCHWEIZER PFEIFE 1' (harmonic) 1$\frac{7}{8}$"

SPITZ FLUTE 8 and 4ft Conical.

8ft CC Diameter at	mouth		5$\frac{1}{2}$"	
8ft CC	"	" top	2"	
4ft C	"	" mouth	3$\frac{3}{8}$"	
4ft C	"	" top	1$\frac{1}{8}$"	length 4'2"

GEMSHORN 4 and 2ft

2ft C Diameter at	mouth	2$\frac{3}{4}$"	
"	" top	1"	length 1' 9$\frac{1}{4}$"

DULCIAN FLÖTE 8ft and 4ft inverted conical

4ft C at mouth 2$\frac{1}{2}$" at top 3$\frac{1}{8}$" length 2'1"

SPITZ QUINT 1$\frac{1}{3}$' at mouth 2$\frac{1}{8}$" at top 1$\frac{7}{8}$"

FLACKFLÖTE 2ft

Pedal	2ft C at mouth	2$\frac{7}{16}$"	at top 1$\frac{7}{32}$"	
Manual	"	"	"	2$\frac{3}{8}$"	at top 1 $\frac{3}{16}$"

GEDACKT POMMER 4ft C 2$\frac{3}{4}$" canister top

All thin light metal at least 60% tin. Light pressure 2$\frac{3}{4}$". All Baroque stops very thin languids practically just metal planes with very slight front bevel to take nicks. Light pressure 2$\frac{3}{4}$"

Diapason types $\frac{1}{4}$ mouths cut up 4 in 1.

Flute types $\frac{1}{4}$ mouths cut up 4 in 1 top arch.

Sparse knifecut nicks in all cases.

"Father" Henry Willis
1821-1901

---

106 Henry Willis to Emerson Richards

8th July, 1935

Senator Emerson L. Richards
Atlantic City,
N.J.
U.S.A.

My dear Richards,

Thanks for your letter of the 26th inst. Glad you are practically all right again now.

Ref. the <u>T.A.O.</u> article etc. and the question of the domination of heavy pressure Solo reeds — Tubas — in full organ this domination is agreed, is expected and sought for in a final "crash" — but the use of such Tubas in <u>ensemble</u> is to be deplored. Because an organ builder provides any given effect is no reason why the effect should be abused.

Full ensemble should, to my mind, be considered as not including the Tubas.

There is, however, no doubt that in my Grandfather's work the reeds predominated in the full ensemble and this dominance became more marked toward the end of his career when owing to the appalling Hope-Jones obsession and H-J's campaign against mixtures (and the appalling mixtures as carried out by Hill's for instance) the anti-mixture gang were very strong in this country and so the old man had great difficulty in keeping the mixture flag flying at all.

Personally I want to hear all ensemble stops pulling their weight in full ensemble — to hear a glowing and lovely tone picture without undue predominance of any particular registers. What undue predominance may be, is difficult to describe as so much depends upon personal taste.

I do not think that a full ensemble dominated by upper work and mixtures to be ideal, nor one dominated by chorus reeds, nor one dominated by unison diapasons.

I certainly do <u>not</u> admire a diapason structure with an Octave (4ft) that dominates the 8ft.

I consider that the full ensemble at Liverpool Cathedral <u>without the Tubas</u> and 32ft Bombarde on 30" wind is the most glorious organ tone — for it sounds as one tone — that I know of. This indicates what I do like. What I don't like, because I wouldn't care to live with it, is a full ensemble as at Ottobeuren or that at Armley. I also feel strongly that "deep-ending" in any direction is undesirable owing to the fact that it creates an inevitable re-action.

Now quite privately to you, Don is not doing what he went to Skinners for, and that was to give Skinner Organs a Willis ensemble. Don is striking out on what might be termed an individual line, <u>obviously influenced by you in the strongest possible way</u>. You will know that Don's Continental European experience is limited to a few French Organs — he has not to my knowledge been in any other European country and most certainly has not heard the various types of German organs Baroque and otherwise. On the other hand he can visualize them perfectly well, especially after hearing Steinmeyer's Altoona job.

Now you know that I appreciate your personal standpoint and ideals, even if I can't go all the way with you sometimes. I consider that you, far more than any other man, have rescued American organ building from the romantic morass it was in when I first visited America in 1924. I consider that my own influence has not been inconsiderable for I did get Skinner interested in a decent ensemble and "sold" him mixtures, although he could not learn how to use them properly. Also if it had not been for me, Don would not have gone to Skinners, for the purpose and object I have named above.

About the use of heavy pressure reeds, I was getting away from the old standard Willis practice of Swell flue work 3½", Chorus Reed 7" <u>before the War.</u>

At Nagpur Cathedral I produced a Swell all on 4½" wind and the Cornopean, which represented a new type, created a lot of interest. Since then I have only used pressures over 5" for Swell reeds for organs on a big scale in big buildings or under exceptional circumstances. I have also for three manuals adhered very largely to a Great flue Chorus only — the

Tromba present being really a Tuba and to be used as such. I consider the organ in the Seventh Church of Christ Scientist, London, to be almost ideal for its size when handled properly. Did you hear it when you were over? I forget.

I was surprised to hear that Austins are going out of business. As a matter of fact I understand that the position of the discerning purchaser is to go to Skinners or if they can't afford Skinners, to Möller for whom Whitelegg is doing good tonal work by all accounts I receive from various quarters. I presume that Möller's prices are about 25% lower than Skinners, so it leaves firms like Austins and Kimballs squeezed out.

How did the two Austin brothers become "independently wealthy" as you phrase it? Not out of organ building surely! I have yet to meet a man who has made anything more than a competence out of the game!

Yours ever,
H.W.

H.W./K.C.

Steinmeyer's Altoona job — see letter 72.
Austins going out of business — see letter 110

---

107 G. Donald Harrison to Henry Willis

July 9, 1935

Mr. Henry Willis,
234 Ferndale Road,
Brixton, London S.W.9
England.

My dear Henry:

Very many thanks for your letter of the 28th of June, and also for the postcard sent from Paris. Curiously enough, the organist of Trinity Church, New Haven, where we have just finished a new organ, was organist for one summer at the American Church in Paris. He was studying with Dupré.

Thanks for your promise to send along particulars of the other Baroque stops. I am anxiously waiting for the details as I am holding up on the manufacture of the pipes until I hear from you.

Regarding next year, I am afraid that August will not be possible, and fear that the trip will have to be made in the spring. The reason for this is that as things work out in this country we are always busy in August and September and the beginning of October installing organs as nearly all churches like to have them put in during this period. I do not desire to make a particularly extended tour either in France or Germany as I wish to spend the majority of the time in England. After all, one or two examples of the best of this type of instrument would be sufficient. It would be fine if the Senator came along, although he is apt to run one ragged in trying to see too much, in which case one is liable to retain but fleeting impressions.

I would like to hear some of the big French organs again, although I have heard them so many times in the past that the impression of them still remains fairly fresh.

I am interested to see that you are running a special train for the Salisbury affair. It will be very enjoyable I am sure. I thought that the conservative rebuild of this organ was the best. . . .

[Balance of letter lost]

the organist of Trinity Church, New Haven — G. Huntington Byles
the manufacture of pipes — for the Groton organ
Salisbury affair — Salisbury Cathedral, dedication of a Henry Willis III rebuild of a Father Willis organ.

---

108 G. Donald Harrison to Henry Willis

July 11, 1935

Mr. Henry Willis,
234 Ferndale Road,
Brixton, London S.W.9
England.
My dear Henry:

I am very much obliged by your letter of July first giving particulars of the Baroque stops. I am having some samples made up at once, and will let you know how they turn out in due course.

I note you say there are no special tips about voicing the Baroque type of Diapason, but if I may worry you just once more, I would like a line from you describing the tone quality of the best Silbermann Diapasons you heard. The reports are very conflicting over here. Do they partake of the old English Diapasons, in other words rather fluty, or are they blown harder than that, and therefore approach Geigen tone.

Since writing you last I had a letter from Richards, who is still recuperating from his operation. He is not at all well yet, and the poisons are still in his system, causing his heart to play up. I feel sure if he could take off about 95 lbs. in weight, he would feel a whole lot better!

Will write again soon.

All the best,

Yours,
Don

GDH:MGM
about 95 lbs. — Richards was seriously overweight for much of his life.

July 18, 1935

Mr. William King Covell,
72 Washington Street,
Newport, R.I.

Dear Mr. Covell:

I am so sorry to have been such a long time replying to your letter of June 12th, but have been exceedingly busy working on the Groton Organ.

Very many thanks for sending me a reprint of your article on Trinity, Newport. When I first read this article in The Organ I found the historical details very interesting, and believe that many in England would enjoy the article from that point of view.

I did not mind the criticism of the organ, though I am not quite certain as to whether it would give a correct impression to English organ enthusiasts. After all, with all its faults, it is a good deal better than many organs in England of similar size.

The details you give are all right since they are all old history from my point of view. I would not care to have, for example, the scales of Groton given in any great detail as I have been to great pains to work out special things, and have also obtained with considerable trouble a lot of data from abroad. After all, why give all this to one's competitors.

The specification of the unenclosed Positif at Groton has been slightly changed. It now reads as follows:

8'	Rohrflöte
4'	Principal
4'	Koppel Flöte
2⅔'	Nazard
2'	Blockflöte
1⅗'	Tierce
1'	Sifflöte
	Scharf (IV Rks.)

The wind pressure has been reduced from 2½" to 2¼". All these stops, and also the 16' Quintaton on the enclosed section of the Choir, will be of the Baroque type absolutely, and I am expecting quite an unusual and beautiful effect from them.

I am not surprised that Verne made some mistakes in last month's Musical Opinion. He saw so many organs that it was practically impossible for him to keep everything straight, although he did make notes each evening, but apparently not detailed enough. He is quite wrong, of course, about the Harvard organ. I am naturally quite pleased with his article in this month's Musical Opinion, which you have doubtless read by now.

The Senator passed through Boston on Tuesday, and I spent a pleasant time with him that evening, and he came over to the factory the next morning. He is intensely interested in the Groton organ naturally. I have not really read his Bach Biography articles sufficiently carefully to give my opinion. He is very keen about the subject, and do not believe he will switch back to organs until it is complete.

Hoping to see you soon, and with kind regards,

Sincerely,

G. Donald Harrison

GDH:MGM

Trinity, Newport — Covell had just published *The Organs of Trinity Church, Newport*, which originally contained a 1733 two manual organ built in England by Richard Bridge and in which Skinner installed opus 800, a small 3-manual, in 1930.

---

110 Emerson Richards to Henry Willis

July 19, 1935

Mr. Henry Willis
234, Ferndale Road
Brixton, London, S.W.9
England

My dear Willis:

This acknowledges yours of June 21st which my secretary forwarded to me at Moosehead Lake, and also yours of the 8th which arrived in Atlantic City on the 17th just before I got back. Had a good rest at the Lake but did not make much progress towards recovery. I was taking the vaccine injections so as to prevent the return of any more carbuncles. It, however, affected my foot and also my heart to some extent, the result being that until I stopped taking the injections a week ago, I was worse off than when I left for Atlantic City. However, after disobeying the local doctor and refusing to take any more injections I began to get better and am feeling very much improved now.

Left the Lake Tuesday morning about 10 o'clock and took it easy into Boston, arriving at six, 275 miles. Don and Mr. and Mrs. Zeuch met me at the hotel and we had dinner together and quite a long talk-fest. Wednesday morning I went out to the factory and ran over the Principal for the Groton job, which is just off the voicing machine. Also the three mixtures, the Tierce, Quint and Octave. All of this material is on 3" wind. I am sure you are going to like that Principal when you hear it. It certainly was a peach on the machine. The organ itself is about complete on the erecting floor and goes to Groton this coming week. The pipe work is only fairly well

John Austin

along. We also had a go at the Koppel Flute on 2½" wind which goes on the Positive.

Our Chicago Doctor, Bill Barnes, was up to hear the Worcester job quite recently. He came prepared to condemn it and his whole attitude on the way up to Boston was that he dared them to make him like it. Bill Zeuch played it to him for an hour. His wife and mother-in-law (Barnes') were along. They voted that they liked it very much which put the Doctor strictly in the middle. He finally agreed that the thing was so new to him that he did not know whether he liked it or not. Finally after another session with Mrs. Bill he said that he did like it but thought that there was not enough contrast between the Great and the Swell. An organ which is to be somewhat a duplicate of Worcester is in the offing for Chicago, hence Bill's visit although both Walter Hardy and Don think that they may be able to sell the organ even if Bill doesn't agree. He is supposed to be experting it.

Left Boston at 12:15 and arrived at my hotel in New York at 6:15 last evening, just six hours. The train takes five. Saw Herbert Brown and went over considerable of the detail of the Austin matter. If you think that the Austins haven't made money out of the organ business, you are vastly mistaken. They admit that they only put $60,000 in the company altogether and the total assets are now $1,570,000 in round figures; of which $123,000 is cash; notes receivable $245,000; accounts receivable $52,000; inventory including work in progress, about $200,000; and investments including stocks, bonds, etc. $905,000. The buildings, machinery, etc. are appraised at $226,000, and which have been written down to $15,000. In addition to which the Austins have been drawing down about $45,000 a year in salaries, cash dividends have approximated 25% a year, and the original $60,000 of stock has been increased by stock dividends to $1,040,000. So that in addition to the moneys already taken out in the organ business in the way of these extensive salaries and dividends, both of the Austins will get about $600,000 a piece out of the liquidation, even if they don't sell the lands and buildings and their patents for anything substantial.

The reason for the liquidation generally appears to be a certain amount of jealousy between the two brothers and their families, plus the fact that they are both tired old men and don't really want to be bothered with business. Herbert Brown, who is their Eastern Sales Manager, is trying to organize a new company. They have offered to sell him the factory and the business for $200,000. He has about two-thirds of this subscribed at the present moment. Wanted me to come in but I have declined because I don't want to be tied up to any one company. Offered to make an arrangement with them for technical advice, etc. which they may accept if the plan goes through to purchase the company. Brown will probably know within the next two weeks if he is going to be successful. The men who will be interested are some of those connected with the Morgan firm whom Brown has been in contact with because of St. George's Church.

Have gone into this in some detail because in talking with Brown Wednesday night the matter was tentatively revived that you and I discussed in London two years ago. This is, of course, all very tentative at the moment and nothing at all may come of it. On the other hand it may, and if so you may find yourself playing that "deep end" tune on the softest stop in your repertoire.

I cannot tell you much about the Convention. Due to my lameness I did not go to New York until Thursday afternoon (the Convention began on Monday and ended Friday night). Heard the five combined choirs do their stuff at St. Bartholomew's. As usual it was pretty awful and that old Skinner was really dreadful. The general report was that the Convention was quite a success. There were about 900 present and most of the program was very interesting. The Round Table affair on Friday morning was somewhat of a dud. Jamison, being just out of a job, talked very much like a hen that had just been pulled out of a pond, and poor Skinner trembled all over so that he could not actually read the paper that he had dictated, and showed that he was all of sixty-nine and not really fit to start out as an independent organ builder next January. Closed the debate myself with some comments upon what the other men had said, kissed the Convention good-bye, and started for Boston. Got up to Moosehead the following afternoon. Fine cool clear weather there the whole time I was there. Cold enough for blankets every night, plenty of sunshine and lots of scenery. The fishing also was good; unable to do any myself but Mrs. Buhrman caught four salmon in one morning's fishing.

This I think is all the gossip up to date. I think you and I agree about the ensemble proposition. Of course we don't want mixtures to dominate the ensemble but we do want them to make it.

Not too seriously. I hardly know how to take your accusation that I am leading Don astray. What really led Don off the reservation was the full Great in the Convention Hall organ in Atlantic City. He has been down here several times and he never pays very much attention to anything except that Great. Undoubtedly it is responsible for his tossing out the Reeds on the Great manual and thinning them out on the Swell.

Senator Richards at the Atlantic City Convention Hall console

Of course I have done quite a lot of talking to him about the unenclosed Choir or Positive. I don't see, however, that we are really deep-ending anything. Up to a certain point the reform was carried out very conservatively. Groton, I will admit, is really the first job that brings it out in the open so far as an ecclesiastical organ is concerned. A design that I made up a year ago is about to be put over by Don in a Boston church, and there are a couple more in the offing of the same kind. All we have really done is to go back to where your grandfather was when he built the Alexandra Palace job, with probably a little less emphasis on the reeds and no high pressure ones.

If these organs are radical it is only by comparison. You yourself would be the first to admit that the Romantic organs of the St. Thomas Skinner period ought to be reformed out of existence. If things have and are moving rapidly over here it is simply because the opportunities are greater. This country is so darned big that there is bound to be more opportunities to build sizable organs, and that gives us reasonable chances to gradually work out theories, which you yourself, I think, fully agree with.

For instance, you mention the matter of the Octave. Where there are two Octaves on the Great, one can afford a big one in order to have a firm foundation for the mixtures. It does not overshadow the unison and of course your smaller Octave is there when you want a small chorus without the mixtures, and fits in perfectly with the unisons.

Of course, if Skinner had only followed your advice all of this would have been accomplished long ago, but the more I learn of E.M. the more I can see that he never intended to follow you. He only pretended to do so in order that he could more surely have his own way. I really think he thought he knew better and that he took your work and so twisted it around so as to make it appear unacceptable in order to prove that his methods were right. As I think you know, he turned on Don just as soon as he discovered that Don was sincerely trying to carry out your ideas. For the last two years he has been practically out of the Skinner Company. He told me this Spring that he was only waiting for his contract to expire on the first of January next to go into business for himself. Marks has tied him up pretty tight but he has been around visiting all his friends and expects to start up in competition with his own company as soon as he can legally do so.

Of course you are right, Don is doing more than putting the Willis Ensemble into the Skinner organ, just as I said in the New Haven article which you have probably read by this time. He has set up for himself, taken all the ideas that he was heir to as well as some others that he has been talked into, and made something which in a shadowy sort of way may be considered American. When Don came over here I don't think he had any intention of leaving England behind, but he told me at breakfast Wednesday morning that he was going to apply for citizenship and that means that the same mental condition that has guided his artistic progress is also continuing in other directions.

I think I told you in one of my previous letters that he had been up to some other things besides organ building. He was confidential then and I don't know whether he has written you of them, but actually he has re-married. It is gradually leaking out so this is no violation of confidence.

I hope your trip to Paris was a success and that you landed the contract. My, how you are changing! I could not conceive of your going to Paris and insisting on coming back the same day. As you know, I don't like the place so I can't blame you, but perhaps then you knew some things about the town that I didn't.

My plans about this fall are still very vague.

With kindest regards, I am,

Cordially yours,

Emerson L. Richards

ER:SSN

the Worcester job — All Saints, Worcester

a duplicate of Worcester — apparently this contract never materialized.

the liquidation — Austin Organs, Inc. was formed January 2, 1937 to purchase the patents, machinery and good will of the the Austin Organ Co. The original firm voluntarily liquidated by recommendation of the Board of Directors on June 12, 1935. Work in the factory never completely stopped. One of the first consoles to be manufactured under the new directorate was installed in the Mormon Tabernacle, controlling 136 stops and 60 couplers.

a design . . . in a Boston church — Church of the Advent, opus 940

St. Thomas Skinner period — a 1913 four-manual, opus 205. Skinner considered it one of his finest.

111　Henry Willis to G. Donald Harrison

22nd July, 1935

Mr. G. Donald Harrison
Technical Director
Aeolian-Skinner Organ Co.
Crescent Avenue, Dorchester,
Boston, Mass. U.S.A.
My dear Don,

Thanks for yours of the 11th instant. The tone of Silbermann Diapasons is somewhat difficult to describe. Loosely, they might be described as being fluty, but owing to the rich metal, thin walls and low cut up there exists an innate harmonic development that is quite definite, giving a "glow" to the tone color. The scaling, also, becomes big in the treble but the character remains the same. The nearest type of tone that you know is the old Renatus Harris type, with a difference.

The best description of this Silbermann tone was in a series of articles by a German-American that appeared in the Diapason, I think, some 18 months or two years ago.

If you like I will make up and send you C's from 4ft up of what I consider a typical reproduction of a Silbermann Diapason, but I would advise you that much depends upon the building in which an individual has heard them.

141

You might make up a stop or stops to particulars I give you and put same in a "difficult" building when Richards or others might say, "nothing like Silbermann tone at all!"

The reproduction of any given type is fraught with difficulties. You know that we used to pooh-pooh the suggestion that age of the metal mellowed the tone; well <u>now I know</u> that it does. The gentle oxidation that takes place has an inevitable effect upon the crystalline structure of the alloy, and you cannot reproduce its effect in new metal. When I reproduced the Schulze Diapason making it exactly the same scale and voicing pipe to pipe, the first stop was excellent but subtly unlike the Schulze in total effect and tone color. I then made another with the same result and to match the new stop tonally had to take certain liberties with the voicing, i.e. nicking on lower lip slightly heavier than the original, cut-up a <u>shade</u> higher and more "blunted" bevel on the top lip with the inside slightly rounded. The reproduction was then just about perfect.

Besides this old metal question there is this fact: the nicking "wears" after many years. The constant passing of the wind wears away the slight burr which is formed in the process of nicking and gives a smoother wind passage. You will remember that the "trade" system of nicking with double edged nickers means that the nicker is pushed in and so forms a definite burr on the lower side which the wind strikes before passage through the flue. Proper nickers for single nicking, and used with a slight "draw" towards you, obviates this as much as it is possible to do so.

So, in view of the above, be <u>very</u> careful to only use the term "on Silbermann lines" etc.

As regards the metal, I would consider that Hoyt metal would give you the desired effect better than any other "new" metal. The Hoyt metal is rolled as you know and this rolling must alter the normal crystalline structure of the metal in a favorable manner <u>for this special purpose</u>, the low tin content (except for the tin surface) helping also.

But the whole proposition of the reproduction of any "old" tone is fraught with difficulties.

I did an Early English Diapason recently that sounded perfect on the voicing machine. In the job — well! not Early English. I had to increase the bevels considerably to get the necessary life into it. The building was the Chapel of S. Katherine's College, Tottenham, quite normal for sound, reverberation period about 1½ seconds empty.

Yours ever,

H.W.

H.W./E.F.

the old Renatus Harris type — Renatus Harris, an 18th-century English builder (ca. 1652-1724)

series ... by a German-American — "The Silbermann Organ," an article by Dr. Oscar E. Schminke in *The American Organist*, May and June 1933, which described Silbermann's scaling methods.

Hoyt metal — sheet lead with a rolled-on tin foil coating which was less expensive than spotted metal. The differing expansion rate in the two metals sometimes deformed the mouths, causing the pipes to go off speech.

---

112 Henry Willis to G. Donald Harrison

26th July, 1935

Mr. G. Donald Harrison
Technical Director
Aeolian-Skinner Organ Co.
Crescent Avenue, Dorchester,
Boston, Mass. U.S.A.

My dear Don,

Reference your letter of the 9th instant and trip to Germany next spring. Will you let me know exactly what jobs you want to try so that I can work out an itinerary, and also obtain the necessary introductions in each case. You must go anyway to Ottobeuren. As you have not been to Germany before, and may not do so again for many years it will be well to do it thoroughly. Do you hope to get Steinmeyer to come around with us? He is an excellent companion and guide and would probably be willing to bring his car and chauffeur for the Southern part of the tour, probably Leipzig and South. He would expect the gas to be paid for and the man given a good tip.

I would be glad to know if you picked up anything useful at Austin's place.

When you try our regulators with "pressure-equalizer" attachment, you will be convinced that it is "the goods."

Yours ever,

H.W.

P.S. Have you tried one of those Hammond "Organs" yet, and if so what is your reaction?

H.W./E.F.

113 G. Donald Harrison to Henry Willis

August 21, 1935

Mr. Henry Willis,
c/o Henry Willis & Sons, Ltd.
Rotunda Organ Works,
234, Ferndale Road,
Brixton, London, S.W.9.
England.

My dear Henry:

Very many thanks for your kind letters of July 22nd and August 6th, which I found awaiting me on my return from a short vacation. The first letter gives me exactly what I need and really confirms exactly what I thought about these old stops. I agree with you entirely about the effect of age on the metal of organ pipes with the resulting modification of the tone quality. I am also very skeptical about many examples which are supposed to be untouched. It seems inconceivable to me that when repairs have been done from time to time that work has not also been done on the pipes which makes them sound quite different from their original quality. There is also the point with all old organs that the toes of the pipes have been gradually closed or altered by the weight of the pipes standing for so many years. Your description of the tone quality of the Silbermann Diapason is exactly as I imagined it, but I wished to have confirmation from a reliable source and from one who can use the words which mean something to an organ builder.

I am not attempting in any way to imitate the Silbermann organ or any Baroque organ for that matter, but am merely reintroducing some of the features of the older organ which have been lost in the modern organs, and using to some extent, the principles utilized by the older builders in the general chorus; the sole object, of course, being to make the instrument a more nearly ideal one for the playing of the best literature written for this particular medium.

Your recent suggestions in regard to the proposed trip next Spring seem excellent, but I must write to you in greater detail about this a little later.

Regarding your letter of August 6th, I was very interested to hear about the London Conference of Organists, and, of course, was aware that John Marshall was going to attend. I know him very well and often get together with him. . . .

[Don]

[The close and signature do not survive; the letter may be incomplete.]

John P. Marshall — (1871-1941) Professor of Music since 1902, organist of Boston Symphony 1896-1902, dean of the College of Music, Boston University, from 1928.

September 19, 1935

Mr. Henry Willis,
234 Ferndale Road,
Brixton, London S.W.9,
England.

My dear Henry:

Very many thanks for your letter of the 4th instant. Since writing you before I have seen Thalben-Ball two or three times, and got a little closer to him than on our previous meetings.

He admits that he could get the Temple organ rebuilt at any time, but at present it would appear that Rothwell is the stumbling block. Apparently the old fellow is well on in his eighties, and taking this contract away from him would be a blow from which he would never recover. As you say, he is waiting for "events."

He is keen to have the organ electrified and the Bombarde section installed, and I also feel that he favors you to do the work. By the way, he seems to feel that when the inevitable happens to old Rothwell that the firm will be absorbed by Walkers.

I don't know whether I was supposed to pass on this information to you or not, so please make use of it tactfully.

I was very interested to hear of Dupré's ovation at the Queens Hall. . . .

I am just in the middle of finishing the Groton organ, which is coming up to my expectations. The acoustics are well nigh perfect — resonant but without distortion or confusion. I will let you know how the whole thing turns out a little later on.

All the best,

As ever,
Don

GDH:MGM

P.S. By the way I got spliced a little time ago! *[handwritten]*

Thalben-Ball — George Thomas Thalben-Ball (1896-1987) organist of the Temple Church, London from 1923.
the Temple organ . . . Rothwell — The Temple Church, London, housed a four-manual Rothwell. The console had stoptab controls in the keyslips between the manuals. This instrument was destroyed in World War II.
I got spliced — Helen Caspari and Donald Harrison were married April 29, 1935.

November 25, 1935

Mr. Henry Willis,
234 Ferndale Road,
Brixton, London, S.W.9.
England.

My dear Henry:

Many thanks for your letter of the 12th instant, and for the enclosures. I was particularly interested to read about your visit to the Brussels Exposition. It must have been quite interesting. I take it the report, a copy of which you enclosed, is part of the dope you sent to the Belgian Government. You do not say what you really thought of these jobs.

You will be interested to hear that the Groton organ continues to win friends. In fact, there have been no serious criticisms from anyone so far. The general impression seems to be that a high-spot has been touched.

The Swell reeds are let out even too much, if anything, and thinner than I would really like to have them. The real trouble is the narrow and deep chamber, and the fact that the Swell has quite a lot of organ to filter through before it gets into the Chapel. Really it would have been better had I used a slightly higher pressure.

I was surprised to see that in your letter to Richards you suggested that I obviously used felt and lead weighting on the reed tongues, and that the latter were thick. This is not the case. The felt and lead weight system of voicing seems to be unknown in this country, and Yours Truly will not introduce it as I have no use for that particular method. In any case, I fear it would not have been permanent as the moths have much bigger appetites here than they do in England, and the felt would disappear in a year or so.

The tongues are the same thickness that you would use on a similar pressure. I have long done away with the thick tongues that used to be used here, and only the 10 lower notes of the 8' and the 22 lower notes of the 16' have any weights of any kind, and these are very small. I have tried using no weights on some of these reeds, but it is nice to have a little control.

I was away when Mrs. Cooms first wrote to me as I had driven down to Memphis, Tenn. to finish a big three manual in Calvary Church. I got in touch with her, however, immediately on my return, and we spent two afternoons together last week. The first day we had lunch, and then visited Groton, and on the second day we went over to All Saints' Church, Worcester. She seemed to be quite favorably impressed with these organs, but she will doubtless tell you all the points in detail on her return.

While driving over to Worcester we had a long talk about the English organ situation, and it seems to worry her considerably, and she is determined to do something about it. All the more power to her, but I fear it will be difficult, but as she says, you never know what you can do until you try. She refers, of course, to Sir Hugh Allen and that bunch. I still feel that the only way is to sell the younger generation.

I do not know whether I told you in my last letter, but if I did so, please forgive me for repeating it, but we have just received a contract for an organ in the Church of the Advent in Boston, a very fine place for sound. This organ will be along the Groton lines, although somewhat smaller. We got the job without competition on the priest in charge, the organist and Wallace Goodrich hearing the Groton instrument. Moreover, they gave me carte blanche within the funds available. Wallace Goodrich, you will probably remember, is the head of the New England Conservatory of Music in Boston, and also happens to be Chairman of the Music Committee at the Church of the Advent. He resembles quite closely the Sir Hugh Allen type, so it was somewhat of a triumph. Of course, he has the advantage that he studied with Widor in Paris in his youth.

The Advent has a beautiful organ chamber, about half as large as Groton, with an opening into the transept as well as the main opening into the Chancel. The church is very lofty and resonant, and the console will be placed in an excellent location immediately opposite the organ. I am enclosing a copy of the specification.

We have quite a few excellent prospects right now; in fact, more than we have had in years, but it seems to be a bad time for actually getting contracts signed, and the factory is very quiet. We expect to pick up again in the New Year, however.

I do hope something will break for you shortly. The cleaning and tuning business is certainly a fine stand-by in such times as these.

I think this is all the news at present.

With all the best,

As ever,
Don

GDH:MGM
Encl.

P.S. *[handwritten]* I would like you to hear our reeds. The voicing technique is as fine if not finer than anything I have seen anywhere. The even results, the margin and the way they stand in tune is remarkable. Of course, the voicers take plenty of time, but in view of the excellent results we have not pressed them. The French reeds have the imported dome-headed shallots (small scale). The other reeds, Willis C sets with varying sizes of openings according to pressure and result desired.

When first I told the head voicer to use Willis thicknesses, he said immediately, and before I had time to tell him, "We will have to change the type of curve for these thin tongues," and went on to describe as nearly as one can in words the Willis curve. I thought that pretty good.

The thicknesses, with a few exceptions, (French Horn, for example) are almost exactly what you would use. For a 32' Bombarde I carried down the ordinary Willis pedal set. It makes a larger shallot than the Willis 32' set and of course, we use a thicker tongue (but in proportion to the 16') and a longer tuning length. This enables you to lay down the curve so that it doesn't stand away nearly so much and makes it possible to get rid of the preliminary "puff" of the thin short tongue type. Moreover, we can regulate them just like a normal 8'.

big three-manual in Calvary Church — Opus 932

The Church of the Advent — The subway that passed the Aeolian-Skinner factory stopped near the Church of the Advent. Although the Groton organ was larger, the Advent was more convenient, and visiting organists were often taken there.

Sir Hugh (Percy) Allen — 1869-1946; Director, Royal College of Music, 1918-38

---

116 Arthur Hudson Marks to Stockholders

SKINNER ORGAN COMPANY

Boston, Mass.   November 25, 1935

To the Stockholders of
SKINNER ORGAN COMPANY:

Since the dividend of five (5) cents per share was declared out of surplus and paid to the Stockholders on October 17, 1933, liquidation of the assets (not transferred to the Aeolian-Skinner Organ Company, Inc.) has been slow, but it is now possible to pay from amounts collected a dividend of five (5) cents per share out of surplus, check for which is enclosed herewith.

We are advised that it is probable that this dividend will be treated as income to the Stockholders both under the Federal and Massachusetts income tax law.

Operations of the Aeolian-Skinner Organ Company, Inc. (60% of the capital stock of which constitutes the principal asset of your Corporation), showed a small operating loss for the year 1934 and will undoubtedly show another small operating loss for the year 1935. The balance sheet of that Company continues in a strong condition and its organization intact. At present the prospects for 1936 appear better than for several years, but are, of course, dependent upon continued improvement in the general business situation.

Very truly yours,
ARTHUR HUDSON MARKS
President

Enc.

148

Arthur Hudson Marks

---

117 Emerson Richards to William King Covell

November 26, 1935

Mr. Wm. King Covell
72 Washington Street
Newport, Rhode Island

Dear Covell:

Both of your letters are in. I don't know that I shall get time at the moment to answer both of them, but shall do so in their order.

I think Buhrman would have published the $15,000 organ scheme had he not been more or less overwhelmed with material at the moment. And unless advertisers become more liberal it is not practical to increase the size of the magazine. I sent you the article largely for the purpose of indication that the ideas suggested are the real basis of the Groton organ. It has these points in common: 1) Mixtures, not Reeds, on the Great; (2) Primary Reed and Mixture chorus on the Swell; and (3) in the case of the Choir a Positive, although it is not called that, and an enclosed section containing modern colors. The theory, not the exact stops, of the lower manual is identical with Groton. The Great is basically the same except that in its details I have had to include some of the straight mutations in the mixtures. The fundamental dominating Flue Chorus is present. The Swell brilliant reeds and mixtures cannot be said to be altogether new, although it is done in a new way. The independent Pedal is, of course, not a novelty since we had already settled this matter and you had used it at Harvard and Harrison had exploited it at Worcester. I have no objection to your writing Buhrman about the article and, while it is as you say more or less a prophecy, it has really reached a stage of realization. Nevertheless, the fact that a 50-stop organ of this type can be bought for $15,000 is undoubtedly news to most readers.

I am glad that you agree with me concerning the Groton organ. I am not sure that I wish to give it the same amount of praise that you have in your letter. Walter Hardy is reported to have said about me that I was the only one in the organ game who knew exactly what I wanted, knew when I had it, and, if necessary, knew how to get it. In the case of a job like the Groton one, or like the classic organ that you and I are thinking about, I know exactly what I want. I know the Groton organ is not that as yet, although it is approaching it. So far as the flue work is concerned I know exactly how to get it. Don didn't believe me and had to go back and do some of the things over again in the factory before they ever got to Groton, and he knows a lot better now. This relates particularly to the scales of the upper work and the pipe treatments of the smaller ranks. So far as the reeds are concerned I am not altogether certain that I do know how to get what I really want in the bass octaves of the 8' and 16' reeds. I have several theories on the subject, but only actual experiment would demonstrate whether they are right. There is still too much body in these bass octaves. Yet when other people have succeeded in eliminating the body they have left little but a rattle that is far from musical when used alone and has too much snare drum effect in an ensemble. I am sure there is a way to get pure tone without the accompanying overbody of tibia tone, but whether I am right in my ideas on the subject only the next organ that I actually superintend will tell. Of course I agree with you that Groton is worthy of praise, more I am willing to concede that designedly or by chance it fell short of the point that I am personally aiming for. For all its paper radicalism it is obviously not offensive to the conservative, and that's a help in practically maintaining our ground. It is after all not so much the length of the step as the direction that counts, so that if I don't give three rousing cheers you'll understand that it is not because I do not appreciate what has been done, but because I envision something which, once it becomes reality, we will agree is ever so much better.

I think that you have rather picked me up on the use of the word "renaissance." To some extent I think your own argument answers itself. You wish to hold the word "renaissance" down to a revival of something that has existed before — "the classic organ has never existed here before." Yet you go on to speak of the classic organ in Germany. We speak of the German and French Renaissance meaning thereby a certain period of Art. Now neither the German nor the French Renaissance were revivals. The same holds true of the parent Italian Renaissance. It was not a revival of any Italian Art, but an examination of the principles of Greek Art, and these fundamental concepts were interpolated with the new ideas which had sprung up with the exhaustion of the Medieval Gothic Art. "Renaissance" has frequently been used as synonymous with "revival" but the dictionary does not make that mistake. The primary meaning is "new birth, resurrection, revival as in Art, and specifically to the revival of letters and art in Europe marking the transition from the Medieval to the Modern." So that when I speak of "a forward step in the Renaissance of the classic organ in America" I am talking about the new birth of the classic organ in the U.S.A. I don't mean to imply that it ever existed here before, but that it is as much a creation of Art based upon classic lines as the work of Michelangelo or Raphael. It was nationalistically Italian and not Greek, so in this case I think the thing will develop as nationalistically American.

I agree that the Harrison work is merely based on the theories of the older organ work. Remember that Don has no first-hand acquaintance with German work whatsoever, unless we can consider the Steinmeyer at Altoona as such, and Henry says that his knowledge of French organs is really not extensive, so that, in reality, he has been working on his own with only a hint from the older work. This is all for the best, since it results in creation, not imitation.

In making the point that Groton is an American achievement I am not trying to overstate the facts as I see them. America has profoundly changed Harrison's mental and artistic makeup. To some extent even Don realizes this. He knows that he now chooses to deliberately do things that he would not have dreamed of doing when he left England ten years ago. He has caught the mobility and restless drive that seems to be characteristic of America. Can't you see this in the Groton organ? Its all-around flexibility, its readiness to take any part in the scheme of things from Scheidt to Ravel, its break with tradition, its vivacity, and its sense of driving power. Of course, it is saved from the less commendable American traits by Don's sense of artistic restraint. It is not a Daily Mirror, but a New York Times.

Regarding the Anglo-Saxonism I am not surprised you feel the way you do. Take Harvard for illustration. What a thorough house-cleaning and fumigation that institution needs! I am inclined to think that Princeton is the real exponent of Anglo-Saxonism, but no matter what the mess is that is boiling within, the shape of the pot that contains the stew is Anglo. . . .

[Emerson Richards]
[The close and signature do not survive; the letter is incomplete.]

Buhrman would have published — Richards' articles often appeared in Buhrman's publication. In September of 1932, Buhrman asked Richards to design an ideal organ. The results were published in September 1933, with an enlarged version following in the October issue. In the summer of 1933, the Senator visited organs in Germany.

His impressions of these instruments were published in eight consecutive issues from September 1934 to April 1935. In 1934, Richards designed a three-manual classic organ to cost about $15,000. This specification was shared with Harrison as the basis of much discussion and also appeared in the *American Organist*.

---

118 Henry Willis to G. Donald Harrison

20th December, 1935

Mr. G. Donald Harrison
Technical Director
Aeolian-Skinner Organ Co.
Crescent Avenue, Dorchester,
Boston, Mass. U.S.A.
My dear Don,

Am sitting down to reply to yours of the 11th October.

The curses of Organ Building here are the Organists, who know little about the traditions of the organ as an instrument and simply think of what happens to please their uninstructed minds, and the organ builders who care less or not at all.

It is simply sickening to advocate a well-reasoned and logical scheme — not deep-end at all — and then to come up against the average "eminent organist" called in to advise who almost openly assesses one as "unbalanced" to suggest such things as two mixtures on a Swell, individual mutations on Swell, Great, Choir, and Pedal, etc. etc. You could hardly imagine the horror with which such specifications as you are putting over would be greeted over here.

Even men like Marchant, Cunningham and Alcock know next to nothing of the ideals that should govern the drawing up of a specification, and care less, they say, "but look at my organ since you rebuilt it, what more could anyone desire." When I say more upperwork and mutations, they say, "I have plenty thank you, and don't want any more "squeakers."

Very few of our young fellows travel, or study. They take their opinions from the old school or else swallow "extension" with the utmost readiness. There are a few, a very few, of the younger school who try to understand, but they are swamped by the others and left crying in the wilderness.

Thalben-Ball is of the old school and knows nothing about Organs really — if he lived and studied for a few months in France and Germany it might alter his attitude, but he has made his name, and a big one, and is settled now. I doubt if anything would change him. Ball was responsible for the big £10,000 job at Southampton Town Hall going to Compton "so much more for the money" etc. etc. The job would otherwise have come here.

You are quite right in saying that the English style and method of playing classical organ music is debased by showmanship and ultra-speed.

I am more than ready to go to the "other extreme" as you put it, but people won't have "advanced specifications" at any price. One of the troubles is that a "classical" specification is more expensive than an ordinary one, and God knows that in these days higher costs are out of the question.

I was delighted to read Richards' article in The American Organist about the Groton job. It is good to build fine organs and better when they are well written up!

The job must be a most interesting one, despite the undue depth of the chamber, but what an awful pity that the console is on the same side of the Chancel and underneath the organ! Usually in America I found it an accepted thing that the Console should be away from the job.

I felt that 3¾" Swell reeds with open shallots would have been altogether too fiery without a pad between the tongue and the weight, such as Skinner (or rather Bolton & Co.) used on French Horns 10 years ago; anyway open and parallel shallots should have tongues quite 50% thicker than the usual standard, to obtain stability.

I did a nice Trompette for a Catholic Church early this year, CC = .032 weight No.10, large scale (CC = 5") French type reeds on 6" wind, but it was too "crackly" with normal brass weights so a thin felt pad was interposed; then it was delightful. If and when you have occasion to use a similar treatment it is quite easy to cover the rim of the felt that is exposed with fish glue or other preservative to keep the moths from chewing the stuff up.

Yes, weights are desirable in the bass for control, the new Choir Trumpet at Salisbury Cathedral on the Choir, 2⅞" wind had 18 weights CC being a No.6. This stop has spotted metal tube CC thickness .028.

I am very glad to hear about the new job for the Church of the Advent, Boston. This should be a heaven-sent opportunity for you.

The specification is most excellent, but I agree with Richards that a metal Stopped Diapason would be more in the picture than the Flute Harmonique of the Cavaillé-Coll Lewis type a la Westminster Cathedral, that you like so much.

I also venture to suggest that in view of their breaking every octave you use a somewhat "grave" composition for your Cymbals. Advent Boston Great Cymbale 22, 26, 29 very grave, especially in view of the top breaks of the Furniture and Cornet. Why not a typical Baroque Quint Cymbale.

C Note	1	¼C	⅙G	⅛C	=	36, 40, 43
C "	13	"	"	"		repeating every octave
C "	25	"	"	"		
C "	37	"	"	"		

```
C    "   49    "      "       "
```
Another Baroque Cymbal of interest for other uses is the Tierce-Cymbal.

```
C  Note  1   1'e    1'g     ½C    =    24, 26, 29 etc.
G   "    8   1'g    1'h     ½d
D   "   15   1'a    ½'d     ½'f#
G   "   20   1'h    ½'d     ½'g
G   "   32   ½'g    ½'h     ¼'d
G   "   47   ¼'d    ¼'g     ¼'h
```

The Advent Boston Swell is normal, relieved by the two Mixtures, without a tierce between the two I note.

The Choir, also, is on ordinary lines. I note the Zauber-flöte — I don't think these stops are worth the trouble and cost.

The high spot of the design beside the Great Organ is, of course, the Positif — delicious.

I note the Scharf Mixture 19, 22, 26, 29 a typical Baroque design of <u>4</u> ranks is

```
C  Note  1   ½'C   ¼'C    ⅙'g    ⅛'C = 29, 36, 40, 43
C   "   13    "     "      "      "
C   "   25    "     "      "      "
C   "   37    "     "      "      "
C   "   49   ¼'C   ⅛'C    ½'g   ¹⁄₁₆'C.
```

or another

```
C  Note  1   1'    c      ½'C    ⅓'g  ¼'C= 22, 29, 33, 36
C   "   13   ½'C   ¼'C    ⅙'g    ⅛'C
C   "   25    "     "      "      "
C   "   37    "     "      "      "
C   "   49   ¼'C   ⅛'C    ½     ¹⁄₁₆
```

Anyway Advent, Boston will be a splendid job and being in Boston should be all the more valuable.

It is the very devil to keep in the Baroque vein for the Swell fluework, the old time stuff was, of course, not enclosed — to meet enclosure Geigen quality becomes desirable but that tone is not the old "flavor" at all.

<u>Reeds</u>. I quite agree with you reference the benefit of the long shallot — i.e. ordinary 16ft taken down. It was my father who started the shorter shallots, with consequent tremendous weight and pneumatic starter. Sheffield City Hall was done in that style with normal results, the starters were especially set but there is a slight preliminary "puff." At Birmingham Town Hall, shortly after Sheffield finding old full-length shallots I retained them — the comparisons are:

<u>Sheffield</u> CCCC thickness .053 Weight 4½ ozs.

<u>Birmingham</u> CCCC thickness .053 Weight 1¾ ozs.

The last example having a flatter curve and less "stand-away" jumps into speech excellently with the aid of the pneumatic starter whose use is still valuable.

The long shallots for me in the future.

At Hereford and Salisbury Cathedrals I had the old shorter shallots and naturally left them, the Hereford reed on 16½" is superb. Salisbury on 9" not so good, "flabby" on the light pressure.

The Germans get excellent speech out of their 32ft. reeds — of comparatively low pressures, long shallot of course — felted surface for the striking part of the shallot and moderate weights. Steinmeyer uses a leather membrane on the side of the wooden socket and claims that it aids quick speech! All rot, of course, but as they "voice" all reeds on the job and under actual speaking conditions the result is all right. The tongues are sent in by trade part makers with the approximately correct curve for the wind pressure already done; the "voicer" simply adjusts slightly to suit local conditions.

I am glad your voicers are doing such splendid work, but keep a sharp eye on them, we all know how fatally easy it is for a voicer to go off the rails! I shall never forget the way Whitelegg used to try and get behind my instructions until he definitely realized that orders were orders.

Had Bonnet over here recently, he stayed with me on both occasions — hated the B.B.C. Organ — and was not at all happy at the Albert Hall. I took him to the Alexandra Palace which delighted him. We also [w]ent to see old Kendrick Pyne — 84 and in retirement at Ilford, very deaf but memory excellent, an entertaining old bird.

André Marchal was over playing for The Organ Music Society at St. Alban's Holborn, I have never heard more perfect playing. I was astounded.

It is very close to Christmas now and we have hardly a man left in the shop owing to the usual pre-Christmas rush.

Have a charming little three-manual for Ireland that has been on exhibition here this month. Specification enclosed, it goes to Portadown, near Belfast, first thing in the New Year: This is my "magnum opus" for the past three months!

I have just returned following a severe chill — colds and a mild form of 'flu very prevalent here at the moment. Weather is typical — fog — wet, a cold night then more fog — warmer again, mist etc. etc. Freezing now.

We are in the throes of a Cabinet crisis as I write, due to the yowlings of our blood-thirsty pacifists mind you!, who long to fight the whole world for the League of Nations. The French must think us a lot of fools — they won't lend a hand to give any practical help any more than the U.S.A. will.

Under such absurd conditions the only sensible thing for us to do is to let Europe stew in its own juice and arm to the teeth for the defence of our own interests. We will not do so, however, our --xx-- pussy politicians seem to consider British interests last of all.

Yours ever,

H.W.

H.W./K.C.

awful pity that the console — eventually the Groton console was repositioned on the opposite side of the chancel.

Or rather Bolton & Co. — There were three Boltons working for the Skinner Company: Ralph, Arthur and Fred. Ralph and Fred were reed voicers when Willis visited America in 1924, 1925 and 1926. Arthur was a pipemaker who later went with E.M. Skinner to Methuen.

The --xx-- is in the original letter.

---

119 G. Donald Harrison to William King Covell

January 13, 1936

Mr. William King Covell,
72 Washington Street,
Newport, R.I.

Dear Mr. Covell:

Thanks for your letter of January 10th. I am awfully sorry but it will not be possible for me to be available on Friday. I have already planned to leave here on Wednesday to go to New Haven, and will be there all Thursday, and I am holding myself in readiness to go direct from there to Philadelphia as I have some important business pending, and expect action any moment.

I am expecting to see Bill Self this evening, and will ask him about Friday, and will telegraph you tomorrow. I will also find out about Mr. Lynes.

Regarding the factory, it would seem to me desirable to postpone the visit until a little later as just now it is rather a sorry looking place, due to a temporary lull in the work, but if you wish to come, it will be quite all right to do so.

I will draw up a specification within the next few days bearing in mind the price of $14,500.

You are right regarding the wind pressure for the Trompette on the Great. It would be desirable to have more than 3", but this could be taken care of without additional cost as I would plan to take the wind in this case from the Pedal reservoir.

I get your point regarding the Pedal flue structure, but still feel that the Pedal Flute is desirable, but not, of course, in place of the 8' Principal. I will try to work one into my scheme.

In reference to mixtures, in latter years I have almost invariably stuck to the rule of breaking mixtures one rank at a time. There have been one or two exceptions, notably at Groton, where the Great Cymbel, being a repeating mixture, breaks every octave. As a matter of fact, I was not entirely satisfied with this arrangement, although it is traditional, and the Cymbel for Advent is arranged rather differently.

I am also in agreement with you regarding the larger Quint mixtures where one would normally break to a 5⅓ Quint to insert a unison rank in place of the Quint, the latter being retarded until the next break. This has been standard with me for two or three years. With the Cornet type of mixtures, or with mixtures which include the Tierce, from a classical standard and also for practical reasons they should not break at all until they are obliged to. Dupré was very strong on this point. The addition of ranks at Tenor C and middle C is not a break after all. In most classical examples the Cornet is a middle C stop — 1,8,12,15,17 running through without a break. It is only within recent times that anything has been done below tenor c with these mixtures, and then it has been usual to run the 12,15,17 to tenor C, and introduce the octave at this point running up to middle C. At the Advent the four and five rank Cornet on the Great, which by the way I am going to call Sesquialtera, is a true Cornet from middle C up, but in the lower two octaves there is a break which occurs at tenor C, and also the addition of the fifth rank. There is no harm at all in having the 17th at the top in a Cornet type mixture, and it can be carried to top C. I used to do this, but have lately made a break either at the C below top C or at top G. I feel it is always well to bear in mind that the classical organ music does not extend into the top octave.

There is a lot to be said for a Larigot in the Positif, particularly as this is a 4' section. In some Baroque examples I note that the Larigot is introduced even before the Nazard.

I am delighted to hear that you received a letter from Fitzsimmons to the effect that he is prepared to take an article on the Groton organ. I will be glad to forward the papers to him with a letter directly you let me have same. It is quite likely we would have some reprints, and I will go into this matter with him at that time.

With kindest regards,

Sincerely yours,
G. Donald Harrison
Technical Director

GDH:MGM

a letter from Fitzsimmons — the editor of *The Organ*
Mr. Lynes — Twining Lynes, organist of the Groton School until 1941

January 22, 1936

Mr. William King Covell,
72 Washington Street,
Newport, R.I.

Dear Mr. Covell:

Thanks for your letter of the 18th of January which interested me greatly. It would seem that the three organs inspected made a deep and very favorable impression on the prospects, and that, therefore, a very fine start has been made.

Of course, if they should desire it, we can give them an exact duplicate of the Harvard key touch, and you can tell them that there will be no thump to the combination action since we are now using a new type which is just as fast as Harvard, but even quieter in operation. The first console of the new type will be at the Church of the Advent.

I have not yet gotten the proposed specification in final shape, but expect to do so very shortly, and will send it along as soon as possible.

I received a long letter from the Senator in which he criticized the Advent scheme pretty harshly in that it did not show much advance over Groton, and I had a three-hour session with him in New York last Friday. As I pointed out to him, there was something to be said for many of his proposed changes if one were considering an organ for one purpose, but if you take into account all that will be required of the instrument in a church such as the Advent, my scheme as it stands is preferable.

He tried to convince me about the necessity of having two super octaves on the Great Organ, but I am still unconvinced. With so many Mixtures, the 15th is naturally repeated several times, and it is quite possible, which is the case at Groton, to have one of them a good hefty stop. That, in my opinion, is a matter of theory rather than practical result.

Regarding the omission of the Pedal Violone, none of the organists have reached the stage where you can convince them that two 16' flue stops on the Pedal are sufficient, and it would be foolishness on my part to try and put it over.

As you know, the Senator is prejudiced against the Great Flute Harmonique, but I feel that the objection is again theoretical rather than practical. I used a stopped Flute at Trinity, New Haven in place of my usual Harmonic Flute, but personally did not feel that it filled the bill nearly as well. I was down at Princeton with Carl Weinrich two or three weeks ago, and it so happened that he mentioned the Great Flute Harmonique as being invaluable to him, and he doubted if anything better could be substituted. This is confirmed by many other of the best organists, and after all they play music.

Richards sent me a layout of mixtures rather more elaborate than those at the Advent which have been used by Steinmeyer, but I did not like them at all, particularly as the principal mixture, the Fourniture, the five rank affair, broke once in the middle of the tenor octave and again right in the middle of the middle octave, and both breaks were of a complete octave. When the Cymbel was added to this it helped it out considerably, but after all, you often play Great to Fourniture without the Cymbel.

When you speak of there being points in the breaks of the Groton Mixtures which appear to be a little abrupt particularly where a 4' or an 8' comes in, this may be so if you play a chromatic scale on a mixture alone, but it must be remembered that they are not used in this way. Whenever you are using a mixture of this kind there is always an independent 4' and 8' already in use, and you will find that these independent ranks completely obscure the introduction of the 4' and 8' in the mixture. The real trouble is to make a smooth break at the top end of the mixture where the top rank falls off. In these cases, in finishing them I always do exactly as you suggest in your letter, namely, taper them off a few notes before the break. If you try any reasonable combination on the Groton Great Organ with one, two or three mixtures in use, you will find an extraordinarily even chromatic scale from top to bottom except at the lower end where the Cymbel goes up to the 36th partial. I do not like those very high pitched ranks at all, and they do little good, and that is why I am eliminating them at the Advent. The mixtures at the Advent will be differentiated to a greater extent than those at Groton.

I fear we will have to leave over further discussions of mixtures until next we meet as it is too long a subject to write about at the moment.

Yes, Mr. Skinner has severed his connection with this organization, and I understand he is starting up at Methuen, but do not know whether he intends to modify the large organ there or not.

We have not done anything for Mr. Lynes yet in connection with the model organ action. We talked about it, but I did not understand him to give me authority to go ahead. When we do get at it, however, I will have some idea of the cost. It is difficult to estimate this ahead of time.

I will certainly save you samples of pipes whenever I get an opportunity. The old Advent pipes have been sold to a junk metal dealer.

With all best wishes,

Sincerely yours,

G. Donald Harrison

GDH:MGM

I do not like those very high-pitched ranks — in the 1964 Aeolian-Skinner rebuild of the Church of the Advent, some of Harrison's mixtures were re-pitched higher.

Skinner has severed his connection — E.M. Skinner had signed a five-year contract with Aeolian-Skinner, which severely restricted his activities outside the company. It expired in January, 1936.

The old Advent pipes — the previous instrument was an 1883 Hutchings-Plaisted, electrified by Hutchings in 1912.

---

121 G. Donald Harrison to Henry M. Channing

March 1, 1937

Mr. Henry M. Channing,
18 Tremont Street,
Boston, Mass.

Dear Mr. Channing:

During the morning of November 23, 1929, Marcel Dupré, the great French organist, Mrs. Dupré, Mr. Skinner and myself were driving out to Methuen from Boston. During the trip Dupré spoke to Mr. Skinner most enthusiastically about the Princeton University Chapel organ which had just been completed, and congratulated him on the fine result. Although I was sitting in the back of the car with Mrs. Dupré, Mr. Skinner did not say a word to Dupré regarding my connection with this instrument. Apparently, Mr. Skinner felt he should have mentioned the matter for when we returned to Boston in the afternoon he dictated and handed to me the enclosed letter.

Yours very truly,

GDH:MGM
Encl.

the enclosed letter — See letter 37.

---

122 Walter Holtkamp to William King Covell

September 13, 1937

Mr. William King Covell,
72 Washington Street,
Newport, R.I.

Dear Mr. Covell:

The Organ and Organmusic Clinic finished last Friday. While I was supposed to be a faculty member, I do believe I learned more than the actual students. Two weeks of intensive application to the music of Johann Sebastian Bach and the requisite instruments for making this music intelligible and also enjoyable, brought out many illuminating facts. I enjoyed every minute of it.

One intensely interesting topic and one which has the greatest significance to all of us who actually design organs, was the matter of the

160

ornaments in the old music. This topic was in charge of John Challis, the harpsichordist. Without intending to do so, he, at least to my mind, made a very clear and conclusive case for the open and harmonically bright organ. To my mind, he also made a good case for slider chest tone.

Please believe me, I have the utmost respect for the work of Harrison. Your letter gave somewhat the impression that you thought I discounted his contribution. I must disagree with him in a number of matters, but in general I would say, and gladly, that he deserves the highest praise. Also I am very grateful to Harrison for the trend his work is taking. Not only are my early efforts vindicated but my future work will be much easier with the Aeolian-Skinner Company doing similar work.

I have never looked upon my work as archaeological. The Cleveland Museum of Art Rückpositiv departed in many respects from the average of its prototypes. Primarily we were not creating a Rückpositiv, that is making a revival, but creating a tonal apparatus to thin out an existing and all-too-heavy ensemble. We applied a corrective treatment, so to speak. The value of a Positiv, located as a Ruckpositiv, has really been made clear to me since then. A more recent Ruckpositiv with a more ideal Great and Swell to work with proved to be even more effective.

We are in the midst of an unusual and unique building program. The last organ out, and the one going out now, and the two to follow are all three-manual instruments with Positivs instead of Choirs. I claim that this fortunate circumstance is a record of consistency or maybe the purchasers were weakminded, who knows?

Keep up your English correspondence. It makes interesting reading. I thought Mr. Skinner's last in <u>The Organ</u> was very revealing.

Sincerely,
Walter Holtkamp
The Votteler Holtkamp Sparling Organ Company

Cleveland Museum of Art — In 1933 Holtkamp had rebuilt the 1920 Skinner at the Cleveland Museum of Art. His unenclosed positiv organ was the first such 20th-century example in America.

Mr. Skinner's last — Skinner hand become an active letter-writer in both American and English organ journals.

Carl Weinrich

---

123 G. Donald Harrison to Carl Weinrich

April 28, 1938

Mr. Carl Weinrich,
Westminster Choir School
Princeton, N.J.
Dear Carl:

I have been studying the three-manual unit classical organ specification which you left with me, and the more I go into it the more certain I feel that the unit principle should only be used in cases where room is at a premium or in an extremely small instrument. The scheme you have outlined necessitates unit chests throughout and four electromagnetic relays, one for each manual and one for the Pedal. This, together with the three manual console and the 49 switches which are involved, runs the cost for the mechanism far too high, and in fact this instrument would cost in the neighborhood of $6000.00. Now for this amount you can get a perfectly straight two manual classical organ with more independent ranks than you have indicated, and which would undoubtedly be more effective musically, and extremely simple mechanically, and, therefore, better suited for practice use.

Will you jot down a two manual straight scheme of what you consider to be the minimum requirements, and let me have it, and I will look into the matter further.

162

I greatly enjoyed my visit with you and Tommy in Boston and both Bill Zeuch and I were bowled over by your playing at the Germanic Museum. I am hoping to arrange a recital for you there this summer, and will look in at Princeton at an early date.

With best wishes,

Sincerely yours,
Donald
Technical Director

GDH:MGM

Tommy — Mrs. Weinrich

---

124 Carl Weinrich to G. Donald Harrison

May 11, 1938

Mr. G. Donald Harrison
Aeolian-Skinner Organ Company
Crescent Avenue
Dorchester, Mass.
Dear Don,

I am submitting to you another specification for a teaching organ. Am I right in believing that it will require only one unit chest — for the reed? In every other case I have confined myself to one borrow per rank. While the scheme will probably cost far too much for our present purpose, it will give us some basis to go on.

As this organ would go into a very small room, I should like to have each manual division in a separate box. It would be interesting to have the organ divided in such a way that we could suggest the alternation between Hauptwerk and Ruckpositiv.

I am not satisfied with the way I have worked out the pedal flue-work. Perhaps we could get together soon to talk this scheme over. At any rate I would appreciate your submitting a price and any suggestions. While I am not yet sure that anything will go through, I would like to be ready with something definite if it does. . . .

I've just picked up an old one-manual Jardine of seven stops. It was built for a private home, has been stored away for thirty years, and is in perfect condition. I'll have a lot of fun this summer setting it up, and making a Positiv out of it.

Should appreciate hearing from you as soon as possible. Have you thought any more about the Baroque organ for New York?

Cordially,
Carl Weinrich

HAUPTWERK		POSITIV	
8'	COPPELFLÖTE	8'	QUINTATON
4'	PRINCIPAL	4'	ROHRFLÖTE
2⅔'	NASAT	2'	PRINCIPAL
2'	NACHTHORN	1⅓'	QUINTE
1⅗'	TIERCE	II	SESQUIALTERA
III	MIXTURE	16'	RANCKETT
	Tremulant	8'	Ranckett
		4'	Ranckett
			Tremulant

PEDAL

		COUPLERS:
16'	BOURDON	Positiv to Hauptwerk 16'-8'
8'	Gedackt	Hauptwerk to Pedal 8'
8'	PRINCIPAL	Positiv to Pedal 8'
4'	Principal	
4'	BLOCKFLÖTE	Hauptwerk and Positiv
2'	Blockflöte	in separate Swell boxes
16'	Ranckett	Pedal in Hauptwerk box
8'	Ranckett	
4'	Ranckett	3 pistons on Hauptwerk
2'	Ranckett	3 pistons on Positiv
		3 pistons on Pedal

---

125 G. Donald Harrison to Carl Weinrich

May 17, 1938

Mr. Carl Weinrich,
Westminster Choir School,
Princeton, N.J.

Dear Carl,

Thanks for your letter of May 15th, from which I am glad to note that things at least look fairly hopeful to get the complete organ right at the start. The instrument as specified in the new specification which you have sent me, together with the double enclosure and the pistons, would cost $5700.00. Originally I had not thought that there would be any combination action.

Regarding the reduction or the preparing at first for some things to reduce the initial cost, it is impossible to get the price down in an organ of this ultimate size to anything like $2500.00.

As I explained when in Princeton, there are certain overhead charges in an organ however small, and which do not increase proportionately as the instrument gets larger. For example, even if you have one stop on each manual, you have the full cost of the console with its case, keys, pedals and contacts, etc., and moreover, you have the cost of building a chest for each stop together with its primary, and if they are separately enclosed, the cost of two swell boxes. Unfortunately, I have not discovered a way of getting around this difficulty by some simplified form of construction. After all, there is a point beyond which one cannot go in this direction. The use of very low wind pressures also necessitates the very highest type of workmanship to insure satisfactory functioning over a long period of years.

The best, therefore, that we can do in this case to reduce the first cost would be to prepare for the swell boxes and the reed unit, which would save $1000.00. Another saving could be effected by omitting the 4' Pedal Blockflöte with its extension to 2'. This would save $300.00. Here we about reach the limit, for to leave off any manual stops would save pipes only, as if there was a chance of their being added later, it would be foolish not to make room for them on the chest. The limit in this type of preparation in an organ of this size would be one stop on each manual, which would save around $350.00. You will, therefore, see that if all these things were done, we could start out with a little more than $4000.00.

Mrs. Loenings's organ cost $2700.00, and to get the price down to $2500.00, we would have to leave out one rank of pipes, probably the Spitzflote.

Anything below this immediately switches to the small type of organ like our three stop unit, which, as you know, is $1850.00. f.o.b. Boston. This price is obtained by a very simplified construction and building many identical instruments to the same design.

If I can be of any further assistance, please let me know, and don't forget to advise about Mrs. Miller's visit.

Cordially,
Don

GDH:MGM

Mrs. Loenings's organ — Aeolian-Skinner opus 973, a small two-manual organ for Mrs. Alfred Loening, Southhampton, NY. It was enlarged in 1940 and fitted with the penultimate roll player Aeolian-Skinner built.

---

126 G. Donald Harrison to Carl Weinrich

July 19, 1938

Mr. Carl Weinrich
Westminster Choir School
Princeton, N.J.
Dear Carl:

Thanks for your letter of the 17th. I am so glad you are more enthusiastic than ever concerning the possibility of the little organ. I am awfully sorry to say, however, that I fear our joint enthusiasm on Friday carried us away, because on checking up at the factory here as to costs, which I could do fairly accurately by looking into Ernest White's organ, I find that your suggestion cannot be built for $2700.00. Actually in your later scheme you have also increased the instrument by one rank of pipes by the introduction of the Sesquialtera.

The thing that runs the price up is the 16' reed extended to 8' and 4' pitches on the Pedal and at 8' on the manual, and I am wondering if we could not prepare for this stop, or whether as an alternative it would be possible for you to get a little extra appropriation to cover this stop. Even without the reed you have one more rank of pipes than Ernest White's organ, but this is balanced by the fact that there is no 16' Bourdon extension on the Pedal.

As an alternative to preparing entirely for the reed at present we might omit the 8' Quintada on Manual I and insert the Ranckett at 8' pitch only on this manual, making provision so that the final scheme as we have it can be realized later without trouble.

I wish I could put the whole thing over for you, but it is too much to ask my company to do as we lost money on both Ernest White's and Mrs. Loening's organs, and with this experience have a very good line as to exactly what the costs are on these little instruments.

Even if a Ranckett was imported, it would run into quite a little money, particularly as we would have to pay a duty on it.

I have been doing a little experimentation with old Vox Humana pipes with a view to making a Ranckett tone, and have gotten some very interesting results. It would seem that the tone is characterized by a very strong 12th, the result being Quintadena-like, only of course reedy.

Will you turn the whole matter over in your mind, and we can talk more about it on Friday when I see you.

All the best,

Cordially yours,
Don

GDH:MGM

---

127 Carl Weinrich to G. Donald Harrison

July 24, 1938

Dear Don:

Your letter was at the school when I went over after lunch. After you called, I was afraid that I didn't make it clear about the appropriation for the organ. In view of the fact that M.K. has put $2500 in the budget, and that the trustees have approved this amount, I don't want to gum up the works by asking for more. At the same time, I don't want to put you in a

The Busch-Reisinger Museum at Harvard University, the "Germanic Museum," and Aeolian-Skinner Op. 951 of 1936

similar position with your company. Hence, it seems as though something will have to come out of the specification. . . .

I am going to try to arrange a trip to Boston on July 31 with my class. If they are interested, I'll write you during the week and perhaps you can arrange to have us see the Germanic Museum organ and drop in at Advent.

Cordially,

Carl

the Germanic Museum — site of Aeolian-Skinner Opus 951, a two-manual Classical organ with Great, Positiv and Pedal. Aeolian-Skinner lent this organ to the Busch-Reisinger Museum at Harvard, where for years it was played by E. Power Biggs for national radio broadcasts on Sundays.

---

128 G. Donald Harrison to Carl Weinrich

August 23, 1938

Mr. Carl Weinrich,
77 Jefferson Road,
Princeton, N.J.

Dear Carl:

You are anxious to hear from me I know, and I did not write to you yesterday because I had not reached a solution to our problem that satisfied me. This morning, however, I had a colossal brainstorm, and I am sure you are going to be delighted at the result.

The storm consisted in suddenly realizing that we have some perfectly fine used chests which were taken out of the Gallery organ of St. Bartholomew's Church, and which will be better than new if the leather work of the pouch valves and primaries is replaced. The two chests I have in mind are those which belong to the Choir Organ and were enclosed so that they have not yet lost their new appearance, and moreover they happen to be just about the right size for our little organ.

I have also discovered a second-hand console, although that is hardly the way to describe it since it has only been used for a short while as a demonstrating organ at the Aeolian Studio. This console is also in new condition, and exactly resembles the one at the Germanic Museum. It has four blind fixed combinations to each manual, and I feel that this should answer the criticism of your associates who feel that pistons are necessary. Suitable combinations could be wired on to them, and I feel they would be entirely adequate for so small an organ. There will also be a crescendo pedal, which will be useful for putting on full organ, if for no other purpose. This is a more handsome console than we would provide for a practice organ if made new so that there is a double advantage in using it. You will remember that at the Germanic there are tablets placed in terraced jambs, which I think is quite in keeping with the German idea.

By using these chests and console I believe I can give you the enclosed specification, which incorporates all we talked of last week. As a matter of fact, I almost feel inclined to throw in a 1' because the chest I would use for the Hauptwerk would have a spare topboard, and a 1' set of pipes costs quite a small sum. The only annoying thing about this is that the 1' should

168

be on the Positiv, but there you are, one cannot have everything when you are adapting materials. . . .

[Don]

[The close and signature of this letter are absent; it is incomplete]
St. Bartholomew's Church — a new 3-manual gallery organ had been added to this instrument in 1937, replacing the previous Skinner.

---

129 Carl Weinrich to G. Donald Harrison

August 24, 1938

Dear Don,

I was quite excited about the new developments in regard to our organ. I see no reason why we shouldn't use the St. B. chests. I wish you could throw in a one foot stop — in which case the Krummhorn could go to the H[auptwerke], and the 1' to the Positiv. In looking over some old registration lists, I think there is an advantage in having the Krummhorn and the Ses[quialtera] on opposite manuals.

The Aeolian console should be very satisfactory. Would it be possible to add the following couplers, even if they were not on the combinations?

Positiv 16'-8'

Hauptwerke 16'-8'

Positiv to Hauptwerke 16'

In your last letter, I believe you mentioned that there would be only one regulator. While I don't question your judgment, my experience with some of these makes me a bit worried. With such small pipes, the slightest robbing and unsteadiness is most annoying. Also, I might want to add a trem[olo] to the P[ositiv] someday. Don't you think it better to use a regulator for each chest?

We also discussed the matter of screening. In measuring the height of the room, I discovered that the chests could not be raised out of arm's reach. Would this revised scheme enable you to include some kind of wire screening?

Carl

August 25, 1938

Mr. Carl Weinrich
77 Jefferson Road
Princeton, N.J.

Re: <u>Westminster Choir School</u>

Dear Carl:

Thanks for your prompt reply to my letter, and for all the information contained therein. It is a very good idea to place the Krummhorn on the Great Organ, thereby giving space for the 1' on the Positiv. I think the whole layout is swell, and could not be better for its size.

I can arrange couplers as you suggest, and the organ will have reservoirs so as to prevent robbing back and forth.

As the organ will extend the whole width of the room, it will be a fairly easy job to arrange a wire screen across the front, and I think I can take care of this.

The St. Bartholomew's chests are larger than I would have made them for this particular organ if they had been new and, therefore, the instrument will take up a little extra space, but actually this is all to the good as every pipe will have an extraordinary degree of speaking room. The organ will lay out something like the rough sketch enclosed, which will mean that the floor will overlap Door B shown on your plan by about 11" or 12". The two chests are 2' 8" and 2' 9" in width respectively, and it will be essential to leave a passage between them so that the primaries and magnet boxes are accessible. The fact that the chests are 8' 6" long makes it impossible to put them end to end. The end-on arrangement, however, would not save much depth because the Pedal chests in that case will have to be placed behind, and the whole thing is more or less as broad as it is long.

In view of the height of the room, my idea would be to keep the chests quite low, giving as much height as possible above the pipes for the development of the tone.

Regarding the position of the blower, I am not altogether encouraged by the fact that the room where it would have to be placed is the boiler room. Surely the atmosphere gets pretty hot in the winter, and it seems to be there would be a liability of dirt being drawn in by the blower and forced into the organ. We can look this over when I come down for the signing of the contract.

I would very much welcome a translation of the chapters of Mahrenholz's book. As you say, there would be many pointers which will be helpful and of considerable interest.

With best wishes,

Cordially yours,

Don

GDH:MGM

Encl. (1)

Mahrenholz's book — Christhard Mahrenholz's *Die Berechnung der Orgelpfeifenmensuren* (Bärenreiter: Verlag Kassel, 1938).

---

131 G. Donald Harrison to Carl Weinrich

September 29, 1938

Mr. Carl Weinrich,

15 Hawthorne Street,

Princeton, N.J.

Dear Carl:

For the last two weeks my time has been fully occupied finishing the Hollins and York organs, but I am now all set to give all my attention to the little job.

Firstly, I have not heard from you, but hope that you have fully recovered and have had no return of the trouble.

I have very carefully checked over the translations you have made regarding the scaling of the Baroque organs, and when you come down to brass tacks the particulars given are rather general indications than anything very specific. On comparing the various scales and the widening or narrowing of those scales in bass or treble to those which I have been using, I find that my various experiments have led me to follow generally along the lines indicated. For example, the Gedackt scale flares out at the upper end, and I find that mine follows suit. I did find, however, that I am using the larger scale or more modern Gedackt described, so for your little job I am going back to the smaller scale as used in the earlier organs.

One has to use a little common sense in applying the method of determining the scales. He suggests, for instance, that the Gedackt should be five or six scales small of the normal scale, and that it should widen out in the treble, but at what point do you attack this normal scale — 16'C, 8'C or 4'C? You will see that where the scale is not constant, the point at which you begin your scale makes a considerable difference, irrespective of the pitch of the stop. Otherwise, if, for example, in a single job you had 16', 8' and 4' Gemshorns, and started at the low C in each case, you would get a very uneven result. All this sounds very involved, and I could explain it much better to you with the scales in front of us to make comparisons.

171

I find also that in my Quintaton I have done exactly what is recommended, that is to say, to fall off in scale very rapidly as you mount the compass.

What I am getting at is this — that I do not know whether it would be worthwhile for you to go to the trouble of translating what he has to say in regard to all the stops we are using, but it might be useful to translate just the parts which come under heading "E" 1-8 inclusive, in connection with the Spitzflöte, Principal and the Krummhorn. It might also be advisable to do the same thing for the Blockflöte and one mutation stop, such as the Nazard. If you are able to do this quickly, and can mail it to me at once, I will be greatly obliged.

Now regarding the various stops, I understand what you are looking for with the Pedal stops and the Quintadena and Gedackt. I feel somewhat in doubt, however, regarding the two Spitzflötes 4' and 2' on the Hauptwerke and Positiv respectively. Don't you think that it might be well not to make them too fluty? In other words, to impart some slight Principal tone to these stops, thereby assisting the ensemble considerably. This seems desirable in view of the fact that we have no 4' Principal anywhere in the organ.

What are your ideas regarding the Sesquialtera? Shall I make the 12th and 17th like mutation stops, or would you rather have them more of the usual Mixture quality? Perhaps you can find some indication of this in your German books.

I am enclosing herewith the layout for the Zimbel. This is similar to the Positiv Zimbel on Bill Hawke's job, and I believe follows along the lines of those we talked over.

I think this is all for the present, and I look forward to receiving an early reply.

With all the best to Tommy and yourself,

Cordially yours,

Don

GDH:MGM

Encl.

Zimbel III Rks		
CC to F	36-40-43	6 notes
F# to B	33-36-40	6 "
C to F	29-33-36	6 "
F# to B	26-29-33	6 "
C1 to F1	22-26-29	6 "
F# to B	19-22-26	6 "
C2 to F2	15-19-22	6 "
F# to B	12-15-19	6 "
C3 to G3	8-12-15	8 "

[last break missing from original]

172

the Hollins and York organs — Opus 975 and 977. First Methodist Episcopal Church, York, Pennsylvania, three-manual; Hollins College, Hollins College, Virginia, three-manual.

Bill Hawke's job — St. Mark's Church, Philadelphia, four-manual, opus 948.

---

132 Carl Weinrich to G. Donald Harrison

October 18, 1938

Mr. Donald Harrison
Aeolian-Skinner Organ Co.
Boston, Mass.
Dear Don,

As I understand it, our specification now is as follows:

GREAT	POSITIV	PEDAL
8' Gedackt	8' Quintadena	16' Bourdon
4' Spitzflöte	4' Rohrflöte	8' Gedacktpommer
2' Principal	2' Nachthorn	4' Koppelflöte
III Scharf	1' Sifflöte	8' Krummhorn
8' Krummhorn	⅙' Zimbel	4' Krummhorn
	II Sesquialtera	

I have been thinking a lot about the Sesquialtera, and if agreeable to you, I am going to suggest that we make the second break at middle C instead of at tenor F. Any melodies which go below this could be done on the Krummhorn, if the break is too noticeable. I rather imagine that in such a small room it would be impossible to make the quint and tierce really blend in the tenor range. Then too, I am secretly hoping to be able to use it somewhat as an ensemble stop, in which case, the middle C break would be better.

I have been wondering about the Nachthorn which you showed me the other day. I have always felt that this stop, as found at Wellesley, for example, was a bit lacking in character, though here it may be owing to the location. In looking at the charts given by Mahrenholz, I notice that the Nachthorn is the widest scaled cylindrical pipe, and that it has a straight upper lip. In view of the experience you have had with the Gedackts, do you think there would be any advantage in experimenting with a Nachthorn along the lines of Mahrenholz?

I enjoyed the visit to the factory the other day, and got a big kick out of the Krummhorn.

Cordially,
Carl

as found at Wellesley — Houghton Chapel, Wellesley College, Wellesley, Massachusetts; opus 943, three-manual. The Nachthorn is in the Choir division.

October 25, 1938

Mr. Carl Weinrich,
15 Hawthorne Street,
Princeton, N.J.

Re: <u>Westminster Choir School</u>

Dear Carl:

Thanks for your letter of October 18th. Your understanding of the specification is exactly in agreement with mine.

Your suggestion for making the second break of the Sesquialtera at middle C instead of tenor F is perfectly all right with me, so we are proceeding on that basis.

Regarding the Nachthorn, I have reduced the scale from those I used originally, but am perfectly prepared to try the large scale again. The large scales rather mean less character than that produced by the smaller scale, but, of course, this can be overcome to some extent by very low cut-up.

I am glad that you liked the Krummhorn, and you will be interested to learn that after you left I made one or two additional changes which improved the tone very considerably. It is now even freer and yet firmer.

I believe it would be a good idea if you could come to the factory next Monday from Wellesley as I have several things to show you, particularly some experimental Quintadena pipes, and I do not care to proceed with the complete stop until you have heard the samples.

The Spitzflöte with a ¼ taper and wide scale at the mouth makes quite an excellent stop. The ¼ mouth and low cutup gives a much better tone that the E.M.S. Erzahler, although the scale is identical. He used a very narrow mouth high cut, which destroyed the true character. The ¼ taper, however, gives the new stop the kind of Erzahler flavor as we expected.

I promised to tell you the cost of the blower. The little machine costs only $60.00, and in some ways I feel that there is some advantage, particularly with delicately voiced stops, to have a blower which is designed for the purpose. If one uses a blower giving a much higher pressure than is desired and you break it down by means of a reservoir, the churning action of the fans is liable to pass through the windtrunks and cause the smaller pipes to dither. It is difficult enough to prevent this even with a blower of correct pressure. However, I will leave this up to you to decide.

While you were here last time we talked about the additional couplers that exist in the console we are to use. On investigation, however, I find that the switches have already been employed for other purposes, so that they will not be available. Therefore, the couplers will have to remain as per contract.

Looking forward to seeing you,

Cordially yours,

Don

GDH:MGM

---

134 G. Donald Harrison to Carl Weinrich

December 2, 1938

Mr. Carl Weinrich,
15 Hawthorne Street,
Princeton, N.J.

Dear Carl:

In further reference to my letter of yesterday's date, do not fail to hear the Krummhorn when you come to the factory. I believe it is going to have a surprising effect as an ensemble stop.

I am anxious to experiment immediately with some other of the Baroque type reeds as I expect to have to use both the Krummhorn and one other stop in a new installation. I particularly want to get a 16' Baroque reed, and am wondering whether you would kindly look through your German books to see which would be the most useful and the best type of reed to employ. There is, of course, the Rankett, but that particular stop does not intrigue me particularly as it is too close to the Vox Humana. I would rather favor the Fagot, or perhaps a Dulzian. There are also the various types of Regals, but I do not remember having seen this class of stop used as a sub unison.

I will be very much obliged if you could look through the specifications and descriptions of pipes and see which would be the best choice. I am also wondering if you would be good enough to write out the descriptions of some of these stops in the same way that you did for the stops of your little organ. The chief thing that I need to know is the general shape, scale, and length of the resonators. Some of these old reeds had ½ length, ¼ length, ⅛ length and ⅔ length resonators.

This is asking an awful lot I know, but it is all in the interests of art!

With best wishes and many thanks in anticipation,

Cordially,

Don

GDH:MGM

December 9, 1938

Mr. Carl Weinrich,
15 Hawthorne Street,
Princeton, N.J.

Re: <u>Westminster Choir School</u>

Dear Carl:

I wired you this morning as per confirmation enclosed herewith. We will have two fast workers on the job, and if all goes well, it would seem to me that the organ should be playing by the 26th. I have John Saul in readiness to send down directly the pipes are in so that there will be no undue delay in getting busy with the finishing, etc. However, with an instrument of this type, as you know, the finishing may take quite a time, and we may want to make adjustments to some of the stops. However, this might be done after the broadcast and the organ used for that event, should it sound well enough in its original shape. I agree with you that it would be a great stunt, and we should try to do it if at all possible.

I was delighted to read your letter of December 6th, and am more than pleased that you like the various stops so well. I think the organ is going to be altogether charming and give quite a great effect in the fairly resonant room.

The fact that we have two men on the job answers your question regarding Mr. Raymond. Normally in cases where we take the assistance of a man who has a large tuning connection, it turns out to be unsatisfactory as naturally the man is subject to constant interruptions, and this would be particularly bad at this season of the year.

Very many thanks for your offer to translate information regarding Baroque reeds out of Mahrenholz.

I am greatly anticipating the time when we hear the first notes out of the little organ, and directly when it is ready for tuning I will be down on the job.

With best regards,

Cordially yours,
Don

GDH:MGM /Encl.

January 26, 1939

Mr. William King Covell,
72 Washington Street,
Newport, R.I.
Dear Mr. Covell:

Thank you for your letter of the 22nd. I am starting out on a long trip this afternoon, and will finish up eventually at Houston where Ned is anxiously awaiting the final touches on the organ.

You are right about the 8' and 4' Principals in the Germanic organ. They were changed early last year, the scales being reduced two notes. I think they are much more in keeping with the rest than the original ones.

I read Holtkamp's article in the <u>American Organist</u>, but cannot agree that his arguments are sound. Of course, the only real test would be to have two complete ensembles side by side, one with a slide chest and the other on the individual valve chest, and some day I hope to do this. While in Germany I asked Steinmeyer about this very thing, and he makes both types of chests according to the tastes of his various clients. He assures me that as far as he can tell there is absolutely no difference in the result, and my own experience rather makes me believe that this is the case. Steinmeyer has absolutely no prejudice one way or the other.

With all best wishes,

Sincerely yours,
G. Donald Harrison

GDH:MGM

at Houston where Ned is — Christ Church Episcopal, Houston, opus 976, three-manual. Edward B. (Ned) Gammons was organist there before becoming the organist at the Groton School in 1941.

April 5, 1939

Mr. William King Covell,
72 Washington Street,
Newport, R.I.
Dear Mr. Covell:

I was very glad to get your letter of April 3rd. It is too bad about St. George's School Chapel, and I was extremely surprised to hear the news which came first as a rumor and then confirmed by the advertisement in this month's <u>Diapason</u>.

It is particularly annoying to me as I have had the organ sold twice, and it was only the lack of funds which prevented the project going through. The first time was some years ago when Bill Strickland was organist at the School, and then later Virgil Toms was all set to do business with us. Mr. Zeuch had many contacts with him, and he was around listening to organs.

I was interested to get your report regarding the little organ at St. Thomas More House, and am delighted that you were so pleased. I built another one for St. Mark's Church, St. Louis, which even turned out better than the New Haven instrument, due to the fact that it was placed on a little West gallery with all the pipework exposed. The full organ sounds like a large instrument and is entirely satisfying. It has one extra stop, a Spitzflöte on the Great, and there is also an 8' Flute in the Pedal, of course extended from the Bourdon. Dan Philippi played the Passacaglia on the organ when I was there and the result was quite amazing.

Yes, I agree with you about the Germanic records. These were quite a help to me on my trip South. I was able to play them to many prospects and gave them at least some idea of how an organ sounded built along classical lines. It convinced many that such an organ need not be all top, which is the usual criticism.

We are now installing the World's Fair organ, and if the acoustics are tolerably good, and if the open end of the building does not make it impossible to keep the organ in tune, I think it should sound fairly well, but I am really quite nervous about it.

Regarding certain questions you raise, the Positiv Salicional is a very soft large scaled string to act as an accompanimental voice for solos on the Swell. Other names are somewhat misleading, for example, the Quintaton on the Pedal is really a quinty Bourdon and not a real Quintaton. The 8' Violon Cello is really an 8' Principal. Many people had a finger in the pie in drawing up this specification, and that is why some of the names seem rather strange, but I have tried in the scaling and voicing to make the instrument regular from our point of view.

Bevo's organ at Columbia will I hope be the finest yet. While the organ is in chambers, they are extremely shallow, and although the case work is heavy, the building is so grand for tone that I think the effect is going to be thrilling. In other words, the acoustics are as good as Groton, but the chambers are much better. You will probably remember there is a dome and the resonance is perhaps a little too great in the empty building, but it is really fine with a congregation assembled.

Yes, the instrument is to have three unenclosed manual departments, and of course the Pedal will also be unexpressive. I carried the latter a step farther than ever before. There are five independent reeds on the Pedal as follows: 16' Posaune, 8' Trumpet, 4' Clarion, 4' Rohr Schalmei and 2'

Edward B. Gammons
Christ Church, Houston,
Aeolian-Skinner op. 976

Cornet. Each reed has a different character imparted to it, and I am expecting quite a surprising result. I am tickled to death with the Rohr Schalmei, sample pipes for which have already been made.

The building is of a type which greatly emphasizes the fundamental tones and the low frequencies generally. This is the reason that the old E.M. job sounded so terribly ponderous. It was entirely the wrong type of thing for such a place. In the new organ I am tapering off all the basses of the Flutes into more or less semi-Quintatons to avoid boom as far as possible.

Ned Gammons' organ really turned out very well considering the awful acoustics of the church and the presence of a very heavy wood screen which imparted a kind of Harvard Chapel effect. Ned, however, has done a splendid job in obtaining a really fine chamber with adequate openings, and this saved the day. The most encouraging thing is the way the people of the South have reacted to the organ. Everybody is crazy about it, and people come from far and wide to hear it. After all, they have heard nothing down there but Pilchers and Wicks, and other instruments of similar type.

Regarding the St. Bartholomew's organ, I can quite understand your feeling that the new West End Organ could be let out a good deal, and naturally it would be more thrilling if this was done. However, it is so close to the people who sit in the back pews and the old organ had annoyed them so much that Dr. Williams was very insistent that the instrument should not be voiced loudly, so that we have a classical organ in miniature. It is extremely effective, however, when played with the other sections of the organ, and seems to tie the whole thing together. Of course, they should have followed my plan to have a console at the West End because the distance is so great that it makes it practically impossible to play trios or other works requiring real rhythm on this section alone. . . .

With best wishes,

Sincerely yours,

G. Donald Harrison

GDH:MGM

St. Thomas More House — Opus 978, six stops, eight ranks

World's Fair Organ — Opus 986, three-manual. Harrison's fears were confirmed. The building, called the "Temple of Religion," was cited as an acoustical failure.

Bevo's organ at Columbia — Lowell P. Beveridge was organist of St. Paul's Chapel, Columbia University. Opus 985, with a fourth manual for the Brustwerk.

Ned Gammons' organ — a Houston installation. At Harvard Chapel, the organ sounded good in the chancel but was difficult to hear from the nave. See "Harvard Buys an Organ," the *American Organist* Vol. 16, No. 3, March 1933 by Emerson Richards.

---

138 G. Donald Harrison to William King Covell

May 10, 1940

Mr. William King Covell,
72 Washington Street,
Newport, R.I.

Dear Mr. Covell:

Thanks for your letter of May 4th. Business is so active at present that I have been too busy to think much about propaganda. However, I have read the letters in the <u>Diapason,</u> and of course those of E.M. are typical.

In my opinion the whole question comes down to one of music. The organ should be designed and voiced so as to be a suitable vehicle for the interpretation of the best literature that has been written for it, past and present. If this is done, it seems to me that the tone more or less takes care of itself. Naturally, voices of beauty are desirable, and the whole trick is to have beautiful voices which will blend one with another, and build up into an ensemble.

The old master organ builders seemed to have arrived at the best solution, for indeed the voices they used may be considered as beautiful <u>per se,</u> and at times even sentimental, although there was no striving after such an effect. To my ears the light pressure open tones are more pleasant than the stuffy thick qualities which have been employed in the modern organ. Sentimentality and the copying of orchestral tones seem to have been the things that have been strived for in recent years, with the neglect of those tones and effects which are peculiar to the organ. As you know, I have no quarrel whatsoever with the introduction of these more or less sentimental sounds and some really good orchestral imitations providing a proper organ is supplied first. I further feel that the number and quality of these sentimental and orchestral voices in relation to the true organ effects must be governed by the other uses for which the organ is required.

It is obviously foolish to put a purely classic organ in a Christian Science Church. Similarly, it would be just as foolish to put an organ suitable for the Christian Science service in the Germanic Museum at Harvard University. These are extreme cases, but I think it makes the point I am striving to get over. The instruments that I have designed for various denominations differ quite considerably in this regard as I have felt it is the proper way of tackling the various problems involved.

With best regards,

Sincerely yours,
G. Donald Harrison

GDH:MGM

---

139 Emerson Richards to Aubrey Thompson-Allen

July 1st, 1941

Mr. Audrey [sic] Thompson-Allen,
Henry Willis & Sons, Ltd.,
London, England.

Dear Audrey [sic]:

Your letter of May 6th reached me while I was vacationing in Moosehead in the latter part of June. I suffered an attack of arthritis so I did not undertake to answer it then and am just back in Atlantic City for a season.

Needless to say, I was very glad to hear from you, although not at some of the news. A letter from Henry about the same time undertook to tell me about the destruction of the factory, but your boss writes on both sides of the paper and the result was that when the censor got through with cutting something out, the story about the destruction of the plant was also eliminated.

Due to the return of prosperity as a result of the huge government expenditures, there is considerable life in the organ business. Don Harrison has about all that he can handle at present. You know, I suppose, that Donald is not only the head of the Company now, but also owns a controlling stock interest in it, and if things go the way they have started, he ought to have a very good year.

He has a large four manual for the University of Texas at Austin, another for Curtis Institute, and a big job for a broadcasting company in

Boston, as well as several two and three-manuals — enough to keep them going at top speed until the end of the year.

I saw Don in Boston on my way north to the camp. He is experimenting with a 32' Bourdon with a chimney that gives him five or six notes in one pipe. Seems to be doing pretty good. I wrote to him and told him about the boys. I know he has written to you and Willis, but says that he is sure all of this mail was destroyed.

All our reports from England show that the people are still in a fighting mood and with no talk of compromise. The Russian business will be all to the good, if the Russians, even if beaten, will only withdraw to the interior with their armies intact. We are afraid that the Germans will cut them up before this can be done, but are hoping for the best. In the meantime I understand you are receiving enough long distance bombers from us to make things very interesting in eastern Germany. Production is up here so that July ought to see at least 2,000 combat planes that can be spared for your use, and an even larger number in August. The new tanks are also rolling off the production line at a rapidly accelerating rate. The exact number is not yet open to discussion, although I understand quite a few have already appeared on the Egyptian front.

Sincerely yours,

Emerson Richards

broadcasting company — the Yankee Network received Opus 1025
top speed until the end of the year — Harrison had received many large contracts; the Curtis Institute organ was a five-manual. But the economic boom in early 1941 was cut short by the Japanese attack on Pearl Harbor six months later.

---

140 Emerson Richards to Aubrey Thompson-Allen

August 22nd, 1941

Mr. Aubrey Thompson-Allen,
Henry Willis & Sons, Ltd.,
London, England.

Dear Aubrey:

Your welcome letter of the 15th finds me just on the eve of returning to Moosehead. Been home for a fishing trip on the cruiser and now back to the camp for two weeks, after which the legal grind will start again.

First of all, let me apologize for the misuse of your name. Defense demands got my last two secretaries, but I am fortunate in having the secretary that I had for a great many years to take pity upon me and return temporarily at least. Unfortunately she had never participated in your correspondence and took the name simply by sound.

I am enclosing in a very condensed form the specification for the organ at the University of Texas as it now stands. In the parallel column is the way Dr. Boner and I sketched it out last December. Both schemes cost the same, and I think you will agree that the original scheme was the better. However, a smart aleck by the name of Gammons butted in and influenced the changes. Now he has quit Texas for another job. Will be glad to know what you think of both schemes. Remember this goes to a part of the country which is still more or less in the musical dark ages. Hence the Harp, Chimes and the original Tibia.

Don is head over heels in work but very much worried at the moment. The new tax bill places a 10% tax on musical instruments and Don faces the loss of over $15,000 on instruments contracted for but not yet delivered. I appeared before the Finance Committee of the Senate on Wednesday representing the various organ companies who had hastily gotten together for this purpose, and I believe that the Committee is willing to take out the retroactive feature at least.

With regard to the Reed articles, it does appear as if the organ had dried up. There is a monotonous level of organ descriptions that leave one cold. I have run over hastily the Harrison-Richards article on the Reeds, but cannot find the statement that you criticize. The only statement I find is not the reason for the invention of the built-in shallot but the statement that the pocket below the opening tends to produce more fundamental tone. I think that you agree that it does.

We did not want to confuse the organ public with too many side issues, and as we were not discussing anything but chorus Reeds we did not go into this pocket feature which is supposed to be important in the case of the French Horn, although you can get a good French Horn without the pocket. I was quite familiar with the type of shallot that you mentioned where the face is carried down below the base of the shallot.

You will remember that Harry Willis worked for Losh during the time that we were building the Convention Hall organ and he actually made a set of these shallots for one of the high pressure reeds. Great things were expected of it but did not materialize, although it cost Losh quite a lot of money. Ultimately Roscoe Evans, another voicer, produced a marvelously fine 100" reed on the Great organ which does not have this feature. The 100" reed in the Gallery organ has never been a success and Evans, who still is with the organ, expects to rebuild it when opportunity permits. Harry Willis did give this type shallot a name but I have forgotten what it was. He claimed that the action of the over-length face and the reed was like hitting a ball with a cricket bat more nearly in the center than at the end. We don't know much about cricket over here, but in the case of a baseball the nearer you hit the ball with the end of the bat the farther the ball is driven.

However, by now you have seen the analysis sheets of the various reeds and I think will agree that the open shallot has many advantages over the closed type. I have just this moment received from Dr. Boner the analysis sheets of the pipes which Willis sent us over a year ago. I haven't had time to more than glance at them, and I will have to reserve until a future time a report to you on their contents. The pipes are safely stored at my home and I am going to keep them until the end of the war because they may be all that is left of the Westminster job as well as the two Schulze's and there is no use of risking them on a return journey at the moment.

And that brings us to the war situation. I found in Washington that the President has confidentially told Congressional leaders that while we are no nearer to war than we have been, that it was a lot nearer to us. An outbreak with Japan is expected almost at any moment. As a matter of fact, it looks as if we had tried to bring it about. Last week Ickes, the War Administrator, publicly announced that we were sending a tanker loaded with aviation gasoline to Vladivostok directly through the Japanese islands. If the tanker goes through it means that Japan's bluff has been called. If it is stopped it unquestionably will mean shooting. Personally I am all for the latter. The Japanese have been a nuisance out of all proportion to their ability, and if we can get a good crack at their fleet I doubt if it will last an hour.

In the meantime, the sentiment here is that you folks cannot relax because of the Russians. As things now stand it doesn't look as if Hitler can break the Russian resistance before Winter sets in. That probably means that his air fleet will be back over England before long. However, you are very much prepared and our own contributions are really getting under way. Production has been stepped up immensely and in another month the tanks will be coming off the assembly line in real quantities. Our own army is sore because they are being deprived of new weapons, but we feel it is better to help you first.

I think R[eginald] W[hitworth]'s book was of real value in that although some of the drawings may be said to be crude, they are clean and understandable to the average individual. Please remember that otherwise intelligent people become terribly confused when they try to read a print. In any event I am sorry that all of this labor has gone for naught. Of course you are right that a lot of it was obsolete, and I am afraid that I never could get very much excited about various kinds of action. It was all right with me if they worked. After all, it is only the tone that counts.

I will tell Don what you say about his boys. Apparently he has no luck in getting his letters across. Also give my regards to Mr. Willis when you see him.

Cordially yours,

Emerson Richards

ER H Enc.

Harry Willis — See note, letter 31.

Dr. Boner — Dr. C.P. Boner of the University of Texas analysed the harmonic content of 18 middle C Diapason pipes collected by Henry Willis III, with additions provided by Harrison and Richards. A pipe by Schulze was chosen as ideal; two of Harrison's Principals came in second and third. In tests on reeds, an E.M. Skinner Tromba showed "less than a dozen harmonics," and the domination of the tone by "fifth sounding harmonics" was shown to be the reason for a "muddying effect" on the flue ensemble. Boner also constructed flue pipes with interchangeable bodies of different materials and demonstrated that the body of the pipe has little effect on the tone. See *Present Trends in Organ Design in the U.S.* by Emerson Richards, published in typescript (undated) by the Organ Club ca. 1952.

Whitworth's book — *The Electric Organ*, Reginald Whitworth. Richards is commenting on the book's second edition.

---

141 Paul Callaway to Ernest Skinner

July 6, 1942

Mr. Ernest M. Skinner
Methuen
Massachusetts

Dear Mr. Skinner:

After three years of constant playing on the instrument which you built for the Washington Cathedral, it is a pleasure to write to you about its excellencies. It incorporates all the fine things for which you are justly honored. I believe that it is a work of art which will always be regarded as a landmark in the history of organ building, and its tonal beauty will afford inspiration to countless numbers of people in the years to come.

Very sincerely yours,

Paul Callaway

Organist and Choirmaster

PC:w

Paul Callaway — Paul Callaway became organist of Washington Cathedral in 1939 and remained until the late '70s.

Leo Sowerby

142 Leo Sowerby to Ernest Skinner (handwritten)

December 1, 1942

Dear Mr. Skinner:

Many thanks for your letter. I am very grateful for your interest in my Symphony for organ, and I'm sorry that I have not been able to hear Miss Crozier play it — particularly that I didn't hear her do it in Washington. I would love to have a copy of your record, as you suggest so kindly, if it is possible for you to let me have it.

It certainly takes all sorts of people and opinions to make up a world! Last week I was in Detroit to play a recital of my own works (on a Möller — terrible instrument!) and I was talking to one of the prominent Detroit organists who had heard Miss Crozier's performance of my Symphony in the Washington Cathedral, and who also is familiar with Mr. Biggs' recording. He said he disliked Miss Crozier's playing intensely, and is greatly taken with Mr. Biggs' recording. So there you are! I do not feel it is proper for a composer to enter into discussion about the various interpretations of his work, particularly when the various performers concerned are his friends. So I say nothing at all, and am glad that everyone can find some performance or other to suit him. As far as I am concerned, I am simply glad that the work is played and continues to arouse interest and discussion. I know what I had in mind when I wrote the work, and were I to play it, might give an interpretation still different from all of the others! But it would be bad manners on my part to criticize others who have devoted themselves to the study and conscientious performance of the work.

I would be very glad to hear Miss Crozier's performance via recording, you may be sure. Thanks again for your letter.

With kindest wishes,

Sincerely,
Leo Sowerby

---

143 Walter Holtkamp to William King Covell

September 15, 1942

Mr. Wm. King Covell
72 Washington Street
Newport, Rhode Island
Dear Mr. Covell:

At the risk of disclosing a colossal ignorance or a very restricted perspective, I am continuing the correspondence; realizing also that it may be more interesting to us, than fruitful; being a believer in the old Mason and Hamlin adage, "No description of the method of construction of a musical instrument can convey to the reader, any idea of the musical result thereby to be obtained."

I believe one of the differences in our points of view as to what aggregations of manual and pedal stops comprise a good organ, is on the one hand (you) a striving for tone per se, as an end in itself, ("the organ plays") and not necessarily subject to keyboards, — and on the other hand (I) probably a tendency to unduly stress the importance of facile response (musical sounds) to keys, — and to allow definite tonal structures or qualities of sounds to be determined by the needs of keys and the nature of keyboard music. (As I understand it.)

This difference is slight, I am sure. And it may be a distinction without a real difference. But it is real enough that you would spend money on, or take up space in an organ by including some stop, to achieve a desired tonal end, which I wouldn't spend the money on or give the space to, even though plenty of money was available. By the same token, I would leave out a stop or an entire chorus, because it did my key responses no particular good, and might do them a lot of harm. And by 'key responses' I mean the facility and grace with which sounds play together like a good dancing team, (trio sonatas) as well as the ease with which they lose themselves in each other and give the player the feeling that they come out as one stop. (fugues) Structure (8'-4'-2⅔'-2' and Mixtures) plays a big part in obtaining these requisite results, but more and more I want the structure to be take-apartable and to work well in most any assembly of the components. Consequently the requirements of structure, the Diapason chorus for example, tend to become compromised to the needs of versatility. Some say no to this, and insist on sticking to the dogma of purity of chorus. And there is something to this viewpoint. I feel that the English with their Diapason chorus (Great) and reed chorus (Swell) are inhibited to a considerable degree. At the same time I recognize that such unanimity of opinion in a people, makes for excellence in certain classes of tone. But at the same time, and from a historical standpoint, any such development may just as well be a trend in a wrong as well as in a right direction. (Cavaillé-Coll, Father Willis and our own E.M.S.)

Just as a matter of interest, think over our differences with the foregoing in mind, and see if you also conclude that we have a somewhat different conception of the end-use of tone. Believe me, the above is not meant to win you away from your point of view, nor is it in any sense derogatory. If we hope to get any place in discussion, we must first establish definitions. All argument finally resolves itself into a discussion of definition.

My sailor boy has long since departed from Newport. From all reports, he became enamored of a cute little button up Boston way. Thanks a lot for having his interests at heart, but I fear he knows by experience that his father's friends are apt to be a bit dusty for his age.

Best regards.

> Sincerely yours,
> Walter Holtkamp
> The Votteler Holtkamp Sparling Organ Co.

WH:ED

sailor boy — Walter Holtkamp, Jr.

---

144 Ernest Skinner to William King Covell

April 17 '43

Dear Mr. Covell,

My business is at an end for the duration. I am personally carrying on elsewhere (from my home) with a couple of men in service work, revoicing &c. but no new work. The big organ is still there but I think the bank has sold the building to a church which uses no organ. So the big organ will have to be taken down and stored or sold. I have written a church about it.

I think an organ without swells is better than one without diapasons. Harrison has placed a three-manual organ in the Brooks School North Andover, without diapasons. None whatever. I don't know whether or not it has swells, perhaps not. Why the organ is selected to be so far as possible an instrument with warmth, color, expression and all poetic implication eliminated is beyond me. I have spent my life trying to make it otherwise. Somehow it has given me the most distinguished clientele any builder ever had in America, so I cannot have been altogether wrong.

I think Jamison's last article was quite sound and have thought of writing a comment upon it. Haven't had time yet. The orchestra of Bach's time was in about the same condition as the organ. No symphonies, tone poems, conductors, fiddle bows more like our cello bows, no French Horns that could ever play chromatic scale, etc. Why was there not protest on improvement in orchestra? Never any protest on bettering the organ 'till I I came along.

Why did Bach supplement organ with orchestral instruments? What has more clarity than contrasting colors? All of which leaves the orchestra with a good ensemble, doesn't it? Why eliminate all color in the interest of that which is used least? The ensemble? Now it's your turn.

Yours sincerely,
Ernest M. Skinner

The big organ— the Walcker organ at Organ Hall, Methuen

---

145 Ernest Skinner to William King Covell

April 25 '43

Dear Mr. Covell,

I believe the hall is to go to a Greek Orthodox Church.

Now as to other questions. I believe the "Baroque" contingent claim that the music of J.S.B. should be played upon an organ of the Bach period. But when they build organs without the most fundamental of all organ voices dating pre-Bach, their claims are obviously spurious. Manual and Pedal Diapasons are of all stops the most peculiar to the organ. Two 32' Pedal Diapasons were thrown away, absolutely cut up. One taken from the Columbia and the other from Cornell University. These stops cost (both) around $7,000, $3,500 each, and were a part of the gifts to these universities.

The Bach organ had an Untersatz 32' and no such overwhelming proportion of mixtures as the present rubbish. You cannot produce synthetic tone with pipes so small that character is eliminated. The qualifying harmonics of a 6" pipe are above audibility. Anyway, is anything synthetic equal to the real thing?

My prime interest is in music. The finest music ever composed is written for definite tone qualities. The tone qualities came first and inspired the symphonies, operas, etc. The modern orchestra and compositions have crystalized tone qualities into a tonal alphabet.

I have so far as possible developed like qualities for the organ, Trombone of real orchestral quality the chief thing yet to be done. If I can get a desired quality like English Horn with one pipe why employ a half dozen to produce a poor imitation? And what would you use to produce a synthetic French Horn?

Now you may say these voices are not desirable in the organ and that is where we can never get together. You stop at the organ. I care nothing for the organ apart from what it can do musically.

The kind of music I want for the organ, now that the organ is given a vast eloquence is coming along as I knew it would. The Sowerby Symphony as heard at the National Cathedral in Washington at last Guild Convention created a sensation in its color and grandeur. 660 organists there to hear it. An organ of the Germanic Museum type in a place like that, in comparison, would be a farce.

I shall never understand why you pick on one of the greatest composers of all time to deny his music tonal charm. To create beauty is the first principle of all art.

I do not see how you can be a real music lover to choose voices destitute of tonal beauty and sound two or three octaves higher than called for in the score.

If I had a son or daughter studying organ in Brooks school and should learn what sort of organ they were employing for instruction, I would sue them for obtaining money under false pretenses. They cannot teach registration for any use except to play on that particular freak organ.

Did I tell you the Aeolian Harrison Co. built a Baroque organ for Williamsburgh [sic], Va. price $16,000. In two years they had all they could stand of it. I put in all new pipes and they cannot say enough in praise of it. It sounds devotional and musical which cannot be so in an organ chiefly squeal and without diapasons. I ask you Covell, if I were to suggest the most extreme violation of classic practice regarding organ design, what can you suggest to outdo the elimination of diapasons?

There you go again with "organ color" — I say music and color whatever the medium.

Sincerely,

Ernest M. Skinner

I believe the hall — The Organ Hall at Methuen, Mass.

146 Ernest Skinner to William King Covell

May 7 '43

Dear Mr. Covell,

Since I found Mr. Buhrman was submitting my advertising copy to the Aeolian-Skinner Co. for their approval, I have had no dealings with him, cancelled advertising and subscription to <u>American Organist</u>. He was naïve enough to tell me of this unethical behavior, <u>not knowing</u> it was unethical.

Richards is an ass. All recitalists who play anything worthwhile are in no trouble for listeners. Thomas Webber at <u>every</u> recital given has a full church and 24 to 25 hundred in the Memphis Auditorium, at <u>every recital</u>. The Cathedral is <u>packed</u> when Virgil Fox plays my organ there. Catherine Crozier has packed houses wherever she plays.

You can find no precedent nor parallel anywhere, at any time, for minimizing the unison tone <u>especially Diapasons</u>, the pitch indicated in the score, outside the present time <u>here in America</u>. First the Mighty Wurlitzer, all unison and no top, now the mighty squeal, all top and no unison, both by Englishmen, Hope J. and Harrison. Germanic Museum, also Tanglewood, by another Englishman, E. Power Biggs. The Boston Symphony had nothing to do with it. This is all I have time for now — leaving for Richmond Va. today.

Yours,
E.M.S.

---

147 T. Frederick H. Candlyn to Ernest Skinner

August 18, 1943

Dear Mr. Skinner,

Your letter of August 13th received today. First of all, don't think that I shall ever allow Aeolian-Skinner to rebuild St. Thomas' organ as a baroque. The name is anathema to me, and I certainly would not tolerate such a travesty in regard to your art.

I have, as you know, only just been appointed at St. Thomas'. Apparently your men have not done a good job there — nor have they at St. Paul's, Albany. The Chimes at St. Paul's — which I very seldom use — are almost unplayable owing to the number of silent notes. Seeing that you installed a new mechanism, the Vestry naturally wonders why the Chimes are so unreliable. Personally, I don't give a damn, but the corporation does, and it is a tough job to explain that "E.M. Skinner gave us a new mechanism in regard to the Chimes, and it just doesn't work!" It is a little bit better since the generator has been changed — but still the Chimes don't function properly.

I shall always stick by the firm of Ernest M. Skinner — that is if E.S. delivers the goods. If he does not — and he didn't in regard to the Chimes at St. Paul's, Albany, I shall certainly look elsewhere, but I shall always stand by you in regard to the tonal scheme at St. Thomas'.

Faithfully yours,

T. Frederick H. Candlyn

Candlyn — Organist and Choirmaster of St. Thomas, New York City from 1943-1954. He was born in 1892 in Cheshire, England, and educated at the University of Durham. For many years prior to his coming to the U.S. he was sub-organist of the famous Schulze organ of Doncaster Parish Church.

---

148 G. Donald Harrison to William King Covell

August 26, 1943

Mr. Wm. King Covell
72 Washington Street
Newport, Rhode Island
Dear Mr. Covell:

Thank you for your good letter of August 4th. I am much interested to hear of your visit to the Church of St. Mary the Virgin in New York City, and am so pleased that you like the effect of the organ. The Pedal Cornet is a honey, and is the second one that I have carried out to date. The first one is in the new organ at the Curtis Institute. In this latter organ there is a true 32' reed so one can actually test the Resultant against the real thing. While the effect of the Cornet is slightly softer than the 32' reed, there is no reason why it should not be of equal strength. Actually I prefer the Cornet to the real 32' reed because, as you suggest in your letter, of its promptness of speech with no preliminary mechanical noise which exists in nearly all 32' registers of this class.

I do not claim to be the originator of the idea of a Resultant of this kind. I got my idea from John Compton in England, but I think I can say without boasting that the two I have made so far are more effective than Compton's, due partly to the particular tone quality given to the ranks, and partly to the fact that Compton so often uses extended ranks which, of course, are not in tune, and which greatly spoils the true Resultant tone.

Glad to hear of news regarding the Channing Church. They have made quite a good start, and I hope more funds will be forthcoming. Whether or not the chests should be used in a rebuild depends entirely on their condition. In the Roman Church in South Boston, St. James, the chests were shot badly, and I substituted pitman chests which were taken out of the old St. Bartholomew's West End organ. This organ turned out very well indeed. There is no difficulty in seeing this organ. The Pastor is very proud of it, and is pleased to let people try it. It will be well to bear in mind that the use of old chests gives one a considerable saving in cost, and there is no reason why the action should not be snappy enough, although one must look for some slight noise as compared with modern chests. Last year we rebuilt a Cole organ in the Episcopal Church at Augusta, Maine. The old chests were used for the Great and Swell, although some added stops on the Great were placed on a new additional pitman chest. This rebuild was very successful.

In regard to your query about the 16' Open Wood, very little can be done to convert same into a Contra Bass. The block is formed incorrectly for this type of tone. I have never seen a successful attempt to date.

Regarding prices, it is pretty difficult to estimate in these times as we have no way of knowing what costs are likely to be after the war. At a guess, $6,000 might do the job very nicely.

Interested to hear of your visit to the West Point organ. I have never been to see it, although Meyer has invited me twice and then cancelled the appointment later for some reason or other.

I will be glad to have the reprints from the <u>Diapason</u> at your convenience.

Yes, I heard of Ned's accident, and in fact saw him in the hospital. I have just received a letter from him, and he seems to be coming along nicely, although now Betty is under the weather.

Sincerely yours,
G. Donald Harrison

GDH:MGM

Ned's accident — "Ned" Gammons

---

149 Emerson Richards to William King Covell

November 29th 1943

Mr. W. King Covell,
Providence, Rhode Island.
My dear Covell:

Don Harrison was here over Thanksgiving and he told me that in a letter from you, you had said that you had not heard from me in a long time. Must be that I was at fault and through some circumstance failed to answer your last letter.

I have suffered rather severely from arthritis since early last spring. The cause of it seems to have been my tonsils, which are now out, but which stirred things up and I have had recurring attacks, but which now seem to be tapering off, and the doctors think that in another three months I ought to be well again. This has confined me to the house most of the time, because the attacks have been centralized mostly in my ankles and knees.

Because of the war conditions there really has not been much to correspond about. All the organ builders are either doing war work or are out of business entirely, and even those who are doing war work are apparently not having a very successful time of it. I hear that some of them are either in for a loss or don't know where they stand financially.

While Harrison was here over the holidays we have been working on an article setting forth the whys and wherefore of the new type of organ for use in one of the English musical magazines. If you have followed Musical Opinion and the Organ you will find that the thing is getting pretty badly mixed up.

Perhaps you have also noted that I have gotten involved in a discussion in the Diapason, more of it to be published in the December issue.

One thing is certain, that as soon as the war is over and materials become available, there is going to be a big demand for either rebuilds or entirely new organs, and I am hoping that we will be able to push the Classic Organ. As you may have noted in the articles on the St. Mary's job, I am endeavoring to give this the name of American Classic, although it is going to be awfully hard to dislodge the word Baroque. I did tag the name Romantic on the old ones, and that has stuck, even in England, but an expressive word for the new organ which is only quasi-Baroque in principal [sic] with some French, English and American practice, makes a new word imperative but difficult to find.

The way things look now it ought not to be long before we will be able to talk organ matters again. I hope so.

With best personal regards, I am,

Sincerely yours,
Emerson Richards

ER H

---

150 Ernest Skinner to William King Covell (handwritten)

January 6, 1944

Dear Mr. Covell:

Why meet Richards, I mean myself — I am not interested in meeting one who is as old as Richards and learned so little. His opinions are fixed and founded on nothing we have in common. My prime interest is in music. All my opinions are based upon music, and I have found myself in sympathy with the greatest composers and musicians of our or my time. I expect I'm much older than you are.

What difference does it make where the Baroque organ is, to which I referred? I have heard it. It is shrill and cold as ice as are all Harrison organs. But you like them, with which fact I have no quarrel. But there is much to be loved in music which you are missing. But if you do not miss it consciously, so much the better for you. The shrill high-pitched stuff you care for means nothing to me but distress. My only kick in the matter is the disappointed public who are led to spend money for the Baroque stuff and then get nothing out of it. I wish I could get a chance to build a Baroque organ. I'll bet I could build one that we would both like and the public as well. But those who build them have a positive genius for building <u>unmusical</u> tone. They don't know how to <u>make pipes</u> to start with.

If I ever do get a chance to build a Baroque organ, I'll give somebody something to think about. I built an organ for Salisbury, Md. and the stop most commented upon was a <u>3 rank mixture</u> which can be used in combination with Flute Celeste and which also is in correct proportion to full Swell. It is a <u>beautiful sound</u> in itself.

Did you ever hear the Washington Cathedral organ, and if so, what was the matter with the 43 ranks of mixture work in this organ which several have spoken of as the greatest in the world?

Very Truly,
E.M. Skinner

---

151 G. Donald Harrison to William King Covell

February 8, 1944

Mr. William King Covell
72 Washington Street
Newport, R.I.
Dear Mr. Covell:

Thank you for your letter of the 1st instant. I have also read the current copy of the <u>Organ</u>, and it would seem that something should be done to try and revise the ideas of the English brethren in regard to this matter, but I fear it is going to be quite difficult as they have such fixed ideas in their minds as to what is essential.

I feel that your suggestion, though good, would appear so extreme to them that they would not take the matter seriously, and I do not think that it would form the basis of any worthwhile discussion. I may be underrating the intelligence of some of those boys, but from reading the British periodicals I see very little change from the old days, and in fact the schemes they suggest and the arguments they put forward are mere repetition of what has been going on for twenty or thirty years.

I do not know what costs are going to be after the war, but my guess would be that your little scheme would be in the neighborhood of $4,500. Personally I am not quite happy with your suggested Great Organ. I would rather have an 8' Spitzflöte, an 8' Bourdon and a 4' Principal.

The couplers you suggest, while they appear to be somewhat lavish for so small an organ, are not costly to install. You have to have some couplers anyway, and the addition of a few more is relatively inexpensive — far less than extension, as you suggest.

Thanks for the news regarding St. George's School and Channing Church. I hope something will come of them in due time. I think you had some good ideas in your suggestions regarding St. George's School in your letter of December 16th, which I see I have not yet answered. . . .

The Rotunda was an interesting magazine, and I am sorry to see it go. You would be surprised, however, the amount of work entailed in getting out such a magazine, and the cost is quite heavy unless you are able to secure advertisements.

I was amazed to read Hunt's articles in the current issue of the Diapason. I think his suggestions are really quite foolish. He must be suffering from senile decay.

I can quite imagine what Skinner says about me and the work I have done, but somehow it does not bother me very much. Some people think I should take some action about it, but I do not believe that would be wise. It all comes about because so many of the organs that we have built have gone into fine places and are admired by musicians who really count. This gets under the old man's skin no end, and I am pretty sure in his heart of hearts he realizes that they do have something to them. That is why he spends his life shooting at them. I feel really sorry for him for after a full and active life he has developed into a disgruntled old man. I certainly hope that I do not develop into that kind of a fellow if and when some younger man appears on the horizon.

Thompson-Allen's approval of Jamison's writings is due entirely I presume to Jamison leaning towards the English school. Jamison is always rushing into print, and this keeps his name before our English friends, but they do not realize that the actual work he has done over here is very small, and there is not one organ of note that has been produced under his guidance.

I think there is going to be considerable prosperity in the organ world immediately after the war. The prospects come in daily, and some of them are most interesting.

With best regards,

Sincerely yours,
G. Donald Harrison

GDH:MGM

P.S. Thanks for the note in T.A.O. re: St. Mary's pedal Cornet.

Hunt's articles — The Rev. Noel Bonavia-Hunt, "Sees Ideal Ensemble in Broadminded Union of Different Schools," *Diapason*, 1 February 1944, p. 20.

---

152 Emerson Richards to William King Covell

August 14th, 1944

Dear Covell:

I am very sorry about missing you in Boston. While up at Moosehead I suffered a return of my old trouble, arthritis, this time in my right arm and had to return home. As I had written to you it was my intention to return to Boston from Maine on Thursday, spend all of Friday on the pedal revoicing, then go on to Atlantic City. As it turned out I was not in condition to travel until Saturday, had to send for a driver from home, and then came straight through. I will have to return to Boston later and will let you know in time in case you want to come up.

Yes, I do own an island up in Moosehead Lake about five miles above Greenville and have a rather extensive camp on it. We have seven bedrooms and can take care of 16 in a pinch, although I try to limit our parties to 10 or 12 at most. The island is kidney shaped, about 600' long, 300' wide, and is about 40' above the lake. It is heavily wooded with tall pines and spruce — our birch have died — and sitting in the surrounding mountains makes a lovely picture. We have our own utilities, a marvelous well, electric light and power, and sewerage. The living room is octangular; the roof, supported on 24" cedars, is 25' high and terminated in a "colonial" belfry. The fireplace takes 4' logs. There is a large dining room, a very large kitchen, ice house, boat house, etc. I have up there a 26' twin screw run-about that does 35 m.p.h., a smaller power boat, a pram, three skiffs, a row boat, a barge, and several outboards. Most of our friends like the place and we have enjoyed the summers there very much. Lack of competent help and gas made it impossible to open the camp last year or this.

You were right, on both counts relating to the design of the mixtures, in my suggestions concerning your seven stop Great. I find that one of the legitimate objections, musically, that is made against mixtures is the confusion that may occur when manual to pedal couplers are drawn. Also there is a tendency for the higher pitches to stick out and not unite with the pedal flues. Remember it is the wrong series of harmonics, dynamically, for the 16' foundation. So it is best not to go too high in the lower octave. Then, since the pipes are larger, there is a decided saving in soundboard space and money by keeping the bottom octave down to two ranks. And I think that the musical effect is better. Those who have handled mixtures most successfully seem to have had this same experience.

The War Production Board is all set to relax L37 but the War Manpower men won't agree, so there may be some delay; there is no shortage of metals.

I have had several letters from Willis and his wife. I had an opportunity to send them a box of fruit by a ferry command officer and they were most grateful, since they had not seen an orange or pineapple for more than four years. Willis is worried about getting started again after the war. He will have to find a new factory and the government insurance may be insufficient to be of much help. His military duties have been exacting and there is worry about the family, especially about the boy who is now eligible for military duty. I have not heard that Alexandra Palace has been destroyed. Although some lines cut out by the censor might have referred to it. I agree that it is the finest organ in England. If you will look at the <u>American Organist</u> for September 1931 you will know better what I think of it.

It does appear that I was not very definite about the sources from which I am drawing the material for my organ. I had originally an Estey built and voiced by Will Haskell. This has a 9 and 11 stop manual chest that when releathered are usable. Later Seibert Losh made some additions. These bass and manual chests are units and are in good condition. Then a short time ago I took a 9 unit 1931 Möller out of the Steel Pier as part of a legal fee. Then there is St. Marks. The Möller chests were in fine condition. It is my intention to use most of these chests and action for the Swell and Choir. Using part of the old pipework from the various sources either as is or revoiced. I revoiced the middle C's on the old work and it sounded to Don and me that this revoiced material will be useful if Goodman can make the whole sets come out that way. If he gets into trouble I will have to go to Boston again. Goodman and Bolton are easy to work with since they say that I know what I want and, what is more important, how to get it. Don and I have ears that are very much alike and instantly know when we have the tone out of a pipe that we want, and when we cannot get it we generally know why. It is this work that I still have to do to the pedal pipes.

All the old material will be used in the Swell and Choir and Pedal. Even here, part of the pipes will be new. The Salicionals and the Violas and all the chorus reeds will be Harrison. As a temporary measure I am revoicing the Losh and Möller reeds in the Willis manner for the Swell chorus and it looks like they may be a success. It will be some time before we can get French reeds made. The Great and Positiv will be all new pipes and chests. Since a large part of the Swell, Choir and Pedal are on unit chests, we have to strongly resist any unit monkey business. But since it will be useful and no extra expense to justify, I will borrow some of the manual 16's to the

Pedal and then do away with the Great and Swell to Pedal couplers. The Pedal will have enough independent choruses to admit of this.

We could not get anything satisfactory out of the St. Mark's Horn Diapason, so we junked it depending upon the Harrison Viola. Since the imitative strings are all Haskell's, they hang together. The Swell flue chorus will be stunning, if it does not prove overwhelming, and we are depending on enclosure to correct this. The Schultz is a beauty and did not have to be touched. Nor did the Mixture, but Don thinks that in the Swell position we may have to ease off the breaks. We had a real battle with the Octave and finally discarded it in favor of the 4th Open. It is a thrilling chorus and with the reeds must make a fine Swell.

I doubt if progress in construction will be made until the Roosevelt is out of the way as they are very short-handed. So I hardly expect to see any of it back in Atlantic City before Christmas.

Don't apologize for your interesting letters, I like them. I am promised a new "Corona" with a bell on it that will help to keep the right hand margin straight, but nothing but the end of the war and a full-time personal stenographer will cure the spelling. I see the mistakes but it is past midnight and I shall not try to make corrections.

Hoping to see you in Boston, I am,

Sincerely yours,

Emerson Richards

this work . . . to the pedal pipes — pipework from a 1926 gallery organ at St. Mark's Church, Philadelphia. This division was an addition to the then-existing Austin organ. Aeolian-Skinner replaced the instrument in 1937.

the Roosevelt — the organ originally installed in the Chicago Auditorium, a large Roosevelt of 1889. William Barnes purchased the organ, and donated it to the University of Indiana. Aeolian-Skinner rebuilt it in 1944, adding a Positiv.

any unit monkey business — Richard's views on unification had changed radically since designing the Atlantic City Convention Hall Organ, where nearly a quarter of the 451 ranks were heavily unified and duplexed.

I see the mistakes — Without a secretary during the war, Richards' typing was filled with mistakes.

---

153 T. Frederick H. Candlyn to Ernest Skinner

February 12, 1945

Dear Mr. Skinner,

I am so glad that your ideas and mine in regard to the improvement of St. Thomas' organ are substantially the same. I don't know what your problems are in reference to space, so I just mentioned what I would like done to make St. Thomas' an outstanding instrument. If we can't have Great

16', 8', and 4' Reeds, then I would much prefer a Great without Reeds, but with plenty of Mixtures, and step-up the Swell Reeds to restore the balance in the ensemble. On the Great, one 8' Flute is too loud, and the other is too soft — also the 4' Flute, and I feel that a second 4' metal stop is necessary.

I am absolutely in accord with you in reference to changing the Pedal Bourdon to a 16' Gemshorn. I found the latter stop to be very useful at St. Paul's, Albany, even though it had to be enclosed. I like your idea of changing the present Violone on the Pedal to a big stop on 10" wind, though I don't know how you will manage this pressure. The Pedal at St. Thomas' simply must have more metal stops or a louder metal stop in order to get some kind of clarity. Perhaps bearding the Small Diapason on the Pedal might help matters.

I most certainly want the Tuba Mirabilis left as it is — a noble stop. The trouble is that much modern church music calls for a powerful <u>enclosed</u> reed, and if one should use the alleged Great Tuba at St. Thomas', the whole Great is tied up. A big enclosed reed must be isolated on the Solo or Choir to avoid such a condition. The Pedal mixture is great. Would that the manual mixtures could compare with it. When the weather gets better, come down to New York and let us talk over the whole thing, including general pistons. Strictly for your own private ear, <u>if you can do the work we may not need to wait until the end of the War to make St. Thomas' organ the outstanding instrument in the country</u>. Let us talk over the whole scheme and be prepared to give me the cost of things.

Sincerely yours,
T. Frederick H. Candlyn

---

154 T. Frederick H. Candlyn to Ernest Skinner

February 17, 1945

Dear Mr. Skinner,

In my first letter to you I suggested a small 4' Principal in place of one of the Great 8' Flutes. I want to retain one 8' Flute, the power to be midway between the two we now have. A combination of Flutes 8' and 4' plus Erzähler gives a very charming old-fashioned effect. A small 4' Principal is very necessary when there are three Opens on the Great. I want to give this stop as a memorial to my son who was killed in action last Christmas week.

I like the idea of the Swell 16', 8' and 4' Reeds being somewhat of the French type as we have a Cornopean to add body. At present the Swell is dull without the 8ve coupler but the use of the latter upsets the balance. However, the things that seem most necessary, tonally, are:

(a) to give brilliance to the Great

(b) "   "   fire to the Swell

(c) " " clarity to the Pedal by the use of more metal stops

(d) to add an enclosed Harmonic Trumpet to Solo in place of one of the existing stops, in order to secure the effect of brass in oratorio accompaniments.

I would prefer to talk over the matter of mixtures with you. You know that I am not afraid of plenty of good mixture work, as it gives something to an organ that no other instrument has. Your Mixture schemes look fine, and I have been trying to find the composition of a five-rank Schulze Mixture I had in England, in order to make a comparison. I hope, therefore, that as soon as the weather improves you can come to New York, examine the situation, and talk over the whole matter with me. I realize that space is limited and nothing can be added unless something is eliminated. For your own private ear, I believe that we may not have to wait until the end of the war for such changes as you and I agree on.

Very sincerely yours,

T. Frederick H. Candlyn

---

155 Document on stationery of St. Thomas Church

March 3, 1945

PROPOSED ALTERATIONS IN REGARD TO THE ORGAN
IN ST. THOMAS CHURCH, N.Y.

1. Change drawstop couplers to tilting tablets.
2. Add following couplers: (a) Solo to Choir, 16', 8', 4'
     (b) Swell to Choir, 16', 4'
     (c) Solo to Great, 16' and 4' for stops on light wind ONLY. Tuba Mirabilis not to be affected by these couplers.
3. Reversible pistons in key-slip for Choir to Pedal, Great to Pedal, Swell to Pedal, Solo to Pedal.
4. Add reversible toe-pistons for each of the three Pedal 32' stops. I prefer the pistons to move the stops, but could tolerate three "blind" pistons if necessary.
5. Add sforzando Pedal with indicator.
6. Great toe pistons to act on Pedal stops only.
7. Add 6 general pistons in Great key-slip, these pistons to be duplicated by toe pistons. Remove Swell toe pistons in order to make room.
8. Silver contacts
9. SWELL. Change both Swell Mixtures. Swell 16' & 4' Reeds to be changed for the French type. French Trumpet to be made bigger. Remove Oboe

T. Frederick H. Candlyn

and substitute Flugel Horn. Remove Claribel Flute (or Gedact) and add a 4' Geigen. Increase tone of the 4' Flute and soften Gamba.

10. GREAT. Change Mixture. Add another rank (19th) to twelfth. Tuba to be re-named Trumpet, and, with the Clarion, re-voiced on Willis lines. Remove Waldflute and substitute a 4' Principal. Increase tone of both 8' and 4' Flutes. Gemshorn for Philomela (See Pedal). Remove Ophicleide.

11. CHOIR. Add one or two mutation stops on special chest. French Horn (Solo) in place of Flugel Horn and so playable on Choir. Louden flue work. Convert Piccolo to Nazard.

12. SOLO. French Horn placed where Flugel Horn was. Harmonic Trumpet added in its place. Could the Contra Fagotto be thinned down in tone and made playable on the Pedal instead of the Swell Dble. Trumpet? It would be infinitely more useful as a soft Pedal stop rather than the Swell 16' reed.

13. ECHO. Remove Flute Celeste and its companion 8' Flute and substitute a big Diapason and 4' Principal. These two stops would be very useful for congregational singing if they would keep in tune with the main organ.

14. PEDAL. Duplex Great 16' Diapason on Pedal preferably at 16' and 8'. Remove Bourdon and substitute Gemshorn 16', with extensions. If possible, brighten the tone of the wooden stops.

15. New music desk.

16. Add one more piston to Great, duplicated by a toe piston.

At present the organ has the following pistons and couplers:

PISTONS. 7 to each manual.

<u>COUPLERS</u>. Choir, Great, Swell, Solo to Pedal, also Solo 4' to Pedal.
Choir, Swell, Solo to Great. Swell 16' and 4' to Great. Swell to Swell, 16' and 4'.
Choir to Choir, 16' and 4'. Solo to Solo, 16' and 4'.
Swell to Choir
Solo unison off

---

156 Emerson Richards to Henry Willis

April Second
Nineteen Forty Five

Captain Henry Willis,
57 Beulah Hill,
London, S. E. 19, England
My dear Willis:

It was a rather odd coincidence that on Friday morning, I stopped at the office on my way down to the railroad station to meet Don and Helen and found your letter, so that it happened that delivery of Don's portion of it was made almost immediately. Don and Helen, as usual, were here over the holidays, leaving Sunday night, so that Don is in Boston Monday morning.

The sad news contained in your letter was anticipated, since someone had written Don, but not too positive a statement, that they had heard of Mrs. Willis' death, and that he had told me the last time that I saw him. However, it still came to both of us with regret and a feeling of sadness. I had rather thought that Mrs. Willis had taken a shine to me on the occasions when I had been entertained at your home. I knew that she was immensely fond and proud of you, and of her family, and the parting is one in which we all felt a loss.

One gets some idea of what you are going through in England from the very fact of this happening. Over here, flu and pneumonia have counted for very few victims this winter. Between the sulfa drugs and penicillin, these diseases have been licked to a point where death from this cause has been reduced to a very small percentage. But the fact that every one of your children is actively engaged in the war as a full time occupation, as well as yourself, shows how badly Britain has been hit. I have many times got out of patience with official Washington because of the many statements that we, over here, don't know that "a war is on," but I can see how our "brass-hats" visiting England and seeing what has gone on there can easily bring home that viewpoint. The reason we do know "a war is on" is that I don't know of a family in this town, which has not got a close member of it actually in the Service and in peril. Many families have two and three children in combat service, but this has not meant with us that we feel obliged to give up either recreations or other comforts, to which we have been accustomed. Much of this has made it appear as if we took the war light-heartedly.

We had our Egg Nog Party yesterday. There were four servicemen, each of whom had lost a leg, and there was not to my knowledge a single person present, who did not have a husband or a son in the service, and there were well over a hundred at the party. Therefore, while we might have our egg nog as usual, it was not without thought that the war is still on. Incidentally, it was some egg nog: 5 qts. of rye liquor, 4 of brandy, 2 of rum, 11 doz. eggs, 12 qts. milk and 8 of cream.

It is a fine thing that your children have all turned out so well. I hope nothing happens to the boy in these last days of this part of the war. Your girls certainly have been a great help and a comfort to you.

As things look now, the last battle of any consequence in Germany is on. By the time you get this, I imagine that organized resistance will have come pretty well to an end, unless we outrun our supplies, as Patton did last fall, when he originally broke the Siegfried Line.

While the Japanese business is looked upon as still a very serious affair, I am inclined to believe that it will turn out a much easier and simpler affair than we have anticipated, and which will be over much sooner. Our occupation of islands so close to Japan, and which now give us control over Japanese communications with the mainland, means that Japan will have to submit or be annihilated. In this situation, I think that they are apt to be more reasonable than the Hitlerites, but even if not, I believe that we can clean up the Asiatic situation with not too great an expenditure of Allied Troops. The Chinese, when properly equipped and led, can be relied upon to take a greater share in mopping up the Japanese-Asiatic Armies than they have heretofore. I, too, believe the Russians will come in, as soon as they can move men and supplies to the East. They want Port Arthur back by the end of April, and next Easter will surely see us sitting in the Emperor's Palace in Tokyo.

Returning again to Mrs. Willis. My own experience with my mother with whom I lived so long, and Adeline's experience of the same type, gives us some idea of what you have gone through, and we both hope that the parting can be somewhat appeased by the continued contact with your children, which will now seem nearer than ever before. Too bad about your home. It will be an awful large house for you to manage by yourself. Unless some of your family are going to be with you, it would hardly seem worthwhile keeping it up for just yourself. I did stick to our house, but, fortunately, I now have someone to take that responsibility. Gradually, we are doing it over and getting it into a much more livable shape than it was before. In your case, it would seem to me that you are doing the sensible thing now. A good rest and changed surroundings, such as you now have, ought to put you in fine condition for the battle ahead.

And now, organ affairs over here. The Organ Builders' Association had a meeting in Washington last week. Officially, they were told that there would be no mitigation of the present orders, and a new man, now in charge of the tin supply, assured them that all of the tin that would be released by the end of the European war would be required to rehabilitate the German railroads. Personally, I think it was lucky for this individual that his statement did not get to the ears of Congress, and it was characteristic of this administration that the head man then sneaked in a back door and privately told the organ builders that they could cheat as much as they pleased and that nobody was going to check up on them, "only don't advertise that you are building new organs." So, the result is that the boys are going ahead with the idea of rebuilding anything that comes along, that's got as much as a Flute d'Amour to start with.

I don't think that Möller will do anything about replacing Whitelegg. It has always been their policy to subordinate individuals to the firm. Whitelegg in their eyes, was merely to set off the Harrison influence. Now, they will have to try some other argument. Incidentally, their success in quantity production was due to the fact that they were in a small, rural community where high priced labor was non-existent. The war has changed that. Other similar industries came in and now they have a higher labor market than almost any place outside of Detroit. The result is that they will have to increase their prices at least 50%. That means that their prices are actually going to be higher than Don's, where there has been no such jump in labor costs. In fact, I doubt if Don will have to pay but a very slight increase for his labor over pre-war times.

I was up in Boston during the third week in March, working on my own organ, checking the revoiced material that was finished and going on setting the C's of the other material that we are using. Don was not there. He was on a trip to the West where he was given a $75,000 contract to replace an Austin rebuild of a very famous organ. The signed contract has not yet come back, so I'll have to leave it to him to tell you what the job is, unless you can guess. My visits to Boston in connection with my own organ always give Don's assistant, Perry Martin, a severe headache, because it invariably results in my picking up some more of the material that we had not used out of St. Marks, or the other jobs, and adding them to the present job. To make room for these additions, I have taken a portion of what is the bathhouse building for organ chambers, and Martin, in speaking to Don, never says that I have added so many more stops to the scheme, but simply says that I have added so many more bathhouses. So on Don's return from the West, Perry told him, "Well, the Senator was here and added three more bathhouses to the organ." Actually, I have finished the chambers for the Swell and Choir, and the Pedal, which is not in a chamber, but an extension of the space between the Swell and Choir chambers and the Great and Positive, which are in the Music Room itself.

Since you may wish to use the specification in an article, for which, of course, you have our permission, I enclose the amended specification, which is now in its final form, and which we do not expect to change. As a matter of fact, Don brought down with him the console drawings and we laid out the order of the stops on the knobs, and while there are one or two blanks left on each division, further enlargements are barred. I, therefore, can tell you that the organ will look like the enclosed.

Taking up the matter that you raise in connection with it, you will see how we have reacted to your suggestion.

THE GREAT ORGAN: The three or four people, who like yourself, are competent to judge, and who have seen the specification, all hit upon the same thing — the absence of the 4' Principal and independent 12th and 15th. Our justification for this was that the 4' Principal was actually in the Grosse Cornet and the 12th and 15th in the Cornet. Consequently, the chorus was complete. However, others, like Covell, have felt that this ruled out the classic "Great to 15th." Therefore, both Don and I have felt obliged to yield to the criticism, and we will, as a part of the Great Organ, add these three stops. I think I know where there is room for them without interfering with the present lay-out. They will have to go on a separate chest. On the Positive, Don's 16' Dulzian is a quarter length reed, more on the Trumpet order, and, of course, light wind. On the Choir, I, too, had felt the need of a softer stop than we were going to have. This became more apparent when we finished the Muted Strings. Their character is very nice, indeed, but somewhat louder than I expected. Therefore, I am finding room for a 2 rank Aeoline, so that there will be at least one voice that will be barely audible with the shutters closed. Our Swell Salicionals are like your Grandfather's. We have run into much the same debate about the mixture combinations on the Great that you have made. My reasons for tapering these mixtures in the bass and treble are two-fold. Up to date, I have stood firmly against the Great to Pedal coupler, but these mixtures might be copied on some other organ where there would be such a coupler, and then I would be fearful of the extra ranks when tied down to the Pedal. My second reason was the matter of room. Cutting down the ranks in the bass, as you realize, narrowed the top boards. Of course, this does not happen to all the mixtures. The Fourniture runs thru as do the two Cornets, and the two mixtures affected are the soft ones, and in the case of the Cymbal, its high pitch is an additional reason for limiting the ranks.

THAT GREAT TO PEDAL COUPLER: Here is an organ of just under 100 stops with 24 wholly independent Pedal voices and there is a stop suitable for almost any purpose. Why, then, try to augment it by using part of the Great Organ, which cannot help but only upset the independence of the Pedal Division? So you see that your criticisms have been constructive and helpful. Will be glad to welcome more, although the console will be past any changes after the next two weeks. You can publish anything you wish about it, and I would be glad to have a copy of the article.

Of course, I do subscribe to the <u>Organ</u>. You mention <u>Musical</u> <u>Times</u>. I have seen a copy or two of this publication, but have never subscribed to it. Does it, too, have an organ department? And should I see it regularly? If so, please give me their address and I will subscribe.

MY ORGAN DESIGN: Perhaps I ought to say with regard to this design that I have made the original design and additions myself. Don has stood by with advice and helpful suggestions, and of course, all the scaling, and much of the voicing details in the Great and Positive will be his, I taking the responsibility for results in the Swell, Choir and Pedal. The general design exemplifies what we both are trying to do, a blending of modern organ practice with classic design. We are not building Baroque organs. We are simply trying to increase the musical possibilities of the modern organ, to clean out the indecision and the fog in favor of greater variety, brilliance and precision. Therefore, the design in general meets with the approval of both of us, but I will have to take the blame for its inception, and Don, for the final result.

SMALL ORGAN DESIGN: The first design is mine. The alternative Swell is as Don actually built it. I think you understood that I was trying to design this organ to be as all-round and useful as possible and at the same time to design it down to a price. Hence, my own and Don's selection of the 16' Quintaton. As Don makes this stop, it has virtually a string-like Bass. It, therefore, gives you your soft pedal stop, completes your Great Organ chorus and when used in an octave position, gives you an additional accompanimental stop. None of these things would be true of the 16' Swell reed. Of course, the first mixture going to the Great completes that division for almost any church work, and adds the necessary power and brilliancy to justify this division as an entity. As I pointed out, the five-stop Swell can easily become a satisfactory Choir, if a true Swell division, even of small dimensions, is to be an added possibility, in which case, of course, the Trumpet would be removed to the Swell and a Clarinet added. As it is, the Swell Trumpet with the couplers added would do much to make up for the absence of the 16' reed. And what is more important is the difference in cost between the reed and the Quintaton. On this question of cost, I think you misread my letter. I did not say that Don could produce the specification for about $7,000, but gave that as my estimated price. Actually, my figures were $6,650.00, and Don figured it at nearer $6,000, at pre-war prices. In reading your letter, he stated that post-war prices would probably run it closer to $8,000. Again, you can use this stop list, if you like, and if you do, I would like to see the articles.

On my organ, we will start the factory erection of the Swell division next week, to be followed by the Choir and the main Pedal section. I hope to have these in Atlantic City by the early part of June and perhaps the console with it. The only bottleneck has been that Don's rack-board man has been ill and this work has been somewhat delayed. We will then go on to the Great and Positive and the balance of the Pedal. As things stand, Don will probably start the chests rather soon, but we cannot do much about the pipes until the tin situation eases up. As you know, Don uses practically pure tin for all the voices in both these divisions, so until your boys pry the Japs out of the Malay Peninsula, we may not get all of the Great and Positive pipes in place for some time to come. We are hoping for at least a few of each by next fall. I think that about covers present organ matters.

I note what you say about supplies. The administration intends to get supplies over to you as fast as possible. The minute that the flow of munitions can be stopped, greater cargo space will be available and this ought to increase your supplies. Perhaps not much of this will actually come from United States. There is a large amount of the supplies due from South America. Also, recently, there has been considerable friction developed between ourselves and Canada. Ration restrictions in Canada have not been anything like those over here. Meat, for instance, has not been rationed. Consequently, there is a feeling that Canada ought to share its supplies in greater degree with Britain. Meat supplies over here have really been getting tough for the last three months, but this, in part, is due to the greater demand for meat occasioned by the fact that people have more money.

The return of part of the expeditionary forces will, of course, ease our problem of supplies, but if a large number of these men are merely going to be trans-shipped to the East, it only increases the headache because of the greater distances involved. Of course, it is our intent to share supplies of all kinds with Britain and in a lesser degree with Russia. There is no enthusiasm for the French over here, and only a few of the pro-German sympathizers will weep if the Germans do starve.

When you do get around to building a new factory, at least you will be able to lay it out efficiently, so that there can be a continuous flow of materials and parts from the various departments to the erecting floor. As you say, undoubtedly, this will have to wait for a while.

Too bad about the Bristol organ. Sorry, but I had never heard it.

The Rotunda Organ Works of Henry Willis & Sons in London bombed April, 1941

Both Don and I would be glad if you could make an early trip over here. Perhaps in the interval between the time passage becomes available and the period when you will be able to resume full scale production. Very likely some time after midsummer, travel restrictions over here will have eased up, so that you could get around. When you do come, I think that between Don and I, we could show you most everything this side of Chicago, at least. I have a car and a good driver and we can do the thing in comfort. I can assure you that your visit will be most welcome.

Poor old Washington Cathedral — they are already talking about rebuilding it.

When last in Boston, I wanted to see Fred White, who has a small pipe factory out at Reading, twelve miles North of Boston. I drove out there, and I found that Skinner had been reduced to renting one small room adjacent to Fred's pipe shop. He has one man working for him and that is all that is left of the once great Skinner Organ Company.

Don, of course, read the letter that you wrote to me and I am now mailing the whole letter to him at Boston, so that he may also reply to it. We were both very glad to get such a detailed letter from you and will surely appreciate hearing from you right soon again.

I should add that I have three extra sets of keys and Don suggests that we might as well make the console a four-manual. So, if the extra keys are nearly a match, this will be done and the couplers arranged accordingly. The Choir then goes to the fourth manual (top), but its position and the Positive (bottom) can be reversed as indicated.

Sincerely yours,
Emerson Richards

ER LB
Enc.

Perry Martin — head draftsman, a cousin of Ernest Skinner, and with the company since the 'teens. Harrison's first position with the firm was in Martin's department.
Mrs. Willis' death — Shortly after the cessation of hostilities in Europe, Mr. Willis took a second wife, Dora Geraldine Lang, who had previously been married to G. Donald Harrison.
replacing Whitelegg — Richard Whitelegg had recently died.
Bristol Organ — Colston Hall, Bristol, which Willis considered his finest concert organ. It burned in January, 1945.

---

157 G. Donald Harrison to Henry Willis

May 17, 1945

Mr. Henry Willis
57 Beulah Road
London, S.E. 19, England
Dear Henry:

I was very glad to read your long letter to Senator Richards of March 20th, and have also received the one to me. Doubtless you have already received my letter of some time ago regarding Clara's death. It is still difficult for me to realize it.

Firstly about lumber, the situation is pretty bad here at present, and in fact you cannot buy California Sugar Pine of first quality without a very high priority, which can only be obtained for defense contracts. We have no way of estimating how soon the restrictions may be relaxed, although it would seem that some consideration will be given to the matter shortly in view of the cutbacks in munitions since the defeat of Germany. One of the difficulties, of course, is due to the dwindling supply from the West Coast caused by a manpower shortage. Obviously, for things to return to normal in this regard some little time must elapse. . . .

In addition to lumber there is a great shortage of tin in this country and, of course, its use is very strictly controlled. Personally, I cannot see of any complete relaxation of the regulations until the Malay Straits are taken back from the Japs. Some supplies of tin are being imported from Bolivia, but apparently they amount to 60% of the requirements of this country, and the other 40% is coming off the stock pile, which is naturally shrinking rapidly. We have tin and alloyed metals in sheet form, but they are all frozen at the moment, and no new organ pipes can be made. In view of this our work consists largely of repairs and rebuilds where no new pipes are required, or where sufficient metals can be salvaged to keep one's inventory up to par.

You had told me about the accidents both to Newman and Deeks, but I am glad to hear that they are now in harness once more.

We have been able to hold our key men, and counting the New York service fellows we have about 25 employees at the present time. Unfortunately, we are in a critical manpower area, and cannot take help for the present. A great many of our ex-employees are in Boston and vicinity defense plants, and will undoubtably return directly once the cutbacks create a layoff.

We have $250,000 worth of post war contracts signed up, before the end of the year I think it will go at least a half a million. I expect to make a trip shortly to sign one of the largest contracts the company has ever had, but it has to be kept confidential for the time being. I will send you the specification in due course.

I was much interested in what you had to say regarding the possible increase in costs of production as discussed with the federation. We hit exactly upon the same percentage after very extensive and careful checking.

I hope you will get a satisfactory settlement for the destruction of the plant so that you can get under way as soon as possible.

I had not heard that Colston Hall was completely destroyed. Too bad, but I suppose it will mean a big job for you in the future when they rebuild.

The Senator's organ is coming along slowly, and we have at last called a halt on the constant increases in size which the Senator demanded weekly. It is now up to over one hundred stops, and I think that is enough for any residence. Your remarks about the lack of a 4' Principal on the Great turned the scale, and this has now been added, together with a 2⅔' independent 12th. The Great and Positiv sections cannot be built at present, and the layouts of the Mixtures of these divisions as sent to you by the Senator are his. I have not given the matter any careful thought and so there may be some changes as they are not in accordance with our usual practice.

I feel as you do about the writings of Dickson and Whitworth, etc. I find it difficult to finish any article I start reading that these boys write. It is hardly necessary to do so for I know exactly what is coming. Just the same old arguments that have been used for 20 years, and which are now completely threadbare. The whole trouble is that they do not tackle the matter from the musical angle, but base their schemes upon theories which seem to appeal to the organ enthusiast, but which have nothing to do with the playing of music. I frankly admit it took me a a long time to rid myself of some of these unwritten theoretical laws about design, but am glad they do not bother me any longer.

Regarding the small organ design, I do not see eye to eye with Senator in all things and, of course, there is no standard that will fit all cases. What I mean is that a small organ suitable for the liturgical service would not be of value to the Christian Scientists. We have built some very radical small organs. As an example, I am enclosing an article on an instrument we built for Brooks School some years ago. I suppose if this was published in any of the English magazines they would know that I am crazy. Not an 8' Diapason to be found anywhere. I should add, however, that there is one prepared for. On the scheme that Senator sent you he was a little bit off on the price we would have charged in 1939. Our figures would have been very close to the £1,250 you mention.

Senator and I were talking over some kind of scheme we could concoct to make it possible for you to pay us a visit, and I would certainly like to have an opportunity to show you some of the jobs I have done, and this would not mean any extensive travelling except around the East here as you could get a fairly good cross-section of my work since I first came over. You would be very well entertained by Senator, and the cost would not be anything to worry about while here. I have been wondering whether I could persuade our Directors that it would be a legitimate expense to pay your round trip fare on the understanding that you wrote some articles upon your return. In other words, it would be a little publicity stunt. Would such a scheme interest you?

We have made various types of Dulzians, some of them having but quarter length conical resonators.

Looking forward to hearing from you again in the near future, and with all the best,

As ever,
Don

GDH:MGM
Encl.

Clara's death — Willis' wife
one of the largest contracts — the Mormon Tabernacle organ, opus 1075. See letters 162, 163.
Brooks School — opus 980, three manual, 1938

4th August, 1945

Mr. William King Covell,
72 Washington Street,
Newport,
Rhode Island,
U.S.A.

Dear Mr. Covell,

Thanks for yours of the 21st July.

As regards costs of organ building over here: Labor is now 55 percent over the 1939 figures, while materials vary from a 100 to 300 percent increase. Costs therefore vary from 50 percent on work that is purely labor, with higher percentages until new work is about 100 percent.

But at present we are not allowed to undertake the construction of new organs or major rebuilds, and even for minor rebuilds government licenses are only obtainable with some difficulty. You will realize that for the present and some months to come, our A-1 priority is the rehabilitation of organs damaged by or as the result of enemy action, and the essential repair and restoration of instruments which could not receive attention during the period of the European war.

I do not know the source from which you assess the cost of replacing the St. Paul's Cathedral Organ before the war at some £15,000, but can assure you that £30,000 was the figure. The St. Paul's Organ was bomb-shattered throughout. Having had no experience you do not realize what bomb-shattered means — I will explain.

After an "incident" an organ may be found to be in all appearance undamaged except for broken and scattered glass and plaster etc. On examination, take an electro-pneumatic magnet machine for example — the exterior of which appears to be normal — you find all the pneumatic membranes and discs split and torn — wires bent, and windings torn off the magnet bobbins or loose, and so it is with every part. Old slider soundboards split from end to end with loose bars and tables; pitman chests similarly deranged; seams of pipes and reeds split, etc. At St. Paul's everything has to be taken apart and remade from start to finish. We brought the 32's out of the Dome Organ a couple of weeks ago — the CCCC of the Open Wood bass nearly fell to pieces in process of being lowered to the floor of the Cathedral. Anyway, we hope to get this grand old job going again in its entirety by Easter, 1946.

Alas! Again you have been misinformed, this time about the Alexandra Palace Organ: a V-1 [flying bomb] fell 150 yards from the Alexandra Palace and blew in the great window behind the organ — the blast forcing the whole instrument forward several inches. All the glass roof went and as no repairs were possible all last winter the rain was pouring through onto the job which is a sodden, rusted up mess. You will say "Why was not the organ sheeted up" — answer — there were no sheets available for such "luxury" purposes.

As regards our own records, most were saved, but much has been lost. My own personal voicing records saved in the form of charred sheets.

At St. George's Hall, Liverpool, the organ was partially destroyed by fire, result of incendiary bombs, in December 1940 — the rest was deluged with water by the firemen. As the roof of the hall was burnt out it will be years before it will be replaced and the organ restored. All building priority is on houses for the people — and rightly so.

Christ Church, Westminster Bridge Road — job was deluged with water by firemen and is <u>hors de combat</u>.

The Colston Hall, Bristol organ was destroyed by fire in January this year — my finest concert hall instrument.

I was released from active service at the end of April, since when I have been and am hard at work to revive a business stricken for the second time in my life by two great wars. I have a piano factory in Stockwell — quite close to the old site — and various other work-shops. Our Liverpool works is intact, and we also have acquired a small factory in Edinburgh to take care of our Scottish connection.

I greatly look forward to another visit to the U.S. to observe developments since I last visited in 1926; I might be able to make the trip next year after 20 years' absence.

It would be a tremendous pleasure to be able to do so.

Yours sincerely,
Henry Willis

---

159 T. Frederick H. Candlyn to Ernest Skinner

August 8, 1945

Dear Mr. Skinner,

How goes it with the new stops for St. Thomas? I am anxious to know how the new 16', 8', and 4' Gemshorn will sound, and if it will brighten up the Pedal sufficiently. Perhaps you can give me an idea when you expect to start the installation of the new stops. Aeolian-Skinner has completed all their repair work, so now you have a free hand. Incidentally I have not forgotten that I owe you for the Great Principal as soon as it is installed. I have put the material for the plate to go in the console, at the foot of this letter.

Sincerely yours,
T. Frederick H. Candlyn

THE GREAT PRINCIPAL IS THE GIFT OF SGT. DONALD S. CANDLYN
1925-1944

---

160 T. Scott Buhrman to Henry Willis,

August 25, 1945

Dear Mr. Willis:

I am heartily sorry to see the photos of damage to your factory. But if we two English-speaking nations don't behave ourselves a lot more intelligently than we have been doing, you and we too can prepare for the third world war made in Germany. If we let the Russians have their way, there won't be another war. It's a compliment to have these photos for reproduction in the <u>American Organist</u> and we'll take care of that in our October issue; perhaps they may help a bit, because they bring the war right home to the organ world.

I hope your business is on the way to recovery, however painfully slow; anyway the period of destruction is now past, and if our two nations can overcome the tremendous handicap of rule by the alleged "working" class. So that men of education and experience can be free to organize for an era of industrial prosperity, everything will be worth working for. Strange, but workmen who don't even own the hammers they work with think they are intelligent enough to run business and factories and government. Thank heaven Providence saw fit to remove Roosevelt; Harry Truman seems, so far, honest and intelligent — two qualities Roosevelt completely lacked.

Our mutual friend Senator Richards is buried in the job of getting that new organ for his home. It looks to me as though it will be the finest thing yet built in America.

Very sincerely yours,
T. Scott Buhrman

TSB/g

October Eleventh
Nineteen Hundred
Forty Five

Mr. Henry Willis,
Oakenshaw
57 Beulah Hill,
Upper Norwood
London, S. E. 19, England.

My dear Willis:

Thanks for your letter of September 24th. I will send you in a few days a final specification of the organ. This is based upon the fact that we have used all of the 108 stop knobs, with the exception of one on the Pedal, and could not, therefore, make any other changes. Indeed, the Swell, Choir and Pedal are now being readied for assembly. There cannot be any additional changes in these departments and I am contemplating no changes in either the Great or the Positive.

One thing, however, has come up as a result of what I am going to tell you. I took another trip up to Moosehead for a couple of weeks and while there, had forwarded to me a letter written by an American Officer in the Occupation Forces, apparently situated at Munich. In the letter, he stated that he had become acquainted with Hans Steinmeyer and was writing this letter at his request. The letter stated that Hans and his wife were well, that Oettingen had been only slightly damaged and the factory not at all; that Fritz, the older son, was back and in charge of the factory, and that the younger boy and his son-in-law were prisoners of war. I had had a letter from this son-in-law, Dr. Franz Winzinger, who is a prisoner of war in England, who wanted to know if I could communicate with Hans, as he had no way of doing so. It appears that the postal system has completely broken down in Germany, and there is no civilian mail. Continuing, the letter from the American officer stated that the factory was now producing furniture for the bombed-out Germans, and that it also had resumed organ manufacture. Hans has been appointed Burgermeister of Oettingen and also of the county. He also acts as interpreter for the American Occupation Forces. It therefore appears that Hans has landed right-side-up and that the family is intact.

I saw Don Harrison on my way back from Moosehead and he was, naturally, pleased with the news, and I am sure that you will be also. For a while, we had no sympathy for the Germans as a whole. I always felt that Hans was more American than German in his attitude towards life and certainly he was not in sympathy with the Nazi régime. The letter also went on to state that the Positives that had been left for reconditioning were intact. This poses a new question, since it had been my intention to locate these two Positives in the lower hall where they could be heard through the stairwell and play them from the new console. Of course, I had no idea that they were still in existence, and, therefore, made no provision for them on the new console, which is virtually complete. The only way we were able to handle this is by putting a series of miniature stop knobs in the extreme end of the stop jambs. They will not be on the combination system, but will be able to control the stops of the two little baroques. I am, of course, taking measures to see if the Army can get them to me. The new console is a really fine example of the organ builders' art, and since we were able for the first time to use the newly devised stop controls, which are very much smaller and more efficient than the old type when used in connection with remote control mechanism, the console is very compact, although there are actually more stop knobs and controls upon my console than on the new console built to control the University of Indiana Organ, although the two organs are about the same size. My console is only about one-half the size; a very important thing in a music room.

Now, for what you say in your letter about public affairs. Your national election was a shock to us, more because of our liking for Churchill than any other reason. Apparently, you are over-confident about your foreign policy, both in the Mediterranean and in India. Your government has not been at all firm and it now begins to look as if the Russians were going to pry their way in.

With regard to the relations between England and America, I am afraid there is much in the way of misunderstanding, that if not checked, will cause a continuance of mutual differences. Perhaps in a way this is due to the fact that we, on our part, have certain fundamental feelings towards Britain, which, for some reason, we never put in the concrete form of words, but which are, nevertheless, a substantial reflection of what we do. If you will go back to one of my very early letters written after the war started, in answer to your plea that we ought to then enter the war, I told you that that could not be expected, because United States would not voluntarily enter a European War. I added that there was an unexpressed, but nevertheless, firm conviction that we would never allow Great Britain to be defeated and overcome by any Continental power. You can see that this statement was a correct appraisal of the situation. After Dunkirk, we did not declare war, but we gave you other means to resist a German invasion to a point of stripping ourselves of every piece of artillery that we possessed. And we got all of this Army equipment by the then undisclosed system of having it convoyed by our Navy. We were sinking German subs long before Pearl Harbor, even as we turned the fifty destroyers over to you. This was all because no matter what the cost in the long run to us, we would not, and, in fact, could not, without great danger to ourselves, permit Great Britain to be conquered.

That is still our policy, but there is a vast difference between preserving the territorial integrity of Britain and our promoting or underwriting its future welfare. And that brings us to what was at the bottom of the lend-lease secession. We recognize that the war effort did drain Britain financially, and that it would be to our ultimate advantage to give her some assistance. However, there is no disposition to hand over to your present labor government several billion dollars to be sunk in governmental, socialistic experiments. Of course, we would not say this publicly. We are too sensitive to appear to interfere in your political domestic affairs to do that. That was, fundamentally, the reason for the sudden stopping of lend-lease. It is generally agreed in Washington that if a method of control could be found whereby the money that we are advancing could be used only for the stimulation of trade between United States and the British Empire, this will be done, and generously. But I think a certain change in British public thinking will have to occur before this can be done with any degree of satisfaction over here. To put it very crudely, we are not particularly impressed by the "sacrifices" that Britain made. Your backs were pressed to the wall with an insane murderer at your throats. To talk of "sacrifices," under the circumstances is to intimate that there was something that you could have done to have stayed his hand. It was his U-Boats which sunk your export trade. It was his Air Force that levelled your cities and it now is revealed how close you were to ultimate disaster.

From your distance, it does not look as we have suffered at all as a result of the war. Materially, we have not, but fifteen years ago an annual budget of a billion dollars was considered as excessive for the Federal Government. Now, it is admitted that we must raise twenty-five billion dollars annually over a long period of time to pay for this war. Of course, we know that had we let you down, we would have had to have dealt with both Germany and Japan with only such help as we could get from Russia. We did do the Japanese job virtually without help and you now know that we could have blasted Germany from the face of the earth without ever having set foot in Normandy, had we been content to wait. We have not starved, as you have. We are not in the same desperate financial condition as you are at the moment, but in the long haul ahead we have a financial situation which is equally as bad as yours. Moreover, we have a million dead and wounded to remind us of the real cost of this war. My home is alongside of the Air Force Hospital that has been taking care of the amputees. It has not been too pleasant to see our Boardwalk filled with young men minus one or two legs or arms, and in some cases, both.

So far as the trade situation is concerned, if we try to tax ourselves all these enormous sums to artificially resuscitate world trade, and at the same time admit world merchandise in competition with our own in our own markets, we naturally cancel out the exports that we might send abroad. And we have this added factor: our cost of living standard is higher than any country abroad, and as a result of the great pressure for even higher labor returns, we can expect our total manufacturing costs to rise to a point where export business will be unable to compete in the world markets. We cannot make our own labor people see this, and, indeed, it is only by a means of some inflation that we can cope with this tremendous debt that we have accumulated. I hope that I have made myself reasonably clear. England will receive help, provided your government is willing to forego about every ideal that put it in power.

Cordially yours,
Emerson Richards

ER LB

---

162 G. Donald Harrison to William King Covell

December 11, 1945

Mr. Wm. King Covell
72 Washington Street
Newport Rhode Island
Dear Mr. Covell:

Thanks for your letter of November 26th. Yes, I was out in Salt Lake City recently, and signed a contract for an entirely new instrument, and the only things from the old organ that will remain are the case, three sets of wood Gedackt pipes, the lower octave of the 32' Open, which is at the back of the instrument, and the ten cylindrical wood pipes in the case, which are also of 32' pitch. All these pipes that are being used were in the original organ, and are all excellent. What happened to the metal pipes of the original seems to be a mystery, for all I could find were Kimball pipes of 1900 vintage, and the remainder by Austin installed in 1915, with some Jamison mixtures of the year 1940. By the way, the latter are very poor.

From the above you will see we are making a really clean sweep, and I would not tackle the job on any other basis. In my opinion, the Austin windchest has no merits whatsoever, for even the one thing that might be considered good is the steadiness of the wind, and actually it is too steady for no decent tremulant can be employed. The Austin action fails in that the pneumatics which operate the valves work under varying loads. When you are playing on one stop they have to pull one stop off. If you are playing on ten stops, the same pneumatic has to pull off ten valves. No key action can possibly work properly with such a system, and as a matter of fact, at Salt Lake I could touch every key from middle C down without getting a single response from the pipes if you had a handful drawn. It was by condemning the mechanism that I was able to persuade them to buy a new organ — at least that was the opening wedge. Of course, the organists were all for the new job anyway, having no illusions as to the glory of the old instrument.

Although the contract has been signed, there are some minor details of the specification to be settled upon, particularly as there may be some extra money available if the tax situation is adjusted, which we hope will be the case in January. Directly when I have the final scheme, I will send you a copy as I am sure you will be interested.

Due to the strength of character of Alexander Schreiner, the chief organist, there was absolutely no competition, and he stuck to one theme — that was that unless one man was placed in charge of the building they would rather carry on with the old instrument with all its faults. Having decided upon the man, he should be given his own way as to the specification after the particular requirements of the Tabernacle were explained to him. Under these conditions, you will see that the whole responsibility has really been placed on my shoulders, and I do not think you will be disappointed with the tonal layout. With the location of the organ and the superb acoustics, there is a real chance to build the most distinguished instrument in the country, and that is what I intend to try to do. Happily, I have plenty of time since the completion date is March 15, 1948. I am glad about this for the flow of materials will be back to normal before we have to commence manufacturing the organ, and there will, therefore, be no restrictions.

I thought your remarks in the November <u>American Organist</u> were to the point, and I am glad they were printed exactly as submitted. As you probably know, the Senator's article produced a contract, so that the smallest scheme, plus some additions, will actually be built, and can be demonstrated, which may do some good. . . .

Yes, I have seen the <u>Organ</u> for October, and of course, noted E.M.'s remarks which referred back to your letter published last spring. While I can understand your desire to go back at him in the interest of truth and to convince the readers that you are an accurate reporter, if it is at all right with you, I would like to see the whole thing ignored and dropped. In the first place, it is of little interest to the English readers, and E.M.'s last remarks are contained in a casual manner at the end of a letter relating to another subject, and I, therefore, doubt if anybody will be looking for a reply. In the second place, it seems to me that it is poor taste to be washing our dirty linen in a foreign magazine, and if you reply, there will be no end to the business, for whatever proofs you bring forth, E.M. will try to disprove them, and you know he is not particular about telling the truth himself. Maybe he has a convenient memory. Thirdly, when first this matter was brought up I wrote to Fitzsimmons a confidential letter explaining the real circumstances to him, and told him that I had the actual proof as to the organs mentioned, but that I would rather see the whole thing forgotten, particularly in view of E.M.'s condition and age. Between us, E.M. has forgotten a letter he wrote to me after the Princeton organ was built and admired by Marcel Dupré. This letter was very flattering as far as I am concerned, and admitted my influence in the tonal part of the instrument. This letter could be readily photostated and printed in The Organ, which would make the old man's hair stand on end. However, I do not wish to hurt him.

I have built too many well-known organs now since E.M. left the company, and upon which he can make no claim whatsoever, so that the matter of the Princeton organ is a very small one anyway. A much better answer to E.M. will be to print the specification and a short description of the Salt Lake City Tabernacle organ when the time comes in the Organ. It will tend to show who is getting the important jobs in this country without giving any offense.

The first load of Senator's organ leaves the plant tomorrow, and installation will commence immediately.

I heard from Willis some little time ago. As far as I can gather, organ building in England is in a poor way, and it is going to be some time before things will return to anything like normal. They are hemmed in with strict government restrictions and, of course, the 100% luxury tax just kills any new work.

With best wishes,

Sincerely yours,
G. Donald Harrison

GDH:MGM

an entirely new instrument — for the Mormon Tabernacle, opus 1075, five-manuals and 188 ranks. Most of the original instrument was likely built in Wm. B.D. Simmons' shop in Boston ca. 1865, and is attributed to Joseph Ridges, a Mormon employee of Simmons who installed it in 1866 and 1867. It was rebuilt by Kimball in 1900 and by Austin in 1915.

E.M. has forgotten a letter — See letter 37.

December 19, 1945

Mr. Henry Willis
57 Beulah Road
London, S.E. 19, England
My dear Henry:

I am sorry to have been so long in replying to your newsy letter of some little time ago, but since the sudden termination of the war I have been simply snowed under, and have been obliged to make long trips, one of which took me as far as Salt Lake City in Utah. There are times when I wish this country wasn't so darn big. On the other hand, however, it does give a very wide field.

There is tremendous activity in the organ field here, and I have closed over half a million dollars worth of contracts already, and there are many more in the offing.

We have over fifty men back in the shop, and in fact we are beginning to have difficulty in absorbing them as quickly as they would wish to return. This is due to the scarcity of materials which we have to procure in small quantities for the time being. We are hoping this situation will gradually ease after the new year for at the present time with the high taxes a great many concerns are reluctant to ship anything until the new year when there will be some tax relief.

In my last letter to you I hinted that I was on the track of a very interesting and important deal. It has now been signed, and is for a completely new organ for the Salt Lake City Tabernacle. The present organ is a typical Austin which has been gingered up from time to time, the last work being carried out in 1940 when Jamison put in some Chorus Mixtures, which by the way are exceedingly poor.

Last spring I was invited to go out there and look over the situation to see what could be done to further improve the organ, but being skeptical about the whole thing I demanded $800.00 fee, which I thought would probably close the matter as far as we were concerned. To my great surprise they accepted the proposition, so I had to make the trip. I gave a written report which, to put it shortly, condemned the present instrument, and told the authorities that we would not touch the job unless a completely new organ was built, with the exception that we were willing to include three original wood stops which were placed in the Tabernacle when it was built. These pipes were made on the spot by Bridges, who was an English organ builder who had been out to Australia, and had become converted to the Mormon faith, and finally wound up in Utah. I think he was trained with the Hill outfit. These pipes are the lower 12 notes of the 32' Wood Open, which by the way, has an inverted mouth, and the famous wood front pipes which look exactly like a 32' Metal Open. They are built up in strips triangular in cross section all glued together, and they appear to be as good as the day they were installed. Even the foot is built up in this way, and the tone is surprisingly good. The other stop we are incorporating is a wooden Gedeckt, which is also excellent. What happened to the original metal pipes in the organ is a mystery. Nobody seems to be able to account for the fact that there are none of them in the present instrument. All the metal stops that are there now are Kimball 1900 vintage and Austin 1915-1940.

You will probably remember that the Mormon Tabernacle is famous for its acoustics. For the edification of visitors they drop a pin, the noise of which is quite audible in the back of the auditorium. The shape of the building is as if one cut an egg shell longitudinally and turned it upside down. There is no absorbent of any kind, and at the same time the reverberation period is not too long to cause confusion. With these magnificent acoustics and the super location of the organ in the open it gives a real chance that one rarely gets.

I was given a free hand with the specification after being told of the requirements that the organ must meet, so that I was able to work out something which more or less carries the ideas on which I have been working to their logical conclusion. I am sure you will be interested in this scheme, which I will let you have at an early date. Although the contract is signed, there are certain details to be settled. For example, the luxury tax situation is to come up in January for settlement, and if this is eliminated, which we rather hope, there will be some more money available to complete one section of the organ which we were obliged to leave partially prepared for, so that I do not want to publish the specification until we know exactly what is going to be possible.

When I was in England in 1936 I was much interested in your all-electric console, and those I saw were quite impressive, but the remote control machine I saw at the back end of the top floor was a tremendous affair, and after I returned I sent to Aubrey working blue prints of our remote control, which was worked on the same principle, but about one-tenth the size. Since that day we have greatly refined that particular remote until it is now extremely efficient and reliable. We have also simplified beyond what I had hoped the pneumatic mechanism in the console for throwing on and off the knobs. During this process we have carried out a great deal of experimentation with all-electric mechanism for the console and remote, have kept tabs on what others have done in that direction, and have come to the conclusion that an all-electric device which will operate as noiselessly and efficiently as our pneumatic console would cost a great deal more with no possible advantage beyond a talking point. We have got to the state here where we don't sell by telling people that something is all-electric. We sell tone pure and simple, and the mechanics of a good organ are taken for granted. Since I received your letter I have questioned several of our best organists about this matter, and they just pass it off with a smile and say "what do we care what agency throws on our combinations providing it is done quietly, efficiently and reliably." The only possible advantage I see in an all-electric console is that you don't have to provide wind for the console. In any case this is not our problem as the churches here bring the wind to the console location. That ad you saw of a suction pump was a kind of fill-in ad. We have only used one in a console where it was impossible to bring wind without cutting through a marble floor.

Wind is very cheap in an organ and, moreover, it is an elastic medium, whereas a solenoid is a harsh action.

Another thing about an all-electric device is the tremendous generator which has to be provided, and my tendency has been to cut down on the action current. Even our large organs are run on a 20 amp. generator. If you have a 75 amp. generator at 15 volts, and it is any distance from the organ or console, you have to provide big mains to carry the current, and it uses up about two horsepower to run the generator, and sooner or later the contacts are going to burn off.

This matter of 15 volts and 75 amps. has another disadvantage in this country in that we are dealing with 48 states, and each State has its own regulations in regard to the fire laws. For example, in New York State even with a 10 volt, 20 amp. generator we have to have all the console wires and those cables that run within the organ enclosed in asbestos fireproof tape. If we are to go in for a system such as you are using, we would be up against all kinds of trouble. Therefore, while I admire greatly your system, which I think is the best that has been produced to date, I am not interested for practical reasons, nor does it do the job any better than a pneumatic system, and in any case costs are out of the question. I think you would be amazed how cheaply we build our remote control combination actions.

Another thing that we are gradually bringing about is considerable simplification of the console. Complications in that regard were running wild before the war, but now we have tonal schemes which do not rely so greatly upon mechanical complications. We have been quite successful in reducing the console to more simple terms, and the mechanism of the organ generally. The Salt Lake City organ will be a tremendous advance in this respect. If you let the organist have his way, he would become gadget-crazy. Where we are spending the money is with the pipe work, which after all with a musical instrument is the chief thing to worry about. We are using extremely rich metals, and for our post-war instruments we are eliminating the disadvantages of the zinc bass, which is something that I have worried about for a number of years. Our bass pipes all have the foot, the whole of the mouth area for about 2' from the languid up made of the same material as the treble pipes. Only the upper end of the pipe will be made of zinc. Boner with his trick pipe where it was possible to substitute various materials from cardboard to pure tin for the upper end of the pipe showed that there was little difference in the tone quality. This means that the critical area from the material point of view is at the business end of the pipe. We made several experimental pipes here and compared them with an all metal pipe, and found that the scheme that I have mentioned above practically eliminates the disadvantage of using zinc. It does not seem to me that it matters whether the zinc is hard rolled or annealed, a zinc pipe is a zinc pipe without any disadvantage and, of course, we will continue to use the material in those cases.

I am not sure what Michael's plans are in regard to organ building, but I have written him today to inquire.

You will be interested to hear that we have shipped the Swell and Choir divisions of Senator's organ, and the men are down there attending to the installation. At the moment Senator is quite sick. He is having one of the worst attacks of his arthritis trouble that he has had to endure in a year or eighteen months. We usually go down for Christmas, but this year it is off.

I hope you and Doe are going along well and are happy. I see no reason why you shouldn't since you have known each other for over thirty years. Regarding all meeting together without embarrassment, this is, of course, perfectly O.K. with me, but I do not know quite how it will set with Helen. We have to remember that she is a newcomer on the scene, and has a different slant than the rest of us.

With all good wishes to you both for Christmas and the New Year,

As ever,

Don

GDH:MGM

P.S. The Wicks organ here is all-electric even to the chest — the results are very poor. You will notice from their ads that they are certainly making a song about it. The quality builder [sic] therefore makes the point that his mechanism is <u>not</u> a cheap electric affair! [handwritten]

Michael's plans — Michael Harrison, Donald's son by his first wife
I hope you and Doe — See note, letter 156.

*Henry Willis III &
Dora Lang Harrison Willis
on their wedding day*

---

164 G. Donald Harrison to William King Covell

January 9, 1946

Mr. Wm. King Covell
72 Washington Street
Newport, Rhode Island
Dear Mr. Covell:

Thanks for your letter of December 15th last, from which I note you agree to allow the E.M. matter to drop. I am sure that is the best thing to do under all the circumstances. I have often heard Courboin tell the story of the time the contract was being drawn for the Princeton organ.

Regarding the St. Patrick's organ, I visit the Cathedral quite frequently, and in fact sat up with Courboin at High Mass last Sunday. His statement about the organ being much better is I should say slightly exaggerated, for all that he has done is to cut off the big flutes and heavy diapasons, etc., from the combinations, crescendo pedal and sforzando. The Plein Jeu to which he refers is the old Ripieno, and all he has done is to re-regulate it and mount the chest to a position where it can speak with greater advantage. All this work was done by the regular service man with Courboin's assistance. Naturally the organ does sound much better, but for all intents and purposes it is still the same old instrument.

Some year or eighteen months ago Courboin and I went through the organ pretty thoroughly, and I prepared a very comprehensive scheme. I think it would have been far better if the matter had been held over for a while as at the time the war was still going strong and all restrictions on organ building were in full force, so that the authorities of the Cathedral had an excellent excuse to shelve the matter. Now they have started complete repairs on the roof and outside walls of the edifice, which is going to take two years to complete, and cost a million dollars a year, so I fear the organ matter will stand over for some time.

I have not yet decided how to deal with the publicity on the Salt Lake City matter, and feel it might be better to have someone else do a short article for me, and in that case I will certainly take advantage of your kind offer. This is a little way off yet, however, as I want to get the specification definitely settled before we go into print.

Regarding the history of the organ, the church issues a little booklet about the Tabernacle, and its instrument, and I am sure Alexander Schreiner would send you a copy if you were to drop him a line.

The old Chicago Auditorium organ has been shipped out to Indiana, and is now being installed.

Red Gaskill has the job at King's Chapel, Boston.

With best regards,

Sincerely yours,
G. Donald Harrison

GDH:MGM

St. Patrick's — St. Patrick's Cathedral, Fifth Avenue, Manhattan
Chicago Auditorium organ — See note, letter 152.

---

165 G. Donald Harrison to William King Covell

July 31, 1946

Mr. Wm. King Covell
72 Washington Street
Newport, Rhode Island
Dear Mr. Covell:

Thank you for yours of the 26th instant. I am glad to say that I already have a contract for doing some work on the Methuen organ, the hall having been recently taken over by a bunch of citizens who are incorporated under the name "Methuen Memorial Music Hall, Inc." By local subscriptions they got together some funds to purchase the whole affair, and intend to carry out the necessary work so that the hall can be used for concerts and recitals. Much work had to be done in the way of providing an adequate heating apparatus, and also making some changes to meet the requirements of the local fire department.

I am glad to say that generally speaking the organ is in excellent shape, and it is surprisingly clean.

I do not know for sure that E.M. ever really owned this organ and hall as it seems to me that I remember hearing there was a $50,000 mortgage on the place. If this is true, I imagine the bank holding the mortgage would still retain title to the instrument, even though E.M. had the use of the place.

There are two E.M. stops in the organ, the first being an 8' spotted metal Principal with zinc bass, which I presume replaced the original Principal, and a Flute Harmonique 8' in the Great Organ also of spotted metal. Unfortunately, however, there are a great many ranks of pipes missing — at least fifteen sets.

Mechanically the instrument is still in first class condition, and the leather work in the chests is as good as new. Naturally, these magnificent chests, reservoirs, etc., will all be retained, but we are to do several things which I hope will increase the efficiency of the action. The repetition is bad, making clean phrasing quite difficult. While I do not believe we can make it as good as one of our modern instruments from this point of view, I think we can improve the present condition to a considerable extent.

Regarding the console, we are building a new remote control combination action and supplying a modern pedal board. We are rather hoping, however, to be able to retain the terraced jambs as at present.

Regarding the tonal side, the fact that many ranks are missing will enable perhaps a better scheme to be realized than if all the pipes were still there, particularly as I have insisted from the start that the general characteristics of the instrument should remain and be restored. When I was first called in, Arthur Howes and I concocted a suggested scheme, and later Ernest White and Carl Weinrich were called in as consultants to repeat the original history. White and Weinrich suggested some improvements to our original plan, and I think we have an excellent specification prepared, although even now it has not reached its final shape as changes may have to be made after a much more critical examination of the pipe work has been carried out, and perhaps after many ranks have been brought here to the plant. Much of the tone work at present is very sluggish in speech, which aggravates the mechanical defects already mentioned, and this we will rectify.

We are going to do the obvious things necessary to improve the organ for the playing of the literature of the instrument, at the same time retaining its present glory. The old Solo Organ is being turned into an enclosed Choir, and the old unenclosed Choir will become a Positiv. The Great will remain more or less as at present, except that we will rearrange the mixtures to some extent, as both of them have faults in their layouts, and both include tierce ranks. There will be some added mixture work to the Great.

The Pedal will be improved by a 2' reed and a mixture. The enclosed Choir (old Solo) will have a Cornet added to it, and there will be three Baroque reeds — Rankett, Cromorne and Rohr Schalmei 16', 8' and 4' respectively. The Swell will have two mixtures instead of the present single Mixture, the old pipes plus some new ones will go to make up this complement. There will also be four new reeds on this division — Fagotto 16', Trompette 8', Hautbois 8' and Clarion 4'.

The Positiv will be typical and quite complete, and will include a 16' Regal, which is the old Vox Humana with the 16' octave added, and the 4' free reed from the present Solo Organ, which is called Vox Angelica. There will be about twenty new sets of pipes to replace those that are missing, and some reeds which are unusable.

When we have the final specification I will be glad to let you have a copy.

I noticed your letter in the Diapason regarding the Germanic Organ, and think it would be a good idea to send a copy to the Harvard Alumni Bulletin, for in the past they have mentioned the Germanic Organ, and I think they will be quite interested.

We are beginning to get supplies and things are going along pretty well. We have greatly increased our help in the factory, and at the moment the future looks very bright.

I hear that Willis has secured a new factory, which is not far from the old place on Ferndale Road. I remember the building, and it would seem to be quite adequate for his purpose. It was originally built for making pianos. The English builders are having terrific difficulties due to the 100% tax, which I understand is still in force for new musical instruments.

Sincerely yours,

G. Donald Harrison

GDH:MGM

the Methuen Organ — See note, letter 57. The stoplist appears in the appendix.
these magnificent chests, reservoirs, etc. — When Edwin F. Searles moved the organ to Methuen from Boston Music Hall, his Methuen Organ Co. built all-new slider windchests to replace the original, German, cone-valve chests which had a long history of malfunctioning.

1st August, 1946

Mr. Wm. King Covell,
72 Washington Street,
Newport,
Rhode Island,
U.S.A.

Dear Covell,

Sorry to have been so long in replying to your letter of the 1st instant, but pressure of work has been, and continues to be, appalling.

I propose to inspire an article descriptive of the rehabilitation of the St. Paul's Cathedral Organ which will appear in the _Organ_ in due course; the task is not yet completed, although a part of the instrument was brought into use last Easter as I advised would be the case.

Further embellishments and improvements are being made, up to date of a minor but important nature, but some major additions are contemplated, have been prepared for, and will be carried out when funds permit and the iniquitious purchase tax, which still exists at a net incidence of 20 percent, is removed.

Christ Church, Westminster Bridge Road: organ was completely ruined by damage consequential to enemy action; salvage only was left.

We have been just over three months in these premises which are twice as commodious as the 'Rotunda' at Brixton, with a fine erecting Hall, but sadly war damaged and rehabilitation proceeds slowly on account of housing having priority over all other work.

You can have little idea of the severity of the housing problem in London. To give one example, there are three families in my own house. The others are relations, it is true, but congestion is awful — mine is not an isolated case. Every step to get back to reasonable condition is cribbed, cabined, and confined by well-intentioned, but non-practical government restrictions of every sort. Here we have government control to the nth degree well-intentioned — operated by a bureaucracy without commercial or business knowledge, hidebound by "regulations" which are sacrosanct despite the complete lack of common-sense in their operation: the result, to say the least, is unfortunate in imposing a brake upon general rehabilitation. But in view of the well-nigh hopeless confusion in countries who attempt to get on without controls, or who having had them attempt to discard them without rhyme or reason, our position is a happy one.

We are still largely engaged upon rehabilitation of war-damaged organs and the restoration work postponed throughout six years of war, but we are now carrying out rebuilds and in another year should be back to something like normal. With costs of new organs 100 percent above pre-war and 20 percent purchase tax, no new organs are being built, and the future in this direction is problematical until the churches become aware of the fact that costs are unlikely to fall for years — if ever.

I would very much like to visit the U.S. again, but this must be for the future — I cannot visualize the possibility of my being free to do so for a long time ahead.

Yours sincerely,
Henry Willis

---

167 Stephen Stoot to Ernest M. Skinner

September 13th, 1946

Mr. Ernest M. Skinner
78 Beacon Street
Chestnut Hill, Mass.

Dear Mr. Skinner,

Our recent letters seem to have the knack of crossing. Yours of the 3rd inst. and the post card arrived the day after I mailed my last letter to you.

Well, we have had the meeting of the directors, and the proposals you outlined, first by letter, and later to me verbally during my recent visit, were discussed in detail. It was felt that your proposals could not very well be entertained by the firm for various reasons, the chief one being the impossibility of our attempting to enter any orders for organ contracts in the U.S.A. in these difficult times due to the dearth of essential materials. We have no less than fifteen Canadian contracts postponed indefinitely from last year — two of them healthy four-manuals. Inquiries keep arriving from the U.S.A. directly to us as well as through our representatives, and we have to explain our inability to enter into any definite negotiations whilst conditions prevail as at present. Block-tin is not the only commodity holding us up over here. Therefore if we are unable to definitely entertain any projects sent in to us by the representatives we already have over the border, it will be obvious to you that it would be as difficult for us to consider the various projects which you so kindly offer to turn in our direction.

Your offer to make metal pipes for us might work out all right for an occasional small job or a re-construction, but the tradition of the Casavant firm has been to erect every job in its entirety (i.e. pipes and all) in our erecting rooms for a thorough test before dismantling and shipping, and the directors felt that this custom and tradition should be maintained.

Then again, another point was raised at the meeting, one that did not even occur to me when we were together recently. Your willingness to associate with us and couple your name with our own is appreciated at its true value, but the fact remains that your name, at least, is already coupled with that of another firm. I understand your hourly and daily chagrin over this fact, and how distasteful it must be to you, but it is so, and the directors wondered what the American public would think of your name being coupled with two firms which may be rivals for honors when the prevailing conditions change and the business of organbuilding be carried on as of yore. However, as we understand and appreciate your interest in our firm, we would value your help in the future in securing any major outstanding job for us through your influence with your old friends, and would endeavor to arrange a remuneration for such service which would be satisfactory to yourself and to us, but this could not apply to ordinary jobs of average size because we would encounter trouble with our other representatives in various sections of the U.S.A.

These, therefore, are the main reasons for the inability of Casavant Frères to enter into the proposals you outlined, and I have endeavored to give them as clearly as they were expressed during the recent discussion in our office.

Re: your need of a slider chest — we would be only too glad to help you out in this respect, but we have not a man in our factory who remembers one being made and how to go about it. The last slider chests of Casavant were made in 1902, and the old chaps who made them have long passed to their reward. Then again we simply have not the suitable lumber to construct one. A reliable slider chest demands the best that can be procured for bars, tables, sliders and topboards, and the method of construction must be considerably different to that which prevailed before the advent of steam-heated churches. If it be only suitable leather for puffs which holds you aloof from making your own style of modern chest, why don't you try to get some from England? We have procured good skins from Brewer & Hardy Limited, Bulwell, Nottingham, England.

Finally many thanks for your kind offer to show me your new remote-control in Washington Cathedral. I am sorry to say that I cannot spare the time to go there with you, enjoyable and interesting though the trip would be. At least as far as the next few weeks are concerned, it must remain a pleasure deferred.

With kindest regards, I remain,

Sincerely yours,

Stephen Stoot

SS/JS

Re: your need of a slider chest — See letter 196.

September 19, 1946

Henry Willis, Esq.
Henry Willis & Sons Ltd.
Rotunda Organ Works
34, Marlborough Grove
Old Kent Road
London, S.E.1, England
My dear Henry:

Thank you for your letter of August 20th, also the personal note of the same date, and also for the copy of the letter you wrote to Senator Richards. Regarding the latter, I must take full blame for the delay in the shipment of the sample pipes which Senator asked me to return to you many months ago. I asked the shipping department to attend to this, but they somehow got sidetracked. I have found them safely placed away in a tray, and they are being placed in a box, and will be shipped immediately.

I am sending you herewith the metal scale sheet according to American standard practice. We do not use this scale ratio exactly as it is, as our trebles widen out, and then we have many mongrel scales even for diapason and mixture ranks, so that if you see on one of our proposed specifications scale references, they will not convey to you exactly what we are using except for the lowest note.

I am glad you have such a good plant which is on the way. The cost of making it over is certainly terrific, but it will only be a matter of time before you work out of it. I went through a terrific upheaval during the war, which cost about $110,000.00, but I hope this will all be wiped off by the middle of next year. It was one of those rare instances where everything seemed to click according to the original plan.

Glad to hear that Dora is looking after you so well, and enjoys going around on inspections.

Helen seems to be somewhat sensitive about mixing up friendships with people who have in the past been so close. It is perhaps a little more difficult for her than the rest of us. Maybe in time she will work out of it. As you say, there is no immediate embarrassment as it will be some time before you can make a trip here, and I guess a long time before I can go to Europe, judging by the amount of work that is piling up.

I will be very glad to let you have our blueprints of the remote control machine. It may be a week or ten days before I can let you have it as our standard drawing will have to be brought up to date with the latest refinements incorporated. There is no guesswork about this machine. There are a great many of them out and they have been giving satisfactory service over a ten-year period.

Our total personnel amounts to about 85, but, of course, we do not have anything like the service business that you have, and only have the New York Branch, with a comparatively few service contracts being attended to by one man in Chicago, and working directly out of the Boston plant. The work on the Coast is handled by Stanley Williams, our representative, but we do not have any connection with it financially or otherwise. Our personnel is, therefore, largely concentrated on new work, and I am rather hoping the gross business for this year will be at least $375,000.00.

You probably noticed from the musical journals that we have the rebuild of the Old Boston Music Hall organ in the works. We are using the old slide chests, which are really magnificently-built affairs. They have the laminated top boards that the old firm used in England. I hope to make this into a really stunning job.

I can quite understand how tired you must be of the English diet, and agree that some of these foreign countries that are supposed to be starving are not too badly off. Recently it came to my notice through the father of an Italian girl who just arrived from Italy that in the North they seem to be doing very well, and in fact the girl was very anxious to immediately return as she seemed to think she was better off in Italy than in Boston. Except for her shoes, she was apparently very well-dressed — unbelievably so according to the father. The father happens to be a waiter in a restaurant I frequent quite often, so the story is quite direct, and not colored in any way.

With my best wishes to you both,

As ever,

Don

DH:MGM
Encl.

a restaurant I frequent — Harrison frequented the Café Amalfi, an Italian restaurant next to Symphony Hall, Boston.

---

169 Emerson Richards to William King Covell

November 12th, 1946

Mr. Wm. King Covell
72 Washington Street
Newport, Rhode Island
Dear King:

. . . Now, in regard to your letter of November 4th. I am afraid I was much harder on Compton than you were. As a matter of fact, Taylor seems to dominate the whole show including Compton and I regard him as the real author of the work they are doing. In the various discussions I had with Compton, he never would open his mouth about anything of an artistic nature unless Taylor was present and he always seemed to look to him to carry the burden of the conversation.

I had a very interesting experience at Downside [Abbey]. I was motoring through southwest England with a man I had hired in Southampton. I was anxious to see and hear the Downside organ. We arrived to put up at night at Bath. Strange to say, nobody at Bath knew where Downside was and my maps did not show it. I was told it lay southeast of the town and after starting in that direction, did pick up someone who said I was on the right road and that I would appear to see the Chapel at quite a distance. I arrived there about ten in the morning, but chapel was not quite completed, so I got my first impression of the organ from the back of the nave.

I asked the Verger to get the organist for me and that my name was Mr. Richards. A few minutes later, the Prior came rushing out to greet me and it was very lucky for me, although the apparent cordiality was a rather ridiculous mistake. It appears that there is a small Welsh organ builder by the name of Richards (my family were Welsh Quakers of the William Penn variety).

However, when he found out who I was, he was exceedingly cordial. He personally took me to the organ and played for me and showed me just what it could do. Compton had gone off with the key and after a good deal of trouble a duplicate was found and we had a look at the organ.

By this time, it was just about noon. The Prior invited me to lunch but I told him I wanted to get on and thanked him. He with a couple of the other brothers who had arrived in the meantime, escorted me out to the car. It was raining and I promised to show him a book of pictures of the big organ. He climbed into the car along side of me and soon became absorbed with the pictures and the two brothers remained in the rain. Perhaps 15 or 20 minutes went by when one of the men reminded him that it was long past lunch time. This did not disturb the Prior too much, but after five minutes he realized he was holding up the lunch. At this point he insisted that I have lunch, and without making it appear that I was ungracious in refusing their hospitality, I accepted.

It was a very novel experience. This is a very strict order and I think silence is one of their vows. In any event, there were at least 150 monks present at the midday meal and if there was any vow of abstinence, it was honored in the breach. It was an exceptionally good meal. I think one of the best I had in rural England, with plenty of wine to wash it down, after which the headmen gathered in the adjacent parlor for coffee and sweets.

I had of course been sat at the head table and the whole affair was a unique experience.

In London, I visited Compton's then-new factory. Taylor showed me the many interesting details of construction, particularly their elaborate use of plastics. He then showed me three or four of their better London jobs. I remember the organs, not the names of the Churches. In the course of our review of these organs, I told Taylor that any criticism would appear ungracious in view of the almost two days time he had taken with me. I also praised both the mechanical work and the individual voicing. I showed him why I could not agree that an extension organ could be successful. (How I had decided to use it in the event of doubling up the center of the extension ranks.) All this was rather new to him, and I told him that we had extension work that was equal to theirs. I told him that if he would come to America, I could show him the Kimball jobs that were as well-voiced as the work they were doing. This was a genuine surprise to him. Sometime after my return, I did state in an article published I think in the American Organist or maybe the Diapason, that English extension work is no better than our own and notwithstanding his attempts, Compton had not succeeded in building an ensemble organ.

It was curious how Willis kept Compton out of the picture, although I was his house guest. He did not take this attitude with other builders and had Walker and some of the others to dinner so that I could meet them and later review their work.

This brings me to the last paragraph of your letter. You should remember that I am a lawyer by profession and that habits of 40 years in viewing facts objectively have left me free of sensitiveness of the kind you evidently envisioned. Nothing makes me more suspicious than unrestrained praise of anything, more particularly of an organ. As I have told you, if I had heard this organ for the first time, I could have given it some critical appraisal, but having lived with the thing from the very beginning, it becomes an almost impossible job. One is too apt to make allowances, for one's ear becomes less critical through repetition. On the whole, I think your letter was on the restrained side and more fault could have been found than you have indicated. On the other hand in most instances we find we are in agreement.

Far from feeling hurt at anything you have said, I feel very grateful for the time you have taken from your other activities and certainly hope you will not be too long in honoring us with another visit. You are welcome at any time as you know, and I do hope that by early next spring we will have more of the organ.

Don seems to be up against a series of bottlenecks. Ralph Bolton is ill and sickness and injuries have seriously upset the pipe shop; while he still lacks sufficient good erection men to get clear of the material that has accumulated in the erecting room. Besides, they have been stuck with three or four rebuild jobs that were musts, including the Methuen Organ, which has delayed making the chest and pipe work for even a part of the Great and Positive. I hope we can clear this right up after the first of the year.

Did you note in this month's <u>Diapason</u> that Möller is going to undertake a Positive? This is something we ought to see.

With kindest personal regards, I am

Sincerely yours,
Emerson L. Richards

Dictated but not read by ELR
ELR/ar

---

170 G. Donald Harrison to William King Covell

November 19, 1946

Mr. Wm. King Covell
72 Washington Street
Newport, Rhode Island
Dear Mr. Covell:

Sorry to have been so long in acknowledging receipt of your letter of October 18th regarding the Senator's organ. I have read your comments with much interest and, of course, a great many of them are well-taken.

As you realize, the time is not yet ripe when one can really criticize the result, for in the first place the organ is incomplete, and no attempt has been made to finish it. The latter work on an instrument of this kind is a much greater task than we usually have to face, due to the use of so many second-hand materials in the first place, and also due to the extreme depth of the organ chambers which during the voicing make it pure guess work as to the proper power to impart to the various ranks. As you know, as the organ developed it has grown in size, and the Senator's ambition has been to produce an ideal tonal layout suitable for any purpose one can think of, and while this is a noble idea, it presents many difficulties under the conditions that exist in this particular case. Inevitably with an organ of this size, even when much second-hand material is used, the cost runs far more than is originally anticipated, and for that reason alone we have had to go somewhat slowly.

Between us, I more and more feel that large organs, except for enormous places, are unnecessary and wasteful. If I was building the organ for myself with the space that is available at Senator's home, I would have been content with a perfect instrument of about thirty-five or forty stops. With all such schemes as Senator's you get into a vicious circle, for if you

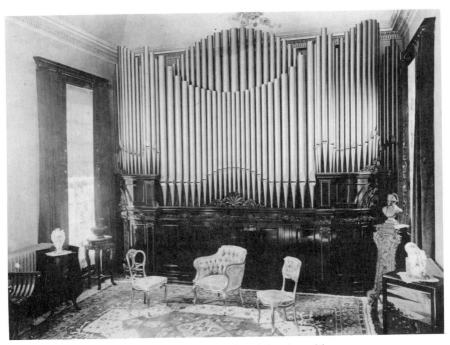

Estey organ of 1904 in the Richards residence.

decide to add to one division, it seems imperative to add to the rest to keep a balance, and so it goes on.

Regarding size of organs, let us just take as an example stops of the Celeste variety. It seems to me that when once you have a good string celeste and perhaps a quiet undulating voice of the Spitz Flute Celeste type, you have all that is necessary, except in an organ of considerable size. In other words, the adding of a pair of Echo strings or a pair of the Grosse Gambe type adds very little to the interpretation of any music that is worthwhile. It is true that when one meets a situation such as the Tabernacle in Salt Lake City, something heroic seems to be in order, but I think organs of that type should be very much the exception.

Many years ago someone of note in England, I forget who it was, made the pronouncement that a fifty stop organ was large enough for all purposes, and I am very sure there is a great deal of truth in the idea. With fifty stops you can provide an adequate Great and Positiv in the open, a Swell and Choir enclosed, and a suitable Pedal, and that kind of an organ will do anything in the way of good music that is available. You can often get by with many less stops with complete musical satisfaction.

The Richards residence organ in the late 1940s.

Of course, when we get the Senator's organ complete and properly balanced, regulated and fine-tuned, he will have an instrument on which you can demonstrate practically anything that has been done in organ building that is worth while, and after all that makes a job of considerable interest, and doubtless an organ that a great many people will want to hear and try. Senator is now engaged in having the organ put into better tune, and I am going down there over the Thanksgiving holiday to get a better idea what has to be done to get it into something like final shape, but I think it is going to be many months before this can be accomplished.

We are moving along at Methuen, and I am trying to get the job ready for the promised date, which is around the middle of February, 1947. I am looking forward to a very grand result, but regret the fact that nearly every pipe in the organ is cut too high and, of course, it is quite impossible to lower the mouth of every pipe. The result could have been much finer if the cutups had been in line with the classical builders.

When you are next in New York, drop in to see Ernest White. He has a new <u>multum in parvo</u> three-manual which has been erected in an old gymnasium, quite a resonant and large room. It is going to be quite something when it is completed. We have a few additions to make, but it will not be very long now before everything is set.

With kindest regards,

Sincerely yours,
G. Donald Harrison
President

GDH:MGM

drop in to see Ernest White — Opus 1080. The divisions included Great, Positiv, Swell I, Swell II, Pedal.

---

171 G. Donald Harrison to Henry Willis

December 4, 1946

Henry Willis, Esq.
Rotunda Organ Works
34, Marlborough Grove
Old Kent Road
London, S. E. 1
England

My dear Henry:

Thanks for your letter of October 7th. Sorry to say I am still not in a position to send you the drawings of our remote control combination action and the console mechanism that goes with it for the reason that we have been so rushed in the drafting room that we have not had time to bring these standard drawings up to date. However, one of our old draftsmen who left us during the war is back with us again, so from now on we will be in better shape and should catch up ere long.

Our force has been built up very considerably since I wrote you last, and we are adding to it all the time. We should have a gross business for 1946 of about $350,000, and we are aiming to jump this to about half a million in '47, and that is about the maximum I feel we can handle and maintain the quality standards we have set up in the last 10 years.

Michael tells me that he hopes to be around your place for a while until he can get out here, and I hope he can make himself of use to you. I will naturally greatly appreciate any facilities you can give him so that he can thoroughly familiarize himself with the technical data of running an organ plant and what goes into making a fine instrument. We have some extremely bright young fellows in our organization at this time, and it will be a great deal better for him if he has all the shop talk at his fingers' ends so that he is more or less in a position where they are not teaching him. It will be an asset also to be able to say that he has worked with you.

240

Regarding wages in our plant, they are running about an average of $1.00 per hour, and the men are paid a week's vacation and the usual holidays. This average is low due to the fact that we have taken on a great many trainees who are ex-servicemen receiving government aid. We work 43.75 hours a week, and, of course, the 3.75 is paid at time and one-half, so that a good week's pay is found in the pay envelopes. We have hourly rate men earning as much as $1.25 per hour and, of course, many salaried employees running as high as $65.00 a week. One advantage that we have in our plant over yours is that female help is allowed, and we find girls very useful for wiring and for small parts work. Their fingers are more nimble, and they are faster and more accurate than men, we find.

As yet no attempt has been made to unionize the shop, and I do not believe if it does come that it will ever originate from inside as our men are very high class people on the whole, and prefer individual bargaining to collective bargaining. It looks as if our new Congress is going to clip the wings of labor to some extent. They were given an outrageous amount of power by the Wagner Act which has been in force about ten years. Unless John L. Lewis and his cohorts ruin the country, it would appear that we are in for a long period of prosperity. The organ business is in better shape than it has ever been, and at present we have a million dollars' worth of untouched contracts protected against inflationary tendencies.

I will write again directly when the drawings are ready.

All the best,

As ever,
Don

GDH:MGM

Michael tells me — Harrison's two sons by his first marriage still lived in England.

---

172 Henry Willis to G. Donald Harrison

January 3rd, 1947

Mr. G. Donald Harrison, President
Aeolian-Skinner Organ Co.
Boston, 25 Mass., U.S.A.
My dear Don,

To reply to your letters of the 4th and 18th December, 1946.

Thanks for the information about wage conditions, etc. With us, the average skilled man now gets 2s./10d. an hour — but 50 percent of the staff are 3s./-, 3s./3d. and higher.

Keys. Our keys have for many years now been made by British Piano Actions (formerly Finnimores) as I found their work as good if not better than Schenstones, who anyway are now absorbed in the Herrburgen centre. British Piano Actions are now finishing the new four-manual set of keys for Canterbury Cathedral and, being the first big post-war job, on a cost basis, as they had no idea how costs will turn out. I have been to them, and they will be very willing to make a five-manual and any other sets of keys for you. Full drawings will be required. State thickness of ivory required, 10 cut or 8 cut (I always use 8 cut for important jobs) and if "heads and tails" or one piece as is the Willis standard; also, if desired, bleached or un-bleached (the latter now very difficult to match up). I will then obtain at least an approximate quotation for you. As it is only the ivories you cannot get in U.S.A. at reasonable thicknesses you may suggest that the ivories only be cut to your requirements and be forwarded for laying by your own keymakers. This latter course would, of course, be much more economical. I do not suppose that you have any difficulty regarding the ebony sharps.

<u>Reference reed shallots</u>. Williams makes ours to our own standards, but is under obligation not to supply our patterns to others. They make normal English trade shallots and would be glad to serve you and your ex-employee now in Sweden. Name and address of Williams given below. Mention my name when writing as that will ensure special attention.

Messrs. W. P. Williams & Co. Ltd.,
61, Hampton Gardens,
Southend-on-Sea,
Essex.

<u>Combination Action</u>. Will be glad to have those blue prints in due course.

<u>Michael</u>. He has a free run here but there is not any modern console work going on at the moment. We cannot get the electrical parts owing to shortage — government regulations, etc. — so he cannot see much of that side of things nor, of course, is he on the staff here, so it will not be possible for him to say that he has been with Willis. I am afraid that walking around the works for a few hours will not help Michael much, especially as most of the work going on is still rehabilitation.

As I was approaching a condition of nervous exhaustion I went away for a cruise — Lisbon-Canary Islands — from 11-31 December and enjoyed a rest and sunshine. Now back again and, as ever, up to the neck in work — three weeks' arrears to catch up.

Yours as ever,
Henry Willis

H.W./J.M.

January 15, 1947

George E. Judd, Esq., Manager
Boston Symphony Orchestra
Symphony Hall
Huntington Avenue
Boston 15, Massachusetts
Dear Mr. Judd:

In further reference to our recent correspondence regarding the Symphony Hall organ, I have made a careful checkup as to the condition of the instrument, and have also considered fully the various points raised in you letter of January 2nd.

I would like to deal firstly with the suggestion of using the organ located in Mrs. Dane's home to replace the present Hutchings instrument. In my opinion such a course would not solve the organ problem for many reasons. In the first place, the Dane organ was scaled and voiced for a residence, and is, therefore, unsuited tonally for an auditorium of the cubic capacity of Symphony Hall. In the second place, the instrument is nearly as old as the Symphony Hall organ, and much of the equipment is obsolete and would have to be replaced. Thirdly, considerable change would be necessary in the layout so as to suit the shallow chamber at Symphony Hall. Finally the cost of dismantling, shipping to our plant, completely rebuilding the mechanical parts and revoicing the pipes and installing in Symphony Hall would amount to close to that of a new organ.

Turning to the Hutchings organ now in Symphony Hall, my recent inspection of the instrument revealed the fact that both the materials and workmanship employed by the original builders were first class in every way, and much of the pipework is still in an excellent state of preservation, and can certainly be rehabilitated. On the other hand, a great deal of the mechanical equipment is obsolete, and must be entirely replaced. You have known for some time that a new console and combination action is necessary, and the blowing apparatus in the basement is also of obsolete pattern.

The wind chests upon which the pipes stand were of a new and unperfected type at the time the organ was constructed, resulting in sluggish action to a degree which makes it impossible for an organist to do fine work. There is at least half a second lag in the attack, and the repetition is extremely poor, which completely defeats the efforts of the finest player. While some of the slowness is due to the obsolete electric action, the chief difficulties are the chests, and unfortunately there is no way of overcoming this without replacement.

E. Power Biggs and G. Donald Harrison with pipes for Symphony Hall, Boston

The total cost of an organ is made up approximately as follows:

Pipes: 25 percent; console and combination action: 15 percent; the balance of 60 percent covers wind chests, reservoirs, windtrunking, electrical equipment, and installation and tone finishing. It will be seen, therefore, that any worthwhile reconstruction will run into at least 75 percent of the cost of a new organ as the only salvage is in the pipework and perhaps a few Pedal chests. Actually the required work amounts to the building of a new instrument, utilizing the best pipes and parts of the present organ. Anything short of this would be an unsatisfactory and patchwork job and in my opinion a waste of money. On the other hand, the new instrument would settle the organ problem for a further long period.

As you pointed out in your letter referred to above, there are many uses for the instrument in Symphony Hall, for example, it should be an ideal instrument for use with the orchestra, it should be suited to recital purposes, for the needs of the Symphony Hall tenants, and finally adapted to the requirements of both radio and recording. I believe that all these desirable functions can be fulfilled by an organ of reasonable size, and I have drawn up and enclose herewith a suggested specification for consideration. Attached to the specification is a description of the tonal layout, making reference to the various types of music which are likely to be played upon it.

Regarding the problem of a movable console, I feel very strongly that if at all possible a detachable union for the cables should be avoided, due to the large number of electrical connections which have to be made at any plug-in system. Even with modern equipment one must expect small failures from time to time, but any failure is irritating and can be disastrous. The suggestion to have an elevator for raising and lowering the console from the basement to the platform level seems to be an excellent one. With an elevator and rubber casters on the console the latter could be rolled off the elevator platform to any desired position on the stage, providing sufficient slack was allowed in the cable. The latter could be permanently attached to the console and extend down through an aperture in a platform of the elevator. This would entirely avoid any kind of plug-in arrangement. Doubtless a scheme could be worked out, and the elevator could be so placed that a minimum of flexible cable would be required, thus eliminating as far as possible failures in the cable due to flexing over the years.

The cost of the scheme outlined in the specification installed in Symphony Hall, but excluding the cost of the elevator, would amount to $52,360.00.

If I can be of any further assistance, please do not hesitate to call upon me.

Sincerely yours,
G. Donald Harrison
President

GDH:MGM
CC to E.P. Biggs

the organ ... Mrs. Dane's home ... the present Hutchings — the Dane residence had a four-manual Frazee with three 32' stops. The Symphony Hutchings was also a four-manual of 1900, built under the supervision of Ernest Skinner.
entirely avoid ... plug-in arrangement — such a system was ultimately adopted

February 6, 1947

Henry Willis, Esq.
Rotunda Organ Works
34, Marlborough Grove
Old Kent Road
London, S. E. 1
England
Dear Henry:

I got your letter regarding the combination action, and only yesterday afternoon I was down in our drafting room looking over the final drawings. I had some criticisms to make, and consequently some revisions are being made with the idea of clarifying as far as possible the whole situation. As I gazed at the drawings I could not help feeling that there may be many difficulties in the way of your making up the remote control action itself, and perhaps more particularly the action behind the knobs as certain essential parts are machine-made from our point of view, and when once we make a setup we are able to turn out many hundreds of small parts without difficulty. The whole action depends on accuracy of manufacture, and when you can make up in bulk small parts by the setting up of a machine you get the necessary accuracy without a lot of hand work.

The more I looked at the drawings the more I realized that it would be desirable to send you as many of the essential parts as possible in the form of models, and I am getting together a box of parts which are being shipped this week. Some of them were made for experimental purposes, and are none too hot as to manufacture, but they will at least give you the idea and explain many of the details which otherwise would seem obscure by merely perusing the drawings. With the drawings I am sending you a description which will explain as far as possible the essential features of the design and the pitfalls to be avoided. After a thorough perusal of the models and drawings please write me for further explanations, and I will give them to you without delay.

While I understand your attitude in regard to the matter of console details I can still appreciate Aubrey Allen's feelings as he has done so much to develop a great many of the all-electric mechanisms you have used, and which I saw during my last trip.

It is quite likely he can take our drawings and use the salient features plus his own ingenious ideas and make perhaps something better or something which is more easily manufactured by hand.

I am grateful for your promise to reciprocate in ideas. There is one thing I would rather like to have, and that is a model of your coupling system. I refer to the multiple contacts and coupler mechanism which I understand you incorporate between the keyboards. I don't know that we will ever employ it, for our own system is so completely reliable that one hates to depart from it, but the development in that direction that you have does seem to be an advance forward, and I would like to know about it.

With best wishes,

As ever,
Don

GDH:MGM

---

175 G. Donald Harrison to Henry Willis

February 6, 1947

Henry Willis, Esq.
Rotunda Organ Works
34, Marlborough Grove
Old Kent Road
London, S. E. 1
England

Dear Henry:

I have received your recent letters. The first one had to do with organ keys, and Michael, and the second about the combination action.

Dealing first with the organ keys, I will send you a drawing which you can submit to the manufacturers, and perhaps by the time they receive it they will be in a position to give at least an approximate price of making and sending us a five manual set with ivories 10-cut to the inch without surface joints. I do not believe the ivories alone would be of much use to us because the extra thickness of ivory would upset our keymakers' normal manufacture procedure and cause them to turn down the job. They have so much business that anything special is a terrific headache, and even to a good customer like ourselves they are not willing to make any concessions. They are frightfully shortsighted, and cannot look forward to the times when business will not be as brisk as it is today. The trouble is that keymaking in this country, large as it is, is almost a monopoly.

Regarding Michael, I understand perfectly that he cannot claim to have worked for you, and I will see to it that he does not use your name in any way when he comes to this country.

With best wishes,

As ever,
Don

GDH:MGM

May 20th, 1947

Dear Willis:

Thanks for your letter of March 13th. I received this letter just before going to Boston to check on the Millville Organ. When I called Don's attention to the experimental pipes he was sure they had been sent as ordered. But upon investigating it developed that they had gotten as far as the shipping department and stuck there because of some customs red tape. They went off at once and hope you have received them by now. I must send you Boner's conclusions about these pipes. The Charterhouse Diapason did the best in the test.

Don and Helen were down for the Easter holidays. They left just in time to meet Michael upon his arrival the following Monday. Later that week, Mrs. Richards and I attended the opening of Ernest White's new semi-Baroque organ and met Michael and his bride. They seemed very happy over their prospective adventure here and I understand that they are now settled in Boston and that Michael seems to be taken up with the organ work very readily.

There is not much new in the organ world. Don has so many orders now that no new ones can be taken under 30 months. Möller wants 24 months but is already more than six months behind on delivery. Prices are very high as I told you before and the situation at present is that on jobs of any size Möller is even higher than Harrison.

We have seen considerable of the Courboins this winter, because when we have been to New York on weekends, we have attended one of the musical services in the Cathedral and then usually going out to dinner afterwards. Consequently, we went out to the dedicatory recital of a new four-manual that Courboin architected and Don built. Charles is a great artist but I cannot agree with him on organ design. There was a very good organ in the west gallery which he removed and put the main organ including the Great and the Pedal in two sound proof chambers that are really a part of the twin towers. The sound struggles to get out but with feeble results. Charles showed me with great delight how the 32' reed could be used to accompany the Unda Maris. I could not concede that this proved anything. However, the church authorities liked the organ very much — so everybody but Don is satisfied.

Harrisburg is in the middle of the Pennsylvania Dutch country, and on our way home stopped in one of the characteristic inns in the neighborhood for a gigantic dinner, in which we counted more than 30 different kinds of food at once on the table — not like England. Charles and his wife have been down for a mid-week visit, and we had a good time with my organ

Emerson Richards, seated, his bride and the wedding party, including Don Harrison.

and also with the Millville job which is nearly finished. Millville is a two manual with 38 stops — a Great and Positive with 2 mixtures all very boldly voiced so that in a resonant church the organ sounds quite thrilling and very much bigger than it actually is. The Swell reeds give a very good account of themselves. The whole organ is quite a success, so that even Charles had to admit it had something that Harrisburg did not have.

I do not know where you got the idea we had so low an opinion of British activities. Of course some people who do not like Britain have said such things, but a great majority of people over here who have any opinion at all on the subject have felt you have done a good job managing backward people not able to take care of themselves. That the present government is kicking this all away is a matter of regret as well as concern to us. Now we have to take up the Greek and Turkish burden and perhaps a lot of other foreign commitments as well. Back of it all is the Russians. Underneath they are the ones who have stirred up India just as they have the Near East and all of our labor unions over here. Our patience is running out. If we must have trouble with Russia, we prefer to have it now while we have plenty of atom bombs and the will to use them.

I heard from Steinmeyer recently — the family is intact. Too bad your boy could not be with you now in this impressionable age.

Ernest White's new organ is all out Baroque and in the large room (formerly a small gymnasium) it kicks up quite a row. Fine for classic music and, when properly managed, for modern stuff as well. The organ is all exposed with a Great over one Swell box housing the reeds and the Positiv over the second Swell box housing the flues. The Great and Positiv pipes are all polished tin and floodlighted. White goes in for some bizarre effects. Even the Swell boxes are decorated in black and Chinese red.

The <u>Organ</u> and <u>Musical Opinion</u> just in, and I read with regret the death of Andrew Freeman. The weather over here has been rather cold and disagreeable. The season is nearly a month behind time. The hot weather is now on its way and I am beginning to think about Maine and the summer vacation.

With kindest personal regards, I remain

Sincerely yours,
Emerson Richards

ER/ar

the Millville organ — First Methodist Church, Millville, N.J., opus 1068, two-manual.
Ernest White's new organ — See letter 178.
a new four-manual Courboin architected — Market Square Presbyterian Church, Harrisburg, Pennsylvania, opus 1048, included two gallery divisions.

---

177 G. Donald Harrison to William King Covell

June 25, 1947

Mr. Wm King Covell
72 Washington Street
Newport, Rhode Island

Re: <u>Methuen Memorial Music Hall</u>
<u>Methuen, Mass.</u>

Dear Mr. Covell:

If I remember correctly, you would like to write up the rebuilt Methuen Organ, particularly as you wrote such a detailed article some years ago for the <u>Organ</u>. The instrument is now practically complete, except for some minor adjustments, so that by making arrangements with Mr. Howes you could probably try it at any time. It would be good to go there before they start their summer school on July 21st.

We do not have a typewritten corrected specification at the moment, and to save additional work, I am sending you the scheme as it appeared on the dedicatory program. Even in this case it was not quite accurate, but I have made the necessary changes so that you can take this scheme as authentic. The couplers and accessories are on a typewritten sheet which is also enclosed.

To save you much trouble, I am also enclosing a list of new stops in each division, together with notes of the rebuilding of some of the old material and the rearrangement of same. Under each division in this list if you do not find a stop mentioned that appears in the specification you will note that it is in its original position, and is virtually unchanged except for tuning and regulation.

As you know, the whole organ is completely straight, and there are no borrows or extensions of any kind.

Regarding the specification in general, although it mentions three consultants, what really happened was as follows:

Before the work was commenced the four of us got together at Methuen and a tentative specification was drawn, but, of course, it was impossible in so short a while to determine whether the substitutions and changes that were brought forward could be accommodated on the top boards, so that when I got down to business I had to completely rewrite the tonal scheme, bearing in mind the main points which we had all agreed upon originally. This latter specification was got out largely in consultation with Arthur Howes, and finally copies were sent to Messrs. Weinrich and White who automatically O.K'd them.

As we worked over the old material even further changes had to be made, as you can well imagine, and even at this late stage there are about 37 pipes to be installed.

As there were so many missing basses and complete stops the door was left open for a much more drastic change in the original instrument than would have been the case had it been complete at the time of the rebuild.

As out of the 112 ranks of pipes about 44 percent of them are entirely new, and most of the other work including all the mixtures have been rearranged and worked over as to be unrecognizable, there is really little of the old quality of sound left, and I think you will agree that it takes on generally an Aeolian-Skinner flavor.

I feel it is one of the most successful jobs I have done to date, and the general effect seems to me to be quite distinguished. There were certain limitations which prevent it from being entirely typical, the first being the size of the chests and the wind pressure. These remarks apply chiefly to the Swell which, from the modern standpoint, is perhaps small, although most people seem to be quite satisfied with it. Personally if the Swell reeds had been on 5", it would have been more in line and in balance with our normal treatment.

Other points of interest I would like to point out are as follows:

1. The new pipe work of the Great Organ in the case of the flue chorus is all of burnished tin, and I think if you will compare a typical sample with the old German work, you will find that our workmanship is superior in every way. Most of the rest of the new pipes are of spotted metal, with the exception of the Nachthorns, which traditionally are made of heavy metal to suit the required tone. The composition of the metals of the old pipes proved to be far less rich in tin than was thought to be the case. Those for example that looked like tin were really of about a spotted metal content. In fact the spots show in many cases on the inside of the pipes. Of course, the fact that they were burnished gives them a more or less bright appearance. Other stops, such as flutes, etc., were all of a composition ranging from 20-25 percent tin.

2. I would like to call your attention to the 4 to 6 rank Cornet on the Great which was made out of the old Great chorus, as you will see in my notes, and the fact that this was fairly large in scale I was able to give all ranks a copious supply of wind, and on the whole I feel it is a very successful stop, and curiously enough does not seem to interfere in counterpoint as is usually the case when mixtures are used that contain a tierce.

3. The four-rank Kleinmixtur on the Great is a new stop, deliberately made of smaller scale to use in lesser combinations and yet add some slight brilliance to the full. I did not want to overdo this so as to retain a good contrast between full Great and full Positiv.

4. Turning to the Positiv, I think you will agree it has turned out very successfully and adds greatly to the Great when coupled to it. If you are at Methuen within the next ten days, you will probably notice that the 8' Gedackt of the Positiv is on the thick side. I am replacing the middle of this stop from tenor C up to the top octave with a lighter type of tone.

5. In the case of the enclosed Choir Organ which plays from the fourth manual, you will see as far as the chest allowed we again followed modern Aeolian-Skinner practice in providing this division with a Baroque chorus of reeds and a small mixture. The 4' Regal seems to take everybody's fancy. Of course, an awful lot of work had to be done on this to make a success of it.

6. The Pedal Organ has been built up to form a bass for the entire instrument, and I think most of the additions and changes will be quite obvious to you. I must give Arthur Howes credit for the suggestion of tuning the top rank of the IV Grand Bourdon as a flat 7th. You will remember it was a 4' originally and did very little. Naturally the flat 7th helps the illusion in giving a 32' Resultant.

7. The 16' Bombarde of the Pedal is virtually new as the only part we used was the upper part of the resonators. This stop had been inserted by

old man Treat, and was quite something with its wooden leathered large scale shallots.

8. Some of the old stops that were used are not perfect or as good as we would have in a new instrument. A typical example is the 2' Waldflote on the Great, which is really too fat in scale in some registers and was cut up far too high. Although we lowered the mouths in some sections, it still leaves something to be desired I feel.

9. Turning to the mechanical improvements, the console accessories, etc., will be quite obvious to you, but in addition to those items we greatly improved the attack and repetition of the manual chests. The attack was improved by inserting lighter and more closely regulated armatures in the magnets, and re-regulating the primary valves. The repetition was improved by substituting new pallet springs, the old ones being on the weak side. Naturally, the draw stop action is still noisy and somewhat slow. That is inherent in the general setup of this type of chest.

One other point of interest is the fact that for the revoicing and voicing of the new work we bought and set up in our plant a slide chest voicing machine which I felt was necessary in view of the type of chest in the instrument. It certainly saved us much time in resetting the speech of pipes on the job.

You will notice that the couplers are so arranged as to be foolproof so that you cannot couple up the entire instrument with 16' and 4' couplers in play. This was done for two reasons. In the first place, I desired to keep up the trebles to a much greater extent than can be done where octave couplers form part of the ensemble. (We are following this same plan at Salt Lake City). Secondly, there is a peculiar acoustical situation in the hall which causes frequencies from pipes above about 6" C or a little longer to be more or less absorbed, causing falling off in strength. More or less heroic methods had to be taken to keep the trebles up.

Finally I would like to tell you that I greatly enjoyed doing this job as I was able to renew my acquaintanceship in a big way with slide chests. They have one advantage in regard to the initial speech for it is possible to voice with a higher position of the languid when a slide chest is used. This is due to the difference in the way the pressure builds up on opening the pallet as compared with the individual pallet chest. Theoretically with a slow pipe the tone is improved, and I think this is the case, and noticeably, when playing in a single register between about 4'C and 3" C. On the other hand, there are so many disadvantages with this type of chest that I have felt no temptation to return to the sliders. There is no doubt in my mind that the modern chest we use gives an attack and cutoff which enables much finer degrees of phrasing to be accurately performed, particularly in these days of high speed playing, so that the result in the long run is more musical, which after all is the real test. The ideal, however, would be to improve our chest so as to get the one advantage mentioned above for at least that section of the compass which is sensitive. This is a problem we hope to tackle in the near future.

If there are any more details that you would like to have, please let me know, and I will try to supply same.

With best wishes,

Sincerely yours,
G. Donald Harrison
President

GDH:MGM

Encls.

P.S. One thing I forgot to mention is the fact that a new set of swell shades giving a much bigger opening were installed.

P.P.S. — Since dictating the above the organ has been completed.

---

178 Henry Willis to G. Donald Harrison

19th August 1947

Mr. G. Donald Harrison
President,
Aeolian Skinner Organ Co.
Organ Builders,
Boston, 25, Mass. U.S.A.
Dear Don,

Ernest White's Organ: I read the specification of this instrument with some interest. White must be an experimentalist. No doubt the 32' reed in the Pedal is one of those German "bee's-in-the-bottle," a normal unit with a comic length resonator. The 32ft. pitch is obtained by "suggestion." I got a CCCC pipe from Germany years ago and found it amusing: the Haskell idea on a much reduced resonator length.

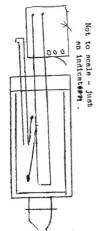

The division of the Swell into two Swell boxes (1) Flues (2) Reeds has its points — Audsley would have given it his approval, but, of course, pointing out that it did not go far enough and that the two Swell boxes should have been enclosed in one larger one. Simple enough to provide a space of say 2ft. in front of the two boxes as a "mixing chamber" with another set of shutters.

I wish I had an enthusiast or two of the Ernest White type over here!

Ernest White

You will be aware that we are facing critical times over here — the Socialist Government has, as Atlee quite correctly suggested, gone "too far and too fast." All the added costs of vastly extended and wholly desirable social services at a time when we have to struggle for economic existence, but it is hard times on the Socialists that this is their second experience of power at a time of severe economic world crisis.

Here, we are still equipping our new works, but it is a slow process, everything is in short supply and most difficult to obtain.

<u>Front drawstop action</u>. We made a model of this on the principle of the drawings you kindly sent, suitably adapted to our longer draw etc. and it is, of course, all right. But it is strange going back to pneumatic draws etc. after many years of all-electric work, but we still cannot obtain all the electrical components for our all-electric drawstop consoles.

Owing to this the consoles we are turning out at the moment, comparatively unimportant two- and three-manual jobs are tilting tablet or stop key, the latter an abomination, but actually selected and chosen by the church. Do you know that we are not allowed to have multiple covered 100 and 200 way, lead sheathed cables? The lead is forbidden.

I had an interesting time in Milan inspecting the big five-manual Mascione-Tamburini organ at the Duomo (Cathedral) there and intend to write a full dress article about it for the <u>Organ</u> when I have time — I hope for the January, 1948 issue.

I am giving a lecture — subject "The Organs of the Middle Ages" to the annual Congress of Organists which meets in London next week. I have dug up much of interest with regard to the re-introduction of registers and separation of ranks, having obtained some useful information from Germany and Italy.

As regards personal matters, old George Sinclair, now 77, has had another series of heart attacks and is in hospital as I write. Ettie left us, as she now lives in Paris after her marriage to Ravet — Chief Interpreter to U.N.E.S.C.O. The last we heard from "son" was from Burma "in transit;" where he is now I don't know, but it is doubtful if he will be demobilised until next year — then he will have to start here at the bottom and learn his job.

As regards living conditions over here, they are drab. There is no actual food shortage but the monotony is appalling. The average egg ration is one a week, when you can get it. Oranges one seldom sees and then for children — bananas likewise. I found the food situation in France to be much worse than ours because they, apparently, cannot organise fair distribution of what they have got. But North Italy does quite well and in Switzerland, well it's a land of plenty — almost at the pre-War level, but we English who go there cannot stomach the rich food and have to go carefully — I found it the same in Ireland.

Yours as ever,
H.W.

H.W./E.T.

George Sinclair — Secretary of the Willis firm at this time. Ettie was Willis' daughter.

---

179 G. Donald Harrison to Henry Willis

October 15, 1947

Mr. Henry Willis
Rotunda Organ Works
34 Marlborough Grove
London, S.E.1
England
My dear Henry:

Thanks for your letter of the 19th of August. The 32' Sakbutt so-called for Ernest White's organ was only prepared for, and I had not decided exactly how I was going to make this stop. It was to be a short length affair, but it will probably wind up being half-length.

I know about the "bee-in-the-bottle" type as per your sketch, but have never tried to make one as it did not impress me favorably enough.

As a matter of fact, I doubt if we will ever put a real 32' reed in this particular organ as Michael, since he has been here, has developed a really magnificent electronic 32' reed, and indeed it is so good that it seems sheer folly to use up all the material and space that one requires for the real thing. His device is capable of giving several 32' effects, such as the 32' Fagotto, 32' Bombarde, 32' Contre Bass and 32' Bourdon and, of course, some intermediate tones if you want them. It is by far the finest electronic device I have heard, and the boy certainly knows his stuff to be able to achieve this wonderful result in an extraordinarily short time compared with the years of experimentation that have been carried on by others.

We are not only making a 32' electronic reed for Ernest, but also 16', 8' and 4' Pedal reeds.

I see now that we could readily make more or less a complete Pedal Organ electronically, saving a great deal of material, expense and space without loss in artistic result. It has always been my idea to go into the electronic field in this way by using electrical equipment for stops one does not normally use alone, and which cost tremendous sums of money, and are, therefore, rarely available to the ordinary church.

I think it will be some time before we will attempt to build a completely electronic organ. We know the art now thoroughly well and all the methods that can be employed, and they all have their drawbacks one way or another unless you are willing to go into a complicated scheme which would cost nearly as much as the real thing. All the electronic organs that have been built in this country, and you will see there are four or five of them from the advertisements, have tremendous compromises in them, and they are all built to a price to capture the wide field that exists in the $1500.00 to $3500.00 class. The more of them that are brought out the merrier because that means that they are competing one with the other and cutting corners to offer a job somewhat cheaper than the others. There is not much to choose between the tone qualities, except that I do prefer the Baldwin and Allen types to the others.

Returning to the Ernest White organ, it is really a stunning instrument. We made some records on it, and when they are issued I will send you a set.

As you suggest, it must be a drab time over in England. I hope the country will get on its feet eventually.

I was much interested to hear of your trip to Milan, and will look forward to seeing an article about the instrument which is to appear in the January issue of The Organ.

George Sinclair has certainly done well to last so long. I am sorry to hear of his recent heart attack.

Old man Frank Taft died the day before yesterday. He had never been ill before. He was 87 and died of a ruptured appendix. The old boy had every tooth in his head, and not one of them was filled, which I think is somewhat of a record.

Will be glad to hear from you in due course.

With all best wishes,

As ever,

Don

GDH:MGM

P.S. Sorry to hear that George S. has passed on. [handwritten]

Frank Taft — Taft was formerly tonal director of Æolian. When Æolian and Skinner merged, Taft came over as a vice president.

---

180 Henry Willis to G. Donald Harrison

11th November, 1947

Mr. G. Donald Harrison
President
Aeolian Skinner Organ Co.
Organ Builders,
Boston, 25, Mass. U.S.A.

My dear Don,

Thanks for yours of the 15th October and news about Michael's success in producing acceptable electronic pedal reed effects. This is, of course, the first step in electronic development because reasonable results are possible without great difficulty and the unit can quite readily give several powers and qualities as named.

The snag, as I see it, is this — over here we service our own Organs, and, candidly, the average tuner, no matter how efficient at his job, would not be able to make the inevitable adjustments that any electronic device will require in time no matter which of the many systems available here are used.

No doubt you are aware of the many try-outs of pedal effects that have been made. Hill & Norman & Beards, for example, fitted a 32' electronic device at the Cinema-type job in the Dome Pavilion, Brighton; it has, so I am informed, been out of use for years by reason of the servicing difficulty.

The same firm fitted a similar device at St. Mary Abbots, Kensington — supplied to give a 32ft. Sub Bass effect. It was satisfactory at the time, as in that church with low reverberation period, it was most difficult to "find" the notes. I have not heard this device recently and, as it is in London, it may have been well-maintained.

If we were to install electronic stops in otherwise normal instruments, special arrangements for servicing would have to be made — otherwise deterioration would be inevitable — and an electronic stop or stops, successful on first installation, would give the entire organ a bad name.

We discussed this question with Michael "en extenso" before he joined you: it may be that he has devised apparatus proof against deterioration and not requiring frequent expert servicing, in which case he is to be most heartily congratulated upon a real triumph.

For the reasons given above my personal feeling is "all or nothing" — i.e. as and when we can produce an electronic instrument as good as a pipe organ we will do so, but at the moment it would cost some £,5000 to develop a successful prototype and I cannot afford it.

The deterioration of electronic instruments, as known over here, is their worst feature.

At Canterbury Cathedral, the Hammond loaned free by that firm as an advertisement no doubt, seems to require frequent servicing — the site of the apparatus is one mass of discarded valves and other components.

We have recently installed a three-manual at St. Michael's, replacing a Compton electronic which had literally worn out, so marked was the tonal deterioration.

But in the U.S.A., where you seldom are able to service your organs, no doubt a really good, reliable and knowledgeable serviceman may be able to give the requisite attention.

Generators: We are now employing transformer-rectifiers in place of generators and have a design which gives approximate results to that of an overcompounded generator. This is valuable and important as generators are now unprocurable. Save 12 to 15 months delay and we can get the transformer-rectifier in seven months — which is good delivery over here in these strange unnerving times.

I have not yet had time to write that article about the Milan Cathedral for the Organ and doubt if I can do it in time for January 1948 issue.

My boy, now a Lieutenant in the Queen's Royal Regiment, and in Ceylon, hopes to repatriated early next year and released shortly after return — February or March we hope. He has a hard time in front of him for he will come into the works and start at the bottom.

The Incorporated Society of Organ Builders: is launched — the council did me the honour of electing me as the first President and Herbert Norman Vice President.

This is a professional body and, of course, disassociated from the F.M.O.B. — which is a trade organization. We have no provision for honorary degrees, but the society is not necessarily limited to British members and if you cared to apply for membership I would be very pleased to propose you and arrange for a seconder: fees as follows:

	Entrance Fee.	Annual Sub.
Fellow: (F.I.S.O.B.)	£21. 0.0	£5. 5.0
Associate: (A.I.S.O.B.)	£10.10.0	£2.12.6.

Member: (M.I.S.O.B.)   £ 5. 5.0   £1. 1.0.

By the way — you remember the two springtype micrometers I had from Skinners for the quick assessment of tongue brass thicknesses. These were destroyed at Ferndale Road: the use of the normal micrometer gauge is a painfully slow process and it would be a great help to have one of the spring type — unprocurable over here.

We are not supposed or allowed to write begging letters asking for gifts from the U.S.A. — whether for food or anything else — and we cannot send money to a hard-currency country, or I would have asked you to send me one. If, however, you did send me one as a wholly unexpected gift it would be greatly appreciated and the time may come when I may be able to repay you in some other way.

If you would like samples of the grid key-contact system I will endeavour to send them — if permitted by controls to do so!

Yours as ever,
H.W.

H.W./J.M.

---

181 Henry Willis to Emerson Richards

10th December, 1947

Mr. Emerson Richards
800 Schwehm Building
Atlantic City,
New Jersey,
U.S.A.

My dear Richards,

Pray excuse delay in replying to your most interesting letter of 16th September — I am quite overwhelmed with work and seem to have no time for personal matters.

Marcel Dupré has been with us and had a most successful tour — he is the colossus of the organ playing world. His public recital at Westminster Cathedral was a stupendous success.

Yes, I read all about the rebuild of the Methuen job and rejoice so much fine old work has been revoiced, improved and is in use again.

Here we continue to carry on chiefly with reparations and rebuilds of various sizes: the conditions are more than difficult and do not seem to be improving. Costs are sky-high — over 125 percent above pre-war, labor alone represents over 70 percent increase and materials — when obtainable — prices are terrific.

How we can carry on and survive appears incredible, but we do.

The personal strain upon me has been eased by the addition to our staff of G.B. Cartright who has taken charge of Maintenance, acts as Office Manager and general duties assisting me. Thompson-Allen is, of course, wholly absorbed in his job in superintendence of works and production. Our branches — Liverpool, Scotland (works in Edinburgh), Sheffield, Nottingham and now Bristol — take care of the maintenance etc. repair, and all voicing and revoicing work is done here under, as ever, my personal direction.

Canterbury Cathedral rebuild is coming along slowly — progress much restricted by lack of material, especially electrical components: we have nothing else of outstanding importance in hand.

At Canterbury the Great, Swell and three-quarters of the Pedal are in use from a temporary console — the new big one, all drawstop, is taking shape here slowly, for the reason named.

My boy is on his way back from Ceylon as I write and there is hope of his demobilization in two or three months.

I have heard from Don with interest of experiments with electronic pedal basses. We have kept off this sort of thing because, chiefly, service difficulties after installation — such servicing being somewhat beyond the ordinary tuner.

There is one thing I wish you could, with delicacy, remind Don about, the experimental pipes sent over before the war have not yet been returned to me and I would be glad to have them. Perhaps a word from you "Oh — by the way have you sent those pipes back to H.W." might have the desired result!

With all best wishes for Xmas and 1948.

Yours as ever,
H.W.

---

182 G. Donald Harrison to William King Covell

January 19, 1948

Mr. Wm. King Covell
72 Washington Street
Newport, Rhode Island
Dear Mr. Covell:

Thanks for your letter of the 1st instant, and for the article on the Methuen organ. I am returning same herewith as requested.

In the text I have made two changes — one has reference to the Pedal 16' Contre Basse. I have cut out the reference to our mutual friend the Senator for he had nothing whatever to do with this development. I used this in 1927 before I was ever friendly with him. The second is in connection with the Pedal Nachthorn. The pipes are cylindrical (not tapered).

Regarding the opinions you express, they are your own, and I wouldn't change them. Of course, I think you have carried the point of "sacrilege" too far for it permeates the whole article, and takes the place of other material that might be of greater interest to the reader. For example, there is nothing describing the flue chorus as a whole, or how it compares with other big organs. Nothing about the general effectiveness or otherwise of the various departments from the point of view of playing the music. There is no comprehensive statement about the general tonal plan which follows the developments that have taken place over here in recent years.

I am not asking you to change it, for it is satisfactory to me as it is, but I feel you have missed the boat, so to speak, and it is not nearly as good an article as you usually write. It is intended for <u>The Organ</u> I take it, and for such use it is not nearly as interesting as it might be.

In Europe, as you know, they are surrounded with much finer organs than this one of the same and earlier periods. These Walckers are looked down upon as being mediocre to say the least.

Naturally my approach was influenced by what I know of British and foreign organs of the same period, and on close examination of many of the pipes I became out of patience with the second rate workmanship of the pipemakers and the poor voicing. High cut-ups with low pressure, they should have known better than that. The high cut wood flutes did not have anything like the charm of a Johnson Stopped Diapason, and their blending capacity was non-existent.

That low octave of the Great String Double was useless for playing any kind of music, the speech being slower than anything I have ever heard. If I could have fixed the speech, it would still be there. The pipes were built like Hohlflötes with inverted mouths, and you simply can't get promptness with this construction even if you are looking for a flute tone.

The above are just samples of things that struck me while reading, and please don't take them too seriously because as I have said above, it suits me without change. I mention them solely because I don't think you have done yourself justice as a fine writer on this subject.

With best regards,

Sincerely yours,
G. Donald Harrison

GDH:MGM
Encl.

May 10, 1948

Mr. Wm. King Covell
72 Washington Street
Newport, Rhode Island
Dear Mr. Covell:

Thanks for your letter of April 23rd giving me the highlights of your recent visit to New Jersey.

Yes, the Convention Hall organ is such a monster that any article would be too long if details are to be considered. There is much good in the organ and the Great Diapason chorus is a heroic sound. I cannot see that the organ need have been so large nor does unification seem to have been necessary or desirable in such a scheme.

I agree with much you have to say about the Bridgeton, Deerfield and Millville jobs. The latter is, of course, the best of the three on all counts. I am sorry a third manual was not provided for the Positiv. The latter does speak out well, due to its location at the top of the organ. Personally, I much prefer a stopped rank as the 8' of a Positiv and have never been able to agree with Senator on that point. I would like to give more careful consideration and carry out certain unusual tests before making up my mind on the matter of the pedal Mixture. I have a very great liking for the unison and quint type.

The Millville organ is now far too crowded and I think this is a pity because an instrument of this kind can never be kept in good shape. It is the worst we have ever done in this regard. The Senator is apt to pour things in. . . .

I remember Mr. Helffrich before the war. He was a very artistic fellow. I didn't know he had passed away.

I will look forward to seeing the Methuen article in the <u>Organ</u> and will let you have my reactions.

Kind regards,

Sincerely yours,

G. Donald Harrison

GDH/MGM

Conventional Hall organ — Atlantic City
Millville — See note, letter 176.

August 3rd, 1948

My dear Willis,

In your last letter you asked me about the various American electronic organs. I had not replied as to this because I had not had heretofore a good opportunity to compare them. This did come at the recent A.G.O. Convention at St. Louis where they were demonstrated. The reaction was much the same as mine with those that discussed them, particularly Walter and Maurice Hardy. Walter as you may remember used to be the head of the Kimball Organ Department and now is the mid-western sales manager for Aeolian-Skinner and an experienced organ man. Maurice has had a lot of organ experience and now is one of the head men in the technical branch of Zenith radio. Maurice has just perfected an improved record changer for Zenith which he says was a waste of time because all record changers will be outmoded by the new long-playing records. Columbia has perfected and already pressed one and a half million of the new records. They play 45 minutes. The records run at less than half speed and the grooves are only .003 of an inch apart. The tone production is better than on the old records, there being less surface noise. Zenith has the jump on the other manufacturers having their new machines ready for the market, and also an adapter for use with old machines. Of course if you can put a whole symphony on one side of a record, there is not much future for record changers.

Returning to the electronic organs, we agreed that they rated about as follows. Taking the Hammond as the standard with which you are familiar, the Allen is the best tonally and the most organ-like. But since it has generators for each tone and pitch, it is almost as expensive as a real pipe organ. A medium sized two manual costs about $15,000 and up and is still not an organ.

The Baldwin rates just a little better than the Hammond, and the Wurlitzer just a little below tonally. They are substantially in the same price range, about $3,000. The Connsonata, made by Conn instruments, is the poorest, having very little harmonic development.

Michael Harrison, now with Aeolian-Skinner, has recently developed a 32' electronic reed which when voiced as a rather smooth Contra Fagotto is quite good. Even the attack and decay are produced. Single pedal notes only are attempted and these match on and extend the 16' reed with good effect. This has been done with Ernest White's new studio organ and is successful. If the amplification is pushed into the Trombone class the illusion appears to me to be lost. Michael has provided a means of converting the tone to the Bourdon class, but this seems to have all the faults of the real pipes (direction & etc.) without the compensating advantages. The construction cost seems to be cheap. I understand that

Harrison intends to limit its use to pedal extensions although they are now experimenting with a 16' octave. It will be useful where either space or funds are limited.

For the first time (this summer) Aeolian-Skinner had two five-manual consoles on the floor at once. One replaces that terrible job that controlled the Riverside (New York) Hook & Hastings. This organ is later to be replaced by an Aeolian-Skinner. The other is for the big organ now being installed in the Mormon Tabernacle, part of which is now playing.

The A.G.O. Convention was a success, although the weather was very hot, as it nearly always is in St. Louis in the summer. The best playing was by Purvis, and the highlight was the organ-orchestra recital. I read a paper on future trends in organ design. Taking the position that the chorus organ with vocal and orchestral combinations would be the ensemble of the future. This will be possible because our younger Americans are taking to orchestral instruments in a big way. We now have 164 really full-sized orchestras, over 100 opera companies, and 22,000 high school and college bands and orchestras.

Organ building is still in about the same condition as when last I wrote. Don is doing by far the best work, both tonally and mechanically. Some of his newest jobs are really distinguished. Möller comes in a poor second tonally, although mechanically their organs are good. Deliveries are slow from both. About two years now. And both are getting extraordinary prices — almost an average of $1,000 a voice. The smaller builders are getting business but not doing anything distinguished, if we except Holtkamp, who has gone off the deep end in the Baroque direction.

Your Westminster article just came in. Thanks. It will be filed with your Rotundas, all of which I have bound. Also interested in the Milan article. Covell, who arrived on Friday for a visit, heard some of these organs and agrees with you. I have been in the Duomo many times and considering the acoustics I think that a low pressure organ, properly voiced and scaled would be successful. I think these Italian builders just don't know how.

I guess this about brings us up to date. Will be glad to hear from you when you have the time. We are here until late in September. Cool and comfortable and only a few visitors. This is an ideal spot for rest amid beautiful surroundings. Lakes and mountains combined. Our St. Louis trip turned into a 3,400 mile auto trip besides two and a half days on the steamer from Buffalo to Chicago. In October we go South to Miami, Florida to attend a military convention and probably also to New Orleans and then home for the winter and apparently a heavy professional schedule.

With best regards,
Emerson Richards

ER H

the best playing was by Purvis — Richard Purvis, for many years the organist of Grace Cathedral, San Francisco

---

185 G. Donald Harrison to E. Power Biggs

August 11, 1948

Mr. E. Power Biggs
c/o Boston Symphony Orchestra
Tanglewood, Mass.

Dear Jim:

Thanks for your letter. Bolton reports you had a marvelous reception at the concert.

You are really great when the members of the public demand an autograph.

I have had a terrific time this summer due to sickness in our engineering department. Three out of four out for weeks! Perry Martin will never return.

I had hoped by now to have working drawings of the new Symphony job, but that must now await a couple of weeks.

This is something we cannot delay longer, and I will look forward to going into the whole thing directly when you return. We must settle what we are going to do about the front. Some nice sketches are required but we will have to wait a short time to get these.

We have checked all measurements and old pipe scales, etc. Also, the materials are mostly procured so we are OK at that end. The elevator seems to be all set. It is to be made now and put in next year.

That center flat of front pipes are awfully heavy to deal with in the way you suggested. Would they stand for (1) eliminating them and showing inside Positive and Great pipes (2) substituting a hinged grill in two halves that could be opened readily.

Be thinking!

I miss you both and look forward to your return.

As ever,

G. Donald Harrison

GDH:AGR

Perry Martin — See note, letter 156.

December 21, 1948

<u>AIR MAIL</u>
Henry Willis, Esquire
34 Marlborough Grove
Old Kent Road
London S. E. l., England
My dear Henry:

I am enclosing herewith a letter which I trust will be helpful to you in the matter of the Concert Hall organ.

The enclosed photographs are of the console of the new Tabernacle organ at Salt Lake City. I have just returned after spending a couple of weeks on the job and I am returning after Christmas to see the finish. It is by far the finest organ in the United States. It has the advantage of a perfect location and ideal acoustics.

You will be interested to note that there are no coupler tablets. The fact that there are comparatively few couplers for so large an organ and that the intramanual couplers are with their own departments, it was decided to use drawknobs for all of them. *[sic]* The pedal couplers form the inner group on the left jamb and the intermanual occupy a similar position in the right jamb. There are 20 general pistons. The fifth manual plays the Antiphonal organ only.

The console case is of solid walnut and was designed and built in our shop. The motifs follow those found in the organ case. It is unnecessarily large, as the couplers and combinations are remote. They wanted an imposing appearance, hence the size and fifth manual! Believe it or not, but a million visitors pass through the Tabernacle each year and must be suitably impressed.

The organ contains Great, Swell, Choir, Positiv, Bombarde, Solo and Pedal divisions, plus a small Antiphonal. The Great, Positiv, Bombarde and Pedal are all unenclosed. There are about 190 independent ranks counting a four rank mixture as four.

A descriptive folder is being prepared and I will forward a copy shortly. It carries my tonal ideas, which started in 1935 in the Groton School instrument, to their logical conclusions. I was given my own way in everything and had to contend solely with two sympathetic organists.

As ever,

Don

GDH:AGR

31st December, 1948

Mr. G. Donald Harrison,
President,
Aeolian-Skinner Organ Co.,
Crescent Avenue
Dorchester,
Boston 25, Mass., U.S.A.
My dear Don,

Thanks for the photo of the Mormon Tabernacle console — a very fine piece of work. Interesting that the couplers are not by tablets but by knobs with the stops. Same as I am doing for Canterbury Cathedral — the new console will be finished in a few weeks when I will send you a photo.

Console,
Riverside
Church

By the way, you approached me about keys with 8 cut ivory on this job, but no developments — so I suppose you are obliged to use the standard "Grand Piano" 16 cut.

But here is a criticism which I know you will accept in the spirit it is offered.

The new console at Riverside for Virgil Fox is, in my opinion, the ugliest, and unhandiest, large drawstop console to which my attention has been drawn.

I say nothing of the stop grouping in threes or twos as fancy — it seems to be liked in U.S.A. — nor of the apparent lack of added vertical space between departments. Nor the two rows of tablets over the fifth manual and no music desk (it would be useless as out of sight) looks strange. But as for the arrangement of the toe pistons — help! You remember Hanley Town Hall toe pistons coming around in a full turning — but square returns!

The swell pedals look ridiculous to me — the wide space in between reminding me of the old console at Wanamakers, Philadelphia.

Of course, this is Virgil Fox's design — not yours — and I suppose you took the line that he could have what he wanted.

But I think that no organist should be allowed to impose his own pet idiosyncrasies on an instrument over which he, temporarily, presides.

Yours as ever,
H.W.

H.W./J.M.

---

188 Henry Willis to G. Donald Harrison

31st December, 1948.

Mr. G. Donald Harrison,
President,
Aeolian-Skinner Organ Co.,
Crescent Avenue
Dorchester,
Boston 25, Mass.,
U.S.A.

My dear Don,

Thanks for your letter of the 21st and prompt reply to mine of the 6th December.

Concert Hall Organ: I can now tell you that the new Concert Hall is part of the 1951 celebrations — the centenary of the 1851 Exhibition. The hall is to be built on the South bank of the Thames between the L.C.C. County Hall and Waterloo Bridge. To seat 3,000 — reverberation period full, 2.2 seconds.

The organ consultant, whose scheme I sent you, is Ralph Downes. He was, as you know, at Princetown [sic] and now at the Brompton Oratory.

At the Oratory there is an old Bishop that had been through Walker's hands. Downes wanted certain alterations carried out of which Walkers did not approve, so Downes went to a small firm named Kingsgate-Davidson & Co. and the principal — Davidson — is engaged in carrying out Downes' wishes.

I met Downes at the Oratory recently to find out what he was doing to his own job — as a guide to his ideas about the Concert Hall.

The general idea is lowering of wind pressures, removing all weights from basses of chorus reeds, toning off the power of all flue stops from about treble F fading away to a 50 percent drop at the top note: the sole exception being a Plein Jeu, 5 ranks. The lower octave only of the Pedal reed — now on 4¼" — has been fitted with French reeds and tongues without weights and [voiced] "all out." The lower octave of the 32ft. reed (an extension of the 16ft.) similarly treated but they do not appear to be able to apply the required voicing technique and the result is — well, irregular — a kindly description. With a few Nazards and Tierces shoved in here and there — made out of old flutes and so forth.

The organ sounds like a very poor imitation of a late 17th century French instrument but without proper upper work.

Downes specializes in the rendition of old organ music and plays it well. Has, so I understand, been to France and heard the ancient job at St. Gervais-sur-l'Ile, Paris, and one or two Cavaillé-Colls — Notre Dame and St. Sulpice for example. He is influenced by the neo-Baroque revival in Germany of the 1920's — of which he knows little — and by your neo-classical designs so well written up by Emerson Richards, but even more by the Parisian school of precious young (and old) men who praise everything pre-Cavaillé-Coll, and want to revert to the late 17th century period. The Society "L'Amis de l'orgue" is the journal of this crowd which is headed by André Marchal. This "school" avowedly wish to convert the superb productions of Cavaillé-Coll to their ideals.

The firm of Gonzales — under the supervision, I regret to say, of Joseph Bonnet — emasculated the Cavaillé-Coll job at the Trocadero (now the Palais Chaillot) in that manner — I heard it after it was butchered.

To return to the new Concert Hall — here is a hall of modern even austere design and, to my mind, nothing could be less suitable to it than an organ on French 17th century lines, with ultra subdued trebles.

I would be most interested to have the specification for the new organ for the Symphony Hall — it would be most useful.

You know that I am not in full sympathy with the designs you and Emerson Richards advocate, preferring to maintain the middle path without extreme swing of the pendulum in either direction — but most certainly utilizing all the best of all periods in a homogeneous whole.

But I am confident that you would not advocate the return to the 17th century or the vandalistic treatment of Cavaillé-Coll or Willis organs.

Your summing up of Downes' scheme damns it with faint praise.

Anyway, Downes is now reconsidering the whole matter and appears to be open to be reasoned with — so let us hope for the best.

Yours as ever,
H.W.

H.W./J.M.
Copy sent to Hon. Emerson Richards

L.C.C. Hall — now known as Royal Festival Hall

---

189 Henry Willis to G. Donald Harrison

31st December, 1948.

Mr. G. Donald Harrison,
President,
Aeolian-Skinner Organ Co.,
Crescent Avenue
Dorchester,
Boston 25, Mass.,
U.S.A.

<u>Strictly Private & Confidential</u>

My dear Don,

<u>St. Peter's, Rome</u>: The position is as follows:

<u>Fernando Germani wants a Willis organ</u>: We drew up the specifications, copy sent you, together. The Vatican decided that opinions should be obtained from the <u>leading</u> organ builders of the world. At my suggestion, the organbuilders invited to consider the specification were: Henry Willis & Sons, Ltd., Aeolian-Skinner, Casavant and Steinmeyer, and in that order they were sent out. Italian organ-builders not asked but later to be invited to cooperate for the provision of basic parts.

The Italian cost of production is just under half our cost of production and this, combined with strong Italian national feeling, is creating difficulty. The upshot may be that I will be called in as consultant and will direct the two Italian firms Mascioni and Tamburini as best I can — supplying all the chorus reeds.

I know St. Peter's, Rome, and the proposed site. Here is a case where light pressure work for the main organ would be useless, and we — that is Ferdy and I — specified the use of really high pressures, and scale in accordance. The siting of the main divisions of the organ in the Apsidal wall — extreme East and well behind the High Altar — leaves no other course possible. In such a case, there could be no drive behind the light pressure work and effect would depend upon glittering upper work <u>in excelsis</u>. This is the Italian style as exemplified at the Duomo, Milan, of which organ I wrote an article in the <u>Organ</u> which you may have seen, and which Ferdy describes as a complete failure.

I understand that you have not yet replied to the letter from Mgr. Inichini inviting consideration of the specification and asking for suggestions.

Anyway, you know the lines I am working upon.

Yours as ever,
Henry

H.W./J.M.

---

190 Emerson Richards to Henry Willis

January 6, 1949

Henry Willis
Rotunda Organ Works
34 Marlborough Grove
Old Kent Road
London, S.E.1, England
My dear Willis,

This comments upon your letter of December 31 to Don. None of us had guessed Downes, perhaps because we would hardly think of him as an organ consultant.

I do remember that he did some vandalistic things to Don's organ at Princeton, such as cutting down the flue trebles and the mixtures until the organ lost all its fire, but I hardly imagine him attempting a thing of this kind.

Evidently the reaction of the various influences that have moved him from time to time has not been in the interests of a critical understanding of the subject or of any clarity of thought either as to cause or effect. There is not much to add to what I have already said except that the background that you now supply indicates an even more questionable success than even we had already predicted.

The average French reed, as made by a Frenchman, and the thing that Don has developed are so radically different that normal experience with French reeds leaves you quite unprepared for the Harrison variety. I can best describe Don's reeds as having all of the refinement and sophistication of a Willis reed plus the aggressive blaze of the French reed. Mechanically, Don's reeds are soundly built. The resonators are in just proportions to the shallots and the reeds. The whole thing is combined together without tension or strain, so that while open shallots are used with a rather light reed, the entire combination is in accord. The result is a very musical thing for all of its harmonic development. The tubes are organ metal even in the lower octaves, with spotted metal bells. They're expensive but they are

William King Covell, William H. Barnes, Frank Bozyan and Edward B. Gammons at Barnes' home in Evanston, Illinois.

really very fine. In my organ we carried down the Trombone to the CCC, without weights, and with very light weights on the 32', but on all such work, slender resonators are required if the whole pipe is to be kept in phase. Consequently, the tone is never going to be extremely loud and the result is more a coloring of the Flues than a domination.

I think I should say that what you call Neo-Classical and what we have been calling American-Classic is nothing quite so radical as you have implied. I only wish I could have you for an hour at the two manual at Millville. I think you would agree with everything we have done. In the Covell, Gammons, Flint, Bozyan party last week they were utterly amazed at the ensemble and this after just hearing a new and larger Möller.

Our contrasting divisions are not new and they are not certainly far from what you yourself habitually do. If we are keeping more of the pipe work out of the Swell boxes, I think you, as an artistic voicer, could well sympathize with our motives. After all, our Positives are nothing more than a complement to the Great, or if you want to look at it in that way, as really part of the Great Organ. The fact that it is on separate chests gives us a chance for greater flexibility, a flexibility that permits the use of this division on the Great at 16' (resulting in a most solid ensemble) as just one example. Also it makes it easier to play certain types of music.

I do not believe that Don has, as yet, finally determined the specification of the Boston Symphony job. You must remember that there is a large four manual Hutchings in there now, that the pipe work of this was really magnificent and some of it Don hopes to use again or failing that to use the material. Therefore, he will not be able to make a final specification of the job until he has removed the old organ and gotten it down to the factory. This will not take place until the end of the concert season, probably in April. For that reason, Don has only discussed his plans in general with nothing too specific.

I know you will think me quite nutty but to help Don out and to make room for another "spree," I have sold my latest organ to a church in Denver, Colorado, Don making the Great and transporting and setting the whole thing up there. They wanted an organ in a hurry and were willing to pay a price that just made it unreasonable not to sell the present instrument. So for the next two or three years, I'll be busy building a new one. Of course, it will show some refinements in design over the other organ.

And speaking of these jobs, you could hardly call the design of my organ really radical. It so happens that I have just finished a design for an organ to be located in Oklahoma and since it is just about the same size as the job you are discussing, I thought you might be interested in a preliminary draft of the stop list. I am therefore enclosing it. In money, this runs around $96,000, more if they add a 32' Fagott to the Swell Chorus.

I think these actual designs go to prove that we have not gotten so far from the "middle of the road" as to be in the gutter.

Don is off today for Denver where my organ goes and then the final finish of the Salt Lake Organ.

With best regards, I am,

Sincerely,

Emerson Richards

ER:af

I have sold my latest organ — It went to First Baptist Church, Denver.

January 7th, 1949

Mons. Guido Anichini,
R. MO Capitolo
Di S. Pietro in Vaticano,
Citta del Vaticano,
Italy.

Dear Mons. Anichini:

I must apologize for the delay in answering your letter regarding the proposed organ for St. Peters. I have been extremely busy with current work and wanted to give the specifications, which you have forwarded, very careful consideration in view of the extreme importance of the matter.

Unfortunately, I have never had the privilege of being in this great Cathedral, so cannot speak with the same authority as I could do if I was completely familiar with all the problems that will arise. Naturally, I am aware of the vastness of the edifice and realize that heroic methods will have to be employed to ensure success.

A great deal depends on the location of the instrument. If at all possible, the main organ should be installed in a dominating position in the open and not enclosed in organ chambers. From long experience, I cannot stress too strongly the importance of this matter. With any organ, proper location is considerably more than half the battle and, in this particular case, it should be made the number one problem. I realize that an open location often calls for much elaborate casework — perhaps a suitable pipe-front could be designed and installed and the woodwork added at a later date.

Turning to the actual specification, I find it to be a very complete and impressive tonal scheme. It follows quite closely some of the larger Willis organs built in England, which have proved to be very successful.

I would like to see at least two additional mixtures added to the Great Organ, comprising Octave and Quint sounding ranks and believe this could be done by leaving out two of the 8' Principals.

I feel the Swell Cornet is an essential mixture to include in the scheme.

In my opinion, the mixture work in the Tuba Organ is essential. There should be two rather than the one proposed; a Fourniture VI and a Grosse Fourniture IV. This will enable the ranks of the 16' harmonic series to be drawn separately. In much contrapuntal music, the 16' series are objectionable.

In the pedal, it would be better if the various ranks could be complete in themselves rather than extended to various pitches. In such an important instrument this should be done.

Regarding the scaling and wind-pressures to be employed, a more intimate knowledge is necessary for me to give a proper opinion. The location of the various divisions will have a bearing on these matters. The layout of the Mixtures is also a matter of paramount importance but particulars are not given of same.

If I can be of further assistance, please let me hear from you.

In closing, may I send a message to Mr. Germani. Please tell him that I had the great pleasure recently of hearing a superb record of the Franck A Minor Chorale, which he made in Westminster Cathedral. The interpretation struck me as being really authentic and the playing is magnificent throughout. I am sure he would receive a warm welcome in the U.S.A. if he should decide to make a recital tour.

With best wishes for 1949.

Very respectfully yours,
G. Donald Harrison

GDH/JB

---

192 G. Donald Harrison to Ralph Downes (handwritten)

January 14, 1949

Ralph Downes
London, England.

My dear Ralph,

Nice to hear from you, and interested to hear of your project. I am in Salt Lake putting the finishing touches to the "giant," see specification enclosed. It is somewhat larger than yours but along the same lines.

Musically speaking, it is the most beautiful organ I have ever heard, partly due, to be sure, to the superb location and acoustics. What you are proposing to do I have been experimenting with since 1935 at the Groton School. That is a modern organ in which the old (Classical) and new are so modified so as to blend into one whole, so that any worthwhile organ music can be played properly. Salt Lake Tabernacle represents the fruit of all my labor rolled into one organ. I can assure you it does something to the nervous system!

Turning to your scheme and your ideas, I think they are generally sound, the second effort is much better than the original. But I shudder to think of the result, for the task is a tremendous one when you are dealing with a builder who doesn't understand and over whom you will have little pressure. The responsibilities are divided and you have to be sure you don't get into a mess. I say this because I know of the difficulties. After all, I have been developing over 20 years with complete command over efficient men. However, more power to you.

Let me warn against the use of imported stops. The tie-in between flues and reeds is an important matter and should be controlled by one person, the builder. After all, the whole thing about French reeds is the dome-headed straight shallot (Trompette Ordinaire). These can be bought in France, but the complete stops voiced — NO! You will be disappointed with them. Something will have appeared to happen to them crossing the English Channel!

To your actual scheme, I think some material is wasted in your Grand department. In the playing of music, I feel the 16' harmonic series are fine on paper but of limited usefulness. Why not put the chief members of your Grand in with the Great? With modern combination action, the separation is less important. Forget theory and be practical musically. You can probably save enough to include an unenclosed Bombarde organ (not 16' series) but rather a super Great. See Salt Lake scheme. The latter has turned out wonderfully. There is a quality about the grand tutti which enables you to put left hand on Bombarde and carry with it full great and anything that may be coupled to it. Your Front and Back Positives seem to be unnecessary. Why not combine them and place in a very forward and prominent position? More independence is necessary on the Pedal, see notes on returned scheme.

On Salt Lake note Swell 32' Fagot and 5⅓' Trompette. All have French shallots. I included the 32' with my tongue in my cheek — but the effect is wonderful. In Salt Lake also I controlled the couplers. In other words, 16' and 4' couplers intra and inter manual only affect selected ranks. By the way, the six rank Cornet of Bombarde 1-8-12-15-17-19 (IV to VI) can be used as a solo stop.

Now in regard to scaling and ratios, you are getting into a deep subject. I have experimented for years with same and have long given up any ratios such as halving on the 17th, etc. throughout the compass. Most of my Classical scales have various ratios throughout, the mutations and flutes especially so. They are big in the treble. The main thing is to keep your cut-up low, lower and lower in the treble as scales increase.

In 1936 I visited Germany complete with drawing equipment. I soon gave up taking measurements and decided it was better to absorb the musical result and then reproduce them in a modern way and in a manner that would be acceptable to modern ears and in our buildings. Providing you obtain clarity in polyphonic music, what more can you ask, providing you add and blend in romantic and modern material.

Salt Lake has proved to me a theory I have had for a long time, namely that the finest ensemble is produced by many ranks, none of which is loud in themselves. The result by these means is terrific and yet does not hurt the sensitive ear.

I hope you can read all this. You seem to be in a hurry and I thought I had better write at once rather than delay. I hope this will be useful to you. Watch your step! If I can be of further help, let me know.

With best of luck,

As ever,
Don

---

193 G. Donald Harrison to Henry Willis (handwritten)

January 16th, 1949

Mr. Henry Willis
Rotunda Organ Works
34 Marlborough Grove
Old Kent Road
London, S.E.1, England
My Dear Henry,

Thanks for your letter of the Dec. 31st last, acknowledging receipt of the Salt Lake City pictures. I am in that City now and the organ was finished today. I am enclosing herewith specification which was prepared by the local Guild. I gave them a talk this evening with demonstrations.

Today I had the great pleasure of a visit from Marcel [Dupré] who was playing at Provo 145 miles from here last night. He came over here especially to see the organ and gave it a good workout. He seemed to be much pleased. It is my finest job and it will be a long time before I get such another chance. Free hand, perfect location and perfect acoustics.

There is always something new. The large towers of front pipes which look like a 32' Violone of metal are made of wood. Some guy in Brigham Young's days built the darned things in the 1860's. They are as good as new and the tone is excellent.

Yes, I did approach you about the 8 cut ivory keys. The cost was too high and the time of delivery too indefinite. After all they don't make the job sound any better.

Your criticism of the Riverside console is well taken but you might modify some of your views if you actually examined it. When you are dealing entirely with detached consoles, if you use the English two rows per department arrangement you would have to build a skyscraper. I see no point to it. The music rack is not nearly as bad as you imagine. The number of couplers is essential when you are dealing with Chancel and West End organs plus a 15 stop Echo all in one instrument. I have no use for the double organ idea.

Regarding the width of the Swell pedals with gaps. We have built one more extreme job than Riverside in this regard, Grace Church New York.

With narrow shoes plus clearance you can get five in where four would normally go with equal safety in clearance. Who cares about appearance and who sees them with the bench in place? It is a matter of efficiency in playing music.

The Riverside console is normal in most respects; the added controls can be ignored by a visiting or future organist. You should hear the results that Virgil Fox can produce with this set up.

Regarding St. Peter's Rome, I am enclosing a copy of my reply which I trust will be useful. The scheme is Liverpool with some additions. That is now 30 years old! I have yet to be convinced that it is the correct solution. The job that you described in the <u>Organ</u> can easily be a failure when carried out in the manner described. I have little faith in the Italian organ builders.

Regarding the concert job in London, I thought of Ralph Downes but couldn't figure how he could be chosen an expert in such a job.

All the best,
Don

Hope you can read this! It is 12:15 A.M. and I am a bit tired after a strenuous day. Can't smoke or drink in Salt Lake City!!!

---

194 G. Donald Harrison to Ralph Downes (handwritten)

January 16, 1949

Ralph Downes
London, England.
My dear Ralph,

In further reference to my recent letter I feel I should have said more about the scales. I think your 8' Principals are O.K., but the 4' Octaves and Mixture scales are all too small. Forget English and French procedure on these scales, for the Germans had them down cold in the Classical period.

The 4' is the crux of the whole thing. It can be at least one scale bigger than your 8' and a slower ratio than the 8'. It can be broad in tone. If you get this right, your 8' can well be a flute! In Salt Lake, the largest scaled pipes of the Diapason type are found in the Fourniture and Cornet, particularly in the trebles. Don't let anybody talk you out of this. You must, of course, keep cut up low. Never more than ¼ of mouth width for a quarter mouth and less in treble. Give them plenty of wind. The English and French systems are poor by comparison.

You want to aim at a satisfactory full organ without reeds (which are useless for polyphonic music) except in the pedal. Glad to see you neatly avoided the 5⅓ in your mixture breaks until well out of the range of fugal passages. The larger the scales used in mixtures, the more the resultant

Ralph W. Downes

effects count. They are very valuable if they reinforce 8' and 4' pitches, but you don't want the undercurrent produced by the 5⅓!

Yours,
Don

P.S. Salt Lake finished today: wish you could hear it! I believe you would be pleased. There is something about it that gets you! Dupré blew in unexpectedly today and tried it out.

---

195 G. Donald Harrison to Henry Willis

February 3, 1949

Mr. Henry Willis
Henry Willis & Sons Ltd.
Rotunda Organ Works
34, Marlborough Grove, Old Kent Road,
London, S.E.1, England
My Dear Henry,

    Thanks for your letter of December 31st re: Concert Hall. I guessed that Ralph Downes may have had something to do with the specifications. How did he get the job?

    I have heard about the Oratory "improvements." One thing, he <u>is</u> a good musician and player.

Yours as ever,
Don

GDH/MOK

February 16, 1949

Dear Mr. Willis;

I am at this moment rather sick at heart. It was a sorry day for me when I ever accepted the services of Donald Harrison. Through the jealousy of Arthur Marks, I was frozen out of the company I had worked so many years to build up, which would not have happened if Harrison were not there to take my place. But that is over and is not what is bothering me now.

Harrison has had contracts for rebuilding three of my organs, built 30 or more years ago. In every instance he has removed and scrapped the 32' Pedal Open Diapasons, one of the most ancient and impressive of all organ voices.

The latest instance regards Symphony Hall Boston, where the Boston Symphony Orchestra holds forth and where all the big choral works are done. What do you think of that, and what would you do about it in my place?

Well, I am doing what I can by writing people of influence and hope something will come of my efforts.

The people of America are very queer. A foreigner always gets the preference. Frankly Henry, will you please write and tell me what you think of discarding 32' Diapasons from big four-manual organs, or three-manuals for that matter?

Never mind the shallots I asked for. It was one scale in particular that I wanted, and I was silly enough to think you might know what it was, forgetting that you were very young when I was over there the first time and got said shallot. I have the dimensions of it, but the tone does not seem the same. I think I shall have to try different scales and stems.

In a year or so I hope to get over there again and have a look around and see what is doing. I have soured on my pitman chest, as the way pneumatic leather (sumac) is tanned now it is only good for about 18 years. So I am back to the slider chest, which I treat as I did the other chest by tubing off the basses, which enables me to reduce all valve motions to about ⅛". I have perfected a pneumatic action for the slider chest which makes it as fast as you can work the knob and with perfect silence.

I never make normal Trumpets larger than 4" but used to make them larger. If I want more power I use greater pressure. But most of my work now is on 5" pressure. If you are in the mind to make me one low C of your standard Trumpets, 4" scale, I should like to have it. The one which gives the warmest tone without being tubby. Do you ever use my French Horn? I heard that you did but were making a tuning roll to reduce the pocket, which is in my opinion a risky thing to do, as the quality of tone depends on the depth of pocket and this permits the passing tuner to put it all out of character. If it is made right in the first place, why change the pocket or make it possible to change it? and by passing tuners?

Good luck to you,

Ernest M. Skinner

The latest instance regards Symphony Hall — although the installation was supervised by Skinner, the original Symphony instrument was a Hutchings. See letter 173.

---

197 Henry Willis to Emerson Richards

16th February, 1949

Hon. Emerson Richards,
800 Schwehm Building
Atlantic City,
New Jersey,
U.S.A.

My dear Richards,

Thanks for yours of the 26th January.

The new L.C.C. Concert Hall is to be a permanent building and the organ likewise.

There has been a rumpus about the proposed importation of French stops. Downes' first specification specified that 21 of the more important stops were to be supplied by a little French organ builder named Rochesson of Pontoise, near Paris. As a matter of interest I obtained his prices and the somewhat surprising admission that he did not make pipes but bought them from a trade maker — Mesure Frères of Paris. Enquiries show that they bought their eschallots, tongues etc., from another part maker — Bertounech of Hery (Yonne). So Rochesson was to be a middleman, but offered his incomparable art for the voicing (at a stiff figure).

Downes had told me that Rochesson was a descendant of Cavaillé-Coll, especially gifted and so forth. I made enquiries from Bouchet of Debièrre et Cie (Nantes) who was Technical Director of the firm of Cavaillé-Coll in its last stages, and he replied that there was no truth in the claim and that Rochesson was "better at the spoken word than for the speaking pipe."

At the beginning of January, the L.C.C. sent around to certain selected firms a list of 78 stops with Rochesson's (high) prices. This was taken as a clear suggestion that the 78 (out of 100) should be obtained from Rochesson. The matter was reported to The Federation of Master Organ Builders, who sent a letter signed jointly by The National Union of Musical Instrument Makers — the Trade Union — protesting against the suggested importation of stops from France that could be produced at least as well, if not better, in this country to the detriment of the skill and labour of our men.

This letter has caused a flutter in the L.C.C. domicile and may shake them on the point. They immediately 'phoned up to say that their list etc. was only sent to aid the British organ builders in case the stops could not be produced in this country in the time available. (Organ to be ready for the 1951 Exhibition.) Whereas, in the first provisional specification, 21 stops were marked R in blue pencil, and when it was asked what it meant the reply was "stops to be supplied by Rochesson."

The amended Specification not yet to hand, this apparently being due to the fact that Downes is suffering from some complaint which interferes with the use of his fingers — can't play or write.

Downes has shown his preliminary specification to other Organists, notably Thalben-Ball (President of the Royal College of Organists), who tried to point out the error of his ways.

It will be most interesting to see what happens. I take a somewhat detached view because it is obvious that I could not work to a specification with which I was not in sympathy, nor suffer deviation on tonal lines.

Salisbury Cathedral. Among my grandfather's bigger jobs this was the only one where the Swell chorus reeds were on the comparatively light pressure of 4½" — with A set reeds unfilled. The norm was 7" and C set reeds.

Hence the effect tends toward French lines although, of course, really very different. I retained them exactly as they were, (non harmonic etc.) in my rebuild of 1934.

Reeds. I sent many sets over to Skinner but have no records — destroyed during the war.

Bonavia-Hunt's latest book was written by an amateur for amateurs — no need to say more.

Oklahoma: As I wrote you, it should prove a very fine instrument. All right — tremolos on unenclosed Positifs — I have just specified one!

I believe in naming a stop Cornet only when it is in the classical tradition.

Production cost. Chief trouble is the awful cost of lumber — all through Government Trade Commission — and so costs far more than it should. Machinery we have. But the staff are not giving even the pre-War output on the same 44-hour week — but quite 20 percent less.

Ever sincerely,
Henry Willis

H.W./J.M.

17th. February, 1949

Mr. G. Donald Harrison,
President,
Aeolian-Skinner Organ Co.,
Crescent Avenue, Dorchester,
Boston, 25, Mass., U.S.A.

My dear Don,

Thanks for yours of the 16th January and specification of the Salt Lake City job. It certainly is a superb specification. Here are some comments:

Great Organ: No reeds. Don't you think that a family of even light pressure reeds would be advantageous? I lost a nice job recently by specifying an all-flue Great without reeds!

Swell Organ: Only one query. Quint Trompette 5⅓ ft. How come? I dislike all such specimens that I have heard.

Choir Organ: Zauberflöte. I personally do not think these harmonic stopped pipes are worthwhile.

Positiv Organ: Delightful — I would have liked to have seen a 16ft. Quintade or similar.

Solo Organ: What! No Cor Anglais 16ft.? I am using a free reed 16ft. Cor Anglais at Canterbury Cathedral.

Bombarde: Pressures seem low. Hall presumed to have a high reverberation period and resonance. Presume reeds all French type shallots.

Antiphonal: Very nice — but seems redundant.

Pedal: A superb stop list.

"Mechanicals": As no mention of an Antiphonal swell pedal, I presume worked from Choir or Solo Pedal. Don't you use swell pedal switch-plates — any pedal on any shoe etc.?

The job must sound superb — I judge on the lines of a refined Cavaillé-Coll — plus. I would greatly like to hear it.

Consoles: A matter of taste. I dislike stopknob grouping in threes. As regards height — well, at the huge 1940 all-electric drawstop console at Liverpool Cathedral, every stop can be conveniently reached without shifting from normal central seating on the organ bench: all stops arranged in standard double-columns.

For big consoles there is much to say for tilting-tablets. I was much impressed by the very neat yet large console at the Duomo, Milan, where tilting-tablets are fitted.

Over here, there is no standardisation whatsoever — all drawstop, drawstop and tablets or stop-keys, all stop knobs, all tilting-tablets, luminous stops, tablets between the keys — all have their protagonists. We have done several all stop-key consoles recently by request and have several

Henry Willis III at a console in the factory

in hand. I am not keen on them but they are certainly small, neat, and much less costly than the drawstop type.

But appearance means a lot here and a majority of organists plump for drawstops for 3 manuals and larger; all two manuals are tilting-tablets or stop-key type.

St. Peter's, Rome: The Liverpool Cathedral job made a tremendous impression on Germani when he was here last year. Playing from the 1940 console you can hear the job perfectly. The specification sent you for St.P/R was, as you say, Liverpool Cathedral Organ with additions — chiefly mutations and mixtures. I expect to be going to Rome shortly for consultation on details. An immense church.

Thanks for sending me a copy of your letter to Monsignor Anichini which will be most helpful to me, and I greatly appreciate the generous spirit shown.

In case you have not heard — I was able to reconcile Germani with LaBerge and G[ermani] has signed a contract to tour the U.S. next fall. F. G[ermani] has developed very greatly since you heard him in execution, registration, style and taste, with an impeccable gift for the translation of the older organ music. One of the greatest artists that the world has produced. G[ermani] is, in my opinion, fully mature, and I can only hope that prolonged and tiring tours will enable him to continue to give of his genius — a genius based on hard thought and hard work.

L.C.C. Concert Hall: Downes brought in by "a very high official" (obviously a Roman Catholic) — it is guessed who this is — but "no names no pack drill."

We are overwhelmed with work but little of an outstanding nature. Now that the flood of rehabilitation work on jobs damaged by enemy action is dying away — and War Damage payments drying up — the money is not available at our awful costs of today.

St. Paul's: I hope to finish this job shortly. Diapason Chorus to install in S.E. Quarter Dome (opposite where the Tubas and most of the Pedal Organ in N.E. Quarter Dome — including a big Cymbale). Choir — with a baby Cymbale — will be finished shortly, and some rounding off, filling in and additions in Solo, Dome and Chancel Pedal sections.

The Dome Diapason Chorus is on 6" wind.

Yours as ever,
H.W.

H.W./J.M
Copy sent Mr. A. T[hompson]-A[llen].

St. Paul's — St. Paul's Cathedral, London. See letter 158.

---

199 Henry Willis to Mr. Möller

28th February, 1949

Mr. Möller,
M.P. Möller Organ Co.,
Hagerstown,
Maryland,
U.S.A.
Dear Mr. Möller,

I read in the <u>Diapason</u> that your firm has recently made some improvements on Willis lines to the old Ernest Skinner Organ in St. Thomas Episcopal Church, New York, and I would be most grateful if you would advise me what has been done. I am particularly interested in this instrument because in 1928 — on one of my visits to the U.S. as consultant to the Skinner Organ Co. — Dr. Tertius Noble asked me to put in some decent upper work and mixtures. I gave Skinner's an exact specification — scales and voicing particulars — but when the stops were ready in the job for finishing I found that the interpretation of my detail not correctly fulfilled, and I did what was possible in the church with the stops concerned.

My personal records were destroyed by enemy action but to my recollection — after over 22 years — in 1926 the new stops were Great 15th and Mixture, Swell likewise, the 4ft. Principals being pulled up in power. Anyway, Dr. Noble was delighted at the freshening up of the upper work.

It would be interesting to learn who is your Technical Director on the tonal side — since Whitelegg's death.

With kindest personal regards,

Sincerely yours,

Henry Willis

H.W./J.M.

in 1928 — Mr. Willis is not known to have visited in 1928. Perhaps he meant 1926.

---

200 Emerson Richards to William King Covell

March 2, 1949

W. King Covell
72 Washington Street
Newport, Rhode Island
My dear King:

I am sending you a carbon of the manuscript as sent to Smets. The footnotes explain themselves. I have made some small suggestions on your copy only for shortening the article. The redlines first, the blue second. It seems hard to leave anything else out.

Now about your letter of February 25 and your post card of February 27th, which both arrived together.

Yesterday, Tuesday afternoon, I called Don and told him, on account of the snow, I would postpone my trip to the factory until next week. He told me that they had plenty of snow and therefore it was wise to postpone it. Therefore, I will not be able to comment on the Positives until next week.

With regard to the article, it can hardly be improved upon. As you say, it can now rest until next summer. Perhaps we can go over it at the camp at our leisure.

Nashua: While I was talking over the phone to Don, I asked him about this job. He told me that Ned was in complete charge of the rebuild, and it was done exactly as he wanted it and he, Don, was not invited to make any suggestions. I told Don you thought the job could have been improved upon but he said that Gammons was alone responsible and that I could tell you that. I read to him your post card about Salt Lake and he was immensely pleased.

Boston Symphony: The reason that the design is still up in the air, although a contract has been executed, is that Don himself has not yet decided many important points. Most of these center around the use of some of the old pipework. Don says that the pipes are well-made and under ordinary circumstances would be considered usable again, but he will not determine this until he actually has the organ at the factory and can put these voices on the machine to see if they can be brought in line with his ideas without too much alteration and cost. If it's going to cost nearly as much to revoice the old set to make and voice a new set, then he prefers to toss the old ones into the melting pot and start anew. This means that the actual size and disposition of the organ cannot be determined by him until this survey has been made. I think Don feels that this organ must be a masterpiece in keeping with the traditions of Symphony Hall. Therefore, whether it will be a three- or four-manual and just what tonal selections will be made depends on the salvage from the old organ. Apparently, the deal is that this organ will be as large as the money plus the salvage will admit, with Don making the mental reservation that the organ will be as perfect as he can make it within the allotted size of money.

So, the actual contract is rather meaningless and the actual organ may vary greatly from the text of the contract. Only one thing is assured. This is one job that will have Don's personal attention in every detail. I do not know how much Don expects to talk to me about this job, but I am to go to the Hall and look it over next week. However, this will settle nothing since Don is determined to take no chances and will do nothing final until the pipes are at the factory, and with this viewpoint I agree. After all, the Millville and Salt Lake results were not obtained by using old pipes and standard procedures. Don must have entire freedom in selecting his materials and in no way be cramped by the inherent qualities of old pipes that no method of revoicing will eliminate. Organ pipes have a personality that can not be gotten rid of, no matter how drastic the treatment. A Hagerstown pipe will smell of Möller and the charm of a Johnson Stopped Diapason will persist in spite of what a voicer may do to them.

I am not arguing that some critical advice might not help Don with this job. I am only pointing out that from his viewpoint, the time is not right to discuss it. After all, Don has taken a lot of advice since he came into authority at Aeolian-Skinner, but in his own way and with regard to his artistic ideals. Of course, there are limitations, some Don's, some forced by the fact that he has a business to preserve and 100 families to support.

Organ Cases: As a matter of principle, both Don and I like to see an organ decently housed. I revel in a beautiful case, but I think Don and I look upon the case problem this way. There is just so much money for the organ and never enough. What goes into the case must come out of the

288

organ. To us a beautifully carved pipe shade is a Nazard or a Tierce lost from the organ. A cunningly designed tower may have cost us a second double on the Great. No factory has its own case makers. Tradition has always separated the two crafts so that the modern German method of grouping the pipes and letting them show has much to commend it.

Running an organ factory for fame is oratorically sound but economically unconvincing. Fame is a moody harlot that counts not upon social security. She may live in a garret with genius one day and depart to live with opulent mediocrity the next. An organ builder gains no credit for his organ by reason of the case, although the case may contribute to destroying an otherwise fine instrument. Organ cases of fine design are much to be desired but if we can't have both the fine case and the fine organ, I say, forget the case.

I have some new books in, all French and German, including Ellerhorst — Handbuch, written in 1936. It runs 825 pages and took me all last evening just to cut them. There are many illustrations and some things of obvious interest. Mostly, however, it deals with German philosophy and mechanics that are pretty well dated now, and Ellerhorst apparently never heard of the United States and only one or two English organs.

Some of the French stuff is very interesting. Many fine pictures of organ cases.

Well, I must quit. Will write you after the Boston trip.

Sincerely,
Emerson L. Richards

ER:af
Enc.

Ellerhorst — a noted German book on pipe scales.

---

201 G. Donald Harrison to Henry Willis

March 8, 1949

Henry Willis, Esq.
Henry Willis & Sons, Ltd.
34 Marlborough Grove
Old Kent Road
London, S.E.1, England
My dear Henry:

Thanks for your letter of February 17th regarding the Salt Lake City organ. Regarding the absence of reeds on the Great Organ, I should say that there is one 16' semi-Baroque reed prepared for, and in fact the chest is already there, but we let it go for something more important elsewhere.

I rather look on the Bombarde reeds as really belonging on the Great but played from a separate manual. However, in this country there is no difficulty in selling somebody a purely flue Great Organ. Incidentally, there is one stop prepared for on the Great, namely, a 32' Montre, which is partially borrowed from the Pedal Montre. This again, which is more or less a theoretical stop, was let go for something else.

Regarding the Swell Organ, I can't agree with you about the 5⅓' Quint Trompette. I do not think you have heard the right kind for if it is small scale and thin, it fits into the ensemble and adds a color which I do not think you can get by other means. I admit I have seen many failures in this regard, and this is the first time I have made one that I consider to be satisfactory.

Choir Organ — I rather like the stopped Harmonic Flute.

Positiv — We look upon the 8's of the Positiv as being doubles. This is why there is no 16' double. There is, however, the Rankett at 16' pitch.

Solo Organ — the boys prefer to have the English Horn at 8' pitch for solo use, both on its own and combined with the 4' Flute. I do not see much advantage in having the 16' Cor Anglais.

The Bombarde reeds are all of the French type as you presume, all placed in a prominent position, and all hooded to speak forward into the very resonant building. The 8', for example, is of just about the same power as the standard Willis type Tuba, which is on 15" wind.

Regarding the Antiphonal, I agree that it is redundant, but they seem to want it.

Regarding the mechanicals, the Antiphonal does have a separate Pedal. The description must have omitted it by mistake. There are no switch plates for the Swell pedals. The organ is used a great deal for broadcasting, and simplicity of console design was the key note to lessen the burden on the minds of the players.

The organ does really sound superb, and I have never heard anything quite like it. Of course, it is of its own particular type. Although the full organ is tremendous, it is very easy on the ears, and you can play it for long periods without fatigue. This is due, I think, to the fact that there are no very loud stops, the effect being obtained by the 188 ranks, all of which add one to another. The large scale Mixtures give quite a powerful resultant effect, which in the resonant hall gives quite a lot of body to the tone, but it is a kind of transparent body, as you can well imagine.

I wouldn't say that the organ sounds anything like a Cavaillé-Coll. It is less reedy than a French ensemble, as the balance between full flues and reeds is entirely different.

I note with pleasure that Germani is coming over here. I certainly look upon him as one of the world's greatest.

G. Donald Harrison &
Alexander Schreiner

I am glad you feel my letter to the good Monsignor in Rome will be helpful to you.

Your letter of the 25th of February has just come to hand. Richards has given an incorrect impression regarding the Princeton organ. When Ralph Downes was there he did move some of the stops into different places with an attempt to make it more of the classic type. However, before he left he had all the pipes replaced in their proper holes so that the organ is just as it was originally. I was there with Carl Weinrich, the present organist, recently, and it all sounded just the same to me. I think Richards has been influenced by hearing so many of our recent jobs that on going back to Princeton the organ seems to be dull. However, I am sure that Downes did not do anything to the organ.

I have had one or two letters back and forth from Downes, and I have tried to steer him a little bit with a view to getting a more normal specification, and it seems to me that the latest version is certainly a great deal more practical than the original. While Downes is somewhat of a peculiar fellow, I think he can be handled, and if I were in your shoes, I would try and play along with him. If, for example, you made up a few sample pipes voiced with typical French dome-headed parallel shallots to show, I think you might be able to overcome the requirements that certain reeds should be imported. He might feel that it was unnecessary to do so to get the effect that he is after.

Glad to hear that Peasgood is coming over. I will see if I can do anything for him in the way of recitals around May 10, 20 & 21st.

With best wishes,

As ever,
Don

one 16' semi-Baroque reed — Harrison had specified a Fagot.
the boys prefer — Alexander Schreiner and Frank Asper, the Tabernacle organists
Peasgood — Osborne Peasgood, assistant organist at Westminster Abbey, London, under Sir William McKie.

March 8, 1949

Henry Willis, Esq.
Henry Willis & Sons, Ltd.
34 Marlborough Grove
Old Kent Road
London, S.E.1, England

My dear Henry:

Thank you so much for your good letter of February 7th regarding Aubrey. I am glad that you feel as you do about the matter, and I think you have shown a very generous spirit as I know that Aubrey must be very valuable to you as he has everything at his finger's ends and can be trusted, and it will mean a lot of training for anybody else to take his place.

I have written Aubrey today assuring him that I do not consider that he is in any way obligated to come to me, but that he should freely choose a concern where he feels he would have the greatest scope and be happy in the long run. Of course, as you have already mentioned to him, the only other real choice is the Möller outfit, but I very much doubt if Aubrey would be happy there, and have told him so. The only advantage from Aubrey's point of view in going to them would be that they might be prepared to pay him a great deal more than we can at the present time. However, although the organ business is very prosperous at the present time and the productive labor is getting high rates, the salaries of officials throughout the industry are all very low, and there are none of the fancy salaries being paid that existed in the lush days of the 1920s. My own salary is, for example, absurdly low for a man in my position, but, of course, when we start to make real profits my income will be greatly increased, together with others who have been underpaid I feel for many years. The trouble with American organbuilding is that they cannot live on their tuning and maintenance business in bad times like you can in England. The country is too large to cover, and if you put out men in a lucrative district, they soon begin to figure that they could make more money if they took the business on their own, and in every instance where I have seen it tried out that is exactly what happens within a few years. The fact that we are a series of states makes it pretty difficult to tie people down like you can in England, and if you did have an ironclad agreement, it would be very costly and difficult to enforce it.

I have advised Aubrey not to burn all his bridges behind him until he passes the medical examination, particularly as your letter reminded me that he was medically unfit during the war, and while I do not know the nature of his disability, it might be one of the things that is frowned on by the U.S. authorities.

All the best,

As ever,

Don

regarding Aubrey — Aubrey Thompson-Allen (1907-1974), who had worked for Willis for more than 30 years, had decided to come to the United States. Originally, he worked with Aeolian-Skinner, but after a few years he moved to Yale University, where he was Curator of Organs from 1951 to 1973. He was succeeded by his son, Nicholas, and Joseph Dzeda.

---

203 T. Frederick H. Candlyn to Henry Willis

March 8, 1949

Mr. Henry Willis,
Rotunda Organ Works,
34 Marlborough Grove,
Old Kent Road
London.

Dear Mr. Willis,

Many thanks for your letter received recently. Möller has done a magnificent job, and the organ at St. Thomas now has life and sparkling upper work. I drew up the scheme and the voicing was done by a pupil of the late Mr. Whitelegg. Many of my New York colleagues refer to the organ as "the Willis at St. Thomas." I am of course familiar with your examples at St. Paul's, Lincoln, and Liverpool as I was born in England.

Here is what Möller has done:

GREAT
(a) all trebles of upper work brightened (this also applies to Swell & Choir)
(b) new four-rank mixture
(c) reeds revoiced on Willis lines
(d) a second Principal added

SWELL
(a) Geigen 4' added
(b) Oboe eliminated
(c) chorus reeds revoiced as Willis reeds
(d) new Mixture four ranks and Cymbal three ranks

CHOIR
Nazard, Tierce, and Larigot added

SOLO
(a) Harmonic Trumpet 8' (in box) added
(b) Tuba Mirabilis (open chest) revoiced
(c) Two soft stops on Echo (West end) replaced by Diapason 8' and Principal 4'

<u>PEDAL</u>

(a) Bourdon replaced by Gemshorn at 16'-8'-4' pitches

(b) The smaller wooden Diapason replaced by a metal Open at 16-8-4 pitches

(c) Reeds brightened (though not very much was possible here)

(d) Bassoon (enclosed Solo) 16', duplexed on Pedal

<u>MECHANICALS</u>

(a) entirely new action

(b) tilting tablets for couplers

(c) eight general pistons duplicated by toe studs

(d) several new couplers added

(e) each manual to pedal by reversing piston in key-slip

(f) reversible toe studs for the three 32' pedal stops

With the brightening of the upper work and the new mixture it is unnecessary to use octave couplers in order to secure brilliance.

I hope that you will eventually be able to hear the instrument, for I am sure that you will approve of the work that Möller has done.

Sincerely yours,
T. Frederick H. Candlyn

---

204 Henry Willis to G. Donald Harrison

15th March, 1949

Mr. G. Donald Harrison,
President,
Aeolian-Skinner Organ Co.,
Crescent Avenue, Dorchester,
Boston 25, Mass.,
U.S.A.

My dear Don,

Thanks for yours of the 8th instant. I quite appreciate the position reference Aubrey, also the salary question. Same applies here. My own salary is lower than before the war — I being the only official of the company who has not had a substantial increase above the pre-war standard. Taxation is so vicious that it is simply not worth while having money above a certain standard.

Aubrey would prefer to go to you because he feels that he would be happy and not so with a soulless crowd as at Möllers — in this preference I can fully sympathize with him, although financially he could no doubt do better with Möllers.

Before the war (1939-1945) Aubrey was troubled by a kidney complaint — had a stone and some reoccurrence and so was unfit for service duties of any sort. But he seems to have got over the kidney trouble completely and no reoccurrence.

Of course I will miss him but, as I said, I would not dream of standing in his way.

Princetown [sic]: Glad to hear that Richards was wrong about Downes messing the job about and toning down the upper work. Of course it must sound dull in comparison with recent practice. I will do my best to "play along" with Downes who, I must say, accepted much strong criticism of his preliminary L.C.C. scheme from me and several others, in good part.

As ever,

H.W.

H.W./J.M.
Copy sent Mr. A.T-A.

---

205 M. P. Möller to Henry Willis

March 18th, 1949

Mr. Henry Willis
34, Marlborough Grove
Old Kent Road
London, S.E.1
Dear Mr. Willis:

Thank you very much for your letter. Our work at St. Thomas Church came through the recommendation of Dr. Noble, who has favored our work the last several years, and for whom we built a small organ in the little Episcopal Church where he is living in retirement in Rockport, Massachusetts. I am enclosing one of our factory copies of the work done at St. Thomas Church. When the work was completed in December 1948 I was present at St. Thomas when Dr. Candlyn demonstrated the work done to the members of the Executive Council of the American Guild of Organists. In his remarks to these organists, Dr. Candlyn said that for the first time in the United States there was a true Willis Great. That was the way he termed the results of the organ in the Great. In addition to the work shown, we also revoiced the entire Diapason structure in the Great and Swell, using the present pipes. We also revoiced all of the reeds in the Swell excepting the Vox Humana. The work of finishing was under the direction of our chief finisher, Mr. John Schleigh, and the supervision of our factory technical engineer, Mr. John Hose.

Under separate cover I am sending you copies of several small folders which we have issued during the past two years and a copy of our current brochure. I would very much appreciate receiving copies of your literature available at this time, and if ever you again come to the United States I hope you will visit us at Hagerstown.

Yours respectfully,
M.P. Möller, Jr.
President

MPM/am

Encl. *[A list of alterations and a stoplist are appended to the letter.]*

---

206 Henry Willis to G. Donald Harrison

21st. March 1949

Mr. G. Donald Harrison,
President,
Aeolian-Skinner Organ Co.,
Crescent Avenue,
Dorchester,
Boston, 25,
Mass.,
U.S.A.

My dear Don,

New York. St. Thomas' Church. Being interested in Möller's announcement, also in the descriptive article in the Diapason to the effect that improvements had been carried out on "Willis" lines, and further, because Tertius Noble asked me to pull the job up in 1926 when, if I remember correctly, new mixtures, 12th and 15th were inserted, all made up incorrectly by the old Skinner metal shop and I did the best I could with incorrect scales, breaks etc. not in accordance with my instructions. But Noble was delighted at the time. I wrote to Möller, also Candlyn — copy of Candlyn's reply enclosed. Nothing from Möller yet.

A pity this work went to Möllers.

As ever,
H.W.

H.W./J.M.

Copy sent Hon. Emerson Richards

207 G. Donald Harrison to Henry Willis

April 5, 1949

Mr. Henry Willis
Henry Willis & Sons Ltd.
34, Marlborough Grove
Old Kent Road
London, S.E.1 England
Dear Henry:

Thanks for your letter of March 21st regarding St. Thomas' Church. The sole reason that Möller got in to do this work was due to the fact that I was unable to tackle it until this year. Möllers offered to get busy on it immediately and, incidentally at a considerably lower price. As you can see from Mr. Candlyn's letter, very little has been done tonally. I haven't heard it so cannot speak from personal experience, but those that have, either heard no difference at all or think that a better job could have been accomplished.

I cannot help getting a kick out of the statement that the reeds have been voiced along Willis lines, as Möller knows nothing about that. Incidentally, as you know, the original reeds were voiced by Brockbank at the beginning of his career in this country, and were not too bad anyway.

Best regards,

Sincerely,
Don

GDH/MOK

Brockbank — Frederick S. Brockbank, died in 1929 at age 46, a former Willis voicer who worked as a reed voicer for Skinner 1904-1914. Also worked for Aeolian, Odell, and lastly with Frazee of Everett, Massachusetts.

---

208 Granville Munson, Jr., to Alexander Schreiner

April 12, 1949

Mr. Alexander Schreiner
The Mormon Tabernacle
Salt Lake City, Utah
Dear Mr. Schreiner:

You will not remember me, I am sure, but I am one of the organists of the Virginia Chapter of the Guild who enjoyed your concert in Richmond so much a year ago. I have recently read how much you liked the work that the Aeolian-Skinner Company did on the Tabernacle organ. I wonder if you would be good enough to help us decide on the building of a new organ we plan for St. Stephen's.

We would like to know why the Aeolian-Skinner organ was decided on for the Tabernacle. There is no doubt in my mind that it is the finest, but we would appreciate your recommendation in this matter.

Thank you so much for your attention to this inquiry.

Yours very truly,
Granville Munson, Jr.

GM:jb

Granville Munson, Jr. — organist at St. Stephen's Episcopal, Richmond, Virginia. The church eventually purchased Opus 1110, 1950.

---

209 Emerson Richards to Henry Willis

April 25, 1949

Mr. Henry Willis
Henry Willis & Sons Ltd.
34 Marlborough Grove
London S.E. 1
England
My dear Willis:

Apparently, the only unanswered correspondence is a series of copies of letters addressed to Harrison and the replies thereto. All relating to St. Thomas Church. While this organ was always considered old man Skinner's best, it never had very much to recommend it in my opinion. You tried to do something with it without very much luck. Thus, after Noble retired the new organist tried again. Unhappily, he either did not understand or did not care and gave the job to E.M. At this time E.M. was already in bankruptcy and [had] no organization, had only a one-room shop to pass as a factory. The work he undertook to do was completely beyond him. I believe that he got advances until he got all the money that was due under the contract and then did not perform half of the agreed work. Candlyn then applied to Don, but he had no inclination to take over this badly mutilated organ and try to do anything with it. Besides, they were money-conscious and Don could not see sufficient remuneration to make up for all trouble the organ was going to cost. The result was that Möller picked the thing up. Just what the result has been, I have no opinion.

I was in Boston recently going over the Symphony Hall organ which is now being taken out to make room for a new organ of Don's. While there, I met Covell by appointment, who knew considerably about the background of the organ and was able to give me some assistance in getting me straight on the historical data. During our meeting, I told him something about the projected organ for the exhibition and about the difficulties that had arisen.

Covell instinctively suggested that he saw no reason why an entirely new organ should be projected at this time. His understanding, as is mine, is that while the Alexandra Palace organ was not destroyed during the war, it was taken down for safety's sake and stored. It was his suggestion, and I think a very good one, that this organ which was in my opinion the finest concert organ in England, could be judiciously revised and perhaps broadened in its scheme and be used with far greater effect than the thing proposed. I agreed to forward the suggestion and I do think that with what modernization would naturally occur to you it would be a far better thing to do than to try an entirely new organ scheme. Has anything like this been explored and if not why not suggest it. As we understand it, the Palace is not likely to ever require this organ again, or to give this famous instrument a proper home of lasting value and of service to the British people.

I saw Don recently and also had a letter from Thompson-Allen. It would be a good thing for American organ people if the both of you came over and started here. Your talents are wasted at home.

With kindest regards, I am,

Sincerely yours,
Emerson Richards

ER:af

projected organ for the exhibition — the L.C.C. (Royal Festival Hall) organ project

---

210 Alexander Schreiner to Granville Munson

April 26, 1949

Dear Mr. Munson,

I have just returned from a long tour of concerts and find your letter awaiting reply.

The reason the Aeolian-Skinner Organ Company was chosen for the new work in the Salt Lake Tabernacle was merely because this company does by all odds the finest work. That we have not been disappointed in the results achieved is clearly shown in the letter which I wrote to the company recently, signed by myself and fellow organists, and published in the recent Diapason.

I wish you well in your efforts to have your contract awarded to this company. In our case we did not even consider any competing bids. Also we did not ask for any reduction in the prices which were quoted. I would always prefer an Aeolian-Skinner organ to any other, even of twice the size.

With every good wish, I am

Sincerely yours,
Alexander Schreiner

9th May, 1949

Mr. G. Donald Harrison,
President,
Aeolian-Skinner Organ Co.,
Crescent Avenue,
Dorchester,
Boston, 25,
Mass.,
U.S.A.

My dear Don,

. . . You have not heard the Liverpool Cathedral job since the central space was opened for use. The organ is now complete as I planned and there is nothing overwhelming about it — every chorus voice plays its part. Ferdy Germani was quite taken aback by its glory and tonal completeness when he heard it again last year and only wants something like it in St. Peter's.

I had an interesting time in Rome. The scheme under consideration is to utilize the service of the leading Italian builders — Mascioni and Tamburini — to do two-thirds of the work (mechanisms etc. under my direction), I to be responsible for the pipework, voicing and, of course, general finishing: Italian costs are less than half ours. Organ builders receive ⅔rds the pay of ours and have a 57-hour week — 9½ hours a day, 6 days a week. They have excellent timber from the Italian Alps, etc.

Now awaiting decision by the Vatican.

Noted about St. John's, New York. What a mess with Ernest Skinner asking for me to send him out some reeds — I have said "cash first!" Poor old chap.

Canterbury Cathedral to be opened next month. It will be a most satisfactory job of a type that would have a strong appeal to you. Moderate pressures, Swell and Great reeds 7" pressure, unenclosed Choir, enclosed Solo Tubas on 17" pressure, Pedal reeds 32' 12" pressure, 16' and 8' 15" pressure.

Of course, the organ is for services, etc. in the Choir and sounds small and remote in the Nave which, in due course, needs an instrument of its own.

Yours as ever,
Henry Willis

H.W./J.M.

*Boston Symphony
Orchestra Conductor
Charles Munch,
E. Power Biggs,
G. Donald Harrison
at Symphony Hall*

---

212 Emerson Richards to Henry Willis

May 23, 1949

Henry Willis & Sons, Ltd.
34 Marlborough Grove
Old Kent Road
London S.E. 1
England
Attention: Mr. Henry Willis
My dear Willis:

Thanks for your letter of the 19th. I had not known of your trip to Rome or the reason therefore. I gather that there must be some organ work in or about that section of Italy which the authorities are afraid to trust to local builders. Is this correct and is the prospective work still in a confidential stage?

If the Alexandra Palace is going to be restored, of course it would be better if the organ were also reinstated.

You do not say whether or not there has been a final decision in the case of the Concert Hall organ. It would seem to me to be the height of absurdity to install a partially French organ in a British exposition. . . .

I'll be interested in the Canterbury job. I am itching to get both to Italy and look around England again before too long.

Nothing very exciting over here except Don's rebuild of the Boston Symphony Hall job. Practically a new organ, since all the chests are new as well as the console, and only about 20 sets of the old pipes are to be used, although entirely revoiced. The interesting thing about this job is that while it was a Hutchings organ, it was voiced so far as the reeds were concerned immediately after Skinner returned from England and with all the dope that he had gotten from your firm. Don and I agree that some of these reeds are very imitative of Willis's work; others are not. Covell, who dislikes E.M. very much, will have none of it — says they do not sound a bit like Willis reeds. A matter of opinion.

Southern Spain will be hot in July but immensely interesting. Many fine organ cases and Seville, Toledo and Granada are worth all the time and trouble. I have done Southern Spain several times and always left with regret. Am just getting my cruiser in commission again after a lapse of six years and likewise preparing for Maine. Some important professional work the early part of June, and then am free until September.

With best wishes, I am,

Sincerely yours,
Emerson Richards

ER:af

Concert Hall organ — the L.C.C. (Royal Festival Hall) project

---

213 Henry Willis to Emerson Richards

22nd. June, 1949

Hon. Emerson Richards,
800, Schwehm Building,
Atlantic City,
N.J.,
U.S.A.

My dear Richards,

Thanks for your letter of the 23rd instant and all the news.

My visit to Rome was due to having been called into consultation by the Vatican authorities to advise about a great instrument for St. Peter's. The high cost of an entirely British built organ makes such impossible from the financial angle, and on my advice the Vatican instructed me to contact the two leading firms of Italian organbuilders — Mascioni and Tamburini — with a view to arranging cooperation. After some difficulty, I was able to overcome the strong feelings of aversion to cooperation, not with me, but between the two Italian firms, and a working arrangement was outlined. I then presented the position to the Vatican with specification and all major details. Basic work to be made by the Italian firms under my direction — I to provide and voice all pipework — also chests for high pressure reeds etc. and to finish. A provisional cost of Lire 72,500,000 — about £37,000 sterling at current exchange.

The Vatican committee of Monsignori, whom I met, approved in principle — but had to refer to a higher committee presided over by a Cardinal who, in turn, would report to a higher committee again — and then obtain the approval of His Holiness. This is, apparently, taking some time, and as the organ is wanted for St. Peter's Day (29th June) in 1950, which is Holy Year, the matter should be settled quickly. But it is nearly two months since I returned from Rome and no response through yet. The project is for a big-four manual on each side of the Choir, each section mounted on movable platforms to be capable of being withdrawn inside the great arches by 3 meters — this to permit of the erection of temporary platforms etc. for certain special services or ceremonies.

Personally, I think that the question of finances is holding matters up, also perhaps the lack of interest in certain quarters to finance a great instrument worthy of St. Peters!

<u>Alexandra Palace</u>: This organ's restoration held up because the roof of the Great Hall still not repaired as the Government refuses to grant the required licenses for labor and material.

<u>L.C.C. Concert Hall Organ</u>: No decision although expected daily. The L.C.C. is run on Government lines and so, of course, moves slowly. The work on the new Concert Hall foundations has commenced. With such protracted delay it will be a rush to get the organ ready for the 1951 Exhibition.

In accordance with municipal practice, three tenders were obtained and it is by no means certain or settled that I build the instrument. The lowest tender is normally accepted for all government and municipal contracts — and my tender was, so I understand, the highest.

In fact, I would have declined to take any interest in the matter, but Don wrote suggesting that I should "string along" with Ralph Downes, and my son was keen on the job — so I tendered.

Off for a motor tour to Southern France and Spain on the 9th July but nothing new in the organ line to see — I have done Spain etc. before. I will take the opportunity of trying the Gonzales "rebuild" of the 17th century organ at St. Merri, Paris — so eulogistically described in the April issue of the <u>Organ</u> which you may have read.

I have written an article about the Canterbury Cathedral organ which will appear in the July issue of the <u>Organ</u>.

Stephen Stoot of Casavant over here recently. I took him to Liverpool Cathedral (he had not heard the finished organ) and he was simply stunned — so indeed am I whenever I hear it. Now that the central space is opened up, the instrument is heard as I designed and voiced it to be heard — and not in the limited East end of the cathedral as you heard it.

J.B. Jamison, the advt. writer for Austin's over here, but so far I have only seen him for half an hour.

I receive <u>piteous</u> letters from Ernest Skinner asking for opinions and for me to send him reeds etc. and I really don't know how to write him in return. I doubt if payment would be made for anything I sent over! The reed stops you refer to were, no doubt, by Brockbank — an assistant reed voicer of ours 1902-1906 or 7.

Aubrey sails on the 25th inst. Don is indeed fortunate in securing so able an <u>aide-de-camp</u> on the technical side. He should get Aubrey to give one of his half-hour extemporisations on the Salt Lake City job over the air.

It is time you revisited us again — why don't you bring Mrs. Richards over for a run-around? Our hospitality is limited because of the food position, but such as we can offer is yours!

I am 60 years of age on 5th June and feel it, but there is life in the old dog yet.

I would much like to revisit the U.S.A. again, but taxation is so high I can't even live on my earnings.

If I could cover expenses by lectures and so forth I might be able to manage a trip next year — but I doubt if such a trip could be arranged.

All the best.

Yours ever sincerely,
Henry Willis

H.W./J.M.
2 copies taken for Mr. G. Donald Harrison

---

214 Joseph Whiteford to Aeolian-Skinner factory staff

July 13, 1949

TO ALL FOREMEN:

Dr. Albert Schweitzer, a world famous authority on organs and organ music, will visit our factory Wednesday, July 20th at 9 a.m. He has particularly requested to see our factory and it will be greatly appreciated if all departments will be as orderly as possible for the occasion. We should like to have the following stops voiced and on the machines, tuned for Wednesday morning, if possible:

8' Trompette
8' Cromorne

4' Principal
4' Koppelflöte
8' String Celeste

Joseph S. Whiteford

JSW/MOK

*G. Donald Harrison,
Albert Schweitzer,
and an unidentified
visitor at the factory*

---

215 Emerson Richards to Henry Willis

July 27th, 1949

Mr. Henry Willis
London, Eng.
My dear Willis,

I have delayed answering your letter of the 22nd June because when it arrived I knew that you were already starting on your journey to Spain. How did you enjoy your trip? I always liked Spain but it is now many years since I have been there and no doubt there are many changes. Are there any new organs and are they any good? I suppose what there is comes mostly from the German commercial shops.

What you say about the Vatican organ is most interesting. A three-way responsibility looks dangerous, particularly with the Italian temperament to reckon with. I do hope something comes of it. There have been some tentative feelers over here but nothing very serious as we viewed it. I would be most interested in seeing what is proposed when a specification becomes available.

I suppose that the L.C.C. organ matter has now been disposed of, and if you did not get it another opportunity wasted.

Jamison talks a good organ; actually he has neither taste or understanding nor technical knowledge. Never made good with any builder he was ever with.

Skinner is without the slightest financial responsibility, badly in debt and in default on what commitments he has. A one room factory in Reading is all that is left. All his own fault. Marks made him, and he repaid Marks by selling his stock (and the control of the company) to outsiders. It cost Marks a very substantial sum to buy the stock back. All because of jealousy of Don. And he has since carried on a campaign of vilification ever since.

I will see Aubrey tomorrow. Have to stop in Boston on a flying trip home and then back here for the rest of the summer. We have had a delightfully cool summer up here but we will be driving into the heat on the way home.

Congratulations on the birthday. I had one too — on the 9th. Sixty five but I don't feel it.

We do hope to see you soon. I must go to San Francisco in September or it would be then.

Yours truly,
Emerson Richards

---

216 Emerson Richards to Henry Willis

7 November 1949

My dear Willis,

The air copy of your letter of October 22 arrived in season, but since the main point of the letter was in the copy of Lady Jeans, I had to await the regular mail.

It seems to me that you gave the Lady a none-too-good brush-off. With regard to the rest of the letter, I think it brings into rather sharp focus the distinct diversion of opinion between American and English organ designs.

I have felt for a good many years that English organ practice, and particularly the opinion of organists, was a full 20 years behind American practice. The things that have been agitating English organ thought are petty things that are dead issues in America today. For instance, extension work is as dead in America as a smoked mackerel, while it still thrives in England. The romantic movement is dead in America but obviously going strong in England. Even the poorest of our builders are adding independent upper work to their Pedals, and certainly in our better jobs we are not making the mistake of dominating flue choruses with high power reeds to the point where nothing but the reeds are left.

Of course, in a way it is somewhat unfair to compare American and English practice today. Over here we are free to build not only the normal 20 or so stop two-manual, but also a goodly number of four-manuals, whereas, thanks to your political and financial difficulties no new work of any substance is going on, (except the Downes fiasco). But if there were it would not rise to the level of your Grandfather's work 100 years ago. We have the means and the initiative with which to experiment and an open mindedness to objectively survey the results. We think the new work, particularly Don's, does show a superior ability to play all kinds of organ compositions, whether it be pre-Bach, Bach, or the most advanced of the moderns. On this score, Leo Sowerby admitted in my presence that he thought some of his compositions came off better on the Germanic Museum organ than on his own.

Underlying your comments, there appears to be a notion on your part that the organs we are building are all right for Bach but not good for the moderns, and that is where you are all wrong. It is a matter of surprise also to us that the most extreme of the modernistic stuff sounds well, often better, on the so-called classical ensembles. This we know from experience and which you would realize once you heard the new jobs.

Tacking labels on things is always dangerous. In a moment of derision I put the word "romantic" to the Skinner organ with the same intent that a small boy ties a tin can to a dog's tail. I hardly expected it to become an accepted term and to travel around the world in a half dozen languages, as it has done. It is, therefore, difficult to use the opposite word, "classical" to cover several schools of organ building. Obviously, there is no relation between the German organs of the Baroque period and the French organs of the same date. The Silbermanns are characteristically in choruses while the French are mostly flutes and reeds. Therefore the word "classical" must be very broadly applied as it is in the case of Beethoven or Mozart, or, if narrowly used, to the particular nationality intended.

By the way, you will find that the Tierce appears in German organs dating from earlier than 1614. The Germans didn't like them in their mixtures for reasons which are sound today. A Tierce has its place even in the chorus but not in normal mixtures. For the reasons stated above, it is easy to understand why English organists and organ enthusiasts now consider "retrograde" stuff to go back 300 years in tonal design. After all, English organ tradition hardly dates half of that time, since both Smith and Harris were foreign builders working on a limited scale.

I don't think that the word "neo-classical" as you apply it to Harrison's organs is at all adequate. I myself have found no word that is sufficiently comprehensive to describe this new organ. Much has been said about the so-called classical tonal structure, but this does not describe the instruments by giving any just idea of their actual character. Don's diapason work is distinctive and not at all even reminiscent of old German practice. His Great Organ chorus is bold and aggressive as a general thing. It has a limited 8' foundation and highly specialized mixture work which dominates the chorus. It is nothing like Schulze, or Schnitger or Silbermann at all. It is somewhat reminiscent of your Grandfather's earlier work, but again the mixture work is as dominant as your Grandfather's reeds.

Against and in contrast with this chorus is his Positiv. This is truly a radical contribution to modern organ design, particularly in view of the fact that Don's Positives have little similarity to their German prototype. Generally speaking, these Positives are merely another Great Organ of higher pitch and greater brilliancy, and also can be joined to the Great Organ with good effect. On the other hand, outside the reeds there is nothing radical about the Harrison Swell. It contains the accepted Geigen chorus supplemented with normal flutes and smoother strings than are usual in England. Don's Choir Organs do tend to have an ensemble of their own so that his general scheme is two open and two enclosed sections, the Great and the Positiv contrasting and complimenting each other, the Swell and Choir doing likewise. The main feature in the Swell is, of course, the employment of the French low pressure reeds and a big mixture which tends to color the Great Chorus without dominating it.

The other main departure is in the independent Pedal. In some of the very big organs of the latest design there is also a Bombarde division consisting of modified French reeds (16'-8'-4') on medium pressure augmented by either one or two very big mixtures. The effect of these Bombarde sections is to somewhat increase the tendency toward reed domination, but nothing like so overwhelming as the high pressure Tubas and Trombas so dear to your English heart.

It is true that Don's ideas in the main are like mine, or you once accused me of having converted his to mine. Somehow, however, we do not seem to get our ideas over to you completely. I cannot seem to shake you loose from the idea that neither of us is intent upon some highbrow ideal of something of iceberg proportions as our idea of the modern organ. Actually, you and Don and I have never been as far apart as you imagine unless it be on the question of reed domination. Don and I are against tonal design in which high power reeds completely dominate the ensemble to the exclusion of the flues. This is not so much because we object to the resultant tone since it may be magnificent and thrilling in effect, but because it is an end in itself and one which we can only appreciate and enjoy as such. Our objection (at least my own and, I believe, Don's) is on an entirely different ground. We find this type of ensemble does not play music as music should be played.

I just talked to Don on the phone. He told me that he had closed the contract for the new organ in the First Church Scientist in Boston. This is the Mother Church and a magnificent building for sound. There is a small II manual and a very big organ for the main church. The total contract is $176,000 with the big job going better than $150,000.

You remember the Boner analysis. High pressure reeds do generate a tibia-like fundamental that dominates the tone, whereas low pressures and open shallots generate a relatively weak fundamental with a series of important harmonics that are stronger and dominate the fundamental. The result is that high pressure reeds have the same effect as fat diapasons and flutes have on the clarity of a musical composition, whereas low pressure reeds, with open or parallel shallots like yours and Don's, have no such effect if properly balanced against flues and mixtures. With this latter setup the music does come off, and that is what we are looking for. We think of an organ as an instrument to play written music, not as a succession of beautiful sounds, or one that comes off in the hands of a clever improviser.

The "Willis tradition." Which one? It is generally agreed that your Grandfather began with a bold flue ensemble with moderately bright reeds and gradually smoothed and restricted the power of his flues. Of course, there is the exception in some of the big jobs, such as St. George's and St. Paul's, where high pressure reeds were employed in the early jobs, but in the average organ you yourself pointed out to me that both you and your Grandfather normally employ reeds on only 3½" to 4½". You cited Salisbury particularly. You seem to imply that you are following your Grandfather's later period, but I do not think it is so in the latest of your organs that I have heard. I think your Diapason showed some Lewis influence, and I do not think the reed domination was deliberate but due somewhat to their distribution. You are inclined to follow the English tradition of three reeds on the Great and three on the Swell with inadequate mixtures, which seems to me to make the Great reeds redundant. We do keep the reeds off the Great for the sake of contrast, clarity and musical flexibility, but where the chance comes to add a second battery of reeds, then Don and I believe, with additional mixtures to support them, they warrant a separate chest. Don calls this a Bombarde organ and plays it from the fourth manual, but of course it couples or transfers to the Great. Don has done this on three jobs recently — Kilgore, Texas; Salt Lake City; and Boston Symphony Hall. The effect is a spine-tingling experience. Power and clarity galore: 16' Bombarde, 8' Trompette Harmonique, 4' Clarion Harmonique, VI Mixture, V Cornet (wind 7").

So much then, for our main difference which you see amounts to little more than a slightly different type of reed differently placed. As to the rest. Don is using your Grandfather's Salicionals — as fine an effect as can be found in any organ. He is using all of the orchestral reeds that you use, and we have to remember that old Skinner's organization did develop this type of reed to the nth degree. Besides, Don is adding the very colorful Baroque reeds.

So far as the flues are concerned, the metal Gedeckts, the Koppelflötes, the Spindleflötes, the Blockflötes and the Zauberflötes are, to a certain extent, revivals that deserve insertion in any organ. As for the rest, Don's diapasons are somewhat more conservative than yours. There is nothing of the Schulze or Lewis about them — 43 and 44 scales with ¼ mouth with spotted metal feet and mouths in the basses. The mixtures are of about the same construction with tin for the smaller ranks and with slide tuners as far as possible — no slots. The mixture scales are the result of a lot of experiments made with playing actual music.

How, then, do we really differ? Not what the British organist thinks or what you can force on them, but what you as an artist with a great tradition to maintain think. You say that with us, "each stop tells little by itself." The implication being that we sacrifice individuality to buildup. On the contrary, we want and expect each stop to be a beautiful voice in itself, capable of individual use. We do not want a collection of pale colors, but we do insist on blend. The two objectives are not irreconcilable. If the wind pressure, scaling and voicing are right, these individual voices will melt together into a satisfactory chorus. We expect a Gedeckt to carry a mixture as well as a Diapason. The Nazard or a Tierce must do something to a flute or a string as well as influence the chorus or we do not want it. Everything must pull its weight in the boat or we toss it overboard. That is our creed to which I think you will agree, and it does not differ from yours.

I long to get to Italy to see what they are doing, but I doubt if it is anything like ours. Aubrey has only been around Boston. He has not seen the best yet. I missed him the last time I was up there looking over the Boston Symphony organ. Only had an hour and a half on Saturday and he was not available. Has he written to you about this job?

I have gone into this at some length because of my feeling that without hearing it you are beginning to get a wrong impression of what Don has been doing. After all, there has been no disposition to take modern voices out of Don's jobs. He still likes two pairs of strings in his Swell and two more in the Choir. His Salicionals are quite reminiscent of your Grandfather's, and there is no cut or edge on his Viols or Gambas. And as far as orchestral reeds are concerned, you can have all you are willing to pay for, and Don will throw in his Rohrschalmeis, Regals and Krummhorns for good luck. Certainly with the amount of mixture work and mutations there is no lack of color in Don's jobs. It is altogether the opposite. The worst that could be said against Don's new work is that he has rejected large scale flutes, diapasons and high pressure smooth reeds, and in this he is certainly in agreement with both your Grandfather and yourself.

I will, of course, respect your wishes about the comment of Fernando Germani. I think this gentleman, with characteristic Latin duplicity, is saying what he thinks will please his immediate audience. Incidentally, I have a hunch, but nothing positive, that it was he who threw the monkey wrench in the St. Peter's project.

Since I wrote you last, I have been all the way to the Pacific Ocean. Mrs. Richards and I drove out to San Francisco via Chicago, Omaha and Salt Lake City. Harrison has a new big three manual in Omaha which is very successful and characteristic. The big organ in the Mormon Tabernacle at Salt Lake is indeed an outstanding achievement. This auditorium has an undeserved reputation for fine acoustics. Actually, they do very little for the organ since the building is rather long and narrow, the roof too high. And because of the curved formation of the roof, the acoustic response is uncertain. Don's Great Organ is somewhat more restrained than his other jobs, but the buildup is very smooth with the mixtures blending into each other and to the foundation to form a very brilliant chorus. The enclosed sections contain many very beautiful effects, both in strings and the reeds. The Bombarde section is terrific, and of course the Pedal is outstanding. There is nothing to compare with it west of the Alleghenies.

We enjoyed our stay in San Francisco very much and our trip down, the side trips to Yosemite and the Big Trees as special events. We were not too much impressed with Los Angeles, which has grown far too much for its own good. We did enjoy our stay around San Diego. We came back through southwestern United States: Arizona, New Mexico, Texas; stopped off for a look at the Grand Canyon. We were gone 24 days and covered 7625 miles without tire or mechanical failure, and had a thoroughly enjoyable time. Back home I have been rather busy with professional matters and an attempt to get a little recreation on my cruiser, but bad weather spoiled most of that.

Next week I am going up to Boston to see the new Symphony Hall organ.

With kindest regards,

Sincerely yours,
Emerson Richards

ER/s
small II manual — Actually, Opus 1202 of 1949 is a small three-manual organ.

Kilgore — First Presbyterian Church, Kilgore, Texas. Roy Perry, an Æolian-Skinner tonal finisher for the Southwest, was organist here. This organ (opus 1173) housed Æolian-Skinner's first Trompette-en-Chamade.

---

217 Henry Willis to *The Diapason*

The Editor, The <u>Diapason</u>
1511 Kimball Buildings
Wabash Avenue & Jackson Boulevard
Chicago 4 Ill., U.S.A.

November 14, 1949

Dear Sir,

In your issue for October, 1949, you publish a letter from my old friend and distinguished Organist Mr. Quentin Maclean, in which he makes reference to the Trompette Militaire that I presented to St. Paul's Cathedral (London) at the time of the rebuild in 1930. Mr. Maclean has been misinformed and he would wish me to state the facts.

I did <u>not</u> invite an orchestral trumpeter to play passages alternating with the stop.

The <u>Rotunda</u> Vol. 1, No. 3, of September, 1930, contained an article by me about the reconstruction of the St. Paul's Organ and I quote the relevant extracts verbatim:

"I had offered to present a further stop, and this offer was approved by Dr. Marchant and approved by the authorities. I refer, of course, to the new Trompette Militaire placed with the Dome section upon the highest pressure of wind available — i.e. thirty inches. The type of tone aimed, and I think approximated, is that of the French Cavalry Trumpet. The tubes are of spun brass and the correct trumpet shape complete with bell is present — the tubes become harmonic at Treble C (c2). The eschallots are of the regular 'Willis' small scale Trumpet class with very long openings. The stop is not, as I think will be evident, intended for use in the general ensemble, but solely for solo purposes, fanfare effects and so forth."

Then, describing the re-opening Service on 25th June, 1930:

"As the procession advanced from the great West door, the opening notes of the "Old Hundredth" were given by Mr. Hopkins, assistant organist (who presided at the organ during the Service) on the Trompette Militaire with thrilling effect. I was sitting in the Organ Gallery on the north side with Dr. Alcock, Mr. Stanley Roper, and others.

Dr. Alcock admitted that he had thought it was a trumpeter who gave the opening notes referred to. This gave me peculiar pleasure, for it showed that my efforts had not been unsuccessful and that the presence of the Trompette was justified."

So that is that.

As I am writing, your readers may care to have information about the improvements and additions to the St. Paul's Organ that I have made following its restoration in 1945/46 after the severe damage sustained as the result of enemy action during the 1939-45 War. These I append. The Dome Diapason Chorus was brought into use in September last and fully justifies its presence.

Much as I dislike entering into a controversial correspondence, as Mr. Ernest Skinner's memory would appear to be at fault, it should be restated that when he was in England in, I think, 1898, he was given the freest possible access to the St. George's Hall (Liverpool) Organ. He also visited London and was taken over the great 'Willis' at the Royal Albert Hall, where he could not have failed to notice the 8ft. French Horn (1870) on the Solo Organ — the earliest example of its kind, and of considerable interest. The stop was, in fact, a big scaled Cornopean, capped as an Oboe and with large scale eschallots. But to suggest that this stop, or any other, was an invention is beside the point. Organ stops are <u>not</u> invented — they are developed. Even the extreme tonalities produced by the skilled (ex-Willis) voicers of Hope-Jones under his direction, were only bizarre developments of known types.

Audsley quotes the Royal Albert Hall example in "The Art of Organ Building" — <u>Solo</u> French Horn 8ft. enclosed. <u>Verb. Sap.</u>!

The English Horn, or Cor Anglais as it is termed over here, was but a development of an early German type of reed stop and, in close approximation to its existing and normal form with double bells, has been used in England, France and Germany for over a hundred years with both free and striking reeds.

A few early examples are as follows:

Notre Dame De Lorrette	Cavaillé-Coll	1836
St. Denis	Cavaillé-Coll	1841
Crystal Palace	Gray & Davison	1857
Leeds Town Hall	Gray & Davison	1859
Royal Albert Hall	Willis	1870
St. Paul's Cathedral	Willis	1872
Salisbury Cathedral	Willis	1876
etc., etc.		

In the United States: Chicago Auditorium, Roosevelt; St. Bartholomew's, New York, Hutchings; etc., etc.

It is now 25 years since I first visited the United States (1924) at the invitation of the late Arthur Hudson Marks, President of the Skinner Organ Company, as a consultant on tonal matters. The company was at that time "in search of ensemble" and during my short visits of 1924, 1925 and 1926,

I did what I could to guide the company and tried to overcome the "romantic" tendency then so obvious. In those years, there was the freest possible exchange of information between my firm and the Skinner Organ Co. to the advantage, I think, of all concerned.

I well remember re-introducing, among others, the Rohrflöte to their notice — this charming type of stop had been "forgotten" — suggesting the re-use of balanced flute mutations and drawing up model specifications embodying diapason and reed choruses on Willis lines; also providing a Flute Triangulaire, which, I think, was installed at the First Church in Boston and was later reproduced by the Skinner Company and other firms.

Since 1926, much development has taken place in the United States — mainly due to the efforts and designs of my old confrère, Mr. Donald Harrison and Hon. Emerson Richards, and to those gentlemen organ design in the States owes profound gratitude for, at least, rescue from the "romanticists."

I am looking forward very keenly to the time — not too far distant, I trust — when I can be free to revisit the U.S. and see and hear for myself the striking progress made since my last visit in 1926.

Yours very truly,
Henry Willis

H.W./J.M.

---

218 Henry Willis to G. Donald Harrison

16th November, 1949

Mr. G. Donald Harrison,
President,
Aeolian-Skinner Organ Co.,
Crescent Avenue,
Dorchester,
Boston, 25,
Mass.,
U.S.A.

My dear Don,

Reference new organ in Boston Symphony Hall. I read in the <u>Diapason</u> that the pitch is set at A444. How is this?

The International Standard Pitch agreed at the conferences in London of 1938 and 1939 is A440 at 68 degrees Fahrenheit, for United States A440 at 70 degrees Fahrenheit, on the grounds that U.S. concert hall temperatures were higher.

But A444 is four (4) vibrations higher, and its use seems to nullify the effort to prevent orchestral conductors forcing up the pitch — as is their tendency.

I was a British Delegate at the International Conference of 1938 and 1939 and am on the Committee of the British Standards Institution whose job it is to implement the decision of 1939.

To learn of A444 being used in the U.S., after U.S. delegates had agreed to A440, is somewhat shattering.

Yours as ever,
H.W.

H.W./R.T.

---

219 Emerson Richards to Henry Willis

21 November 1949

Henry Willis, Esq.
Old Kent Road
London, England
My dear Willis:

With reference to your letter of November 16, addressed to Don, copy to me, relative to the pitch of the Boston Symphony Hall organ, this pitch was established by Koussevitzky and the organ had to conform. A.440 is the established pitch, almost universally adhered to in the United States. All the musical instruments as turned out by their manufacturers are so tuned, and all the organs that I know of, except for a few very old ones, are now so tuned. This is also the pitch established for radio, motion pictures and records. Notwithstanding this uniform practice, some of our prima donna conductors have not hesitated to adopt other pitches, some lower and some higher. Koussevitzky has been the most serious offender and in forcing the pitch to 444 it has been necessary for the performers on all of the wind instruments to have their instruments altered accordingly. I have also heard some objection from people who are very sensitive to pitch changes that they objected to records made by the Boston Symphony Orchestra on this account.

Don has apparently run into some trouble by reason of the pitch change, particularly in the trebles in his 8' and 4' reeds. He told me over the phone this week that he had to take some back to the factory and rebuild the trebles because they were somewhat unstable, an effect that has not appeared in Don's new reeds at all. He agreed that the pitch change was probably responsible.

He also agreed that this change in pitch was unfortunate, but he felt that he could not oppose Koussevitzky who is responsible for the organ, particularly in view of the fact that a return to the 440 pitch meant new instruments for a considerable part of the orchestra. Munch, who is the new conductor, succeeding Koussevitzky who is retiring, accepted the Koussevitzky pitch for this reason.

We all agree that the Boston Symphony business is unfortunate, but under our system of free enterprise nobody can be put in jail for implementing an opinion.

I have to make an official inspection of the Boston Symphony Hall organ on December 3, but I have been told by men like Covell that the organ is magnificent.

With best regards,

Sincerely yours,
Emerson Richards

ER/s

---

220 Ernest Skinner to T. Scott Buhrman

Mr. T. Scott Buhrman,
The American Organist

Your poverty of ethical sense permits you to open your column to the vilest calumnies any pole cat is in the mind to say.

Emerson Richards in your September issue makes statements which are destitute of truth or fact. Richards speaks of my "romantic atrocities." He is too completely dumb to realize that I have had the most distinguished and conspicuous clientele in America, if not in the world, for whom I built organs because they asked me.

I never in my life called upon any church for a contract except that they sent for me. Richards therefore implies that all my clientele are damned fools, because they happen to like my work and that his judgment is superior. Well, I have seen that Atlantic City monstrosity and so have some others. It is the windiest, worst-voiced monstrosity on the face of the earth as everybody knows.

I haven't said a word in print or spoken about Richards. Why is he making his outrageous statements about me? I'll tell you Buhrman: it is because he has the most unethical publication on the face of the earth open to him. You told me once that the Aeolian-Skinner Co. demanded that you submit my advertising copy to them before publication. You said you did this. Any decent disposition would have told them to go to Hell where Marks now resides, if there is any such place.

Now as soon as I get time, I am going to write a reply to Richards. I am asking you if you will publish it in the next issue after you receive it. There will be nothing unethical about it, though I have reason to know you are not posted on ethics. If you won't publish it, I will prepare a statement which I will read to the American Guild of Organists to be held in Boston next summer.

Gruenstein would not publish such tripe as you permit in your columns at any price whatever. You remember perhaps why you are not the Guild representative as you once were.

Please let me know at once if you will publish what I say in reply to Richards, exactly as I say it.

Yours truly,
E.M. Skinner

---

221 Emerson Richards to T. Scott Buhrman

25 November 1949

My dear Buhrman:

I have read the Skinner letter. I agree that to associate a pole cat with Skinner is a vile calumny, but as I see it there is nothing effective that the pole cat can do about it. Mr. Skinner already stinks worse than anything the cat could dish out. The word <u>ethics</u> loses all sense of meaning when mouthed by this disappointed, irresponsible, artistically and financially bankrupt old man.

I knew Skinner could not hear, but I didn't know he could not read. Romantic atrocities refer to the reeds (after he lost Brockbank) and not to his organs as a whole, although some of these were no better than the contemporary Wurlitzers.

Mr. Skinner's "distinguished" clientele consisted mostly of trusting old ladies who fell for his high-power salesmanship. Did the authorities at the San Francisco Cathedral send for Skinner, or at Princeton, or the Hartford Seminary, to mention just a few that come to mind? And who had to finish his last fiasco at St. Thomas'?

Skinner lies when he says that he has even seen the Auditorium organ, and of course his hearing is too defective for him to have even heard it. Since it was built and voiced by men who originally made Skinner's reputation for him, it could hardly be any worse than his own jobs. Skinner is too full of malice, envy and egotism to be a critic of any organ.

I don't presume to know about your own dealings with Aeolian-Skinner and with Skinner, but there is certainly nothing unethical about censoring advertising copy in the interest of truth and accuracy, particularly when one pays for his advertising and the other does not. You have always insisted on truth in advertising, and that is something that Skinner would neither understand nor appreciate.

I have never made any personal statements about Skinner, outrageous or otherwise, although this is a fertile field that I am now tempted to explore. I have criticized his organs and in this I have been justified by the musically informed everywhere. It is characteristic of Mr. Skinner that he now would forget that he sought and I gave him several thousand dollars' worth of legal advice which in his arrogance and spleen he failed to take and which has ultimately resulted in his present misfortune.

As for your publishing Skinner's tripe, I say do it, although it is a waste of good white paper of no practical interest to the general organ public. I would only ask for the privilege of having my reply printed in parallel columns.

In conclusion, let me observe that Hell will never really be Hell until Skinner joins Marks in that resort for unpleasant characters.

Sincerely yours,

Emerson Richards

ER H

San Francisco Cathedral . . . Princeton . . . Hartford Seminary — Grace Cathedral, San Francisco, opus 910, 1934. Skinner had gone on his own to San Francisco and tried to alter a contractual stipulation that Harrison would personally finish the organ. Hartford Seminary (actually, Trinity College) and Princeton were other well-known organs that bore Harrison's mark. Skinner and Harrison collaborated on Princeton; Hartford was Harrison's own design and finishing.

---

222 Henry Willis to Emerson Richards

5th December, 1949

Hon. Emerson Richards,
800, Schwehm Buildings,
Atlantic City,
N.J.,
U.S.A.

My dear Richards,

Many thanks for your letters of the 7th and 21st November.

I think that you and I in correspondence can eliminate from discussions the stupid things done in this country by some organ builders — just as when you write about modern American practice you do not think of or refer to some of the silly specifications that appear from time to time in the Diapason, etc. You and I discuss matters on a high level.

When you write "we" — it, of course, means you and Don Harrison — for the use of the term cannot cover the productions of other than the Aeolian-Skinner Company, or, perhaps, Holtkamp.

If you and Don like and pursue the method of tonal design by which each stop tells little by itself — effect and buildup being cumulative — and hold up your hands in horror at a reed chorus dominating the flues, well and good. Excellent results can be obtained on these general lines which are simply those of the old German builders of the 17th century and those followed by the Italians today, including weak 16ft. stops on the Pedal — scaling becoming large in the Treble (halving on the 22nd note!) except that, I think and trust, the Ripieno do not stand out so much as with the Italian.

I cannot help thinking that if you heard and tried the large Organ at the Duomo, Milan, you would find it to be almost exactly on the lines you now recommend — including a weak pedal foundation and all the rest.

Aubrey wrote me a description of two jobs on the "new" lines and he might have been writing following his first hearing of two modern Italian instruments.

It is all a matter of opinion — I carry on the Willis traditions which are similar — a chorus reed dominating in full ensembles — as were the masterpieces of Cavaillé-Coll.

The modern French school decries Cavaillé-Coll, reverts to 17th Century French practice (as opposed to German) and openly calls for the destruction of Cavaillé-Coll organs by redesigning on 17th Century lines. This school of thought is headed by André Marchal — who is hand in hand with Gonzalez — who is the humble camp follower who does the work! Marcel Dupré opposes the retrograde attitude of the "17th Century" School. Fernando Germani thinks on similar lines to myself — combining the glories of our own tradition and development with those of earlier times. Germani's "pet" organs are, avowedly, Liverpool Cathedral and Westminster Cathedral.

Correspondents in the U.S. — and many organists who look me up when over here — deplore the ideals to which you subscribe, mention the acidity of tone developed, and always ask me "why cannot we get reeds and diapasons like these in America?"

In my opinion, the violent swing of the pendulum from "romanticism" to Don's creations of today will correct itself in time.

I have been told that the Möller rebuild at St. Thomas', New York "on Willis lines" is overdone — hard and screaming tone.

I agree that the use of the term "classical" as applied to any School is unwise and even meaningless.

What you seem not to understand is that here the Willis tradition built up from 1851 onward is the standard on which sound work was and is based. 99% of organists here do not want to go back beyond the period named and so hidebound are they that it is difficult to persuade them that there are some pre-1851 ideas of tonal design and apportionment that are worthy of incorporation alongside the now accepted English tradition.

I think that you are wrong about Fernando Germani. I know the whole story — F.G. is mad keen on a Willis at St. Peters, Rome.

To sum up this question of tonal designs and ideals, I feel that if a representative "Willis" Organ of reasonable size — say a biggish three manual — was installed in the U.S., suitably housed in good organ chamber and a church with a reverberation period of, say, 3 seconds, it would create the greatest interest.

I have had many inquiries from the U.S. and Canada since the war — but costs have proved too high for would-be clients to face.

Now that the pound has been devalued, there is a practical possibility of sending organs over and I propose to make a suitable announcement in the appropriate press in the U.S. to that effect. An agent will be required — could you recommend anyone?

I figure that with the pound at $2.80 I could ship instruments O.I.F. to an Eastern Port, U.S., including the U.S. 15 percent tariff, at about $1150 a stop. Some basic and obvious requirements such as blowers and low voltage units could, of course, be acquired in the U.S. to cut down shipping costs and tariff. It might well be possible to have other basic parts such as consoles, chests, reservoirs, swell boxes etc. made by suppliers in the U.S., so still further cutting down costs.

Our Government brings considerable pressure upon all here to export — especially to dollar areas — and every facility is given to help in that connection. We are doing some export work for British Crown Colonies etc. — and will, for example, be shipping a small organ to Malta very shortly — but these are sterling transactions and not very helpful to our serious dollar deficiency.

In short, I look forward to sending a representative instrument to the U.S. and think that it would create much artistic interest.

It would give me an opportunity (and an excuse) for me to visit America and see and hear for myself what has happened in the past 25 years — I have not been over since 1926 — and also and equally important see many old friends again.

I would be very glad to have your reactions to the above — and especially your advice about an agent.

Yours ever sincerely,

Henry Willis

P.S. I have just received two amazing letters, copies enclosed, from Scott Buhrman and Gruenstein respectively, declining to accept announcements (advertisements) in their papers. S.B. on political grounds; G. that it would offend American organ builders. I cannot believe that political discrimination against British manufacturers exists to the extent S.B. suggests, or that American organ builders are so petty-minded as G. suggests.

By and large, how can this country overcome our dollar shortage unless British goods are accepted in the U.S.A.? The only other solution is to give us the dollars. Strangely enough, we British would rather work for the dollars!

Buhrman and Gruenstein — then editors of the *American Organist* and the *Diapason*, respectively

---

223 Emerson Richards to Henry Willis

December 21, 1949

Henry Willis, Esq.
34 Marlborough Grove
Old Kent Road
London, S.E.1,
England.
My dear Willis,

Your letters are always welcome, but I confess that part of that of December 5th upset me completely. I immediately called Buhrman on the office telephone and gave him hell. I fear I did not mend matters to make him eat his words. I pointed out that he and Gruenstein take Casavant ads, and that Casavant was serious competition to U.S. builders. We cannot sell an organ in Canada under any circumstances. The trade barriers are so arranged that we cannot even get paid if by some chance we did sell an organ up there. Ernest White took his practice organ up to Toronto and now he cannot pay Don the balance due on it because of currency restrictions. I did not get an immediate reversal of his letter to you, but I think I will. He is sore on your government and that is understandable. But he won't separate you from that government. However, I think the spring elections will settle that.

Gruenstein is different. His half Semitic blood will tell. I have this suggestion — write to Lewis Odell, 1404 Jesup Avenue, New York, NY, Secretary of the Organ Builders Association, and ask him if the Association has any objection to your advertising in the Diapason. That will put them on the spot, and I am sure they will say that there is no objection. You may not know this, but Walker was put down before you applied on the same grounds. In any event, there are other musical journals such as The Étude which would take your ad and give it more of a circulation than the Diapason and the American Organist combined. I think the whole thing is silly.

Personally, I think one of your organs over here would be a good thing, an influence, and a half dozen more a salutary effect. You know I might not approve of them entirely, but they would still be better than most of the work done over here. Most of the organs of yours that I have heard, I like.

Now about an agent. I want to give that some thought. I have only one or two people in mind, but I want to think it over.

Now, to the main part of your letter. "We" does not always mean me and Don, and never Holtkamp. Success is making Don somewhat impatient of advice. The program article accompanying the Symphony Hall organ is a crack at "sidewalk superintendence being kept at arm's length." The words are supposed to be Biggs', but while the organ is magnificent, it could have been better if Don's ears had not been closed to suggestions.

In listening to visitors from the United States, remember that Skinner's venom is still working. He is getting more violent and vindictive all the time. Because of his age everybody hesitates to go after him, but the situation is becoming intolerable.

I have not seen the St. Thomas rebuild. As far as "acidity of tone," certainly there is no such defect in Don's Diapason work. It is more restrained than yours — perhaps too much that way. This is just more Skinner propaganda.

You may have heard that Ridgely was spreading the story that Don was bankrupt. Recently I saw a special auditor's report. Not a bill unpaid; a big inventory; two years work on order; over $100,000 in the bank clear. Yet Möller was trying to get business by telling customers that Don could not finish their organs. This is the least vicious of what some of them will try to do.

My only fear is that too much success will do what it has done for most people, although I think Don is too level-headed for that. But for that reason, among many others, I welcome your decision to try for some jobs over here. As it is Don has no real competition and you would do him a lot of good, and yourself as well. On the larger organs Möller is asking as much money as Don. Möller is somewhat cheaper on the small two-manuals.

Returning to the question of an agent. My first thought was Courboin. He has had experience, is now quite influential in the Catholic Church, and is widely known on account of his recitals. To that extent he would make an ideal salesman if he could spare the time. His job at the cathedral keeps him pretty busy, even with two assistants. What you seem to want is a practical organ man who can erect your organs as well as sell them. To get a reliable man of this type is a problem. Nobody that I would want to recommend comes to mind at the moment, but I will give it plenty of thought.

In your letter you speak of "weak" 16' stops on the pedal. Where did you get this idea? Most of the builders still use the open wood much the same as yourself, although Möller is trying to get away on his cheaper jobs with a metal 16' extension of the Great 8' Diapason. Don's Contra Bass is really a big tone, although the scale looks small. It has plenty of power and precision, and to that extent is better than the old wood "Diapason." The Bourdons are about the same and the reeds are about the same power, although Don opens them up more. Also, Don uses 5" wind on the pedal flues and about 7" on the reeds. In addition to the 16' stops Don adds more independent 8's and 4's, mutations and mixtures than you do. There are practically no extensions of the 8's and 4's, and the mutations are also separate. Consequently, these pedals are not only more independent but actually more powerful than the English pedal.

With sincere best wishes to you and yours for a Happy Holiday Season, I am

Faithfully,
Emerson Richards

ER/af

Courboin . . . at the Cathedral — St. Patrick's Cathedral, Manhattan

---

224 G. Donald Harrison to Henry Willis

December 29, 1949

Mr. Henry Willis
Henry Willis & Sons Ltd.
34, Marlborough Grove
Old Kent Road,
London, S.E.1, England
My dear Henry:

I have not written to you for an awfully long while, in fact, my correspondence generally is way behind due to terrific pressure of work.

Aubrey seems to be settling down all right and he and his family live in the home they have purchased not too far from the plant. He seems to be making plenty of friends. While he has plenty of ideas we have not changed any of our production methods to date and usually we have found the time to do anything drastic is during a period of slackness where matters can be developed and properly watched. Making changes during a period of great activity is apt to throw a monkey wrench into the wheels and retard the completion of jobs to a considerable extent.

We have just obtained a very large contract, in fact, the largest the Company has ever received, from the Mother Church, Christian Scientist here in Boston. It involves two organs; a medium size three manual for the Original Church and an organ somewhat bigger than the Salt Lake City instrument for the big Edifice. While we have all kinds of business with plenty in the offing, it is difficult to say how long it is liable to keep up. If the information I receive is correct, some of the other builders are beginning to draw in their horns to some extent.

I have your letter regarding the pitch at the Boston Symphony Hall. I agree with you that it's a very unfortunate thing that they should have retained their old pitch at A444 instead of reverting to the standard of A440. As far as I know, they are the only important orchestra which is out of step with the standard pitch. It is something of rather long standing and was introduced by Koussevitzky. We were all hoping that when the new conductor came in that the pitch would be brought back to A440. However, he decided to retain the sharper pitch and there was nothing we could do about it. To have changed the pitch would have cost all the wood wind players quite a little, as their instruments have all been changed to suit the sharp pitch and it is very difficult, if not impossible, to flatten them again and this is undoubtedly one of the reasons for retaining A444.

There are plenty of musicians here who strongly object to it, and I have heard criticisms from many people who listen to the records made by this orchestra. For some reason or other the sharpness seems to sharpen up a good deal more on records than listening to the performance in the Hall. It is, of course, the string players who have gradually pushed the pitch up, as they seem to think it gives a more brilliant tone in the string section. There is a constant fight going on between the string players and the wood winds as all the time there is a tendency to sharpen even more.

The authorities were thoroughly warned about the organ, and it was pointed out if after it was decided to lower the pitch from the standard, it would be a terrific job from the organ point of view.

I understand that Harrison and Harrison got the contract for the Exposition organ, and I cannot help wondering about the final result. I hope they got a big enough price to make the whole transaction worth while.

I was interested to hear from Aubrey that the new dome section of St. Paul's Cathedral is all completed. I saw some pictures in an illustrated magazine and one of them showed the Low C of the 16' Open being hoisted up to the quarter gallery. It is surprising how one's memory works at times, for the appearance of this pipe was so familiar to me that there was no question as to where it came from.

I was very surprised that Piper came over to go to Austins but I understand he has a very good job there and they are very nice people to work with but I imagine he will not relish the Austin chest. I have not seen him since he arrived.

Germani, as you know, has been here and I heard him give his recital on the Methuen organ and he certainly did a fine job. He seemed quite indefinite as to when any contract would be let for St. Peter's but I gathered that you are sitting pretty in connection with the matter and I hope it will develop into something tangible before too long.

I trust you had a Merry Christmas and wish you all the best for 1950.

Yours, as ever

Don

GDH/MOK

the Mother Church — four-manuals, eight divisions, 237 ranks. Opus 1203.
retained their old pitch — See letter 218.
Exposition Organ — Royal Festival Hall, see following letter.
contract . . . for St. Peter's — This organ never materalized. The Basilica uses two portable organs and an electronic.

---

225 G. Donald Harrison to Ralph Downes

January 13, 1950

Ralph Downes
London, England

Re: <u>L.C.C. Organ</u>

My dear Ralph:

I have read your letter of November 29th and enclosures with great interest, and I have made a close study of the layout of the auditorium and the remarks about the acoustics, also the specification of the instrument and the mixture layouts and scales.

For your sake, and also for the sake of the art of organ building, I am very anxious that a really fine instrument shall be produced, as it may start a new style of tonal schemes in England and they certainly need it. Of course, however good the organ may be, you and Harrison and Harrison have to be prepared for a flood of criticism, and the arguments pro and con will be endless!

You will need much patience with Harrison and Harrison, for this is so unlike anything they have ever dreamed of that it will be quite a shock. In my own case, the matter has been a gradual development over a long period of nearly 20 years — one step at a time. I would not have liked to have been suddenly confronted with such a piece of work and with the grave responsibilities that are involved. From Aubrey, I understand the present head of Harrison and Harrison is a nice chap and not too old and set (<u>in tonal matters</u>). It seems that you have made a wise choice as to builder.

G. Donald Harrison

I am wondering if slide chests are to be used, as I understand Harrison and Harrison are quite conservative (<u>mechanically</u>). If so, make sure plenty of room is given to the slides carrying the mixtures. The larger ones should have more than one slide. This will prevent much robbing and drawing and simplify the regulation and tuning.

Are these mixtures going to have slide tuners or be cone-tuned? If the latter, the regulation will have to be done with the utmost care, and it will take hours, for they have to be cut into tune and regulated simultaneously. Once you cut a pipe too short you are sunk!

I hope all reservoirs will be of the double rise weighted type with winkers on all chests to keep wind steady. With so many small pipes a really steady wind is essential. A separate reservoir for the Great and Positiv basses that are set off the main chest would be very helpful in this regard.

Don't forget that old organs which are so impressive on the continent are nearly always speaking under ideal conditions acoustically, and the location is always perfect. The few I have heard where there is little reverberation, the places have been small and intimate, but the instrument has been right in the room. If one of these organs could be transplanted into a typical American church or to many in England and also located in typical fashion in what we would consider a good chamber, the difference in the effect of the instrument both as to individual voices and in ensemble would not only amaze you but you would insist that the pipework had been tampered with. Unless you have had much experience in handling pipes under different conditions, you cannot appreciate this phenomenon. You can be terribly fooled, and it is well to remember that things are relative. Even the most experienced can rave about a particular stop in an inferior instrument. All this means is that by comparison with the rest it is good. How often I have included in a new organ a favourite stop from the old instrument on the request of the organist, and later to be accused of having tampered with the "beautiful pipes" or requested to substitute a new one. I examined the Flentrop organ in the World's Fair. It was a nice piece of work, but out of its proper environment. Individually and collectively, the tone was strident, windy in spots and spiky. There were some pleasant stopped flutes which interested me, the rest was decidedly unpleasant and they could not sell it over here. They had failed to adapt the instrument to its surroundings, which I feel is inartistic.

So often when I was in Germany I was given one reason or another for the beauty of a particular organ only to find it to be untrue on examining the pipes. As a typical example, I was told by the organist at Freiburg that the mixtures were unnicked, hence the beautiful effect. I went inside and although I lifted out numerous pipes I failed to find an unnicked one. True, they had the typical 18th century knife cuts for nicks similar to those used by Father Smith in England. Here and there was a pipe with modern nicks added to make the pipe speak properly. The hand of some restorer. I have made unnicked pipes, and what it really does is to add some enharmonic sounds. Whether or not they are desirable is a matter of debate. In certain places yes, and in others no.

I have written at length on such matters because you are really placing yourself in the position of the master organ builder in this job. I don't want you to be misled by what you hear in certain places with your own ears or by advice given by "experts" who have theory down pat and can quote scales and ratios ad infinitum, but possess little or no practical experience. This can only come by years of building and experimentation. The proper way of going about a job of this kind is to decide by a mental picture exactly the effect of each stop, the general color to be imparted to each division, the relative dynamic level of each division, the office of the Pedal, and finally the effect of the full organ. You must have a mental vision of all this, and then every step you take almost subconsciously will tend to bring about the realization of the dream. Of course, this needs experience, and I may be able to help you in this, plus the practical experience of H.&H. may be valuable.

At Salt Lake my dream came true, except there was one pleasant surprise in the toute ensemble. There is a fullness of tone, yet transparency,

I had missed. I had not realized that the many large scaled mixtures would create such valuable resultant effects in that acoustical environment. I have never heard anything just like it, and, to me anyway, it has quite an exciting effect on the nervous system.

It has been my custom to try out certain pipes in the building, both flue and reed, to confirm or otherwise one's judgment. When you know the effect of certain specimens, it is easier to scale and voice the entire organ with greater confidence.

Now in this job, we are dealing with a set of blueprints, which is unfortunate. However, let us see what we may reasonably expect on considering the plans:

1. The auditorium is large and can seat a large number of people. I would say the number of people is large for the total cubic capacity as compared with many existing buildings in which organs are placed.

2. The instrument will be fairly well-placed, but there is an orchestral deflector which provides interference.

3. The orchestra is in a much better position, and in front of the organ.

4. The auditorium has planned acoustics. Acoustics is far from an exact science, but at the least the <u>very latest</u> theories are being employed, and many of the pitfalls have been avoided. It is a good thing they are arranging to take the boom and undue prolongation of the low frequencies. However, the absorbent material will adversely affect the high frequencies. Also in all probability there will be less reverberation when judged by ear than is specified. Unfortunately, they do not specify the frequency for the prolongation period. I judge the auditorium will be somewhat inferior to Boston Symphony Hall, where we have just finished an organ.

Now, all four of the above points mean that the instrument has to have considerably authority, otherwise it will be feeble in effect when heard by the audience. It must have an ensemble that balances the dynamic level of the full orchestra playing ff. (The latter has a better location.) Also, there may be a choir added at times. To help we have a large number of ranks, which is very important, and they are well distributed over the departments, which means a large area. We feel, therefore, that forcing of the tone is unnecessary to make the instrument fill the bill, but it must be full and moderately bold in its various ranks. It will be well to keep all ranks within narrow limits as to dynamic level. Very loud and very soft ranks should be avoided. All must pull some weight in the ensemble. The engineers have taken care of excessive bass boom so we can voice normally at the lower end of the Pedal Organ. On account of condition 4, we must build up the trebles of each rank partly by scaling and partly by voicing. If they are too small and we have to blow them hard, they will become spiky. We must be careful about the top octave however. This is where real trouble starts. The classical builders had no problem here! You must be able to hear your right hand little finger at all parts of the compass on individual ranks and collectively. On account of condition 1, and particularly the latter part of 4, a well developed harmonic development is indicated throughout.

All the above indicates that we cannot rely upon copies of stops we have heard under entirely different conditions, neither can we expect small variations in basic scaling, or the ratios of the same, to make any appreciable difference. Rather it is going to be the tonal design, the voicing methods, dynamic levels and balance between bass and treble, together with the final finishing that is going to make for success. We must ensure getting off to a good start, so let us examine first the specification.

I find this to be excellent in every way, and it represents a good balance between classical and modern ideals. It follows fairly closely many organs that exist and have proved to be successful. (See enclosed re: Symphony Hall.) May I make just one point. I am not sold on the arrangement of the Pedal mixtures. I do not like to see the 3⅕ Tierce tied to the 5⅓ Quint. The use of the Tierce is often dangerous while the 5⅓ Quint properly treated and bold adds great depth without weight to the Pedal. Why not tie the Tierce and Septième together and leave the Quint on its own.

You have a very fine tonal scheme. I have examined carefully the layout of all the mixtures, and I like them. In some you have doubled up on the ranks, which will be quite helpful under the conditions. Where you double a rank I have found it advantageous to use longer feet on one rank in addition to changing the scale. This is a further safeguard against sympathy.

Now, let us examine the scaling of the flue pipes. If we make a start with the Great 4' Octave and get that right, we can base the rest on this rank, and make certain of a successful job.

The scale at 4' C is excellent. I used approximately the same at Salt Lake. The ratio, however, seems uneven.

Think this over and consult H.&H. The pressure is 3½", and I take it the metal will be 50 percent tin. The pipes should not be too heavy, and I hope a ¼ mouth will be used. The languid should not be too thin, and the bevel retreating. This should give ample control. Do not try to make the pipes too quick and have the flues narrow. The toe should be opened to give a copious wind supply (at least 7/16" for a 2' C pipe). The tone will be natural and unforced, and the stop will be found to have a beautiful singing quality. If you could try this sample in a building of equivalent size, it might be helpful in giving you confidence to proceed further. When you have all C's in correct balance, I would recommend you voice all other C's of the Great and other departments, balancing them against your octave C's. Of course, you must determine on the Great, for example, whether you are going to reduce in power for ranks of higher unison pitch, and how the off-unisons are to be treated in this regard. The way this is done will give the instrument its peculiar personality, its clarity and transparency or otherwise. Whether it will be pointed or round generally speaking. You will realize that it will also greatly influence the power and blend of the complete department. I fear this is something you must decide upon, for what I say might mislead you. If I could be there for a few hours with some pipes that might be different. Suffice it to say you can make it like this $\wedge$ or $\vee$ or a variation of all. One thing, have a plan and stick to it. The possibilities are infinite, and most of them can be successful in varying degrees.

When you have the Great set up, you can set the C's of other departments, having determined to what extent the general dynamic levels of departments are to vary. Don't overlook that you should compensate for enclosed stops. Enclosure cuts down power and harmonic development. Compensate for same.

I take it the Pedal is to balance the manuals without Pedal couplers as far as possible. Now let me comment on some other individual scales.

Great Diapason 8. I notice you have flared out the bass. A copy I guess. Don't forget the basses of diapasons were usually in the front, and were made to suit the proportions of the case rather than the tone. Use a lower cut-up for the big bass. Personally I feel a much better blend would be obtained between 8' and 4' diapasons if the 8' was smaller. Don't take my word for it though!

Now my remarks regarding the 4' Octave, about a kind of hollow scale [at] about 1' C holds good in your 15th and mixture scales, and in the latter they are exaggerated by your scheme of dropping three scales to prevent.[sic] I fear you have overdone this anyway for my taste. It will be more French than German, and you will be more dependent on reeds. I would suggest further consideration on this. I am enclosing separate sheet giving some scales of the Great Organ at Groton School. This flue chorus is acknowledged by all to be the best in the country — many say the best they have heard anywhere. You will note the big scales employed.

Now let us look at your Bourdons 8'. Take the Great. I have a special scale I worked out. Yours falls off too much in treble. You will find a beautiful stop will result, and one that will support the 4' and upperwork without having to use the 8' Diapason. A much better blend and clarity are obtained in this way.

I feel your strings, etc., are O.K., also flutes, except a Rohrflöte similar to above makes a beauty. Your Koppel treble could be bigger. This does not mean fat tone, providing the cutups are lowered. It gives bloom.

Now about reeds, I hope your French friend is O.K. I fear the divided responsibility, and would suggest he gives scales of pipes and shallots and tongue thickness only, and let H.&H. do the voicing.

I hope you will find all this of help and not too unsettling. I want to give you confidence. Don't forget to make allowance for the fact that you are not used to hearing things constantly in a small room against a voicing machine. Make allowances and try odd pipes in a bigger place. Try to have everything as perfect as possible in the shop. The fewer changes you have to make on the site (when you are rushed) the better. Always leave well enough alone, and avoid second guesses. Make up your mind and stick to it.

Now in all this I hope you will take my remarks in the spirit in which they are offered. I don't want to dictate and cannot take any responsibility. I have tried just to be helpful and perhaps prevent some pitfalls. You can show this to H.&H. or any part of it if you should wish; provided it won't give any offense. It is so different from the normal practice, and they are diving in all at one jump!

Let me hear from you and ask any questions you wish, and I will try to answer.

All the best for 1950,

Yours,
Don

P.S. I would keep dynamic level of departments fairly close. Let them contrast in color rather than power. By the way, an 8' Quintadena would be much more useful in the Positiv than the 8' Diapason. How do you use the latter in a Positiv?

I trust the examples of scaling will be sufficient for your purpose. If you want more, let me know.

Commentary by Ralph Downes:

"The significance of this letter is that it is unique, among all the advice and correspondence I received, in giving a real, practical down-to-earth lead regarding the building of a neo-classical organ for a large, essentially modern concert auditorium — and this at a time when such things were only <u>beginning</u> to be considered in the English-speaking world.

As Don knew, I had not in any way "angled" for the job as consultant; I was virtually pushed into it and only consented because I realized that no other organist here had at that time had the practical experience of, or given the same concentrated thought to, the problems involved.

Once the builders had been chosen (on my considered advice), <u>they</u> looked to <u>me</u> for complete guidance for everything except the construction and mechanism (of which they were past masters). Hence, Don's typically generous attitude as shown in this letter.

I have considered the idea of handing over all (or as much as I have of) our correspondence to you, but decided that to make it all public property would be unfair not only to Don (because, amongst other things, I eventually rejected his conception of pipe scales, voicing, even specification), as also to the numerous other people who provided me with equally generous advice and moral support, whose contribution was publicly acknowledged in the organ builder's brochure and included the late Walter Holtkamp, Robert Noehren, Louis-Eugène Rochesson, Dr. Maarten Vente, Fritz Abend, Susi Jeans and very especially, Dirk Flentrop; and of course, the entire staff of Harrison and Harrison, the builders, who had the "nitty gritty" to deal with at every turn and who generously cooperated down to the last detail.

In the end, the completely integrated plan was mine alone, specification, location, materials, pipe construction and scales, wind pressures, voicing and tonal finishing. The final batch of scales was not put in hand until 2½ years after Don's letter, in late 1952. The building period lasted from 1949 to late 1953 — in the hall from 1952. Every pipe was finally voiced in the building, all the work being done overnight, six nights a week, with direction from me in a selected position in mid-auditorium. We discovered at first hand all the acoustical problems and dealt with them on the spot as perfectly as we could. In the past 32 years, the reputation of the organ has increased as its many-sided excellence has been demonstrated over and again by a great number of the most distinguished performers — not to mention its constant use in choral and/or orchestral concerts of many assorted dimensions.

Ralph Downes
Curator-Organist, Royal Festival Hall,
London SE., October, 1986

---

226 Emerson Richards to Henry Willis

January 30, 1950

Henry Willis, Esq.
Rotunda Organ Works,
34, Marlborough Grove,
Old Kent Road, London, S.E.1
My dear Willis:

Thanks for the copy of the letter of January 16 sent to Don in which you enclosed a copy of the L.C.C. Concert Hall organ specification.

It looks to me as if Downes had tried to copy Don Harrison's and Holtkamp's specifications with a few individual ideas thrown in for luck. The whole thing resembles nothing in the heavens above nor the earth beneath nor the waters under the earth. I am curious to know how much money your Socialistic government is spending on this atrocity. Are you not trying to kid Don when you suggest that he might approve of this thing? Of course he would not.

Perhaps one of the worst things about this job is the extraordinary composition of the mixtures, and while we do not know where they break or how they are to be voiced, they are obviously much too acute in the bass to be at all satisfactory and they are sure to put a stop to any suggestion of a mixture revival in England. When Aubrey was here we had a chance for quite a long talk about this proposed organ. Partly from what Aubrey said and partly from what he left unsaid, I gather that Downes has almost reached a state of nervous exhaustion over this job, and that personal disaster might result.

Incidentally, I presume the specification is rather inaccurate when it claims that even the 16' basses are made of 50 per cent spotted metal — and why was not tin used in the mixture at least?

Perhaps Don has sent you a specification of the new 224 rank job for the First Church of Christ, Scientist. If not and you are interested I will send you a copy.

This is all for the moment.

Sincerely,
Emerson Richards

ER/s

even the 16' basses — the 16' basses are indeed of spotted metal
the new 224 rank job — eventually 237 ranks

---

227 G. Donald Harrison to William King Covell

February 15, 1950

Mr. William King Covell
72 Washington Street
Newport, Rhode Island.

Dear Mr. Covell:

Thank you for your letter of the 7th instant and for the draft of the letter you propose to send to the <u>Organ</u> in London.

Of course I read E.M.'s recent letter in the past issue and it is full of mis-statements — as usual. Some years ago when Fitzsimmons was still alive, E.M. was writing a great many letters to the <u>Organ</u> and I suggested to Fitzsimmons that it was a very bad thing to have us washing our dirty linen in a foreign magazine. Fitzsimmons did not tell me whether he tipped E.M. off or not, but the fact remains that for quite a while there were no further letters from E.M.

I have never answered any of E.M.'s letters, feeling that it would simply start an endless correspondence back and forth, and we would finally get to the brick-bat throwing stage. Of course E.M. has done everything he possibly can to get me to answer him, but I have never fallen.

Undoubtedly, it is a good thing to have someone point out that all E.M. says is not true and I greatly appreciate your effort in this regard. I think your letter is fine, and the only criticism I can find is that it may be on the long side. I wonder if it could be boiled down to about two pages and still retain all the kick it has in the present, more lengthy document. However, whatever you decide is all right with me.

With best wishes,

Sincerely yours,

G. Donald Harrison
President

GDH:AGR

P.S. I am returning the draft herewith in case you need it.

Fitzsimmons — then-editor of *The Organ*.

---

228 G. Donald Harrison to Carl Weinrich

AIR MAIL - SPECIAL DELIVERY
November 9, 1951

Dr. Carl Weinrich
Princeton University
Princeton, New Jersey

Dear Carl:

I am sending this Special Delivery because if it ever got lost it would break all of our hearts. We have spent many alcoholic and non-alcoholic hours pouring over this trying to figure out how we could do what you want done and still keep from getting fired by the Directors when they discover what we have done.

I do hope we have it now. Frankly the four-manual scheme is simply out of the question for $10,000.00. I am even amazed that I am able to give in to this figure for a three-manual but it does all depend on the fact that we will be doing only factory work. As you know, outside work is very expensive for us. I do hope you can persuade Raymond to do all of this work for this amount. I am certain we couldn't do it.

I am enclosing the new specification and I have attempted to work out everything that you want. In the Great organ all the chests will remain the same and the new 16' reed will go where the old 16' Posaune is. If the Pedal borrow is moved from 10⅔' to 16, you will have a nice, soft 16' reed on the Pedal to use without tying up the Great. How's that for throwing something in? In the Brustwerke, I agree that you would have a better use for that old Choir chest than the useless mutations now on it. Therefore, if Raymond can move this we can supply a two-stop chest for the Rohrgedackt and the mixture. The winding of this may be difficult. It probably could be winded from the Great. If it needs a new reservoir, however, this would have to be extra.

There will be one compromise which is somewhat amusing. You will note that we are taking back the old French Horn, that magnificent stop, as you have suggested. Why don't you then move the English Horn to the Swell to replace the useless First Open Diapason. The pressures are just the same and it would work well. It would not work where the French Horn was because the pressure is too high. Instead, we will voice the main part of the Positiv organ on very low pressure and have one stop, the Larigot 1⅓' on 15" pressure along with the Tubas. This also allows you to leave the Tuba Mirabilis chest the way it is. What more could we do? It seems to me now that you have just about everything. I hope I have written this down intelligently so that you can get from it what Raymond has to do.

This pricing is so tight that we will have to be free to use old materials whenever they are satisfactory. I am sure you have no objection to this because old pipes are just as good as new if the voicing can be accomplished that we want and I know you'll be very particular about that. For instance, the 16' Quintaten on the Great can well be made out of an 8' Diapason. I don't know whether you have heard the one in Bronxville or not, but that is one of the best Quintatens that we have ever made and it was made out of the old First Open of the Great capped. In the same way, the Rohrgedackt in the Brustwerke can be made out of the Swell 8' Principal with chimneys and caps modified considerably. We plan to do this sort of thing all the way through to save material costs. I just hope we can squeak by.

You are going to have to make an awful lot of records for M.G.M. to get over this.

If you agree with all this we had better get going because time has been fleeting since we have considered this and I am being so pressed for early promises that I am getting worried about the time necessary to complete this unless we can finally settle on something and get into the planning of it.

With all best wishes from both of us,

Sincerely,

AEOLIAN-SKINNER ORGAN COMPANY

Don

President

GDH/MOK

---

persuade Raymond to do all this — Chester A. Raymond, an organ technician, formerly with A. Gottfried in Erie, PA, before establishing his own business in 1933 in Princeton, NJ. He died in 1970 at the age of 72.

I hope we have it now — a reworking of the Princeton University Chapel organ, opus 656, 1927, the first significant job with which Harrison was involved.

records for M.G.M — Weinrich's survey of Bach works on MGM Records, Volume II of which had been released by February, 1952, according to advertising in *The Diapason*.

229 G. Donald Harrison to Carl Weinrich

May 1, 1952

Professor Carl Weinrich
University Chapel, Princeton University
Princeton, New Jersey
Dear Carl:

I have been checking up with Joe in regard to the pipes for the Chapel organ and I find it will be utterly impossible for us to have the work done by June. Due to the 237 ranks belonging to the Christian Science organ here, our voicing has become so behind that we have two jobs now already installed waiting pipes. I have never seen such a situation in this plant before. Those tremendous jobs, like the Christian Science organ, are terrific unbalances, so to speak, of one's shop because the number of pipes involved is so much greater in relation to the rest of the organ, than with a normal instrument.

We will be able to complete your work during the summer, however, but I hope you will be patient with us. I will arrange to get together with you real soon. I fear I am tied up this coming Friday.

With all best wishes,

> Cordially yours,
> AEOLIAN-SKINNER ORGAN COMPANY
> Don
> President

GDH/MOK

---

230 G. Donald Harrison to Carl Weinrich

May 21, 1952

Mr. Carl Weinrich
Princeton Chapel, Princeton University
Princeton, New Jersey
Dear Carl:

As we are now gradually coming to the time when we must get the pipes voiced etc. for the changes in the Chapel organ, I would very much appreciate it if you could possibly take time out to run up to Edgar Hilliar's Church which is St. Mark's Mount Kisco, New York. There we have just finished a three-manual organ which I believe is right down your alley in regard to the voicing, particularly in connection with the Mixturs. There is also an unenclosed Positiv organ on the opposite side of the chancel to the main division which I think is particularly interesting.

If you could take a look at this organ and try it out very carefully, I think it would go a long way to straightening out the matter at Princeton

Chapel, and we can have a complete meeting of the minds in the situation. Hilliar has the same feeling that you do about Mixturs of the Fourniture type, so we avoided them in his particular case. Most of the Mixturs he has are of the higher pitch variety, and I must say from the contrapuntal angle, it is about the clearest instrument I have ever heard.

Mount Kisco is not difficult to get to via the Saw Mill River Parkway and is not more than about thirty-six miles out of New York City.

With best wishes, as ever

Yours,
Don

GDH/MOK

St. Mark's, Mt. Kisco — Opus 1201: Great, Swell I, Swell II, Positiv, and Pedal.

Joseph S. Whiteford

---

231 Joseph S. Whiteford to Carl Weinrich

June 9, 1952

Dr. Carl Weinrich
Princeton University
Princeton, New Jersey
Dear Carl:

Thanks so much for your letter of June 2, 1952. It was good to hear from you and good to know that you have been to Mt. Kisco. I am sorry you had such a time locating us. We have been out of town a great deal recently and Mother Mary Baker Eddy's Opus has been wound up during their week's conclave here so that we have that off our shoulders.

It's been awfully good of you to be so patient with us about time but, honestly, an organ like that Mother Church organ just simply puts us in an impossible situation with reference to pipes and voicing. You will be glad to know that we recently got in two superb voicers from Europe, thus doubling our capacities in flue voicing and have been able to acquire some skilled workmen in other fields. This makes it possible for us to go ahead very soon now and after the next conference you have with the boss, I am sure we would be ready to go ahead.

Mr. Harrison will be in New York this coming Friday, and he will call you this week with reference to an appointment.

With all best wishes and kind regards to you both,

Sincerely,
AEOLIAN-SKINNER ORGAN COMPANY
J.S.W.
Vice President

JSW/MOK

---

232 Emerson Richards to Henry Willis

August 5th, 1952
Confidential

My dear Willis,

I have just received the copy of your letter of July 15th to Thompson-Allen. I already owed you a letter but in the middle of June I became aware that something was wrong with the rear universal of my chassis and upon investigation the surgeons said immediate repair was indicated.

So to the hospital on June 23rd and two of the A.M.A.'s prize pets spent forty-five minutes on a complete overhaul and now, to change the metaphor to one more familiar, my West End organ is completely renovated, tuned and revoiced, and is in service again.

By July 11th I was able to get rid of the nurses and come up here by plane. Where it was cool and comfortable. Aubrey arrived the next day and later Covell, and matters organistic got a good going over. Sumner's book we agreed was, despite its obvious defects, about the best thing of its kind since Hopkins.

By now I have quite recovered and am very thankful that it was not as serious as inconvenient.

I was naturally interested in your German visit. Glad Steinmeyer is doing so well. I should like to visit with him again. Mrs. Steinmeyer has

Hans Steinmeyer with a 32' pipe at Passau Cathedral

been over here on a visit but when she was in the East I was up here. Ad and I were sorry we missed her.

I agree with you about the Holtkamp cases. Too bad that Don cannot build the organs and Holtkamp the cases. I don't think too much of the new Æolian-Skinner booklet. Whiteford.

Methuen. You use the wrong adjective. It is not a mongrel. It is and always was a bastard. It followed Ulm, and you remember what that was like. It was conceived in a miscegenation of German pseudo classic-romanticism wherein its reputed . . . *[remainder missing]*

If Don thought that he could make a silk purse out of a sow's ear, it only goes to prove that overconfidence may overthrow the canons of Art, but it cannot overcome the laws of genetics.

I do think that Don's efforts did invest it with a certain amount of genteel respectability, just as the honest American case served to screen the misalliance within. But bastardy is not so much an accident of birth as a physical disorder of the hereditary system that cannot be exactly defined but in moments of crisis exposes this spiritual feebleness. The aphorism "once a bastard, always a bastard" is founded upon ages of human experience. Therefore we must credit Don's generosity even if we do question his judgment.

I have been enjoying the camp as usual. Have an excellent cook and a household team of three that makes living quite comfortable. Better than we can do at home.

All over the East the heat has been terrific all summer, but up here a blanket at night has been necessary. And a blazing log fire is mighty cheerful. Because of the lack of rain, forest fires have been quite destructive up here.

There is not much organ news. I have not yet heard the Christian Science job. No competent reports from others as these very odd people do not encourage visitors or possible critics.

I do hope you will find time for a more detailed report on German organs and organ building. It would be interesting.

Ad is here for a couple of weeks and sends her love to Dora and our best to you.

Sincerely,

Emerson Richards

Sumner's book . . . since Hopkins — W. L. Sumner, *The Organ* (London: MacDonald & Jane, 1952. Edward John Hopkins, *The Organ* (London: R. Cocks, 1870).
It followed Ulm — In the 1860s, Walcker built a large organ at Ulm Cathedral.

August 5, 1952

Dr. Carl Weinrich
Princeton University
Princeton, New Jersey

Dear Carl:

Thanks for your letter of July 22nd, 1952. It would be impossible for me to tell you what a stew we are in here on the matter of pipes. We are at the point now where we have three organs installed complete with consoles, swell shades, tremolos, chests and absolutely no pipes made. Sometimes I wonder how we can get into these situations but on the other hand, there are such unavoidable things as people dying, people quitting, training of new personnel and Mary Baker Eddy which gang up on one every so often. Last year it seemed to be consoles. We had organs and pipes but no consoles. You can see what with so many organs out and installed with the exception of pipes, we really are in a difficult position and for you, of all people, I want to do my best and do it as fast as possible knowing your plans in the Fall.

Right now we are getting together everything we can on the mechanical side to send it down to Mr. Raymond. We will tackle the Great first and undoubtedly ship that down there first. Don't worry about the pipes taking too long to put in. They will all be set here in the racks and the only work to do is to screw down the top and rack boards and set the pipes in and then start to work tuning and finishing. Thank God you have some other organ there that you can be playing on. Little by little as the stops are finished you can bring them into your work. I can't tell you how sorry I am that things have been delayed this long but you have been so good, so patient with us.

All the best to you.

Sincerely,

AEOLIAN-SKINNER ORGAN COMPANY

Don

GDH/MOK

---

get into these situations — Roy Perry, the Aeolian-Skinner representative in the Southwest and a finisher, related how fretful Harrison was over the Mother Church — "Tying up the shop only to accompany a tenor soloist singing 'Shepherd, show me how to go.'"

Aubrey Thompson-Allen, Dora Willis, Emerson Richards, Henry Willis III during the American visit of the Willises

---

234 Henry Willis to G. Donald Harrison

18th. August, 1952

Mr. G. Donald Harrison,
President, Aeolian-Skinner Organ Co.,
Crescent Avenue, Dorchester,
Boston 25, Mass., U.S.A.

Personal and Private.

My Dear Don,

I have been working at high pressure since my return, have had no time before now to write you of my impressions gained during my recent visit. I write you quite frankly as I know you would wish me to do.

Following my visits in 1924, 1925, and 1926 and E.M's incapacity, combined with unwillingness, to carry out the tonal indication I had given, as you know, you went out to do that. Frustration by Skinner limited your progress for, I gather, about five years, for it was not until 1932 — so I understand — that you secured a free hand in tonal matters, so that I can take it from 1932 onwards Aeolian-Skinner Organs were your productions.

From 1932 to 1935 from my observation, you were doing work on general lines with which you were well-acquainted here. But with a wider scope you introduced more upper-work and again — with a bigger palate — reduced wind pressures, relying on massed tones for ensemble in the older tradition. Your excellent specifications were and are a godsend to others. In or about 1937 you, very naturally and properly, began to express your own convictions not only in specifications but in the manner of carrying them out.

Diapasons had less importance — greater accent on the 4ft. line shown, with a healthy abundance of upper-work and mixtures. You developed pedal organ design logically, eschewing extension whenever practicable, and later departed from the use of closed shallots for chorus reeds. The French type Bombardes or similar type took the place of Tubas. A typical "Donald Harrison" came into being, and I do trust that you will appreciate my point of view when I say that, in my opinion, your work between 1937 and 1942 represented an individual expression that might well have continued without basic alteration.

Since then some feeling of restlessness together with the strongly expressed views of the extremists on your side has resulted in certain developments beyond the safe and excellent norm you had established, and in which you could have remained secure and supreme in the U.S.

Parallel eschallots of the French type have their uses, and with comparatively light pressures and tubes of correct scale can and do have a splash and thrill of their own. But to cut down the scales until you have a Swell Trompette 8ft. scale CC 3-9/16" results in a crackly blare that becomes most wearisome, to my ear. The use of the French type of eschallots for <u>all</u> chorus reeds, Bombardes, and pedal reeds gives a "sameness" of result that, while invigorating for a time, becomes tiring to the ear. From MF to FF is a growing blaze of extreme toned reeds and very brilliant mixtures, and this effect is repeated in organs large, medium and small.

Take that nice little job at Millville — a good, basic specification marred by some odd ideas from Richards. The snarly Swell Trompette, to my ears, mars the ensemble from the point of view of the primary use of a church organ — the accompaniment of services.

Your early Positif sections were quite delightful; you used suitable scaling and secured charming results.

Later Positif sections show, to me, extremes in scaling <u>not</u> found in the German Organ of the 17th century or early 18th, but similar to the extraordinary perversions introduced in Germany at the time of the so-called Baroque revival 1920 onwards.

Gedackts of enormous scale and very low cut-up — so fundamental in tone as to be difficult to differentiate from the very wide scale open pipes used in the same department, e.g. Gemshorn-type stops of wide scale, again very low cut-up giving a tone very close to that of the wide scaled Gedackts — and so on.

In addition, the fitting of canister stoppers with thick felt packing takes away virility and life. I find metal to metal essential if the format not be damped. These Positifs treated in the manner indicated have their several voices of muffled tone without individuality. Blend is impaired and, although a pleasant effect is obtained, it is without the distinction and beauty that your earlier Positifs had.

I, imbued with the Willis tradition, have not stood still as you know, but I have avoided violent change or departure from a reasonable norm.

Now for the plaudits. Your development of pedal organs as entities somewhat in the old German style is wholly admirable. I have been trying to induce clients in that direction for years, but with little success. To suggest a pedal mixture to the organist or consultant (usually an exceptionally conservative cathedral organist) is looked upon as sheer mania when an Orchestral Oboe could be added to a scheme at less cost. I tried to get a pedal mixture in Southwark Cathedral, but no luck. It is, of course, prepared for — so is Principal 8ft. and Super Octave 4ft. (your Choral Bass). You must be grateful that with you it is more necessary to restrain the exuberance of the extremists.

Another point — I really cannot appreciate your revival and use of the old German reed stops which give tonality that to my mind is positively undesirable and indeed harmful. But at the Mother Scientist Church at Boston judging from the C's I heard, you modified extreme tonalities to something possibly useful in the rendition of ancient organ music.

But you have done wonders for American organ building, and it is a great tribute that others are imitating you as closely as they can — or dare. That Möller at Central Presbyterian Church, New York is a close copy indeed of your later work, and therefore a really fine instrument — far better than I thought it possible for Möller to produce.

Having got the above off my chest, the following will amuse you. After visiting you and our discussion about no starters for 32ft. reeds, on my return I countermanded my orders for starters on the 32ft. reed for Southwark Cathedral and decided to take a chance without them. The Lewis stop, a 42 note unit Posaune 32 and 8ft. [sic], was on 3¾" wind: wooden tubes CCCC 10½" square, long wooden eschallots in the Lewis style which you know, and light felt weights. This unit was revoiced on 12" wind, using the old tubes and the old tongues with appropriate weights. These brought the tuning wire more forward, shortening the vibrating length, and by suitable curve prompt speech was secured. This was all done in the works <u>without the tubes</u> of the 32ft. octave, which could not have been got out of the organ without cutting them in half. The revoicing was done on 16ft. tubes.

When assembling in the organ we had only two or three notes to adjust further and the tonality was distinctly on the smooth side with perfectly prompt speech. The other pedal reed unit, Bombarde and Trumpet 16ft. and 8ft. were revoiced on 12" wind very much on the free side, in fact I thought too much so for English taste, but I got away with it.

So the second Willis 32ft. reed without starters — the first as you know was that one of Diaphonic type at Huddersfield Town Hall 1920.

By the way, your original report on this job, accurate in every way, said, "Solo Flutes (harmonic 8ft. and 4ft.) should be let out." They were, and are now very beautiful indeed.

I did appreciate your giving Aubrey leave to be with me for so many days when I was over — and for everything. It was very nice to be back in Crescent Avenue again and find things so little changed and to see the old faces again.

Yours as ever,
Henry

H.W./R.G.

since my return — Willis was in America in February of 1952 for three weeks.

---

235 Joseph Whiteford to Carl Weinrich

August 21, 1952

Mr. Carl Weinrich
Princeton University
Princeton, New Jersey
Dear Carl:

We're having walkie-talkies installed where our pocketbooks used to be (sic!) so we can get your calls wherever they come — inside a 32' Untersatz, at the top of a Vox Humana, or even down the hall in that little room provided with a sign!

We are splattering our guts out to get the Great to you in two weeks and also the Brustwerk chest and the remainder of the switches, etc.

Have faith!

Best,
Joe
Vice President

JSW:AGR

236 Henry Willis to William E. Zeuch

22nd August, 1952

Mr. William E. Zeuch,
1440, Beacon Street,
Brookline, Mass., U.S.A.

<u>Private.</u>

My dear Bill,

Very many thanks to Margory and yourself for the smaller photo received; this is for my home.

I was sorry to hear the news about Aubrey. What is to be the future of Aeolian-Skinner without a really capable technician to direct that side of the work?

Joe Whiteford is but an amateur and will never be anything else. And, when Don goes — as he must in time — J.W. will, in my opinion, play "old Harry" with the company. A poor outlook, especially for you, after so many years devoted service.

Yours as ever,
Henry

H.W./M.P.

the news about Aubrey — Aubrey Thompson Allen had left Æolian-Skinner for Yale. See letter 202.

---

237 G. Donald Harrison to E. Power Biggs

September 4, 1952

Mr. E. Power Biggs
53 Highland Street
Cambridge, 38, Massachusetts

Dear Jim:

Thanks for yours of August 24th which arrived at the office during my absence. Your letter is marked, "arrangements have been made to take care of all the items you mention," so that everything will be O.K. I will follow it up anyway.

I hope we may get together real soon. Now, it looks as though it will have to be next week.

I do want to take Peggy and you to the Greek Cathedral to see our <u>magnum opus</u> — a one-manual with four octaves and no pedalboard. It is an expansion of your little Steinmeyer job and gives an extraordinary account of itself for the purpose for which it was intended. It is all very lightly blown, and I think you will get quite a kick out of it.

It won't be long now before we will have something bigger to show at St. Paul's Cathedral here, complete with its Ruck-Positiv.

See you next week. All the best,

As ever,

Don

GDH/MOK

St. Paul's Cathedral — Opus 1207 in Boston's Episcopal cathedral has Brustwerke and Ruck-Positiv divisions. The Ruck-Positiv is on the gallery rail, behind the console.

Aeolian -Skinner Op. 1247 for the Greek Cathedral, Boston

31st October, 1952

Hon. Emerson Richards,
800, Schwehm Buildings,
Atlantic City, New Jersey,
U.S.A.

My dear Richards,

Sorry to have been so long in replying to your letter of the 5th August. Note that you had an operation and glad it proved successful.

Sumner's book very good on the whole, but much repetition and some factual errors which will, no doubt, be corrected in the second edition. It seems strange that the proof reader did not point out the somewhat wearisome repetition that is so evident.

I have not seen the new Aeolian-Skinner (Whiteford) booklet. Apparently I am not on the A.S. mailing list.

Your strictures on Methuen noted and agreed, but as Walckers left the job it was their product. Now it is neither fish, flesh, fowl or good red herring.

Reference our German visit — I heard several post-War Steinmeyers, and his tonal work has improved greatly. He, as others, have one long fight with the State Organ Architects, but Steinmeyer wins more often than not. He over does his mixtures! Tried new and big Walcker at the Radio Hall at Stuttgart: dreadful. Slider soundboards, slow drawstop action (to keep the noise down), a shocking console (although a copy of a Willis pedalboard). No two notes in any one stop of equal tonality, and reeds put in, tuned and apparently not regulated at all. I also visited Walcker's works, met young Werner Walcker. He is a Walcker — name was Werner Meyer and has assumed the Walcker — who looks like a South American "spiv" and knows little of organs and organ building. Also has a works manager who was for years a manufacturer of furniture in Poland. Visited Weigle's works — all small stuff of low quality.

All except Steinmeyers have gone over to slider chests at the orders of the State Experts. Hans gets away with it by demanding 15% more for slider-chests and tracker action, and so gets away with his standard types.

Went to Weikersheim and saw Laukhuff. He has built up again from almost nothing to 200 men; makes parts of any quality desired — and some of it looks awful. Saw only slider-soundboards being made. Standard Swell engine has 6 stations. Hans uses 14. Walckers at Radio Hall, Stuttgart, 10 stations, all on light pressure wind and slow.

As, I regret to say, in U.S. and Canada, I found nothing to learn but much to avoid! Everything now in Germany is 2¼" to 2⅜" wind — nicking as little as possible so to ensure imperfect speech – the "lisp" or "chiff" being worshipped. But anyway, no extension, and even derivation of manual doubles to the pedal frowned upon.

No special news here. I have the usual run of two- and three-manuals, a fair sized three-manual going to a "coloured" Church in Nigeria in two or three months. I feel lost without a four-manual to play with.

I found my house at Hampton Hill, to which we moved just over two years ago, too far from the office, and am buying another in Dulwich, only 3½ miles from the works — in place of 17½ miles.

Got a new car, a little Morris, lovely little job, and we are very pleased with it — done 3,500 miles without a hitch. Went in it to the "Three Choirs" at Hereford Cathedral, and finished jobs at Malvern and Felinfoel and Cadoxton in South Wales.

Now "the season" is in full swing, and it is one long round of recitals, concerts, lectures, dinners and so forth.

Kindest regards to Ad and yourself from Dora and

> Yours as ever,
> Henry Willis

H.W./R.G.
Copy for Mr. A. Thompson-Allen

---

239 William E. Zeuch to Dora and Henry Willis (handwritten)

Nov. 12, 1952

Dear Dora & Henry:

It's a helluva friend who lets nearly three months slip by without answering so nice a letter as yours, Dora, 20 Aug. 27. Anyway, it mustn't happen again. True, we have been busy what with our summer at the Cape and fixing up our new apartment in town.

What did you say about dividends? I can hardly realize it is 20 years since I've had a Skinner and Company dividend. 20 tough years, what with the depression and then the war, and after the war the accursed inflation. And what is going to happen when the long awaited deflation sets in? It's enough to make one take to liquor!

Of course, Dora, you miss your boys, and you can indeed be proud of both. I know Stephen is doing a swell job in Chicago and as for Michael, he certainly didn't choose the easy path and ride easily along on his father's shoulders (that comes under the head of a somewhat mixed metaphor). He rose in everyone's estimation when he decided he wouldn't let his dad's reputation make it easy for him.

Henry, I recently saw in our Boston paper where a local citizen had won $140,000.00 on the Cambridgeshire race. When Uncle Sam's merchants got through with him, all he had left was a measly $40,000.00. Well,

William E. Zeuch

I'll even settle for that! So put the 10 "bucks" on any Sweepstakes gamble, and I'll be grateful.

Aubrey seems very happy in his new work, which keeps him busy. I know he hasn't sold his Boston house as yet, so Violet and the kids are still here.

It was a good move for him. He's his own boss and the financial returns are much better than anything he could have made with us. Besides, it is a depression-proof business, and goodness knows what a Hell-on-Earth organ building is in times of a business stir-up. The best proof of it is that Goeckler, from whom Aubrey bought the business, is able to retire at the early age of 52. Look at me, 85 and still working!

Please write soon — I have a deep and abiding affection for you both!

As ever,

Bill Zeuch

you miss your boys — Dora's boys are Stephen and Michael Harrison, sons of Donald.
Goeckler — Arthur Goeckler, Curator of Organs at Yale University prior to the A. Thompson-Allen Company.

January 15, 1953

Mr. Henry Willis
31 Underhill Road
Dulwich S.E. 22
London, England
My dear Henry:

I was shocked to hear from Doe of your operation, but am glad to hear that you are coming out of it in fine shape. I saw Mary and she gave me the latest news.

I hope that this will give you a new start for I am sure that ulcer has been bothering you on and off for years. It is a good thing to get behind you and no doubt the new drugs helped to make your recovery more rapid. I suppose you are itching to get back to the works to see how things are going.

In recent months work seems to have piled up worse than ever. Glad that First Church of Christ, Scientist, Boston, is all done and accepted.

I have been working at St. John the Divine, New York. For Christmas I finished the new Great, all but one mixture. The Tubas 8 and 4', also about half the Pedal, including the 16' Ophicleide on 20", wind are finished. This is the old 10" x 10" at CCC wood stop. I made new blocks and shallots and it sounds very fine. Have yet to tackle the 32' reed. The old Swell and Choir and part of the Pedal are still playing. The pitch of same is A435, the new 440! Of course they don't try to use them in the same piece although, strangely enough, you can jump from one pitch to the other in an unrelated key without it sounding too bad.

I never did seem to get time to write you about your reactions to my work. It all seems to be very reasonable to me, and the criticisms are taken in good part. What you have to say about the metal stopped flutes with felt packing is very true. Done to save time after the war with big demand and too few in help. We are gradually returning to our original methods. People here, even the more sane organists, like some Baroque reeds in their jobs, while the demand for orchestral reeds is practically nil.

Aubrey seems to be making out in his new surroundings, and I don't doubt that he will do well.

By the way, we adopted all-electric tablets like yours in a couple of jobs. Aubrey got them imported. Just because they don't tilt like the old ones, there is violent opposition to them here. We also had considerable difficulty in keeping them in regulation.

It seems like the old Ferndale Road days. Here I am alone — everyone left both from plant and office as it is 6:15 p.m. I am making some headway with correspondence and without the telephone ringing every half hour.

I am greatly interested in the location of your new house. When I was at Dulwich I walked from Honor Oak along Wood Vale and eventually down Dulwich Common past St. Peters Church each day. I was often on Underhill Road.

At 8 o'clock this evening I have to meet Ned Gammons and George Faxon at St. Paul's Cathedral here in Boston. A last going over of the new job. No wonder my hair is white!

All the best to both of you.

As ever,
Don

GDH/MOK

meet Faxon and Gammons — a last finishing of the job. Faxon had been organist at the Church of the Advent from 1946-49, and left the Cathedral in 1954 to go to Trinity Church, Boston.

St. John the Divine — Cathedral of St. John the Divine, New York, opus 150-A. The rebuilding of this 1910 E.M. Skinner took more than 18 months, leaving it 141 ranks on four manuals with a floating Bombarde Organ.

---

241 Henry Willis to G. Donald Harrison

February 4, 1953

Mr. G. Donald Harrison,
President, Aeolian-Skinner Organ Co.,
Crescent Avenue, Dorchester,
Mass., U.S.A.

My Dear Don,

Many thanks for yours of the 15th January.

I had been in poor and deteriorating health and at the beginning of last December a series of X-ray photos revealed a very large stomach ulcer and certain nebulous shadows. Treatment failed to improve matters and I got to the point when I could eat nothing without vomiting afterwards. A further X-ray resulted in my entering the hospital on 23rd December at 24 hours' notice. Three doctors out of four suspected cancer, fortunately not so, no malignancy being found. I was operated upon Christmas Eve. One third of stomach removed, including the chronic ulcer which had penetrated the stomach wall and adhered to the liver causing complications. The first three days after the operation were more than unpleasant. I could not drink anything and food was out of the question. Water was "rectal water." On the fourth day I had four ounces of milk and water. And then recovery was rapid, and I was out of the hospital the eleventh day after the operation — on normal diet. But, of course, have had to take things easily since. I was back at the office in just over four weeks from date of operation. Am told

I have "a new stomach and can eat anything in reason" — a change after 35 years of tummy trouble.

So all's well that ends well.

Boston, First Church of Christ Scientist. You must be relieved to have finished that job. I read article by . . . in the Diapason — what pseudo-scientific nonsense.

New York, St. John the Divine. This will be a really fine job when you have finished the rebuild.

I hope to hear both the above instruments in good time, also St. Paul's Cathedral, Boston. You will have a job in resisting what I suspect are wild suggestions from Gammons and Faxon.

Electric tablet units. I do not know what type Aubrey got for you or where they were from. Bear in mind that Kimber-Allen make our type for us only — and do not supply our model to others, but a cheaper "trade" type not good enough for us, or for you. Our type costs more, but worth it.

Electro drawstop solenoids. New type, first used at Southwark Cathedral last year. A sweet and simple job drawing less current than the old twin-solenoid type, good as that was, for consoles so equipped are as good as ever after over 20 years use and are not taken apart at cleanings.

For the larger jobs with capture system combinations, all combination mechanism and couplers are in separate case and remote control so that there are no moving parts in the console at all beyond keys, drawstops, tablets, piston-touches, pedals and toe pistons, and, of course, no wind.

After sending a medium sized two-manual to Lagos (Nigeria) some 18 months ago, we are now doing a fair sized three-manual for Ebute Metta (Nigeria), which is costing this "coloured" church over £12,000. Also doing another two-manual in Lagos.

These jobs for the tropics are a bit of a nuisance, as everything has to be tropicalised including all electrical components. In Nigeria, for eight and a half months in the year the average humidity is 93 percent, remaining three and a half months 25 percent, so you will appreciate the allowance for expansion and contraction that is necessary.

I am continuing my long fight for independent pedal organs, but not with much success. The average organist and "consultant" (usually a dyed-in-the-wool cathedral organist) is non-understanding. But I have in hand a biggish three-manual concert organ for St. George's Hall, Bradford, where there will be a straight pedal but — alas — no mixture, although I pressed it very strongly.

A Dutch "expert" Dr. Vente, came to see me two or three weeks ago. I did not realize he was the Vente who had written to the Methuen Institute Bulletin and to whose article I had replied with vigor. These so-called experts with their advocacy of slider-soundboards, tracker action etc. etc.

make me tired, yet there is a small gang of the "precious" type over here which is endeavoring to spread this gospel or part of it — ultra light wind pressures, "no nicking" and so forth. (The wretched finisher has to do the nicking on the job — as at Battell Chapel, Yale!)

On the other hand quite a lot of work passes me, because I will not use manual extension in any shape or form, as quite a number of organists still think there is no harm in it if judiciously planned and carried out. You know all the meretricious arguments.

Over here we are awaiting the completion of the Festival Hall Organ by Harrison and Harrison to Ralph Downes' specification, orders, instructions and finishes.

Rochesson, the French "expert" is over here to finish some 40 stops supplied by him (made and voiced by Masures of Paris), six weeks work is alleged. Beuchet, who you may remember acted as technical Director in the last days of the firm of Cavaillé-Coll told me that Rochesson "was better at the speaking word than the speaking pipe" — in other words a gas-bag of low technical ability.

I also, as ever, find an hour and a half after the works closes at 5:45 p.m. (overtime — normal closing down is 4:45) invaluable, indeed essential. No interruptions as you say.

New house: 31 Underhill Road, Dulwich, is four minutes walk from St. Peter's, Dulwich Common in Lordship Lane. A new house built on a bombed site and, fortunately, there was room to build a second garage. Three and a half miles from the works and, despite traffic, 12 minutes run in the car. A real boon after Hampton Hill, which distance — 17 miles — was too much for me.

Standaart. What happened to this concern? No advertisements noticed of recent months.

As ever,

H.W.

P.S. We are to rebuild the 1897 Hope-Jones four-manual at Edinburgh Univ. McEwan Hall: much of the pipes & reeds will be scrapped.

Copies sent: Hon Emerson Richards and Mr. A. Thompson-Allen

(P.S. and copy note handwritten)

Dutch "expert" Dr. Vente — Maarten A. Vente (1915-1989), the noted musicologist and authority on Dutch and Belgian tracker organs. An early proponent of the tracker revival.

Battell Chapel, Yale — The organ is a 1951 Holtkamp.

Standaart — Adrian V. Standaart had acquired the A. Gottfried Co. of Erie, PA, in 1950 to form the Standaart Organ Co. The firm went into receivership in 1953.

Feb. 20, 1953

My Dear Willis:

Replying to your letter of Feb. 10th regarding Paul Haggard, I am sorry that I cannot give you too much definite information about him, I have only met him once, and have known about his activities down in Oklahoma for some years. It is easy to see why he is very much dissatisfied with his connection with Aeolian-Skinner. Their three year deliveries, total lack of cooperation, "we know it all, you know nothing" attitude annoys me, and I am sure it would if I were representing them, as Mr. Haggard has been doing.

The situation at Aeolian-Skinner has emphatically not improved with the ascendancy of Joe Whiteford. He is cocky, dictatorial and arbitrary. He will never build an organ for me. Even Ned Gammons, who has worshipped at the Aeolian-Skinner shrine for years, is completely fed up.

I couldn't possibly tell you whether or not Haggard would be able to sell Willis organs in the Southwest. So far as I know he is honest, conscientious and reliable, and has something of a following among the organists in his territory. The success or failure would depend on many things, including price, when freight, duty and installation are paid.

A certain number of Dutch and Rieger organs have been sold in this country in the past four years. They are mostly very extreme baroque types, suitable for museums, music schools, morons, and the like. There might be some demand for normal, first class church organs such as Willis makes.

There still is a demand in some quarters for the Casavant in this country, with which I do not sympathize in the least, as they are far too conservative in tonal ideals.

As a matter of honest fact, today's best organs in America are being made by Austin, with your ex-employee, Richard Piper in charge. No greater revolution ever occurred in tonal ideals with any builder, after Piper's entrance on the scene. Then, the present day work of Reuter satisfies me nearly as well. Their improvements have been phenomenal in the past ten years. So long as we have two such excellent builders, no church need wait three years for Aeolian-Skinner to get around to them, and be insulted in the meantime.

If organists around the country would ever get themselves up to date in what is going on in organ building, there wouldn't be any need to import.
. . .

[William Barnes]

26th February, 1953

Dr. William H. Barnes,
8111, North St. Louis Avenue,
Skokie, Illinois,
U.S.A.

My Dear Barnes:

Thanks a lot for your letter of the 20th. instant, which is greatly appreciated.

Your remarks about the Aeolian-Skinner setup of today indicates an unfortunate position. When I was in Boston last February I spent some time at Crescent Avenue, chiefly with Don Harrison. I met Joe Whiteford and found him a very nice young man socially. I did not discuss organ matters with him.

It was a pity that owing to divergence of views Thompson-Allen felt obliged to leave Aeolian-Skinner. That man knows organ building on the grand scale from A to Z. I let him go with some reluctance and thought he would settle down with Aeolian-Skinner and be an invaluable assistant to Don Harrison.

I would very much like to send at least one organ to the U.S. — in a worthy edifice — and think it would create great interest. All the excellent chaps who were trained here tend to develop individual ideas!

I am glad you have so high an opinion of Piper's work. I saw and tried some of his work in and about Hartford etc. Of course, he has revolutionized Austin tonal productions. A pity his work is allied to the Austin consoles and mechanisms.

Interesting to hear of Reuter's progress. I did not hear any of their recent work.

In view of your favourable comment I will investigate the Haggard proposition. A difficulty is that some two years ago Gruenstein of the <u>Diapason</u> and Scott Buhrman of the <u>American Organist</u> declined to accept a Willis announcement on the grounds of not offending old clients. Yet Casavant's advertisements are accepted and they are just as much a foreign firm as mine is! Could you help them to change their minds?

I was sorry that my three weeks in the U.S. in February last did not allow me time to contact you in Chicago.

Ever sincerely,
Henry Willis,

H.W./R.G.

G. Donald Harrison, Peggy Biggs, E. Power Biggs, Joseph Whiteford
at Symphony Hall, Boston

244 G. Donald Harrison to E. Power Biggs

April 21, 1953

Mr. E. Power Biggs
53 Highland Street
Cambridge 38, Massachusetts
Dear Jimmie:

Thanks for your letter and check. Formal receipt for the latter is enclosed herewith.

Some of the things you say may be justified. However, other things hurt me not a little. Let me go through the various items in the light of our records and time sheets:

1. Re: <u>Tuning of Symphony Hall organ</u>. The bill originally sent to the hall included the tuning October 14th and 19th and the stand-in for recording October 20th to 25th. These two items were based on our regular charges and amounted to $144.88 and $164.26 respectively. When the hall advised that these items should be charged to you I gave instructions to reduce them to $84.53 and $56.94 respectively as same represented actual wages paid out and nothing for overhead or profit. As our overhead expense amounts to 80 percent on labor this meant that the company was out, or absorbed, $129.17.

It seemed to me that you could probably use this expense against income. However, you told me over the telephone that it was too late for that. I don't know on what basis you figure your tax, accrual or cash basis. Most professional men use the latter and if you figure that way these amounts are still usable. Frankly, I would rather write off these amounts than have any hard feeling about them.

2. <u>Germanic Museum</u>. In Joe's letter to you of October 19th, six items were mentioned which it was felt would improve this instrument and an estimated actual cost of $750 was quoted which included some factory overhead. The English Salicional was to be a swap. According to our time sheets, metal shop order, etc., the following are the facts:

We commenced cleaning the organ and Krummhorn January 19, 1951. Walter Doucette spent 17½ hours on the 19th and 22nd of January. For the week ending January 29, 1951, Herbert Pratt spent 62 hours, George Steinmeyer 54¾ hours and Walter Doucette 12 hours. This time was for tuning and mechanical adjustments.

The English Salicional and chest for bass of 16' Quintaten were ordered on shop order A-732 dated October 31, 1950. The cost of the Salicional labor and material amounted to $143.52. The allowance for the old Principal was $169.06. Therefore this was not an even swap for the pipes, as there was a difference in your favor of $25.54. There is no question that this stop was made specially for Germanic, and it may easily be stamped Viole-de-Gambe, as we often use this name for this particular scale.

On the hours mentioned above and spent on the organ, only actual wages were charged and no overhead whatever. Although this was mentioned in our original letter of October 19, 1950.

To sum up, this is how it worked out:

Labor at Germanic	$198.50
New Salicional	143.52
New Quintaten	64.86
	406.88
Allowance Old Principal	169.06
Amount of Bill	$237.82

All this shows, I think, that we showed reasonable cooperation and interest in the work and certainly kept the cost to a minimum.

After the above work was completed, further work was suspended and according to the shop, this was at your request through Joe. Joe is away at the moment and I cannot confirm this. However, the chest for the Quintaten bass has been made and is still here awaiting installation, together with the switches to complete the other items.

Now, if you wish me to do so, I will proceed immediately and finish all the items, or if you prefer, put the Quintaten chest in some other job and give credit for it. The fact that you do not like the new stop is something else again and I certainly agree that you must have exactly what you want in this regard. If we could get together and decide exactly what it should be for your purpose, we can make another swap. Perhaps you will let me know about this.

3. Symphony Hall. There have been troubles, 90 percent of which have been with the cables. You will remember that part of the cable was used that had been installed by Mears quite recently. This was a stranded wire cable and was supposed to be better than a single wire cable, and as it was impossible to obtain these now, it was used. All cable troubles have been with this cable and we put in added mains to relieve same, and indeed are now considering replacing it entirely as there have been no broken wires in our cables.

There was some trouble with a swell pouch board, and this was removed and rebuilt. You know the way the console is banged up and pushed around there are bound to be some troubles.

Finally, regarding what the company has done, you refer to this as a small cost, but you would be surprised how this has added up through the years. How many years did we completely maintain the Germanic organ and stood the depreciation, etc.? I think it was very much worthwhile, for in past years you were very good in insisting on script credits.

Sorry for the length of this letter.

All the best to you both.

Very sincerely yours,
Don
President

GDH/MOK

P.S. Regarding your question on the memorandum of bills you sent to me, Larry Mogue's time sheet shows Symphony Hall Friday, October 24th, seven hours and Saturday, October 25th, six and a half hours. He does not indicate whether or not the stand-in at the concerts was included in these hours. I have just asked him about it and he states that on the 24th he spent half an hour at the concert as the organ was used once only. He cannot remember Saturday. It is safe to assume that these hours did include both concerts as he was at the hall.

G.D.H.

---

245 T. Frederick H. Candlyn to Henry Willis

May 22, 1953

Mr. Henry Willis
34 Marlborough Grove
Old Kent Road, London.
Dear Mr. Willis,

It seems almost yesterday when we had lunch at the Lotus Club in New York. Actually I suppose it was at least a year ago. However, I plan to be in England during the summer, arriving about August 8th. I expect to fly back to the U.S.A. early in September. During my stay in the "Old Country," I wish to hear some of your glorious instruments including the one in St. Paul's Cathedral. I think that you will be pleased to know that after the rebuild, organists refer to the organ at St. Thomas as "Candlyn's Willis." No higher praise is possible. I will write you from the home of my sister as soon as my plans mature. I might add that my time is free, and that I can conform to whatever arrangements you may have made for the Summer.

Sincerely yours,
T. Frederick H. Candlyn

---

246 G. Donald Harrison to William King Covell

May 27, 1953

Mr. William King Covell
72 Washington Street
Newport, Rhode Island
Dear King:

Thanks for your letter of the 16th instant. Glad you like the leaflets. I note what you have to say about the setting out of the stop lists. I am inclined to agree with you on this.

Regarding the lack of mention of Larry Phelps' name, this was none of our doing. You will notice that no names are mentioned except that of the Company. This seems to be the desire of the authorities and we had to submit our proofs for O.K. before the leaflets were printed.

Regarding St. Paul's, the curtains, as you probably know, are really a temporary expedient and it was done to save money for the time being. As I understand it, the real intention is to have grille work there in place of the curtains at some time in the future.

360

I will look forward to getting together with you and Dr. Conant later on in the year.

Glad to hear that you have added the Mixture to your little organ. I can quite imagine it is a charming instrument.

I do wish I could get away to Europe just for a change but work is so pressing and we have so many important jobs to complete that it is quite out of the question this year.

I will certainly be glad to hear all about your trip when you return. With best wishes,

Sincerely yours,

Don

President

GDH:MOK

Larry Phelps' name — Lawrence Phelps had acted as a consultant on the First Church of Christ, Scientist, organ. At the time, he was married to Ruth Barrett Phelps, Mother Church organist.

St. Paul's — Cathedral, Boston. The unexpressive divisions were functionally exposed, but curtains were used to conceal the shades of the Swell and Choir.

Dr. Conant — consulted on the physical design of the organ for St. Paul's Cathedral, Boston.

---

247 Henry Willis to T. Frederick H. Candlyn

4th June, 1953

Mr. T. Frederick H. Candlyn
St. Thomas Church
Fifth Avenue and West Fifty-First Street
New York, New York
U.S.A.

Dear Candlyn,

I was glad to have your letter of the 22nd, May and to learn that you will be over here in August.

Here in London the organs you must hear and try are St. Paul's Cathedral, Westminster Catholic Cathedral, Southwark Cathedral and All Souls, Langham Place.

On your arrival get in touch with me, and I will arrange in accordance.

If you can manage Liverpool Cathedral you should do so, as the organ is my personal "magnum opus."

Yours sincerely,
Henry Willis

August 9, 1953

Mr. Henry Willis,
Rotunda Organ Works
34 Marlborough Grove
Old Kent Road
London, S.E.1
England
Dear Mr. Willis:

There is a great deal of discussion and writing over here today about the supposed behavior of the bar and slider chest vs. the pitman type — with its pouchrails close up to bottom of top-board. Piper has told me of your experience with expansion boxes and downward extension of pipe hole by plastic tube so as to increase the space (and airflow) between rail and topboard. You are probably the best qualified of anyone to answer some of the questions that perplex me, and I wonder if you can find time to do so.

In the "Organ Institute Quarterly," a small magazine brought out by a group of organists most of us connect with the Aeolian-Skinner propaganda department (a good one by the way) Lawrence I. Phelps, the "expert" retained by the Christian Science Mother Church in Boston, tells in great detail of his difficulty in getting prompt response from the Great and Hauptwerk flue choruses. He was forced to make new topboards with expansion boxes for the Great. Then, though the Hauptwerk chorus was smaller scale and voiced in a "sprightly manner," it also had to have boxes, in order to duplicate the prompt speech of the Great. In other words the pitman chest, unaided, would not deliver this speed of speech.

Everybody over here is laughing at his naïvete, and I wonder Aeolian-Skinner has not had him slaughtered by some hired assassin. He let the cat out of the bag in wonderful style. The glacial coldness of the Aeolian-Skinner fluework sounds "quick" in all the jobs I have heard — new work. Scaling, balance etc., all are good but there is no warmth — no radiance. They also stress the off-unison mixture ranks, which is anathema to me — I hear a Trompette in the fluework! Now Mr. Harrison has entered the lists — in the last number of the "Quarterly" and writes of several things I cannot reconcile with my version of the facts.

Evidently following the line put out by Ernest Skinner in his book, and quoted in the last number of the London Organ Club pamphlet, Mr. Harrison speaks of the gradual attack (rather than the so-called "pneumatic blow") delivered by a B & S chest. Ernest (and Donald) says that when the big pallet first tries to drop, a tendency towards partial vacuum is generated in space above valve (and in pipefoot), so that this atmospheric air first leans to minus, then normal then plus pressure, as the chest air invades it. It seems to me this is assuming a lot. I wonder if actual tests substantiate it. Do you know of any? If a split-pallet were used, the initial tendency to partial vacuum would of course be very small (comparatively) and I wonder if your experience covers this. Does a split-pallet steady the attack of the B & S chest? My guess is that it does not — for I do not believe there is any appreciable variation in pressure such as Skinner describes.

When a double handful of notes is struck on a B & S chest the tone "gasps" because of the terrific robbery of chest pressure caused by the total opening to atmosphere. It takes a perceptible (very perceptible) instant to recover. This is the wobble we all hear. If there were a partial vacuum created by the sudden drop of the pallet, the pipe does not speak till the pressure is readjusted and the pipe gets pressure wind. By that time, and flowing up through an inverted conical pipe foot, I feel that the pressure is righted — stabilized — before it reaches the vital FLUE and languid. The gasp is real — the vacuum is fanciful, for real, not fanciful reasons.

The huge oversupply of pressure air below pipefoot and above valve passes through the short boring of the slide without skinfriction — much less friction than if through an attenuated boring or approach.

Mr. Harrison says reeds do not respond to the expansion box treatment. I disagree with this. I believe a well curved reed takes a jolt of air to start it, rather than the gradual pressure build-up Mr. Harrison says the B & S chest affords. I believe the B & S chest does not gradually build up pressure but jolts it with a fast, copious, unblocked attack.

The close-up pouchrail of the normal pitman type chest compels the chest wind to squeeze through a narrow slit to get to and past the valve. This would surely mean a gradual — not instant attack. We all recognize the virtue of the short boot for reeds. It would seem this reduction of cubic content was meant to make the pressure build up inside the smaller boot faster than if the cubic content were larger. So I cannot reconcile short boots and Harrison's statement that expansion boxes do not help reeds.

I believe the B & S chest, or expansion boxes that approximate its effects, or such a valve as the Austin chest provides — permit slowside voicing with at least acceptable key-pipe response speed. I believe such attack starts a reed with a curve that a pitman chest valve will not start — am I right? If, as I understand you use — a plastic tube extension permits rail to be farther down from topboard — with plenty of room for chest air to get past the valve, then the term "pitman" does not apply. It is not the pitman — it is the cramp of the rail to topboard.

I am writing a book on design and take up this matter of chest attack. I cannot afford to make any mistake. I would appreciate your help. I shall not quote you. I know you have friends in both camps — but I also feel you hew to the line and let the chips fall where they may. I am sure I do. I don't give a whoop for any firm including my own — if the truth is involved.

Any good flue voicer realizes the merit of slowside tone. The only reason I can see for an otherwise good firm to turn out quick chorus flues is that its chest will not yield prompt enough speech — so they voice things "quick."

Have you Barnes' Fifth Edition of <u>The Contemporary American Organ</u>? If not let me send you a copy. I hope you have read my article on the Lodi organ — pages 305-10. The Lodi organ has turned out more than good. Church almost totally dead (about ⅔ second). Yet for <u>what it will do</u> — this organ tops any of my experience. 34 registers, 42 rks. Voicing is good, balance more than good, subsurface utility remarkable. It will play anything — authentically. There are three real secondary flue choruses, VERY different in color, mood and pitch — all about same power. Automatic manual-pedal balance for any stratum of power. (Made for that purpose).

We are about ready to spring a surprise on the organ world and I shall write you all about it soon as I can. The stepless engine is coming along — about ready for the market. I shall see that you get it if it can be arranged — export — etc.

Piper is helping us tremendously. He has improved our work immeasureably. He is a good man and an honest friend. He admires you very greatly — has told me so.

Hope trade is good with you and send my thanks and regards. Please answer questions and tell me where I am wrong.

Yours truly,

J. B. Jamison

B & S Chest — slider chests

---

249 Henry Willis to James B. Jamison

19th August, 1953

Mr. J.B. Jamison,
Sleepy Hill,
Los Gatos, (P.O. Box 151)
California
Dear Jamison,

Reference your interesting letter of the 9th instant.

<u>Slider-vs-Sliderless Chests</u>. In my opinion the assessments by Laurence [sic] Phelps consisted of amateur nonsense. To suggest that the speed of speech is greater on a slider chest than on a well-designed sliderless chest is errant nonsense. Donald Harrison's article is on practical lines although

he hedges somewhat by giving a small slider chest virtues that it does not possess.

Donald Harrison is quite correct when he says that reeds speak best when right over the pallet and that an expansion chamber is not necessary. The Austin chest is ideal for reeds and quite acceptable for flues in view of good valve openings and great volume of wind available.

The "partial vacuum" theory is pure rubbish — a build up of pressure to fill the channel is inevitable and for prompt speech pipes voiced on a pitman type chest without expansion chamber have to be quickened to speak correctly.

I have recently returned from an exhaustive tour of Holland and Denmark, observing the use by the various builders of slider chests in accordance with the dictates of self-appointed "experts" and noted the quaint efforts made to render these chests less susceptible to climatic changes, efforts which indicate no knowledge or appreciation of hundreds of years experience!

Split or relief pallets only reduce the pluck on the bass and have no other value — only desirable on tracker actions. The Willis relief pallet, invented by my Grandfather in 1861 is the best of its type.

Before I switched over to sliderless chests 30 years ago, I examined every type of chest in conjunction with pipe speech. I tended to favor the Tauschellade, but decided on the pitman type by reason of the superior drawstop action.

The chests were made with small expansion chambers in the top-boards but this was dropped about 1926 as there was no advantage in their use. Pipes voiced on the sliderless type of voicing machine and on identical bores etc., took care of the situation, with pallet rails scalloped in the bass, there was no wind restriction.

This necessitated two different types of voicing machines: we had to retain the slider type — B & S as you call it — for we do so much revoicing of old instruments with that type of chest. This became a bit of a nuisance, and after many tests I adopted the tube expansion chamber. Then it was immaterial on what type of voicing machine flue pipes were voiced upon — the performance being identical.

Much verbiage has flowed about the languid position — a high languid necessitates a forward top-lip and vice-versa. The "norm" is best adhered to. The flow of vortices must be divided by the top lip in correct order and proportion and the voicer should voice for correct articulation and assuming the correct manufacture of the pipes this must be on orthodox lines.

With cheaply made pipes with flat (not dubbed) lower lips, the pipes are very sensitive and must be voiced on the slow side, i.e. instead (for open pipes) of blowing to the first upper partial on doubling the wind pressure, they blow into a 'bubble' and so — if unbearded — are slow. If the early English Diapason tone is desired this type of lower lip is essential — with a low angled languid.

Our improved type chest with plastic tubes, ensures against any possible wind restriction.

The "Back to Methusaleh" cranks really believe that there is some mystical connection between one pipe and another on a barred chest that enhances sympathetic blend and talk about the "tone channels." What nonsense: the "sympathetic blend" is simply one pipe pulling on another as the number of stops drawn increases — hence the "drawings" and "pullings" so well-known and deplored.

The very light pressure fans firmly believe in the 16th and 17th century practise of huge tip bores and regulation at the flue, disregarding the high value of the pipe foot as an expansion chamber and air-stabilizer. This ancient system was, of course, due to inability to obtain any but low pressures and endeavoring to obtain maximum power in the manner indicated.

I read all the stuff that appears in your organ press — often with great amusement tempered by regret at the amateurish and incorrect views expressed.

We have a similar bunch over here!

I will be interested to hear more about the stepless swell engine about which you have been whetting my appetite for years.

Yours sincerely,
Henry Willis

H.W./D.N.
Copy sent to Mr. Willis Jr.

huge tip bores — open-toe voicing

---

250 G. Donald Harrison to Henry Willis

August 25, 1953

Mr. Henry Willis
Rotunda Organ Works
34 Marlborough Grove
Old Kent Road
London, S.E.1
England
My dear Henry:

I was very interested to read your letter of July 31st last, particularly your report on your recent Continental tour.

I am sure you have summed up the whole business accurately, and I am certain I would have about the same opinions could I have been along with you.

From reports received from some of our younger organists who are not too extreme, they tell me that they prefer the Marcussen organs to any. My friend Fenner Douglass of Oberlin College seems to admire Marcussen reeds. You do not mention these specifically. I would be glad to have your opinion of same.

I will look forward to seeing copies of your lectures when you give them, and also will, of course, read what you have to say in the <u>Organ</u>.

We can get away with considerable chiff in flutes, and we have voiced some high-pitched small-scale mixtures without nicks, although we do not make a regular practice of doing this.

Much interested to hear of the degree given to Henry Goss-Custard. I am writing to him by this mail.

The prospect at St. Paul's Cathedral, Boston, is unfinished, hence the somewhat poor appearance. Money ran out, and it could not be finished until more is in hand.

You are right, the four manual keys at the First Church of Christ, Scientist, Boston, are all flat. We have only occasionally made tilting manuals. We have no particular call for them, and personally, I do not like them.

All the best,
Don

GDH/MOK

prospect at St. Paul's — the organ façade

---

251 Walter Holtkamp to E. Power Biggs

October 20, 1953

Mr. E. Power Biggs
53 Highland Street
Cambridge 38, Mass.
Dear Jimmie:

Yes indeed!!! I shall look for a call from Harry Gabb. Thanks for your thoughtfulness in putting him on my trail. If you know his itinerary please drop him a line and ask him to try to reserve time enough to see an organ or two while in Cleveland. I wish I could induce the choir to visit an organ or maybe stage a rehearsal with a good organ. When these people get home they will talk and it is all good propaganda. The English "at home" are so uninformed about what is really going on over here.

Walter Holtkamp

Jimmie, me boy, there is much too much talk going around about the parting of the ways of one E.P.B. and G.D.H. I don't like it. You both have too much meaning for each other and together, you have too much meaning for the American organ scene to so upset your public. If I may, I would suggest an arms around the shoulder picture in Father Gruenstein's paper. You are clever. You can contrive it.

Sincerely,
Walter Holtkamp

Harry Gabb — then assistant organist of St. Paul's Cathedral, London
Father Gruenstein — Samuel Gruenstein, then editor of the *Diapason*

---

252 G. Donald Harrison to William King Covell

December 31, 1953

Mr. Wm. King Covell
72 Washington Street
Newport, Rhode Island
Dear King:

Thanks for yours of December 28th. The Steamboat Christmas leaflet arrived and I am always interested in reading descriptions of those old ships. They were quite something in their way. . . .

Very glad you enjoyed the record but you are in error about the example which illustrates mixtures having tierces, etc. The example which immediately followed my statement was played on purely mixtures and no reeds were employed. I admit it certainly sounds like reeds. There are otherwise one or two relatively minor things that could be better. I left out a word in one place which resulted in the statement being somewhat incorrect. However, nobody has noticed it to date unless perhaps you have.

I would like to send many records abroad, including one to Bonavia-Hunt. I am finding out from the Customs people what is involved as I don't want the receivers to be charged with an enormous duty.

All the best,

Very sincerely,
AEOLIAN-SKINNER ORGAN COMPANY
Don
President

GDH:MOK

enjoyed the record — King of Instruments, Volume I, a demonstration record in which Harrison narrated fundamentals of the organ, interspersed with brief examples played on Æolian-Skinner organs. Subsequently, the company produced other records; these were in a normal format and featured individual artists playing major works. See letter 287.

---

253 G. Donald Harrison to William King Covell

January 12, 1954

Mr. Wm. King Covell
72 Washington Street
Newport, Rhode Island
Dear King:

Thanks for yours of the 10th instant.

I think you have something in a Christmas card dealing with some organ but along the lines of your Steamboat card. I remember Willis's effort in that direction. . . .

Glad you like the State Trumpet. [Norman] Coke-Jephcott resigned from the Cathedral several months ago and no new organist has been definitely appointed. His old assistant is carrying on as acting organist. The rebuilding work is not yet completed but we are trying to get this finished before Lent starts, and I do hope this will be possible. It would be a good thing to wait until everything is in ship shape order before trying out the instrument. As I understand it, the State Trumpet is used at every service each Sunday morning, by order of the Bishop, and that would be a good time to hear it. The acting organist's name is John Upham.

I was interested in the big mixture layout which you sent. As a matter of fact, there is some idea of placing an independent organ at the west end some time in the distant future. In that case a console at the west end would definitely be necessary so it could be played properly. The distance is so great that artistic playing of compositions presents great difficulties. Any individual stop like a Trumpet can be used effectively after some practice.

You will be interested to know that many of the ranks in the Great organ are doubled. For example, the 2' Doublette has two pipes per note on the top 24 notes and in the big Mixtures the ranks are doubled and even trebled in some cases. Of course we used different scales for the extra pipes and had special feet on them. In these large buildings I am convinced that doubling of this sort is very beneficial to the general feeling. You can get a big tone, and a very interesting one, without forcing.

With best wishes,

Sincerely yours,
AEOLIAN-SKINNER ORGAN COMPANY
Don
President

GDH:MOK

the State Trumpet — at St. John the Divine, Harrison added a 50" pressure trumpet stop, *en-chamade*, at the West End of the Cathedral.
the big mixture layout — Covell's idea was to install a large mixture with the State Trumpet, to aid in filling the room.

---

254 G. Donald Harrison to William King Covell

May 20, 1954

Mr. Wm. King Covell
72 Washington Street
Newport, Rhode Island
Dear King:

Thank you for your letter of May 12th and for the copy of the suggested reply to E.M.'s letter which appeared in the April issue of The Organ. I think it is perfectly all right to let this go through just as you have it. I realize, of course, that E.M.'s mind is not exactly working 100 percent and therefore it is difficult to be too hard with him but I think your letter is O.K. from that point of view.

I always get a big laugh about this voicing proposition. I suppose E.M. refers to the practical side of this work. If that is the case I would gladly go into a competition with E.M. on the voicing of any kind of flue pipe. I don't know if you have ever seen any of the work he attempted to do in that direction. As a matter of fact, our pipes are cut up, nicked and the toe holes adjusted by young, intelligent girls who can learn to do this work in about six weeks and, incidentally, do an extremely neat job. This leaves for the actual voicer the job of making the pipes speak properly on the machine.

Of course these girls work to very definite instructions. However, this is a matter that is not worthwhile going into.

I hope you will have some luck at the Cathedral and Saint Bartholomew's.

Thank you also for your letter of May 7th from which I note with much interest your satisfaction with the Dutch pipes. I will be happy to see prints of your photographs in due time.

I was, of course, extremely interested to hear of your letter from Cecil Clutton. The remarks are just about what one would expect. I have just received a letter from Henry Willis on the same subject and I will quote his remarks exactly as they appear in his letter.

"Royal Festival Hall, London. This organ, carried out by Harrison and Harrison to the dictates of Ralph Downes, is a washout. Hard in tone, mixtures all wrong, so-called French reeds thin and wiry in tone. One Great diapason. All absurdly unsuited to this hall, with its low reverberation period. The appearance of the instrument is awful."

This is quite funny and I do not believe the organ is quite as bad as that.

I expect to be at the plant both on Monday and Tuesday of next week.

Looking forward to seeing you,

Sincerely yours,

Don

President

GDH:MOK

the Cathedral and Saint Bartholomew's — Cathedral of Saint John the Divine, Saint Bartholomew's Church, both in Manhattan

---

255 G. Donald Harrison to Henry Willis

June 30, 1954

Mr. Henry Willis
Henry Willis & Sons, Ltd.
Rotunda Organ Works
34, Marlborough Grove
Old Kent Road
London, S.E.1
England

Dear Henry:

I received your letter and copies of what you sent to Möller quite awhile ago and was much interested.

I was also interested to hear your report on the Royal Festival Hall organ in London. Perhaps after all you were right to keep out of that mess. I see Archibald Farmer of the <u>Musical Times</u> gives it quite a black eye in the May issue.

Curiously enough, just from the point of view of curiosity, I ordered a Trumpet Ordinaire from Paris from the maker who made these reeds that went into the Royal Festival organ. I just wanted to see what kind of things they were turning out. I must say the workmanship of the pipes was very fine indeed but tone left much to be desired and the basses were so darn slow that the whole thing is unusable from our point of view. Of course, it can be revoiced into a good stop for some special job.

I don't know if you know Alec Wyton; he has been over here about three years and has just been appointed to the Cathedral of Saint John the Divine in New York. I have not met him so far.

My life is rapidly becoming a burden, due to the enormous amount of work we have and the constant pressure of people to obtain deliveries. The first six months of this year we have closed $600,000.00 worth of new contracts, which constitutes a record. The funny thing is, we don't go out and try to sell them, people just come in to buy. I look back with much pleasure to the depression days when one could take things easily and give a lot of time to every job. I am just leaving for Texas for three weeks and thought I would drop you a line before I get too far away.

All the best,

As ever,

Don

GDH:MOK

---

256 Henry Willis to G. Donald Harrison

7th July, 1954

Mr. G. Donald Harrison,
President,
Aeolian Skinner Co., Inc.,
Boston 25,
Mass. U.S.A.

<u>Personal</u>

Dear Don,

Thanks for yours of the 30th June.

<u>Royal Festival Hall</u>. Following protests by recitalists, Downes has had the mixtures softened and they are less screamy; but the job is tonally unsatisfactory.

It now seems that Downes has narrow aural receptivity and can hear nothing below 100 cycles or above 5000 cycles — which explains much!

Reference the Trompette Ordinaire you obtained from France "from the maker who made the reeds that went into the R.F. organ" — who was this? If Rochesson, he does not make anything. The reeds are made by Masure Frères of Paris and the Eschallots and tongues by Bertouneche — usually voiced by Masures — of which little firm of pipe makers the technical brother died some three years ago and, so Marcel Dupré and others tell me, their work is not up to their old and good French standard.

Rochesson is regarded with contempt in France. Gonzalez out of action — half paralyzed. His son-in-law, not an organ builder, is carrying on with a staff of ten to twelve.

Organ building in France is in a sad state.

Congratulations on your heavy program of work, a very comfortable state of affairs. In view of the well nigh intolerable burden upon you personally it is a pity that you have not a personal assistant with high technical and tonal knowledge to relieve your personal burden. I had thought and hoped that Aubrey would have served that purpose, but it was not to be.

Here we are overwhelmed with work at the moment, but no really big new jobs. Money is very tight.

"Son" has gone to Liverpool to take charge of the branch for two years and to supervise the restoration of the St. George's Hall Organ, so seriously damaged during the War — £26,000 job.

Our Scottish Branch has developed greatly since the War, extremely busy and doing fine work.

As ever,
Henry

H.W./J.P.

---

257 G. Donald Harrison to Henry Willis

August 13, 1954

Mr. Henry Willis
Rotunda Organ Works
34 Marlborough Grove
Old Kent Road
London, S.E.1, England.
Dear Henry:

Thanks so much for your letter of the 7th of July. I've been so long answering it as I have only just returned from a five-week trip to Texas and Louisiana. I experienced the hottest weather that has come my way so far.

In Austin, Texas on one day it was 113 degrees. I can assure you that is really hot and you feel as if you are in an oven. Even the wind that blows is hot. There is one saving grace, however, the humidity is extremely low, about 20 percent, so that it is not nearly as unbearable as it might sound. I much prefer it to about 95 degrees in Boston with a 97 percent humidity — that is hard to take.

I was checking up on several jobs that have been installed in recent months in Texas and Louisiana and found them to be excellent, due largely to the installation crew we have down there and the excellent finisher who is in charge of that territory.

I was interested to hear your remarks about the Royal Festival Hall. I cannot quite imagine how this sounds, but I'm sure it cannot be right from what you have to say and from just reading the specification and knowing the kind of scales that Downes used.

A man with such narrow aural receptivity should not be allowed to have anything to do with the finishing of an organ.

The Trompette Ordinaire, of which you speak, did come from Masure Frères of Paris, and as I think I told you in my earlier letter, it is a beautifully made stop, but the voicing leaves so much to be desired. The trebles are terribly weak and the bass as slow as molasses. It can be revoiced into a good stop.

The organ at St. John's is practically finished. I'm enclosing a folder which may interest you.

I was much interested to hear that the organ in St. George's Hall is to be restored. Henry IV is going to have a good time up in Liverpool looking after that work.

Best wishes,

As ever,

Don

GDH:AGR
Encl.

excellent finisher — Roy Perry. See letter 274.
the organ at St. John's — Cathedral of Saint John the Divine, Manhattan

August 26, 1954

Dr. Carl Weinrich, Director of Music
University Chapel
Princeton University
Princeton, New Jersey
Dear Carl:

Thanks for your letter. At the foot of this one you will find the layout of the Great Plein Jeu III-VI ranks, which I trust will enable you to go ahead with loudening it.

I have been fussing a great deal with your pipes here and have discovered that one of our Koppelflötes even of larger scale will <u>not</u> do the job on your Positiv organ. Neither of us realizes, I am afraid, that what we are trying to do is to make a Schnitger scaled and voiced organ form part of an American instrument of the period of 1927 and 1928. In other words, we are actually trying to get too much out of the Schnitger scale pipes. One has to remember that the actual Schnitger organs were always in the open and usually placed against the west wall in much smaller surroundings than Princeton Chapel, and without any absorbent material. They had quite an impact, but you simply cannot expect the same impact from similarly treated pipes under the conditions we have at Princeton University Chapel. In addition to this, we have part of the organ, like the Positiv, in a box which muffles it to some extent.

Another thing which we are contending with, which is a natural law of physics, is that if you have a sound of so many decibels going on in a room, it takes a tremendous additional percentage of sound to make any practical difference to what you are listening to. This is what we are up against when we add to the full Great flue work, for example, the Swell or Brustwerke mixtures. They don't seem to do anything. This situation is aggravated by the fact that <u>all</u> the mixtures are high pitched. In addition to all this, we are also expecting this flue work to cope with the high pressure work which exists in the organ. In other words, from what I have heard in the Chapel, and what I have seen here, on the voicing machine, I think we are asking the impossible — reaching for the moon, so to speak, and there seems to be no possible advantage in making new mixtures because we cannot do anything more than we have already. I tried sample Mixtur pipes just to see, and the same thing applies to the 4' Blockflöte on the Positiv organ. As I say, the Koppelflöte is simply too soft to do anything with the bunch of pipes such as we have in the Positiv, and which make up the Cornet.

The only way we could change this, would be to go to something entirely different — either have Mixturs of a much greater variation in pitch

375

and much larger scales, and probably cut higher, but that is not what we are after. What I have done, anyway, is to revoice these stops and I am sending them down to Princeton, together with a Cromorne and, here again, this is the maximum that can be got out of a Cromorne, and trust that they will work out all right. I am also sending a new treble for the Larigot so that we can see how that works.

When you have these pipes in I will certainly come down to Princeton and we will regulate and tune them. This cannot be until after the 7th of September, as I am going away next week for a vacation.

All the best,

As ever,
AEOLIAN-SKINNER ORGAN COMPANY
Don
President

GDH:MOK

[Handwritten] Plein Jeu III to VI Rks

22-26-29	18 notes
1-15-19-22	19 notes
1-5- 8-12-15	6 notes
DQ-1-5-8-12-15	18 notes

---

259 Ralph Downes to G. Donald Harrison

September 1, 1954

Mr. G. Donald Harrison,
Aeolian-Skinner Organ Co.,
Dorchester,
Mass., U.S.A.

Dear Don Harrison:

It is a very long time since we corresponded, and "much wind has gone through the pipes since then." I don't remember whether I finally thanked you for a great deal of very valuable help you offered and gave me in the early stages of the organ venture at the Royal Festival hall — anyway, I do now.

You may have heard some echoes of the stir caused by its first hearing. The verdict has been about 50/50. However, it represents the best that I personally could produce, and on the whole I think it very fine, except possibly for the Pedal Bombardes, which are too prominently placed and do not blend well. The pressure on these has had to be lowered, and needs to come down to the flue level — about 3¾". The scale of the 32' part is too large, and I personally think (still) that the 32' extension would have been better from the Great 16' instead of the Pedal. There Rochesson disagreed with me, and I think he slipped up there.

The recording companies will have nothing to do with the hall; they like heaps of atmosphere. (How times have changed! They used to take the opposite line!) And of course the organ is not their idea of an instrument. They prefer H.W. For myself, I can no longer see any merit in that type of instrument!

The scales at the R.F.H. and at the Oratory have all followed the general Baroque principle of wide flutes and narrow principals, and there is no doubt that the blend and tonal synthesis is remarkable. All the same, the scales are a good deal larger than at Brompton, at the R.F.H. The Solo diapason is 2½" at middle C, if not more. But it tapers off in the bass to about 5¾", and the treble C 49 is only about ¾". I am of the opinion that the variations in scale used by the 18th century builders were purposeful. We have proved their efficacy in these two organs.

I hear news of you from time to time: I saw Harold Gleason this summer, also Paul Callaway, and Noehren writes occasionally. I hope all is well with you. What a thrill it must be to hear the St. John the Divine organ now. It must be like Liverpool should have been. However, my own taste is increasingly in favour of smaller organs. My visits to the fine old Dutch organs convinced me, and I regard even the R.F.H. as ideally too large, though of course not in view of its chief requirement as a "Universal-Orgel." It can certainly do César Franck, with all the high mixtures and sharp tierces cut off; it sounds equally well like that.

We hope to see you someday. Any prospects?

Yours,

Ralph Downes

---

260 G. Donald Harrison to Ralph Downes

September 29, 1954

Mr. Ralph Downes
9 Elm Crescent
Ealing, W5
London, England
Dear Ralph:

I was delighted to get your letter of September 1st, for it is a long time since I heard from you. I don't believe that I was of any great help to you in the organ venture at the Royal Festival Hall, but if any of the things I said during our somewhat long correspondence of the early days produced some results, I am, of course, happy.

You can well imagine that I have followed all of the articles and criticisms about the organ that I could find and, reading between the lines, I came to the conclusion that it must be a very fine instrument. One cannot expect the die-hards in England to fall for such an instrument right away, and it will take many years before the instrument is generally really appreciated. After all, you have done in one fell swoop what has been done here over a period of 15 or more years, going one step at a time, so that the conservative fellows got used to things over a long period.

I would very much like to hear the instrument for myself, and it may possibly turn out that I will make a trip to Europe next year and, of course, if I do so my first stopping place will be to see you.

I have often toyed with the idea of some recitals for you in this country — not that they would be any financial bonanza, but you might be able to pick up enough money to pay for the trip and see some of the things we have done since you left. What do you think of such a scheme? I have just received a letter from Susi Jeans, and she tells me she is going to Canada in the spring and hopes to come to the U.S. for a few dates. I will certainly do everything I can for her as I would do for you.

What a pity about that 32' reed extension. I can quite imagine how it sounds. For many years now I have never extended a 32' reed from the major 16' Pedal reed, but have rather taken down one of the other reeds. At Saint John's in New York, for example, I carried down the manual 16' Bombarde of the Bombarde organ, which is of comparatively small scale and it is very effective. In Salt Lake City and at the First Church of Christ, Scientist here in Boston, I carried down a secondary Pedal reed to form the 32'. In other cases I have had much success in smaller jobs in carrying down the Swell 16' reed with half-length resonators, but with French dome-headed shallots and, while they are not exactly nice to listen to by themselves, they are really effective musically. After all, you do not play solos on a 32' Bombarde.

You will be interested to know that I imported a French Trumpet from Masure in Paris and asked him to send me a typical Trumpet Ordinaire, and I did not give him any particulars to work to whatsoever. Probably what he sent is something like the kind of thing you have in the Festival Hall organ. The pipes themselves were beautifully made with spotted metal resonators down to 8' C. The workmanship was extremely beautiful. The general tone of the stop is excellent, but the slowness of speech throughout, and particularly in the bass, is something I just can't understand. I am using this stop in a rebuild of the Hill Auditorium organ at the University of Michigan, where Bob Noehren is the Professor, but I found it necessary to completely revoice it. Those long boots, which are typical of French reeds, are very bad, I feel, and we cut them off as short as possible and put a new tip on the end of the socket, with greatly improved results. The tone becomes much more steady under those conditions. The general tone of the stop is not as good as those we produce, and, in fact, I do pride myself on one thing — that our reeds are the best in the world, whether they be of the English, French or German Baroque variety. I have not slavishly copied anything, but have worked every stop through to get proper balance between bass and treble and a stability, so that the stops will stay in tune and not be so crazily unreliable as those one finds in Europe. I bought a Rankett in Europe and it was the most uneven and unreliable kind of a thing I have ever seen, although, again, beautifully made. With suitable revoicing we were able to turn it into a stop, however. Now, having blown my own Trompette-en-Chamade, I will get on with the letter.

I was interested to hear of the scale of the Solo Diapason in the R.F.H. organ. I note the middle C is 2½" or perhaps a little more, which is really a big scale. The largest 8' Principal I put into Saint John's is only 2³⁄₁₆" at middle C. I am very interested to note that you pinched in the bass, for I did exactly the same thing on this particular stop at Saint John's and the CC measures 5⁵⁄₁₆". With my somewhat smaller scale at middle C, I did not find it necessary to pinch the trebles which you have done with your Solo Diapason. Obviously, with such a scale at middle C, you would have to do that. I agree with you entirely that the variations in scale instead of the straight progressions certainly work, and I have been doing that for many years.

Generally speaking, I think I could say that we have done what you believe in, wide scale flutes and narrow scale Principals. Although I have varied very considerably from the pure Schnitger-type organ and have broadened out my treble scales perhaps more so than you would consider proper, but I think now we have settled down to a more reasonable arrangement. I have not felt it was desirable to try and make an absolute Baroque organ, but rather to take the principles of the builders of the period and adapt them for the kind of buildings we usually meet in this country and, of course, adding more modern and romantic material to the instrument duly modified so as to form part of the whole.

The late Fritz Heitmann came to America several times after the war and I was tremendously impressed with his artistry as a player. At the Church of the Advent here in Boston, he played most of the Bach Catechism and I do not believe I have ever been so moved by organ music. It was a real, religious experience. Fritz was familiar of course with all the well-known Continental organs, German, Scandinavian and Dutch, and he seemed to feel they all had their points. At the same time I was very flattered when he told me that he found the organ at the Advent a perfect vehicle for his style of playing, and he was just as happy with our electric action with a tracker touch, and although he preferred pure tracker and slide chest actions for small organs, he felt the larger ones should have electric control. That brings up a big matter and I feel that some of our friends are going overboard in returning purely to a mechanical action. I would be very glad to hear what you think about that.

Very interested to hear that you have seen Harold Gleason recently and also Paul Callaway and Bob Noehren. The Great, Positive and Pedal organs of Noehren's rebuilt instrument are along pure Baroque lines, and I will be very interested to see how it will turn out.

I still think that Salt Lake City is the finest organ that I have built so far and will probably remain that way. Of course, the place has marvelous acoustics from the organ point of view.

I am very, very happy with the results at Saint John's, although it does not go as far as I would like to have gone, because of the lack of funds. The Solo organ is a kind of a mess except for the 8' Tuba and Clarion, which are of the Willis type. While one does not find any great musical use for a thing like our Trumpet at the west end, nevertheless there are occasions in a big cathedral when it can be used with stunning effect. It is quite electrifying. It is a modified type of French Trumpet placed horizontally and cut dead in tune.

I am in complete agreement with you about the size of organs and I much prefer instruments of medium size to these great, big fellows. It seems to fall to my lot, however, to have built most of the large organs in this country.

We have been making some records and they are really quite good, I think. The third one is coming out shortly and when they come to hand, I am going to send you all three in one fell swoop. I will also send you a money order to pay for the duty. It cannot be paid at this end, but it is terrific. I wouldn't stick anybody with that. Doubtless you have a chance to use a high fidelity machine which, of course, is necessary to play these records properly.

Well, I seem to have run on at great length. Please let me hear from you from time to time.

With all best wishes,

Yours,
Don

GDH/MOK

September 28, 1954

Mr. Henry Willis
Henry Willis & Sons, Ltd.
Rotunda Organ Works
34, Marlborough Grove
Old Kent Road
London, S.E.1
England

Dear Henry:

Thanks for yours of the 2nd instant, from which I am interested to hear that there has been an Organists Conference in Norwich somewhat similar to our A.G.O. Conventions here. It is amusing to hear about what is happening to the Hill, Norman and Beard concern.

You are right about Saint John the Divine, but I did not really keep too much of the old Skinner pipe work because it was absolutely hopeless, as you can well imagine, for use in the kind of effect I was attempting to produce.

If the Festival Hall chorus reeds are all of the type sent over here by Masure, I can understand that they need some revoicing. Since I wrote you last, we have revoiced the sample I got over from Paris and we have made it into quite a decent reed. Incidentally, we cut off all the sockets to shorten them and found we obtained a much more steady effect as one could readily imagine.

I am sorry that French organ building is at such a low ebb, and there doesn't seem to be any bright spark on the horizon which might rejuvenate the whole thing. It has been going downhill for an awful long time.

Still slugging along here with the daily routine, which includes writing letters of excuses as to why this or that job is not yet completed. One thing about it, we are having gorgeous weather now — cool, but sunny and very clear.

I don't know whether you know it, but Joe's house on the beach burned down last fall, and he has built himself an absolutely modern structure which is nearly all plate glass. I have been staying there for a few days and am completely sold on this contemporary design. It has been very cleverly worked out. Work is reduced to a minimum and the chores which have to be done almost seem to be a pleasure in the surroundings. All the furniture is modern in addition to the structure and there are some curious looking chairs, but, funnily enough, they are all extremely comfortable.

Joe has a grand piano in the living room, which has an 18' 6" ceiling, which gives the room excellent acoustics and, in addition to the piano, organ records sound superb and one is able to get far enough away to get a real effect. The house is only 44 miles from the plant, so it is very accessible.

    With best wishes,

As ever,

Don

GDH:MOK

---

262 G. Donald Harrison to Henry Willis

December 8, 1954

Mr. Henry Willis
Rotunda Organ Works
34, Marlborough Grove
Old Kent Road
London, S.E.1
England
Dear Henry:

    I was very glad to get your letter of the 1st of November and to hear the news about the National Association of Organists but particularly Birmingham Town Hall and St. George's Hall Liverpool. The latter is some job I would imagine. I hope that they have not interfered with the acoustics of the hall in the restoration.

    I know that you have always been interested in hard rolled zinc Geigens and also strings. I remember those strings that were developed by your Uncle years ago. I would certainly like to hear one of them and am much interested to hear that you feel you obtain a more singing quality than with spotted metal.

    Of course Fernando Germani is one of the best organists we have today. I have missed him so far in the States.

    Harry Goss-Custard is certainly wonderful. I had a very nice letter from him after I wrote and congratulated him on his honorary degree. It is impossible to think that the Liverpool organ is now 30 years old. How the time slips by.

    I agree entirely with you that a visit to Europe is sadly overdue and, frankly, I have been toying with the idea of making one next summer. There are so many things I would like to see both in England and on the Continent. More of this later when I see how I can work things out.

    The best news in your letter is the fact that your health is standing up so well. I suppose you have to be a bit careful with the intake, so to speak.

    There is one matter on which I would like to take your advice, and that is, once again, about the English keys with thick ivories without surface joints. We have been getting keys from the British Piano Action Ltd., but in recent shipments it does seem to me that their quality has slipped badly. They are inaccurate in many instances, will not follow one's drawings and it means that we have to do an awful lot of work on the keys after they are received here. One of our troubles has been that the ivories are not securely cemented on the key itself.

I am wondering if you could put me onto anybody else who might prove to be more satisfactory. I forget if you buy your keys from this concern. I know we talked about it when you were here but I cannot remember exactly what you said about the matter. Any dope you can give me on this matter will be thankfully received.

With all the best,

As ever,
Don

GDH:MOK

---

263 Henry Willis to William King Covell

16th December, 1954

Mr. Wm. King Covell,
72 Washington Street,
Newport, Rhode Island,
U.S.A.

<u>Channing Memorial Church, Newport</u>

Dear King Covell,

Thanks for yours of the 18th November and the interesting photos. That of the Koppelflöte reveals the pernicious practice of either felting or leathering the canister top which damps down the harmonic development. This is done to avoid the necessity for the meticulous workmanship essential for metal to metal fitting — as carried out here. I observed a similar treatment, use of heavy felt, for similar canister topped pipes in modern Aeolian-Skinner organs — pointed out to D.H. who entirely agreed with me. Earlier A.S. work for which I gave full chapter and verse was metal to metal and so much better.

Regulation of Willis chorus reeds:

The tuning tongues set at an angle of approximately 35° and the stop rough tuned at the spring. Fine regulation then takes place — when, for those not fully versed in such matters, the "tuning" wire is tapped down until the note begins to grunt and then tapped up to a clear note, no more. Tuning is then and henceforth at the tuning tongue. The chief regulation control is at the spring and, once set, must not be altered, tuning must be at the tuning tongue provided for that purpose, treble only excepted, which is cut to dead length.

Owing to shading on the job, all tuning tongues will not finally be at an angle of 35° , but vary slightly one way or the other. Tuning at 70° F. This is well known to A[ubrey] T[hompson]-A[llen].

Yours very sincerely,
Henry Willis

H.W./T.F.

---

264 Ralph Downes to G. Donald Harrison

December 10, 1954

My dear Don,

Thank you for your long letter of September 29, and for all the extremely interesting enclosures. I did feel a queer sensation when I read about your 50" trumpet — seems rather like a kind of retrogression! But then you've never gone the whole hog about the classical organ in the way that some of us have. I expect you are right really. There are people here who clamour for Tubas at the Royal Festival Hall and needless to say, "British diapasons" too. My view is that one kind of tone would kill the other, and in any case the whole tonal ideal of many mild ranks making a big sound would go by the board.

I am prompted to write to you now, having just seen in the <u>Diapason</u> that you have overhauled the Princeton organ. How I wish I could see and hear it! That, however, is impossible for the present, at any rate. I am most curious to know the exact arrangement now; I remember the old layout very clearly. Could you spare time to tell me? Surely you still found the acoustics and the generally bad position of the organ a great drawback? I note that the pedal is still mostly "augmented" — i.e., "diminished!"

Thank you also for your promise to send me the three recordings of your productions; I will be <u>most</u> interested to hear them. I cannot reciprocate, for none of the recording firms will look at the Festival Hall because of its lack of reverberation! (How times do change; it doesn't seem long since it was the other way 'round!)

I am interested to hear you had a French reed from Masure; personally I've only seen their flue pipes and was not impressed. Ours here are much better made, in my opinion. All the R.F.H. reeds were made by H.&H. at Durham, but French moulds were used for the blocks; the globe-shaped type are used from about 4' f up to the top. This does make a more solid pipe. It is true that the reeds at the R.F.H. are a little unstable, but I attribute this entirely to the enormous amount of very fluffy dust floating about the place. My reeds at the Oratory have the usual English blocks, but they vary a little too, in the middle and treble. I haven't got to the root of this matter at all.

The R.F.H. 32' reed extension mystery is solved. H.&H. broke the shallot progression at BBBB, using a cut-off bevelled end instead of the dome-end, and the openings are much wider. (How Rochesson let this pass, I cannot understand. I was too tied up myself to be able to go and worry out <u>every</u> detail at Durham. One does expect experienced organ builders to know the <u>elements</u> of their trade. But no! Nobody noticed it.) In the end, Rochesson came back and leathered the shallots, also the pressure on these reeds has been reduced on to 3¾", and it all fits in very much better. In fact, the 16' Bombarde can be used with Great to Mixtures though I don't recommend it; I stop at the 8' Trumpet in such a combination.

This is about the end of the sheet, so I will stop, with heartiest greetings and good wishes.

Yours,
Ralph Downes

---

265 G. Donald Harrison to Ralph Downes

January 13, 1955

Mr. Ralph Downes
9 Elm Crescent
Ealing, W5
London, England
My dear Ralph:

Thank you so much for your letter of December 10th. I can quite imagine the queer sensation you had when you read that the west end trumpet is on 50" wind. It does have a gorgeous tone and of course is not part of the organ, but used solely for certain fanfares used at Easter, etc. Of course we do have Tubas 8' and 4' in that organ also. With Coke-Jephcott as organist at the time the instrument was built, it would have been quite impossible to have left out stops of that nature. They can be ignored, after all, and the new organist, Alec Wyton, who is an enlightened Englishman, only uses them occasionally and never in the ensemble. These were the first Tubas we voiced in years.

The work done at Princeton was a terrific chore as you can well imagine, due to the rather poor location of the instrument with its heavy casework, and again aggravated by the Gustoveno tiles which are plastered all over the ceiling and upon much of the side walls, making the chapel a bass-heavy place acoustically.

Carl Weinrich is one of my best friends and one of the nicest fellows in the world, but he really did want a kind of Baroque effect, using very light pressures and that is where the rub came in such a place. I had to re-scale some of my mixtures for this job, as they did not come off in the distressing acoustical environment. However, finally the job turned out quite well and, indeed, the effect is in many ways quite surprising. They had very little money to improve the organ so Carl decided that he would like to have a Baroque section spread over three manuals and pedal. This was done, as you will see by the enclosed specification, to which I have attached the mixture layouts, as I thought they might interest you. The latter I do not consider as ideal, but Carl wanted them that way. Please excuse the fact that these particulars have not been typed, but we are so busy in our office at the moment that I am sure you will not mind.

The weak part of the scheme is of course the Pedal Organ. You will notice that the Solo Organ flue work and fancy reeds have all disappeared. The shades have been taken off the box and this is now the Positiv Organ. The old Tubas are still there, however, although Carl does not use them.

The Choir now, of course, is much reduced due to the fact that we yanked out one of the chests. The Swell remains much the same as it was except that four or five years ago I did revoice the 16', 8' and 4' Trumpets, making them a great deal better than they were originally.

You may well ask "Does the new and old mix?" There, of course, is the rub, although it is much better than you would realize. For the Classical works, one can restrict the registration to the three manual Baroque section, together with the Pedal.

Probably the organ that I have recently done that you would like the best is the rebuild of the Ann Arbor organ for Bob Noehren, specification of which is enclosed herewith. The old Ann Arbor organ was almost a sister of the Princeton instrument and built around the same time. Here the face-lifting has been much more drastic, as you will note from the layout. The general effect is extremely mild, perhaps a little bit overdone in that direction, although Bob likes it and so do his students.

Regarding the records, I now find that some dealer is arranging to sell these records in England and rather than go through all the paraphernalia one has to to send them directly, I think I will wait until I can find out where they can actually be purchased in the old country.

You may see me in May or June this year. I am thinking of taking a trip for a rest. I will visit Holland, Germany and, of course, England. I look forward with keen interest to hearing the Festival Hall instrument.

Glad to hear that you have the 32' Bombarde straightened out. Regarding your other reeds, I am sure you would find an amazing difference in their stability if you shortened the sockets. As the French type has a double block, this has to be done by cutting off about 2" at the lower end and then soldering on a new toe. With the regular English block one can just use a shorter socket. Try one, I think you will be amazed.

Looking forward to seeing you soon and with all good wishes for 1955,

As ever,
Don

GDH/MOK

---

266 Henry Willis to Arthur Howes

19th January, 1955

Mr. Arthur Howes,
Director, Organ Institute
Andover, Massachusetts, U.S.A.

<u>Organ Institute Quarterly</u>

Dear Mr. Howes,

References appear in your journal from time to time to the effect that tracker touch is the only perfect touch, suggesting that this "can only be obtained with tracker action which gives an intimacy between the player and the speech of the pipes unobtainable by other means."

It is agreed that tracker or top-resistance touch is the ideal, but this is

readily obtained with electric action by simple means known and used by your own best firms, and by me for over 30 years.

The standard average use is that the key supports a weight of four ounces and is held down by a weight of two and three-quarter ounces — the four ounces touch is overcome when the key is depressed by 3/32".

I am well aware that there are some firms both in this country and in the U.S. who do not fit "tracker touch" to their electric key actions because of the added cost, and this may give the unversed the impression that all electric touches are of the spring type, lacking crispness in use.

To suggest that tracker action gives the intimacy etc., only shows a lack of knowledge of the facts. These are that with tracker action, the pluck of the pallet has first to be overcome, then the key falls readily. The pallet does not and cannot "follow the finger" — there is only one form of mechanism which achieved that result, the Vincent Willis Floating Lever.

I hope that the above will make it clear that the agreed perfect touch can be and is achieved with electric action even better than with tracker action for the reason that with the latter the weight of touch is heavier in the bass and lighter in the treble, therefore not even throughout the manual compass — to say nothing of the implied use of mechanical intermanual couplers and the added weight of touch when they are in use.

I would observe that your leading firm — the Aeolian-Skinner Organ Co., use electric actions only, with "tracker touch" and, incidentally, do not use slider chests!

Yours sincerely,
Henry Willis

H.W./M.P.

the Vincent Willis Floating Lever — introduced in the Willis organ at the 1885 Inventions Exhibition in London, the floating lever was an ingenious pneumatic servo mechanism that actually caused the pallet to duplicate the movement and speed of the key. It was difficult to keep in adjustment and never widely used.

---

267 Emerson Richards to William King Covell

Jan. 21st., 1955

Dear King,

Before answering your last letter there were some questions unanswered from that of Jan 7th. Color pictures will wait until the front is finished. The 16' Spitz Principal is not in and I think that I will put a fiber glass curtain (it is not supposed to obstruct the high frequencies) in front of the Swell shades. I think they are going to be annoying when they move and they don't look too well — although worse in the picture than in the room. We have two spotlights on the pipes in the room now and it looks better than the harsh light of the picture.

Of course we are NOT going to put the towers back. If you look hard you will see that it would be impossible as the Positiv sits on them. Everything shows as in the picture.

The slotting is on the Steinmeyer pipes and is only on the flutes and like material. All of Don's Principal chorus has slide tuners.

When the Spitz Principal 16' is in there will be 3104 pipes showing. I have made a deal with Chester Raymond, of Princeton, to do the wiring. He has done quite a bit of work for Don and has been satisfactory. He is nearby and fairly reasonable. I did ask Whalon for a price but he left without giving me a reply so I judged that he was not interested. Raymond has just done all the erection work for Don on the rebuild at Princeton Chapel. He also has a good tonal man if I get stuck in that direction.

The console is at the factory and is being worked upon. Don says that it should be done the first week in February and ready to come down then. If so the wiring to the junctions will be finished and it will be only a question of wiring from the junction board to the console until we will be hearing something. Don is trying to push the console through but he tells me that already the men are doing work that we did not contemplate in our contract but that they think necessary. I hope he does not lose on it.

Now for your last letter. I return the Channing list. I will forget Whalon and Channing in this letter for lack of time. If I am to answer you about San Diego. I had to talk to Don on some matters about my organ so I know about what he has answered in a letter about this job although it has not yet arrived and may not until Monday (I am going to Washington tomorrow). This is what he said. First the scheme you suggested he thought academic and not very practical for an Episcopal Church. No accompanimental material on the Great at all. TWO similar 8's on the Choir and the three manual business on so small an organ.

Because you know nothing of actual costs you chose to ignore them. Organs are now averaging, with Don, about $1100 per stop. But that Choir organ [is] better than $2600 per stop! Don did not say on the phone what he would want for the two manual I suggested [but] what he did say was that they just were so overwhelmed with orders that they just could not take small contracts at reasonable prices. [And] that they were so set up that a small organ taken at their regular prices invariably resulted in a loss to them so that only in the case where a client insisted and was willing to pay for it would they, at this time, take a small job.

He suggested that Möller was better adjusted for this kind of thing than they were. But he pointed out that the last financial statement on Möller's showed that on $2,000,000 of business (1954) they had a profit of less than 2½ percent.

Also California is so far away. Work that is close to the factory is so much more manageable. Only a very large job warrants attention out there — one that can absorb the extra travel as well as freight charges.

So all this boils down to a point that unless these people had a church that was important enough and large enough and rich enough to want an organ about twice the size (in money) than they contemplated, an Aeolian-

Skinner is not for them at this time. Want me to try Möller on a two-manual for you? Austin might be your next best bet. Schantz is financially shakey. You know what a Wicks is. And a Casavant can be just as lousy.

This may all sound as if success had gone to Don's head. Nothing of the kind. They have done a lot of work and increased their prestige, but they have not made a lot of money. Some of this is, in my opinion, their own fault. They do things in a wasteful way. But as Don says, the men are used to doing things in a fine way and refuse to do it any other. Also they have burnt their fingers on some of the important jobs that they undertook and these cut into their profits seriously.

So while it is easy to stand on the side lines and kibitz, it is something else to create a work of art. And that is what we expect every organ of Don's to be.

So it don't [sic] look like your friends out in San Diego can count on an A-S and if this organist MUST have a three manual, he will have to find more money for it or have an organ that is all keys AND NO PIPES.

I guess this about brings us up to date except if there is anything further in Don's letter that is to arrive I will pass it on.

Sincerely,

Emerson

ER/af

Color pictures will wait until the front is finished — The new organ, op. 1269, for the Senator's home replaced the instrument sold to a Denver church.

---

268 G. Donald Harrison to Henry Willis

January 27, 1955

Mr. Henry Willis
Rotunda Organ Works
34 Marlborough Grove
Old Kent Road
London, S.E.1
England.
Dear Henry:

Thanks so much for your letter of December 29th and for the information you give us about the keys. I presume we may as well try to worry along with British Piano Actions as to start out with a new outfit — might be inadvisable at this time.

Regarding my trip to England, I expect to leave on about May 21st and am going to Holland, and then expect to visit Denmark and will come to

England. I will certainly be in England about the middle of June and will leave at the end of the third week for the U.S. once more.

Of course, things can arise which will upset these calculations but I hope to follow through with them. I have to leave town today for a couple of weeks, so this is a hurried letter just to give you a little information about the trip.

All the best,

As ever,
Don

GDH:AGR

---

269 Henry Willis to G. Donald Harrison

3rd February, 1955

Mr. G. Donald Harrison,
President,
Aeolian Skinner Organ Co.,
Organ Builders,
Boston 25,
Mass. U.S.A.
Dear Don,

Glad to have yours of the 27th February and to learn of your coming visit. Reference Holland, Dr. Vente can be invaluable to you in arranging any visits you want to make; he is not only enthusiastic but knowledgeable and was with us on our extended organ tour in Holland, N. Germany, Denmark and Malmö (Sweden) in 1953. He is a school master at Utrecht and will not be free to accompany you in term time. Write him mentioning my name:

Dr. M.A. Vente,
Stolberglaan 17,
Utrecht,
Holland.

Denmark. Can I give you any introductions? I know Marcussen's and Frobenius — stayed with the latter for a week. Firm now run by two youngish brothers who are completely "back to Methuselah." Also introductions to Danish organists, also an enthusiast at Malmö who could arrange access to interesting local instruments. (Malmö readily accessible by ferry from Copenhagen and the trip there and back readily done in a day if prior arrangements have been made.)

By far the best way to do Holland, North Germany and Denmark is by car, as many interesting churches are "off the map" and/or not readily accessible by train or bus.

England. Please say when you may arrive and what you would like to see. Three days in London would give a general idea of the more important jobs since 1934.

Willis, London. Southwark Cathedral, All Souls Langham Place, St. Dunstan's, Fleet Street with some 18th century pipework, Training College Chelsea etc. and as many revisits as you wish.

Provinces. Edinburgh is a <u>must</u>. St. Giles' Cathedral 1940. McEwan Hall, University of Edinburgh 1953. Coatsbridge Town Hall 1954, and others as time is available.

Other Builders. London. Westminster Abbey Harrison and Harrison. St. Michael's Chester Square and St. Peter's Eaton Square — Walker post-war rebuilds.

An experiment in the quasi-baroque by H[ill], N[orman] and B[eard] at Crouch End; the "Downes" job — neo-quasi-Baroque at Brompton Oratory (Walker's); and Festival Hall (H & H) just about covers the ground.

I should very much like to go with you to Edinburgh, and would, of course, look after you in London and get some fun in accompanying you to the non-Willis jobs. I can readily arrange all the visits.

As ever,
H.W.

H.W./M.P.

---

270 Henry Willis to Martin Wick

26th February, 1955

Mr. Martin M. Wick,
President, The Wicks Organ Company
Highland,
Illinois, U.S.A.
Dear Mr. Wick,

Thank you for your letter of the 13th January and booklet with it.

It is gratifying to hear of the expansion of your company and your need especially for a voicer.

There is a very good youngish man, now about 30, trained here as a flue voicer, who left to tonally supervise the productions of a firm making electronic imitations of pipe organs and, not finding this artistically satisfying, set up in business for himself. He might be interested if you made a really attractive proposition including cost of his travel, and I suggest that you write him direct offering say, $250 a month for a 40-hour week, overtime rates beyond that, travelling and removal expenses to Highland, usual guaranteed covering entry to the U.S.A. and a guaranteed three-year engagement.

No less would induce a first-rate voicer!

R.J. Piper, who went to Austins and is now their Tonal Director, had Mr. Hyatt as his assistant, and he also worked under me very successfully after Mr. Piper left for the U.S.

> Mr. Clifford Hyatt,
> Messrs. Williamson & Hyatt
> Crunch,
> North Walsham,
> Norfolk.

> Yours sincerely,
> Henry Willis

---

271 William E. Zeuch to Dora and Henry Willis (handwritten)

March 10, 1955

Dear Dora & Henry:

. . . I derive a measure of self satisfaction that it was I who convinced Arthur Marks that organ building in America greatly needed a renaissance or house cleaning or whatever word expresses the thought best. Your first visits to us are among my happiest memories.

So pack up the old bags and come again soon. Surely Dora would love to see Michael & Stephen and their progeny again.

> All the best for you both
> from Margie & Bill Zeuch

Bill Zeuch — was then 87.

---

272 G. Donald Harrison to Henry Willis

April 14, 1955

Mr. Henry Willis
Rotunda Organ Works
34, Marlborough Grove
Old Kent Road
London, S.E. 1
England

Dear Henry:

Thanks for your two letters of February 3rd and March 31st.

My plans are now pretty well complete and we propose to leave New York on May 20th on the New Amsterdam. I think the ship takes about seven days. We sail from Southampton on the Liberté June 21st, so that you see we have very little time but I cannot stay away longer, due to so many important commitments to meet.

I do not think we will go into Germany or to France on this trip. It's all too much of a rush. I would like, however, to visit Denmark in addition to Holland, and I would be much obliged for introductions to Marcussen and Frobenius. Will you kindly send me their addresses.

I am writing to Dr. M.A. Vente.

The exact date of our arrival in England depends on how much of interest we find in Holland and Denmark. In England, of course as I said originally, I must spend some time with my brother and my sister but I imagine we will have a week in which to look at organs. Thanks for your offer of help in this regard. There is one thing that I would rather like to do and that is to go to Liverpool. I would like to see Harry Goss-Custard once more and also see the Liverpool organs again. I did not go there last time, you will remember.

Thanks a lot for your offer to arrange hotel accommodations in London. I suppose for the most part we will be staying with my brother, and I do not know exactly when or how long we will be staying in London, so it is pretty difficult to make a definite reservation. I can tell much better when I get over there.

Of course, I will have to see Ralph Downes and the organ at South Bank and I hope also to see Cecil Clutton. I have had one or two letters from him recently.

I will, of course, write you again before we leave and try to give you some more specific dates.

Many thanks for all your help,

As ever,

Don

GDH:MOK

the organ at South Bank — Royal Festival Hall

---

273 Emerson Richards to William King Covell

April 19th, 1955

Mr. Wm. King Covell
72 Washington Street
Newport, Rhode Island
Dear King,

This letter will have to go off in sections if you are to get an answer to the Harvard matter in time. I would be glad to accept an invitation, if extended, to address the club at any convenient time and provided that my health permits. I have not had too good a winter. Not really sick but just not as vigorous as I used to be.

Now to answer your letter. METHUEN. I doubt if any prolonged discussion of this subject will get us anywhere. Neither facts nor logic will serve to alter your point of view. Your contention that a bad organ should remain a bad organ is unique and cannot be altered by argument. But let us take up as made your statements and reply to them. Is the organ still 50 percent Walcker? That depends on how you figure it. ALL the chests and mechanical parts are Searles and that is more than 50 percent of the organ. Then Don says that 40 percent of the pipe work is new. So that leaves about 10 percent of the organ Walcker. But if you limit yourself to the pipe work alone, then a half is still Walcker. But here all the important parts like the reeds have been radically revoiced, so that the ensemble is much less Walcker than 50 percent.

I agree that the organ is not a characteristic Harrison. He was limited by the chests and the material available and the MONEY. Neither is Symphony Hall a true Harrison although it is different from Methuen. I agree that if there had been a place for them, a 16-8-4 reed chorus on the Great would have been in order — or placed so as to be available on the Great. But again the new Principal Chorus would have been sacrificed to make room for a new chest and MONEY would have been required.

Regarding your Par.IV-Pg.1: the argument that a mid 19th century German [organ] is EVER worth saving leaves me very cold. They did not have a single redeeming character. Compared to the Willis and the Cavaillé-Colls they were, as the Germans admit, the very depth of the decadent German period.

If this organ had been a Roosevelt or a Hutchings or a Hook and Hastings of the "good" period, then I would say preserve them, but when you start with an inferior instrument that has no right to survive except as a horrible example, then it is not a "museum piece" that deserves to be preserved. A museum is for worthy ART and historical objects. But what is neither art nor history has no place there. A storage house or the junk pile is its proper environment.

I do not agree that the Walcker had any influence on American organ building. You overlook the real influences that governed organ building during the last quarter of the 19th Century.

I got the first page off at 3:00 P.M. and after a session with the organ am now back to your letter.

We now have the organ wired through to the console and playing from the Great and Positiv. Tomorrow we will wire in the stop action on these divisions and can then play individual stops. And by tomorrow night we ought to have the Swell to the console and perhaps the Choir. They are all to the junctions. Right now we are getting various assorted squeals because nothing is tuned, but the 8' Principal seems like it is going to come up to expectations.

Now to get on with your letter. The Roosevelts were NOT influenced by German design. Hilborn's [sic] notebooks show that it was the English flue ensemble and the French reeds that took him. Now there IS a certain amount of German influence to be found in his work, but it was like all the other builders in America. Due to the German workmen who emigrated here in the 70's and earlier. For example the elder Haskell was the superintendent at the Philadelphia works for the Roosevelts during the time that they were turning out the most organs. And Haskell was very German. (Quite a bit of the action is due to him.) So that while ON PAPER the Roosevelts were not at all German, they did have a distinctive flavor acquired from the men who did the work. This same thing also applied to several other American builders, as I can remember when I first came in contact with organ building just about the beginning of the century. Even some of E.M.'s men were Germans.

So I say that the German influence did come from the workmen and not from the isolated Walcker. No one can say that Johnson was influenced by the Walcker, but he did produce a chorus WITH MIXTURES. Newspaper items are notoriously silly when dealing with organs so I don't think we can rely on them for evidence.

The American organs of the three last decades of the 19th Century were on paper English in design, but actually American in reality and most of them were mighty good organs too! Left to develop without E.M.'s bum ear we might never have gone so far astray.

You ask me (Pg.2) if I really think the [Methuen] organ has been an outstanding musical success? As I say, from the whole text, I think what I said is accurate. Compared to what it was before, it is. Then, it was silent and nobody wanted to hear it. Now it does have a following, and people do come to hear it. Yes, there are other factors to be sure, but here is the main one. You must remember it was playable when Skinner moved in 1940, and it could have been used before that but nobody wanted to play it or hear it. Of course it could not have been rebuilt in 1920 as you suggest.

Now as to my real feelings about the organ. I think it is a good organ considering its genesis. It was and still is a bastard. And I have discovered that a bastard is not so much an accident of birth as of the circumstances that engendered the creature. And that the world's dislike of b's is based on experience, not morality.

With that explanation I would say that as organs go, it is still an outstanding organ. But as to my feelings, do you remember one of the recent times that we visited it together, you and I and several others went directly to Groton. While there I said to Ned, and I thought you heard me, that I would not trade his organ for a dozen Methuen organs. And that is my real feeling about the organ. Don has contrived a silk purse out of the sow's ear, but you can still smell the hog and hear the grunt.

I am a bit amused about your reference to Willis. ALL Henry knows about German organs he learned with me. He has only been to Germany once to my knowledge and that is when he went with me and over the same ground that I had traversed before. And all I heard was "It's all very well, Old Man, but it would never do over here." But he did get all the dope possible from Hans down at Oettingen while we were there, and when he got home he tried desperately to sell it (the Baroque stuff), but the British just would not buy it. In return he did try to show Hans' voicers how to do an English Diapason and also a Willis reed, but that got nowhere either. So I would not count Henry as an authority on 19th century romantic German organs. As I remember it, he heard only two on that trip. One in Berlin (a real stinker) and the big one in Hamburg, and that one he did not like. These were both Walckers as you know. He did hear some others, but they were all bad.

I did not try the old organ at Methuen to really know it. I have a dim recollection of hearing it privately, but I cannot recall the circumstances. All I do remember is we got admission through the man at the white house above the Hall. I can't even remember who was with me. I thought it to be just another German organ and wrote it off. . . .

I think you brush off the MONEY problem without giving it due weight. What used to be done is no criterion of what goes now. Taxes and other conditions have cut into the patrons' fortunes to the point that they cannot write those checks for $50-100,000 like they could in the 1920's. That kind of money no longer exists. If it were not for the big corporations and the Foundations, Yale and Harvard and the like could not now exist. I will be much surprised if Frank can come up with the money sufficient to do this job. The resumption of your answer. I did NOT make the distinction you do not seem to understand. It was made by Biggs in the letter he wrote to you, and I suspected there was a reason for it.

I have covered the money angle but this does not interest you. You have a supreme disdain for such matters that fascinates me. . . .

[The remainder of this typewritten letter from Emerson Richards is absent.]

May 10, 1955

Mr. Henry Willis
Rotunda Organ Works
34 Marlborough Grove
Old Kent Road
London, S.E.1, England
Dear Henry:

During this summer our representative in Texas, Mr. Roy Perry, will be visiting England with a friend of his and would naturally very much like to meet you and see some of your organs. Also he would like some advice as to those instruments he should see generally in the middle and southern part of the country.

Roy Perry, or Perriola, as he is affectionately referred to in our organization, has supervised, with the aid of Jack Williams and his son, most of our important installations in Texas. He is an accomplished organist and has a wonderful ear. He is a top notch finisher and during my periodic visits to Texas I cannot remember a time when I have had to suggest that something might have been done a little differently. He just has that kind of organ sense.

I think you will also enjoy him as a personality. He knows some good southern stories and, by the way, he is an expert at southern hospitality. I always look forward to my trips down to his neck of the woods as we have a glorious time just waiting for sundown to start on a little nourishment.

I would be particularly grateful for any courtesy you can show Perriola and with many thanks in advance,

As ever,
Don

GDH:MOK

May 11, 1955

Mr. Henry Willis
Rotunda Organ Works
34 Marlborough Grove
Old Kent Road
London, S.E.1, England
Dear Henry:

Thank you very much for your letter of the 19th of April and for the introductions to Marcussens and Frobenius. I had already written to Dr. Vente and Flentrop.

We are all set to sail May 20th, going direct to Holland. I do not know exactly what date we will arrive in England but I will certainly communicate with you from the Continent but you can count on it being somewhere around the 10th or 11th of June. I am greatly looking forward to the trip although I am having great difficulty clearing up matters here so that I can feel happy about sailing.

I will keep all further news until I see you.

As ever,

Don

GDH:MOK

---

276 G. Donald Harrison to Henry Willis

July 11, 1955

Mr. Henry Willis
Rotunda Organ Works
34 Marlborough Grove
Old Kent Road
London, S.E.1
England

Dear Henry:

We got back to the United States and the voyage was again very smooth and except for fog, which persisted for four days, we had a very nice time.

I want to thank you for all the time you gave us while in London and for the marvelous hospitality which you showed to us. It was really nice to get together with you again and talk over old times. I hope it will not be long before we can meet again, and perhaps you will decide to take a trip to the United States in the near future.

I am glad to say I got the shallots through the customs without the slightest hitch.

I found a mountain of work awaiting me on my return as you can well imagine, but I have a fine chance to get rid of some of my correspondence as the shop is closed this week for the annual vacation. Next week when the shop is open again and we have the wind on, I will test out the shallots and also let you know how you could help us out with pipes, etc.

With all good wishes,

As ever,

Don

President

GDH:MOK

277 G. Donald Harrison to Ralph Downes

July 11, 1955

Mr. Ralph Downes
9 Elm Crescent
Ealing, W5
London, England
My dear Ralph:

We are now back once more in the United States, but are looking back with a great deal of pleasure to our visit to the Continent and especially to England.

I cannot tell you what a joy it was to be able to talk with you again and we certainly had a wonderful time with Mrs. Downes. We were so happy to see you both looking so fit and well. I wish our time could have been doubled and even that wouldn't have been enough to cover everything that we want to talk about.

I want to congratulate you once more on the success of the two organs — the large one at the Royal Festival Hall and the smaller one at Brompton Oratory. There is no doubt that both these instruments show a great step forward in organ design and voicing, and I do hope they will have a large influence on other British builders to follow suit.

At the Royal Festival Hall I was not entirely happy with the chorus reeds, as they seemed to be very slow and the balance between bass and treble is a little bit unfortunate, I feel.

As I believe I told you during our last talk, in a way I prefer the Brompton Oratory organ in spite of its poor location. The acoustical environment, however, suits an instrument of this kind much better than the awful acoustics at the Festival Hall and the complete instrument seemed to me to be much more of an entity.

I was much impressed with Henry Willis's mechanical work, but he does not seem to be in sympathy with the present trend in tonal ideas. I imagine there is too much family pride to cause him to change in this regard. That seems to me to be a great pity.

It would be great if we could somehow work out a trip for you to the United States. I would be so happy to show you what I have been trying to do since you left. Let us keep up a correspondence from time to time. In the meantime, we both thank you and Mrs. Downes for your hospitality and look forward to seeing you both as soon as possible.

With all best wishes,

As ever,
Don

GDH/MOK

400

G. Donald Harrison

---

278 G. Donald Harrison to Henry Willis

July 20, 1955

Mr. Henry Willis
Rotunda Organ Works
34 Marlborough Grove
Old Kent Road
London, S.E.1
England
Dear Henry:

In further reference to my recent letter, I am now enclosing herewith a list of flue pipes and reed shallots upon which I would like to receive a definite quotation from you. You will notice that in the list of flue pipes there is only one set, the 8' Geigen, that I would like to have voiced. The fact that this is of your new zinc construction seemed to necessitate your voicing treatment.

You will notice I have mentioned that the cut-ups shall be low on the flue pipes. I do not remember what your metal shop cut-ups are, but we use somewhat lower cut-ups than your standards, so that I want them to be low enough so that we can make them anything we want. Your standard foot lengths for the flue pipes will be perfectly satisfactory.

You will notice that in the matter of the 8' Principal I have suggested a half dubbed lip in view of the low cut-up that will be used in the light pressure. It seems to me that you have a half dub arrangement on some of your pipes.

Regarding the reed shallots, you can readily give me a quotation on those which are standard Willis practice and which you probably have in stock.

Regarding the French shallots, I am not entirely satisfied with the bronze set which I brought home with me. They are perfectly O.K. from 2' C up, but in the lower two octaves we cannot get the exact tone that we get with our dome headed French shallots which we have been making ourselves. It is a great chore to make these French shallots here, but I do believe that Williams can make them, because it seems to me that Herbert Norman told me while I was in England that he had some made by Williams. You will notice that we have a shallot called 909C, which was specially developed, and which we use occasionally. The others run very close to the normal French Trumpet Ordinaire, except that in the lower two octaves of the 16 and the lower octave of an 8, we insert a plate at the inner end of the shallot as shown on the sketch. This we find to be beneficial for obvious reasons. There are also some other English type shallots to scales that we have produced here and upon which I would like to get a price.

I am not quite sure whether for our own special scales that we should not deal direct with Williams, but it would be very convenient for us if you could make the contact with him and see what he is able to do for us. We are prepared to give very substantial orders for all the French type of shallot and also our special English shallots. I think it would mean considerable business for Williams. Naturally, delivery is of paramount importance, and I would like to know what he could offer per month on a large order. Would he be willing to give us the same undertaking not to use our scales for other British builders, except in the case of your firm should you want to try any of them.

Regarding the 32' French type of shallot, which is included on our list, we would probably order three of them at this time.

Under separate cover I am sending you all the records we have produced to date. I am having the package marked "Unsolicited Gift," with the hope that the customs will let them through without you having to pay any duty on them. I just heard yesterday from one source that this can be done.

I hope to hear from you very shortly and providing everything seems to be all right, an order will be forthcoming immediately.

Hope you had a good time on the Continent and with best wishes,

As ever,

AEOLIAN-SKINNER ORGAN COMPANY

Don

President

Encl.

GDH:MOK

P.S. Regarding the French shallots, it would seem obvious that the thing to do would be to order them directly from France. This applies particularly to the standard 16, 8 & 4' sets even without the plates which we can add. However, we have heard nothing from our old supplier A. Bertouneche of A. Hery (Yonne) France, since 1946. At that time he said he was getting back on his feet again. I have written him today by Air Mail. Recently we wrote to Masure about this matter but no reply. Is there any other reliable supply house or do you know anything of Bertouneche?

G.D.H.

PIPES FROM
HENRY WILLIS & SONS LTD.
London, England

<u>8' Geigen</u>   CC to G 68 pipes

Willis standard zinc construction

Scale: 5½" @ CC

3⅛" @ C

Mouth: Standard for zinc Geigen

Pressure: 5"

Pitch: A 440 @ 70 degrees F.

Voicing: Normal strength for this scale.

<u>8' Lieblich Gedeckt</u>   61 pipes

Scale Willis large, solid stoppers.

<u>Material</u> Spotted metal throughout

Pipes unvoiced. Please keep cut up low.

Pitch A 440 @ 70 degrees F.

<u>8' Rohrflöte</u>   61 pipes unvoiced

Scale Willis large tulip stoppers.

Spotted metal throughout.

Low cut-up. Unvoiced.

Pitch A440 @ 70 degrees F.

8' Cor-de-Nuit   61 pipes Cavaille-Coll scale. Tin.

Unvoiced pitch A 440 @ 70 degrees F.

8' Principal   61 pipes

Scale: CC 6"   C 3½"   ½ 17th note.

Mouth – ¼ low cut up half dubbed.

Material Zinc lower 12, rest spotted.

Tuning – Lower 12 slotted, rest tuning slides

Pitch A 440 @ 70 degrees F.

Unvoiced.

16' Principal   32 pipes mouth 2/9

Scale: CCC   10¼"
          CC   6"
          C   3½"

Lower 24 standard construction

Zinc, with slotting for tuning

4'C up spotted with slide tuners

Unvoiced.

Reed Shallots 61 notes

Willis – 16', 61 notes B set unfilled as per sample
          already received.

Willis – 8' Trumpet 61 notes
          B set unfilled.

French – Aeolian-Skinner special 909C
          (See separate sheet for particulars, also sketch)

16' French Bombarde – Aeolian-Skinner Regular
          (see separate sheet for particulars) Dome heads.

8' French Trompette – Aeolian-Skinner Regular, same as 16'
          Regular from CC to top G, 56 notes. Dome heads.

4' French Clarion – Aeolian-Skinner Regular, same as 8' from
          4' C up 44 notes. Dome heads.

16' Trombone – 56 notes. Aeolian-Skinner, light pressure
          (see patterns enclosed)

8' Trumpet – Aeolian-Skinner English small (see pattern)

32' Bombarde – Aeolian-Skinner Regular (see separate sheet)

279 Henry Willis to W. P. Williams & Co.

15th August, 1955

Messrs. W.P. Williams & Co.,
61, Hampton Gardens,
Southend-on-Sea,
Essex.

Dear Sirs,

The Aeolian-Skinner Co., of Boston, Mass., U.S.A., have written asking if we could get you to make brass reeds for them to their own scales — which are their own — and if you did make for them would require your guarantee not to make for any other firm.

They are prepared to give very substantial orders for both their French and English types.

Delivery is of paramount importance, and they would like to know what delivery you can offer.

The 32' French type of shallot — would be ordered three sets at a time.

We are sending you all the information sent us by the Aeolian-Skinner Co. You will no doubt find it necessary to construct a comprehensive scale for each of these special types.

Yours faithfully,
For and on behalf of
Henry Willis & Sons Ltd.
Henry Willis
Governing Director

---

280 Emerson Richards to Henry Willis

Aug. 28th, 1955

Mr. Henry Willis
Rotunda Organ Works
34 Marlborough Grove
London S.E. 1
England

Dear Willis

Your card dated July 22nd. showing the . . . organ finally caught up with me at my Island summer 'camp' in Moosehead Lake. Thanks to you and Dora.

The people up here call it a 'camp,' although it has eight bedrooms and four baths. The living room has a 25' ceiling, supported on eight perfectly straight cedar logs, each more than two feet in diameter and 20' long. The fireplace burns six-foot logs — mostly oak and birch. We have our own

Emerson Richards in his boat at "camp"

electric plant and 137' well. I enclose a picture of the Island. The big trees hide the camp.

In the cities and at home they had a very hot summer, 90 degrees and above, but up here with a 1400' elevation, the Lake and the mountains, we never had a night that a blanket was not welcome. So we had a good summer.

I do not have too much organ news. I had to go down to near Boston to pick up Ad and then talked to Don who had just come back. He said that you looked ever so much better. And that was good news.

I had some correspondence with a committee chairman in Atlanta about an organ deal. When I last heard from them it had narrowed down to you, Steinmeyer, and Don. They did not want to wait 30 months for Don so I suggested you — provided they let you dictate the specifications. A Steinmeyer in a non-conformist church in the deep South would be ridiculous. Erection might cause difficulties. I am not sure that Whalon could do it. But there is a man who has done work for both Don and I *[sic]* who might be safe. His name is Chester Raymond, Princeton, N.J. He has, I understand, a branch in Atlanta.

My own organ is mostly up, but now comes the tuning and regulating. I hope to resume when I return home this September.

Ad and I are well and we are always glad to hear from you and Dora. On account of Ad's eyes it is hard for her to write so I have to do for both.

With our very best regards,
Emerson Richards

ER/ag

a committee chairman in Atlanta — See letter 284.

---

281 Henry Willis to G. Donald Harrison

5th September 1955

Mr. G. Donald Harrison,
President,
Aeolian Skinner Organ Co.,
Boston 25,
Mass., U. S. A.
My dear Don,

Thanks for yours of the 20th July.

Shallots. Shorthanded owing to holidays and I am overwhelmed with personal work. Will go into these as soon as I can. Meantime, the obvious source for French type is France. If you do not hear from Bertouneche I will ask my daughter, Ettie, who lives at Montmorency just outside of Paris, to make inquiries as to whether the firm is alive or not.

Pipes. I will be glad to help you personally as desired with voiced stops. I understood that any stops you asked for would be on that basis so that you would have our voicing.

I do not see that my supply of unvoiced stops would serve a useful purpose, beyond giving you another source of supply, and I do not think that you would ask me to accept that position especially as our metal shop is as overloaded as yours is.

You will appreciate that our metal shop costs are high, this by reason of my insistence on maintenance of the Willis tradition for perfect pipework. Our costs are some 20 percent higher than trade suppliers, who make a profit, here for that reason.

Costs vary quite considerably because every stop is made especially for the organ for which it is required. There is little exact repetition.

To take your list seriatim.

1. Geigen 8ft. The last made of scale CC 5½", C 3⅛", 4th mouth was in November last year. A Swell organ stop, no front pipes. Zinc construction and special voicing. Stop will be made and invoiced on cost.

2. <u>Lieblich Gedackt 8ft</u>. Willis large scale, 8ft. CC would be 4¾". 4ft. C 2 $1\frac{1}{16}$". Spotted metal, in my opinion, absolute waste. Our norm is:

8ft. octave. Zinc CC. 3½" scale merging to Willis large at 4ft. C. 4ft. C up regular scale, zinc bodies. Solid wooden stopper or, preferably for large scale, with zinc canister tops, fitted without felt or paper hence fitting must be impeccable. The cut up must be in accordance with the harmonic development required, and pressure must be known.

I would like to send one of our Gedackts to you as above with zinc canisters, <u>voiced</u>.

3. <u>Rohrflöte 8ft.</u> See 2. Perforated Willis tulip stoppers — add to the cost.

4. <u>Cor-de-Nuit 8ft</u>. Again <u>better</u> results obtained in zinc, solid wooden stoppers, Cavaillé-Coll type.

5. <u>Principal 8ft</u>. CC, 6". You can get this from Stinkens and quite good, except for the baked zinc in lower octave, at less than ⅔ our costs but I would do one for you in zinc, voiced. The cut up of ¼ is low for a ¼ mouth and the power would, of course, be low in proportion.

6. <u>Principal 16ft</u>. Here again you would get no advantage except the use of hard rolled zinc.

Candidly, I think that Stinkens can give you what you want for 5 and 6 anyway, unless you want hard rolled zinc. As you know Stinkens is using soft Electrolytic zinc, to my mind the tone is poor, as must be expected from such material.

Stinkens also using those machines which shave the sheets down to a uniform thickness and they are apparently used as such, no slight reduction of thickness at the top and bottom of the pipes, as necessary to leave each pipe slightly thicker at the node. This is common commercial practice in Germany; Walcker, Steinmeyer, Laukhuff all using the same process.

Steinmeyer is now purchasing metal sheets in 70 foot rolls all thickened and, in his opinion, ready for cutting out. The metal I saw was 60% tin and thin in proportion, suitable for the production of the light yet bright tone which they like. The aim seems to be to use as thin metal as possible, concomitant with the pipes standing up!

Surely the scales, reinforcing pieces, everything, on parallel shallots should be to a regular graduating scale, and not in groups of threes, fours, fives, &c. there would be no true scale at all. Some years ago you complained that French suppliers were doing this and you could not get regular scaling.

<u>Willis Shallots</u>. Noted that you want additional sets, 16ft. B set 61 notes unfilled.

8ft. B set unfilled, 61 notes, for a Trumpet.

A "B" set is, in my opinion, unsuited for a Trumpet, the openings are too short, surely what you want is an A set, same scale as a B, but longer openings.

Many thanks for sending records, they are excellent recordings.

I sent the patterns to Williams, he cannot undertake this special work, too busy. His letter enclosed.

Walcker-Meyer has been here, and told me about his visit to U.S. in October. He does not speak English very well, and without an interpreter, this limits conversations on technical matters especially.

As ever,
H.W.

H.W./T.D.

<u>P.S.1.</u> I will have the Geigen put in hand as soon as possible, I usually use a graduated bass, from bottom B down, but I suppose you want the normal scaling. Please confirm.

<u>P.S.2.</u> You will be sorry to hear that Harry Goss-Custard retires from Liverpool Cathedral as from 30th September, sight too bad to carry on. Do write to him, especially as you missed him on your visit here.

Dr. H. Goss-Custard, M.A., F.R.C.O.
20 Gambier Terrace,
Liverpool, 1.

His pupil and assistant, Noel Rawsthorne is appointed in his stead, a young man of about 28, and a very good player and accompanist.

---

282 Emerson Richards to William King Covell

September 16th, 1955

Mr. William King Covell,
72 Washington Street
Newport, Rhode Island

Dear King,

More about Oberlin. Just talked to Don who is just back from there. It is much as I told you. It is the old E.M. done over — but radically.

The Montre 16' is new as is all of the Great except the 16' Fagotto which is from the old Choir. He says the two reeds color but don't dominate the flue chorus. 3½" wind.

The Choir is what it is because of lack of money. He admits the organ should have more string tone. The Positiv is new. Cannot account for the lack of an independent 2⅔', but the Sesquialtera is 12-17.

The Great and Positiv VI Mixtures are an octave apart. They have repeats of the same pitch but do run to the 29th.

The Pedal 32's are old as is the metal 16' Principal. The reed 32' is half length and extension of the Swell, but Don says it is good. I wonder.

Don is very much pleased with the job and says it is really a fine organ.

I do hope you see the Barnes opus. As I guessed, Don saw him last before he wrote it. If you can't get a copy I will lend you mine.

Best regards,

Emerson

Oberlin — opus 230-A, Finney Chapel, Oberlin college, originally a four-manual E. M. Skinner of 1916

Barnes opus — Barnes had just completed a tour of Holland, Germany, and Denmark conducted by Arthur Howes. He wrote an article on this, which later became a supplement to his book *The Contemporary American Organ*, in the 1956 edition. See letter 289.

---

283 Henry Willis to G. Donald Harrison

29th September, 1955

Mr. G. Donald Harrison,
President,
Aeolian-Skinner Organ Co.,
Crescent Avenue,
Dorchester,
Boston 25,
Mass., U. S. A.

My dear Don,

Many thanks for yours of the 23rd instant and very generous contribution to the Harry Goss-Custard Testimonial — Harry will be given a list of all donors.

Reference: records "The King of Instruments." I have had a further opportunity to try this out exhaustively. Will you tell me what organ was used for Record One and who is the player? Whoever it was did a good piece of work. Your explanatory words were excellent and fully descriptive. But to reproduce your voice to correct timbre I had to turn on both treble and bass controls to "full" when your characteristic speech was obtained with fidelity. Before that it was not recognizable.

As ever,

HW

P. S. I enclose Harry's *[Goss-Custard]* programme for 22nd October.

284 Henry Willis to Emerson Richards

29th September 1955

Hon. Emerson Richards,
800, Schwehm Building.
Atlantic City, N.J.,
U.S.A.

My dear Richards,

Many thanks for yours of the 28th August.

<u>Atlanta, Peachtree Road Presbyterian Church</u>. I enclose copies of letter received from them and of our reply. The specification sent us was an effort in the direction of the 'Classic American Organ' by someone who had not fully digested the basic principle involved.

For this job I could better Don's 30 months by about half. Pressure of work is very heavy indeed, and the absorption of several small firms in the last two years has made increased demands upon this H.Q.

By the way, I heartily dislike the term <u>Viola Pomposa</u> when a normal Geigen is provided, it sounds not only pompous but misleading. But "what's in a name."

I note that Chester Raymond would be a suitable erector for an organ sent over. . . .

Sorry Ad's eyes are troublesome.

Kind regards from us both,

As ever,
Henry

H.W./T.D.

---

285 G. Donald Harrison to Henry Willis

October 5, 1955

Mr. Henry Willis
Rotunda Organ Works
34 Marlborough Grove
Old Kent Road
London, S.E.1
England

My dear Henry:

Thank you for your letter of September 5th which was in reply to mine of July 20th.

Regarding shallots, I am glad to say that Bertouneche in Paris is now back in business and is very anxious to do our work, so from that angle we would be taken care of from now on I hope.

Regarding the Willis shallots, we would like to have additional sets of your 16' B sets unfilled. Regarding the 8' B set unfilled that I mentioned for a Trumpet, I guess I made an error. Naturally I want the longest and widest opening you make on these shallots. I wanted, however, the smaller diameter of the A and B set rather than the usual Trumpet C shallots.

Regarding the flue stops, I misunderstood you. I did not know that you wanted to voice the pipes you made, and thought that you had some spare room in your metal shop to make some additional pipes for us. As our metal shop is now a real bottleneck, I was obliged to make some commitments to take pipes from Stinkens and we have here a couple of trade makers who are now doing good work. One of them works for us and can make pipes that are indistinguishable from ours. Of course, he charges us a higher rate than for the trade.

In view of this situation, why not for the time being make and voice an 8' zinc Geigen, ¼ mouth, scale CC 5½" and tenor C 3⅛. This should be voiced on 5". This is regular construction as it will go into a Swell organ.

I would also like you to make a Lieblich Gedackt 8' Willis, large scale, and this can also be made of your regular construction, zinc bass and zinc bodies above 4' C all as specified in your letter. The solid wooden stoppers will be O.K. in this regard. We like as much color as possible out of our Gedackts and this particular stop should be of medium power and voiced on 3" wind. Of course both these stops will be used for the standard pitch, A440 at 70° Farenheit.

Let us just try out those two first, and see how we get along.

I notice that Williams cannot take over any work for us, but I think will be pretty well taken care of without his help.

Glad you enjoyed the recordings.

Walcker-Meyer was here yesterday. I was not too impressed by him. He is a bit of a lightweight, I feel.

With best wishes,

As ever,

Don

GDH:MOK

Williams — the English shallot suppliers

12th October 1955

Mr. G. Donald Harrison,
President,
Aeolian-Skinner Organ Co.,
Crescent Avenue,
Dorchester,
Boston 25,
Mass., U. S. A.

My dear Don,

Thanks for yours of the 5th instant, in reply.

French shallots. Glad that you can get what you want from Bertouneche.

Willis shallots. Both our B and A sets are the same basically. B set has a short opening, used for Oboes (not Orchestral). A opening is longer and is a standard use for small scale Trumpets, CC 3¾", and when I want a fiercer tone than normally given, by a C set which shallot is larger scale than A.

Sometimes I use an A set with a C (longer) opening, and again, for special use, an A set with opening to the "back mark," this gives a tonality verging upon that of a parallel shallot.

Say what you want.

How many 16 B set unfilled do you require? Note the use is for Contra Oboes, my type of Dulzian, and Clarinets. (Corno-di-Bassettos and Vox Humanas are B set filled in.)

Flue Pipes. (1) Geigen 8ft. Zinc construction. CC 5½". C 3⅛" (our No. 6 scale), ¼ mouth. C 523.3. 5" wind. I will have this made and voiced on our normal lines for you.

Lieblich Gedackt 8ft. Our regular zinc construction, nicking and voicing, large scale from 4ft C; zinc scaled bass. Our standard production. Solid stoppers.

As regards keeping up the "color," it depends how much "chiff" you want left in. On 3" wind, I use what is, to us, a comparatively low cut up, and nick to give the amount of color required. I will give you slightly more "chiff" than I normally give them, if you find the "chiff" too great you can either (1) cut up a little more, (2) deepen the nicking slightly (not advised) or a combination of the two.

Pressure of work on our metal shop is very high, so do not expect early delivery of these two stops. I am glad that your position has improved somewhat. Ours tends to become worse. Two promising young improvers have been called up for National Service just as they were getting into first-class production.

<u>Walcker-Mayer</u>. *[sic]* I entirely agree with your summing up. In my opinion he has but superficial knowledge of organ building and little of scaling and voicing. His training was at <u>Saver's</u>, as you know, and their tonal work li[v]ed up to their name.

It is common talk in Germany that the firm of Walcker is going down-hill with some rapidity and, judging from their recent work, that is my impression also. I took Mayer to three typical Willis jobs, St. Paul's Cathedral, All Souls Langham Place (a big three manual) and College of St. Mark and St. John, Chelsea (a small three manual) and he did not show any signs of really intelligent understanding, but was obviously deeply impressed at St. Paul's Cathedral. But quite a pleasant person.

I wonder what took him to America? If he sent over one of his typical present day productions it would be his last, unless low prices secured orders for German connections. Not a patch on Steinmeyer who is doing interesting tonal schemes with a tendency to over-brilliance, especially in mixture work.

Marcel and Jeanette Dupré are now with us. He plays at the Royal Festival Hall this evening.

<u>H.G.C. Fund</u>. Coming on nicely. Your gift the biggest yet received. Harry is retiring to St. Leonards-on-Sea.

I hope to have a tape-recording made of his last recital at Liverpool Cathedral on the 22nd instant.

As ever,
Henry Willis

H.W./T.D.

P.S. Claire Coci gave a really superb recital at All Souls', Langham Place.

---

287 G. Donald Harrison to Henry Willis

October 19, 1955

Mr. Henry Willis
Rotunda Organ Works
34, Marlborough Grove
Old Kent Road
London, S.E.1, England
Dear Henry:

Thanks for your letter of September 29th. I will send Harry a cablegram which will arrive before his recital on the 22nd of this month.

Glad that you had another opportunity to try out the record. The instruments used are as follows:

Symphony Hall, Boston, Mass.
St. Paul's Cathedral, Boston, Mass.

Cathedral of Saint John the Divine, New York
First Presbyterian Church, Kilgore, Texas
First Unitarian Church, Boston, Mass.
(This is Bill Zeuch's job.)

The latter organ was used to demonstrate the romantic instrument in the second rendition of the last part of the St. Anne Fugue. There were several players used — Thomas Dunn did the examples played at Symphony Hall, Boston. George Faxon, who was then organist at St. Paul's Cathedral in Boston, did a major part of the examples played on that instrument and also the Trio Sonata which concludes the second side of the record. Roy Perry played the examples at Kilgore. There were just two of them (1) the opening to the reed section of the record where he used his Trompette-en-Chamade. There is also an excerpt of the Flute Celeste played by him on the same organ.

Joe Whiteford played some of the examples, particularly those made at Saint John the Divine. This included the last part of the B Minor Chorale of César Franck.

It is peculiar that you had difficulty with my speech because we do not have to change our setting of the record player to have a normal voice. Of course all these machines differ and it depends on the curve which is used in the make-up of the machine. Here most of them have what is known as the LP curve and the records are therefore made in accordance with same. If you have trouble with my voice, I just wonder how authentically the tonal examples were reproduced.

As ever,
Don

GDH:MOK

---

288 Henry Willis to G. Donald Harrison

26th October, 1955

Mr. G. Donald Harrison,
President,
Aeolian-Skinner Organ Co., Inc.,
Boston 25, Mass., U.S.A.
Dear Don,

Many thanks for yours of the 19th instant — and information about the first "King of Instruments" record: all the players named did very good work indeed.

Reference to the reproduction of the record — I can assure you that they came through excellently on normal settings except for your voice, which required both bass and treble settings to be at maximum setting to reproduce your voice correctly as I know it. Such setting for the organ tone was quite impossible — the bass and treble being so exaggerated as to be intolerable.

H.G.C. farewell recital at Liverpool Cathedral on the 22nd instant. A packed congregation; Harry played superbly — I enclosed his program. Afterwards there were nearly 400 guests for tea at our Liverpool Works, when I made a short speech, followed by the Bishop of Liverpool and Canon Dillistone (acting Dean, as Dwelly left on 30th September) who made the presentation — a check for £250 — not bad and largely helped by your generous gift, which was the largest received.

In replying Harry nearly broke down and his speech was somewhat incoherent — he was overcome by emotion.

It was a great and historical occasion.

As ever,
Henry Willis

H.W./M.P.

---

289 G. Donald Harrison to Carl Weinrich

December 22, 1955

Mr. Carl Weinrich
Office of Director of Music, University Chapel
Princeton University
Princeton, New Jersey
Dear Carl:

Thanks so much for your good letter of December 9th. I was not around when that date was given to you for the installation of the Antiphonal Organ. I will take steps to get this pushed forward so that we can do it while you are around.

I am most interested to hear that you have made some good records and I certainly want to meet you to talk over the European jaunt. I think you got a wrong impression, perhaps from Bill Barnes' article. I was much impressed, but I am afraid chiefly with the old organs although I admire some of the present organ builders, but I am afraid I cannot say I found much that was worth copying. I feel they are trying to live in the past to a great extent. This may go in a country like Holland or Denmark but it certainly would not go here in our churches. One must be practical, I feel.

I will try to get in touch with you soon and in the meantime, best Christmas Greetings to you, Tommy and the whole family.

As ever,
Don

GDH:MOK

---

290 Henry Willis to G. Donald Harrison

27th January, 1956

Mr. G. Donald Harrison,
President,
Aeolian-Skinner Organ Co.,
Boston 25,
Mass., U. S. A.

My dear Don,

Sorry that intense pressure of work, sickness and shortage of staff have delayed the manufacture of the stops you want. Apart from normal demands we have had to replace nearly half the pipework for St. George's Hall and nearly all the reeds and are sadly behind schedule. I will push them through as soon as possible.

I noted in a recent specification published in the Diapason there is a Swell Trumpet (Willis) 8ft. stated. You have not asked me to send you one. I will be glad to do so if scale and pressure advised. I recommend CC 4½" our standard middle scale Trumpet for all wind pressures. But it may be that you have found one of the Trumpets I sent over some 25 years ago!

Transference Rectifier units. Our people here cannot provide automatic voltage regulation on the output side. Orgelectra say that they can and you confirmed this although you do not use all-electric consoles and so your maximum requirement is probably met by a 30 amp unit or less. I use 50 amp units for big jobs at 15 volts output and the voltage drop on full load — i.e. up to 90% of the rating drop of 2 volts — is a nuisance.

If Orgelectra can provide what I want there is the currency trouble — our Board of Trade will not give permits for importation. I wonder if it could be arranged by a "contra" in conjunction with the stops I am sending you?

I am sending you a copy of the brochure on the organ at McEwan Hall, University of Edinburgh. You may have seen the article in the Organ.

I am rebuilding and modernizing the old Willis at Huddersfield Town Hall — to be ready in September. You will remember the improvements of 1919, when among other improvements, we added a 32ft. reed with wide scale wooden shallots. I tried the organ recently and this stop is an excellent example which I will not alter.

Francis Jackson of York Minster is the Consultant to the Corporation. He is a "bright" boy and wants this Willis diapason work and mixtures brightened up. Pipes full of dirt and not speaking properly — only needs cleaning — but I will fit Compensator-Amplifier on the Great No.1 which is on the small side as regards output.

We are jammed up with work. It is difficult to keep up with requirements of our manufacturing Branches at Liverpool, Edinburgh, Nottingham and Southhampton in addition to London demands, Liverpool, where "Son" is stationed — are now making their own consoles, which is a relief.

The truth over here is shortage of trained staff, the older men are passing out and retiring and the younger men not of quite the same calibre and, of course, experience — but we carry on.

I would very much like to attend the convention in New York next June — but lack of dollars forbids — no Bank of England dispensation for attending a convention!

No word from Emerson Richards for months — except a Christmas card. I hope he is not fading out.

I see Ernest Skinner is 90 — 22½ years older than we are. Poor old boy — he has been his own greatest enemy.

All well here — my health excellent in view of advancing years.

As ever,

H.W.

wide scale wooden shallots — unusual construction compared to Skinner practice of making 32' wooden Bombardes with brass shallots, as almost all other reeds.

Compensator-Amplifier — a metal cowl or hood on the top of a pipe, fitted to increase and project the tone

---

291 G. Donald Harrison to Henry Willis

February 15, 1956

Mr. Henry Willis
Rotunda Organ Works
34, Marlborough Grove
Old Kent Road
London S. E. 1, England
Dear Henry:

Thanks for yours of January 27th. I know that you are busy but would like to have the stops you are making for us at your convenience.

I do not know which job to which you refer which calls for a Swell Trumpet (Willis), as we have had no request for an imported Willis Trumpet, to the best of my knowledge. I will look through the recent Diapasons. As a matter of fact, I do not have them in my office at the moment. I think they are in my assistant's office, and I have just walked to the door and find he has three people in there so I don't want to barge in. I will let you know what I find, however.

Regarding the rectifier units, we will be very happy to work out a method of paying for these in the manner you suggest. I hope you can make a suitable deal with Orgelectra, as they seem to be the best people in the business and really understand what is required. Of course normally they are working at 60 cycles and on a 10 volt system, but undoubtedly they can do what you require.

These rectifying units act somewhat like a very fine over-compounded generator. In other words, as you put the load on there is a rising tendency in the voltage which levels off again at the rated D.C. voltage when you reach full load, but I am sure they would be very helpful to you with the old electric consoles.

I am most interested to hear about Huddersfield Town Hall, as that was always one of my favorite organs from boyhood. I well remember the work we did in 1919, including the 32' Bombarde. I also remember the two strings which I think we put in the Solo Organ and which were Lewis stock pipes which were spotted metal down to 8' C.

Of course we are constantly plagued by lack of good help and have the same situation that you have — that the really good men are growing older.

Yes, old man Skinner is 90 and still going strong. It looks as if he may live as old as his mother. He always used to boast that he would. I think his mother was 94 or 95 when she passed away. He said "If she can live that long there's no reason why I can't" and I think sheer determination will keep him going. Of course his brain is a little bit muddled.

Emerson Richards caught pneumonia and has been very sick but is coming around slowly. He is far from well, however and anything could happen at any time.

Glad you are all well — we are here.

As ever,
Don

GDH:MOK

---

292 Henry Willis to G. Donald Harrison

22nd. February, 1956

Mr. G. Donald Harrison,
President,
Aeolian-Skinner Organ Co. Inc.
Boston 25,
Mass., U. S. A.
Dear Don,

Thanks for yours of the 15th instant.

In the <u>Diapason</u> for December, 1955 on page 10 there appeared the specification of new Aeolian-Skinner organ for St. Mark's Episcopal Church, Shreveport, and the Swell includes:

| Trompette | 8ft. | (French) | 68 pipes |
| Trumpet | 8ft. | (Willis) | 68 pipes |

The indication is clearly that a Willis Trumpet is to be used. I will let you have a standard Trumpet if you advise wind pressure and if to be hooded or not and height for mitering.

Will write later ref Orgelectra.

I have written to Richards wishing him a complete recovery.

As ever,
H.W.

---

293 G. Donald Harrison to Henry Willis

March 22, 1956

Mr. Henry Willis
Henry Willis & Sons Ltd.
Rotunda Organ Works
34, Marlborough Grove
Old Kent Road
London S.E.1, England
Dear Henry:

Thanks for yours of the 2nd instant, from which I note that you used our No. 1 record at a meeting of the Incorporated Society of Organ Builders.

Yes, that particular record has sold extremely well and more than paid for itself. The others which we have produced have also done extremely well, so we have looked upon it as very good advertising which costs nothing, except of course, a lot of extra time put in by people like Joe and our engineer.

I am going to spend the weekend with Senator Richards over Palm Sunday and I will let you know how he is when I get back. Talking to him on the phone he sounds as if he is coming along very well.

All the best,

As ever,
Don

GDH:MOK

---

294 Emerson Richards to William King Covell

April 5th, 1956

Dear King,

When I got your last letter I wanted to answer it at once as a kind of supplement to my last one, but the house was a merry-go-round with Ad all excitement and the phone ringing constantly. But yesterday, in the fog, we started off at dawn for N.Y. and the Queen Elizabeth. Fog and delay at the Lincoln Tunnel made us jittery and a mob due to the sailing of the Kelly party made additional trouble at the dock, so we just had time to stow the girls comfortably aboard and were chased off, because they were sailing in a few minutes. So as there was nothing else to do and the dock is so enclosed that you cannot wave farewell to those on board, we left and after lunch drove home. Imagine my surprise last night when Ad called and said that they were still at the dock. The British Captain lacked the guts to back out in the Hudson in the fog as the American Captain on the Constitution did, and so lost the tide and had to wait until 1 a.m. last night. I guess they got off then. It sure is quiet around here.

Now for your letter. Had a letter today about the new edition. Bill [Barnes] did not say that he was sending me one. So knowing Bill I replied and, after condolences on the death of his Mother, I reminded him that he had sent me an autographed copy of the last edition — as he had the others — and had returned my check so I asked for a copy and said I would send the check when he agreed to take it. So as yet I do not know what is new in the book and cannot comment.

Chestnut Hill: The organist is Thomas Dunn. There is to be an A.G.O. dinner and recital at the church on April 14th at 6:30 p.m. Don says the organ is quite mild and the church non-resonant. But that it comes off well. Don was hampered by the fact that the job is a rebuild of the old Skinner and is limited by the chests that were used. Some old work remains, like the strings, and hence the d'Celeste. But ALL the choruses and mixtures are new as are the reeds. The church can be reached by Broad Street subway to Erie Avenue and bus route 23 to Bethlehem Pike or by Reading or Pennsylvania R.R. The church is a block from the station. I expect to go up and will report later.

About the factory. You are dreaming again. The State of Massachusetts is building the new road and has no interest in Art. At first they only offered Don a fishcake for the damage. The Irish Mayor of Boston stepped in when Don threatened to leave Mass. for a site in the Southwest, saying that any cultural activity that would stay in Boston ought to be encouraged. So while the state did not allow Don enough in damages to build a good backhouse (for your antique house) the Mayor found them this concrete building (four stories) on a hill in South Boston that was vacant because of zoning restrictions on manufacturing, got it for Don at a low price and has had the zoning restrictions waived so that when all is concluded this week they can begin to move in June without too much disruption of the work in progress. Also there is plenty of ground for parking and future additions, and they are away from the noise of the railroad, but near the subway station so that

the men are not inconvenienced. I will tell you more as soon as all is settled.
. . .

The thing that I wanted to supplement in our discussions about progress in design and especially Don's part in it is occasioned by the arrival of the <u>Diapason</u> on Monday. On the front page were two specifications for rather large and expensive organs. How do they compare with Don's? The Casavant could be considered old stuff 25 years ago. The only concession is a bow toward Don with the Great Principal and the TWO Mixtures. That horrible 4' Harmonic Flute is still there and the rest is of the Dark Ages. No 16' flue on the Swell, an extended Pedal and chimes, harp, and orchestral . . . Why no Vox? The Schantz is somewhat better simply because it borrows more from Don. The Great could have been his except for the Hohlflute. The Swell is conventional A-S. The Choir an enclosed Positiv. The Positiv Don's. The Pedal a bit less badly extended. But it all goes back to my argument that Don is still the most progressive builder in America and no thanks to any "expert" either.

I see that the tracker argument is getting a foothold in England. The Dutch builders are putting up a sales talk that is making an impression in some quarters. Note the comment and the program of the International Organ Week, Copenhagen, May 28th, where ALL the organs played upon for a week will be tracker action. The program is printed in the Journal of the Organ Club for February, just in.

I think this about brings us up to date.

With best wishes,
Emerson

the Kelly party — Actress Grace Kelly (later Princess Grace of Monaco) was also at the dock.
Chestnut Hill — St. Paul's Chestnut Hill, opus 724-A. The three-manual organ had been rebuilt in 1953 and enlarged in 1956. Its stoplist appears in the appendix.

---

295 G. Donald Harrison to Carl Weinrich

April 12, 1956

Dr. Carl Weinrich
Princeton University
Princeton, New Jersey
Dear Carl:

I have been away finishing an organ in St. Paul's Church, Philadelphia, hence the delay in replying to your letter of March 23rd.

Since I wrote you last, many things have been going on around here. I believe you already know that our factory is going to be interfered with to a considerable extent by a new expressway which is to be built close by.

We have had several plans about rebuilding the plant or entirely moving it to another location. This matter has only just been settled in the last few days and it does mean a big moving job very shortly. There is going to be some loss of time as you can well imagine, although we are doing everything we possibly can to minimize this.

I am sure you want to be in Princeton at the time we are making this installation and that would mean it would have to be done before Commencement which, I regret to say, is entirely impossible. Incidentally, it is down on our production schedule for shipment in July of this year and we will go ahead and build it anyway, but it might be August before it is ready for shipment in view of this move we have to make. If you want us to go right ahead with the installation we will do so, but if you would prefer that we hold up the actual installation in the Chapel until you return, that we can also do. Please let me have your good word on this.

All the best,

As ever,

Don

President

GDH:MOK

P.S. Sometime take a look at the rebuilt organ in St. Paul's Church Chestnut Hill. There is an instrument I think you would really like. As you know, Tommy Dunn is the organist and he is quite a fine musician.

G.D.H.

this installation — the Antiphonal division at Princeton Chapel

---

296 Henry Willis to G. Donald Harrison

30th April, 1956

Mr. G. Donald Harrison
Aeolian-Skinner Organ Company Inc.
Organ Architects, and Builders,
Boston 25, Mass., U.S.A.

<u>Personal and Confidential</u>

Dear Don,

Thanks for yours of the 24th instant.

The Biggs dined with us last night after his recital at St. Paul's Cathedral — two Mendelsohn Sonatas and two Mozart Fantasias — similar period romantic stuff.

What annoyed me — although I did not show it — was Biggs' attitude to your work — more than deprecatory. Why is this? He said, for example, St. Paul's Cathedral, Boston organ absurdly large for the Church and a retrogression from the Church of the Advent; Mormon Tabernacle success solely due to the wonderful acoustics; and so forth.

Perhaps he is going in for organ building — like Noehren?

As ever,

H.W.

H.W./E.T.

---

297 G. Donald Harrison to Henry Willis

May 29, 1956

Mr. Henry Willis
Rotunda Organ Works
34, Marlborough Grove
Old Kent Road
London, S.E.1, England
Dear Henry:

I have your personal and confidential letter of April 30th and am interested by the contents although, of course, it does not surprise me as this is nothing to what has been said around the United States by the gentleman in question. I think the real answer is that he is probably tied up with another builder in Buffalo. The whole matter is a very long story and when I get time after the Convention I will write you more fully on this subject.

I am at present very busy at Saint Thomas Church and have little time for correspondence. I have been in Boston just yesterday and today and am off again tonight to New York to carry on with the good work. I think the organ is going to be a honey!

I appreciate your letter very much and with best wishes,

As ever,

Don

GDH:MOK

St. Thomas Church — opus 205-A. The rebuild of this 1913 Skinner was unusual. The Great organ was on the first manual, the Positiv (separate enclosed and unenclosed divisions) on the second. The fourth manual was a "Grand Choeur" manual, with both chancel and gallery divisions. The organ had only 12 intermanual couplers — all at unison pitch.

298 Willis & Sons to Aeolian-Skinner

11th June 1956

The Aeolian-Skinner Organ Co. Inc.
Boston 25,
Massachusetts, U.S.A.

Dear Sirs,

We have much pleasure in advising you that we have today received a draft for £232.19.11 in full settlement of our account dated 14th May 1956.

Yours faithfully,
For and on behalf of
HENRY WILLIS & SONS LTD
N.D. Watkins
Secretary

NDW/PH

---

299 Aeolian-Skinner Co. to Henry Willis

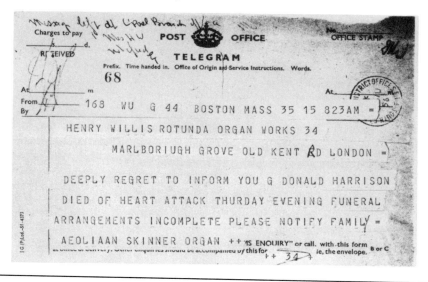

---

300 Rector, St. Thomas Church, to Congregation

ST. THOMAS CHURCH
New York City

The sudden death of Mr. G. Donald Harrison, on the very day the last pipes of our new organ were delivered at the church, was a tragic loss to the world of music as well as to his many friends and to his family.

President of the Aeolian-Skinner Organ Company, he was regarded by many as one of the greatest organ builders of all time. For over a year he has been constantly in and out of St. Thomas Church personally supervising the installation of the organ which was a project especially dear to his heart. He was heard to say that he wanted this organ to be a monument to his career. Fortunately, he was able to play it when it was practically complete and he expressed himself as happily satisfied.

We at St. Thomas Church thank God that he lived to insure the high quality of this great instrument and we express our deep sympathy to his family in their bereavement. Our organ will be an enduring reminder of him and of his genius. His funeral will be on Monday, June 18, at 2 p.m. in St. Mary's Church, Hampton Bays, Long Island. At that same time the Burial Office will be read in our church. You are invited.

Frederick M. Morris
Rector

---

301 Henry Willis to Joseph S.Whiteford

19th June, 1956

Mr. Joseph S. Whiteford
Vice President,
Aeolian-Skinner Organ Co.,
Boston, 25,
Mass. U.S.A.
Dear Whiteford,

Your cable conveying the sad news of Don's sudden passing arrived here in my absence — the information was passed to Mrs. Willis who immediately took steps to advise all Don's relatives over here.

To me, the sad news was a great shock as when Don was over here in June last year he seemed in the best of health and spirits, but a heart condition is seldom diagnosed in a man who has shown no signs.

To me, Don's death has been a real shock as you will appreciate — knowing of our long and close friendship.

It was a great source of satisfaction to me to follow and to note the artistic success of an old pupil.

The blow to the Aeolian-Skinner Co. is, of course, a serious one — I hope all difficulties will be overcome.

Yours very sincerely,
Henry Willis

H.W./B.R.

302 Henry Willis to Aubrey Thompson-Allen

19th June, 1956

Mr. A. Thompson-Allen,
30 Walden Street
Hamden,
Connecticut,
U.S.A.

<u>Personal</u>

Dear Aubrey,

Many thanks for your letter of the 15th inst. which arrived on the 18th inst. when I was in Liverpool. A cable arrived in my absence on the 15th inst. signed Aeolian-Skinner Co. announcing Don's passing and asking me to advise relatives in this country — Mrs. Willis performed this sad task. See copy of my letter to Joe Whiteford.

I do not know how the Aeolian-Skinner Co. will carry on without Don's name and prestige behind it. I fear that Joe, who has the dollars, will nominate himself President and attempt to carry on as Don's pupil and confidante. Of course, he is not capable and should have a Technical Director. If he has the sense to appreciate this there is only one person in the U.S.A. that I could recommend, and that is you. In view of past friction (?) with Joe would you be prepared to accept such a position? If so and with your assent, I will write Joe a fatherly letter of advice in accordance. Let me know for it is a matter for immediate action.

We will look forward to seeing Violet and the children the week after next. Fortunately I expect to be in London until the 10th July, when we go on an organ tour in Switzerland and North Italy with Dr. Vente.

All the best,
H.W.

---

303 Emerson Richards to Henry Willis

June 19th, 1956

My Dear Willis,

It is with a very heavy heart indeed that I write this note. Yesterday Ad and I made the 225-mile journey down to Southampton to see Don for the last time and to see him laid away on the shores of the Atlantic that he had selected and which he looked upon, perhaps, as a sort of bond between his old and his new home.

It was a very simple funeral. Only a few of his closest friends were there, and in the church only the voice of the priest was heard. No organ sounded. But at the same moment in New York it was a different story. A memorial service at St. Thomas, with the organ that he had literally given his life to finish mourned for him.

I think Aubrey has written the details. He overworked trying to finish St. Thomas in time for the A.G.O. convention. I think he looked upon this organ as his reply to all the abuse that E.M. had heaped upon him in the past.

He was suffering from angina and the heat and the exhaustion of walking home, because of a subway strike, exhausted him. And the nitro tablets were no longer effective. Still he seemed all right, Helen says, but while watching and laughing at a TV show he suddenly gasped and was gone.

It was about 10:30 p.m. Because of a stupid police regulation, he could not be moved from the chair where he had died until the following morning.

Somehow I cannot think that he is gone. AND HE HAD SO MUCH TO LIVE FOR and so much to do before his work was to be finished. We have lost more than a friend — we have lost the only man who could carry on the advance in tonal work that he had started.

I am sending to you a little booklet that I had printed for the opening of my organ on June 9th. Also the program. Elmore is a young and coming man and the Philadelphia Chapter is my home chapter of the A.G.O., so that is why the recital was for and by them. About 90 came down by bus and the recital was a success. The organ behaved, was approved, and so was the dinner that I gave them afterwards.

With best regards,

Sincerely,
Emerson

---

304 Henry Willis to Emerson Richards

22nd. June, 1956

Hon. Emerson Richards,
Counselor-at Law,
800, Schwehm Building,
Atlantic City, N.J.
U.S.A.

Personal

My dear Emerson,

Many thanks for yours of the 19th instant. I received the sad news of Don's passing by cable from the Aeolian Skinner Co. on the 15th instant and in accordance all relatives in this country were advised.

Aubrey wrote me with some details, your letter is fuller and more explanatory and it is now clear that Don was in New York working on St. Thomas's and returned to his home on Long Island and died there.

The police regulation you mention seems to me to be one that is callous and disgraceful.

You say "the nitro tablets were no longer effective." So it is clear that Don had suffered previous mild attacks of angina. This I did not know. When he was here last June he appeared to be in the best of health and spirits and made no mention to me of any heart trouble.

The news came as a dreadful shock to me. As you know Don and I were as brothers.

I also am greatly concerned about the future of the Aeolian-Skinner Co. I do not know what the financial setup is and if Helen will hold a controlling interest. I fear that Joe Whiteford will make a bid to be president on the grounds of having been Don's "pupil and confidante." As you know he is incapable of giving artistic direction and even with a really capable Technical and Tonal Director, the Company's production and prestige would under his general level descend to a combination of the Austin, Holtkamp and Möller level within five years — an appalling thought in view of Don's work.

If Joe Whiteford was prepared to delegate technical and artistic design and supervision wholly to a capable Technical Director, all may be well, but the only man I know of in the U.S.A. is Aubrey. And after his previous experience with Joe it is unlikely that he would accept the appointment.

<u>Your organ</u>. Glad to hear of its successful completion and opening.

Ever sincerely,

Henry

H.W./E.T.

returned to his home on Long Island — Willis' assumption is incorrect. The Harrisons had an apartment at 1019 Third Avenue in Manhattan, and a subway strike forced Harrison to walk from St. Thomas' to this residence. He was buried in Hampton Bays, Long Island.

June 22, 1956

Mr. Henry Willis
Rotunda Organ Works
34, Marlborough Grove
Old Kent Road
London, S.E. 1
England
Dear Mr. Willis:

I am grateful for your thoughtful letter of June 19th. I can well imagine that the news was a great shock to you. He was extremely fond of you and grateful for all of the many favors and the background that you offered him as a basis for his work in this country.

My only solace is that I was privileged to work closely with him technically for so many years and that he taught me all that could be taught about carrying on the ideals that he laid down. I am determined to carry those ideals forward to the best of my ability and appreciate deeply your sympathetic consideration.

Sincerely,
AEOLIAN-SKINNER ORGAN COMPANY
Joseph S. Whiteford
President

JSW:MOK

June 23rd 1956

Henry Willis, Esq.,
Rotunda Organ Works,
34 Marlborough Grove,
Old Kent Road
London.S.E.1.
ENGLAND
Dear Henry,

Many thanks for yours of the 19th instant received today. Don's passing is a sad business and somehow has been a tremendous shock to me. I think I knew him longer than anyone alive today in this country, and you must have been his oldest friend.

I had a pleasant day with Don a few weeks ago at Trinity College, Hartford. The organ is in my care, and for some while I have been pressing for its rebuild. The three of us, Watters, Don and myself got together on a preliminary, confidential discussion and after lunch I drove Don to New

Haven where I put him on the train for New York. While I still think this stepping stone of 1931 is a fine job, the consensus of opinion is very much against this kind of organ nowadays. Three Diapasons on a Great are unmentionable and where they still exist no one ever uses a No.1 any more and rarely a No.2! A mixture with a flat twenty-first is a thing of the past and that rank is usually cut off with cotton-wool. Big wood Pedal Opens also belong to the past. Generally speaking, English-style organs are no longer popular among the younger generation of brilliant organ students here. Don had succeeded in the last few years in developing an American instrument which is not at all English, German or anything else.

King Covell joined us on Sunday evening and together Violet, he and I drove down to New York and up to Hampton Bays on Monday where the funeral took place from St. Mary's Episcopal Church at 2 p.m. It was a beautiful day. About 40 people were present. Poor old Bill Zeuch was frightfully upset, naturally. The first car contained Helen, Mike and Mary, Stephen, a relative and Joe Whiteford. We had a chat with them all and others afterwards and then when everybody left, Violet, Covell and I sat in Richards' car for awhile.

I appreciate very much your thought as to me and the future of Aeolian-Skinner. Of course others outside the company have been having the same idea. I have given it a great deal of thought. Only full control from the top would satisfy me now and even so I feel very, very dubious about the whole thing. I never liked the set up. Violet will explain when she sees you next week. On the other hand I am happy in my present work, enjoy the University atmosphere and people around me and without too much stress and strain. Remember, when Don came to Skinner's, although he had old E.M.S. to put up with, he had a wonderful and steady aide in old Bill Zeuch (now retired). A very different situation would obtain were he to go there today. All things considered, I suggest you do not write to Whiteford about me. If I were not happy here it would be different.

Strange that you should mention poor old Reggie Goss-Custard. Only Monday I was thinking of him and asked Covell if he knew if he were still alive. I am sorry to hear of his passing.

You must see Violet and the children. I am seeing them off from Idlewilde Airport N.Y. today, Saturday, June 23rd for London. Violet will 'phone either you or Dora.

As ever,
Aubrey

307 Henry Willis to Joseph Whiteford

25th June, 1956

Mr. Joseph S. Whiteford
Aeolian-Skinner Organ Co.
Boston 25,
Mass. U.S.A.
Dear Joe Whiteford,

Thanks for your letter of the 22nd instant the contents of which are noted and appreciated.

You have undertaken a great and onerous burden and I wish you every possible success in bearing it.

Very sincerely,
Henry Willis

H.W./E.T.
Copy sent Hon. Emerson Richards
      A. Thompson-Allen

---

308 Henry Willis to Emerson Richards

25th June, 1956

Hon. Emerson Richards,
Counselor at Law,
800, Schwehm Building,
Atlantic City,
New Jersey,
U.S.A.
Dear Emerson,

I enclose copy of letter received from Joe Whiteford which speaks for itself — he has assumed the crown!

Ever sincerely,
Henry

H.W./E.T.

---

309 Helen Harrison to Eric Harrison

June 28, 1956

1019 Third Ave.
New York City

My dear Eric:

I know you will want to know more about Don, since he was with me the past three weeks finishing St. Thomas organ. There were many interruptions like going to Buffalo, Philadelphia etc. He was so pleased with his work. Then Mr. Bell took ill and was home in bed with prostate gland trouble and poor old Don had to make up the payroll. It seems he couldn't get anyone interested to take over for him. They also got Don upset one day. When he told them in the factory to send all in the truck, only a few pipes came, and G. Donald lost his temper, phoned Boston and he hoped the operator didn't hear what language he used. He was just doing everything.

When he left for Buffalo to sign a $75,000 contract, he lost two days going there. Then tried to make it up by working as late as eleven o'clock. Well, he did not sleep in the train and working late lost another night's sleep. Thursday he promised to come home for dinner. It was hot and a subway strike was on, so it took Don over an hour to walk a few blocks.

He said even his pills did not work anymore. But I gave him a drink, he relaxed and we had a light dinner which he thoroughly enjoyed. About eleven o'clock he wanted to see Victor Borge on the television, got into a bathrobe and comfortable so we could go right to bed afterwards. He so enjoyed it, laughed, and in a second he was gone. You might be interested about the pills. He took Phenobarbitol at night and some relaxing pills after meals. After the funeral I had to see Dr. Bellows, who told me that the defective artery was hard as an egg shell and just broke.

Hope you, Rene and family are well.

With love,
Helen

My dear Eric — Eric Harrison, a medical doctor in Sussex, England, G. Donald Harrison's brother

---

310 Emerson Richards to Henry Willis

July 12th, 1956

My Dear Willis,

I have not answered your last letters because I have been waiting to find out what has really happened in Boston. As yet no results. Phone calls to Boston and Whiteford only bring the response that he is not expected in that day or that he has left for the day. Apparently he does not spend much time at the factory.

In the mean time the general opinion is that Joe will not be able to hold Don's clients nor the factory personnel together. I think that he has more ability than he is given credit for but he is impatient and for some reason does not inspire confidence — just why I cannot say. It would be a tragedy if all that Don has built up goes down the drain.

But right now I do not think it is the time to make any suggestions such as contained in your first letter, but let things develop a bit until the picture is clearer. While your idea might be a solution, it might be only a temporary one and it might not work at all. And for this reason. The attitude of the key men at the factory has always been one of great independence and only Don had their confidence. Even with Don they resented innovations or anything that smacked of a speed up or use of new materials. They utterly refused to work with Aubrey, and this was the real reason he did not get on at A-S. He just could not understand this and blamed Joe, but Don himself told me that Allen just did not fit into the organization and that he was glad that he had found something more acceptable. I know this to be true from what the men themselves told me and the comments made. In my presence Aubrey said to one of the men, "This is not the way we do it in England." The man glared at him, turned and walked away. Later the same man told me where he could go and what he could do when he got there! You can see what I mean.

From this you can see that the problem has aspects which you may not have contemplated when you made the suggestion contained in your first letter. You may not quite understand what I mean by the above but even Don could not always get them to change a time-honored procedure even for the better and found it difficult to get them to change routines, although it might have been a relic of the Skinner days and they all hated E.M. and all his works.

Don only put over his own ideas because of their personal liking for him and his tactful way of leading them into the new ways. So I am more afraid of the men's reactions to any new direction (including Joe) than any other factor in continuing the work that Don left undone. If a number of the key men quit, and they may, since they are all "prima donnas" it is curtains for A-S.

The pity of it all is that if Don would have only listened to me, he would have been with us now. I kept warning him but he told me he would not "quit until he fell off an organ bench" and that is almost literally what happened.

I think St. Thomas was his reply to Skinner and he drove himself beyond endurance.

Now about your last letter. As I said in the 'forward' I don't go in for pipes with defective speech and I can assure you there are no 'chiffs' in the diapason chorus of Don's. Not in the Steinmeyer pipes either. While the cut up is low we have not sacrificed prompt speech and the chorus is clean and stays well together. The wonder is that the Steinmeyer stuff fits in so well. When Don was here last (Palm Sunday weekend) he had to admit that it was pulling together altho at that time we had only rough tuned and no regulation had been done. He was surprised and I think just a little bit upset that I had done so well. He spent a lot of time going over the pipes and then saying he ought to find some way to help finish it. A rather interesting comparison is the organ he had just finished at St. Paul's, Philadelphia, with mine. The A.G.O. Chapter had just heard the opening recital on it the month before mine and they all said that they thought mine was by far the better altho St. Paul had the advantage of the church acoustically.

I do hope you will get a chance to hear it soon. Of course it is not quite all in because now that Don is gone. I may have trouble getting the upper work of the Choir and the remainder of the Swell but what I have does give a good account of itself. It is big and brilliant but it also has guts and that counts.

About Biggs. Helen showed me your letter written to Don (April 30). I thought you knew that after all Don had done for Biggs he had turned on Don and is now busy promoting Schlicker and condemning all of Don's work. It even went so far that after suppressing the fact that Don had rebuilt Boston Symphony Hall and also Methuen he implied on the jackets of the Columbia records that it was the original organs that were being heard. Don got so mad he threatened to sue Columbia and Columbia's lawyers made Biggs retract. But he loses no opportunity to run down Don and does not mind twisting the facts to do it. Take St. Paul's Cathedral which you mention. He knows that this job was a promotion of Whiteford, Gammons, and the organist and Don had nothing to do with it and would not go near it when it threatened to turn out poorly until I talked him into going down there and straightening it out. The church is lousy for sound and the organ is not too big but the specification could be better but that is not Don's fault and Biggs knows it.

I must have tired you with this long letter but no fishing to day on account of rough seas and I am doing this at home as you can see from the typing and these electrics are misherable spellers.

I will keep you informed of what goes on and in the meantime Ad and I are always glad to hear from you and please give our best to Mrs. Willis.

Sincerely yours,
Emerson

311 Henry Willis to Emerson Richards

19th July, 1956

Hon. Emerson Richards,
Counselor-at-Law,
800, Schwehm Building,
Atlantic City,
New Jersey,
U.S.A.

My dear Emerson,

Thanks for your interesting letter of the 12th instant.

I am amused at your reference to the "prima donnas" at the Aeolian-Skinner Works. When I was trying to help them in 1924, 1925 and 1926 I found the key men all keen and cooperative — but Ernest Skinner was the obstacle.

I can quite understand Aubrey not getting on with the A.S. staff — he always lacked tact in handling men and, as I found out later, this was the cause of several of my good men resigning.

I had not failed to note that Don could not get the staff to depart from time-honored procedure and, being easygoing by nature, he left the mechanism side to carry on as before and concentrated on the tonal side.

It seems deplorable that the so-called key-men should appear to "rule the roost!"

I have been told that since Don's passing three important contracts have been cancelled by the clients on the ground that they were promised a Don Harrison organ.

I fear the outlook for A.S. is pretty grim in the existing circumstances.

. . .

[H.W.]

---

312 Ernest Skinner to Henry Willis

Feb. 18 1958

My dear Henry Willis:

Since I discovered that the wind stream issuing at the flue remains entirely outside the upper lip, otherwise something over 50 years ago, I have never in a single instance skived or sharpened the upper lip of flue pipes except in the top octaves of stops of two foot pitch and now Henry, will you please take a Diapason pipe such as a two foot C and while it is speaking, as on a voicing chest, drop some sawdust into the top of said pipe and see what happens. The sawdust will fall to the bottom, or to the languet and remain there undisturbed, as I think you will find. Now one more thing; look in your dictionary at the word spelled LANGUET and see what you see. It may be and probably is a fact that a long time usage of spelling or usage will justify a colloquial spelling or pronunciation of a word but do you think that justifies discontinuing the original spelling or pronouncing of a word. Well all my life, until recently I called that partition on a flue pipe LANGUID, but should that stop me from correcting an error, when I discovered that it was an error?

For example, I have a short time ago, completed a book which I named, "The Composition of the Organ" and which manuscript is now in the hands of my son who is in conference with a publisher. I have a fine book by an English publisher who I was in the mind to send it to, but my son is in conference with an American university who may decide to publish it. Anyhow I'll let you know how it turns out, but I'll be ninety-two years old and that's no chicken is it. When that book is published I can really relax I guess.

Henry, will you please take a two foot C diapason pipe and put it on a voicing chest and then fasten the key down and hold a chisel in the wind stream and note as I have many years ago, that the said wind stream is way outside the upper lip. By moving a chisel blade back and forth parallel to the upper lip and through the wind stream you can locate its position precisely and then you will see as I did, that said wind stream is way outside the upper lip and that the tonal vibrations in reaching said wind stream must necessarily pass the lip absolutely horizontally and for this reason I have left the upper lip absolutely square which as I think you will agree, is more in consonance with the movement of the sound wave than is the universal practise of skiving said lip. Anyway I haven't skived the lips of flue pipes for over fifty years and as far as I know I have got the name of building the most musical toned organs in America. If you like I will send you a report of a music critic relative to a recital given on my big organ in the Washington Cathedral. But one thing I well know and that is that the finest chorus reeds in the world are built by the Willis Co. of England and how I would love to hear those marvelous Trumpets again. But though I am as far as I know, in perfect health, nobody lives very long after reaching ninety as far as I know, so I am wondering how old my friend Henry Willis happens to be? Wish I could get to England again but don't believe that will ever happen. I'm sending you sketches of upper lips such as I have used for the last fifty years. . . .

Feb. 28 1958

I just saw your ad in <u>Musical Opinion</u> and so as I am sick of sitting around and doing nothing reading ads in <u>Musical Opinion</u> I am writing you to see if you have any need for a flue voicer?

I am personally as adept at that branch of the organ business and also have developed a total of thirty-four entirely new stops, such as the French

Horn, English Horn, and Orchestral Oboe, which are exact reproductions of their orchestral prototypes, and also a perfect orchestral Bassoon, muted strings, a Pedal Gemshorn and a Pedal 32 ft. Fagotto, a Flauto Dolce and Flute Celeste, which combined with a two rank 4 ft. Unda Maris, "make the most beautiful sound in music." I once had a printed page of my developments both mechanical and musical, but gave them all away.

I really wish I could leave my tonal developments to some organ builder of a technical capacity such as yours, but as it happens, I know of no such builder here in the U.S. so why not the Willis Company of England?

If it happens that I do come to England I mean to bring sample pipes of some of my personal developments. If you don't happen to have them yet as it seems to me you would like them very much. Anyway, why not write and tell me if you want me to bring them as a gift of course. There are many others I have not named that are, to me, of similar musical value, which could be made in your factory under my direction, if I happen to come and as for ME I want to hear those glorious Trumpets again which I heard on my last visit to you. I have never heard anything like them.

Well, I was cleaned practically out of cash during the last war and may not be able to come and see you until my book is out, after which I suppose I'll have all the money I need for the rest of my life. Have been out of the organ building business now for a couple of years, so all I do now is write letters and read and am now physically very inactive, but darned if I wouldn't like that flue voicing job for which I think you advertised. If I could spare the money I would come immediately, but guess I'll have to wait a little longer.

My best to you Henry.
Ernest M. Skinner

Appendix

Concluding Notes and Commentary

Ernest M. Skinner Although Ernest Skinner did little work for Aeolian-Skinner after mid-1933, he was under contract until January, 1936. Subsequently, he moved to the old Methuen Organ Company factory, which adjoined what is now the Methuen Memorial Music Hall. As the Ernest M. Skinner & Son Company, he continued to build organs until 1943, when the factory burned. The highlight of Skinner's Methuen period was the 1938 instrument for Washington Cathedral. Skinner died in 1960 at age 94.

William King Covell Covell continued to write about organs, and kept up lively correspondence with Senator Richards. But his writing in the post-Harrison years shows that he was unsympathetic to the direction organ "reform" was taking. Troubled by diabetes and a weakened heart, he died in his sleep on February 23, 1975.

Henry Willis III At the outbreak of war in 1939, Henry Willis III was called to service as a Reserve Officer and served for almost six years as a captain. During this time organ work consisted solely of tuning, repair work and rescue of organs in bombed churches. On the night of April 16, 1941, the Willis factory in the Brixton section of London was destroyed by bombs. Aubrey Thompson-Allen, a director of the firm, ran the business for the remainder of the war from his home in Upper Norwood. After the war, a new plant was established in Marlborough Grove, off the Old Kent Road in Southeast London.

In his last decade, Willis became known to a new generation of English organists, not so much for his new organs, which were not well received, as for his habit of attending the opening recitals of other builders' organs, sitting in the front pew, and leaving in disgust during the first piece. Like Skinner, he was a notoriously bad driver; miraculously, they both managed to survive serious automobile accidents and live to old age. Perhaps with the current reassessment of Skinner's work, a retrospective of Willis III's achievements is in order as well.

Emerson Richards Richards met G. Donald Harrison soon after the Englishman immigrated to the United States. Possibly they had met even earlier in the Willis factory in London. They found common ground in the desire to tonally improve the American organ, and by the early '30s, they had become close friends. At that time, Harrison had traveled only briefly in France and never in Germany, and it was Richards who encouraged him to hear the old instruments for himself. Harrison's first visit to Germany in 1936 altered his outlook and the tonal direction of Aeolian-Skinner.

Richards' friendship with Donald Harrison spanned more than 30 years, but in hindsight it is somewhat perplexing. Michael Harrison, son of the organbuilder, has said that he was never able to understand the relationship, because the two men were so unlike each other. On the surface, the association might be comparable to the relationship of Arthur Harrison and Colonel Dixon, the wealthy musical amateur who brought much business to the Durham firm of Harrison and Harrison. Senator Richards' influence was equally helpful to Aeolian-Skinner, as was his encyclopedic knowledge of organ building theory and practice. Lawrence Phelps has gone so far as to state that Richards' technical knowledge was "the most comprehensive I have ever seen in an individual not employed as an organ builder." Exactly how much influence Richards exerted on Harrison's designs is hard to determine. If asked, Richards doubtless would have claimed credit for much more than the concept and naming of the American Classic Organ, and would have argued his case persuasively.

The relationship with Harrison was social as well as professional, as the Harrisons often visited the Richardses for holidays, both in Atlantic City and at Richards' summer retreat on Squirrel Island in Moosehead Lake in Maine. When Richards finally married in 1944, at the age of 60, he asked Donald Harrison to be his best man. Whatever the ramifications of the friendship, Richards was one of Harrison's prominent admirers and staunch advocates.

As a writer, Richards expressed himself exactly and succinctly, even when describing organ tone. Harrison seemed to prefer picturesque analogies such as a "bouquet of tone" which did not really convey what he he had in mind. Perhaps Harrison realized this, and preferred to let his organs (and Richards) articulate his ideas. Through extensive articles in the organ journals and as consultant in many organ projects, Richards brought a significant number of contracts to Aeolian-Skinner.

Athough overweight and arthritic, Richards traveled all over the country in his plush, well-appointed, chauffeur-driven limousine to try out Harrison's latest instruments. The late Roy Perry told of a visit by the Senator to Kilgore, Texas, early in the 1950s. As the Southwestern Aeolian-Skinner representative, Perry took Richards to play the company's newly installed organs. It soon became apparent that the older man's active repertoire was limited to the first inversion of a G-minor triad. Helped onto the bench by his chauffeur-bodyguard, Richards tried each stop individually with the same G-minor chord, commenting over and over, "Don's on the right track," "Don's doing just what I taught him." In this manner, Richards progressed inexorably through all the Great stops, and then reached for the

Swell. Expecting more G-minor, Perry excused himself and walked to the nearby Western Union office to cable Harrison:

DEAR BOSS: THE SENATOR IS HERE. STOP. HE SAYS HE TAUGHT YOU ALL YOU KNOW ABOUT ORGAN BUILDING. STOP. IN RETURN, DID YOU TEACH HIM ALL YOU KNOW ABOUT ORGAN PLAYING? SIGNED ROY.

Perry insisted that Harrison laughed so much over this telegram that he carried it in his wallet until the day he died.

By 1956, Richards' residence organ had gone through seven major rebuilds and emerged as a four-manual, 100-rank Aeolian-Skinner. Pipework was incorporated from several instruments, as well as new pipes by Aeolian-Skinner and Steinmeyer of Germany. Unfortunately, Richards' home, including his extensive organ library, two pianos and the organ, was destroyed by fire in 1958. Despite this misfortune, as well as health problems which might have destroyed a lesser man, Senator carried on valiantly. Typically, one of his last projects was overseeing the enlargement of the Aeolian-Skinner organ in the First Methodist Church of Millville, New Jersey. Senator Richards died from a heart attack in October, 1963, at the age of 79.

G. Donald Harrison Until the end of his life, Harrison constantly experimented with new ideas and sonorities, different ways to build an organ. This was nothing new, for he had been quietly developing his ideals since 1927. Michael Harrison characterizes his father as a man who tended to be conservative at first, in order not to appear radical. He took very small steps over careful amounts of time, and he was extremely diplomatic and tactful.

At first, Harrison's organs differed little from Skinner's post-1924 works. Orchestral voices were maintained, but the ensemble was strengthened. Leather-lipped diapasons were discarded, and more upper-work was added. Harrison first experimented with mixtures including tierce and septième ranks, but later excluded these from chorus mixtures altogether. He gradually reduced wind pressures, slowly experimented with scaling, and gave reeds new brilliance over time.

Relations between Marks and Skinner had been strained since the mid-'20s, and soon Skinner began to question Harrison's ideas as well. An increasing number of clients requested organs to be built under Harrison's supervision; this was a blow to Skinner's pride. Harrison himself felt that the organ built for Trinity College, Hartford, in 1931 was the real starting point in his work.

Coming to America was, from Harrison's point of view, the best thing that happened to him. It gave him his own route, and liberated him from the traditions of his country. By the mid-'30s, the departure of Ernest

Skinner gave Harrison an open field to develop a new type of organ. In 1936, he visited Germany with Carl Weinrich, where, according to Weinrich, the men did the playing and the ladies did the pumping. A quote from a 1937 interview in *The American Organist* illuminates Harrison's thinking at the time:

> To me, all art is international; one can draw from the best of all countries. I have used the technique at my disposal to produce instruments which I consider suitable for expressing the best in organ literature. I have no use for copying successful works of the past; such a method is doomed to failure. I have seen many so-called exact copies of the old work which are but weak shadows of the original. There are many factors which enter into the tone produced by an organ's pipes; some of them seem to be intangible.
>
> It seems to me that the only way to build artistic and successful instruments is to have knowledge of what has gone before, and to thoroughly understand the underlying principles upon which the great works of the past have been based. The works produced are then originals, and while they can possess all the advantages of other good work, they have their own personality and reflect their own good time."

Harrison's identification with the United States was strengthened by his naturalization as an American citizen on July 25, 1938.

Following the death of Arthur Hudson Marks in 1939, Harrison acquired controlling interest in the Aeolian-Skinner Company, perhaps with the financial assistance of his second wife, Helen, whom he had married on April 29, 1935. An American of Italian descent, Helen Caspari had been married earlier, and maintained an apartment on Third Avenue in New York City as well as a summer residence in Hampton Bays, Long Island. After his marriage, Harrison began to spend Monday through Thursday in Boston at the factory, leaving late Thursday night for New York, where Aeolian-Skinner maintained a Fifth Avenue office. Whenever Harrison finished an instrument, he would spend days and sometimes weeks on-site. With a voicer in the organ, Harrison would sit at the console or at a specially-wired keyboard in the middle of the room.

With the 1941 tonal revisions at the Church of St. Mary the Virgin, Manhattan, Harrison and Aeolian-Skinner reached a turning point in the development of the "American Classic Organ," as the new type of instrument was termed. In December, with the bombing of Pearl Harbor, the United States entered World War II. Two months later, the War Board restricted the production of all musical instruments. By 1944, there were only 12 men in the factory, making cases for artillery shells and crates for military coffins. The few organs built in the war years were rebuilds, which used metal pipes of older instruments, since no new metal could be used.

Harrison was too old for military service, so he occupied his time directing the work of the company, such as it was, and experimented with the development of new baroque-style reeds. Not until December, 1945, did the Civilian Production Administration relax a few of the restrictions on manufacturing pipe organs by authorizing the use of tin from old organs or taken from inventory. A year later, permission was given for the purchase of tin in the open market, at greatly increased prices. The five-year hiatus in organ building, considerable post-war inflation and lack of contractual escalation clauses severely affected Aeolian-Skinner finances as the company returned to organ building in 1946.

Since early in World War II, a ten percent federal tax was levied on new organs. When this tax was finally eliminated in July, 1948, its repeal was actually a rider on another abolition: tax that breweries paid on "waste beer" — beer lost through bottle breakage or leakage.

Some of the company's largest and most important organs were produced during Harrison's final decade. Despite Aeolian-Skinner's high prices, financial statements show that the company often lost money, especially on large organs. After the completion of the Mormon Tabernacle organ, which Harrison considered his finest, he consulted Tabernacle organist Alexander Schreiner about the severe financial loss. Schreiner took Harrison to see the Mormon authorities, who reviewed the balance sheets, reimbursed Aeolian-Skinner for the loss incurred, and added a percentage for profit.

In the early '50s, Harrison suffered a heart attack, which he kept secret from all but his closest friends. He feared any effect on the firm if others found out. By 1954, he had developed degenerative heart disease. Like his first attack, he did not discuss his condition with associates for fear of alarm. According to his son Michael, many years of heavy drinking and smoking had weakened his heart and hardened his arteries. He relied on vasodilators, which he consumed more and more frequently; by 1956, he taking them "like candy."

Despite the emphasis on the American Classic, Aeolian-Skinner continued to produce instruments more in the Ernest Skinner style when requested. Harrison's willingness to produce these more romantically-inclined instruments was a result of his desire to please clients, and also his awareness of the needs of his employees. Michael Harrison recalls his father's sense of responsibility toward his employees (who numbered at times over a hundred) and their families. While Harrison was not willing to lower the company's standards by turning out poor organs, he was capable of admitting that there were other viewpoints than his own.

In the mid-50s, many leading organists desired even further brilliance in the ensemble. Toward the end, Harrison experimented with narrower scaling and higher mixtures, using two last organs as tests: St. Paul's Church, Chestnut Hill, Philadelphia, and St. Thomas'. During the finishing at St. Paul's, Harrison remarked to finisher Donald Gillett, "Some of this is a little way out, Donald," referring to the organ's many high-pitched mixtures. Whether he would have continued in this style is questionable. In a conversation with Ned Gammons, Harrison remarked, "Mixtures are like taking dope. Your tolerance goes up, and you have to increase the dose until at last you don't want substance any more."

It was this leaner, thinned ensemble which Harrison's successors cultivated after his death. The mixture-work began to dominate rather than clarify. The Aeolian-Skinner Organ Company, like the concept of the American Classic Organ, was a product of a time which is now history. Time adds perspective and wisdom to judgment, and will tell us that the work of Harrison, like Father Willis, Cavaillé-Coll and Ernest Skinner, was noble indeed.

Stoplists

Liverpool Anglican Cathedral, England

Henry Willis & Son, 1924

GREAT flues 5", 6", 10" reeds 15"

32'	Contra Violone
16'	Double Open Diapason
16'	Contra Tibia
16'	Bourdon
10²/₃'	Double Quint
8'	Open Diapason I
8'	Open Diapason II
8'	Open Diapason III
8'	Open Diapason IV
8'	Open Diapason V
8'	Tibia
8'	Doppelflöte (open)
8'	Stopped Diapason
5¹/₃'	Quint
4'	Octave I
4'	Octave II
4'	Principal
4'	Flute Harmonique
4'	Flute Couverte
3¹/₅'	Tenth
2²/₃'	Twelfth
2'	Super Octave
2'	Fifteenth
V	Mixture
V	Fourniture
16'	Double Trumpet
8'	Trumpet
8'	Trompette Harmonique
4'	Clarion

SWELL flues 5", soft reeds 7", horns 10", trumpets 15"

16'	Contra Geigen
16'	Contra Salicional
16'	Lieblich Bordun
8'	Open Diapason I
8'	Open Diapason II
8'	Geigen
8'	Salicional
8'	Echo Viola
8'	Vox Angelica FF
8'	Tibia
8'	Flauto Traverso
8'	Waldflöte

8'	Lieblich Gedackt
4'	Octave
4'	Octave Geigen
4'	Salicet
4'	Lieblichflöte
2²/₃'	Twelfth
2'	Fifteenth
1³/₅'	Seventeenth
V	Mixture
16'	Double Trumpet
16'	Waldhorn
16'	Contra Hautboy
8'	Trumpet
8'	Trompette Harmonique
8'	Cornopean
8'	Hautboy
8'	Krummhorn
4'	Octave Trumpet
4'	Clarion
	Tremulant 5"
	Tremulant 7"

CHOIR 4" wind, trumpets 7"

Unenclosed

16'	Contra Dulciana
8'	Open Diapason
8'	Dulciana
8'	Rohr Flöte
4'	Dulcet
4'	Flute Ouverte
2'	Dulcina
	Tremulant

Enclosed

16'	Contra Viola
8'	Violin Diapason
8'	Viola
8'	Claribel Flute
8'	Unda Maris FF
4'	Octave Viola
4'	Suabe Flöte
2'	Lieblich Piccolo
V	Dulciana Mixture
16'	Bass Clarinet
16'	Baryton
8'	Trumpet (orchestral)

8'	Corno di Bassetto		**PEDAL ORGAN**
8'	Cor Anglais		**Unenclosed**
8'	Vox Humana	64'	Resultant Bass
4'	Clarion	32'	Double Open Bass
	Tremulant 4"	32'	Contra Violone Great
SOLO 7" wind, trombas 20"		32'	Double Open Diapason
Unenclosed		21¹/₃'	Double Quint
16'	Contra Hohlflöte	16'	Open Bass I
8'	Hohlflöte	16'	Open Bass II
4'	Octave Hohlflöte	16'	Open Diapason
Enclosed		16'	Contra Basso
16'	Contre Viole	16'	Dolce
8'	Viole de Gambe	16'	Tibia
8'	Viole d'Orchestre	16'	Bourdon
8'	Violes Celestes FF	10²/₃'	Quint
8'	Flute Harmonique	8'	Principal open diapason
4'	Octave Viole	8'	Octave
4'	Concert Flute Harmonique	8'	Stopped Flute bourdon
2'	Violette	5¹/₃'	Twelfth
2'	Piccolo Harmonique	4'	Fifteenth open diapason
III	Cornet des Violes	III	Mixture
16'	Cor Anglais	V	Fourniture
8'	French Horn	32'	Contra Bombarde
8'	Bassoon (orchestral)	16'	Ophicleide
8'	Oboe (orchestral)	16'	Bombarde ext.
8'	Clarinet (orchestral)	8'	Clarion
16'	Contra Tromba	8'	Bombarde ext.
8'	Tromba Réal	4'	Bombarde ext.
8'	Tromba	**Enclosed in Pedal box**	
4'	Tromba Clarion	16'	Geigen
	Tremulant 7"	16'	Violone
	Solo Trombas on Great	8'	Violoncello
BOMBARDE Manual V		8'	Open Flute
6", tubas 30", magna 50"		4'	Flute Triangulaire
X	Grand Chorus 610,	32'	Contra Trombone
	SU.1.5.8.12.15.19.22.26.29	16'	Trombone
16'	Contra Tuba	16'	Fagotto
8'	Tuba	8'	Octave Bassoon
4'	Tuba Clarion		
8'	Tuba Magna		

Source: Willis photographs of the 1926 console & a Cathedral publication

Princeton University Chapel, Princeton, New Jersey

Opus 656 E. M. Skinner, 1927-8

GREAT:		8'	Second Diapason 61
Unenclosed:		8'	Third Diapason 61
32'	Quintaton TC 49	8'	Principal Flute 61
16'	Diapason 61	5¹/₃'	Quint 61
16'	Bourdon [5 Ped]	4'	Octave 61
8'	First Diapason 61	4'	Principal 61

$3^1/5'$ Tenth 61
$2^2/3'$ Twelfth 61
2' Fifteenth 61
V Harmonics 15, 17, 19, 21, 22 305
III-VI Plein Jeu 268
Enclosed with Choir
8' Doppelflöte 61
4' Flute 61
16' Contra Tromba 61
8' Tromba 61
4' Octave Tromba 61
SWELL
16' Bourdon 73
8' Diapason 73
8' Geigen Diapason 73
8' Gamba 73
8' Gamba Celeste 73
8' Salicional 73
8' Voix Celeste 73
8' Flauto Dolce 73
8' Flute Celeste TC 61
8' Rohrfloete 73
8' Cor-de-Nuit [A] 73
4' Octave 73
4' Fugara [B]
4' Flute Triangulaire 73
$2^2/3'$ Nazard [C]
2' Flautino [D]
2' Piccolo 61
$1^3/5'$ Tierce [E]
V Chorus Mixture 305
V Cornet [draws A-B-C-D-E] 305
16' Posaune 73
8' Cornopean 73
8' French Trumpet 73
8' Oboe 73
8' Vox Humana 73
4' Clarion 73
Tremolo
CHOIR
16' Gamba 12
8' Diapason 73
8' Viole d'Orchestre 73
8' Viole Celeste 73
8' Dulciana 73
8' Dulciana Celeste TC 61
8' Concert Flute 73
8' Quintadena [no pipes, synthetic]
4' Violina 73

4' Flute Harmonic 73
$2^2/3'$ Nazard 61
2' Piccolo 61
$1^3/5'$ Tierce 61
$1^1/7'$ Septième 61
16' Fagotto 73
8' Trumpet 73
8' Corno di Bassetto 73
8' Orchestral Oboe 73
Tremolo
SOLO
8' Stentorphone 73
8' Gamba 73
8' Gamba Celeste 73
8' Flauto Mirabilis 73
4' Octave 73
4' Orchestral Flute 73
V Mixture 305
16' Contra Tuba 73
8' Tuba Mirabilis 73
8' Tuba 73
8' French Horn 61
8' English Horn 61
4' Clarion 73
Tremolo
PEDAL
32' Diapason [open to GGGG] 12
16' Diapason 32
16' Contra Bass 32
16' Diapason (Great)
16' Gamba (Choir)
16' Bourdon 32
16' Echo Lieblich Swell
$10^2/3'$ Quint 12 [sic]
8' Octave (Open) 12
8' Principal 12
8' Gedeckt (Bourdon) 12
8' Still Gedeckt (Swell)
$5^1/3'$ Twelfth
4' Flute (Bourdon) 12
V Harmonics 15, 17, 19, 21, 22 160
32' Bombarde 12
32' Fagotto 12 (Choir)
16' Trombone 32
16' Tuba (Solo)
16' Fagotto (Choir)
$10^2/3'$ Quint Trombone 12 [Great]
8' Tromba 12
4' Clarion 12

Source: *Stop, Open &*
Reed, Vol. 5, No. 1

448

St. Paul's Cathedral, London, England

Rebuilt Willis 1900, Willis & Sons 1930

GREAT

16'	Double Open Diapason
16'	Lieblich Bourdon
8'	Open Diapason No. 1
8'	Open Diapason No. 2
8'	Open Diapason No. 3
8'	Open Diapason No. 4
8'	Tibia
$5\frac{1}{3}$'	Quint
4'	Principal No. 1
4'	Principal No. 2
$2\frac{2}{3}$'	Twelfth
2'	Fifteenth
3 rks.	Fourniture
3 rks.	Mixture
16'	Trombone (heavy wind)
8'	Tromba (heavy wind)
4'	Clarion (heavy wind)

SWELL

16'	Contra Gamba
8'	Open Diapason
8'	Lieblich Gedeckt
8'	Salicional
8'	Vox Angelica (bass from Sal.)
4'	Principal
2'	Fifteenth
3 rks	Cornet
16'	Contra Posaune (heavy wind)
8'	Cornopean (heavy wind)
8'	Hautboy (heavy wind)
4'	Clarion (heavy wind)

CHOIR

16'	Contra Viola
8'	Open Diapason
8'	Violoncello
8'	Clarabella
8'	Lieblich Gedeckt
8'	Dulciana
4'	Gemshorn
4'	Flute Harmonique
$2\frac{2}{3}$'	Nazard
2'	Flageolet
$1\frac{3}{5}$'	Tierce
8'	Corno di Bassetto
8'	Cor Anglais
8'	Trumpet

SOLO (Enclosed)

8'	Open Diapason
8'	Viola da Gamba
8'	Flute Ouverte
8'	Flute Harmonique
4'	Concert Flute
2'	Piccolo
16'	Contra Posaune
16'	Contra Fagotto
8'	Trumpet
8'	French Horn
8'	Corno di Bassetto
8'	Cor Anglais
8'	Orchestral Oboe (unenclosed)

ALTAR

16'	Quintaton
8'	Cor de Nuit
8'	Sylvestrina
4'	Fern Flöte

TUBA

Dome:

16'	Double Tuba
8'	Tuba harmonic (heavy wind)
4'	Clarion harmonic (heavy wind)
8'	Trompette Militaire (har. trebs.)

Chancel:

8'	Tuba harmonic (heavy wind)
4'	Tuba Clarion harmonic (hvy wnd)

PEDAL

Dome:

32'	Double Open Bass
32'	Contra Violone
16'	Open Bass No. 1
16'	Open Bass No. 2
16'	Open Diapason
8'	Principal
8'	Violoncello
3 rks	Mixture
32'	Contra Posaune
16'	Bombarde (heavy wind)
8'	Clarion (heavy wind)

Chancel:

16'	Open Bass
16'	Contra Bass
16'	Violone
16'	Bourdon

16' **Open Metal** (from Gt.)
16' **Viola** (from Choir)
8' **Octave**
8' **Flute**

4' **Octave Flute** (ext.)
16' **Ophicleide** (heavy wind)

Source: *Diapason*, 1 Sept. 1930, p. 18.

Trinity College Chapel, Hartford. Connecticut

Aeolian-Skinner Opus 851, 1931

GREAT 61 notes
16' **Diapason**
8' **First Diapason**
8' **Second Diapason**
8' **Third Diapason**
8' **Principal Flute**
8' **Erzähler**
5^1/3' **Quint**
4' **Octave**
4' **Flute**
2^2/3' **Twelfth**
2' **Fifteenth**
5 rks **Harmonics**
8' **Tromba**
4' **Clarion**
Chimes

SWELL 73 notes
16' **Bourdon**
8' **Geigen Diapason**
8' **Rohrflute**
8' **Salicional**
8' **Voix Celeste**
8' **Echo Gamba**
8' **Echo Gamba Celeste**
4' **Octave Geigen**
4' **Flute Triangulaire**
2' **Fifteenth** (61)
5 rks **Mixture**
3 rks **Carillon**
8' **Oboe**
8' **Vox Humana**
16' **Waldhorn**
8' **Trumpet**
4' **Clarion**
Tremolo

CHOIR 73 notes
16' **Contra Spitzflute**
8' **Spitzflute**
8' **Concert Flute**
8' **Dulciana**
8' **Unda Maris** (61)

4' **Flute** (reported in *The American Organist*, July, 1933)
4' **Gemshorn**
2^2/3' **Nazard** (61)
2' **Piccolo** (61)
4 rks **Sesqialtera**
8' **Clarinet**
8' **Trumpet**
Tremolo

SOLO 73 notes
8' **Orchestral Flute**
8' **Gamba**
8' **Gamba Celeste**
4' **Concert Flute**
8' **French Horn**
8' **English Horn**
8' **Tuba Mirabilis**
Tremolo

PEDAL 32 notes
32' **Contra Bass**
16' **Diapason** (bearded)
16' **Metal Diapason** (Great)
16' **Bourdon**
16' **Echo Bourdon** (Swell)
16' **Spitzflute** (Choir)
8' **Octave**
8' **Gedeckt**
8' **Still Gedeckt** (Swell)
4' **Super Octave**
4' **Flute**
32' **Bombarde** (metal)
16' **Trombone**
16' **Waldhorn** (Swell)
8' **Tromba**
4' **Clarion**
Chimes (Great)

Source: Advertisement, *Diapason*, 1 August 1932, p. 5.

450

Royal Albert Hall, London, England

Harrison & Harrison, Durham, England, 1933

GREAT

32'	Contra Violone
16'	Double Open Diapason
16'	Contra Gamba
16'	Bourdon
16'	Double Claribel Flute
8'	Open Diapason I
8'	Open Diapason II
8'	Open Diapason III
8'	Open Diapason IV
8'	Open Diapason V
8'	Geigen
8'	Viola da Gamba
8'	Hohl Flöte
8'	Harmonic Flute
$5^{1}/_{3}$'	Quint
4'	Octave
4'	Principal
4'	Viola
4'	Harmonic Flute
$2^{2}/_{3}$'	Octave Quint
2'	Super Octave
2'	Fifteenth
6 rks	Harmonics 10, 15, 17, 19, 21, 22
5 rks	Mixture 8, 12, 15, 19, 22
7 rks	Cymbale 19, 22, 26, 29, 31, 33, 36
16'	Contra Tromba
8'	Tromba harmonic
4'	Octave Tromba harmonic
8'	Posaune
8'	Harmonic Trumpet
4'	Harmonic Clarion

SWELL

16'	Double Open Diapason
16'	Bourdon
8'	Open Diapason
8'	Viola da Gamba
8'	Salicional
8'	Vox Angelica
8'	Flûte à Cheminée
8'	Claribel Flute
4'	Principal
4'	Viola
4'	Harmonic Flute
4'	Octave Quint
2'	Super Octave

2'	Harmonic Piccolo
5 rks	Mixture 8, 12, 15, 19, 22
5 rks	Fourniture 15, 19, 22, 26, 29
16'	Contra Oboe
8'	Oboe
16'	Baryton
8'	Vox Humana
16'	Double Trumpet
8'	Trumpet harmonic trebles
4'	Clarion harmonic trebles
8'	Tuba harmonic
4'	Tuba Clarion harmonic

CHOIR AND ORCHESTRAL

First division Choir, unenclosed:

16'	Double Salicional
8'	Open Diapason
8'	Lieblich Gedeckt
8'	Viola da Gamba
8'	Dulciana
4'	Gemshorn
4'	Lieblich Flute
2'	Flageolet
3 rks	Mixture 12, 19, 22
8'	Trumpet harmonic trebles
4'	Clarion

Second division Orchestral, enclosed

16'	Contre Viole
8'	Violoncello
8'	Viole d'Orchestre I
8'	Viole d'Orchestre II
8'	Viole Sourdine
8'	Violes Celestes 2 rks
4'	Viole Octaviante
5 rks	Cornet de Violes 12, 15, 17, 19, 22
16'	Quintatön
8'	Harmonic Flute
4'	Concert Flute
2'	Harmonic Piccolo
16'	Double Clarinet
8'	Clarinet
8'	Orchestral Hautboy
8'	Cor Anglais

SOLO AND BOMBARDE

First division Solo, in a swell box

16'	Contra-Bass
8'	Flûte à Pavillon

8' Viole d'Amour
8' Doppel Flöte
8' Harmonic Claribel Flute
8' Unda Maris (2 rks)
4' Wald Flöte
4' Flauto Traverso
2' Piccolo Traverso
16' Double Bassoon
8' Corno di Bassetto
8' Hautboy
8' Bassoon
16' Double Horn harmonic
8' French Horn harmonic
Carillons
Tubular Bells
Second division Bombarde, enclosed
16' Bombardon
8' Tuba harmonic
8' Orchestral Trumpet harmonic
8' Cornopean harmonic trebles
5¹/₃' Quint Trumpet
4' Orchestral Clarion harmonic
5 rks Sesquialtera 12, 15, 17, 19, 22
16' Contra Tuba harmonic, unenc.
8' Tuba Mirabilis harmonic, unenc.
4' Tuba Clarion harmonic, unenc.
PEDAL
64' Acoustic Bass 20 from Double Open Wood; lower 12 acoustic
32' Double Open Wood
32' Double Open Diapason
32' Contra Violone from Gt.
21¹/₃' Double Quint from Dbl Opn Dia
16' Open Wood I
16' Open Wood II 20 from Dbl Open Wood
16' Open Diapason I

16' Open Diapason II 20 from Dbl Open Diapason
16' Violone
16' Sub-Bass
16' Salicional from Choir Dbl Sal
16' Viole from Choir Contre Viole
10²/₃' Quint
8' Octave Wood 20 from Opn Wd I
8' Principal 20 from Opn Dia I
8' Violoncello
8' Flute
5¹/₃' Octave Quint
4' Super Octave
7 rks Harmonics 10, 12, 15, 17, 19, 21, 22
5 rks Mixture 15, 19, 22, 26, 29; in Solo box
32' Double Ophicleide 20 from 16' Ophicleide
32' Double Trombone 20 from 16' Trombone
16' Ophicleide
16' Bombarde
16' Trombone in Swell box
16' Fagotto
16' Trumpet from Swell Dbl Trumpet
16' Clarinet from Orches Clar
16' Bassoon from Solo, in Solo box
10²/₃' Quint Trombone
8' Posaune 20 from 16' Ophicleide
8' Clarion
4' Octave Posaune 20 from Ophicleide & Posaune
Drums

Source: *Diapason*, 1 November 1933, p. 3, which reports the original organ to have been built by "Father" Willis in 1872 and that the work by Harrison & Harrison, begun in 1923, "completely transformed" the organ.

St. John's Chapel, Groton School, Groton, Massachusetts

Aeolian-Skinner Opus 936, 1935

GREAT (3" wind)
16' Sub Principal 61 pipes
8' Principal 61 pipes
8' Diapason 61 pipes
8' Flute Harmonique 61 pipes
8' Gemshorn 61 pipes
5¹/₃' Gross Quint 61 pipes
4' Octave 61 pipes

4' Principal 61 pipes
3¹/₅' Grosse Tierce 61 pipes
2²/₃' Quint 61 pipes
2' Super Octave 61 pipes
1³/₅' Tierce 61 pipes
4 rks Full Mixture 244 pipes
4 rks Fourniture 244 pipes
3 rks Cymbel 183 pipes

SWELL ($3^3/4$" wind*)
- 16' **Flute Conique** 73 pipes
- 8' **Geigen** 73 pipes
- 8' **Gedeckt** 73 pipes
- 8' **Viola da Gamba** 73 pipes
- 8' **Viole Celeste** 73 pipes
- 8' **Echo Viole** 73 pipes
- 4' **Octave Geigen** 73 pipes
- 4' **Fugara** 73 pipes
- 4' **Flute Triangulaire** 73 pipes
- $2^2/3$' **Nazard** 61 pipes
- 2' **Fifteenth** 61 pipes
- $1^3/5$' **Tierce** 61 pipes
- 6 rks **Plein Jeu** 366 pipes
- 8' **Vox Humana** 61 pipes
- 16' **Bombarde** 73 pipes
- 8' **First Trompette** 73 pipes
- 8' **Second Trompette** 73 pipes
- 4' **Clarion** 73 pipes

PROCESSIONAL (old Processional, revoiced and relocated; plays on Swell)
- 8' **Viole**
- 8' **Gedeckt**

POSITIF (unenc., $2^1/4$"* wind, Ch. man.)
- 8' **Rohrflöte** 61 pipes
- 4' **Principal** 61 pipes
- 4' **Koppel Flöte** 61 pipes
- $2^2/3$' **Nazard** 61 pipes
- 2' **Blockflöte** 61 pipes
- $1^3/5$' **Tierce** 61 pipes
- 1' **Sifflöte** 61 pipes
- 4 rks **Scharf** 244 pipes

CHOIR ($3^3/4$" wind*)
- 16' **Quintaton** 73 pipes
- 8' **Viola** 73 pipes
- 8' **Orchestral Flute** 73 pipes
- 8' **Dulciana** 73 pipes
- 8' **Unda Maris** 61 pipes
- 4' **Lieblichflöte** 73 pipes
- 2' **Zauberflöte** 61 pipes
- 16' **English Horn** 73 pipes
- 8' **Clarinet** 73 pipes
- 8' **Trompette Harmonique** 73

PEDAL (4" wind*)
- 32' **Contre Basse** 12 pipes
- 16' **Principal** 32 pipes
- 16' **Contre Basse** 32 pipes
- 16' **Bourdon** 32 pipes
- 16' **Flute Conique** (Swell)
- $10^2/3$' **Grosse Quint** 32 pipes
- 8' **Octave** 32 pipes
- 8' **Flute Ouverte** 32 pipes
- 8' **Gedeckt** (Swell)*
- 8' **'Cello** 12 pipes
- $5^1/3$' **Quint** 32 pipes
- 4' **Super Octave** 32 pipes
- 4' **Flute Harmonique** 32 pipes
- 4' **Klein Gedeckt** (Swell)*
- 3 rks **Mixture** 96 pipes
- 3 rks **Fourniture** 96 pipes
- 16' **Bombarde** 32 pipes
- 16' **English Horn** (Choir)
- 8' **Trompette** 32 pipes
- 4' **Clarion** 32 pipes

Sources: *Diapason*, 1 August 1935, p. 1; *pipe shop notes, July 7, 1935

Church of the Advent, Boston

Aeolian-Skinner, Opus 940, 1936

Contract signed November 1935,
Organ installed February, March 1936,
Dedicated April, 1936

GREAT 3" wind
- 16' **Diapason** 61
- 8' **Principal** 61
- 8' **Diapason** 61
- 8' **Flûte Harmonique** 61
- $5^1/3$' **Grosse Quint** 61
- 4' **Principal** 61
- 4' **Octave** 61
- $2^2/3$' **Quint** 61
- 2' **Super Octave** 61
- IV-V **Sesquialtera** 293
- IV **Fourniture** 244
- III **Cymbel** 183

SWELL $3^3/4$" wind
- 16' **Lieblich Gedeckt** 73
- 8' **Geigen** 73
- 8' **Viol-de-Gambe** 73
- 8' **Viole Celeste** 73
- 8' **Echo Salicional** 73

8' **Stopped Diapason** 73
4' **Geigen Octave** 73
4' **Fugara** 73
4' **Flauto Traverso** 73
2' **Fifteenth** 61
III **Grave Mixture** 183
III **Plein Jeu** 183
16' **Bombarde** 73
8' **Trompette I** 73
8' **Trompette II** 73
8' **Vox Humana** 73
4' **Clairon** 73
Tremolo
CHOIR 3³/4" wind
8' **Viola** 73
8' **Dolcan** 73
8' **Dolcan Celeste TC** 61
8' **Orchestral Flute** 73
4' **Zauberflöte** 73
8' **Clarinet** 73
8' **Unenclosed Trumpet** 73
POSITIV 2¹/4" wind
8' **Rohrflöte** 61
4' **Principal** 61

4' **Koppel Flöte** 61
2²/3' **Nazard** 61
2' **Blockflöte** 61
1³/5 **Tierce** 61
1' **Sifflöte** 61
IV **Scharf** 244
PEDAL 4" wind
32' **Sub Bass FFFF** 7
16' **Principal** 32
16' **Contre Basse** 32
16' **Bourdon** 32
16' **Echo Lieblich** Swell
8' **Principal** 32
8' **Flûte Ouverte** 32
8' **Still Gedeckt** Swell
5¹/3' **Quint** 32
4' **Principal** 32
4' **Flûte Harmonique** 32
III **Mixture** 96
II **Fourniture** 64
16' **Bombarde** 32
8' **Trompette** 32
4' **Clairon** 32
Source: pipe shop notes, Nov. 12, 1935

Washington Cathedral, Washington, D. C.

Ernest M. Skinner & Son, Methuen, Mass., 1937

GREAT
16' **Diapason** 61 pipes
8' **First Diapason** 61 pipes
8' **Second Diapason** 61 pipes
8' **Third Diapason** 61 pipes
5 rks **Muted String Ensemble**
(four 8' and one 4' rank)
8' **Principal Flute** 61 pipes
8' **Clarabella** 61 pipes
8' **Viola** 61 pipes
8' **Erzähler** 61 pipes
5¹/3' **Quinte** 61 pipes
4' **Octave** 61 pipes
4' **Principal** 61 pipes
4' **Harmonic Flute** 61 pipes
2²/3' **Twelfth** 61 pipes
2' **Fifteenth** 61 pipes
7 rks **Plein Jeu**
(15, 19, 22, 26, 29, 33, 36), 427 pipes
4 rks **Harmonics**
(17, 19, 21, 22) 244 pipes
3 rks **Cymbale***

16' **Posaune** 61 pipes
8' **Tromba** 61 pipes
8' **Tuba Mirabilis** (Solo)
8' **Trumpet** 61 pipes
4' **Clarion** 61 pipes
SWELL
16' **Dulciana** 73 pipes
16' **Bourdon** 73 pipes
8' **First Diapason** 73 pipes
8' **Second Diapason** 73 pipes
8' **Gedeckt** 73 pipes
8' **Claribel Flute** 73 pipes
8' **Viol d'Orchestre** 73 pipes
8' **Viol Celeste** 73 pipes
8' **Salicional** 61 pipes
8' **Voix Celestes** 73 pipes
8' **Flauto Dolce** 73 pipes
8' **Flute Celeste** 61 pipes
Muted String Ensemble
8' **Aeoline** 73 pipes
8' **Unda Maris** 73 pipes

454

4' **Octave** 73 pipes
4' **Gemshorn** 73 pipes
4' **Unda Maris** (2 rks) 122 pipes
4' **Violin** 73 pipes
4' **Flute Harmonique** 61 pipes
2²/₃' **Twelfth** 61 pipes
2' **Fifteenth** 61 pipes
5 rks **Full Mixture**
(15, 19, 22, 26, 29) 305 pipes
5 rks **Cornet** (1, 8, 12, 15, 17) 305 pipes
3 rks **Carillon** (12, 17, 22) 183 pipes
16' **Posaune** 73 pipes
8' **Trumpet** (light wind) 73 pipes
8' **Cornopean** 73 pipes
8' **Flügel Horn** 73 pipes
8' **Vox Humana** 73 pipes
4' **Clarion** 61 pipes
Tremolo

CHOIR
16' **Gemshorn** 73 pipes
8' **Diapason** 73 pipes
8' **Concert Flute** 73 pipes
8' **Gemshorn** 73 pipes
8' **Kleine Erzähler** (2 rks) 134 pipes
8' **Viol d'Orchestre** 73 pipes
8' **Viol Celeste** 73 pipes
Muted String Ensemble
4' **Harmonic Flute** 73 pipes
4' **Gemshorn** 73 pipes
4' **Violin** 73 pipes
2' **Piccolo** 61 pipes
2²/₃' **Nazard** 61 pipes
1³/₅' **Tierce** 61 pipes
1¹/₇' **Septième** 61 pipes
3 rks **Carillon**
(12, 17, 22) 183 pipes
8' **Trumpet**
(small orchestral type) 73 pipes
8' **Clarinet** 61 pipes
16' **Orchestral Bassoon** 61 pipes
8' **Orchestral Oboe** 61 pipes
Celesta 61 bars

SOLO
8' **Flauto Mirabilis** 73 pipes
8' **Gamba** 73 pipes
8' **Gamba Celeste** 73 pipes
4' **Orchestral Flute** 61 pipes

7 rks **Mixture** 427 pipes *[called "Compensating Mixture" in firm brochure]*
16' **Ophicleide** 73 pipes
8' **Tuba Mirabilis** 73 pipes
8' **Trumpet** 73 pipes
4' **Clarion** 61 pipes
8' **French Horn** 61 pipes
8' **Cor d'Amour** 61 pipes
8' **English Horn** 61 pipes
16' **Corno di Bassetto** 12 pipes
8' **Corno di Bassetto** 61 pipes

PEDAL
32' **Diapason** 12 pipes
32' **Violone** 12 pipes
16' **Diapason** 32 pipes
16' **Diapason (metal)** 32 pipes
16' **Contra Bass** 32 pipes
16' **Violone** 32 pipes
16' **Gemshorn** 32 pipes
16' **Dulciana** (Swell)
16' **Bourdon** 32 pipes
16' **Echo Lieblich** (Swell)
8' **Octave** 12 pipes
8' **Principal** (metal) 12 pipes
8' **Gemshorn** 12 pipes
8' **Gedeckt** 12 pipes
8' **'Cello** 12 pipes
5¹/₃' **Quinte**
8' **Still Gedeckt** (Swell)
4' **Super Octave** 32 pipes
4' **Still Flute** 32 pipes
5 rks **Mixture** (12, 15, 19, 22, 26)
5 rks **Harmonics**
32' **Bombarde** 12 pipes
32' **Fagotto** 12 pipes
16' **Trombone** 32 pipes
16' **Fagotto** 32 pipes
8' **Tromba** 12 pipes
8' **Fagotto** 12 pipes
4' **Clarion** 12 pipes
4' **Fagotto** 12 pipes

Full complement of couplers
10 combinations for Swell, Great, & Ped.
9 combinations for Choir and Solo
12 general pistons
Sources: *Diapason*, 1 March 1947, pp. 1-2;
* Ernest M. Skinner & Son brochure

Busch-Reisinger Museum of Germanic Culture ("Germanic")
Harvard University Cambridge, Massachusetts

Aeolian-Skinner Opus 951, 1936

HAUPTWERK
- 16' **Quintade** 61 pipes
- 8' **Principal** 61 pipes
- 8' **Spitzflöte** 61 pipes
- 4' **Principal** 61 pipes
- 4' **Rohrflöte** 61 pipes
- 2²/₃' **Quinte** 61 pipes
- 2' **Super Octave** 61 pipes
- 1¹/₃' **Fourniture** (4 rks) 244 pipes

POSITIV
- 8' **Koppel Flöte** 61 pipes
- 4' **Nachthorn** 61 pipes
- 2²/₃' **Nasat** 61 pipes
- 2' **Blockflöte** 61 pipes
- 1³/₅' **Terz** 61 pipes
- 1' **Sifflöte** 61 pipes
- ¹/₂' **Cymbel** (3 rks) 183 pipes
- 8' **Krummhorn** 61 pipes

PEDAL
- 16' **Bourdon** 32 pipes
- 8' **Gedeckt Pommer** 32 pipes
- 8' **Principal** 32 pipes
- 4' **Nachthorn** 32 pipes
- 2' **Blockflöte** 32 pipes
- 4' **Fourniture** (3 rks) 96 pipes
- 16' **Posaune** 32 pipes
- 8' **Trompete** 12 pipes
- 4' **Krummhorn** (from Pos.)

COUPLERS
- **Pos. to Ped.**
- **Haupt. to Ped.**
- **Pos. to Haupt.**
- **Pos. to Haupt. 16'**
- **8 general pistons**
- **Crescendo pedal**

Source: *Diapason*, 1 May 1937, p. 1.

Church of St. Mary the Virgin, New York City

Rebuilt Aeolian-Skinner 1943 from Aeolian-Skinner Opus 891, 1932

GREAT
- 16' **Principal** 61 pipes
- 16' **Quintaton** (Ped.)
- 8' **Montre** 61 pipes
- 8' **Bourdon** (metal) 61 pipes
- 8' **Quintaton** 61 pipes
- 5¹/₃' **Quint** 61 pipes
- 4' **Prestant** 61 pipes
- 4' **Flute Couverte** 61 pipes
- 3¹/₅' **Grosse Tierce** 61 pipes
- 2²/₃' **Octave Quint** 61 pipes
- 2' **Doublette** 61 pipes
- 5 rks **Harmonics** 305 pipes
- 3-5 rk **Fourniture** 245 pipes
- 3 rks **Cymbale** 183 pipes

SWELL
- 16' **Flûte Conique** 73 pipes
- 8' **Bourdon à Cheminée** 73 pipes
- 8' **Salicional** 73 pipes
- 8' **Voix Celeste** 73 pipes
- 8' **Viole Sourdine** 73 pipes
- 8' **Voix Aeolienne** 73 pipes
- 4' **Flûte Couverte** 73 pipes
- 4' **Salicet** 73 pipes
- 2²/₃' **Nazard** 61 pipes
- 2' **Salicetina** 61 pipes
- 3 rks **Cornet** 183 pipes
- 5 rks **Plein Jeu** 305 pipes
- 16' **Bombarde** 73 pipes
- 8' **Trompette** 73 pipes
- 4' **Clarion** 73 pipes
- 8' **Oboe** 73 pipes
- 8' **Vox Humana** 73 pipes

POSITIF
- 16' **Salicional** 73 pipes
- 8' **Flûte Traversiere** 73 pipes
- 8' **Viole** 73 pipes
- 8' **Viole Celeste** 73 pipes
- 8' **Gambe** 73 pipes
- 8' **Gambe Celeste** 73 pipes
- 4' **Principal** 73 pipes
- 4' **Flute d'Amour** 73 pipes
- 2²/₃' **Nazard** 61 pipes
- 2' **Piccolo** 61 pipes
- 1³/₅' **Tierce** 61 pipes
- 1¹/₃' **Larigot** 61 pipes

4 rks   **Cymbale** 244 pipes
  16'   **Musette** 73 pipes
   8'   **Cromorne** 73 pipes
   8'   **Clarinet** 73 pipes
   4'   **Chalumeau** 73 pipes
BOMBARDE
Prepared for, ten knobs
PEDAL
  16'   **Contre Basse** (wood) 32 pipes
  16'   **Principal** (Gt.)
  16'   **Quintaton** 32 pipes
  16'   **Salicional** (Pos.)
  16'   **Flûte Conique** (Sw.)
   8'   **Contre Basse** 12 pipes
   8'   **Quintaton** 12 pipes
   8'   **Salicional** (Pos.) 12 pipes
   8'   **Flûte Conique** (Sw.) 12 pipes
$5^{1}/3$'   **Octave Quint** 32 pipes

   4'   **Doublette** 32 pipes
   4'   **Contre Basse** 12 pipes
   4'   **Quintaton** 12 pipes
   4'   **Salicional** (Pos.) 12 pipes
   4'   **Flûte Conique** (Sw.)
   2'   **Quintaton** 12 pipes
4 rks   **Grand Cornet** 128 pipes
4 rks   **Fourniture**
2 rks   **Carillon**
  32'   **Contre Bombarde** lower octave
       Grand Cornet
  16'   **Bombarde** 32 pipes
  16'   **Musette** (Pos.)
   8'   **Trompette** 12 pipes
  16'   **Musette** (Pos.) *[sic, 8'?]*
   4'   **Clarion** 12 pipes
   4'   **Musette** (Pos.)
Source: *Diapason*, 1 March 1943

Cleveland Museum of Art, Cleveland, Ohio

E. M. Skinner Opus 333, 1922; Rebuilt Walter Holtkamp, 1946

GREAT
  16'   **Quintadena**
   8'   **Principal**
   8'   **Gedackt**
   8'   **Salicional**
   4'   **First Octave**
   4'   **Second Octave**
   4'   **Spitzflöte**
$2^{2}/3$'   **Quinte**
   2   **Super Octave**
4 rks   **Mixture**
4 rks   **Harmonics**
  16'   **Dulzian**
   8'   **Schalmey**
POSITIV (1933 reused)
   8'   **Copula**
   4'   **Principal**
   4'   **Rohrflöte**
$2^{2}/3$'   **Nazard**
   2'   **Doublette**
$1^{3}/5$'   **Tierce**
3 rks   **Fourniture**
CHOIR
   8'   **Concert Flute**
   8'   **Dulciana**
   8'   **Erzähler Celeste** (2 rks)

   4'   **Fugara**
   2'   **Flautino**
   8'   **Flugel Horn**
SWELL
   8'   **Geigen Principal**
   8'   **Flute à Cheminée**
   8'   **Gamba**
   8'   **Gamba Celeste**
   8'   **Quintaton**
   4'   **Octave Geigen**
   4'   **Bourdon**
   2'   **Octavlein**
   2'   **Blockflöte**
3 rks   **Dolce Cornet** ($2^{2}/3$, 2, $1^{3}/5$)
5 rks   **Plein Jeu**
  16'   **Contra Fagott**
   8'   **Trompette**
   8'   **Vox Humana**
   4'   **Clarion**
PEDAL
  32'   **Contrabass**
  16'   **Major Bass** (open wood)
  16'   **Subbass** (from Contrabass)
  16'   **Quintedena** (from Gt.)
  16'   **Lieblich Gedackt**
   8'   **Octave**

8' Gemshorn
8' Gedackt
5^1/$_3$' Quinte (stopped)
4' Choral Bass
4' Nachthorn (stopped)
2' Piccolo
3 rks Mixture (2^2/$_3$, 2, 1^1/$_3$)
16' Posaune

8' Dulzian (from Gt.)
8' Trumpet
4' Cromorne

Source: John Allen Ferguson, *Walter Holtkamp: American Organ Builder* (Kent, OH: Kent State University Press, 1979), pp. 112-113.

Methuen Memorial Music Hall, Methuen, Massachusetts

Rebuilt Aeolian-Skinner Opus 1103, 1947

GREAT
16' Principal 61 pipes
16' Viola Major 61 pipes
16' Bourdon 61 pipes
8' Principal 61 pipes
8' Gemshorn 61 pipes
8' Gedeckt 61 pipes
5^1/$_3$' Quint 61 pipes
4' Octave 61 pipes
4' Spitzflöte 61 pipes
4' Koppelflöte 61 pipes
4' Flute d'Amour 61 pipes
3^1/$_5$' Terz 61 pipes
2^2/$_3$' Quint 61 pipes
2' Super Octave 61 pipes
2' Waldflöte 61 pipes
1^3/$_5$' Terz 61 pipes
1^1/$_7$' Septième 61 pipes
4-6rk Cornet 311 pipes
4 rks Fourniture 244 pipes
4 rks Scharff 244 pipes
4 rks Kleine Mixtur 244 pipes

SWELL
8' Principal 61 pipes
8' Viole de Gambe 61 pipes
8' Viole Celeste 49 pipes
8' Flûte à Cheminée 61 pipes
8' Aeoline 61 pipes
4' Prestant 61 pipes
4' Flute Couverte 61 pipes
2^2/$_3$' Nazard 61 pipes
2' Piccolo 61 pipes
2' Octavin 61 pipes
1^3/$_5$' Tierce 61 pipes
4 rks Plein Jeu 244 pipes
16' Basson 61 pipes
8' Trompette 61 pipes

8' Hautbois 61 pipes
4' Clairon 61 pipes

CHOIR (enclosed)
16' Quintaten 61 pipes
8' Viola 61 pipes
8' Unda Maris 49 pipes
8' Konzert Flöte 49 pipes
4' Traverse Flöte 49 pipes
2' Gemshorn 49 pipes
3 rks Cymbel 171 pipes
16' Dulzian 61 pipes
8' Krummhorn 61 pipes
4' Regal 61 pipes

POSITIV (unenclosed)
8' Gedeckt 61 pipes
8' Quintaten 61 pipes
4' Principal 61 pipes
4' Nachthorn 61 pipes
2^2/$_3$' Nazard 61 pipes
2' Oktav 61 pipes
2' Blockflöte 61 pipes
1^3/$_5$' Tierce 61 pipes
1^1/$_3$' Quinta 61 pipes
1' Super Octave 61 pipes
3 rks Scharff 183 pipes
3 rks Zimbel 183 pipes

PEDAL
32' Principal 30 pipes
16' Principal 30 pipes
16' Contre Basse 30 pipes
16' Bourdon 30 pipes
16' Quintaten 30 pipes
16' Lieblich Gedeckt 30 pipes
8' Octave 30 pipes
8' 'Cello 30 pipes
8' Spitzflöte 30 pipes
5^1/$_3$' Quint 30 pipes

4'	Super Octave 30 pipes	16'	Bombarde 30 pipes
4'	Nachthorn 30 pipes	16'	Basson 30 pipes
3¹/₅'	Terz 30 pipes	8'	Trompette 30 pipes
2'	Waldflöte 30 pipes	4'	Clairon 30 pipes
4 rks	Grand Bourdon 120 pipes	2'	Rohr Schalmei 30 pipes
4 rks	Mixtur 180 pipes		Sources: *Diapason*, 1 August 1947, p. 1.
32'	Contre Bombarde 30 pipes		OHS *Convention Handbook*, 1978

Symphony Hall, Boston, Massachusetts
Aeolian-Skinner Opus 1134, 1950

GREAT

16'	Violone 61 pipes
8'	Principal 61 pipes
8'	Geigen 61 pipes
8'	Grossflöte 61 pipes
8'	Spitzflöte 61 pipes
5¹/₃'	Quint 61 pipes
4'	Principal 61 pipes
4'	Gemshorn 61 pipes
2²/₃'	Quint 61 pipes
2'	Super Octave 61 pipes
4 rks	Fourniture 244 pipes
3 rks	Cymbel 183 pipes

SWELL

16'	Contra Gamba 68 pipes
8'	Diapason 68 pipes
8'	Gedeckt 68 pipes
8'	Viole de Gambe 68 pipes
8'	Viole Celeste 68 pipes
8'	Aeoline 68 pipes
4'	Octave 68 pipes
4'	Flauto Traverso 68 pipes
2'	Fifteenth 61 pipes
3 rks	Grave Mixture 183 pipes
3 rks	Scharff 183 pipes
16'	Bombarde 68 pipes
8'	Trompette 68 pipes
8'	Hautbois 68 pipes
4'	Clarion 68 pipes
	Tremulant

CHOIR

8'	Viola Pomposa 68 pipes
8'	Viola Celeste 68 pipes
8'	Concert Flute 68 pipes
8'	Dulciana 68 pipes
4'	Prestant 68 pipes
4'	Koppelflöte 68 pipes
3 rks	Plein Jeu 183 pipes

16'	Serpent 68 pipes
8'	Trompette 68 pipes
4'	Cromorne 68 pipes
	Tremulant

POSITIV

8'	Spitzflöte 61 pipes
8'	Singend Gedeckt 61 pipes
4'	Nachthorn 61 pipes
2²/₃'	Nasat 61 pipes
2'	Blockflöte 61 pipes
1³/₅'	Terz 61 pipes
1'	Sifflöte 61 pipes
3 rks	Zimbel 183 pipes

BOMBARDE

6 rks	Plein Jeu 366 pipes
16'	Bombarde 61 pipes
8'	Trompette Harmonique 61 pipes
4'	Clarion Harmonique 61 pipes

PEDAL

32'	Contre Violone 12 pipes
16'	Contre Basse 32 pipes
16'	Montre 32 pipes
16'	Violone [Great]
16'	Bourdon 32 pipes
16'	Contra Gamba [Swell]
8'	Principal 32 pipes
8'	'Cello 32 pipes
8'	Spitzflöte 32 pipes
5¹/₃'	Quint 32 pipes
4'	Choral Bass 32 pipes
4'	Nachthorn 32 pipes
2'	Blockflöte 32 pipes
4 rks	Fourniture
32'	Contre Bombarde 12 pipes
16'	Bombarde 32 pipes
8'	Trompette 32 pipes [*sic, 12 pipes*]
4'	Clarion 32 pipes [*sic, 12 pipes*]

Source: *Diapason*, 1 September 1949, p. 1.

Royal Festival Hall, London, England

Harrison & Harrison, Ltd. Durham, England, 1954
Ralph Downes, Consultant

GREAT
- 16' Prestant
- 16' Bourdon
- 8' Diapason
- 8' Spitzgamba
- *8' Flute Harmonique
- 8' Bourdon
- 5¹/₃' Quintflöte
- 4' Octave
- 4' Gemshorn
- 4' Gedecktflöte
- 2²/₃' Quint
- 2' Octave
- 2' Blockflöte
- 1³/₅' Tierce
- 5 rks Mixture (15, 19, 22, 26, 29)
- 4 rks Scharf (26, 29, 33, 36)
- 5 rks Cornet* (1, 8, 12, 15, 17, mid C)
- *16' Bombarde
- *8' Trumpet
- 4' Clarion

SWELL
- 16' Quintadena
- 8' Major Principal
- 8' Holzprincipal
- *8' Rohrgedeckt
- 8' Viole de Gambe
- 8' Voix Celestes (AA)
- 4' Octave
- *4' Koppleflöte
- *2²/₃' Nazard (F)
- 2' Octave
- *2' Nachthorn
- *1³/₅' Tierce (F)
- 1' Flageolet
- 4 rks Mixture (22, 26, 29, 33)
- 3 rks Zimbel (38, 40, 43)
- *8' Hautbois
- *8' Vox Humana
- *16' Bombarde
- *8' Trumpet
- *4' Clarion

CHOIR (enclosed)
- 16' Salicional
- 8' Barpyp

- 8' Quintadena
- 8' Salicional
- 8' Unda Maris
- 4' Fugara
- 4' Rohrflöte
- 2' Waldflöte
- 1¹/₃' Quintflöte
- 1' Sifflöte
- 2 rks Sesquialtera (26, 31)
- 4 rks Mixture (29, 33, 36, 40)
- 16' Dulzian
- *8 Cromorne

POSITIV (unenclosed)
- 8' Prestant
- 8' Gedeckt
- 4' Prestant
- 4' Open Flute
- 2²/₃' Quintflöte
- 2' Octave
- 1³/₅' Tierce
- 1¹/₃' Larigot
- 5 rks Cornet (1, 8, 12, 15, 17, middle C)
- 5 rks Mixture (15, 19, 22, 26, 29)
- 5 rks Scharf (22, 26, 29, 33, 36)
- *8' Regal
- *8' Trumpet

SOLO
- *8' Flute Majeure
- 8' Violoncello
- 8' Violes Celestes (CC)
- 4' Flute Harmonique
- 2' Piccolo
- 8' Corno di Bassetto
- 8' Orchestral Oboe
- 8' French Horn
- 8' Trompette Harmonique
- 4' Clarion Harmonique

PEDAL
- 32' Prestant (20 from Gt.)
- 16' Major Bass
- 16' Prestant
- 16' Sub Bass
- 16' Quintadena (from Sw.)
- 16' Salicional (from Ch.)
- 10²/₃' Quintflöte

8' Open Flute
8' Gemshorn
8' Rohrgedeckt
8' Quintadena (from Sw.)
4' Open Flute
2' Nachthorn
2 rks Sesquialtera (12, 17)
2²/7' Septième
2 rks Rauschpfeife (19, 22)
4 rks Mixture (26, 29, 33, 36)
*32' Bombarde (20 from Gt.)
*16' Bombarde
16' Dulzian (from Gt.)
*8' Trumpet
*8' Regal (20 from Pos.)

*4' Clarion
*4' Regal (from Pos.)
*2' Kornett

Mechanicals: 8 pistons for each manual and eight generals. Gt., Sw., and General pistons duplicated by foot pistons. Wind pressures: Pedal: 3-4¹/2"; Pos.: 3¹/4"; Ch.: 3¹/4- & 3³/4"; Gt.: 3¹/2"; Sw.: 3³/4"; Solo, flue work, corno di bassetto and Orchestral oboe: 4"; trompette and clarion harmonique: 7"; French horn: 12".

* To be designed and voiced by M. Rochesson of Paris

Source: *Diapason*, 1 April 1950, p. 8.

Princeton University Chapel, Princeton, New Jersey
Aeolian-Skinner Opus 920, 1954, Rebuilt from Opus 656

GREAT

16' Diapason 61 pipes
16' Bourdon 61 pipes
16' Quintade 61 pipes
8' Principal 61 pipes
8' Geigen 61 pipes
8' Gedeckt 61 pipes
5¹/3' Quint
4' Octave 61 pipes
4' Doppelflöte 61 pipes
4' Principal Flute 61 pipes
4' Lieblich Flöte 61 pipes
3¹/5' Tenth 61 pipes
2²/3' Twelfth 61 pipes
2' Fifteenth 61 pipes
3-4rk Fourniture 267 pipes
3-6rk Cymbale 330 pipes
16' Basson 61 pipes
16' Contra-Tromba 61 pipes
8' Tromba 61 pipes
4' Octave Tromba 61 pipes

SWELL

16' Bourdon 73 pipes
8' Diapason 73 pipes
8' Principal Flute 73 pipes
8' Gamba 73 pipes
8' Gamba Celeste 73 pipes
8' Salicional 73 pipes
8' Voix Celeste 73 pipes

8' Flute 73 pipes
8' Flauto Dolce 73 pipes
8' Flute Celeste 73 pipes
8' Cor de Nuit 61 pipes
4' Flute Triangulaire 73 pipes
4' Principal 73 pipes
4' Cornet Eighth 61 pipes
2²/3' Cornet Twelfth 61 pipes
2' Piccolo 73 pipes
2' Cornet Fifteenth 61 pipes
3¹/5' Cornet Seventeenth 61 pipes
[sic 1⅗']
5 rks Mixture 305 pipes
5 rks Cornet [draws five stops]
16' Posaune 73 pipes
8' Trumpet 73 pipes
8' Cornopean 73 pipes
8' Oboe 73 pipes
8' Vox Humana 73 pipes
4' Clarion 73 pipes
Tremolo

CHOIR-BRUSTWERK

16' Gamba 12 pipes
8' Concert Flute 73 pipes
8' Dulciana 73 pipes
8' Dulciana Celeste 73 pipes
8' Viole d'Orchestre 73 pipes
8' Viole Celeste 73 pipes
4' Harmonic Flute 73 pipes

<table>
<tr><td>4'</td><td>Violina 73 pipes</td></tr>
</table>

4' Violina 73 pipes
16' Fagotto 73 pipes
8' French Trumpet 73 pipes
8' Orchestral Oboe 73 pipes
8' Corno di Bassetto 61 pipes
8' English Horn 61 pipes
Tremolo
(unenclosed)
8' Gedeckt 61 pipes
4' Quintadena 61 pipes
2' Principal 61 pipes
1^1/3' Nineteenth 61 pipes
1' Sifflöte 61 pipes
4 rks Cymbel 244 pipes
POSITIV-BOMBARDE
8' Gedecktpommer 61 pipes
4' Principal 61 pipes
4' Blockflöte 61 pipes
2^2/3' Nazard 61 pipes
2' Nachthorn 61 pipes
1^3/5' Tierce 61 pipes
1^1/3' Larigot 61 pipes
5 rks Scharf 305 pipes
8' Krummhorn 61 pipes
16' Contra Tuba 73 pipes
8' Tuba 73 pipes

8' Tuba Mirabilis 73 pipes
4' Tuba Clarion 73 pipes
PEDAL
32 Diapason 12 pipes *[open to GGGG]*
16' Diapason 32 pipes
16' Contra Bass 32 pipes
16' Diapason (Great)
16' Quintade
16' Gamba (Choir)
16' Echo Lieblich (Swell)
8' Principal Octave
8' Octave
8' Pommer
8' Quintade
8' Still Gedeckt *[Swell]*
5^1/3' Twelfth
4' Super Octave
5 rks Mixture 160 pipes
32' Bombarde 12 pipes
32' Contra-Fagotto 12 pipes
16' Tuba *[Solo]*
16' Trombone 32 pipes
16' Fagotto *[Choir]*
8' Tromba 32 pipes
4' Clarion 12 pipes

Source: *Diapason*, 1 November 1954, p. 1.

St. Paul's Church (Episcopal), Chestnut Hill, Philadelphia, Penn.

Aeolian-Skinner Op. 724-A, 1953, Enlarged 1956 Rebuilt from Op. 724, 1928

MANUAL I (unenclosed)
16' Quintaton 61 pipes
8' Prinzipal 61 pipes
8' Bourdon 61 pipes
4' Oktav 61 pipes
2^2/3' Quinte 61 pipes
2' Principal 61 pipes
1^1/3' Mixtur (IV-VI rks) 294 pipes
Scharff (IV rks) 244
16' Rankett 61 pipes
(enclosed)
Cornet (III rks) 183 pipes
16' Serpent 61 pipes
8' Cromorne 61 pipes
8' Régale 61 pipes
Tremulant (enclosed portion only)

MANUAL II
8' Gedeckt Pommer 61 pipes
4' Prinzipal 61 pipes
4' Koppelflöte 61 pipes
2' Blockflöte 61 pipes
2' Oktav 61 pipes
1^1/3' Larigot 61 pipes
1' Prinzipal 61 pipes
Sesquialter (II rks) 122 pipes
Zymbel (III-V rks) 263 pipes
8' Rohr Schalmei 61 pipes
Zymbelstern
Tremulant
MANUAL III
16' Gambe 61 pipes
8' Viole 61 pipes
8' Voix Éolienne (II rks) 110 pipes

462

8' **Flûte à Cheminée** 61 pipes
4' **Flûte Harmonique** 61 pipes
4' **Voix Éolienne** (II rks) 24 pipes
Plein Jeu (III rks) 183 pipes
Tremulant (Flue)
16' **Bombarde** 61 pipes
8' **Hautbois** 61 pipes
4' **Clarion** 61 pipes
Grand Cornet (IV-VI rks) 306
Tremulant (Reed)
Pedal
32' **Soubasse** 12 pipes
16' **Contre Basse** 32 pipes
16' **Violone** 32 pipes
16' **Quintatön** (Man. I)
16' **Gedeckt** 32 pipes

8' **Montre** 32 pipes
8' **Bordun** (Man. I)
4' **Prestant** 32 pipes
4' **Recorder** 32 pipes
2' **Cor-de-Nuit** 32 pipes
Rauschquinte (II rks) 64 pipes
Fourniture (II rks) 64 pipes
32' **Bombarde** 12 pipes
16' **Bombarde** 32 pipes
16' **Rankett** (Man. I)
8' **Trompette** 12 pipes
4' **Clarion** 12 pipes
2' **Zink** 32 pipes

Source: Advertisment, *Diapason*,
1 November 1955, p. 3.

Kresge Auditorium, Massachusetts Institute of Technology, Cambridge

Walter Holtkamp, 1955

GREAT
16' **Quintadena** 61 pipes
8' **Principal** 61 pipes
8' **Flute** 61 pipes
8' **Gedackt** 61 pipes
4' **Octave** 61 pipes
4' **Spitzflöte** 61 pipes
2' **Doublette** 61 pipes
$1^1/_3$' **Octave Quinte** 61 pipes
4 rks **Plein Jeu** 244 pipes
16' **Dulzian** 61 pipes
8' **Trumpet** 61 pipes
SWELL
8' **Rohrflöte** 61 pipes
8' **Gambe** 61 pipes
8' **Gambe Celeste** 56 pipes
8' **Dulciane** 61 pipes
4' **Octave Geigen** 61 pipes
4' **Bourdon** 61 pipes
2' **Flautino** 61 pipes
1' **Piccolo** 61 pipes
3 rks **Cymbal** 183 pipes
8' **Fagott** 61 pipes
4' **Clarion** 61 pipes
8' **Voix Humaine** 61 pipes

POSITIV
8' **Copula** 56 pipes
4' **Praestant** 56 pipes
4' **Rohrflöte** 56 pipes
$2^2/_3$' **Nazard** 56 pipes
2' **Flute** 56 pipes
2' **Octava** 56 pipes
$1^3/_5$' **Tierce** 56 pipes
3 rks **Fourniture** 168 pipes
8' **Cromorne** 56 pipes
PEDAL
16' **Principal** 32 pipes
16' **Subbass** 51 pipes [sic?]
16' **Quintadena** (from Gt.)
8' **Octave** 32 pipes
8' **Gedackt** 32 pipes
4' **Choralbass** 32 pipes
4' **Nachthorn** 32 pipes
3 rks **Mixture** 96 pipes
32' **Cornet** 160 pipes
16' **Posaune** 32 pipes
16' **Dulzian** (from Gt.)
8' **Trumpet** 32 pipes
4' **Schalmey** 32 pipes

Source: *Diapason*, 1 December 1955, p. 1.

Preface to
Skinner & Aeolian-Skinner Pipe Shop Notes

The scale sheets are taken from factory records of "pipe shop notes" — instructions to pipe shops and voicing rooms. They provide a view not of complete instruments, but of organs under construction. Just as the letters of Willis, Harrison and Skinner illustrate their personalities, these shop notes show how their tonal designs differed over thirty years. Occasionally, an organ's design was altered in the factory; more often, individual ranks were replaced on the job and pressures changed by the designers. Hence, specifications appearing in organ journals do not always provide the details of a finished organ. Additionally, most organs had a full complement of couplers and accessories which were seldom listed in printed accounts. Nomenclature and spelling also sometimes differed slightly on the drawknobs.

Skinner and Aeolian-Skinner Pipe Shop Notes

Opus 584 — Holy Trinity Episcopal Church, Havana, Cuba

Source: pipe shop notes dated February 17, 1926

Great Organ — 61 pipes

8'	Diapason	43 sc
8'	Gedeckt	(Swell)
8'	Aeoline	(Swell)
4'	Flute	(Swell)
	Chimes	20 tubes, prepared for

Swell Organ — 73 pipes

8'	Gedeckt	com. wood
8'	Salicional	64
8'	Voix Celeste	64
8'	Aeoline	60
4'	Flute	common
	Tremolo	

Pedal Organ — 32 notes

16'	Bourdon	#2 wood
8'	Gedeckt	ext. wood
	Chimes	prepared for

Opus 699 — St. Luke's Cathedral, Portland, Maine

Source: pipe shop notes dated February 27, 1928

Great Organ — 61 pipes, 6" pressure

16'	Bourdon	(Pedal extension)	
8'	First Diapason	42 sc, 1/5	Metal
8'	Second Diapason	42 sc, 1/4	Metal
8'	Flute Harmonique	new scale	Metal
8'	String Celeste II	60 sc, in Choir, 15" wind	Metal
4'	Principal	57 sc	Metal
4'	Flute		Metal
2'	Fifteenth	70 sc	Metal
8'	Tuba	in Choir, 15" wind	Metal
8'	French Horn	in Choir, 15" wind	Metal
	Chimes (prepared for)		

Swell Organ — 73 pipes, 7½" pressure

16'	Bourdon	D B	Wood
8'	Diapason	45 sc, 1/4	Metal
8'	Rohrflute	com.	Metal
8'	Salicional	64 sc	Metal
8'	Voix Celeste	64 sc	Metal
8'	Flute Celeste II	com., 134 pipes	Metal
4'	Octave	58 sc	Metal
4'	Flute Triangulaire	com.	Wood
V	Mixture	15.19.22.26.29 C-4	Metal
16'	Waldhorn		Metal
8'	Cornopean	Eng.	Metal

8'	Oboe d'Amore	com.	Metal
8'	Vox Humana	com.	Metal
4'	Clarion	Eng.	Metal
	Tremolo		

Choir Organ — 73 pipes, 6" pressure

8'	Geigen	46 sc	Metal
8'	Concert Flute	#1	Metal
8'	Dulciana	56 sc	Metal
8'	Unda Maris	56 sc, 61 pipes	Metal
4'	Flute	com.	Metal
2⅔'	Nazard	61 pipes	Metal
8'	Corno di Bassetto	com.	Metal
8'	Harp		
4'	Celesta	61 bars	
	Tremolo		
8'	Tuba (Great) not subject to Choir to Great coupler		

Pedal Organ — Augmented — 32 pipes

32'	Resultant		
16'	Diapason	52x56	Wood
16'	Contre Basse	58x62 com., bearded	Wood
16'	Bourdon	#2	Wood
16'	Lieblich	(Swell)	
8'	Octave	12 pipes	
8'	Cello	12 pipes	
8'	Gedeckt	12 pipes	
8'	Still Gedeckt	(Swell)	
16'	Trombone	8" sc, 12" wind	Metal
16'	Waldhorn	(Swell)	
	Chimes		

CHAPEL ORGAN — with separate console and also playable from Swell and Great manuals of main organ

Great Organ — 73 pipes

8'	Diapason	45 sc	Metal
8'	Gedeckt	(Swell)	
8'	Vox Angelica II	(Swell)	
4'	Flute	(Swell)	

Swell Organ — 73 pipes

16'	Bourdon	#2	Wood
8'	Gedeckt	com. Rohr.	Metal
8'	Vox Angelica II	60, 134 pipes	Metal
4'	Flute	#2	Metal
8'	Trumpet	com. Eng.	Metal
	Tremolo		

Pedal Organ — 32 pipes

16'	Bourdon	#3	Wood
16'	Lieblich Gedeckt	(Swell)	

Opus 718 — Charles E. Bedaux, Château de Candé, Monts, France

Source: pipe shop notes dated November 20, 1928

Manual I — 73 pipes, 7½" pressure

8'	Diapason	44sc, ¼	Expression I	Metal
8'	Gedeckt	Rohrflute	Expression I	Metal
8'	Salicional	64sc	Expression I	Metal
8'	Voix Celeste	64sc	Expression I	Metal
8'	Flute Celeste II	new GDH	Expression I	Metal
4'	Octave	58sc	Expression I	Metal
III	Mixture	C-14	Expression I	Metal
8'	Cornopean	Eng.	Expression I	Metal
8'	Harp	61 bars	Expression I	
4'	Celesta	--	Expression I	
	Tremolo			

Manual II — 7½" pressure

8'	Diapason	48sc, ¼ spotted	Expression II	Metal
8'	Chimney Flute	com	Expression II	Metal
8'	Cello	60sc	Expression II	Metal
8'	Cello Celeste	60sc	Expression II	Metal
4'	Flute Harmonique	new	Expression II	Metal
2'	Piccolo	common	Expression II	Metal
8'	Corno d'Amore	common	Expression II	Metal
16'	Bassoon	common	Expression II	Metal
8'	French Horn	residence org sc.	Expression II	Metal
8'	English Horn	common	Expression II	Metal
8'	Clarinet	common	Expression II	Metal
8'	Tuba	harm. Tenor F#, 10" wind	Expression II	Metal
8'	Vox Humana	common	Expression II	Metal
	Carillon Chimes	electric 20 notes		
	Tremolo			

Manual III

8'	Diapason	Expression I
8'	Gedeckt	Expression I
8'	Salicional	Expression I
8'	Voix Celeste	Expression I
8'	Flute Celeste II	Expression I
4'	Octave	Expression I
III	Mixture	Expression I
8'	Cornopean	Expression I
8'	Harp	Expression I
4'	Celesta	Expression I
8'	Diapason	Expression II
8'	Chimney Flute	Expression II
8'	Cello	Expression II
8'	Cello Celeste	Expression II
4'	Flute Harmonique	Expression II
2'	Piccolo	Expression II
8'	Corno d'Amore	Expression II

16'	Bassoon	Expression II	
8'	French Horn	Expression II	
8'	English Horn	Expression II	
8'	Clarinet	Expression II	
8'	Tuba	Expression II	
8'	Vox Humana	Expression II	
	Carillon Chimes		
	Tremolo		

Pedal Organ — 32 pipes

16'	Bourdon	#2	Wood
8'	Gedeckt	ext.	Wood
16'	Contra Bass	42 metal Violone pipes	Metal
8'	Cello	ext.	Metal
16'	Bassoon	Manual II	
16'	Trombone	6" sc, 10" wind	Metal
	Carillon Chimes		
	Drum — roll		
	Drum — strike		

Note: *Marcel Dupré played this organ at the wedding of the Duke of Windsor and Wallace Simpson in June, 1937.*

Opus 886 — Memorial Church, Harvard Univ., Cambridge, Mass.

Source: pipe shop notes dated March 12, 1932

* = prepared for

Great Organ — 61 pipes, 4½" main chest pressure, 3¾" offsets, 7" reeds

32'	Violone*	#28 at CCCC	Metal
16'	Diapason	#44 at CC, 2⁄9 mouth throughout	Metal
16'	Bourdon	Unit A Bass, Rohrflote from 4'C up	Std. Wood & Metal
10⅔'	Double Quint*	Com. Rohr. to 4'C, #2 wood bass	Std. Wood & Metal
8'	Diapason I	#42 — ¼ mouth, full, spotted	Metal
8'	Diapason II	#43 — ⅕ mouth	Metal
8'	Diapason III	#44 — 2⁄9 mouth, spotted	Metal
8'	Gemshorn	Erzahler, common	Metal
8'	Viola*	#50 — ⅕ mouth, spotted	Metal
8'	Flute Harmonique	Gt. type similar to Girard	Metal
8'	Stopped Diapason	as at Sacred Heart, Pittsburgh	Std. Wood
5⅓'	Quint	#52 — 2⁄9 mouth spotted open	Metal
4'	Octave	#54 — ¼ mouth spotted	Metal
4'	Principal	#57 — 2⁄9 mouth spotted	Metal
4'	Flute Couverte	common wood Gedeckt scale	Std. Metal
3⅕'	Grosse Tierce	#67 — 2⁄9 mouth spotted	Metal
2⅔'	Octave Quint	#69 — ¼ mouth spotted	Metal
2²⁄₇'	Grosse Septieme*	#72 — 2⁄9 mouth spotted	Metal
2'	Super Octave	#70 — ¼ mouth spotted	Metal
2'	Fifteenth*	#70 — ⅕ mouth spotted	Metal
VI	Harmonics	12.15.17.19.21b.22 366 pipes D-10	Metal
V	Fourniture	19.22.24.26.29 305 pipes E-9	Metal
16'	Double Trumpet	Eng. Waldhorn spotted 4'C up	Metal
8'	Tromba*	5" scale harm. at mid. F# Eng. sh.	Metal

8'	Trumpet	Eng. 4½ New sc. sh. spotted 4'C	Metal
4'	Clarion	Eng. 4½ New sc. sh. spotted 4'C	Metal

Swell Organ — 73 pipes, 6" pressure

16'	Contra Geigen	#39 for lower 18, then #56 at No.19	Metal
16'	Double Melodia*	#2 open throughout	Open Wood
8'	Diapason	#44 — 2⁄9 mouth	Metal
8'	Geigen	#46 — ¼ mouth spotted	Metal
8'	Salicional	#64 — ⅙ mouth	Metal
8'	Voix Celeste	#64 — ⅙ mouth	Metal
8'	Claribel Flute	#3	Open Wood
8'	Flute a Cheminee	common chimney flute	Std. Metal
8'	Melodia pp	#3 melodia	Open Wood
8'	Flute Celeste pp	#3 melodia	Open Wood
8'	Aeoline ppp	#56	Metal
8'	Unda Maris ppp	#56	Metal
5⅓'	Quint Flöte	Com. Rohr. carried down 5 in metal	Metal
4'	Octave	#57 — ¼ mouth spotted	Metal
4'	Viola	#66 — ⅕ mouth spotted	Metal
4'	Flute Triangulaire	common	Metal *(sic)*
2⅔'	Nazard	(Gem. mp) common gemshorn scale	Metal
2'	Octavin	(Gem. mp) common gemshorn scale	Metal
IV	Mixture	12.15.19.22 244 pipes C-8	Metal Diapason
VIII	Plein Jeu	12.15.19.22.26.29.33.36 488 E-8	Metal Reed Chorus
16'	Double Trumpet	Eng. spotted 4'C up as Hartford	Metal
8'	Trumpet (French)	New 4½ slightly larger in treble than recent samples	Metal
8'	Cornopean	Eng. original scale shallots with English openings	Metal
8'	Oboe	common	Metal
8'	Vox Humana*	lift cap, 61 pipes	Metal
4'	Clarion	English, same as Cornopean	Metal
		Tremulant	

Choir Organ — 73 pipes, 5" pressure

16'	Contra Dulciana	changed to 16' Gemshorn for 24 lower #40, 4'C up as at Trinity, Hart.	Metal
16'	Lieblich Gedeckt	Unit A, lower 24 Rohrflote 2 small tenor C up with solid stoppers	Std. Wood & Metal
8'	Diapason	#43 — ⅕ mouth	Metal
8'	Viola	#52 — ⅕ mouth spotted changed to 52 sc. Gems.	Metal
8'	Dulcet II	as in old organ, common	Metal
8'	Erzahler	common Kleine type	Metal
8'	Erzahler Celeste	ditto, 61 pipes	Metal
8'	Concert Flute	common, as in old organ	Wood
8'	Lieblich Gedeckt	com. Rohrflote, solid bungs	Std. Metal
4'	Octave	#58 — ⅕ mouth	Metal
4'	Viola	#66 — ⅕ mouth changed to #64 gemshorn	Metal
4'	Lieblichflote	Rohrflote 2 small, solid bungs	Std. Metal
2⅔'	Nazard	Rohrflote 4 small, 61 pipes	Std. Metal
2'	Flautino	Gemshorn common scale, 61 pipes	Metal
1⅗'	Tierce	Gemshorn common scale	Metal
1⅓'	Larigot	Rohrflote 6 small, 61 pipes	Std. Metal

1'	Piccolo	common gemshorn scale	Metal
V	Sesquialtera	12.15.17.19.22, H-2	Metal
16'	Contra Fagotto	common fagotto, not orchestral	Metal
8'	Trompette	common 4½" French with Cavaille-Coll shallots, spotted 4'C up	Metal
8'	Corno-di-Bassetto	common	Metal
8'	Corno d'Amore	common	Metal
4'	Clarion	Eng. original scale shallots	Metal
		Tremulant	

Solo Organ — 73 pipes, 7½" pressure, chorus reeds and F. Horn 12" wind

8'	Diapason	#42, ¼ mouth spotted from tenor C	Metal
8'	Major Flute	Flauto Mirabilis	Wood
8'	Gamba*	#60	Metal
8'	Gamba Celeste*	#60	Metal
4'	Octave	#56 — 2⁄9 mouth	Metal
4'	Orchestral Flute*	common	Wood
8'	French Horn	extra smooth, com. large scale	Metal
8'	English Horn*	common	Metal
VII	Grande Fourniture	12.15.17.19.22.26.29 F-3, 427 pipes	Metal
16'	Posaune	6½" at CCC, Eng. wald shallots	Metal
8'	Tuba	similar to Yale Solo Tuba common Eng. harmonic tenor F#	Metal
5⅓'	Quint Horn	com. Eng. Trumpet 12"	Metal
4'	Tuba Clarion	similar to Yale Solo Tuba common Eng. harmonic low F#	Metal
8'	Trompette en Chamade*		
4'	Clarion en Chamade*	5" scale as Tuba, harmonic tenor F# French shallots, spotted metal from 4'C up as Tuba. Tubes to be hooded.	Metal

Pedal Organ — 32 pipes, 3-¾" pressure flues, 12" pressure reeds

32'	Open Wood	bearded, same as Trinity Hart. 12 pipes from Contre Basse	
32'	Soubasse	Major Bass scale	12 pipes
32'	Violone*	Great	
21⅓'	Double Quint*	Unit A carried down	12 pipes
16'	Open Wood	very large scale, 14" x 16"	32 pipes
16'	Diapason	open metal, #26 — 2⁄9 mouth	32 pipes
16'	Contre Basse	10" x 12" bearded	32 pipes
16'	Bourdon	1-A	32 pipes
16'	Dulciana	Choir	
16'	Violone*	Great	
16'	Geigen	Swell	
16'	Lieblich Bourdon	Choir	
10⅔'	Quint*	Unit A scale	32 pipes
8'	Octave	from Contre Basse, metal at 4' C	12 pipes
8'	Principal	#40 — ¼ mouth spotted	32 pipes
8'	Cello*	Great	
8'	Flute	#2 Melodia	32 pipes
8'	Octave Geigen	Swell	
8'	Lieblich Gedeckt	Choir	
6⅖'	Tierce*	#52 — 1⁄5 mouth spotted	32 pipes

5⅓'	Octave Quint*	from Quint	12 pipes
4'	Super Octave	#54 — ¼ mouth spotted	32 pipes
4'	Flute	from Bourdon	24 pipes
4'	Lieblichflote	Choir	
2'	Waldflote*	#3 Melodia, wood open	32 pipes
V	Harmonics	15.17.19.b21.22 K-6	160 pipes
32'	Bombarde	metal 12", shallots like Hartford	12 pipes
16'	Trombone	8" metal common	32 pipes
16'	Bombarde	8" metal E.M.S. #2	32 pipes
16'	Posaune	Solo	
16'	Trumpet	Swell	
8'	Tromba	5" metal E.M.S. #2 shallots	32 pipes
8'	Trumpet	Swell	
4'	Clarion	English Trumpet harmonic treble	32 pipes
2'	Clarino*	ditto harmonic treble	32 pipes

SPECIAL PROVISIONS

General Considerations

1. The agent for the Skinner Company shall be G. Donald Harrison.
2. The organ is to be finished to the satisfaction of Dr. Davison.
3. The quality of the craftsmanship shall be equal; and, as indicated, below, superior to that of the best Skinner work in the past.
4. The ensemble shall be generally less brilliant in the trebles and upper work than that of recent Skinner work — i.e. less brilliant than that at St. Peter's, Morristown; the west-end organ, Grace Church, N.Y.C., Dwight Chapel, New Haven.

Mechanical Considerations

5. There shall be no noisy action and no sluggish and windy basses.
6. All contacts in the organ, whether for keys, couplers, stops, swell-shoes, or relays, shall be made of sterling silver.
7. There shall be no off-set tubular action. All off-set basses shall be operated electrically from relays through stop switches. The relays shall be located at, or near, the chest primary valve.
8. The Swell Organ shall be fitted with a double set of swell shutters — one behind the other.
9. All swell motors shall have at least 16 stations.

Console Design

10. The console shall be similar in size to that at Grace Church, N.Y.C. The Skinner Co. shall submit drawings for the console before beginning its construction. A model of the key action shall also be submitted.
11. The contract price shall cover space in the console for an Antiphonal Organ of not less than two manuals with forty manual stops and fifteen Pedal stops. The particulars about the Antiphonal Organ shall be arranged before the construction of console begins. It is understood that this provision covers the employment of the main organ couplers to control the Antiphonal Organ.

Completion of the Organ

12. Subject to delays in the construction of the Chapel, the installation shall begin on the 20th of June and the rough tuning shall be completed by the 20th of September, 1932.

The organ was dedicated by Clarence Watters:

Fantasia and Fugue in g minor	Bach
Noels sur les Flutes	d'Aquin
Chorale in b minor	Franck

Scherzetto in f# minor		Vierne
Variations sur un Noel		Dupré
"A Rose Breaks Forth"		Brahms
Vivace from Sixth Trio Sonata		Bach
"Christ Lay in Bonds of Death"		Bach
Passacaglia and Fugue		Bach

Opus 892 — Northrop Auditorium, Univ. of Minnesota, Minneapolis

Source: pipe shop notes dated October 1, 1932

Great Organ — 61 pipes, 4" pressure, *enclosed

16'	Diapason	#28 to #45 at mid. C
8'	Diapason I	#40 — 2/9 common metal
8'	Diapason II	#42 — 1/4 spotted metal
8'	Diapason III	#43 — 1/5 common metal
8'	Viola	#50 — tapered 2 scales, spotted 2/9 mouth
8'	Gemshorn	Erzahler, common
8'	Flute Harmonique	#1
8'	Gedeckt*	#2 new stopped diapason, 16 wood 45 metal
5 1/3'	Quint	#50 at mouth, 2/3 at top, 2/9 spotted
4'	Octave	#54
4'	Second Octave	#56
4'	Flute*	same as Great Principal Flute #2
3 1/5'	Tenth	#65 — 2/9 mouth spotted
2 2/3'	Twelfth	#69
2'	Fifteenth	#70
IV	Harmonics	D-7
VII	Plein Jeu*	same as Severance Hall E-6 special
16'	Contra Tromba*	common, 12" wind
8'	Tromba*	common, 12" wind
4'	Octave Tromba*	common, 12" wind
	Harp	Choir
	Celesta	Choir
	Chimes	Solo

Swell Organ — 73 pipes, 6" pressure

16'	Bourdon	A Unit
16'	Gemshorn	#34, 2/3 taper, 1/5 mouth spotted 4'C up
8'	Geigen Diapason	#44, 1/4 mouth, common metal
8'	Salicional	#60
8'	Voix Celeste	#60
8'	Echo Gamba	#64
8'	Echo Celeste	#64
8'	Flauto Dolce	common
8'	Flute Celeste	common
8'	Hohlflute	#1 Melodia
8'	Rohrflute	4 scales larger than normal
4'	Octave Geigen	#57, 1/4 mouth, spotted
4'	Violina	#72, 1/6 mouth
4'	Flute	common triangulaire

2⅔'	Twelfth	#65, ¼ mouth
2'	Fifteenth	#68, ¼ mouth
V	Dolce Cornet	8.15.19.22.24 12 pipes, then 1.8.12.15.17, all #50
V	Chorus Mixture	C-3
16'	Posaune	E.M.S. #2
8'	Cornopean	E.M.S. #2
8'	French Trumpet	same as Aeolian
8'	Oboe	common
8'	Vox Humana	lift cap
4'	Clarion	E.M.S. #2
	Harp	Choir
	Celesta	Choir
	Tremolo	

Choir Organ — 73 pipes, 6" pressure

16'	Contra Viole	#50
8'	Diapason	#46
8'	Dulcet II	two #75 scales
8'	Dulciana	#56
8'	Unda Maris	#56
8'	Concert Flute	common
8'	Cor de Nuit	common <u>thin</u> spotted metal
4'	Gemshorn	#56 at mouth, ½ taper, ¼ mouth
4'	Flute	d'amour
2⅔'	Nazard	rohr 4 small
2'	Piccolo	common
1⅗'	Tierce	gemshorn common
1⅓'	Larigot	new tapered scale like 936 Tierce
III	Dulciana Mixture	15.19.22
16'	Fagotto	common, not orchestral
8'	Trumpet	English low pressure
8'	Clarinet	Corno scale without bells
8'	Orchestral Oboe	common
	Harp	Skinner
	Celesta	Skinner
	Tremolo	

Solo Organ — 73 pipes, 10" pressure, Tubas and French Horn 20" pressure

16'	Contra Gamba	#48, 2/9 spotted
8'	Gamba	#54, 2/9 spotted
8'	Gamba Celeste	#54, 2/9 spotted
8'	Ætherial Cel. II	#64, 1/6 spotted
8'	Flauto Mirabilis	common with let in metal mouth
4'	Octave Gamba	#68
4'	Orchestral Flute	common with let in metal mouth
III	Cornet des Violes	10.12.15 no breaks, all #50 scale at 8' CC
16'	Corno di Bassetto	as Girard College
8'	English Horn	common
8'	French Horn	common, 20" wind
8'	Tuba Mirabilis	French shallots, harmonic trebles
4'	Tuba Clarion	" "

	Tremolo	
	Chimes	
	Harp	Choir
	Celesta	Choir

Pedal Organ — 32 pipes, 6" pressure, reeds 15" pressure

32'	Dbl. Open Diapason	bearded Contre Basse 40x44
32'	Sub Bourdon	A1 carred down 5 pipes, rest resultant
16'	Diapason	48x52
16'	Contre Basse	24 metal trebles
16'	Metal Diapason	5" pressure, #26, 2⁄9 low cut up, foot 50% longer
16'	Diapason	from Great
16'	Bourdon	1A
16'	Contra Viole	from Choir
16'	Gamba	from Solo
16'	Echo Lieblich	from Swell
16'	Gemshorn	from Swell
8'	Octave	from 16' wood
8'	Cello	from Contre Basse
8'	Gedeckt	1A carried up
8'	Viole	from Choir
8'	Still Gedeckt	from Swell
4'	Super Octave	from Metal Diapason, 24 pipes, #58 scale
4'	Flute	1A carried up
V	Harmonics	15.17.19.b21.22 on #50 scale
32'	Bombarde	Metal 12" scale and shallots, from 16'
32'	Contra Fagotto	from Choir, 8" CCCC, pocket in shallots, 6" pressure
16'	Trombone	8" metal
16'	Fagotto	from Choir
16'	Posaune	from Swell
8'	Tromba	ext. 16'
4'	Clarion	ext. 8'

Opus 948 — St. Mark's Church, Philadelphia, Pennsylvania

Source: pipe shop notes dated June 24, 1936

Great Organ — 61 pipes, 3" pressure

16'	Principal	lower 24 old, #34 sc. ¼m, spotted, ½ 17th note
8'	Principal	lower 12 old, #43 sc. ¼m, spotted, ½ 18th note
8'	Diapason	#45 sc., 2⁄9 m, spotted, ½ 17th note
8'	Gemshorn	Flauto Dolce spotted
8'	Flute Harmonique	new metal Std. Diap. 2 sc. small, wood bass, ¼m, spotted, low cut *[called Bourdon in* The Diapason, *April, 1937]*
4'	Principal	#54 sc. ¼m, spotted, ½ 18th note, 1'C up coned
[4'	Octave	*This stop appears in addition to the other two 4' stops in* The Diapason, *April, 1937, but not in the shop notes.]*
4'	Gemshorn	common Flauto Dolce
2⅔'	Quint	#66 sc., ¼m, spotted, ½ 17th note, 1'C up coned
2'	Super Octave	#68 sc., ¼m, spotted, ½ 17th note, 1'C up coned

III-V	Cornet	unisons and quints #44sc @ 8'CC, ¼m, ½ on 19th, tierce #74, ⅕m, ½ on 19th, all tin, 1'C up coned

12.15.17	12
8.12.15.17	12
1.8.12.15.17	24
SU.1. 5. 8.12	13

[The III-V Cornet is called "Full Mixture, 3 to 5 rks.," 8 ft." but its composition is not specified in The Diapason, *April, 1937.]*

IV	Fourniture	#48 sc @ 8'CC, ¼m ½ on 19th tin, 1'C up coned

15.19.22.26	12
12.15.19.22	18
8.12.15.19	6
1.8.12.15	18
SU. 1. 5. 8	7

III	Cymbel	#50 @ 8'CCsc, ¼m, ½ on 19th tin, 1'C up coned

22.26.29	18
19.22.26	12
15.19.22	6
12.15.19	6
8.12.15	12
1. 8.12	7

| | String Organ |
| | Chimes |

Swell Organ — 73 pipes, 5" pressure +3¾" pressure

16'	Flute Conique	3¾", as Groton, #36 at mouth, ⅔ taper at top
8'	Geigen	3¾", #46sc, ¼m spotted ½ on 18th note
8'	Viole-de-Gambe	3¾", #56sc, ¼m spotted
8'	Viole Celeste	3¾", #56sc, ¼m spotted
8'	Rohrflöte	5", common metal Std. Diap. ¼m
4'	Octave Geigen	3¾", #58sc, ¼m, spotted, ½] on 18th note, 1'C coned
4'	Fugara	5", #65sc, ⅕m, spotted
4'	Flute Triangulaire	5", common, new large bass
2⅔'	Nazard	5", com. Std. Diap. ¼m, tapered treble at open pipes
2'	Fifteenth	5", #70 sc, ⅕m. ½ 18th note, top 5 notes break back
1⅗'	Tierce	5", #66-78-90-106 (straight pipes)-120 (top octave repeats) <u>very low</u> cut-up, ⅔ diam. at top, spotted
III	Mixture	#48sc @ 8'CC, ¼m ½ on 19th tin, 1'C up coned

19.22.26	12
15.19.22	18
12.15.19	12
8.12.15	6
1.8.12	13

III	Cymbel	#50sc @ 8'CC, ½ on 18th, ¼m, spotted-coned

29.33.36	12
26.29.33	6
22.26.29	6
19.22.26	6
15.19.22	6
12.15.19	6
8.12.15	19

16'	Bombarde	3¾" as Advent, CCC=4⅞", CC=3¾" (small sc)
8'	Trompette	5" new small sc. French shallots 4'C up spotted
8'	Trumpet	3¾" Eng. small sc. Trumpet light pres. opening in shal.

4'	Clairon	5" as 8' Trompette. French shallots
	String Organ	
	Tremolo	

Choir and Lady Chapel Screen Organs
Choir section (enclosed) — 73 pipes, 5" pressure

16'	Contra Viola	Old Swell Contre Gambe, #40sc
8'	Viola	#52 sc., ¼m, spotted
8'	Dolcan	#52 sc., ⅕m, spotted
8'	Dolcan Celeste	61 pipes, #52 sc., ⅕m, spotted
8'	Nachthorn	as Gt. Nachthorn for Wellesley 2 sc large, wood Mel. open bass
4'	Viola	#64 sc., ⅕m spotted
4'	Zauberflöte	as Advent Choir
[16'	Krummhorn	*This stop appears in addition to the other reeds in* The Diapason, *April, 1937, but replaced proposed 8' Clarinet.]*
8'	Trompette	small French Trompette from Choir of op. 943 *[Wellesley]*
8'	Clarinet	Common, no bells *[organ built with 16' Krummhorn instead]*
	String Organ	
	Tremolo	

Screen Section (unenclosed) — 61 pipes, 4 ⅛" pressure, old

8'	Diapason	
8'	Dulciana	
4'	Gemshorn	
2⅔'	Nazard	
2'	Piccolo	

Positiv and Bombarde Organ (4th manual)
Positive section (unenclosed) — 61 pipes, 2 ½" pressure

8'	Singend Gedackt	#1 stopped wood bass. Tenor C up 4 scales larger than common wood gedackt. Low cut-up. stopped wood to 4'C.
4'	Prinzipal	#56 sc., ¼m, ½ 18th note. very low cut-up
4'	Koppel Flöte	Tin. all as Advent, very low cut-up
2⅔'	Nasat	#60-66-78-90-102-120. All ⅔m. diam at top except top octave which has straight pipes. very low cut-up, tin.
2'	Blockflöte	#68, ¼m, ½ 17th, long flats, extremely low cut. Tin., 1'C up coned.
1⅗'	Terz	#66-78-90 ⅙ m, very low cut throughout, ⅔ diam at top coned
1⅓'	Larigot	as Nazard, one octave higher. Top Octave repeats
1'	Sifflöte	⅙m. Very low cut. Tin, all straight pipes coned. #75-87-99-114-130. Top octave repeats.
IV	Scharff	all #48sc, ½ on 19th, ¼m, tin, coned, in the top octave where there are two drops and two octaves, the scale should be varied 2 scales for the respective similar ranks

19.22.26.29	12
15.19.22.26	6
12.15.19.22	12
8.12.15.19	6
1. 8.12.15	12
1. 1. 8. 8	13

476

III	Zimbel	all #48sc ½ on 17th, ⅕m tin, coned	
		36.40.43	12
		29.33.36	12
		22.26.29	12
		15.19.22	12
		8.12.15	13

Bombarde Section (enclosed in Choir) — 61 pipes, 7" pressure

16'	Posaune	English small scale with light pressure shallots
8'	Trumpet	English small scale with light pressure shallots
4'	Clarion	English small scale with light pressure shallots
	String Organ	

String Organ (floating and enclosed in separate box) — 73 pipes, old

All pipes to be revoiced.

16'	Viole	
8'	Orchestral Strings II	
8'	Dulcet II	
8'	Muted Strings II	
8'	Dulciana	
8'	Flute	
4'	Viole	
16'	Vox Humana	12 pipes
8'	Vox Humana	
		Tremolo

Pedal Organ — 32 pipes, 5" pressure

16'	Principal	#26 graduating to #42sc @ 8'C., 4'C up spotted, 2/9m, long feet	
16'	Contre Basse	changed to new by GDH	
16'	Violone	changed to new by GDH	
16'	Sub Bass	old	
16'	Flute Conique	from Swell	
16'	Viola	from Choir	
16'	Viole	from String	
8'	Principal	#43sc, 2/9m, spotted 4'C up	
8'	Viola	from Choir	
8'	Nachthorn	#2 Mel. open bass 4'C up open as #943 *[Wellesley]*, special slow scale (60-68), ½ on 19th	
8'	Flute Conique	from Swell	
5⅓'	Quint	#52 sc, straight pipes ¼m, zinc and spotted	
4'	Principal	#54 sc, ¼m spotted	
4'	Flute Harmonique	#2 EMS harm. fl.	
2'	Blockflöte	¼m, coned 1'C up. Very low cut-up. 62-74-98 at mouth, ⅔ at top	
III	Mixture	17.19.22	32
		17th: 64 scale, ¼m, ½ on 19th, spotted	
		19th: 66 scale, ¼m, ½ on 19th, spotted	
		22nd: 68 scale, ¼m, ½ on 19th, spotted	
II	Cymbel	26.29	32
		26th: 80 scale, ¼m, ½ on 19th, spotted	
		29th: 82 scale, ¼m, 1/2 on 19th, spotted	
32'	Posaune	ext. of 16', CCCC=10" sc. metal, graduating to meet 16' Eng. shallots with long and wide openings	

16'	Bombarde	6" scale. Eng. Ped. shallots with long and wide openings
8'	Trompette	English small scale with Eng. light pressure shallots
4'	Clairon	English small scale with Eng. light pressure shallots
	Chimes	

Opus 980 — Chapel, Brooks School, North Andover, Mass.

Source: pipe shop notes dated August 16, 1938

Great Organ — 61 pipes, 2-½" pressure

8'	Spitzflöte	com. 3 sc. large
8'	Bourdon	com. metal Std. Diap. #1 bass
4'	Principal	#57sc, ½ on 17th note
2'	Octave	#69sc, ½ on 18th note
IV	Fourniture	same as 951 ["Germanic Museum"] Great Fourniture

Swell Organ — 61 pipes, 3½" pressure

8'	Viola	#56sc
8'	Stopped Diapason	common metal stopped diapason
4'	Gemshorn	#58sc, as 927 [Trinity, New Haven] Choir 4' Gemshorn
III	Cymbel	as 951 ["Germanic"] Positiv Cymbel
8'	Trompette	small scale

Positiv Organ — 61 pipes, 2½" pressure

8'	Koppelflöte	common Positive type, #1 bass
4'	Nachthorn	common Positive type, 2 scales small
2⅔'	Nasard	common Positive type
2'	Blockflöte	common Positive type
1⅗'	Tierce	common Positive type

Pedal Organ — 32 pipes, 3½" pressure

16'	Bourdon	#1A
8'	Gedackt	metal throughout — solid caps, zinc bass
4'	Principal	#56sc
III	Mixture	5⅓'–2⅔'–2' #53, #65, #70 respectively, all ½ on 17th
16'	Fagotto	special 5" diameter

Opus 985 — St. Paul's Chapel, Columbia University, New York, NY

Source: pipe shop notes dated 1938

Great Organ — 61 pipes, 3" pressure

16'	Quintade	exactly as for #976 [Christ Church, Houston, TX] Choir — spotted metal
8'	Principal	#45, ¼m, ½ 17th, tin
8'	Spitzflöte	#56 at 4'C, ¼m cut in, diam. at top ¼ of mouth diam., cone tuned, lower 12 with ears. Tin. Bass #44 graduated to meet #56 at tenor C 2/9m, same taper to pipes as treble. Zinc
8'	Bourdon	Standard metal std. diap., ¼m, spotted metal from 4'C. Solid canister tops felted. Bass to be of zincs to match scale
4'	Principal	#56, ¼m, ½ 17th, tin, semitone long for slotting coned from 1'C up
4'	Rohrflöte	common metal std. diap. with chimneys and felted caps, ¼m spotted metal, no wood pipes. Scale C to be D# regular, no. 18 up, all as #981 [Westminster Choir College]
2⅔'	Quint	#66, ¼m, ½ 17th, tin, coned 1'C up

2'	Super Octave	#68, ¼m, ½ 17th, tin, coned 1'C up	
IV	Fourniture	all #48sc @ 8'CC, ¼m, ½ 18th, tin, 1'C up coned	
		15.19.22.26	12
		12.15.19.22	18
		8.12.15.19	6
		1.8.12.15	18
		1.5.8.12	7
II-IV	Cymbel	all #50 @ 8'CC, ¼m, ½ 18th, tin, cone tuned	
		26.29	18
		19.22.26	12
		12.15.19.22	9
		8.12.15.19	6
		1.8.12.15	16
III	Cornet	12.15.17, #64, #68, #76 respectively, tin, ¼m, cone tuned	
16'	Fagot	Special	

Positiv Organ — 61 pipes, 2½" pressure

8'	Nason Flute	as 981 [Westminster Choir College]	
4'	Nachthorn	as 981 [Westminster Choir College]	
2'	Italian Principal	#70, ½ 18th, ¼m, tin, coned	
1⅓'	Larigot	#76, ½ 17th, straight pipes, tin, coned	
1'	Sifflöte	Common Positive type	
II	Sequialtera	Standard Sifflöte scale	
		26.31	12
		19.24	6
		12.17	43
III	Zimbel	all #50sc @ 8'CC, ½ 17th, tin, ¼m, coned	
		36.40.43	12
		29.33.36	6
		26.29.33	6
		22.26.29	6
		19.22.26	6
		15.19.22	6
		12.15.19	6
		8.12.15	6
		1.8.12	7
8'	Krummhorn	Special	

Brustwerk Organ — 61 pipes, 2½" pressure

8'	Muted Viole	56sc, ⅙m, spotted, tapered ¼	
8'	Gedackt	981 [Westminster Choir College] Great Gedackt	
4'	Spitzflöte	981 [Westminster Choir College] Great Spitzflöte	
2⅔'	Nasat	Positiv type	
2'	Blockflöte	Positiv type	
1⅗'	Terz	Positiv type	
III	Scharf	all #48sc @ 8'CC, ¼m, ½ 17th note, tin, cone tuned	
		29.33.36	12
		26.29.33	6
		22.26.29	6
		19.22.26	6
		15.19.22	6
		12.15.19	6
		8.12.15	19

Swell Organ — 73 pipes, 5" pressure

16'	Lieblich Gedackt	Low 24 zinc, rest spotted, CC up new small sc #55 (as 981), ¼m, solid felted caps, bass #43 at CCC.
8'	Diapason	#47, ¼m, spotted, ½ on 17th
8'	Viole de Gambe	
8'	Viole Celeste	
8'	Stopped Diapason	
4'	Octave	#58, ¼m
4'	Flauto Traverso	
2'	Fifteenth	
IV	Mixture	spotted metal, ¼m slided, all as Trinity New Haven [#927] Unisons #48sc @ 8'CC, ½ 18th, Quints #50sc @ 8'CC, ½ 18th

19.22.26.29	15
15.19.22.26	12
12.15.19.22	12
8.12.15.19	12
5.8.12.15	10

16'	Bombarde	small scale French Trompette open shallots
8'	Trompette	
8'	Hautbois	all as 976 [Christ Church, Houston, TX] French shallots
4'	Clairon	
		Tremolo

Choir Organ — 73 pipes, 5" pressure

16'	Contra Viole	#50, ⅙m
8'	Viole	#64, ⅙m, spotted
8'	Dulciana	#56, old
8'	Unda Maris	#56@8'CC, old, 61 pipes
8'	Orchestral Flute	wood harmonique, metal mouths, std. bass
4'	Fugara	#66, ⅕m, spotted
4'	Flute Triangulaire	common
2'	Zauberflöte	976 Choir
III	Carillon	
8'	Clarinet	old
8'	Orchestral Oboe	old
		Tremolo

Pedal Organ — 32 pipes, 3¾" pressure

16'	Principal	#28, long feet
16'	Bourdon	Unit A
16'	Viole	Choir
16'	Lieblich Gedeckt	Swell
8'	Principal	#44sc, ¼m, spotted from 4'C up, ½ 17th
8'	Gedacktpommer	#55sc, solid caps felted, make like quintaten
8'	Viole	Choir
8'	Lieblich Gedeckt	Swell
5⅓'	Quint	#52sc, ¼m, spotted straight pipes, ½ on 17th
4'	Choralbass	#57sc, ¼m, ½ on 17th, semitone long for slotting
4'	Koppelflöte	positiv type, tin
2'	Blockflöte	positiv type, tin

480

III	Mixture	3⅕'--2⅔'--2' no breaks, 32 notes, slided #63, #63, #68 respectively, all ¼m, ½ on 17th
II	Cymbel	1⅓'--1' no breaks, 32 notes, slided #75, #80 respectively, all ¼m, ½ on 17th
16'	Posaune	like Brooks School
8'	Trompette	small Choir Trompette French shallots
4'	Clairon	small Choir Trompette French shallots, 32 pipes
4'	Rohr Schalmei	32 pipes
2'	Cornet	32 pipes

985B — St. Paul's Chapel, Columbia Univ., New York, NY

Source: pipe shop notes Jan. 11, 1962

Choir Organ

8'	Flauto Dolce	new on old Dulciana, common
8'	Flute Celeste	t.c., 56 pipes, new on old Unda Maris, common
8'	Viola	old lower 12, #64, new 4'C up #73
4'	Prestant	new special scale on old Fugara
4'	Musette	Old Orchestral Oboe moved down on 8'CC hole
8'	Concert Flute	revoiced from 2'C up

Swell Organ

8'	Aeoline	old Choir Dulciana 56sc set on old 8' Diapason, gate blocks on 10 offsets cut off toes 56 sc
4'	Fugara	⌠ and old Choir Fugara pipes, increase scale 1 pipe per
2⅔'	Nazard	⌡ octave, tune in perfect fifths to unison, unit stop
8'	Hautbois	revoice
8'	Vox Humana	Old pipes from stock revoiced on new chest with Solo
8'	Trumpet	10" in dome. Tremulant to operate with Swell
	Tremulant	to cut out when trumpet stop is drawn.
32'	Bombarde reversible	

Brustwerk Organ

8'	Spitzgeigen	all new on Muted Viole topboard, 6 offset, 61 pipes
		8' CC — #56, ¼m
		4' C — #68, ¼m
		2' C — #78, ¼m
		1' C — #88, ¼m
		6" C — #98, ¼m
		3" C — #108, ¼
		Return and put old 56 scale muted Viole in stock, use as Dulciana or Unda Maris elsewhere
4'	Montre	new 61 pipes & chest, 4'C = 60, ½ taper, ¼m compound magnets from 25 to 44 — 3" pressure, trunk to Great Reservoir

Positiv Organ

| 8' | Nason Flute | revoice 4'C up bigger and more body |
| 4' | Nachthorn | revoice |

Pedal Organ

16'	Montre	low 18 pipes in case, trunk to suit on job FF# up new 53 sc. Ext. Brust. Montre
8'	Montre	ext.
16'	Quintade	Great
16'	Bombarde	Swell

8'	Solo Trumpet	4th Manual
32'	Bombarde	electronic, control only 32 notes
32'	Bourdon	electronic, control only 32 notes

Fourth Manual Dome Organ

16'	Solo Trumpet (T.C.)	
8'	Solo Trumpet - 61	10" pressure #2 French, harmonics at #37
4'	Solo Trumpet - 12	

New pipes, chest, reservoir, blower, cable, swell folds and box.
Swell engine, tremulant cut out.
Cable from electronic stops located in dome.

8'	Vox Humana (Swell)
32'	Bombarde reversible

Opus 988 — St. Mary's R.C. Church, Jersey City, New Jersey

Source: pipe shop notes, April 22, 1939

Great Organ — 61 pipes, 4" pressure

16'	Quintaten	CCC=43, CC=45
8'	Principal	45
8'	Gemshorn	44 to meet 46 at ten. C
8'	Bourdon	52 stopped diapason
4'	Principal	57
4'	Cor de Nuit	com. French, solid canisters
2⅔'	Quint	66, ½ on 18th
2'	Doublette	69
IV	Fourniture	all #45 @ 8'C, ½ on 18th note

19.22.26.29	18
15.19.22.26	9
12.15.19.22	12
8.12.15.19	7
1.8.12.15	15

Positiv Organ — 61 pipes, 3" pressure

8'	Gedeckt	Koppelflote with #1 bass
4'	Nachthorn	60
2⅔'	Nasard	Positiv type
2'	Blockflote	Positiv type
1⅗'	Tierce	Positiv type

Swell Organ — 73 pipes, 5" pressure

8'	Rohrflote	54 sc, common Pommer
8'	Viole de Gambe	56
8'	Viole Celeste	56
4'	Octave	58, ½ on 18th
2'	Fifteenth	70, ½ on 18th
III	Cymbale	all based on #49 @ 8'C, ½ on 18th, as 951 *["Germanic" Museum]* Positiv

29.33.36	12
26.29.33	6
22.26.29	6
19.22.26	6
15.19.22	12
12.15.19	6
8.12.15	13

16'	Bombarde	French small
8'	Trompette	French small
4'	Clairon	French small
		Tremolo

Pedal Organ — 32 pipes

16'	Montre	
16'	Quintaten	Great
8'	Nachthorn	4'C = #60, 1-12 #2 open Melodia bass
8'	Quintade	Great
4'	Principal	56
4'	Quintade	Great
IV	Mixture	5⅓'–#56
		3⅕'–#60
		2⅔'–#65
		2' –#68 All ½ on the 17th
16'	Bombarde	Swell
8'	Trompette	Swell

Opus 1002 — The Shed at Tanglewood, Stockbridge, Mass.

Source: pipe shop notes dated April 8, 1940

Great Organ — 61 pipes, 3½" pressure

16'	Quintaten	as 946 [Central Congregational, Jamaica Plain, MA] Choir Quintaten, also Columbia Gt. Quintaten special note lower 36 zinc, rest spotted
8'	Principal	45, ¼ mouth, ½ on 17th, tin, slided
8'	Spitzflote	as 985 Gt. Spitz, ¼ mouth, tin
4'	Principal	low C=58, ten C=70, mid C=82, treb c=92, high c=100 Top c=118, ⅕ mouth bass, ¼ treble semitone long for slotting throughout
4'	Rohrflote	#8 Rohrflute, ¼ mouth, special note lower 24 zinc, rest spotted
2⅔'	Quint	low C=65 scale, then follows a special layout as job #995 principal, tin, ¼ mouth, slotted throughout
2'	Super Octave	low C=70 scale, then follows 995 as above, tin, ¼m
III-V	Fourniture	#995 [studio of Ernest White] principal scales

15.19.22	12
12.15.19.22	18
8.12.15.19	6
1.8.12.15	12
1.5.8.12.15	13

all tin, ¼ mouth, semitone long for slotting and sliding throughout

Positiv Organ — 61 pipes, 3½" pressure

8'	Nason Flute	wood throughout, "Green" type
4'	Koppelflote	standard baroque tin, ¼ mouth
2⅔'	Nazard	Koppelflote, ¼ mouth, tin, as Bradford organ
2'	Nachthorn	Special ⅙ mouth, 4 scales large of standard bar. tin
1⅗'	Tierce	Standard tapered baroque tin, ⅙ mouth
1'	Italian Principal	70, ¼ mouth, ½ on 18th note, tin
III	Cymbel	as Germanic

Enclosed section — 5" pressure

8'	English Salicional	exactly as 995, this tapers 2 scales
8'	Gedackt	#6 metal Gedackt, ¼ mouth, solid caps special 24 zinc, rest spotted
4'	Gemshorn	#60, ¼ mouth spotted, tapered ⅔rds, slided
8'	Trompette	French type, imported shallots

Pedal Organ — 32 pipes, 5" pressure

16'	Geigen Principal	#33 scale, 2/9 mouth, 24 zinc, rest spotted, short feet and large toes, long ears for large beards, pressure 6"
16'	Salicional	ext of enclosed 8', CCC=#38, ⅕ mouth
16'	Quintaten	Great
8'	Spitzprincipal	standard flute conique, ¼ mouth, spotted 4'C up
4'	Nachthorn	standard baroque type tin, ⅕ mouth
IV	Mixture	5-⅓ 4 2-⅔ 2 all #45 @ 8'C, ¼m, ½ on 17th, spotted
32'	Bombarde	low CCCC, one pipe, use Willis pipe in reed room
16'	Posaune	as 980

Opus 1007 — Christ Church, Cambridge, Massachusetts

Source: pipe shop notes dated June 5, 1940 and contract
Comments in parentheses are thought to be notations of Ernest White,
consultant to Christ Church, and are typed, rather than handwritten, on the contract.

Great Organ — 61 pipes, 3 ¼" pressure

16'	Violone	(keen) #44, lower 24 zinc, rest spotted, ⅕m
8'	Spitzprincipal	(beards) #44, tapered 3 scales, ¼m, slide tuners, ½ on 17th, lower 12 zinc, rest spotted
8'	Cello	(tapered) #54, tapered 3 scales, ¼m, ½ on 17th, spotted, lower 12 zinc
8'	Bourdon	(small scale bass - large scale treble - bright tone), #6, very low cut up
4'	Principal	(slotted throughout) #995 *[studio of Ernest White]* principal scale, 2 large, slotted through with slide tuners, ¼m, tin
4'	Koppelflote	(bright tone - smallish scale - large treble) common Positiv type, tin, ¼m, very low cut up in bass
2⅔'	Quint	(fluty) #65, ¼m, tin, ½ on 18th, slided
2'	Super Octave	(slotted - not coned) #68, ½ on 18th, slotted and slided
IV	Fourniture	(8' Series) all as #995 *[studio of Ernest White]* Principal scale, tin, ¼m slotted and slided

15.19.22.26	12
12.15.19.22	18
8.12.15.19	6
1.8.12.15	18
1.5. 8.12	7

III	Scharff	(4' Series) as 951 *["Germanic"]* Positiv, ¼m, tin, all #49 at 8'CC, ½ on 18th, ¼m tin

29.33.36	12
26.29.33	6
22.26.29	6
19.22.26	6
15.19.22	12
12.15.19	6
8.12.15	13

8'	Bombarde	Pedal ext., 17 pipes

Swell Organ — 73 pipes, 5" pressure

16'	Flute Conique	(Narrower scale than at St. Mary the Virgin) common type, but 4 scales smaller, ¼m, lower 24 zinc, rest spotted
8'	Viole de Gambe	(tapered) new English Salicional scale, tapered, spotted, ¼m, all as #1002 *[Tanglewood]*, #50 at 8'CC, 62 at 4'C
8'	Viole Celeste	as Viole de Gambe
8'	Rohrflote	(small scale in bass) zinc and spotted throughout, 4'C up #3, bass #7
4'	Principal	(tapered) as 1004 *[Druid Hills Presbyterian, Atlanta]* Swell Gemshorn, 2 larger, spotted, ¼m, 1004 was 60 scale Flute Conique, standard mouth
4'	Nachthorn	(fluty) Positiv type, spotted, slided, 1/6m
2'	Super Octave	(slotted) as 995 Principal scale, spotted, ¼m, slotted and slided
III	Plein Jeu	to be given greater topboard space than for regular III rank mixture
16'	Bombarde	(thinner and brighter than 8' rank) regular Fagotto as 976 *[Christ Church, Houston, TX]* 4" diam, with French shallots
8'	Trompette	French small
4'	Clairon	as Trompette
	Tremolo	

Choir Organ — 73 pipes, 5" pressure

16'	Dulciana	(stringy - narrow bass scale) 50 at 16'C, graduating to #56 at 8'C, ⅕m, lower 24 zinc, rest spotted
8'	Nachthorn	(narrow mouth) special scale, 8'C=50 4'C=56 2'C=66 1'C=76 6"C=86 3"C=98, ⅙m, very low cut up, spotted, lower 12 zinc
8'	Viola	(keener than Swell - straight sided pipes) #60, ⅕m spotted
8'	Viola Celeste	as Viola
4'	Rohrflote	#5, spotted metal, ¼m
2⅔'	Nazard	(Koppelflote) Koppel Flute type, tin, ¼m
2'	Blockflote	Positiv type, tin, ¼m
1⅗'	Tierce	Positiv type, tin, ⅙m
8'	Schalmei	Krummhorn like 998 *[Bradford College, Bradford, MA]*
	Tremolo	

Pedal Organ — 32 pipes, 5" pressure

16'	Principal	(with beards throughout) as 1002 with large toes and short feet, 33 scale
16'	Quintaton	as 998 *[Bradford College, Bradford, MA]* Great Quintaton
16'	Violone	Great
16'	Flute Conique	Swell
16'	Dulciana	Choir
8'	Spitzgeigen	as 1002 *[Tanglewood Music Shed]* Pedal Spitzprincipal
8'	Quintadena	(fluty) #7 stopped diapason, low cut
8'	Flute Conique	Swell
8'	Dulciana	Choir
4'	Choral Bass	(tapered slightly) #57 principal, spotted metal, ¼m slotted and slided
4'	Rohrflote	#4 spotted metal, ¼m
4'	Flute Conique	Swell

2'	Blockflote	Positiv type, 1/4m, spotted metal
III	Mixture	no breaks, 995 *[studio of Ernest White]* principal scale ¼m slotted and slided 5⅓'--2⅔'--2'
16'	Bombarde	as 998 *[Bradford College, Bradford, MA]*
8'	Trompette	ext. 16
4'	Clarion	ext. 8'

GALLERY ORGAN — prepared for in console only

Hauptwerk — 61 pipes (placed with Great stops)

8'	Gedackt	
4'	Principal	
2⅔'	Nasat	
2'	Principal	
1⅗'	Terz	
	Tremolo	

Positiv — 61 pipes (placed with Choir stops)

8'	Nason Flute	
4'	Rohrflote	
2'	Nachthorn (German style)	
1⅓'	Larigot	
1'	Oktav	
III	Scharf 22.26.29	

Pedal — 32 pipes (placed with Pedal stops)

16'	Quintaten	
8'	Spitzprincipal (narrow mouth - beards)	
5⅓'	Rohrquint (normal Gedackt pipes)	
4'	Koppelflote (open throughout)	
II	Mixtur 2-2⅔'-2'	

Note — Hauptwerk and Positiv both play from top manual without coupling.

Opus 1075 — The Mormon Tabernacle, Salt Lake City, Utah

Source: pipe shop notes dated September 15, 1947

Great Organ — 61 pipes, 3¾" pressure

16'	Sub Principal	#36, 1/4m, 18h, 24 zinc, balance spotted
16'	Quintaten	standard Gt. Quintaten, 12 zinc, balance spotted, solid metal caps
8'	Principal	#44, ¼m, 18h, burnished tin, slided, low 9 regular zinc, with spotted metal mouths, AA-AA#-BB spotted feet and mouths
8'	Diapason	#43, ¼m, 17h, spotted to AA#, spotted feet and butts low 10
8'	Spitzflote	regular Gt. type, ¼m, coned, spotted
8'	Bourdon	#1 metal stopped diapason, solid felted caps, spotted, ¼m
8'	Flute Harmonique	common Gt. type, #50, spotted
8'	Bell Gamba	tapered with bells, #60, tapered 2 scales
5⅓'	Grosse Quinte	#56, 18h, 1/5m, spotted
4'	Octave	#57, 2/9m, 17h; however, new Octave 2 scales larger sent Dec. 2, 1948, semitone long for slotting and sliding
4'	Principal	#55, ¼m, 18h, burnished tin, 1-24 slided, 25-61 coned
4'	Gemshorn	common, ¼m, spotted, slided, 2/3 tapered
4'	Koppelflote	standard Baroque, burnished tin

486

3⅕'	Grosse Tierce	like #1047 *[Sen. Richards res.]* Choir Blockflote scale, ¼m
2⅔'	Quinte	#66, ⅕m, 18h, burnished tin, slotted and slided
2'	Super Octave	#68, ¼m, 18h, burnished tin
2'	Blockflote	Baroque Blockflote, tapered, ⅕m, spotted
1⅗'	Tierce	#74, ¼m, 18h, burnished tin
1⅐'	Septieme	standard Zauberflote scale, stopped harmonic throughout, 2/9m, spotted, felted solid caps, top 12 break back an octave
IV	Full Mixture	spotted, #45 @ 8'C for all ranks, ¼m on unisons, ⅕m on quints, semitone long for slotting and sliding
		12.15.19.22 — 18
		8.12.15.19 — 12
		1.8.12.15 — 31
IV	Fourniture	burnished tin, slided, #46 @ 8'C, 18h, ¼m
		15.19.22.26 — 18
		12.15.19.22 — 12
		8.12.15.19 — 12
		1.8.12.15 — 12
		1.5. 8.12 — 7
III	Acuta	burnished tin, #47 @ 8'C, 18h, ¼m
		22.26.29 — 12
		19.22.26 — 12
		15.19.22 — 12
		12.15.19 — 12
		8.12.15 — 13
IV	Klein Mixtur	burnished tin, based on #995 scale, slotted and slided, 2/9m throughout
		19.22.26.29 — 12
		15.19.22.26 — 12
		12.15.19.22 — 12
		8.12.15.19 — 12
		8.8.12.15 — 13
	Chimes	

Swell Organ — 68 pipes, 5" pressure

Swell Organ chests are divided in such a way as to allow sub and super couplers to affect only the flue stops up to 4' pitch, the Harmonic Trumpet, the Hautbois and the Voix Humaine. The stops not affected by octave couplers are of 61-note compass.

16'	Gemshorn	#44
16'	Lieblichgedeckt	from old organ *[Bridges-Simmons]*
8'	Geigen	#44, ¼m, 17h, slotted and slided, zinc basses, bearded from 4'B down
8'	Claribel Flute	from old organ *[Kimball stop]*
8'	Gedeckt	#9 stopped diapason, wood
8'	Viole de Gambe	#56, ¼m, spotted
8'	Viole Celeste	#56, ¼m, spotted, basses of both ranks have spotted butts and feet
8'	Salicional	#60, ⅙m, spotted
8'	Voix Celeste	#60, ⅙m, spotted, basses of both ranks have spotted butts and feet
8'	Orchestral Strings II	#64, ⅙m, spotted butts in bass
8'	Flauto Dolce	common scale, common metal, zinc basses, bearded from 8'A
8'	Flute Celeste	(TC), common scale, common metal
4'	Prestant	#56, ¼m, 18h, slotted and slided, bearded from 4'B down

4'	Fugara	#64, ¼m spotted
4'	Flauto Traverso	#50 @ 8'C Great type, spotted, upper 12 larger scale Cavaille-Coll Harmonic Flute type
2⅔'	Nazard	Koppel type, spotted, ¼m
2'	Octavin	#70, ¼m, 18h, spotted, slotted and slided
III	Cornet	unisons and quints #46 @ 8'C, tierce #48 @ 8'C, all ¼m, 18h, slotted and slided

	12.15.17	49
	8.12.15	5
	1. 8.12	7

VI	Plein Jeu	unisons and quints #44 @ 8'C, 17h, slided

12.15.19.22.26.29	12
8.12.15.19.22.26	12
1.8.12.15.19.22	12
1.8. 8.12.15.19	12
1.5. 8. 8.12.15	6
1.1. 5. 8. 8.12	7

IV	Cymbale	unisons and quints #48 @ 8'C, ¼m, 18h, slided, where 15th repeats, second 15th to be two scales smaller

26.29.33.36	12
22.26.29.33	6
19.22.26.29	6
15.19.22.26	6
12.15.19.22	6
12.15.15.19	6
8.12.15.15	19

32'	Fagot	regular Sw. 16' Fagotto type, lower 12 like #1047 [Richards], graduated to meet scale at 16'C, softly voiced, spotted tips and bells on lower 36 pipes, above that all spotted, mitred and hooded
16'	Contre Trompette	#2 French shallots, lower 12 regular tapered shallots with slant head. Resonators all spotted to 8'C, basses have spotted tips and bells, mitred and hooded, lower 12 shallots of new construction as Oscar Pearson worked out for Methuen [#1103]
8'	Trompette	#2 French shallots, wide openings, resonators, all spotted to CC and hooded
8'	Harmonic Trumpet	#2 English, Harmonic from tenor F#, CC-3 ¾", spotted throughout
8'	Hautbois	French shallots, regular scale, spotted bells
8'	Voix Humaine	regular lift cap Vox Humana on separate chest with its own tremulant
5⅓'	Quinte Trompette	#3 French shallots, spotted throughout
4'	Clarion	as 8' Trompette

Choir Organ — 68 pipes, 5" pressure

Choir organ chests are divided in such a way as to allow sub and super couplers to affect only the flue stops up to 4' pitch. Stops not affected by octave couplers are of 61-note compass.

16'	Gamba	#46, ⅕m, slided, lower 24 zinc, balance spotted
8'	Principal	#48, ¼m, 17h, slotted and slided, lower 12 zinc, rest spotted
8'	Viola	Christ Church Cambridge [#1007] Swell 8' Viole de Gambe, tapered, #50, slotted
8'	Viola Celeste	same as Viola, except lower 12 to be regular #60 Gamba

8'	Dulcet II ranks	two #75s, ⅕m, slided, burnished tin, low octaves tin butts and feet, 136 pipes
8'	Kleine Erzahler II	only one rank below tenor C, common scale, spotted
8'	Concert Flute	common wood with harmonic metal treble, #1 large scale upper 7 pipes
4'	Prestant	as 8' Montre as to scale, etc.
4'	Gambette	#72, ¼m spotted
4'	Zauberflote	common stopped harmonic through to top C, spotted, upper 7 larger scale
2'	Piccolo Harmonique	common Gt. Harmonic Flute type, spotted, upper 24 larger scale
III	Rauschpfeife	scales all based on #995 Principal scale, ¼ spotted

15.19.22	18
12.15.19	12
8.12.15	31

III	Carillon	all Baroque Sifflote scale, ⅙m, spotted, slided

12.17.22	49
8.12.15	12

16'	Dulzian	½ length 16' Fagott, all like #1080 [second organ for Ernest White], spotted tubes, mitred and hooded
8'	Trompette	#3 French, spotted throughout, mitred and hooded
8'	Orchestral Oboe	common, voiced loudly
8'	Cromorne	common Baroque, hooded
4'	Rohr Schalmei	common Baroque
	Harp	61 notes Skinner harp
	Celesta	

Positiv Organ — 61 pipes, 2¾" pressure

8'	Cor de Nuit	common French, burnished tin
8'	Quintade	wood from tenor C up, Nason Flute scale, lower 12 zinc metal quintadena
4'	Principal	#995 scale, ¼m, burnished tin, slotted and slided
4'	Nachthorn	standard Baroque, ⅙m, #54, spotted, slided
2⅔'	Nazard	Baroque tapered, ¼m, burnished tin, slided
2'	Principal	#70, ¼m, 18h, burnished tin
2'	Spillflote	Like #1047, burnished tin
1⅗'	Tierce	Baroque tapered, ⅙m, burnished tin, slided
1⅓'	Larigot	Baroque Sifflote scale, ⅙m, burnished tin
1'	Sifflote	Zauberflote, stopped harmonic to top note, repeat top octave, burnished tin
II	Septerz	flat 21st-#76, 24th #72, both Zauberflotes, stopped harmonic to top, burnished tin
III	Scharf	all #46 @ 8'C, 18h, ¼m, burnished tin

22.26.29	12
19.22.26	12
15.19.22	12
12.15.19	12
8.12.15	6
1.8.12	7

III	Zimbal	all #48 @ 8'C, 17h, ¼m, burnished tin

29.33.36	18
26.29.33	6
22.26.29	6

19.22.26	6
15.19.22	6
12.15.19	6
8.12.15	6
1.8.12	7

| 16' | Rankett | as per sample in Oscar Pearson's room |

Solo Organ — 68 pipes, 10" and 15" pressure

8'	Gambe	#56 flared two scales to make #54 at top, slotted rolled tuners, $\frac{1}{5}$m, zinc basses with butts spotted, balance all spotted
8'	Gambe Celeste	same as Gambe
8'	Viole Celeste II	two #60s, $\frac{1}{4}$m, spotted, bass has spotted butts and feet, slided, 136 pipes
8'	Flauto Mirabilis	wood, harmonic, common open bass, larger scale for upper 7 pipes
4'	Concert Flute	Gt. Type, harmonic, two scales larger, spotted, upper 19 larger scale
8'	French Horn	common
8'	English Horn	special, see samples in Oscar Pearson's room, loud treble
8'	Corno di Bassetto	special, with double tongues, see samples in Oscar Pearson's room, spotted
8'	Tuba	15" wind, English Tube #2 scale, harmonic from tenor F#, spotted resonators 8' C up, special shallots, see samples in Oscar Pearson's room
	Chimes	25 tubes, unenclosed
	Harp and Celesta	from Choir

Bombarde Organ — 61 pipes, 7" pressure, unenclosed

| 8' | Diapason | #42, lower 9 regular zinc construction, burnished tin down to AA, $\frac{1}{4}$m |

4' C — #54	
2' C — #66	
1' C — #78	
$\frac{1}{2}$' C — #89	
$\frac{1}{4}$' C — #100	

| 4' | Octave | same as 8', but one scale smaller at all C's, $\frac{1}{4}$m burnished tin, slided |

| VI | Grande Fourniture | all #44 @ 8'C, $\frac{1}{4}$m, 18h, burnished tin |

12.15.19.22.26.29	12
8.12.15.19.22.26	12
1.8.12.15.19.22	12
1.5.8.12.15.19	12
1.1.5.8.12.15	13

| IV-VI | Grosse Cornet | all $\frac{1}{4}$m, spotted, slotted and slided, unisons and quints #43 @ 8'C, 18h, tierce #45 @ 8'C, 18h |

12.15.17.19	12
8.12.15.17.19	12
1.8.12.15.17.19	25
1.8.12.15	12

16'	Bombarde ⎫	all #2 French shallots, harmonic from tenor #F up,
8'	Trompette ⎬	resonators spotted to 8' C, lower 12 of 16' to have
4'	Clairon ⎭	spotted tips and bells, all mitred and hooded and arranged on the chest so hoods project the tone forward

Note: All but Bombarde Organ finished (pipes voiced) Oct. 11, 1948; Bombarde finished Dec. 24, 1948.

Antiphonal Organ — 68 notes, 5" pressure

8'	Diapason	#44, ¼m, 17h, spotted
8'	Gedeckt	unchanged from old organ *[Bridges-Simmons]*
8'	Salicional	#60, ⅕m, spotted, bass has spotted butts
8'	Voix Celeste	as Salicional
4'	Principal	#56, 18h, ¼m, spotted, slotted and slided
III	Klein Mixtur	all as #995 scale, slotted and slided, ¼m, spotted

15.19.22	18
12.15.19	12
8.12.15	24
1.8.12	7

8'	Trompette	#2 French shallots (standard openings), spotted tubes from 4'C up, lower octave spotted tips
8'	Vox Humana	as Yankee Network organ scale, spotted *[#1025]*

Pedal Organ — 32 notes, 5" and 7" pressure

32'	Flute Ouverte	12 old pipes and blocks fitted to new chest action, ext. 16'
32'	Montre	10 old fronts, AAAA# and BBBB new, ext. 16' Principal
32'	Soubasse	12 old Bourdon pipes with new chest and action, ext. 16'
16'	Flute Ouverte	regular Pedal Wood Open, but bellied two scales both ways and lengthened for slotted slide tuners, regular Pedal Open block and cap. Inside scale CCC-10"x12"
16'	Principal	metal, same as Tanglewood (feet 50% longer than normal) lower 24 normal zinc construction with long feet, AA up spotted, #33 @ 16'C
16'	Contre Basse	wood, special scale new wood bellied Violone #1
16'	Violone	#2 new wood bellied Violone
16'	Bourdon	new #1-A (fat scale)
16'	Gemshorn	Swell
16'	Gamba	Choir
16'	Lieblichgedeckt	Swell
10⅔'	Grosse Quinte	based on #1-A Pedal Bourdon, all wood
8'	Principal	#42, ¼m, 17h, low 12 normal zinc construction, the latter 50% longer than normal, 4'C up slided
8'	Violoncello	#54, ¼m, Gamba, lower 12 spotted butts and feet, rest all spotted
8'	Spitzprincipal	#1080 Spitzprincipal, regular construction, spotted 4'C up
8'	Flute Ouverte	#2 wood Melodia, open basses, low 12 made long enough for slotted slide tuners
8'	Flauto Dolce	regular Swell Flauto Dolce, spotted
8'	Gamba	Choir 16'
8'	Lieblichgedeckt	Swell 16'
5⅓'	Quinte	#54, ¼m, 17h, spotted
4'	Choral Bass	#53, ¼m, 18h, spotted, slotted and slided
4'	Nachthorn	standard Baroque, plain metal (30%), ⅙m
4'	Gamba	Choir 16'
4'	Lieblichgedeckt	Swell 16'
2'	Blockflote	Baroque, ¼m, spotted, slided
V	Grande Harmonics	5.10.14b.16.17 no breaks

1. 10⅔'	Unit A wood bass, 17 lower wood
2. 6⅖'	#54, ¼m, 18h, spotted, slided
3. 4⁴⁄₇'	regular manual Gemshorn scale, ¼m, spotted

	4. 35⁄9'	based on #1 stp. dia., solid metal tuners, felted,¼m , spotted
	5. 31⁄5'	as 2nd rank, one octave higher
IV	Full Mixture	all #43 @ 8'C, ¼m, 18h, spotted, slided 2⅔'–2'–1⅓'–1' no breaks
IV	Cymbal	all #44 @ 8'C, ¼m, 17h, spotted, slided ⅔'–½'–⅓'–¼' no breaks
32'	Bombarde	5" pressure, 12" scale, French shallots, unweighted tongues. Pipes of new construction: metal tips ¼ length, then zinc with 4' bell of metal, spotted at 8' C up, 32 pipes
32'	Contra Fagot	Swell
16'	Ophicleide	7" pressure, 7" @ CCC, French shallots, small weights on tongues, tubes to have metal tips ¼ length, then zinc, then 2' bell of metal, all spotted 8' C up
16'	Trombone	7" pressure, 6" @ CCC, English light pressure shallots, screwed on weights for tongues, pipes constructed as Ophicleide
16'	Fagot	Swell 32'
16'	Dulzian	Choir
8'	Posaune	7" pressure, 4-½" scale, French shallots with small weights, spotted tubes throughout
8'	Trumpet	7" pressure, similar to 16' Trombone
8'	Cromorne	Choir
4'	Clairon	7" pressure, similar to 8' Posaune
4'	Chalumeau	special new Baroque (to be developed), topboard space required as Clarinet
2'	Kornett	5" pressure, standard #2 English Trumpet, light pressure shallots
	Chimes	Great

Opus 1110 — St. Stephen's Episcopal Church, Richmond, Virginia

Source: pipe shop notes dated July 25, 1950

Great Organ — 61 pipes, 3 ¾" pressure

16'	Quintaten	#42 spotted, etc.
8'	Principal	#44, ¼m, ½ 17th, spotted
8'	Spitzflote	Great type, spotted
8'	Bourdon	#6 spotted
4'	Principal	#56, ¼m, ½ 18th, spotted
4'	Rohrflote	#4 spotted
II	Rauschquinte	12th & 15th #66 & #68, respectively, ¼m, ½ 18th, spotted
IV	Fourniture	all #46 @ 8'C, ½ 18th

15.19.22.26	18
12.15.19.22	12
8.12.15.19	12
1.8.12.15	19

Chimes (prepared for)

Swell Organ — 68 pipes, 5" pressure

8'	Geigen Principal	#46, ¼m, ½ 18th (pinch bass one pipe)
8'	Stopped Diapason	wood #9
8'	Viole-de-Gambe	#58, ¼m ½ 18th
8'	Viole Celeste	(tc) same as Gambe
4'	Principal	#58, ¼m, ½ 18th

4'	Flauto Traverso	Great type Cavaillé-Coll
4'	Flute Celeste II	common (unison 68 pipes, sharp 61 pipes), one scale bigger at 4'C, increasing one more at 1'C and one more at 6" C as per JSW
IV	Plein Jeu	all #47 @ 8'C, ½ 18th

19.22.26.29	12
15.19.22.26	12
12.15.19.22	12
8.12.15.19	12
5.8.12.15	13

16'	Contre Hautbois	French shallots
8'	Trompette	#2 French
4'	Clairon	#2 French
Tremulant		

Choir Organ — 68 pipes, 5" pressure

8'	Viola	#50, ¼m tapered 2 scales
8'	Viola Celeste	#60 at 8' CC #62 at 4'C tapered 2 scales
8'	Erzahler	common
8'	Kleine Erzahler	common, tenor C
8'	Singend Gedeckt	as 1134 [Symphony Hall, Boston] Positiv Cor-de-Nuit
4'	Koppelflote	common Baroque
2⅔'	Nazard	common Baroque
2'	Blockflote	common Baroque
1⅗'	Tierce	common Baroque
8'	English Horn	common
Tremulant		
Harp		
Celesta		

Pedal Organ — 32 pipes, 5" pressure

16'	Principal Bass	wood and metal, #1 Contre Basse
16'	Bourdon	#1 A
16'	Quintaten	Great
16'	Echo Lieblich	Ext. Swell 8' Stopped, 12 pipes
8'	Principal	#44 ¼m ½ 18th spotted
8'	Flute	ext. 16', 12 pipes
4'	Super Octave	ext. 8', 12 pipes
IV	Fourniture	prepared for, 5-⅓', 4', 2-⅔', 2'
16'	Bombarde	6" scale English low pressure
16'	Contre Hautbois	Swell
8'	Trompette	ext.
4'	Clairon	ext.
	Chimes	Great (prepared for)

Note: In 1967-68, Aeolian-Skinner added a Positiv and Antiphonal divisions, several new stops to Pedal, Great and Swell, and a new four-manual console.

Opus 1118B — The Riverside Church, New York, New York

1930 Hook-Hastings, 1948 new 5-manual console, 1955 rebuild
Source: pipe shop notes dated January 20, 1955

Great Organ — 61 pipes, 3¾" pressure

16'	Violone	#40 at 16' CCC, #52 at 8'CC, #63 at 4'C, #73 at 2'C; #80 at 1'C; #92 at 6" C (old Choir Gamba)
16'	Quintaton	new #42, enlarge treble
8'	Diapason	#43 2⁄7m ½ 18th
8'	Principal	#45 ¼m ½ 18 (old Sw. Geigen bass)
8'	Holzgedackt	#9 with ORG sub bass
8'	Gemshorn	Great type 44
8'	Flute Harmonique	old Great 4' revoiced #48 at 8'CC, 57 at 4'C and bass added
5⅓'	Quinte	#53 ¼m ½ 17th
4'	Octave	#55 2⁄7m ½ 18th
4'	Spitzprinzipal	#56 tapered ½, ½ 18th
4'	Flute Couverte	#4
2⅔'	Twelfth	#65 2⁄7m ½ 18th
2'	Fifteenth	#68 2⁄7m ½ 18th
[2'	Blockflote	*This stop appears in addition to the others in an advertisement of May, 1955, in* The Diapason.]
1⅗'	Seventeenth	#74 ¼m ½ 18th
IV	Kleine Mixtur	19.22.26.29 #48 at 8'CC
IV-VI	Fourniture	12.15.19.22 #44 at 8'CC
IV-VIII	Cornet	15.17.19.22.24 #45 at 8'CC
III	Cymbel	29.33.36 #45 at 8'CC
16'	Rankett	common

Swell Organ — 68 pipes, 6" pressure

32'	Contre Gambe	#32, #44 at 16'C, ⅕m, ext. 8' Viole de Gambe
16'	Flute Conique	as 1075 [M. Tabernacle] Swell, 42 at CCC, 50 at CC, slow
16'	Rohr Bordun	old (6 ⅜" x 8", 4" x 4 ¾")
8'	Geigen Principal	#46, 2⁄7m old lower 12
8'	Bourdon	old Gedackt (4 ¾" x 5 ¾")
8'	Viole de Gambe	#54 (old rescaled)
8'	Viole Celeste	#54 (old rescaled)
8'	Salicional	#57 (old rescaled)
8'	Voix Celeste	#57 (old rescaled) (to GG)
8'	Flauto Dolce	#50 (old)
8'	Flute Celeste	#59 (old) (T.C.)
4'	Prestant	#58 2⁄7m tin
4'	Fugara	#65 old Violina rescaled
4'	Flauto Traverso	old 3 'x 3 ¼" 12 wood, 2' C = 2 ¼ metal
4'	Unda Maris II	old Choir Dolce & Unda Maris rescaled to #67
2⅔'	Nazard	New Baroque type
2'	Doublette II	1st rank = #68 2⁄7m, 2nd rank = old Flageolet, #72
2'	Spillflote	new common
1⅗'	Tierce	New Baroque type

III-V	Dolce Mixture	all #49 at 8'CC, ¼m unisons, ⅕m quints, ½ 18th old pipes

15.19.22	18
12.15.19	12
8.12.15.19	12
5. 8.12.15	12
1.5.8.8.12	7

IV	Plein Jeu	All #45 at 8'C, ¼m ½ 18th

19.22.26.29	12
15.19.22.26	12
12.15.19.22	12
8.12.15.19	12
5.8.12.15	6
1.5.8.12	7

IV	Scharff	all #48 at 8'CC, ¼m, ½ 18th

26.29.33.36	12
22.26.29.33	6
19.22.26.29	6
15.19.22.26	6
12.15.19.22	6
8.12.15.19	12
5.8.12.15	13

16'	Contre Trompette	16' C = 4¼

8' C = 3¼
4' C = 2½
2' C = 1¾
1' C = 1¾
Harmonic at 1' F#
6" C = 1¾

8'	Trompette	#3 French
8'	Hautbois	Common French
8'	Oboe d'Amour	Old Choir, 8'C = 3¾ 4'C = 3" 2'C = 2½
8'	Menschenstimme F	old Vox Humana
8'	Menschenstimme P	in separate masonite box as 1201 [*St. Mark's, Mt. Kisco, NY*], action to operate lid cover of Menschenstimme F
4'	Clairon	#3 French
4'	Octave Trumpet	#4 English
	Tremulant	

Choir Organ — 68 pipes, 5" pressure

16'	Contre Viole	#56 at 16'CCC

64 at 8'CC
71 at 4'C
80 at 2'C
88 at 1'C
98 at 6"C

8'	Viola Pomposa	#50 tapered 2 etc.
8'	Viola Celeste	#60 etc, meeting unison
8'	Erzahler	Kleine type
8'	Erzahler Celeste	Kleine type
8'	Dulcet II	#70 with one new bass added from old 1173 [*1st Presbyterian, Kilgore, TX*]
8'	Concert Flute	old wood revoiced (4¼x5¼)
8'	Cor de Nuit	2 larger than common from 4'C up, tin
4'	Montre	#60 slotted and slided, tin

4'	Koppel Flote	common, not felted
2⅔'	Rohr Nasat	#7 Rohrflote, tin
2'	Zauberflote	common, spotted
1⅗'	Terz	Common tin
1⅓'	Larigot	Common tin
1'	Sifflote	Common tin
III-IV	Mixtur	All #48 at 8'CC, ¼m ½ 18th tin long feet
		19.22.26 12
		15.19.22 12
		12.15.19 12
		8.12.15 12
		5.8.12.15 5
		1.5.8.12 8
III	Zimbel	all #48 at 8'CC, ¼m, ½ on 18th tin
		36.40.43 6
		33.36.40 6
		29.33.36 6
		26.29.33 6
		22.26.29 6
		19.22.26 6
		15.19.22 6
		12.15.19 6
		8.12.15 6
		1.8.12 7
16'	Serpent	½ length Fagot
8'	Petite Trompette	#4 French, bass 2 smaller
8'	Cromorne	common
4'	Rohr Schalmei	common
	Tremulant	

Note: device to be installed to cut the stop action of the Zimbel whenever Choir 4' or Choir to Great 4' is drawn. The same should apply to the 1-⅗', 1⅓' and the 1'.

Solo Organ — 68 pipes, 10" pressure

8'	Gamba	old Solo revoiced, #53 at 8'C, 62 at 4'C, ½ 18th
8'	Gamba Celeste	old Solo revoiced, #53 at 8'C, 62 at 4'C, ½ 18th
8'	Doppel Flote	old Gt. Bass (4'C 4-¾x3-¼) plus old Solo Hohl Pfeife
4'	Orchestral Flute	old wood from 1203 old Choir new
2⅔'	Quint Flute	2 large Baroque
2'	Fife	old Great Doppel
16'	Corno di Bassetto	old with new lower 12, 16'=5" dia new 8'CC 4" dia bell, 4'C = 3" bell, 2'C= 2-¼" bell
8'	French Horn	old 8' CC
8'	English Horn	old with new lower 12 as 1203 Solo
8'	Orchestral Oboe	old Swell Oboe revoiced 2" at 8'CC
8'	Tuba Mirabilis	new on 15" pressure
2'	Regal	½ length Fagot with cap
	Zimbelstern	6 bells
	Tremulant	

Triforium Bombarde — 61 pipes, 7" pressure, unenclosed

IV-VI	Mixture	all #44 at 8'CC ½ 18th	
		19.22.26.29	12
		15.19.22.26	12
		12.15.19.22	12
		8.12.15.15.19	12
		5.8.8.12.15.15	13
8'	Trompette	Harmonic at middle C #2 French shallots as 1254 [*St. Michael & All Angels, Baltimore*]	
4'	Clarion	#2 as 8'	

Pedal Organ — 32 pipes, 6" pressure

32'	Contre Basse	old 32 open, cut up lowered, ext. 16'
32'	Bourdon	old, as is, ext. 16'
32'	Contre Gambe	Swell
16'	Contre Basse	old #31 revoiced
16'	Principal	old Violone 8" x 9-½"
16'	Bourdon	old 10x11-¾
16'	Violone	Great
16'	Gamba	Swell
16'	Flute Conique	Swell
16'	Rohr Bordun	Swell
16'	Contre Viole	Choir
16'	Quintaton	Great
10⅔'	Gross Quint	old as Unit A scale
8'	Principal	#43 old
8'	Spitzprincipal	#48 old Great Viole d'Amour
8'	Cello	Great
8'	Rohrflote	Swell
8'	Quintaton	Great
8'	Bourdon	ext. 8'
5⅓'	Quinte	Old Swell Geigen #53
4'	Choral Bass	Old Swell Octave #56
4'	Nachthorn	Old #58
4'	Rohrflote	Swell
2'	Blockflote	Old Great 15th #70
III	Fourniture	All #46 at 8'CC, old 3/5, 2⅔, 2
III	Cymbale	all #46 at 8'C ¼m old 2, 1⅓, 1
32'	Contre Bombarde	ext. 16' Bombarde of Bombarde organ (as 1134) CCCC=10", 7" pressure
16'	Ophecleide	8" at 16'CCC old 7" pressure
16'	Contre Trompette	Swell
16'	Serpent	Choir
16'	Bombarde	Bombarde
8'	Trumpet	4¾" at 8'CC old 7" pressure
8'	Bombarde	Bombarde
4'	Clarion	ext. 8'
4'	Bombarde	Bombarde
2'	Regal	Solo

Opus 1136 — The Chapel, Westminster Church, Buffalo, New York

Source: pipe shop notes dated November 13, 1950

Great Organ — 61 pipes, 3/4 pressure

8'	Gedackt Pommer	#1
8'	Gemshorn	Great type
8'	Viole Sourdine	Swell
4'	Principal	#58 ¼m ½ 18th
III-IV	Fourniture	#46 at 8'CC, ¼m ½ 18th spotted

19.22.26	18
12.15.19.22	12
8.12.15.19	12
1.8.12.15	19

	Chimes	from Aeolian Organ

Great 4' will not come on when Fourniture is on.

Swell Organ — 61 pipes, 4" pressure

8'	Holzflote	old, #1 Melodia from 4'C
8'	Viola Pomposa	#50 ¼m tapered 2
8'	Viola Celeste	#60 at 8'CC, #62 at 4'C
8'	Viole Sourdine	old Aeoline enlarged 2, 60 at 8'CC
4'	Spitzflote	old, to be 58 scale
2'	Zauberflote	(topboard big enough for III ranks)
8'	Trompette	#4 French
	Tremulant	

Positiv Organ — 61 pipes, 2½" pressure

8'	Nason Flute	common mahogany fronts
4'	Koppelflote	common spotted
2⅔'	Nazard	Special Rohrflote (small) chim #7
2'	Blockflote	common tin, coned
1⅗'	Tierce	common tin, coned
1'	Sifflote	common tin, coned
8'	Rohr Schalmei	prepared for in Great chamber
	Tremulant	

Pedal Organ — 32 pipes, 3¼" pressure

16'	Bourdon	old 2 pipes
16'	Sanftbass	Swell Ext, #48, ⅕m, 4" wind
8'	Principal	old Great
8'	Bourdon	ext. 16'
4'	Choral Bass	ext. 8'

This specification contemplates the usage of the suitable old pipes from the present Aeolian organ, in such a manner as not to compromise in any way the tonal result. The Builder is to remove the present instrument, prepare the chambers and complete the organ in every detail.

Opus 1247 — Greek Orthodox Cathedral, Boston

Source: pipe shop notes dated November 27, 1951

Compass F - F, 49 notes, Pitch A 440

MANUAL — 2¾" pressure

8' Spitzflöte	49 pipes, lowest pipe - 5-2/3' F 3 smaller than Gt. type 4' C - 2 smaller 2' C Gt. type etc. spotted with butts to 5-1/3' G, coned throughout 1/4 m
4' Octave Flöte	12 pipes - Extension of 8'
4' Montre	49 pipes Lowest pipe = 3' F = 66 carry up to 2' C. Then as #60 at 4' C ½ 18th tapered 2 scales, slotted and roll tuned. 80% tin 1/4m

Rausch-Zimbel (II - V rks.)

Scales all #50 ½ 18th
spotted and coned ¼m

12.15	12
12.15.19	8
8.12.15.19	12
1. 8.12.15	12
1. 5. 8.12.15	5
	49 notes

Pedal Effect (Played on lower 12 keys)

16' Spitzbass	12 pipes Lowest pipe = 11' F = Quintaton = #48 scale 8' CC = 3 smaller than Gt. type Spitzflöte
8' Montre	12 pipes Lowest pipe 5-2/3' F = 55. 4' C = 62, tapered 2, slotted and roll tuned
Pedal Effect only	(releases four switches of 12 notes each, controlling lower 12 of manual stops, so that pedal switches only operate on lower 12 keys)

Notes on construction:

1. Bass pipes to be racked with pins.
2. Pipes to be voiced in Cathedral.
3. No top boards except for mixtures.
4. All wood to be stained per sample.
5. Console to consist of one manual mounted separate from chests.
6. Reisner switches to be installed at keyboard.
7. Stop controls to be mechanical reversibles with light indicators.

Opus 1151 — Chapel of Grace, Grace Cathedral, San Francisco

Source: Pipe shop notes, reed voicing dated June 9, 1952

The present Aeolian organ #1738 is to be rebuilt to the following specification:

Great Organ — 73 pipes, 4½" pressure

8'	Principal	#45, ¼m ½ 17th in old 8' Diapason
8'	Gedeckt Pommer	lower 15 as #7. Then merge to #8, chimneys from 5⅓' G, on old Gemshorn
8'	Gemshorn	Flute Conique scale to 1'C. Then increase gradually 4 scales. In old 8' Clarabella
8'	Gemshorn Celeste	T.C., 2 smaller than Flute Conique scale, trebles increasing to Flute Conique scale after 1'C. In old Dulciana, block off lower 12.
4'	Prestant	#57, ½ 18th, ¼m in old 4' Octave
4'	Gemshorn	extension

III	Plein Jeu	all #48 ¼m	
		15.19.22	18
		12.15.19	24
		8.12.15	12
		1.8.12	7
	Tremolo		

Swell Organ — 73 pipes, 4½" pressure

16'	Lieblich Gedackt	old rohrflote, ext. 8'
8'	Viola Pomposa	#50 ¼m tapered 2 scales, in old Horn Diapason
8'	Viola Celeste	#60 etc in old Voix Celeste
8'	Koppel Flote	lower 12 from old Rohrflote, from 4'C Koppel 4 scales smaller, merging to regular in 14 notes
4'	Spitzprincipal	#60 slotted, etc., in old Salicional
4'	Koppel Flote	ext. 8', enlarge trebles
2'	Octavin	#70, ½ 18th, in old 2-⅔' Nazard
2'	Koppel Flote	ext. 8', enlarge trebles
II	Sesquialtera	2⅔ Rohrflote as 1136 Positiv
1⅗	Baroque Tierce	on old Cornet Mixture
8'	Trompette	#4 French on old Cornopean
4'	Rohr Schalmei	per 1203 *[The Mother Church, Boston]* sample, on 8' Oboe
	Tremolo	

Pedal Organ — 32 pipes, 5" pressure

16'	Montre	on old 16' Diapason
16'	Gemshorn	ext. Great 8', as 1075 Swell, merging to Flute Conique, on old Bourdon
16'	Lieblich Gedeckt	Swell
8'	Principal	ext. 16'
8'	Flute	Swell
4'	Choral Bass	ext. 8'
16'	Contre Trompette	Sw. Ext. ½ length, 5" scale, new chest
8'	Trompette	Swell
4'	Clairon	Swell

Opus 825-A — St. Paul's School, Concord, New Hampshire

Hutchings Op. 176, 1888, Rebuilt by Skinner in 1930 as Op. 825 and Aeolian-Skinner in 1953 as Op. 825-A. Source: pipe shop notes dated May 21, 1953

Great Organ — 61 pipes, reduce pressure to 4"

16'	Quintaton	old Great 2nd Open capped, new from 4'C based on #42	
8'	Principal	new #44 on 1st open, use old bass in case	
8'	Bourdon	new #1 on Principal Flute	
8'	Gemshorn	Erzahler revoiced	
4'	Octave	new #56 on Octave	
4'	Flute Harmonique	old, as is	
2⅔'	Twelfth	new #65 on 12th	
2'	Fifteenth	new #68 on 15th	
III	Fourniture	all #48 at 8'CC, ½ 18th, on old III Mixture	
		15.19.22	18
		12.15.19	12
		8.12.15	12
		1.8.12	19

III	Scharff	all #46 at 8'CC, ½ 18, new on new chest	
		22.26.29	12
		19.22.26	12
		15.19.22	12
		12.15.19	12
		8.12.15	13

8' Trompette-en-Chamade new on Tromba, French, harmonic at #25
4' Clairon-en-Chamade 12 pipes, ext.
Trompette not subject to couplers

Swell Organ — 68 pipes, 7½" pressure

16'	Bourdon	old, as is
8'	Geigen	old Choir Diapason on 8' Diapason
8'	Salicional	old, rescaled and revoiced from 4'C
8'	Voix Celeste	old, rescaled and revoiced from 4'C
8'	Gedeckt	old, with new canister tops
8'	Flute Celeste II	old, as is
8'	Echo Gamba	old, revoiced
4'	Prestant	old octave as is
4'	Flute Triangulaire	old as is
2'	Octavin	old Flautino rescaled and revoiced, break back top octave

IV	Plein Jeu	all #48 at 8'CC, ½ 18th on old Mixture V	
		19.22.26.29	12
		15.19.22.26	12
		12.15.19.22	12
		8.12.15.19	12
		1.8.12.15	7
		1.5.8.12	6

16'	Fagot	New ½ length on Waldhorn
8'	Trompette	new #4 on Cornopean
8'	Oboe	old, as is
8'	Vox Humana	old, as is
4'	Clairon	new #4 on Clarion
	Tremulant	

Choir Organ — 68 pipes, 7½" pressure

8'	Viola Pomposa	new #50 on Diapason
8'	Viola Celeste	old Gamba rescaled to #60 etc. as Viola and revoiced
8'	Concert Flute	old, as is
8'	Dulciana	old, as is
4'	Flute	old, as is
2'	Piccolo	old, rescaled and revoiced
II	Sesquialtera	old and new on old Carillon III
8'	Clarinet	old, as is
8'	English Horn	old, as is
	Tremulant	
	Harp	
	Celesta	

Solo-Antiphonal Organ — 61 pipes, 5" pressure

8'	Gedeckt Pommer	new 2 larger than #8 on Diapason
4'	Principal	new #60 on Octave

III-V	Mixture	new on Tromba	
		15.19.22	18
		12.15.19	24
		5.8.12.15	12
		1.5.8.12.15	7

8'	Trompette-en-Chamade	Great, not subject to couplers
8'	French Horn	in Swell Box
	French Horn Tremulant	

Positiv Organ — 56 pipes, 2" pressure

All new and new chest. All as 1207 (St. Paul's Cathedral, Boston) Positiv. The Singend Gedeckt is to be of Oak and stained per the color sample for the console. Wood throughout as 1207.

8'	Singend
4'	Koppelflote
2'	Italian Principal
1⅗'	Terz
1⅓'	Larigot
III	Zimbel
	Tremulant

Pedal Organ — 32 pipes, 5" pressure

32'	Resultant	
16'	Principal	old great 16' metal Diapason revoiced on job
16'	Violone	new #44 on 16' Diapason. Provide foot blocks.
16'	Bourdon	old, as is
16'	Echo Lieblich	Swell
8'	Octave	borrowed from 16' Principal, make borrow action for 12 in Great chest 12 pipes
8'	Gedeckt	old as is, 12 pipes
8'	Still Gedeckt	Swell
4'	Choral Bass	old Great Octave #57 on new chest
III	Fourniture	new on new chest, all #46 at 8'CC 10.12.15
32'	Contre Fagot	Swell Ext., ½ length, 7½" pressure
16'	Posaune	Trombone revoiced on 4" pressure
16'	Fagot	Swell
8'	Trumpet	ext. 16', 4" pressure, old
4'	Clarion	new chest for 12 notes, 4" pressure, 12 pipes

Notes: remove French Horn reservoir and wind from Swell. Remove Tromba reservoir and wind from Great. This specification contemplates the usage of such materials from the old instrument as will in no way compromise the result. The entire organ is to be releathered (except console).

Opus 330-A — Fifth Church of Christ Scientist, New York, New York

Source: pipe shop notes dated March 26, 1954 (Op. 330 originally built 1921)

Great Organ — 61 pipes, 5" pressure

16'	Quintaton	old 2nd Diapason, capped and revoiced on old 16' Diapason topboard lower 32 on new chest
8'	Principal	new #43 ¼m, spotted, ½ 17th on old 1st Diapason tb
8'	Harmonic Flute	new #50 scale spotted metal on old 2nd diapason tb

502

8'	Spitzflote	new 2 - 52 etc type spotted metal on old Harm. Flute tb
8'	Gedeckt	old revoiced
4'	Principal	new #56 ¼m, ½ 18 spotted metal on old 4' Octave tb
4'	Flute	old revoiced
2⅔'	Quint	new #66 ¼m, ½ 18th spotted metal, new chest
2'	Super Octave	new #68, ¼m, ½ 18th spotted metal, new chest
IV-VI	Fourniture	new on new chest, all #46 at 8'CC ¼m, ½ 18th spotted metal, doubled ranks two scales smaller, long feet

19.22.26.29	12
15.19.22.26	12
12.15.19.22	12
8.12.15.15.19	6
1.8.12.12.15.15	19

III	Cymbel	new on new chest, all #48 at 8'CC ¼ ½ 18th spotted

26.29.33	12
22.26.29	12
19.22.26	12
15.19.22	6
12.15.19	6
8.12.15	13

	Chimes	

Swell Organ — 73 pipes, 7" pressure

16'	Bourdon	old as is
8'	Geigen	new #46 ¼m, ½ 18th spotted metal on old 8' Diapason
8'	Viole de Gambe	new #54 ¼ spotted metal on new chest
8'	Viole Celeste	new #54 ¼ spotted metal on new chest
8'	Echo Viole	old Viol d'Orchestre revoiced
8'	Echo Viole Celeste	old Voix Celeste revoiced
8'	Aeoline	old revoiced
8'	Unda Maris	old revoiced, t.c.
8'	Gedeckt	old revoiced
8'	Quintadena	old revoiced
4'	Octave Geigen	new #60 ¼m, ½ 18th spotted metal on old 4' Octave
4'	Flute	old revoiced
2⅔'	Nazard	new pipes Baroque, ¼m spotted metal on new chest
2'	Fifteenth	old piccolo revoiced
IV	Plein Jeu	new on old 3rk Mixture tb, all #46 at 8'CC, ¼ ½ 18th spotted metal

15.19.22.26	12
12.15.19.22	12
8.12.15.19	12
1.8.12.15	25

III	Scharff	new pipes on new chest, all #48 at 8'CC ¼ ½ 18th spotted metal

22.26.29	12
19.22.26	12
15.19.22	12
12.15.19	6
8.12.15	19

16'	Contre Trompette	new #4 French on old Posaune tb
8'	Trompette	new #3 French on old 8' Cornopean
8'	Flugel Horn	old revoiced

8'	Vox Humana	old revoiced
4'	Clairon	New #3 French on old 4' Clarion tb
	Tremulant	

Choir Organ — 73 pipes, 6" pressure

8'	Viola	new #50 ¼m, tapered spotted metal on new chest
8'	Viola Celeste	new #60 at 8'CC, at no.22, #50 reg at 8'CC on new chest
8'	Concert Flute	old as is
8'	Kleine Erzahler II	new common, on old Flute Celeste
4'	Nachthorn	old 4' Flute as is
2⅔'	Nazard	new Rohr type spotted metal on old 8' Dulciana
2'	Blockflote	old 2' Piccolo revoiced
1⅗'	Tierce	new Baroque ⅙ mouth on new chest
8'	Clarinet	old revoiced
	Harp	
	Celesta	second hand to be used
	Tremulant	

Positiv Organ — 61 pipes, 2½" pressure, new pipes, reservoir and chest

8'	Nason Flute	common wood, as #1136 [Westminster Pres., Buffalo, NY]
4'	Koppel Flute	common, spotted metal
2'	Principal	#70, ¼m, tin ½ 18th
1⅓'	Larigot	#75 ¼m tin, ½ 18th
1'	Sifflote	common Baroque, ⅙ mouth
III	Cymbel	as 1207 [St. Paul's Episcopal Cathedral, Boston] Positiv, all #48 at 8'CC

36.40.43	6
33.36.40	6
29.33.36	6
26.29.33	6
22.26.29	6
19.22.26	6
15.19.22	6
12.15.19	6
8.12.15	13

8'	Cromorne	common
	Tremulant	

Solo Organ — 73 pipes, 10" pressure

8'	Gamba	old revoiced
8'	Gamba Celeste	old revoiced
8'	French Horn	old revoiced
8'	English Horn	old rebuilt and revoiced
8'	Tuba	old revoiced (15" pressure)
	Tremulant	

Echo Organ — 73 pipes, 5" pressure (enclosed and floating)

16'	Dulciana	old as is
8'	Viole	old as is, on present tb
8'	Viole Celeste	old as is, on new chest
8'	Flute Celeste II	new common 2 - 56, on new chest
8'	Gedeckt	old as is
8'	Vox Humana	old as is
	Tremulant	

504

	Chimes	(old 20 plus 1 new F)

Antiphonal Organ — 61 notes, 5" pressure (enclosed and floating)

8'	Diapason	new #44, ¼m, ½ 17th spotted metal
4'	Octave	new #56, ¼m, ½ 18th spotted metal
III	Plein Jeu	all #48 at 8'CC ¼m ½ 18th

15.19.22	18
12.15.19	24
8.12.15	12
1.8.12	7

8'	Trompette	new #4 French

Pedal Organ — 32 pipes, 5" pressure

32'	Bourdon	old as is, ext. 16'
16'	Contre Basse	new #1 on new chest
16'	Principal	metal, old revoiced
16'	Bourdon	old as is
16'	Violone	new #42 zinc and spotted metal on new chest
16'	Quintaten	Great
16'	Echo Lieblich	Swell
8'	Principal	Old Swell 8' Diapason on new chest
8'	Cello	ext. Violone, 12 pipes
8'	Gedeckt	ext. 16', old
8'	Still Gedeckt	Swell
5⅓'	Quint	Old Great 4' Principal and 5 old basses on new chest
4'	Choral Bass	old Swell 4' Principal on new chest
4'	Nachthorn	new common Baroque on new chest
2'	Blockflote	new common Baroque on new chest
III	Fourniture	all #44 at 8'CC ¼m ½ 17th spotted 15.19.22 16' Series
II	Cymbel	all #46 at 8'CC ¼m ½ 17th spotted 26.29 16' Series
32'	Bombarde	new Swell extension CCCC=7" as 1196 [Covenant Presbyterian, Charlotte, NC] 7" pressure new chest
16'	Bombarde	old Trombone revoiced on 7" pressure
16'	Trompette	Swell
8'	Trumpet	old revoiced, ext. 16'
4'	Clarion	new pipes and chest, ext. 8'
	Chimes	

Antiphonal-Echo Pedal — 32 pipes, 5" pressure

16'	Principal	new #36 merging to meet #44 on new chest, ext. Antiphonal 8' Diapason
16'	Bourdon	new #1-A on new chest
16'	Dulciana	Echo
8'	Principal	Antiphonal
8'	Flute	ext. 16', new on new chest
8'	Dulciana	Echo
16'	Posaune	old Swell 16' Posaune on new chest
8'	Posaune	ext. 16'

Opus 664-A — Hill Auditorium, University of Michigan, Ann Arbor

1892 Farrand & Votey Op. 700, 1913 Hutchings, 1927 Skinner Op. 664
Source: pipe shop notes dated May 26, 1954

This job is to be undertaken in two parts as follows:
Phase 1. Tonal changes to be done this summer.
Phase 2. New console and pedal relays to be installed January of 1955.

PHASE I
The tonal changes are listed in the specification. The specification also contains notes regarding certain Swell folds, chests, reservoirs, bass chests, stop actions, etc., listed under each division.

General Procedure
1. Send to Ann Arbor sufficient trays to pack up all unused stops and stops to be re-voiced.
2. Remove pipes as above and return to plant. Leave 32' Octave of Bombarde in place at present.
3. Remove and return to plant all top and rack boards upon which new pipes are to be set.
4. Make test examination of chest pouches and primary leathers to ascertain condition. Report to plant as to those parts which may require releathering. Examine present switch work.
5. Pressures on Great and String organs are to be lowered considerably, in fact to 3". Chest pouch springs may be found too heavy in some cases, although a test made recently on Great seemed to show the reverse. Doubtful valve boards should be removed and one coil cut off bottom of springs. Examine all reservoirs.
6. Clean organ thoroughly. Special attention to be given to reeds not to be returned for revoicing.
7. Replace pipes of Solo and Choir organs. Regulate and fine tune.
8. Revised top boards and new pipes will be supplied as soon as possible.

Great Organ — 61 pipes, 3" pressure
Voicing   1. Flues — unforced, with flue ensembles equal in power to Swell, Positiv and Pedal flue ensembles.
      2. Reeds — Great reeds mild, with German type for 16' reed

16'	Principal	new #33 scale, 2⁄9 ¼ mouth, ½ 17th, long feet. 8' Octave spotted metal butts. Bass zinc, treble spotted on old 16' Diapason top board
16'	Quintaten	old 2nd Diapason capped, use present top board provide inside caps
8'	Principal	new #46, ¼, ½ 17th spotted on old 1st Diapason top board
8'	Rohrflote	new #4, ¼ spotted on old 8' Erzahler top board
4'	Principal	new #59, ¼, ½ 18th spotted on old 4' Octave top board
4'	Spitzflote	new Flute Conique scale ¼ spotted on old 4' Principal top board
2'	Octave	New #70 ¼ ½ 17th spotted on old 15th top board
2'	Waldflote	new common Baroque Nachthorn plain metal. On old 5⅓ Quint top board

2⅔'	Rauschquinte	new II ranks on old Twelfth and tenth top boards. Rank I = 12th = 67 on old 12th tb Rank II = 15th = 72 ¼m, ½ on 17th, spotted on old 10th tb
2'	Mixture IV-VI	all #49 @ 8'CC ¼ mouth ½ 18th tin

15.19.22.26	12
12.15.19.22.26	12
8.12.15.19.22.22	12
8.12.15.15.19.19	12
8.8.12.12.15.15	13

1'	Scharff IV	all #47@8'CC ¼ mouth ½ 18th tin

22.26.29.33	12
19.22.26.29	12
15.19.22.26	12
12.15.19.22	12
8.12.15.19	6
5.8.12.15	7

16'	Posaune	Old Swell 16' Posaune revoiced new German type shallots use old Great 16' Trombone top board. Note old great #3 bass chest to be replaced with a new chest
8'	Trumpet	Old Swell 8' Cornopean revoiced on old Great 8' Tromba top board
4'	Clarion	old as is, revoiced

Note: the old Great reed chest is on a separate reservoir with 7½" wind. This is to be lowered to 5" wind.

Positiv Organ — 61 pipes, 3" pressure

Voicing: Flues — unforced, with flue ensembles equal in power to Swell, Great and Pedal flue ensembles.

This division will use the old enclosed Great chest and the string organ chest. The shades and box panels are to be removed and returned and reservoirs lowered to new wind pressure.

8'	Principal	new #47 ¼ ½ 17th spotted metal butts, on old Great 3rd Diapason topboard
8'	Gedeckt	(Nason Flt.) new Nason Flute, wood, with old Clarabella basses (replaced with #1 Metal stopped diapason, #57 sc @ 4'C)
4'	Octave	New #60 ¼ ½ 18th
4'	Koppelflote	New common spotted
2'	Octave	New #71 ¼ ½ 18th tin on old Great 4' Flute
2'	Blockflote	new common Baroque spotted 65 scale on old String Voix Celeste
1⅓'	Quint	new Baroque Sifflote scale #66 on string organ 8' Gamba Celeste top board
1⅓'	Mixture IV-VI	all #49 @8'CC ¼ mouth ½ 17th tin

19.22.26.29	12
15.19.22.26.29	12
12.15.19.22.26.26	12
8.12.15.19.22.22	12
8.12.12.15.15.19	6
8.8.12.12.15.15	7

⅔'	Scharff III	all #50 scale @8'CC, ¼ mouth ½ 17th tin

40.43.45	5
36.38.40	7
33.36.38	5

29.31.33	7
26.29.31	5
22.24.26	7
19.22.24	5
15.17.19	7
12.15.17	5
8.12.15	8

Swell Organ — 73 pipes, lower pressure to 3 ¾", open toes of old stops to compensate

Voicing 1. Flues — unforced, with flue ensembles equal in power to Great, Positiv and Pedal flue ensembles.

2. Reeds — fiery

16'	Dulciana	old as is
8'	Principal	new #46 ¼4½ 17th, spotted on old Diapason top board
8'	Flute Harmonique	new 49 scale, one large of Great type, spotted on old Clarabella top board
8'	Rohrflote	new #4 spotted on old Rohrflote top board
8'	Viole de Gambe	new #54 1/4 spotted on old 16' Bourdon top board
8'	Viole Celeste	new (tenor c) ¼ spotted on old Viole d'Orchestre top board
8'	Voix Celeste II	old as is
8'	Quintadena	old as is
8'	Flauto Dolce	old as is
8'	Flute Celeste	old as is, tenor C
4'	Octave	new #58 ¼ ½ 17th spotted on old 4' Octave top board
4'	Flute Harmonique	new great type, spotted, 62 scale, on old Flute Triangulaire top board
4'	Unda Maris II	old as is
2'	Octavin	new #70 ¼ ½ 18th spotted on old Flautino top board
2⅔'	Mixture VI	Unison: #48@8'CC ½ 18th ¼ mouth
		Quint : #50@8'CC ½ 18th¼ mouth
		Tierce: #52@8'CC ½ 18th ¼ mouth

15.22.24.26.36.43	12
15.22.24.26.29.36	12
15.19.22.24.26.29	12
8.12.15.17.19.22	12
8.12.15.15.17.19	6
1.8.10.12.15.15	7

8'	Cornet V	from tenor C up only, no lower octave
		4' - 2' - 1⅓' - 1' - ⅘'
		57 - 64 - 72 - 76 - 80
16'	Bombarde	new as 909C (All Saints Worcester)
		16'=3¾", 8'=2¾", 4'=2", 2'=1⁹⁄₁₆" on old Posaune top board, lower 6 mitred to 12'0".
8'	Trompette	new #3 French shallots on old French Trumpet top board
8'	Oboe	old revoiced on new pressure on old top board
8'	Vox Humana	install present Echo Vox Humana on present Swell vox top board. Put Swell Vox Humana into Echo organ.
4'	Clarion	new #3 French shallots on old Clarion top board
	Tremulant	

Note: the old reeds were on 10" pressure with separate reservoir. Reduce to 5".

Choir Organ — 73 notes, 6" pressure

16'	Gamba	old as is
8'	Diapason	old as is
8'	Concert Flute	old as is
8'	Dulcet II	old as is
8'	Gamba	old as is, ext. 16'
8'	Gedeckt	#7 new in place of Dulciana 8'
8'	Kleine Erzahler II	old as is
4'	Gemshorn	old as is
4'	Flute	old as is
2⅔'	Nasat	new common Baroque spotted
2'	Blockflote	new common Baroque spotted in place of 2' Piccolo
1⅗'	Terz	new common Baroque spotted
1'	Sifflote	new common Baroque in place of 1⅐' Septieme
16'	Bassoon	old as is
8'	Bassoon	old as is, ext. 16'
8'	Cromorne	common in place of 8' Clarinet
4'	Rohr Schalmei	common in place of 8' English Horn
	Tremulant	
	Harp	old as is
	Celesta	" " Physharmonica to be removed and returned

Solo Organ — 73 notes, 3 pressures

10" pressure

8'	Stentorphone	old as is
8'	Flauto Mirabilis	old as is
8'	Gamba	old as is
8'	Gamba Celeste	old as is
4'	Octave	old as is
4'	Orchestral Flute	old as is
16'	Heckelphone	old as is
8'	Heckelphone	old as is, ext. 16'
8'	Corno di Bassetto	old as is
8'	Orchestral Oboe	old as is

15" pressure

16'	Contra Tuba	old as is
8'	Tuba	old as is
8'	French Trumpet	old Swell 8' French Trumpet revoiced on 15" to take place of French Horn
4'	Clarion	old as is

25" pressure

8'	Tuba Mirabilis	old as is
	2 Tremulants — 10" and 15"	

[Chimes, 25 tubes, advertisement of June, 1955, The Diapason]

Echo Organ — as is except noted [61 notes]

8'	Gedeckt	
8'	Muted Viole	
8'	Unda Maris	
8'	Vox Humana	(Swell Vox Humana to be moved to Echo)
	Tremulant	

Pedal Organ — 32 pipes, 5" pressure

32'	Diapason	old as is, ext. 16' Diapason
32'	Violone	old as is, ext. 16' Violone
16'	Diapason	old 2nd Diapason wood, as is
16'	Principal	new #31 scale, 2/9, 1/4 mouth, zinc and spotted, long feet, in place of 1st wood Diapason
16'	Violone	old as is
16'	Bourdon	new throughout, ext. 8 Gedeckt

$$\begin{array}{ll}
CCC & =37 \\
CCC\# & =38 \\
DDD & =39 \\
DDD\# & =41 \\
EEE & =42 \\
FFF & =43 \\
FFF\# & =45 \\
GGG & =46 \\
GGG\# & =47 \\
AAA & =48 \\
AAA\# & =50 \\
BBB & =52
\end{array}$$

(CC =54), at 8' C #6 metal stopped diapason. Use present chest.

16'	Dulciana	Swell
16'	Gamba	Choir
8'	Principal	new #45, 1/4 1/2 17th, butts for lower 12 spotted. See note below for chest.
8'	Gedeckt	#54 scale Gedeckt Pommer, new 56 pipes extension
8'	Cello	ext 16' Violone, as is
4'	Octave	new 32 pipes #58, 1/4 1/2 17th spotted, see note below for chest
4'	Gedeckt	ext. 8'
2'	Gedeckt	ext. 8'
2 2/3'	Rauschquinte II	12th=#65, 15th=#70, 1/4 1/2 17th spotted, see note below for chest
1 1/3'	Mixture IV	all #46 at 8'CC, 1/4 1/2 17th spotted, on old Pedal Mixture chest, 19.22.26.29 no breaks
1'	Scharff	all #50 at 8'CC, 1/4 1/2 17th spotted 22.26.29.31
32'	Bombarde	old revoiced on light pressure, ext. Ophicleide
16'	Ophicleide	old revoiced on light pressure
16'	Posaune	Great
16'	Bombarde	Swell
8'	Trumpet	old revoiced on light pressure, ext. 16'
4'	Clarion	old revoiced on light pressure, ext. 16'

[Chimes, source noted in Solo Organ, above.]

Note: a small 32 note pitman chest will be required for 8' Principal, 4' Octave, 2 2/3' Rauschquinte II, and 1' Scharff IV.

Opus 1269 — Residence, Senator Emerson Richards, Atlantic City, New Jersey

Source: pipe shop notes May 13, 1953 and October 11, 1954 (stop spellings as in source)
* = stops voiced under the direction of G. Donald Harrison. Balance of Great and all of the Positiv by Hans Steinmeyer, Bavaria.

Great Organ — 61 pipes, 3" pressure

16'	Spitz Principal*	spotted metal, spotted metal butts in bass, based on a #46 at 8'CC, ¼ taper, ¼ mouth, cut-up ⅕, ½ 19th
8'	Gedeckt Pommer	spotted metal, copper basses
8'	Principal*	spotted metal, spotted metal butts in bass, #44, ¼m, ½ 17th, cut-up ⅕
8'	Dolce Principal*	spotted metal
8'	Bell Gamba*	spotted metal
8'	Gemshorn	tin
8'	Kleingedeckt	tin
8'	Holzgedeckt	stopped wood
5⅓'	Quint	spotted metal
4'	Prestant*	spotted metal, #55, ¼ mouth, ½ 18th, cut-up ⅕
4'	Spitzprincipal*	spotted metal
4'	Blockflote	tin
4'	Rohrflote	spotted metal
2'	Spillflote	tin
II	Rauschquint*	12.15 no breaks, tin Twelfth=#64, ⅕ mouth, cut-up about ⅕, ½ 19th Fifteenth=#66, ¼ mouth, cut-up about ⅕, ½ 19th
IV-V	Fourniture*	tin, all based on #44 at 8'CC irregular. ¼ mouth, cut up about ⅕, ½ 19th-20th

15.19.22.26	12
12.15.19.22	12
8.12.15.19	12
1.5.8.12.15	25

III-V	Kleinmixture	tin

19.22.26	12
15.19.22	12
12.15.19.22	12
8.12.15.19	13
5.8.12.15	12

IV	Cymbal	tin

22.26.29.33	12
19.22.26.29	12
15.19.22.26	12
12.15.19.22	7
8.12.15.19	6
5.8.12.15	6
1.5.8.12	6

III-V	Cornet	spotted metal and tin

1.12.15	12
1.8.12.15.17	49

Positiv Organ — 61 pipes, 2-¾" pressure

8'	Violflote	tin
8'	Quintaton	spotted metal

4'	Holzprincipal	open wood		
4'	Viola d'Gambe	tin		
4'	Koppleflote	tin		
4'	Nachthorn	spotted metal		
2⅔'	Nazard	tin		
2'	Italian Principal	tin		
2'	Gemsleine	tin		
1⅗'	Tierce	tin		
II	Quartain	tin		
			19.22	49
			12.15	12
IV	Terzian cymbal	tin		
			24.26.29.33	12
			22.24.26.29	12
			19.22.24.26	12
			15.19.22.24	13
			15.17.19.22	12
IV	Zartcymbal tin			
			15.19.22	12
			12.15.19.22	12
			8.12.15.19	12
			5. 8.12.15	13
			1.5.8.12	12
	Tremulant			

Swell Organ — 61 pipes, 5" pressure

16'	Contra Dolce	open metal, prepared for		
8'	Montre	spotted metal, prepared for		
8'	Clarabella	open wood		
8'	Viola Pomposa*	spotted metal, spotted metal butts in bass		
8'	Viola Celest*	to GG, spotted metal, spotted metal butts in bass		
8'	Salicional*	spotted metal		
8'	Vox Celest*	to DD, spotted metal		
8'	Dulciana	spotted metal		
8'	Unda Maris	to GG, spotted metal		
8'	Stopped Diapason	stopped wood		
4'	Geigen Octave*	spotted metal		
4'	Flute Traverso	Har.open wood		
4'	Dolce	spotted metal, prepared for		
4'	Aeolines Celeste II	tin, prepared for		
3⅕'	Tenth*	spotted metal		
2⅔'	Twelfth*	spotted metal		
2'	Flautino*	spotted metal		
III	Sesquialtera*	tin		
			31.33.36	15
			29.31.33	7
			22.24.26	15
			17.19.22	4
			12.15.17	20
III	Dolce Cornet	tin		
			12.15.17	49
			10.12.15	12

IV	Plein Jeu*	tin		
			19.22.26.29	17
			15.19.22.26	19
			12.15.19.22	6
			8.12.15.19	11
			5.8.12.15	8

16'	Bass Clarinet*	common metal
8'	Trumpette Harmonic*	spotted metal
4'	Hautbois*	spotted metal
	Tremulant	

Choir Organ — 61 pipes, 5" pressure

16'	Quintaton	stopped metal, prepared for
8'	Diapason	spotted metal, prepared for
8'	Hohlflute	open wood
8'	Gamba*	spotted metal
8'	Gamba Celest*	to EE, spotted metal
8'	Dulcett II*	celeste rank to EE, spotted metal
8'	Stillgedeckt	stopped wood
4'	Fugara*	spotted metal
4'	Blockflote	tin, prepared for
4'	Flute d'Amour	stopped wood
4'	Orchestral Violes II	tin, prepared for
2⅔'	Nassat*	spotted metal
2'	Flagolet*	spotted metal
1⅗'	Tierce*	spotted metal
III-IV	Petite Fourniture	tin, prepared for

		12.15.19	12
		8.12.15.19	17
		5.8.12.15	20
		1.5.8.12	12

16'	Contra Fagotto*	
8'	Petite Trumpette	spotted metal, prepared for
8'	English Horn*	common metal
8'	Vox Humana*	common metal
4'	Rohrschalmi	spotted metal
	Tremulant	

Pedal Organ — 32 pipes, 5" pressure

32'	Untersatz	stopped wood, ext. 16' Bourdon
16'	Contra Bass	open wood
16'	Spitzprincipal	Great
16'	Violone	common metal
16'	Contra Dolce	Swell
16'	Bourdon	stopped wood
16'	Lieblichbass	stopped wood
10⅔'	Sub Quint	common metal
8'	Principalbass	common metal and spotted metal
8'	Geigenprincipal	spotted metal
8'	Dolce	Swell
8'	Flute Overte	common metal
6⅖'	Terz	common metal

5⅓'	Quint	spotted metal
4'	Choralbass	spotted metal
4'	Prestant	spotted metal
4'	Harmonic Flute	spotted metal
2'	Super Octave	spotted metal
IV	Mixturebass*	metal and spotted metal 4'–3⅕'–2⅔'–2' no breaks
III	Scharf	spotted metal 2'–2⅔'–1' no breaks
16'	Trombone*	common metal
16'	Contra Fagot	to Choir
16'	Bass Clarinet	Swell
8'	Trumpet*	spotted metal
4'	Clarion*	spotted metal
4'	Fagott	Choir 16'
2'	Kornet*	spotted metal

Note: *In the dedication booklet, Emerson Richards writes:* "Principal Chorus planned and voiced by G. Donald Harrison (Aeolian-Skinner Organ Co., Boston), in consultation with Emerson Richards. All pipes have slide tuners. Details of the Steinmeyer pipe scales and voicing are not given because they are not based on American practice. The cut-up is less and the nicking very fine or absent in many ranks."

Opus 1273 — St. Paul's Episcopal Church, Chester, Pennsylvania

Source: pipe shop notes dated January 10, 1955

Great Organ — 61 pipes, 3" pressure

8'	Principal	#45, ¼m, ½ 17th
8'	Gedeckt	exactly 1254 [St. Michael & All Angels, Baltimore], special wood (Nason Flute)
8'	Flute Conique	Swell
4'	Octave	#57, ¼m, ½ 17th tin
4'	Rohrflote	as 1254 and 1207, #8, 4'C= 59, etc.
2⅔'	Twelfth	#68
2'	Fifteenth	#70
III-V	Fourniture	Special J.S.W (Stinkens), tin

19.22.26	12
15.19.22	12
12.15.19.22	12
8.12.15.19	12
1.5.8.12.15	13

Chimes
Tower Bells
Tremulant

Swell Organ — 68 pipes, 4" pressure

16'	Quintaton	#44
8'	Rohrbordun	#4
8'	Viola Pomposa	#50 tapered 2
8'	Viola Celeste	#60, then as Viola
8'	Flute Conique	#48, 4'C=#60
4'	Spitzflote	#60

514

2⅔'	Nasat	#7 Rohrflote
2'	Zauberflote	common
III	Plein Jeu	common, 15.19.22
16'	Contre Hautbois	as #1110 [St. Stephen's, Richmond], 4" diam.
8'	Trompette	#4
8'	Vox Humana	prepared for
4'	Rohr Schalmei	common
	Tremulant	

Pedal Organ — 32 pipes, 4" pressure

16'	Contre Basse	exactly as #1272 [Juilliard Recital Hall], #40 at CCC

CCC	=40		CC	=47		C	=57	
CCC#	=41		CC#	=48		C#	=58	
DDD	=42		DD	=49		D	=59	
DDD#	=42		DD#	=50		D#	=60	
EEE	=43		EE	=50		E	=61	
FFF	=43		FF	=51		F	=61	
FFF#	=44		FF#	=52		F#	=61	
GGG	=44		GG	=53		G	=62, etc.	
GGG#	=45		GG#	=53				
AAA	=45		AA	=54				
AAA#	=46		AA#	=55				
BBB	=46		BB	=56				

16'	Quintaton	Swell
8'	Spitzprincipal	ext. 16'
8'	Quintaton	Swell
4'	Choral Bass	ext. 8'
II	Fourniture	2⅔'- 2', #66 and #68 respectively
16'	Contre Hautbois	Swell
8'	Hautbois	Swell
4'	Hautbois	Swell

Opus 1285 — Washington Hebrew Congregation, Washington, D.C.

Source: pipe shop notes dated November 1, 1954

Great Organ — 61 pipes, 3¾" pressure

16'	Violone	#42, #50 tapered 2, etc.
8'	Principal	#43, 2/7m, ½ 18th
8'	Holzflote [sic]	Great type Gemshorn
8'	Bourdon	#9
4'	Gross Octave	#55, 2/7m, ½ 18th
4'	Flute Harmonique	Great type 2 larger
2⅔'	Twelfth	#64
2'	Fifteenth	#67
IV-VI	Fourniture	All #45 at 8'CC, ¼m, ½ 18th

19.22.26.29	12
15.19.22.26	12
12.15.19.22	12
8.12.15.15.19	12
1.1.5.8.12.15	13

III-V	Cymbel	all #46 at 8'CC, ¼m, ½ 18th	
		29.33.36	12
		26.29.33	12
		22.26.29	12
		19.22.26	6
		15.19.22	6
		12.12.15.19	6
		8.8.12.15.15	7
8'	Trompette-en-Chamade	French, Harmonic at #19, 7" pressure	
4'	Clairon-en-Chamade	ext. 8, neither subject to couplers	

Swell Organ — 68 pipes, 5" pressure

16'	Rohrgedeckt	Unit A, ext. 8'	
8'	Geigen Principal	#45, ¼m, ½ 18th	
8'	Viole-de-Gambe	#54	
8'	Viole Celeste	#54	
8'	Rohrflote	#4	
8'	Flauto Dolce	common	
8'	Flute Celeste	t.c., common	
4'	Prestant	#57, ¼m, ½ 18th	
4'	Waldflote	#58, ⅔ taper Spitzflote	
2'	Octavin	#68, ¼ ½ 18th	
IV	Plein Jeu	all #45 at 8'CC, ¼m, ½ 18th	
		15.19.22.26	18
		12.15.19.22	12
		8.12.15.19	12
		5.8.12.15	12
		1.5.8.12	7
III	Scharff	all #48 at 8'CC, ¼m ½ 18th	
		26.29.33	12
		22.26.29	12
		19.22.26	12
		15.19.22	12
		12.15.19	6
		8.12.15	7
16'	Bombarde	as 1118C Swell (Riverside)	
8'	Trompette	#3	
8'	Hautbois	common and French	
8'	Vox Humana	common	
4'	Clairon	#3	
	Tremulant		

Choir Organ — 68 pipes, 5" pressure

8'	Concert Flute	Great type 3 larger	
8'	Cor-de-Nuit	common	
8'	Viola Pomposa	#50 tapered 2, etc.	
8'	Viola Celeste	#60, then as Pomposa at 4'C	
8'	Unda Maris II	1st rk.= #56 Dulciana	
		2nd rk.= #68 TC Unda Maris	
4'	Montre	#60, slotted ¼, ½ 18th	
4'	Koppelflote	common	
2⅔'	Nazard	common	
2'	Blockflote	common	

1³⁄₅'	Tierce	common	
1'	Sifflote	common	
III	Zimbel	as 1118B (Riverside) all #48 at 8'CC, ¼m, ½ on 18th	

36.40.43	6
33.36.40	6
29.33.36	6
26.29.33	6
22.26.29	6
19.22.26	6
15.19.22	6
12.15.19	6
8.12.15	6
1.8.12	7

16'	English Horn	common
8'	Cromorne	common
4'	Rohr Schalmei	common
8'	Trompette-en-Chamade	Great
4'	Clairon-en-Chamade	Great
	Tremulant	

Pedal Organ — 32 pipes, 6" pressure

32'	Bourdon	to GGGG, quints to CCCC — upper 5 pipes are 1A scale carried down, ext. 16'
16'	Contre Basse	special
16'	Violone	Great
16'	Bourdon	1-A
16'	Rohr Bass	Swell
16'	Sanftbass	Ext. Choir Cor-de-Nuit = #44 Quintaton
8'	Octave	#43, ¼m
8'	Cello	Great
8'	Pommer Gedackt	#1 std. Diapason
4'	Choral Bass	#55, ¼m
4'	Spitzflote	#60, ¼m, ⅔ taper
III	Fourniture	all #45 at 8'CC, 5⅓'--2⅔'--2' no breaks
32'	Contre Bombarde	Swell ext., ½ length as Longview, CCCC=6½"
16'	Ophicleide	7" scale
16'	Bombarde	Swell
8'	Trompette	ext. 16' Ophicleide
4'	Clairon	ext. 16' Ophicleide

Opus 205-A — St. Thomas Church, New York City, New York

Source: pipe shop notes dated October 12, 1955; built 1913 by Skinner as Op. 205,
Note: Wherever there are two names for a stop the name [in brackets] is for knob engraving only. The other name is for chest orders, blueprints, pipe orders, etc.

Great Organ — 61 pipes, 3¼" pressure

16'	Quintaton	(Quintade 16) lower 17, old first diapason in case. Provide inside bungs. 18 and up, new spotted. FF=#59
8'	Principal	(Montre 8) #45, ¼m, ½ 17th, tin (tenor C)
8'	Viola	(Violoncelle 8) #50, spotted
8'	Gemshorn	new #46, ¼, ⅔ taper

8'	Bourdon	#51 metal stopped diapason, spotted, ¼m, solid caps, "S"
8'	Flute Harmonique	#48 at 8'CC, spotted, zinc bass for lower 8
4'	Principal	(Prestant 4) #58, ¼m, ½ 18th, tin
4'	Rohrflote	#59 with chimneys, ¼m, spotted "SS"
2⅔'	Quinte	#67, ¼m, ½ 18th, tin
2'	Doublette	#70 ¼m, ½ 18th, tin "SS" - top 24 doubles, 85 pipes in all, 2nd rank based on #70 at 2'C, ½ 17th
1'	Fife	(Octave 1) #82, ¼m, ½ 19th, spotted, top octave repeats
(Cornet de Recit V)		starts on g below middle C (#20) and goes to C #49, future, knob only–no pipes
IV	Kleine Mixtur	all #48 at 8'CC, ¼m, ½ 18th tin

19.22.26.29	12
15.19.22.26	12
12.15.19.22	12
8.12.15.19	12
1.8.12.15	13

IV-VI	Mixtur	all #46 at 8'CC, ¼m, ½ 18th tin "SS"

19.22.26.29	12
15.19.22.26	12
12.15.19.22	12
8.12.15.15.19.19	12
1. 8.12.12.15.15	13

IV	Scharff	all based on #48 at 8'CC, ¼m ½ 18th tin "SS"

22.26.29.33	12
19.22.26.29	12
15.19.22.26	12
12.15.19.22	6
8.12.15.19	6
1.8.12.15	13

16'	Rankett	from Positiv
8'	Krummhorn	from Positiv
4'	Rohr Schalmei	from Positiv
	Cymbelstern	

Grand Choeur Organ — Grand Choeur is the top manual on the console and controls the following divisions: Grand Choeur (chancel), Grand Choeur (Antiphonal). The antiphonal is in 3 parts — enclosed, unenclosed and pedal.

Grand Choeur (Chancel) — 61 pipes, 5" pressure

32'   Quintaten   (Quintaton 32) from CCCC 31 sc. To BBBB 42 sc., in left pedal chamber at 5" pressure, with compound magnets. From #13 to #17, old Great 3rd Open, on old Great bass chest, with new compound magnets, at 5" pressure. Organ build on job to provide inside diameter information for bungs. From #18 to #24 in front as old case pipes, (right side) at 5" pressure, with new compound magnets. Organ builder on job to provide inside diameter information for bungs. From #25 to #32, new, 55sc., spotted, on new chest inside right side with compound magnets, 5" pressure. From #33 to #61, new, 63sc., spotted, on old great 3rd open topboard for 29 trebles, pressure 5".

16'	Principal	61 pipes in left Pedal chamber on 5" pressure, as 150A (St. John the Divine), spotted

CCC	=40
CC	=48
C	=60
2'C	=70
1'C	=80
6"C	=90

8'	Octavebass	#46 graduating to #56 at 4'C, ¼m, ½ 17th, spotted. On 8' Gross Flute. New butts for bass.
8'	Flute Ouverte	future, knob only — when it goes in it will be a #50 open metal flute, on old 2nd diapason
5⅓'	Grosse Quint	(Quinte 5⅓) old Erzahler cut to length on old Erzahler topboard
4'	Octave	#56, ¼m, ½ 18th, spotted "S" on old 4' Principal topboard
3⅕'	Grosse Tierce	(Tierce 3⅕')#62, ¼m ½ 18th spotted, on old Flute Harmonique topboard "S"
	(Principal 2)	knob only
V-IX	Tierce Mixture	376 pipes, as 150A (St. John the Divine) Bombarde Mixture 4 scales smaller. First three ranks on old 4' Octave, fourth through ninth on old 3 rank Mixture.
IV-VII	Grosse Fourniture	(Grand Fourniture IV-VII) all #45 at 8'CC "S" ¼m, ½ 18th spotted

15.19.22.26	12
12.15.19.22	12
8.12.15.15.19	12
1.8.12.12.15.15	12
1.5.8.8.12.12.15	13

16'	Bombarde	French #4 scale on old Great Tuba unit
8'	Trompette	(Trompette Harmonique 8) #3 French, harmonic at middle F# on old Trumpet topboard
4'	Clairon	(Clairon Harmonique 4) #3 French, harmonic at tenor f# on old Clarion
8'	Trompette en Chamade	In gallery. Provide extra contacts in manual keys and Positiv manual keys. Does not go through couplers.

Grand Choeur (Antiphonal) — 61 pipes, 5" pressure

Enclosed Portion (old Echo chest)

8'	Flute	(Flute Ouverte 8) 61 pipes, old as is on Concert Flute
8'	Salicional	old revoiced on Salicional
8'	Voix Celeste	old revoiced on 8' Diapason
4'	Aeoline	old revoiced on old Aeoline
4'	Flute	(Flute Douce 4) knob only
	(Piccolo 2)	knob only

Unenclosed Portion (new chest)

16'	Bourdon	old pipes from stock
8'	Principal	(Diapason 8) old for low 12, from 4'C up #56, ¼m, ½ 17th, plain metal, can be old
4'	Principal	#57, ¼m ½ 17th, spotted, can be old
IV	Plein Jeu	all (not marked) at 8'CC, ¼m, ½ 18th "S"

15.19.22.26	12
12.15.19.22	12
8.12.15.19	12
1.8.12.15	25

| III | Cymbel | (Cymbale III) all #48 at 8'CC, ¼m, ½ 18th spotted |

22.26.29	12
19.22.26	12
15.19.22	12
12.15.19	12
8.12.15	13

| 16' | Bombarde | #3 French |

| 8' | Trompette | #3 French |
| 4' | Clarion | (Clairon 4) #3 French |

Pedal Portion — please mark these Pedal pipes "Antiphonal" so they will not get mixed up with the regular Pedal pipes.

16'	Principal	CCC=32sc, old chancel pedal principal on new chest, pipes to have flanges
16'	Bourdon	from manual
8'	Principal	CC=42sc, old chancel Pedal principal, new chest
V	Mixture	knob only, for future
16'	Posaune	½ length, new pipes and chest, like #1036

Positif Organ — This is the next to the bottom manual on the console and controls the following divisions:
Positif Unenclosed = Positiv
Positif Enclosed = Choir

Positiv — 61 pipes, 2¼" pressure flues, 5" pressure reeds

8'	Spitzgamba	(Viole Conique 8) #54, ¼m, ½ taper, spotted. Lower 6 pipes on 5" pressure
8'	Nason Flute	special wood, mahogany as #1207 (St. Paul's Cathedral, Boston). Use manual type stoppers.
4'	Principal	#63, ¼m, ½ 19th, tin
4'	Koppelflote	common spotted
2⅔'	Nasat	(Nasard 2⅔) Rohr type as #1207, spotted
2'	Principal	(Octave 2) #72 ¼m, ½ 18th, tin burnished
2'	Blockflote	common Baroque, tin
1⅗'	Terz	(Tierce 1-⅗) common Baroque, ⅙m, tin
1⅓'	Larigot	#77, ¼m ½ 18th, tin, principal pipes
1⅐'	Septieme	no pipes, knob only. Will go in later as a #80, ⅕m, ½ 19th, tin, set of principal pipes
1'	Oktav	(Principal 1) no pipes, knob only. Will go in later as a #84, ¼m, ½ 19th, tin, with top octave repeating
IV-VI	Mixture	(Fourniture IV-VI) all #50 at 8'CC, ¼ ½ 19th tin burnished

26.29.33.36	12
22.26.29.33	12
19.22.26.29	6
15.19.22.22.26	6
15.15.19.19.22	6
12.12.15.15.19.19	6
8.8.12.12.15.15	13

| III | Zimbel | (Cymbale III) as #1207 St. Paul's Cath. Boston, tin polished |
| II | Jeu de Clochette | unison: Baroque Sifflote scale
tierce: #50 ¼ ½ 18th burnished tin |

36.38	12
29.31	6
22.24	31
15.17	12

16'	Rankett	¼ length Vox Humana with long boots, solid caps, ⅓ slot at top, slided 5" pressure
8'	Cromorne	(Krummhorn 8) common, French shallots, 5" pressure
4'	Rohr Schalmei	common, keep up treble, 5" pressure

Choir — 61 pipes, 5" pressure

16'	Quintaton	old 8' Swell Quintadena, 57 scale at 8'CC, lower octave made from old Geigen Principal. Provide internal bungs. On old Geigen
8'	Principal	knob only
8'	Viola Pomposa	#50, ¼m, tapered, spotted, on Grosse Gamba celeste topboard
8'	Viola Celeste	as Viola Pomposa, pinched bass to #60, on old Grosse Gamba
8'	Rohrflote	4'C=#59 "S", lower octave = old bass, 12 pipes. On old Concert Flute topboard
8'	Dulciana	old rescaled to #54 at 8'CC on old Flute Harm. topboard
8'	Unda Maris	new #54, on old Kleine Erzahler topboard
4'	Prestant	#60, ½ 18th, spotted, no slots, on old 4' Gemshorn topboard
4'	Nachthorn	common Baroque 30% metal "S" on old 16' Gamba
2'	Principal	knob only
2'	Hellflote	old Piccolo revoiced (2" diam.) on old 4' Fl. Harm. topboard
1'	Piccolo	knob only
IV	Plein Jeu	all #49 at 8'CC, ¼m, ½ 18th, spotted "S"

15.19.22.26	12
12.15.19.22	12
8.12.15.19	12
1.8.12.15	13
1.5.8.12	12

16'	Buccine	½ length fagot, new 4" diam. On old Fagotto
8'	Petite Trompette	(Trompette 8) no pipes, knob only, to be extra small French Clarion on old Tr. Harm.
8'	Chalumeau	½ length Clarinet like #1203 Pedal Chalumeau (First Church of Christ Scientist Extension, Boston) on old Bassoon topboard
4'	Clairon	extra small French Clarion on Orchestral Oboe
	Tremulant	
	Super Coupler 4'	
	Sub coupler 16'	

NOTE: these couplers to affect Choir only. The Positiv and Choir will have to have individual key plates with some of the switches in duplicate.

Swell Organ — 61 pipes, 6" pressure

16'	Quintflote	new on old Lieblich, lower 12 old revoiced 8'CC up 53sc.
8'	Geigen	(Diapason 8) #45, ¼m, ½ 18th spotted, on old 1st open
8'	Flute Ouverte	(Flute Traversiere 8) #50 new on old G.G.
8'	Rohrflote	#4, ¼m, spotted chimneys, revoice old bass, on old 8' Gedeckt topboard
8'	Viole de Gambe	#54, ¼m spotted "SS" on old Aeoline
8'	Viole Celeste	#54, ¼m spotted "SS" on old Vox Celeste
8'	Flauto Dolce	(Flute Douce 8) old or common 2-56 etc., on old 2nd Open, provide foot blocks
8'	Flute Celeste	old or common 2-56 etc., on old Dulciana
4'	Geigen	(Octave 4) #57, ¼m, ½ 18th, spotted, on old Octave tb "M"
4'	Fugara	#66, ¼m, spotted "SS" on old Fl. Harm.

4'	Spillflote	(Flute a Fuseau 4) common spotted Baroque, on old Geigen Principal 4'
4'	Dulciana	#68 on old Salicional
4'	Unda Maris	tenor C, 49 pipes old, on old Unda Maris
2⅔'	Nasard	#65 on old 8' Quintadena
2'	Principal	knob only, no pipes
2'	Octavin	#68, ¼m, ½ 18th spotted, on old Flautina
1⅗'	Tierce	#76, ¼m ½ 18th, Principal pipes, on old Flugel Horn
VI	Plein Jeu	all #47 at 8'CC, ¼ ½ 18th spotted "S"
		15.19.22.22.26.29 — 12
		12.15.19.22.22.26 — 12
		8.12.15.15.19.22 — 12
		1.8.12.15.15.19 — 6
		1.8.8.12.12.15 — 19
III	Cymbel	(Cymbale III) all #49 at 8'CC, ¼ ½ 18th spotted "S"
		26.29.33 — 12
		22.26.29 — 12
		19.22.26 — 12
		15.19.22 — 6
		12.15.19 — 6
		8.12.15 — 13
16'	Contre Trompette	(Bombarde 16) #909C *[All Saints, Worcester, MA]*, 3-¾" diam., on old 16' Trumpet
8'	Trompette	#3 French on old Cornopean
8'	Hautbois	French shallots, old stock Oboe, place on old French Trumpet
8'	Vox Humana	old lift cap revoiced, on old Vox Humana
4'	Clairon	#3 French, on old Clarion topboard
	Tremulant	

Pedal Organ — 32 pipes, 5" pressure flues, 5" and 10" pressure reeds

32'	Contre Basse	12 pipes, Symphony 50x58 Violone E.M.S to match 60x64 (Schenectady)
32'	Quintaton	Grand Choeur
32'	Contre Bourdon	(Bourdon 32) 12 pipes, present old
16'	Contre Basse	#1 sc. Contra Basse (Symphony)
16'	Principal	Grand Choeur
16'	Bourdon	old pipes, 1-A scale, use stock #149, 22 pipes, plus 10 more from misc. stock
16'	Quintade	Great
16'	Quintflote	Swell
10⅔'	Grosse Quinte	CCC=42, use old 16' Ped. Gemshorn rebuilt, per J.S.W., 6-1-55, zinc, slotted
8'	Principal	#44, 2/9m, ½ 17th, zinc bass with butts to GG
8'	Spitzflote	Flauto Dolce 2-56 common
8'	Gedeckt Pommer	#55 zinc with spotted "S"
6⅖'	Grosse Tierce	#50, ¼ zinc and plain
5⅓'	Quinte	#57 old or new
4'	Choral Bass	#56, ¼m, ½ 17th slot, slide "S"
4'	Nachthorn	#56 plain metal "S"
2'	Blockflote	common "S"

III	Grosse Cornet	(Cornet III) 5.8.10 no breaks 5⅓' = #52 ¼ plain metal, 4' = #56 1/4 plain metal 3⅕' = tapered based on Flute Conique scale, spotted ¼ mouth
IV	Fourniture	2-⅔'—2'—1-⅓'—1' no breaks All #46 at 8'CC, ¼m ½ 18th spotted
III	Scharff	(Cymbale III) 1'—½'—¼' no breaks, All #48 at 8'CC, ¼m, ½ 18th
32'	Bombarde	12 pipes, 10" scale, 10" wind, French shallots, ext.
16'	Bombarde	7-½" scale, 10" wind, French shallots
16'	Posaune	(Buccine 16) ½ length like Pedal reed at #1036 (Worcester Art Museum) = 4" diam. 5" wind pressure
8'	Trompette	#3 French, 5" pressure
8'	Krummhorn	Positiv
4'	Clairon	#3 French, 5' Pressure
4'	Rohr Schalmei	Positiv
2'	Zink	Special, 5" pressure

NOTE: Pedal Pitman, pipes are exposed

April 24, 1956

It has been decided to leave out the 16' Pedal reed of the Antiphonal organ and put in the Cornet-de-Recit of the organ. This is a short compass stop, runs from tenor G to high C 30 notes in all. Its composition is:

1.8.12.15.17 no breaks 150 pipes in all 30% tin

8' Tenor G 64 ¼ mid. C 70 Treble C 81 high C 91 all capped with solid canisters low cutup

4' Tenor G 69 ¼ mid. C 75 Treble C 87 high C 96 low cut straight pipes no ears from 2'G up, slided

2⅔' Tenor G 71 2/9m, mid C 79 Treble C 89 high C 98 tapered 2 scales up to Mid. C 1 scale at Treble C top octave straight no ears slided, low cutup

2' Tenor G 77 ¼ Mid. C 82 Treble C 94 high C 108 no ears all straight pipes slided, low cut

1⅗' Tenor G 83 ⅕m Mid. C 88 Treble C 100 high C 114, tapered 2 scales slided low cutup

Magnet chest about 3'8" x 2'6" wide. Please RUSH. Would like to have chest delivered as soon as possible — G.D.H.

Index of Letters

39	William H. Barnes to Henry Willis	March 25, 1930	45
40	Henry Willis to Lynnwood Farnam	March 28, 1930	47
41	Henry Willis to William H. Barnes	April 7, 1930	48
42	Edwin H. Lemare to Henry Willis	April 12, 1930	48
43	G. Donald Harrison to Henry Willis	April 22, 1930	51
44	Henry Willis to G. Donald Harrison	April 25, 1930	51
45	Emerson Richards to Henry Willis	May 2, 1930	53
46	Henry Willis to Emerson Richards	May 17, 1930	54
47	Henry Willis to Edwin H. Lemare	July 16, 1930	55
48	Lynnwood Farnam to Henry Willis	August 3, 1930	55
49	Henry Willis to Charles M. Courboin	September 9, 1930	56
50	Charles Courboin to Henry Willis	September 17, 1930	57
51	Henry Willis to Charles Courboin	October 1, 1930	58
52	Henry Willis to Basil Austin	October 2, 1930	59
53	Bernard Laberge to Henry Willis	October 6, 1930	59
54	Emerson Richards to Henry Willis	October 16, 1930	60
55	Henry Willis to Bernard Laberge	October 20, 1930	61
56	Emerson Richards to Henry Willis	October 27, 1930	62
57	Ernest Skinner to Archibald T. Davison	November 8, 1930	63
58	Henry Willis to Emerson Richards	November 21, 1930	65
59	Henry Willis to James B. Jamison	November 21, 1930	66
60	Emerson Richards to Henry Willis	November 22, 1930	68
61	Henry Willis to Alexander Russell	November 25, 1930	69
62	Henry Willis to Emerson Richards	December 3, 1930	70
63	Emerson Richards to Henry Willis	December 8, 1930	70
64	Emerson Richards to Henry Willis	December 15, 1930	71
65	Henry Willis to Emerson Richards	December 19, 1930	73
66	Henry Willis to Emerson Richards	December 29, 1930	73
67	Emerson Richards to Henry Willis	January 8, 1931	75
68	Emerson Richards to Henry Willis	March 13, 1931	76
69	Henry Willis to Emerson Richards	April 28, 1931	78
70	Emerson Richards to Henry Willis	May 8, 1931	78
71	Henry Willis to Emerson Richards	May 19, 1931	80
72	Emerson Richards to Henry Willis	June 19, 1931	81
73	James B. Jamison to Henry Willis	June 21, 1931	82
74	Henry Willis to Emerson Richards	June 29, 1931	84
75	Emerson Richards to Henry Willis	July 9, 1931	85
76	Henry Willis to Emerson Richards	July 20, 1931	87
77	Emerson Richards to Henry Willis	July 29, 1931	88
78	Henry Willis to Robert Pier Elliot	December 29, 1931	89
79	Emerson Richards to Henry Willis	January 15, 1932	91
80	Robert Pier Elliot to Henry Willis	January 26, 1932	92
81	Henry Willis to Emerson Richards	February 1, 1932	95

211	Henry Willis to G. Donald Harrison	May 9, 1949	300
212	Emerson Richards to Henry Willis	May 23, 1949	301
213	Henry Willis to Emerson Richards	June 22, 1949	302
214	Joseph Whiteford to Aeolian-Skinner factory staff	July 13, 1949	304
215	Emerson Richards to Henry Willis	July 27, 1949	305
216	Emerson Richards to Henry Willis	November 7, 1949	306
217	Henry Willis to *The Diapason*	November 14, 1949	312
218	Henry Willis to G. Donald Harrison	November 16, 1949	314
219	Emerson Richards to Henry Willis	November 21, 1949	315
220	Ernest Skinner to T. Scott Buhrman	1949	316
221	Emerson Richards to T. Scott Buhrman	November 25, 1949	317
222	Henry Willis to Emerson Richards	December 5, 1949	318
223	Emerson Richards to Henry Willis	December 21, 1949	321
224	G. Donald Harrison to Henry Willis	December 29, 1949	323
225	G. Donald Harrison to Ralph Downes	January 13, 1950	325
226	Emerson Richards to Henry Willis	January 30, 1950	332
227	G. Donald Harrison to William King Covell	February 15, 1950	333
228	G. Donald Harrison to Carl Weinrich	November 9, 1951	334
229	G. Donald Harrison to Carl Weinrich	May 1, 1952	336
230	G. Donald Harrison to Carl Weinrich	May 21, 1952	336
231	Joseph Whiteford to Carl Weinrich	June 9, 1952	337
232	Emerson Richards to Henry Willis	August 5, 1952	338
233	G. Donald Harrison to Carl Weinrich	August 5, 1952	341
234	Henry Willis to G. Donald Harrison	August 18, 1952	342
235	Joseph Whiteford to Carl Weinrich	August 21, 1952	345
236	Henry Willis to William E. Zeuch	August 22, 1952	346
237	G. Donald Harrison to E. Power Biggs	September 4, 1952	346
238	Henry Willis to Emerson Richards	October 31, 1952	348
239	William E. Zeuch to Dora and Henry Willis	November 12, 1952	349
240	G. Donald Harrison to Henry Willis	January 15, 1953	351
241	Henry Willis to G. Donald Harrison	February 4, 1953	352
242	William H. Barnes to Henry Willis	February 20, 1953	355
243	Henry Willis to William H. Barnes	February 26, 1953	356
244	G. Donald Harrison to E. Power Biggs	April 21, 1953	357
245	T. Frederick H. Candlyn to Henry Willis	May 22, 1953	360
246	G. Donald Harrison to William King Covell	May 27, 1953	360
247	Henry Willis to T. Frederick H. Candlyn	June 4, 1953	361
248	James B. Jamison to Henry Willis	August 9, 1953	362
249	Henry Willis to James B. Jamison	August 19, 1953	364
250	G. Donald Harrison to Henry Willis	August 25, 1953	366
251	Walter Holtkamp to E. Power Biggs	October 20, 1953	367
252	G. Donald Harrison to William King Covell	December 31, 1953	368
253	G. Donald Harrison to William King Covell	January 12, 1954	369

Sources of Letters

The letters in this book are from the Willis American Correspondence file, with the following exceptions:

Letters 57, 93-99, 109, 117, 119, 120, 122, 136-138, 143-146, 156, 158, 162, 164, 165, 169, 170, 177, 182, 183, 200, 219, 220, 221, 227, 237, 244, 246, 251-254, 267, 273, 282 and 294 are located in the E. Power Biggs Organ Library at Boston University, from the collections of E. Power Biggs and William King Covell.

Letters 192, 194, 225, 259, 260, 264, 265 and 277 were most generously loaned especially for this book by Mr. Ralph Downes.

Letters 123-135, 228-231, 233, 235, 258 and 289 were kindly permitted publication from the collection of Carl Weinrich.

Letters 208 and 210 are from the files of St. Stephen's Church, Richmond, Virginia through the gracious cooperation of Mr. Neal Campbell.

Letters 116 and 121 were cordially provided by the Organ Literature Foundation.

Letter 20 is found in *The Diapason*, January, 1928.

Letter 30 is found in *The American Organist*, June, 1929.

Charles Callahan *is a native of Cambridge, Massachusetts, where he began his musical studies with Theodore Marier while a student at the Boston Archdiocesan Choir School. Further study with George Faxon, Clarence Watters, and Julius Chaloff preceded study at the Curtis Institute of Music in Philadelphia under Alexander McCurdy. Following graduation from Curtis, Callahan was awarded a grant to study in Belgium with Flor Peeters. During his European stay, he also studied Gregorian Chant at Solesmes Abbey in France. Returning to the United States, Callahan taught at the Catholic University of America in Washington D. C., where he earned his doctorate in 1978 at age 26.*

He is currently on the music faculty of Rollins College in Winter Park, Florida, and organist at Knowles Memorial Chapel at Rollins. He was recently Composer in Residence and Director of the Choir at Middlebury College, Middlebury, Vermont.

In the past decade, Charles Callahan has become one of the leading performers and composers of organ and choral music in America. His works have received premieres at the Spoleto Festival, the Smithsonian Institution, the Kennedy Center, the Organization of American States, and the International Organ Festival in Morelia, Mexico. Simon Preston played the world premiere of his "Partita on Hyfrydol," Opus 42, at Westminster Abbey in 1986.

Dr. Callahan has been extremely active as a recitalist and lecturer throughout the United States, Canada, England, and Germany. He presented the complete organ works of Franck in a series of recitals at the Kennedy Center in Washington, D. C. in 1979 and was featured artist at the University of Wisconsin in 1988.